Reference Manual on SCIENTIFIC EVIDENCE

Second Edition

WEST GROUP
ST. PAUL, MN
2000

ISBN 0–314–25077–8

TEXT IS PRINTED ON 10% POST CONSUMER RECYCLED PAPER

Reference Manual on Scientific Evidence

Second Edition

Federal Judicial Center 2000

This Federal Judicial Center publication was undertaken in furtherance of the Center's statutory mission to develop and conduct education programs for judicial branch employees. The views expressed are those of the authors and not necessarily of the Federal Judicial Center.

Westlaw online/westlaw.com

To access the *Reference Manual* on Westlaw,
enter this dedicated database:
RMSCIEVID

For Federal Judicial Center publications generally, this database:
FJC

Customer Support: For general or technical questions, call West Group Customer & Technical Services at 1-800-WESTLAW (1-800-937-8529). For search assistance, call the West Group Reference Attorneys at 1-800-REF-ATTY (1-800-733-2889). Assistance is available 24 hours a day. You can also send an e-mail message to:

support@westgroup.com

Federal Judicial Center

An electronic version of the *Reference Manual* can be found at the Federal Judicial Center's site on the World Wide Web. Go to
http://air.fjc.gov/public/fjcweb.nsf/pages/16

For the Center's overall homepage on the Web, go to
http://www.fjc.gov

Summary Table of Contents

A detailed Table of Contents appears at the front of each chapter

Preface

Thomas Henry Huxley observed that "science is simply common sense at its best; that is, rigidly accurate in observation and merciless to a fallacy in logic."[1] This second edition of the *Reference Manual on Scientific Evidence* furthers the goal of assisting federal judges in recognizing the characteristics and reasoning of "science" as it is relevant in litigation. The *Reference Manual* is but one part of a series of education and research initiatives undertaken by the Center, in collaboration with other professional organizations, and with support by a grant from the Carnegie Corporation of New York, to aid judges in dealing with these issues. The *Reference Manual* itself responds to a recommendation of the Federal Courts Study Committee that the Federal Judicial Center prepare a manual to assist judges in managing cases involving complex scientific and technical evidence.[2]

The first edition of the *Reference Manual* was published in 1994, at a time of heightened need for judicial awareness of scientific methods and reasoning created by the Supreme Court's decision in *Daubert v. Merrell Dow Pharmaceuticals, Inc.*[3] *Daubert* assigned the trial judge a "gatekeeping responsibility" to make "a preliminary assessment of whether the reasoning or methodology underlying the testimony is scientifically valid and of whether that reasoning or methodology properly can be applied to the facts in issue."[4] The first edition of the *Reference Manual* has been republished by numerous private publishers and used in a variety of educational programs for federal and state judges, attorneys, and law students. The Center estimates that approximately 100,000 copies have been distributed since its initial publication.

This second edition comes after recent decisions that expand the duties and responsibility of trial courts in cases involving scientific and technical evidence. In *General Electric Co. v. Joiner,*[5] the Supreme Court strengthened the role of the trial courts by deciding that abuse of discretion is the correct standard for an appellate court to apply in reviewing a district court's evidentiary ruling. In a concurring opinion, Justice Breyer urged judges to avail themselves of techniques, such as the use of court-appointed experts, that would assist them in

1. T.H. Huxley, The Crayfish: An Introduction to the Study of Zoology 2 (1880), *quoted in* Stephen Jay Gould, Full House: The Spread of Excellence from Plato to Darwin 8 (1996).

2. Federal Courts Study Comm., Report of the Federal Courts Study Committee 97 (1990). *See also* Carnegie Comm'n on Science, Tech., & Gov't, Science and Technology in Judicial Decision Making: Creating Opportunities and Meeting Challenges 11 (1993) (noting concern over the ability of courts to manage and adjudicate scientific and technical issues).

3. 509 U.S. 579 (1993).

4. *Id.* at 589 n.7, 592–93.

5. 522 U.S. 136, 141–43 (1997).

making determinations about the admissibility of complex scientific or technical evidence.[6] Last year, in *Kumho Tire Co. v. Carmichael*, the Supreme Court determined that the trial judge's gatekeeping obligation under *Daubert* not only applies to scientific evidence but also extends to proffers of "'technical' and 'other specialized' knowledge," the other categories of expertise specified in Federal Rule of Evidence 702.[7] Also, the Supreme Court recently forwarded to Congress proposed amendments to Federal Rules of Evidence 701, 702, and 703 that are intended to codify case law that is based on *Daubert* and its progeny.

This second edition includes new chapters that respond to issues that have emerged since the initial publication. The Introduction by Justice Breyer reviews the role of scientific evidence in litigation and the challenges that trial courts face in considering such evidence. Supreme Court cases subsequent to *Daubert* are summarized in a chapter by Margaret Berger. The philosophy and practice of science are described in a chapter by David Goodstein. New reference guides on medical testimony and engineering will aid judges with the broader scope of review for cases involving nonscientific expert testimony following *Kumho*. Reference guides from the first edition have been updated with new cases and additional material. The Reference Guide on DNA Evidence has been completely revised to take account of the rapidly evolving science in this area. To make room for the new material, essential information from the chapters on court-appointed experts and special masters was condensed and included in the chapter on management of expert evidence.[8]

We continue to caution judges regarding the proper use of the reference guides. They are not intended to instruct judges concerning what evidence should be admissible or to establish minimum standards for acceptable scientific testimony. Rather, the guides can assist judges in identifying the issues most commonly in dispute in these selected areas and in reaching an informed and reasoned assessment concerning the basis of expert evidence. They are designed to facilitate the process of identifying and narrowing issues concerning scientific evidence by outlining for judges the pivotal issues in the areas of science that are often subject to dispute. Citations in the reference guides identify cases in which specific issues were raised; they are examples of other instances in which judges were faced with similar problems. By identifying scientific areas commonly in dispute, the guides should improve the quality of the dialogue between the judges and the parties concerning the basis of expert evidence.

6. *Id.* at 147–50.

7. 119 S. Ct. 1167, 1171 (1999) (quoting Fed. R. Evid. 702).

8. Much of the information in those two chapters is available in Joe S. Cecil & Thomas E. Willging, *Accepting* Daubert*'s Invitation: Defining a Role for Court-Appointed Experts in Assessing Scientific Validity*, 43 Emory L.J. 995 (1994), and Margaret G. Farrell, *Coping with Scientific Evidence: The Use of Special Masters*, 43 Emory L.J. 927 (1994).

This Reference Manual was begun and furthered by two of my predecessors, Judge William W Schwarzer and Judge Rya Zobel. Their work in developing the Center's program on scientific evidence established the foundation for the Center's current initiatives. In developing the *Reference Manual* we benefited greatly from the encouragement and support of David Z. Robinson, former executive director of the Carnegie Commission on Science, Technology, and Government, and Helene Kaplan, chair of the Commission's Task Force on Judicial and Regulatory Decision Making. A number of persons at the Center have been instrumental in developing this second edition of the *Reference Manual*. Joe Cecil and Dean Miletich served as editors of the *Reference Manual*. They profited from the advice and assistance of the following members of the Center's Communications Policy & Design Office: Geoffrey Erwin, Martha Kendall, Kris Markarian, and David Marshall. Rozzie Bell of the Center's Information Services Office offered great assistance in locating much of the source material. Finally, we are grateful to the authors of the chapters for their dedication to the task, and to the peer reviewers of the chapters for their thoughtful suggestions.

FERN M. SMITH
Director, Federal Judicial Center

Introduction

STEPHEN BREYER

Stephen Breyer, L.L.B., is Associate Justice of the Supreme Court of the United States.

Portions of this Introduction appear in Stephen Breyer, *The Interdependence of Science and Law*, 280 Science 537 (1998).

IN THIS AGE OF SCIENCE, SCIENCE SHOULD EXPECT TO find a warm welcome, perhaps a permanent home, in our courtrooms. The reason is a simple one. The legal disputes before us increasingly involve the principles and tools of science. Proper resolution of those disputes matters not just to the litigants, but also to the general public—those who live in our technologically complex society and whom the law must serve. Our decisions should reflect a proper scientific and technical understanding so that the law can respond to the needs of the public.

Consider, for example, how often our cases today involve statistics—a tool familiar to social scientists and economists but, until our own generation, not to many judges. Only last year the U.S. Supreme Court heard two cases that involved consideration of statistical evidence. In *Hunt v. Cromartie,*[1] we ruled that summary judgment was not appropriate in an action brought against various state officials that challenged a congressional redistricting plan as racially motivated in violation of the Equal Protection Clause. In determining that disputed material facts existed regarding the motive of the state legislature in redrawing the redistricting plan, we placed great weight on a statistical analysis that offered a plausible alternative interpretation that did not involve an improper racial motive. Assessing the plausibility of this alternative explanation required knowledge of the strength of the statistical correlation between race and partisanship, understanding of the consequences of restricting the analysis to a subset of precincts, and understanding of the relationships among alternative measures of partisan support.

In *Department of Commerce v. United States House of Representatives,*[2] residents of a number of states challenged the constitutionality of a plan to use two forms of statistical sampling in the upcoming decennial census to adjust for expected "undercounting" of certain identifiable groups. Before examining the constitutional issue, we had to determine if the residents challenging the plan had standing to sue because of injuries they would be likely to suffer as a result of the sampling plan. In making this assessment, it was necessary to apply the two sampling strategies to population data in order to predict the changes in congressional apportionment that would most likely occur under each proposed strategy. After resolving the standing issue, we had to determine if the statistical estimation techniques were consistent with a federal statute.

In each of these two cases, we judges were not asked to become expert statisticians, but we were expected to understand how the statistical analyses worked. Trial judges today are asked routinely to understand statistics at least as well, and probably better.

But science is far more than tools, such as statistics. And that "more" increas-

1. 119 S. Ct. 1545 (1999).
2. 119 S. Ct. 765 (1999).

ingly enters directly into the courtroom. The Supreme Court, for example, has recently decided cases involving basic questions of human liberty, the resolution of which demanded an understanding of scientific matters. In 1997 we were asked to decide whether the Constitution contains a "right to die."[3] The specific legal question was whether the federal Constitution, which prohibits government from depriving "any person" of "liberty" without "due process of law," requires a state to permit a doctor's assistance in the suicide of a terminally ill patient. Is the "right to assisted suicide" part of the liberty that the Constitution protects? Underlying the legal question was a medical question: To what extent can medical technology reduce or eliminate the risk of dying in severe pain? The medical question did not determine the answer to the legal question, but to do our legal job properly, we needed to develop an informed—although necessarily approximate—understanding of the state of that relevant scientific art.

Nor are the right-to-die cases unique in this respect. A different case in 1997 challenged the constitutionality of a state sexual psychopath statute. The law required a determination of when a person can be considered so dangerous and mentally ill that the threat he or she poses to public safety justifies indefinite noncriminal confinement, a question that implicates science and medicine as well as law.[4]

The Supreme Court's docket is only illustrative. Scientific issues permeate the law. Criminal courts consider the scientific validity of, say, DNA sampling or voiceprints, or expert predictions of defendants' "future dangerousness," which can lead courts or juries to authorize or withhold the punishment of death. Courts review the reasonableness of administrative agency conclusions about the safety of a drug, the risks attending nuclear waste disposal, the leakage potential of a toxic waste dump, or the risks to wildlife associated with the building of a dam. Patent law cases can turn almost entirely on an understanding of the underlying technical or scientific subject matter. And, of course, tort law often requires difficult determinations about the risk of death or injury associated with exposure to a chemical ingredient of a pesticide or other product.

The importance of scientific accuracy in the decision of such cases reaches well beyond the case itself. A decision wrongly denying compensation in a toxic substance case, for example, can not only deprive the plaintiff of warranted compensation but also discourage other similarly situated individuals from even trying to obtain compensation and encourage the continued use of a dangerous substance. On the other hand, a decision wrongly granting compensation, although of immediate benefit to the plaintiff, can improperly force abandonment of the substance. Thus, if the decision is wrong, it will improperly deprive the public of what can be far more important benefits—those surrounding a drug

3. Washington v. Glucksberg, 521 U.S. 702 (1997); Vacco v. Quill, 521 U.S. 793 (1997).

4. Kansas v. Hendricks, 521 U.S. 346 (1997).

that cures many while subjecting a few to less serious risk, for example. The upshot is that we must search for law that reflects an understanding of the relevant underlying science, not for law that frees companies to cause serious harm or forces them unnecessarily to abandon the thousands of artificial substances on which modern life depends.

The search is not a search for scientific precision. We cannot hope to investigate all the subtleties that characterize good scientific work. A judge is not a scientist, and a courtroom is not a scientific laboratory. But consider the remark made by the physicist Wolfgang Pauli. After a colleague asked whether a certain scientific paper was wrong, Pauli replied, "That paper isn't even good enough to be wrong!"[5] Our objective is to avoid legal decisions that reflect that paper's so-called science. The law must seek decisions that fall within the boundaries of scientifically sound knowledge.

Even this more modest objective is sometimes difficult to achieve in practice. The most obvious reason is that most judges lack the scientific training that might facilitate the evaluation of scientific claims or the evaluation of expert witnesses who make such claims. Judges typically are generalists, dealing with cases that can vary widely in subject matter. Our primary objective is usually process-related: seeing that a decision is reached fairly and in a timely way. And the decision in a court of law typically (though not always) focuses on a particular event and specific individualized evidence.

Furthermore, science itself may be highly uncertain and controversial with respect to many of the matters that come before the courts. Scientists often express considerable uncertainty about the dangers of a particular substance. And their views may differ about many related questions that courts may have to answer. What, for example, is the relevance to human cancer of studies showing that a substance causes some cancers, perhaps only a few, in test groups of mice or rats? What is the significance of extrapolations from toxicity studies involving high doses to situations where the doses are much smaller? Can lawyers or judges or anyone else expect scientists always to be certain or always to have uniform views with respect to an extrapolation from a large dose to a small one, when the causes of and mechanisms related to cancer are generally not well known? Many difficult legal cases fall within this area of scientific uncertainty.

Finally, a court proceeding, such as a trial, is not simply a search for dispassionate truth. The law must be fair. In our country, it must always seek to protect basic human liberties. One important procedural safeguard, guaranteed by our Constitution's Seventh Amendment, is the right to a trial by jury. A number of innovative techniques have been developed to strengthen the ability of juries to consider difficult evidence.[6] Any effort to bring better science into

5. Peter W. Huber, Galileo's Revenge: Junk Science in the Courtroom 54 (1991).
6. *See generally* Jury Trial Innovations (G. Thomas Munsterman et al. eds., 1997).

the courtroom must respect the jury's constitutionally specified role—even if doing so means that, from a scientific perspective, an incorrect result is sometimes produced.

Despite the difficulties, I believe there is an increasingly important need for law to reflect sound science. I remain optimistic about the likelihood that it will do so. It is common to find cooperation between governmental institutions and the scientific community where the need for that cooperation is apparent. Today, as a matter of course, the President works with a science adviser, Congress solicits advice on the potential dangers of food additives from the National Academy of Sciences, and scientific regulatory agencies often work with outside scientists, as well as their own, to develop a product that reflects good science.

The judiciary, too, has begun to look for ways to improve the quality of the science on which scientifically related judicial determinations will rest. The Federal Judicial Center is collaborating with the National Academy of Sciences in developing the academy's Program in Science, Technology, and Law.[7] This program will bring together on a regular basis knowledgeable scientists, engineers, judges, attorneys, and corporate and government officials to explore areas of interaction and improve communication among the science, engineering, and legal communities. This program is intended to provide a neutral, nonadversarial forum for promoting understanding, encouraging imaginative approaches to problem solving, and conducting studies.

In the Supreme Court, as a matter of course, we hear not only from the parties to a case but also from outside groups, which file briefs—thirty-page amicus curiae briefs—that help us to become more informed about the relevant science. In the "right-to-die" case, we received about sixty such documents from organizations of doctors, psychologists, nurses, hospice workers, and handicapped persons, among others. Many discussed pain-control technology, thereby helping us to identify areas of technical consensus and disagreement. Such briefs help to educate the justices on potentially relevant technical matters, making us not experts, but moderately educated laypersons, and that education improves the quality of our decisions.

Moreover, our Court recently made clear that the law imposes on trial judges the duty, with respect to scientific evidence, to become evidentiary gatekeepers.[8] The judge, without interfering with the jury's role as trier of fact, must determine whether purported scientific evidence is "reliable" and will "assist the trier

7. Letter from Richard E. Bissell, Executive Director, Policy Division of the National Research Council, to Judge Rya W. Zobel, Director, Federal Judicial Center (Oct. 27, 1998) (on file with the Research Division of the Federal Judicial Center). *See also* Anne-Marie Mazza, Program in Science, Technology, and Law (Oct. 1999) (program description) (on file with the Research Division of the Federal Judicial Center).

8. General Elec. Co. v. Joiner, 522 U.S. 136 (1997); Daubert v. Merrell Dow Pharms., Inc., 509 U.S. 579 (1993).

of fact," thereby keeping from juries testimony that, in Pauli's sense, isn't even good enough to be wrong. Last term our Court made clear that this requirement extends beyond scientific testimony to all forms of expert testimony.[9] The purpose of *Daubert*'s gatekeeping requirement "is to make certain that an expert, whether basing testimony upon professional studies or personal experience, employs in the courtroom the same level of intellectual rigor that characterizes the practice of an expert in the relevant field."[10]

Federal trial judges, looking for ways to perform the gatekeeping function better, increasingly have used case-management techniques like pretrial conferences to narrow the scientific issues in dispute, pretrial hearings where potential experts are subject to examination by the court, and the appointment of specially trained law clerks or scientific special masters. Judge Jack B. Weinstein of New York suggests that courts should sometimes "go beyond the experts proffered by the parties" and "appoint independent experts" as the Federal Rules of Evidence allow.[11] Judge Gerald Rosen of Michigan appointed a University of Michigan Medical School professor to testify as an expert witness for the court, helping to determine the relevant facts in a case that challenged a Michigan law prohibiting partial-birth abortions.[12] Judge Richard Stearns of Massachusetts, acting with the consent of the parties in a recent, highly technical genetic engineering patent case,[13] appointed a Harvard Medical School professor to serve "as a sounding board for the court to think through the scientific significance of the evidence" and to "assist the court in determining the validity of any scientific evidence, hypothesis or theory on which the experts base their testimony."[14]

In what one observer describes as "the most comprehensive attempt to incorporate science, as scientists practice it, into law,"[15] Judge Sam Pointer, Jr., of Alabama recently appointed a "neutral science panel" of four scientists from different disciplines to prepare testimony on the scientific basis of the claims in the silicone gel breast implant product liability cases consolidated as part of a multidistrict litigation process.[16] This proceeding will allow judges and jurors in numerous cases to consider videotaped testimony by a panel of prominent scientists. The use of such videotapes is likely to result in more consistent decisions

9. Kumho Tire Co. v. Carmichael, 119 S. Ct. 1167 (1999).

10. *Id.* at 1176.

11. Jack B. Weinstein, Individual Justice in Mass Tort Litigation: The Effect of Class Actions, Consolidations, and Other Multiparty Devices 116 (1995).

12. Evans v. Kelley, 977 F. Supp. 1283 (E.D. Mich. 1997).

13. Biogen, Inc. v. Amgen, Inc., 973 F. Supp. 39 (D. Mass. 1997).

14. MediaCom Corp. v. Rates Tech., Inc., 4 F. Supp. 2d 17 app. B at 37 (D. Mass. 1998) (quoting the Affidavit of Engagement filed in Biogen, Inc. v. Amgen, Inc., 973 F. Supp. 39 (D. Mass. 1997) (No. 95-10496)).

15. Olivia Judson, *Slide-Rule Justice*, Nat'l J., Oct. 9, 1999, at 2882, 2885.

16. *In re* Silicone Gel Breast Implant Prods. Liab. Litig., Order 31 (N.D. Ala. filed May 30, 1996) (MDL No. 926).

across courts, as well as great savings of time and expense for the individual litigants and the courts.

These case-management techniques are neutral, in principle favoring neither plaintiffs nor defendants. When used, they have typically proved successful. Nonetheless, judges have not often invoked their rules-provided authority to appoint their own experts.[17] They may hesitate simply because the process is unfamiliar or because the use of this kind of technique inevitably raises questions. Will use of an independent expert, in effect, substitute that expert's judgment for that of the court? Will it inappropriately deprive the parties of control over the presentation of the case? Will it improperly intrude on the proper function of the jury? Where is one to find a truly neutral expert? After all, different experts, in total honesty, often interpret the same data differently. Will the search for the expert create inordinate delay or significantly increase costs? Who will pay the expert? Judge William Acker, Jr., of Alabama writes:

> Unless and until there is a national register of experts on various subjects and a method by which they can be fairly compensated, the federal amateurs wearing black robes will have to overlook their new gatekeeping function lest they assume the intolerable burden of becoming experts themselves in every discipline known to the physical and social sciences, and some as yet unknown but sure to blossom.[18]

A number of scientific and professional organizations have come forward with proposals to aid the courts in finding skilled experts. The National Conference of Lawyers and Scientists, a joint committee of the American Association for the Advancement of Science (AAAS) and the Science and Technology Section of the American Bar Association, has developed a pilot project to test the feasibility of increased use of court-appointed experts in cases that present technical issues. The project will recruit a slate of candidates from science and professional organizations to serve as court-appointed experts in cases in which the court has determined that traditional means of clarifying issues under the adversarial system are unlikely to yield the information that is necessary for a reasoned and principled resolution of the disputed issues.[19] The project also is developing educational materials that will be helpful to scientists who are unfamiliar with the legal system. The Federal Judicial Center will examine a number of questions arising from such appointments, such as the following:

- How did the appointed experts perform their duties?
- How did the court, while protecting the interests of the lawyers and the

17. Joe S. Cecil & Thomas E. Willging, *Accepting* Daubert*'s Invitation: Defining a Role for Court-Appointed Experts in Assessing Scientific Validity*, 43 Emory L.J. 995, 1004 (1994).

18. Letter from Judge William Acker, Jr., to the Judicial Conference of the United States et al. (Jan. 2, 1998).

19. Information on the AAAS program can be found at Court Appointed Scientific Experts: A Demonstration Project of the AAAS (visited Dec. 23, 1999) <http://www.aaas.org/spp/case/case.htm>.

parties they represent, protect the experts from unreasonable demands, say, on their time?

- How did the court prepare the experts to encounter what may be an unfamiliar and sometimes hostile legal environment?

The Private Adjudication Center at Duke University is establishing a registry of independent scientific and technical experts who are willing to provide advice to courts or serve as court-appointed experts.[20] Registry services also are available to arbitrators and mediators and to parties and lawyers who together agree to engage an independent expert at the early stages of a dispute. The registry has recruited an initial group of experts in medicine and health-related disciplines, primarily from major academic institutions, and new registrants are added on a regular basis. As needed, the registry also conducts targeted searches to find experts with the qualifications required for particular cases. Registrants must adhere to a code of conduct designed to ensure confidence in their impartiality and integrity.

These projects have much to teach us about the ways in which courts can use such experts. We need to learn how to identify impartial experts. Also, we need to know how best to protect the interests of the parties and the experts when such extraordinary procedures are used. We also need to know how best to prepare a scientist for the sometimes hostile legal environment that arises during depositions and cross-examination.

It would undoubtedly be helpful to recommend methods for efficiently educating (that is, in a few hours) willing scientists in the ways of the courts, just as it would be helpful to develop training that might better equip judges to understand the ways of science and the ethical, as well as practical and legal, aspects of scientific testimony.[21]

In this age of science we must build legal foundations that are sound in science as well as in law. Scientists have offered their help. We in the legal community should accept that offer. We are in the process of doing so. This manual seeks to open legal institutional channels through which science—its learning, tools, and principles—may flow more easily and thereby better inform the law. The manual represents one part of a joint scientific–legal effort that will further the interests of truth and justice alike.

20. Letter from Corinne A. Houpt, Registry Project Director, Private Adjudication Center, to Judge Rya W. Zobel, Director, Federal Judicial Center (Dec. 29, 1998) (on file with the Research Division of the Federal Judicial Center). Information on the Private Adjudication Center program can be found at The Registry of Independent Scientific and Technical Advisors (visited Mar. 8, 2000) <http://www.law.duke.edu/pac/registry/index.html>.

21. Gilbert S. Omenn, *Enhancing the Role of the Scientific Expert Witness*, 102 Envtl. Health Persp. 674 (1994).

The Supreme Court's Trilogy on the Admissibility of Expert Testimony

MARGARET A. BERGER

Margaret A. Berger, J.D., is Suzanne J. and Norman Miles Professor of Law, Brooklyn Law School, Brooklyn, New York.

CONTENTS

I. Introduction

On March 23, 1999, the U.S. Supreme Court decided *Kumho Tire Co. v. Carmichael,*[1] the third in a series of cases dealing with the admissibility of expert testimony. The trilogy began in 1993 with *Daubert v. Merrell Dow Pharmaceuticals, Inc.,*[2] a toxic tort action, in which the Court promulgated a new test for federal courts to use when ruling on the admissibility of scientific evidence. The second case, *General Electric Co. v. Joiner,*[3] decided in 1997, likewise dealt with the admissibility of scientific evidence in the context of a toxic tort suit. In *Kumho,* the Court extended the approach of these prior opinions to nonscientific expert testimony proffered in a product liability action. In doing so, *Kumho* provides new insights into the meaning of *Daubert* and *Joiner,* and offers guidance on how federal trial and appellate courts can appropriately respond when a party seeks to exclude an opponent's expert testimony. Because of its broad scope, *Kumho* is likely to play a significant role in all future rulings on the admissibility of expert proof.[4]

The opinions in the trilogy are so interrelated that *Kumho*'s significance and potential impact emerge much more clearly when viewed in conjunction with the Court's analyses in the earlier cases. Consequently, section II of this chapter examines the *Daubert* and *Joiner* opinions. Section III begins with a survey of the lower courts' opinions in *Kumho* and then turns to the Supreme Court's opinion. Section IV examines the current state of the law with regard to expert testimony in light of *Kumho* and addresses some of the more troublesome questions that are likely to arise in connection with requests to exclude expert testimony. As in the Evidentiary Framework chapter that appeared in the first edition of the *Reference Manual on Scientific Evidence,* the aim of this discussion is to provide a starting point for analysis by highlighting issues that the courts will have to resolve.

1. 119 S. Ct. 1167 (1999).
2. 509 U.S. 579 (1993).
3. 522 U.S. 136 (1997).
4. David L. Faigman et al., *Preface* to 3 Modern Scientific Evidence: The Law and Science of Expert Testimony at v (David L. Faigman et al. eds., 1999) ("The importance of this decision cannot be overstated, and it ranks with *Daubert* in the likely effect it will have on the practice of admitting expert testimony.") [hereinafter Modern Scientific Evidence].

II. The First Two Cases in the Trilogy: *Daubert* and *Joiner*

A. *Daubert v. Merrell Dow Pharmaceuticals, Inc.*

In the seminal *Daubert* case, the Court granted certiorari to decide whether the so-called *Frye* (or "general acceptance") test, which was used by some federal circuits in determining the admissibility of scientific evidence, had been superseded by the enactment of the Federal Rules of Evidence. The Court held unanimously that the *Frye* test had not survived. Six justices joined Justice Blackmun in setting forth a new test for admissibility after concluding that "Rule 702 . . . clearly contemplates some degree of regulation of the subjects and theories about which an expert may testify."[5] While the two other members of the Court agreed with this conclusion about the role of Rule 702, they thought that the task of enunciating a new rule for the admissibility of expert proof should be left to another day.[6]

The majority opinion in *Daubert* continued by setting forth major themes that run throughout the trilogy: The trial court is the "gatekeeper" who must screen proffered expertise, and the objective of the screening is to ensure that what is admitted "is not only relevant, but reliable."[7] There was nothing particularly novel about a trial judge having the *power* to make an admissibility determination. Federal Rules of Evidence 104(a) and 702 pointed to such a conclusion, and federal trial judges had excluded expert testimony long before *Daubert*. However, the majority opinion in *Daubert* stated that the trial court has not only the power but the *obligation* to act as "gatekeeper."[8]

5. *Daubert*, 509 U.S. at 589.

6. Chief Justice Rehnquist, joined by Justice Stevens in an opinion concurring in part and dissenting in part, stated: "I do not doubt that Rule 702 confides to the judge some gatekeeping responsibility in deciding questions of the admissibility of proffered expert testimony." *Id.* at 600. However, Chief Justice Rehnquist and Justice Stevens would have decided only the *Frye* issue and left "the further development of this important area of the law to future cases." *Id.* at 601. The Chief Justice raised a number of questions about the majority's opinion that foreshadowed issues that arose in *Joiner* and *Kumho:*

> Does all of this dicta apply to an expert seeking to testify on the basis of "technical or other specialized knowledge"—the other types of expert knowledge to which Rule 702 applies—or are the "general observations" limited only to "scientific knowledge"? What is the difference between scientific knowledge and technical knowledge; does Rule 702 actually contemplate that the phrase "scientific, technical, or other specialized knowledge" be broken down into numerous subspecies of expertise, or did its authors simply pick general descriptive language covering the sort of expert testimony which courts have customarily received?

Id. at 600.

7. *Id.* at 589.

8. "The primary locus of this obligation is Rule 702 . . . ." *Id.*

The Court then went on to consider the meaning of this two-pronged test of relevancy and reliability in the context of scientific evidence.[9] With regard to relevancy, the Court explained that expert testimony cannot assist the trier in resolving a factual dispute, as required by Rule 702, unless the expert's theory is tied sufficiently to the facts of the case. "Rule 702's 'helpfulness' standard requires a valid scientific connection to the pertinent inquiry as a precondition to admissibility."[10] This consideration, the Court remarked, "has been aptly described by Judge Becker as one of 'fit.'"[11]

To determine whether proffered scientific testimony or evidence satisfies the standard of evidentiary reliability,[12] a judge must ascertain whether it is "ground[ed] in the methods and procedures of science."[13] The Court, emphasizing that "[t]he inquiry envisioned by Rule 702 is . . . a flexible one,"[14] then examined the characteristics of scientific methodology and set out a nonexclusive list of four factors that bear on whether a theory or technique has been derived by the scientific method.[15] First and foremost the Court viewed science as an empirical endeavor: "Whether [a theory or technique] can be (and has been) tested" is the "'methodology [that] distinguishes science from other fields of human inquiry.'"[16] Also mentioned by the Court as indicators of good science are peer review or publication, and the existence of known or potential error rates and standards controlling the technique's operation.[17] Although gen-

9. *Id.* The majority explicitly noted that "Rule 702 also applies to 'technical, or other specialized knowledge.' Our discussion is limited to the scientific context because that is the nature of the expertise offered here." *Id.* at 590 n.8.

10. *Id.* at 591–92.

11. *Id.* at 591. Judge Becker used this term in *United States v. Downing*, 753 F.2d 1224, 1242 (3d Cir. 1985), in the course of discussing the admissibility of expert testimony that pointed to particular factors that make eyewitness testimony unreliable. On remand, the district court rejected the proffered expert testimony on the ground of "fit" because it found that factors discussed by the expert, such as the high likelihood of inaccurate cross-racial identifications, were not present in the case. United States v. Downing, 609 F. Supp. 784, 791–92 (E.D. Pa. 1985), *aff'd*, 780 F.2d 1017 (3d Cir. 1985).

12. Commentators have faulted the Court for using the label "reliability" to refer to the concept that scientists term "validity." The Court's choice of language was deliberate. It acknowledged that scientists typically distinguish between validity and reliability and that "[i]n a case involving scientific evidence, evidentiary reliability will be based upon scientific validity." Daubert v. Merrell Dow Pharms., Inc., 509 U.S. 579, 590 n.9 (1993). However, the Court also explained that by its reference to evidentiary reliability, it meant trustworthiness, as that concept is used elsewhere in the Federal Rules of Evidence. *Id.*

13. *Id.* at 590.

14. *Id.* at 594.

15. *Id.* at 593–94. "[W]e do not presume to set out a definitive checklist or test." *Id.* at 593.

16. *Id.* at 593 (quoting Michael D. Green, *Expert Witnesses and Sufficiency of Evidence in Toxic Substances Litigation: The Legacy of Agent Orange and Bendectin Litigation*, 86 Nw. U. L. Rev. 643, 645 (1992)).

17. *Id.* at 593–94.

eral acceptance of the methodology within the scientific community is no longer dispositive, it remains a factor to be considered.[18]

The Court did not apply its new test to the eight experts for the plaintiffs who sought to testify on the basis of in vitro, animal, and epidemiological studies that the drug Bendectin taken by the plaintiffs' mothers during pregnancy could cause or had caused the plaintiffs' birth defects. Instead, it reversed the decision and remanded the case. Nor did the Court deal with any of the procedural issues raised by the *Daubert* opinion, such as the burden, if any, on the party that seeks a ruling excluding expert testimony, or the standard of review on appeal.[19]

B. General Electric Co. v. Joiner

The Supreme Court granted certiorari in *General Electric Co. v. Joiner,*[20] the second case in the trilogy, in order to determine the appropriate standard an appellate court should apply in reviewing a trial court's *Daubert* decision to admit or exclude scientific expert testimony. In *Joiner,* the 37-year-old plaintiff, a longtime smoker with a family history of lung cancer, claimed that exposure to polychlorinated biphenyls (PCBs) and their derivatives had promoted the development of his small-cell lung cancer. The trial court applied the *Daubert* criteria, excluded the opinions of the plaintiff's experts, and granted the defendants' motion for summary judgment.[21] The court of appeals reversed the decision, stating that "[b]ecause the Federal Rules of Evidence governing expert testimony display a preference for admissibility, we apply a particularly stringent standard of review to the trial judge's exclusion of expert testimony."[22]

All the justices joined Chief Justice Rehnquist in holding that abuse of discretion is the correct standard for an appellate court to apply in reviewing a district court's evidentiary ruling, regardless of whether the ruling allowed or excluded expert testimony.[23] The Court unequivocally rejected the suggestion that a more stringent standard is permissible when the ruling, as in *Joiner,* is "outcome determinative."[24] In a concurring opinion, Justice Breyer urged judges to avail themselves of techniques, such as the use of court-appointed experts,

18. *Id.* at 594.

19. The Ninth Circuit panel thereafter found that the experts had been properly excluded and affirmed the grant of summary judgment dismissing the plaintiffs' case. Daubert v. Merrell Dow Pharms., Inc., 43 F.3d 1311 (9th Cir. 1995).

20. 522 U.S. 136 (1997).

21. Joiner v. General Elec. Co., 864 F. Supp. 1310 (N.D. Ga. 1994).

22. Joiner v. General Elec. Co., 78 F.3d 524, 529 (11th Cir. 1996).

23. General Elec. Co. v. Joiner, 522 U.S. at 141–43.

24. *Id.* at 142–43.

that would assist them in making determinations about the admissibility of complex scientific or technical evidence.[25]

With the exception of Justice Stevens, who dissented from this part of the opinion, the justices then did what they had not done in *Daubert*—they examined the record, found that the plaintiff's experts had been properly excluded, and reversed the decision without remanding the case as to this issue.[26] The Court concluded that it was within the district court's discretion to find that the statements of the plaintiff's experts with regard to causation were nothing more than speculation. The Court noted that the plaintiff never explained "how and why the experts could have extrapolated their opinions"[27] from animal studies far removed from the circumstances of the plaintiff's exposure.[28] It also observed that the district court could find that the four epidemiological studies the plaintiff relied on were insufficient as a basis for his experts' opinions.[29] Consequently, the court of appeals had erred in reversing the district court's determination that the studies relied on by the plaintiff's experts "were not sufficient, whether individually or in combination, to support their conclusions that Joiner's exposure to PCBs contributed to his cancer."[30]

The plaintiff in *Joiner* had argued that the epidemiological studies showed a link between PCBs and cancer if the results of all the studies were pooled, and that this weight-of-the-evidence methodology was reliable. Therefore, according to the plaintiff, the district court erred when it excluded a conclusion based on a scientifically reliable methodology because it thereby violated the Court's precept in *Daubert* that the "'focus, of course, must be solely on principles and

25. *Id.* at 147–50. Justice Breyer also mentioned narrowing the scientific issues in dispute at Rule 16 pretrial conferences, examining proposed experts at pretrial hearings, and appointing special masters and specially trained law clerks. *Id.*

26. *Id.* at 143–47. Justice Stevens expressed doubt as to whether the admissibility question had been adequately briefed, and in any event, he thought that the record could be studied more efficiently by the court of appeals than by the Supreme Court. *Id.* at 150–51. In addition, he expressed concern about how the Court applied the *Daubert* test to the reliability ruling by the trial judge. *Id.* at 151. *See infra* text accompanying note 32.

27. *Id.* at 144.

28. The studies involved infant mice that had massive doses of PCBs injected directly into their bodies; Joiner was an adult who was exposed to fluids containing far lower concentrations of PCBs. The infant mice developed a different type of cancer than Joiner did, and no animal studies showed that adult mice exposed to PCBs developed cancer or that PCBs lead to cancer in other animal species. *Id.*

29. The authors of the first study of workers at an Italian plant found lung cancer rates among ex-employees somewhat higher than might have been expected but refused to conclude that PCBs had caused the excess rate. A second study of workers at a PCB production plant did not find the somewhat higher than expected incidence of lung cancer deaths to be statistically significant. The third study made no mention of exposure to PCBs, and the workers in the fourth study who had a significant increase in lung cancer rates had also been exposed to numerous other potential carcinogens. *Id.* at 145–46.

30. *Id.* at 146–47.

methodology, not on the conclusions that they generate.'"[31] The Supreme Court responded to this argument by stating that

> conclusions and methodology are not entirely distinct from one another. Trained experts commonly extrapolate from existing data. But nothing in either *Daubert* or the Federal Rules of Evidence requires a district court to admit opinion evidence which is connected to existing data only by the ipse dixit of the expert. A court may conclude that there is simply too great an analytical gap between the data and the opinion proffered.[32]

Justice Stevens, in his partial dissent, assumed that the plaintiff's expert was entitled to rely on such a methodology, which he noted is often used in risk assessment, and that a district court that admits expert testimony based on a weight-of-the-evidence methodology does not abuse its discretion.[33] Justice Stevens would have remanded the case for the court below to determine if the trial court had abused its discretion when it excluded the plaintiff's experts.[34]

III. *Kumho Tire Co. v. Carmichael*

A. The District Court Opinion

Less than one year after deciding *Joiner*, the Supreme Court granted certiorari in *Kumho*[35] to decide if the trial judge's gatekeeping obligation under *Daubert* applies only to scientific evidence or if it extends to proffers of "technical, or other specialized knowledge," the other categories of expertise specified in Federal Rule of Evidence 702. A split had developed in the circuits on this issue. In addition, there was uncertainty about whether disciplines like economics, psychology, and other "soft" sciences counted as science; when the four factors endorsed in *Daubert* as indicators of reliability had to be applied; and how experience factors into the gatekeeping process. Although Rule 702 specifies that an expert may be qualified through experience, the Court's emphasis in *Daubert* on "testability" suggested that an expert should not be allowed to base a conclusion solely on experience if the conclusion can easily be tested.

In *Kumho*, the plaintiffs brought suit after a tire blew out on a minivan, causing an accident in which one passenger died and others were seriously injured. The tire, which was manufactured in 1988, had been installed on the minivan

31. *Id.* at 146 (quoting Daubert v. Merrell Dow Pharms., Inc., 509 U.S. 579, 595 (1993)).
32. *Id.* at 146.
33. *Id.* at 153–54.
34. *Id.* at 150–51.
35. Carmichael v. Samyang Tire, Inc., 131 F.3d 1433 (11th Cir. 1997), *cert. granted sub nom.* Kumho Tire Co. v. Carmichael, 118 S. Ct. 2339 (1998), *and rev'd,* 119 S. Ct. 1167 (1999).

sometime before it was purchased as a used car by the plaintiffs in 1993. In their diversity action against the tire's maker and its distributor, the plaintiffs claimed that the tire was defective. To support this allegation, the plaintiffs relied primarily on deposition testimony by Dennis Carlson, Jr., an expert in tire-failure analysis, who concluded on the basis of a visual inspection of the tire that the blowout was caused by a defect in the tire's manufacture or design.

When the defendant moved to exclude Carlson's testimony, the district court agreed with the defendant that the *Daubert* gatekeeping obligation applied not only to scientific knowledge but also to "'technical analyses.'"[36] Therefore, the district court examined Carlson's visual-inspection methodology in light of the four factors mentioned in *Daubert*—the theory's testability, whether it was the subject of peer review or publication, its known or potential rate of error, and its general acceptance within the relevant scientific community.[37] After concluding that none of the *Daubert* factors was satisfied, the court excluded Carlson's testimony and granted the defendant's motion for summary judgment.[38]

The plaintiffs asked for reconsideration, arguing that the court's application of the *Daubert* factors was too inflexible. The court granted the plaintiffs' request for reconsideration, and agreed that it had erred in treating the four factors as mandatory rather than illustrative.[39] But the plaintiffs were not aided by this concession, because the court went on to say:

> In this case, application of the *Daubert* factors did operate to gauge the reliability of Carlson's methods, and all of the factors indicated that his testimony was properly excluded. The Court's analysis revealed no countervailing factors operating in favor of admissibility which could outweigh those identified in *Daubert*, and the parties identified no such factors in their briefs. Contrary to plaintiffs' assertions, the Court did not convert the flexible *Daubert* inquiry into a rigid one; rather, the Court simply found the *Daubert* factors appropriate, analyzed them, and discerned no competing criteria sufficiently strong to outweigh them.[40]

The district court then reaffirmed its earlier order, excluding Carlson's expert testimony and granting summary judgment.[41]

36. Carmichael v. Samyang Tire, Inc., 923 F. Supp. 1514, 1522 (S.D. Ala. 1996) ("The plaintiffs may be correct that Carlson's testimony does not concern a scientific concept per se; however, it certainly is testimony about an application of scientific concepts involved in physics, chemistry, and mechanical engineering. In other words, Carlson's method is necessarily ground in some scientific foundation . . . ."), *rev'd*, 131 F.3d 1433 (11th Cir. 1997), *cert. granted sub nom.* Kumho Tire Co. v. Carmichael, 118 S. Ct. 2339 (1998), *and rev'd*, 119 S. Ct. 1167 (1999).

37. *Id.* at 1520–21.

38. *Id.* at 1522, 1524.

39. Carmichael v. Samyang Tires, Inc., Civ. Action No. 93-0860-CB-S (S.D. Ala., June 5, 1996), App. to Pet. for Cert. at 1c (order granting motion for reconsideration discussed in *Kumho*, 119 S. Ct. at 1173).

40. *Id.*

41. *Id.*

B. The Court of Appeals Opinion

The Eleventh Circuit reversed the district court's decision in *Kumho,* holding, as a matter of law under a de novo standard of review, that *Daubert* applies only in the scientific context.[42] The court of appeals opinion stressed the difference between expert testimony that relies on the application of scientific theories or principles—which would be subject to a *Daubert* analysis—and testimony that is based on the expert's "skill- or experience-based observation."[43] The court then found

> that Carlson's testimony is non-scientific . . . . Carlson makes no pretense of basing his opinion on any scientific theory of physics or chemistry. Instead, Carlson rests his opinion on his experience in analyzing failed tires. After years of looking at the mangled carcasses of blown-out tires, Carlson claims that he can identify telltale markings revealing whether a tire failed because of abuse or defect. Like a beekeeper who claims to have learned through years of observation that his charges always take flight into the wind, Carlson maintains that his experiences in analyzing tires have taught him what "bead grooves" and "sidewall deterioration" indicate as to the cause of a tire's failure. . . . Thus, we conclude that Carlson's testimony falls outside the scope of *Daubert* and that the district court erred as a matter of law by applying *Daubert* in this case.[44]

The Eleventh Circuit did not, however, conclude that Carlson's testimony was admissible. Instead, it directed the district court on remand "to determine if Carlson's testimony is sufficiently reliable and relevant to assist a jury."[45] In other words, the circuit court agreed that the trial court has a gatekeeping obligation; its quarrel with the district court was over that court's assumption that *Daubert*'s four factors had to be considered.

C. The Supreme Court Opinion

All the justices of the Supreme Court, in an opinion by Justice Breyer, held that the trial court's gatekeeping obligation extends to all expert testimony[46] and unanimously rejected the Eleventh Circuit's dichotomy between the expert who "'relies on the application of scientific principles'" and the expert who relies on

42. Carmichael v. Samyang Tire, Inc., 131 F.3d 1433, 1435 (11th Cir. 1997), *cert. granted sub nom.* Kumho Tire Co. v. Carmichael, 118 S. Ct. 2339 (1998), *and rev'd,* 119 S. Ct. 1167 (1999).

43. *Id.* at 1435.

44. *Id.* at 1436 (footnotes omitted).

45. *Id.* The court noted that the defendant had raised "a number of potentially troubling criticisms of Carlson's alleged expertise and methodology, including his rendering of an opinion regarding the Carmichaels' tire before he had personally inspected its carcass." *Id.* at 1436–37.

46. Kumho Tire Co. v. Carmichael, 119 S. Ct. 1167, 1171 (1999) ("*Daubert*'s general holding—setting forth the trial judge's general 'gatekeeping' obligation—applies not only to testimony based on 'scientific' knowledge, but also to testimony based on 'technical' and 'other specialized' knowledge.").

"'skill- or experience-based observation.'"[47] The Court noted that Federal Rule of Evidence 702 "makes no relevant distinction between 'scientific' knowledge and 'technical' or 'other specialized' knowledge," and "applies its reliability standard to all . . . matters within its scope."[48] Furthermore, said the Court, "no clear line" can be drawn between the different kinds of knowledge,[49] and "no one denies that an expert might draw a conclusion from a set of observations based on extensive and specialized experience."[50]

The Court also unanimously found that the court of appeals had erred when it used a de novo standard, instead of the *Joiner* abuse-of-discretion standard, to determine that *Daubert*'s criteria were not reasonable measures of the reliability of Carlson's testimony.[51] As in *Joiner*, and again over the dissent of Justice Stevens,[52] the Court then examined the record and concluded that the trial court had not abused its discretion when it excluded Carlson's testimony. Accordingly, it reversed the opinion of the Eleventh Circuit.

The opinion adopts a flexible approach that stresses the importance of identifying "the particular circumstances of the particular case at issue."[53] The court must then make sure that the proffered expert will observe the same standard of "intellectual rigor" in testifying as he or she would employ when dealing with similar matters outside the courtroom.[54]

The crux of the disagreement between the parties was whether extending the trial judge's *Daubert* gatekeeping function to all forms of expert testimony meant that the trial judge would have to apply *Daubert*'s four-factor reliability test in all cases. The defendant had stated at oral argument that the factors discussed in

47. *Id.* at 1176 (quoting Carmichael v. Samyang Tire, Inc., 131 F.3d 1433, 1435 (11th Cir. 1997), *cert. granted sub nom.* Kumho Tire Co. v. Carmichael, 118 S. Ct. 2339 (1998), *and rev'd,* 119 S. Ct. 1167 (1999)). "We do not believe that Rule 702 creates a schematism that segregates expertise by type while mapping certain kinds of questions to certain kinds of experts. Life and the legal cases that it generates are too complex to warrant so definitive a match." *Id.*

48. *Id.* at 1174.

49. *Id.*

50. *Id.* at 1178.

51. *Id.* at 1171 ("the law grants a district court the same broad latitude when it decides *how* to determine reliability as it enjoys in respect to its ultimate reliability determination" (citing General Elec. Co. v. Joiner, 522 U.S. 136, 143 (1997))).

52. Justice Stevens objected that this question had not been raised by the certiorari petition and would have remanded the case to the court of appeals for a review of the record. *Id.* at 1180. He noted, however, that he did "not feel qualified to disagree with the well-reasoned factual analysis" of the question in Part III of the Court's opinion. *Id.*

53. *Id.* at 1175. "In sum, Rule 702 grants the district judge the discretionary authority, reviewable for its abuse, to determine reliability in light of the particular facts and circumstances of the particular case." *Id.* at 1179.

54. *Id.* at 1176.

Daubert were "always relevant."[55] Justice Breyer's opinion rejects this notion categorically:

> The conclusion, in our view, is that we can neither rule out, nor rule in, for all cases and for all time the applicability of the factors mentioned in *Daubert*, nor can we now do so for subsets of cases categorized by category of expert or by kind of evidence. Too much depends upon the particular circumstances of the particular case at issue.[56]

The *Daubert* factors "*may*" bear on a judge's gatekeeping determinations, however.[57] The four *Daubert* factors "'may or may not be pertinent'"; it will all depend "'on the nature of the issue, the expert's particular expertise, and the subject of his testimony.'"[58] Determining which factors are indicative of reliability in a particular case cannot be accomplished solely by categorical a priori characterizations about the particular field in question. The Court explained: "Engineering testimony rests upon scientific foundations, the reliability of which will be at issue in some cases. . . . In other cases, the relevant reliability concerns may focus upon personal knowledge or experience."[59] In all cases, a court must exercise its gatekeeping obligation so that the expert, whether relying on "professional studies or personal experience," will, when testifying, employ "the same level of intellectual rigor" that the expert would use outside the courtroom when working in the relevant discipline.[60]

How this extremely flexible approach of the Court is to be applied emerges in Part III of the opinion when the Court engages in a remarkably detailed analysis of the record that illustrates its comment in *Joiner* that an expert must account for "how and why" he or she reached the challenged opinion.[61] The Court refused to find that the methodology Carlson was advocating could never be used by an expert testifying about tire failures:

> [C]ontrary to respondents' suggestion, the specific issue before the court was not the reasonableness in general of a tire expert's use of a visual and tactile inspection to determine whether overdeflection had caused the tire's tread to separate from its steel-belted carcass. Rather, it was the reasonableness of using such an approach, along with Carlson's particular

55. *See* Official Transcript at 11–16, Kumho Tire Co. v. Carmichael, 119 S. Ct. 1167 (1999) (No. 97-1709). Counsel for petitioner, after a series of questions based on the *Daubert* standards, finally responded by saying, "The questions are always relevant, absolutely. That's our point." *Id.* at 16.

56. *Kumho,* 119 S. Ct. at 1175. Indeed, as is discussed further below, the Court stated that the *Daubert* factors "do not all necessarily apply even in every instance in which the reliability of scientific testimony is challenged." *Id.*

57. *Id.* The Court answered the question of whether the four specific *Daubert* questions may be considered by replying: "Emphasizing the word 'may' in the question, we answer that question yes." *Id.*

58. *Id.* (quoting Brief for United States as *Amicus Curiae* Supporting Petitioners at 19, Kumho Tire Co. v. Carmichael, 119 S. Ct. 1167 (1999) (No. 97-1709)).

59. *Id.*

60. *Id.* at 1176.

61. *See supra* note 27 and accompanying text.

> method of analyzing the data thereby obtained, to draw a conclusion regarding the particular matter to which the expert testimony was directly relevant. That matter concerned the likelihood that a defect in the tire at issue caused its tread to separate from its carcass.[62]

The Court then discussed numerous case-specific facts that made it reasonable for the district court to conclude in this case that Carlson's testimony was not reliable because "[i]t fell outside the range where experts might reasonably differ, and where the jury must decide among the conflicting views of different experts, even though the evidence is 'shaky.'"[63] The tire was old and repaired, some of its treads "had been worn bald," and Carlson had conceded that it should have been replaced.[64] Furthermore, although Carlson claimed that he could determine by a visual and tactile inspection when a tire had not been abused, thereby leading him to conclude that it was defective, the tire in question showed some of the very marks that Carlson had identified as pointing to abuse through overdeflection.[65] Perhaps even more troublesome to the Court was the fact that

> the expert could not say whether the tire had traveled more than 10, or 20, or 30, or 40, or 50 thousand miles, adding that 6,000 miles was "about how far" he could "say with any certainty." The [district] court could reasonably have wondered about the reliability of a method of visual and tactile inspection sufficiently precise to ascertain with some certainty the abuse-related significance of minute shoulder/center relative tread wear differences, but insufficiently precise to tell "with any certainty" from the tread wear whether a tire had traveled less than 10,000 or more than 50,000 miles.[66]

The Court further noted that the district court's confidence in Carlson's methodology might also have been lessened by "Carlson's repeated reliance on the 'subjectiveness' of his mode of analysis" when questioned about his ability to differentiate between an overdeflected tire and a tire that looks overdeflected,[67] and by the fact that Carlson had called the tire defective after looking at photographs of it and before he ever inspected it.[68] Finally, the Court remarked that there is no indication in the record that other experts, papers, or articles support Carlson's theory,[69] and that "no one has argued that Carlson himself, were he still working for Michelin, would have concluded in a report to his employer that a similar tire was similarly defective on grounds identical to those upon which he rested his conclusion here."[70]

62. *Kumho,* 119 S. Ct. at 1177.
63. *Id.* (quoting Daubert v. Merrell Dow Pharms., Inc., 509 U.S. 579, 596 (1993)).
64. *Id.*
65. *Id.*
66. *Id.* (citation omitted).
67. *Id.*
68. *Id.*
69. *Id.* at 1178.
70. *Id.* at 1179.

IV. The Implications of the *Kumho* Opinion

A. A Comparison of Kumho *and* Daubert

1. Differences in emphasis between Daubert *and* Kumho

Nothing the Supreme Court said in *Kumho* is explicitly inconsistent with what it said in *Daubert.* As Justice Breyer's opinion stated, *Daubert* described "the Rule 702 inquiry as 'a flexible one,'"[71] and made "clear that the factors it mentions do not constitute a 'definitive checklist or test.'"[72] Nevertheless, *Kumho* may indicate that the Court has somewhat backed away from laying down guidelines for particular categories of expert testimony. Certainly the Court's opinion does not support those who construed *Daubert* as creating a four-factor test for scientific evidence, or those who thought that the Court might in subsequent cases articulate classification schemes for other fields of expertise.[73]

The Court seems less absorbed in epistemological issues, in formulating general rules for assessing reliability, or in fleshing out the implications of its having singled out testability as the preeminent factor of concern. It appears less interested in a taxonomy of expertise and more concerned about directing judges to concentrate on "the particular circumstances of the particular case at issue."[74] This flexible, nondoctrinaire approach is faithful to the intention of the drafters of the Federal Rules of Evidence, who viewed Article VII as setting forth flexible standards for courts to apply rather than rigid rules.

In *Kumho,* the Court contemplated that there will be witnesses "whose expertise is based purely on experience," and although it suggested that *Daubert*'s questions may be helpful in evaluating experience-based testimony, it did not single out testability as the preeminent factor of concern, as it did in *Daubert.*[75] The Court offered the example of the "perfume tester able to distinguish among

71. *Id.* at 1175 (quoting Daubert v. Merrell Dow Pharms., Inc., 509 U.S. 579, 594 (1993)).

72. *Id.* (quoting *Daubert,* 509 U.S. at 593).

73. Arvin Maskin, *The Impact of* Daubert *on the Admissibility of Scientific Evidence: The Supreme Court Catches Up with a Decade of Jurisprudence,* 15 Cardozo L. Rev. 1929, 1934 (1994) ("some courts are applying the four factors as if they were the definitive checklist or test."); Bert Black et al., *Science and the Law in the Wake of* Daubert*: A New Search for Scientific Knowledge,* 72 Tex. L. Rev. 715, 751 (1994) ("Some commentators have read these observations as essentially constituting a new four-factor test . . . ."). The oversimplification of *Daubert* as embodying a four-factor test may have been furthered by commentaries that noted the nondefinitive nature of the factors but used them to organize their discussion. *See* 1 Modern Scientific Evidence, *supra* note 4, § 1-3.3. The 1999 Pocket Part added a new § 1-3.4[2], *The Four-Factors of* Daubert.

74. *Kumho,* 119 S. Ct. at 1175. The Court expressed agreement with the Brief of the Solicitor General that the factors to use in making reliability determinations will depend "'on the nature of the issue, the expert's particular expertise, and the subject of his testimony.'" *Id.* (quoting Brief for the United States as *Amicus Curiae* Supporting Petitioners at 19, Kumho Tire Co. v. Carmichael, 119 S. Ct. 1167 (1999) (No. 97-1709)).

75. *Id.* at 1176.

140 odors at a sniff" and stated that at times it will "be useful" to ask such a witness "whether his preparation is of a kind that others in the field would recognize as acceptable."[76] However, this is somewhat different, and much less rigid, than conditioning testimony by perfume testers on objective standards that establish whether perfume testers can do what they claim to be able to do.

It may also be significant that in *Kumho* the Court was silent about the distinction between admissibility and sufficiency. In the interim between *Daubert* and *Kumho,* disputes involving expert testimony have increasingly been addressed as questions of admissibility. Because *Daubert* requires judges to screen expert testimony, civil defendants make *Daubert* motions to exclude plaintiff's experts prior to trial instead of waiting to move for judgment as a matter of law if the verdict is unfavorable. Such an approach furthers both case-processing efficiency and economy, as the in limine exclusion of expert proof may eliminate the need for trial by making possible a grant of summary judgment.

In *Daubert,* the Court observed that when expert testimony is admitted, the trial court "remains free to direct a judgment" if it concludes "that the scintilla of evidence presented" is insufficient.[77] The Court did not contemplate that a district judge could exclude testimony that meets the "scintilla" standard if the judge concludes that the proponent will not be able to meet its burden of persuasion on the issue to which the testimony relates. Nevertheless, the benefits of economy and efficiency that accrue when expert proof is considered in the context of admissibility determinations may tempt courts to consider sufficiency when ruling on admissibility.[78] Moreover, some opinions have held that the "fit" prong of the *Daubert* test and the helpfulness standard of Rule 702 require courts to exclude a plaintiff's expert testimony that does not satisfy the plaintiff's substantive burden of proof on an issue.[79] In *Kumho,* the Supreme Court showed no discomfort with this trend toward assessing issues regarding expert proof through admissibility determinations; there is no reminder, as there is in *Daubert,*

76. *Id.*

77. Daubert v. Merrell Dow Pharms., Inc., 509 U.S. 579, 596 (1993).

78. In his book on the Bendectin litigation, Joseph Sanders suggests that such decisions may "undermine a sophisticated approach to the question of scientific validity" and become troublesome precedents in cases in which the issue in dispute is considerably closer. Joseph Sanders, Bendectin on Trial: A Study of Mass Tort Litigation 195 (1998).

79. *See, e.g.,* Daubert v. Merrell Dow Pharms., Inc., 43 F.3d 1311, 1320 (9th Cir.) *(Daubert* on remand) ("In assessing whether the proffered expert testimony 'will assist the trier of fact' in resolving this issue, we must look to the governing substantive standard, which in this case is supplied by California tort law."), *cert. denied,* 516 U.S. 869 (1995); Hall v. Baxter Healthcare Corp., 947 F. Supp. 1387, 1398 (D. Or. 1996) ("Under Oregon law, the plaintiffs in this litigation must prove not merely the possibility of a causal connection between breast implants and the alleged systemic disease, but the medical probability of a causal connection.").

that if the admissibility test is satisfied, questions of sufficiency remain open for resolution at trial.[80]

2. The role of "general acceptance" and the "intellectual rigor" test

Some early comments predicted that *Kumho* may result in a retreat from *Daubert* and a resurrection of *Frye* because *Kumho*'s flexible approach and abuse-of-discretion standard authorize trial courts to rely on "general acceptance" as the chief screening factor.[81] Such an effect certainly does not seem to have been intended by the Court. The enormous detail with which Justice Breyer described steel-belted radial tires like the Carmichael tire (a sketch is appended to the opinion), the particular characteristics of the ill-fated tire, and Carlson's proposed testimony would all have been unnecessary if the Court's only consideration was "general acceptance." All the Court would have needed to say was that workers in the tire industry did not use Carlson's approach.[82] Although the Court in *Kumho* endorsed an extremely flexible test, it manifested no inclination to return to *Frye*.

This misunderstanding about the role of "general acceptance" may have been enhanced by a passage in which the Court acknowledged the significance of the *Daubert* gatekeeping requirement:

> The objective of that requirement is to ensure the reliability and relevancy of expert testimony. It is to make certain that an expert, whether basing testimony upon professional studies or personal experience, employs in the courtroom the same level of intellectual rigor that characterizes the practice of an expert in the relevant field.[83]

This reference to "the same level of intellectual rigor that characterizes the practice of an expert in the relevant field" is not synonymous with *Frye*'s insistence on "general acceptance" of "the thing from which the deduction is made . . . in the particular field in which it belongs."[84] The difference between these

80. It should also be noted that as of this writing, a proposed amendment to Rule 702 is pending before the Judicial Conference. It would require expert testimony to be "based upon sufficient facts or data." A possible interpretation of this phrase is that the expert's testimony may be excluded if it would not suffice to meet the profferor's burden of persuasion on an issue. The advisory committee notes accompanying the amendment include the following clarification: "The emphasis in the amendment on 'sufficient facts or data' is not intended to authorize a trial court to exclude an expert's testimony on the ground that the court believes one version of the facts and not the other."

81. *See, e.g.*, Michael Hoenig, *New York "Gatekeeping": "*Frye*" and "*Daubert*" Coexist,* N.Y. L.J., July 12, 1999, at 3 ("Kumho Tire says the general acceptance standard could be pivotal for trial judges even when non-science or experience-based expert testimony is proffered."); Joseph F. Madonia, Kumho Tire *Steers New Course on Expert-Witness Testimony*, Chi. Daily L. Bull., July 2, 1999, at 5 ("Thus, while superficially appearing to extend *Daubert* to an additional class of expert witnesses, *Kumho Tire* could just as easily end up being an excuse for courts to avoid *Daubert* altogether.").

82. *See supra* note 70 and accompanying text.

83. Kumho Tire Co. v. Carmichael, 119 S. Ct. 1167, 1176 (1999).

84. Frye v. United States, 293 F. 1013, 1014 (D.C. Cir. 1923).

two formulas—which epitomizes the contrast between *Daubert* and *Frye*—becomes apparent if one looks at two Seventh Circuit opinions by Chief Judge Posner in which the "intellectual rigor" standard was first employed.

In *Rosen v. Ciba-Geigy Corp.*,[85] the plaintiff, a heavy smoker with a history of serious heart disease, sued the manufacturer of a nicotine patch that his physician had prescribed in the hope of breaking the plaintiff's cigarette habit. The plaintiff continued to smoke while wearing the patch, despite having been told to stop, and he suffered a heart attack on the third day of wearing the patch.

The district court dismissed the action, after excluding testimony by the plaintiff's cardiologist, Dr. Harry Fozzard, a distinguished department head at the University of Chicago, whose opinion was that the nicotine patch precipitated the heart attack. The court of appeals affirmed the decision. Chief Judge Posner stated that *Daubert*'s object "was to make sure that when scientists testify in court they adhere to the same standards of intellectual rigor that are demanded in their professional work,"[86] and he went on to explain why the district judge had rightly concluded that the cardiologist's proposed testimony did not meet this standard:

> Wearing a nicotine patch for three days, like smoking for three days, is not going to have a significant long-run effect on coronary artery disease; that much is clear. In the long, gradual progression of Rosen's coronary artery disease those three days were a blink of the eye. The patch could have had no significance for Rosen's health, therefore, unless it precipitated his heart attack in June of 1992. That is an entirely different question from whether nicotine, or cigarettes, are bad for one's arteries.
>
> . . . Nowhere in Fozzard's deposition is there an explanation of how a nicotine overdose (for remember that Rosen was smoking at the same time that he was wearing the patch) can precipitate a heart attack, or a reference to a medical or other scientific literature in which such an effect of nicotine is identified and tested. Since Fozzard is a distinguished cardiologist, his conjecture that nicotine can have this effect and may well have had it on Rosen is worthy of careful attention, even though he has not himself done research on the effects of nicotine. But the courtroom is not the place for scientific guesswork, even of the inspired sort. Law lags science; it does not lead it. There may be evidence to back up Fozzard's claim, but none was presented to the district court.[87]

The difference between the "intellectual rigor" standard and the "general acceptance" standard is revealed even more clearly in *Braun v. Lorillard, Inc.*[88] In *Braun*, the plaintiff, who had mesothelioma, sued the manufacturer of his brand of cigarettes on the ground that crocidolite asbestos fibers in the cigarettes' filters had caused his illness. The plaintiff died before trial, and his attorney sought to introduce expert testimony that crocidolite asbestos fibers, the type of asbestos

85. 78 F.3d 316 (7th Cir.), *cert. denied*, 519 U.S. 819 (1996).
86. *Id.* at 318.
87. *Id.* at 319.
88. 84 F.3d 230 (7th Cir.), *cert. denied*, 519 U.S. 992 (1996).

fibers most likely to cause mesothelioma, were found in the decedent's lung tissues. The plaintiff's expert, Schwartz, regularly tested building materials; he had never tested human or animal tissues for the presence of asbestos fibers, or any other substance, before he was hired by the plaintiff's lawyers. The expert was hired after the plaintiff's original experts, who regularly tested human tissue, found nothing. The district court refused to permit testimony at trial concerning the presence of crocidolite asbestos fibers, and the court of appeals affirmed the decision. Chief Judge Posner explained that the Supreme Court in *Daubert* held

> that the opinion evidence of reputable scientists is admissible in evidence in a federal trial even if the particular methods they used in arriving at their opinion are not yet accepted as canonical in their branch of the scientific community. But that is only part of the holding of *Daubert*.[89]

After quoting the "intellectual rigor" test articulated in *Rosen*, Judge Posner stated that "[t]he scientific witness who decides to depart from the canonical methods must have grounds for doing so that are consistent with the methods and usages of his scientific community."[90] That this is a different requirement than the *Frye* test is shown by the sentences in the opinion that immediately follow:

> The district judge did remark at one point that *Daubert* requires that the expert's method be one "customarily relied upon by the relevant scientific community," which is incorrect. But she did not rest her decision to exclude his testimony on that ground. Her ground was that Schwartz had testified "that he really didn't have any knowledge of the methodology that should be employed, and he still doesn't have any information regarding the methodology that should be employed with respect to lung tissue. It seems to me that this witness knows absolutely nothing about analyzing lung tissue and [for?] asbestos fibers."[91]

The court explained further:

> If, therefore, an expert proposes to depart from the generally accepted methodology of his field and embark upon a sea of scientific uncertainty, the court may appropriately insist that he ground his departure in demonstrable and scrupulous adherence to the scientist's creed of meticulous and objective inquiry. To forsake the accepted methods without even inquiring *why* they are the accepted methods—in this case, why specialists in testing human tissues for asbestos fibers have never used the familiar high temperature ashing method—and without even knowing *what* the accepted methods are, strikes us, as it struck Judge Manning, as irresponsible.[92]

It is not enough, therefore, under the "intellectual rigor" test for experts to venture hunches that they would never express or act upon in their everyday

89. *Id.* at 234.
90. *Id.*
91. *Id.*
92. *Id.* at 235.

working lives. Experts must show that their conclusions were reached by methods that are consistent with how their colleagues in the relevant field or discipline would proceed to establish a proposition were they presented with the same facts and issues.

Chief Judge Posner's exposition of the "intellectual rigor" test should not be read as meaning that once a "canonical method" is identified, a court may never inquire further into reliability. Clearly, in *Kumho* the Supreme Court wished to avoid the result sometimes reached under *Frye* when testimony was admitted once experts pointed to a consensus in a narrow field they had themselves established.[93] In the course of discussing the inapplicability of *Daubert* factors in every instance, the Court noted, "[n]or . . . does the presence of *Daubert*'s general acceptance factor help show that an expert's testimony is reliable where the discipline itself lacks reliability, as, for example, do theories grounded in any so-called generally accepted principles of astrology or necromancy."[94] The problem of determining when a discipline lacks reliability is discussed further below.[95]

B. *The Reaffirmation and Extension of* Joiner*'s Abuse-of-Discretion Standard*

1. *The scope of the standard*

In *Kumho*, the Supreme Court extended the *Joiner* abuse-of-discretion standard to all decisions a trial judge makes in ruling on the admissibility of expert testimony, including the procedures it selects to investigate reliability:

> Our opinion in *Joiner* makes clear that a court of appeals is to apply an abuse-of-discretion standard when "it reviews a trial court's decision to admit or exclude expert testimony." That standard applies as much to the trial court's decisions about how to determine reliability as to its ultimate conclusion. Otherwise, the trial judge would lack the discretionary authority needed both to avoid unnecessary "reliability" proceedings in ordinary cases where the reliability of an expert's methods is properly taken for granted, and to require appropriate proceedings in the less usual or more complex cases where cause for questioning the expert's reliability arises.[96]

The adoption of one standard of review for all determinations means that the abuse-of-discretion standard applies even with regard to issues that transcend

93. *See* discussion of the development of voiceprint evidence in Andre A. Moenssens, *Admissibility of Scientific Evidence—An Alternative to the* Frye *Rule*, 25 Wm. & Mary L. Rev. 545, 550 (1984) ("The trend in favor of admitting voiceprints continued until a group of lawyers discovered that, in each case, the same two or three experts had been the proponents who bestowed 'general acceptance' on the technique.").

94. Kumho Tire Co. v. Carmichael, 119 S. Ct. 1167, 1175 (1999).

95. *See infra* text accompanying notes 110–13.

96. *Kumho*, 119 S. Ct. at 1176 (citations omitted).

the particular case, such as the validity of a new DNA typing procedure or marker, or whether a particular substance is capable of causing particular diseases or injuries. Some commentators believe that it is unwise to allow conclusions about the soundness of a scientific theory or a theory's general applications to vary on a case-by-case basis; consequently, they advocate a de novo standard of review for such issues.[97] For now, however, the standard of review required by the Supreme Court is the same regardless of whether the trial court decided an issue that may be common to many different cases,[98] such as general causation, or an issue that relates only to the particular case, such as specific causation. Ultimately, of course, a court may resort to judicial notice pursuant to Federal Rule of Evidence 201 if a matter is sufficiently well established.

2. *The possibility and consequences of intracircuit and intercircuit conflict*

Since it is the trial court that is afforded this broad latitude to decide "*how* to test an expert's reliability" and "*whether* that expert's relevant testimony is reliable,"[99] in theory judges are free to select different procedures and apply different factors to a particular expert or type of expertise than their colleagues do in the same district or circuit. As a consequence, similar cases could be resolved differently on the basis of inconsistent determinations about admissibility.[100] The extent to which this will occur within circuits is not clear at this time. Even though the abuse-of-discretion standard mandates deference to the trial court, it remains to be seen to what extent the courts of appeals will acquiesce in district court rulings on the admissibility of expert testimony.

Of particular interest is whether the appellate courts will exert more supervision, and reverse more frequently, when a ruling below admits rather than excludes evidence. Justices Scalia, O'Connor, and Thomas joined in a brief concurring opinion in *Kumho* to warn that the abuse-of-discretion standard "is not discretion to abandon the gatekeeping function" or "to perform the function inadequately."[101] Because the Supreme Court docket is so limited, it is the courts of appeals that will have the final word on the proper exercise of discretion by

97. *See* 1 Modern Scientific Evidence, *supra* note 4, § 1-3.5, at 19–20 (Supp. 1999).

98. Even with regard to an issue like general causation, the evidence being introduced may well vary over time because science does not stand still. Furthermore, the issue in two individual cases may not be the same. If in Case A the court allowed the plaintiff's expert to testify on the basis of published research that the plaintiff's leukemia was caused by his 10-year exposure during childhood to Agent X, this does not necessarily mean that the plaintiff's expert in Case B should be allowed to testify that the plaintiff's leukemia was caused by a one-year exposure to Agent X when she was in her forties. The research on which the expert purports to rely still has to fit the facts of the case.

99. *Kumho*, 119 S. Ct. at 1176 (emphasis added).

100. *See, e.g.*, the discussion in text accompanying notes 126–46 *infra* about opinions on causation offered by clinical physicians.

101. *Kumho*, 119 S. Ct. at 1179. Justice Scalia's opinion continued:

trial judges in their circuits. Depending on the issue, deference to the trial court may well be exercised differently from circuit to circuit.

What is more likely than intracircuit conflicts, and indeed was possible even under *Daubert* and led to the grant of certiorari in *Kumho*, is that the courts of appeals will reach divergent conclusions about some of the unresolved issues discussed in subsection C *infra*. A consequence of the latitude endorsed by *Kumho* may be an increase in forum-shopping as plaintiffs seek a congenial circuit and a sympathetic district judge. Defendants may also engage in forum-shopping by removing cases to federal court that were originally brought in state court. Ultimately, if outcomes in federal court differ substantially from those in state court, forum-shopping may arouse *Erie* concerns about deference to state substantive policy which the courts have ignored up to now.[102] Of course, if rulings on the admissibility of expert testimony lead to different outcomes in federal cases brought under the diversity jurisdiction than in similar cases litigated in state courts, state legislatures may react by modifying the applicable substantive law on what has to be proved and thus bypass exclusionary evidentiary rulings.[103]

3. Procedures a trial judge may use in handling challenges to expert testimony

The Court explained in *Kumho* that applying the abuse-of-discretion standard to determinations of "*how* to test an expert's reliability"[104] gives the trial judge broad latitude "to decide whether or when special briefing or other proceedings are needed to investigate reliability."[105] This standard also allows the trial court to make other choices about how to respond to a request to exclude expert testimony, and to use mechanisms that would provide the court with needed information in making its relevancy and reliability determinations.

In civil cases, a court might respond to a motion in limine by refusing to undertake any reliability–relevancy determination until the movant has made a prima facie showing of specific deficiencies in the opponent's proposed testi-

> Rather, it is discretion to choose among *reasonable* means of excluding expertise that is *fausse* and science that is junky. Though, as the Court makes clear today, the *Daubert* factors are not holy writ, in a particular case the failure to apply one or another of them may be unreasonable, and hence an abuse of discretion.

Id.

102. *See* Michael H. Gottesman, *Should Federal Evidence Rules Trump State Tort Policy?: The Federalism Values* Daubert *Ignored*, 15 Cardozo L. Rev. 1837 (1994).

103. In product liability design defect cases, for instance, if courts insist on too rigorous a standard for technical experts, such as requiring absolute proof that an alternative design prototype exists, this might garner support for a less demanding consumer expectation test. *See* James A. Henderson, Jr., & Aaron D. Twerski, *Intuition and Technology in Product Design Litigation: An Essay in Proximate Causation*, 88 Geo. L.J. (forthcoming 2000).

104. *Kumho*, 119 S. Ct. at 1176 (emphasis added).

105. *Id. See* William W Schwarzer & Joe S. Cecil, Management of Expert Evidence, § IVA.A., in this manual.

mony.[106] Although the burden of persuasion with regard to showing the admissibility of expert testimony is clearly on the proponent, shifting the burden of production to the party seeking to exclude the expert testimony may at times be expeditious and economical. As the Court noted in *Kumho*, quoting from Federal Rule of Evidence 102, "the Rules seek to avoid 'unjustifiable expense and delay' as part of their search for 'truth' and the 'just determination' of proceedings."[107]

Certainly, a trial court need not hold a full pretrial hearing in every case, and, indeed, the trial judge in *Kumho* did not. However, in complex civil litigation that has the potential to affect numerous persons, the trial court may conclude that extensive evidentiary hearings are the most efficacious way for the court to inform itself about the factors it will have to take into account in ruling on admissibility. The facts of the case and the consequences of losing the in limine motion will determine the extent of the opportunity the proponent of the expert must be given to present its case.[108]

Trial judges also have discretion to avail themselves of the techniques Justice Breyer described in his concurring opinion in *Joiner*: using court-appointed experts, special masters, and specially trained law clerks, and narrowing the issues in dispute at pretrial hearings and conferences.[109]

In a criminal case in which the defense challenges the prosecution's expert testimony, a trial court may choose to proceed differently than it would in a civil case, in light of factors such as the narrower scope of discovery, the defense's lack of resources and need for expert assistance, and the government's role in developing the expertise that is now in question. As in civil cases, the court must take into account the particular facts of the case. Whatever the district court does, a clear message that emerges from the Court's remarkably detailed factual analysis in *Kumho* is that the district court must explain its choices so that the appellate court has an adequate basis for review.

C. Persistent Issues

The discussion below considers a number of difficult and recurring issues that courts have had to face in ruling on the admissibility of expert testimony. The impact of *Kumho* is considered.

106. *See generally* Margaret A. Berger, *Procedural Paradigms for Applying the* Daubert *Test*, 78 Minn. L. Rev. 1345 (1994).

107. Kumho Tire Co. v. Carmichael, 119 S. Ct. 1167, 1176 (1999) (quoting Fed. R. Evid. 102).

108. *See, e.g.*, Padillas v. Stork-Gamco, Inc., No. CIV.A.97-1853, 1999 WL 558113 (3d Cir. 1999) (trial court abused its discretion in excluding expert's report without holding an in limine hearing even though plaintiff failed to request hearing).

109. *See supra* note 25.

1. *Determining if the expert's field or discipline is reliable*

As mentioned earlier,[110] in *Kumho*, the Supreme Court anticipated that at times proffered expert testimony may have to be excluded because the field to which the expert belongs lacks reliability. However, other than singling out astrology and necromancy as examples of disciplines whose theories would not be admissible,[111] the Court offered no guidance on how a court can properly reach this conclusion.

a. Challenging an expert from a nonorthodox branch of a traditional discipline

One context in which the problem of reliability arises is when practitioners of a traditional discipline, such as medicine, find untenable claims by a nonconformist branch, such as clinical ecology. Thus far, federal courts have sided with the orthodox group and rejected the clinical ecologists' theory that environmental insults may cause people exposed to them to develop a "multiple-chemical sensitivity" that makes them hypersensitive to certain substances.[112] Since *Daubert*, decisions excluding the proposed testimony of a clinical ecologist have usually been justified on the ground that the multiple-chemical sensitivity theory has not been validated by testing. Although *Kumho* does not "rule in" testability as a factor to be considered in all cases, neither does it "rule out" testability as a reasonable criterion of reliability in an appropriate case.[113] It is unlikely, therefore, that courts will handle clinical ecologists any differently than before, unless, of course, new research substantiates their theories.

In the future, courts will have to deal with other theories put forth by nonorthodox factions in an established field. For instance, new claims resting on postulates of alternative medicine are sure to arise. It may be in this context—determining the reliability of a novel hypothesis vouched for by a splinter group of self-anointed experts whose views are not acceptable to the traditional majority—that courts will find the full range of *Daubert*'s factors most helpful.

b. Challenging the reliability of a traditional field of expertise: the forensic sciences

A somewhat different question arises when challenges are made to a field whose practitioners have in the past routinely been permitted to testify as experts. How much of an obligation does the Supreme Court's emphasis on gatekeeping place

110. *See supra* note 94 and accompanying text.

111. 119 S. Ct. at 1175.

112. *See* surveys of federal case law in Summers v. Missouri Pac. R.R. Sys., 132 F.3d 599, 603 (10th Cir. 1997); Bradley v. Brown, 42 F.3d 434, 438–39 (7th Cir. 1994); Coffin v. Orkin Exterminating Co., 20 F. Supp. 2d 107, 109–11 (D. Me. 1998).

113. *See supra* note 56 and accompanying text.

on the trial court? When, if ever, must the judge analyze proffered traditional expertise to see whether it really is capable of furnishing reliable answers to questions before the court?

In the wake of *Daubert*, with its emphasis on empirical validation, challenges to reliability have been raised with regard to numerous techniques of forensic identification, such as fingerprinting, handwriting analysis, ballistics, and bite-mark analysis. DNA typing may well be the only area of forensic identification in which research has been conducted in accordance with conventional scientific standards.[114] In other areas, experts have in large measure relied on their experience to arrive at subjective conclusions that either have not been validated or are not objectively verifiable.[115]

These post-*Daubert* challenges to forensic identification have been largely unsuccessful if looked at solely in terms of rulings on admissibility. Courts have by and large refused to exclude prosecution experts. For instance, although a number of scholars have challenged the ability of forensic document examiners to identify the author of a writing,[116] courts have permitted such experts to testify even while expressing concern about the reliability of their methodology.[117] Before *Kumho*, some courts reached this result using an approach not unlike that of the court of appeals in *Kumho:* The courts concluded that handwriting analysis is not a science, and that, therefore, *Daubert*—and the need for empirical validation—is inapplicable.[118]

That courts continued to allow forensic identification experts to testify is not, however, the whole story. It is clear that in the aftermath of *Daubert*, empirical research has begun to examine the foundation of some forensic sciences.[119] It would be a great pity if such efforts cease in the wake of *Kumho* because trial judges have discretion to admit experience-based expertise. Even though the Court's opinion clearly relieves a judge from having to apply the *Daubert* factors in a given case, it does not eliminate the fundamental requirement of "reliability." The post-*Daubert* debate on forensic techniques has identified many hypotheses that could be tested. A court has the power since the *Kumho* decision

114. *See* David H. Kaye & George F. Sensabaugh, Jr., Reference Guide on DNA Evidence, § IV.A–B, in this manual.

115. For a detailed examination of these various techniques of forensic identification, see 1 & 2 Modern Scientific Evidence, *supra* note 4, §§ 15-1.0 to 26-2.3.

116. A widely cited article by D. Michael Risinger et al., *Exorcism of Ignorance as a Proxy for Rational Knowledge: The Lessons of Handwriting Identification "Expertise,"* 137 U. Pa. L. Rev. 731 (1989), had questioned the reliability of handwriting analysis prior to *Daubert*. The Court's analysis in *Daubert* seemed tailor-made for continuing the attack.

117. *See, e.g.*, United States v. Starzecpyzel, 880 F. Supp. 1027, 1028–29 (S.D.N.Y. 1995).

118. *See* United States v. Jones, 107 F.3d 1147 (6th Cir.), *cert. denied*, 521 U.S. 1127 (1997).

119. *See* 1 & 2 Modern Scientific Evidence, *supra* note 4, §§ 1-3.4, 22-2.0 (commenting on the solicitation of research proposals on the validity of handwriting analysis by the United States Department of Justice, Office of Justice Programs, National Institute of Justice).

to decide that particular *Daubert* factors, including testability and publication, apply under "the particular circumstances of the particular case," given the significance of the issue to which the expert opinion relates and the ease with which the reliability of the expert's conclusions can be verified.[120]

If research continues and courts focus more on the particular circumstances of the case, as *Kumho* directs, they will perhaps draw more distinctions than they generally do now in ruling on the admissibility of forensic identification expertise. A court could rule, for instance, that a document examiner is capable of reaching certain conclusions but not others. In other words, the issue might be recast: rather than appraising the reliability of the field, courts would instead question the ability of experts in that field to provide relevant, reliable testimony with regard to the particular contested issue.[121]

2. *Challenging an expert's testimony to prove causation*

a. Is evidence used in risk assessment relevant?

Not surprisingly, each of the cases in the Supreme Court's trilogy involved the proof of causation in either a toxic tort or product liability case. Causation is frequently the crucial issue in these actions, which have aroused considerable controversy because they often entail enormous damage claims and huge transaction costs. Particularly in toxic tort cases, proving causation raises numerous complicated issues because the mechanisms that cause certain diseases and defects are not fully understood. Consequently, the proof of causation may differ from that offered in the traditional tort case in which the plaintiff details and explains the chain of events that produced the injury in question. In toxic tort cases in which the causal mechanism is unknown, establishing causation means providing scientific evidence from which an inference of cause and effect may be drawn. There are, however, numerous unresolved issues about the relevancy and reliability of the underlying hypotheses that link the evidence to the inference of causation.

The facts of the *Joiner* case illustrate a number of issues that arise in proving causation in toxic tort cases. Justice Stevens' separate opinion assumes that evidence that would be considered in connection with risk assessment is relevant in proving causation in a toxic tort action, although the standard of proof might be higher in a court of law.[122] Consequently, he would have found no abuse of

120. *See supra* note 74 and accompanying text.

121. This issue is also certain to arise with respect to social scientists. The split in circuits about the extent to which *Daubert* applies to the social sciences is also resolved by *Kumho* in the sense that the trial court has a gatekeeping function with regard to this type of evidence as well. However, the extent to which courts will choose to apply the *Daubert* factors to social scientists' testimony remains an open issue.

122. General Elec. Co. v. Joiner, 522 U.S. 136, 153–54 (1997) ("It is not intrinsically 'unscientific'

discretion had the district court admitted expert testimony based on a methodology used in risk assessment, such as the weight-of-evidence methodology (on which the plaintiff's expert claimed to rely), which pools all available information from many different kinds of studies, taking the quality of the studies into account.[123] Combining studies across fields is even more controversial than pooling the results of epidemiological studies in a meta-analysis, a statistical technique that some find unreliable when used in connection with observational studies.[124] Of course, even if a court has no objection to the particular methodology's relevance in proving causation, it may disagree with how it was applied in the particular case. As the Supreme Court said in *Joiner*, "nothing . . . requires a district court to admit opinion evidence which is connected to existing data only by the ipse dixit of the expert."[125]

However, not all would agree with Justice Stevens' assumption that whatever is relied upon in assessing risk is automatically relevant in proving causation in a court of law. Proof of risk and proof of causation entail somewhat different questions because risk assessment frequently calls for a cost–benefit analysis. The agency assessing risk may decide to bar a substance or product if the potential benefits are outweighed by the possibility of risks that are largely unquantifiable because of presently unknown contingencies. Consequently, risk assessors may pay heed to any evidence that points to a need for caution, rather than assess the likelihood that a causal relationship in a specific case is more likely than not.

There are therefore those who maintain that high-dose animal studies have no scientific value outside the context of risk assessment.[126] These critics claim that although such studies may point to a need for more research or extra caution, they are irrelevant and unreliable in proving causation because of the need to extrapolate from the animal species used in the study to humans, and from the high doses used in the study to the plaintiff's much lower exposure.

Both *Kumho*'s insistence on "the particular circumstances of the particular case at issue"[127] and *Joiner*'s discussion of animal studies suggest, however, that

for experienced professionals to arrive at a conclusion by weighing all available scientific evidence. . . . After all, as Joiner points out, the Environmental Protection Agency (EPA) uses the same methodology to assess risks, albeit using a somewhat different threshold than that required in a trial.") (footnote omitted) (citing Brief for Respondents at 40–41, General Elec. Co. v. Joiner, 522 U.S. 136 (1997) (No. 96-188) (quoting EPA, Guidelines for Carcinogen Risk Assessment, 51 Fed. Reg. 33992, 33996 (1986))).

123. For a discussion of the weight-of-evidence methodology and arguments supporting its use to prove causation in toxic tort cases, see Carl F. Cranor et al., *Judicial Boundary Drawing and the Need for Context-Sensitive Science in Toxic Torts after* Daubert v. Merrell Dow Pharmaceuticals, Inc., 16 Va. Envtl. L.J. 1, 67–75 (1996).

124. *See* Michael D. Green et al., Reference Guide on Epidemiology § VI, in this manual.

125. *Joiner*, 522 U.S. at 146. *See supra* text accompanying note 32.

126. *See, e.g.*, Phantom Risk: Scientific Inference and the Law 12 (Kenneth R. Foster et al. eds., 1993).

127. *See supra* note 53 and accompanying text.

the Court does not have a doctrinaire view on the risk-assessment-versus-causation debate. The Court is more interested in focusing on "how and why" causation could be inferred from the particular evidence being proffered than in formulating per se rules about the admissibility or inadmissibility of categories of evidence to prove causation. In *Joiner,* the district court had refused to allow the plaintiff's experts to testify on the basis of animal studies because the studies varied so substantially from the facts of Joiner's exposure. They had been done with infant mice, who had been injected with much higher doses of PCBs than those in the fluids the plaintiff had been exposed to at work, and the mice developed a different type of cancer than the plaintiff did. The Supreme Court stated that Joiner failed to explain how the experts could have extrapolated from these results, and instead chose "'to proceed as if the only issue [was] whether animal studies can ever be a proper foundation for an expert's opinion.'"[128] The Supreme Court said that "[o]f course . . . was not the issue.[129] The issue was whether these experts' opinions were sufficiently supported by the animal studies on which they purported to rely."[130]

Obviously the match between the results in the animal studies and Joiner's disease would have been closer if the studies had been conducted on adult mice who had developed tumors more similar to his. However, reliance on animal studies is always going to require some extrapolation—from animals to humans, from the high doses the subjects are given to the plaintiff's much lower exposure. Does this mean that a district court will always be justified in exercising its discretion to exclude animal studies? Would the decision of the district court in *Joiner* have been affirmed if the court had admitted the studies? How does the nature and extent of other proof of causation affect the admissibility determination? Is such a ruling appropriate if no epidemiological studies have been done and the plaintiff's proof consists almost exclusively of animal studies that match the plaintiff's circumstances far more substantially than did those in *Joiner*? In such a case, is it appropriate to exclude testimony about animal studies because the court has concluded that it would grant judgment as a matter of law on the ground of insufficiency?

b. May clinical physicians testify on the basis of differential diagnoses?

Judges disagree on whether a physician relying on the methodology of clinical medicine can provide adequate proof of causation in a toxic tort action. Recent cases in the Fifth and Third Circuits illustrate very different approaches to this issue.

128. *Joiner,* 522 U.S. at 144 (quoting Joiner v. General Elec. Co., 864 F. Supp. 1310, 1324 (N.D. Ga. 1994), *rev'd,* 78 F.3d 524 (11th Cir. 1996), *and rev'd,* 522 U.S. 136 (1997)).

129. *Id.*

130. *Id.*

In the Fifth Circuit, two single-plaintiff toxic tort cases, one decided before *Kumho* and one after it, suggest that the court will permit a medical expert to testify about causation only if sufficient proof exists that the medical establishment knows how and at what exposures the substance in question can cause the plaintiff's alleged injuries or disease. In *Black v. Food Lion, Inc.*,[131] which was decided after *Kumho*, the appellate court reversed the decision of a trial judge who admitted testimony by a medical expert that the plaintiff's fall in the defendant's grocery store had caused her to develop fibromyalgia, a syndrome characterized by chronic fatigue, insomnia, and general pain. The expert had followed the approved protocol for determining fibromyalgia, but the appellate court found that there is no known etiology for fibromyalgia, which the expert conceded.[132] It was therefore scientifically illogical, and an instance of "post-hoc propter-hoc reasoning" for the expert to conclude that the disease must have been caused by the fall because she had eliminated all other possible causes.[133] The court then stated:

> The underlying predicates of any cause-and-effect medical testimony are that medical science understands the physiological process by which a particular disease or syndrome develops and knows what factors cause the process to occur. Based on such predicate knowledge, it may then be possible to fasten legal liability for a person's disease or injury.[134]

The court then held that since neither the expert nor medical science knows "the exact process" that triggers fibromyalgia, the expert's "use of a general methodology cannot vindicate a conclusion for which there is no underlying medical support."[135]

Furthermore, the Fifth Circuit found that it was not an abuse of discretion to exclude the expert's opinion even when the expert pointed to some support for finding causation. In *Moore v. Ashland Chemical, Inc.*,[136] the plaintiff claimed that he developed a reactive airways disorder (RAD) after a defendant negligently caused him to clean up a chemical compound spill without proper safety precautions. The district court entered judgment for the defendants after the jury

131. 171 F.3d 308 (5th Cir. 1999).

132. *Id.* at 313.

133. *Id.*

134. *Id.* at 314. This language would seemingly rule out proof through epidemiological or animal studies unless the disease process is understood. Of course, this was a single-plaintiff case, so perhaps the court is limiting itself to that kind of case.

135. *Id.* The court faulted the trial court's exercise of its discretion:

> If the magistrate judge thought he was applying *Daubert*, however, he fatally erred by applying its criteria at a standard of meaninglessly high generality rather than boring in on the precise state of scientific knowledge in this case. Alternatively, if the magistrate judge decided to depart from *Daubert*, he failed to articulate reasons for adopting the test he used. In particular, he failed to show why an alternate test was necessary to introduce "in the courtroom the same level of intellectual rigor that characterizes the practice of an expert in the relevant field."

Id. (quoting Kumho Tire Co. v. Carmichael, 119 S. Ct. 1167, 1176 (1999)).

136. 151 F.3d 269 (5th Cir. 1998) (en banc), *cert. denied*, 119 S. Ct. 1454 (1999).

found that the plaintiff's injury had not been caused by the defendants' negligence. A divided panel of the Fifth Circuit reversed the decision because the trial court had not allowed one of the plaintiff's medical experts to state his opinion that exposure to the spill had caused the plaintiff's illness.[137] On a rehearing en banc, a divided court found that the district court had not abused its discretion in excluding the opinion.

The majority stated that the trial court could properly conclude that the material safety data sheet that warned that the solution in question could cause respiratory problems had limited value because it did not specify the level of exposure necessary to cause injuries, and in any event, the plaintiff's expert did not know how much exposure there had been.[138] A study showing the effects of fumes could be discounted because the level and duration of the exposure were greater.[139] The temporal connection between the spill and the onset of symptoms was entitled to little weight.[140] The expert's opinion, based on his experience, that any irritant could cause RAD in a susceptible subject was inadequate because it had not been confirmed by the *Daubert* factors.[141] The court assumed that in resolving an issue of medical causation, a court must apply the scientific method, and "[t]his requires some objective, independent validation of the expert's methodology. The expert's assurances that he has utilized generally accepted scientific methodology is [sic] insufficient."[142]

Although *Kumho* suggests that there is no scientific method that must be applied to a particular issue without taking the circumstances of the case into account, the Fifth Circuit in *Black* stated that *Kumho*'s "reasoning fully supports this court's en banc conclusion in *Moore* that *Daubert* analysis governs expert testimony."[143] Do *Moore* and *Black* read together mean that a trial court will always be found to have abused its discretion if it permits a treating physician to testify about general causation in a case in which no consensus exists about causation on the basis of prior studies? The dissenting judges in *Moore* apparently thought so; they objected that under the majority's approach, a plaintiff will never be able to win a case involving chemical compounds that have not been

137. Moore v. Ashland Chem., Inc., 126 F.3d 679 (5th Cir. 1997) (panel opinion). The trial court had admitted the second treating physician's causation opinion even though it relied heavily on the opinion of the expert whose causation testimony was excluded and relied essentially on the same data. *Id.* at 683. The appellate court sitting en banc supposed that the district court had done so because the second physician was the actual treating physician and because he had relied on one study in a medical journal. In view of the verdict, the defendants had not raised the propriety of this ruling on appeal. 151 F.3d at 273–74.

138. 151 F.3d at 278.

139. *Id.* at 278–79.

140. *Id.* at 278.

141. *Id.* at 279.

142. *Id.* at 276.

143. Black v. Food Lion, Inc., 171 F.3d 308, 310 (5th Cir. 1999) (citing Moore v. Ashland Chem., Inc., 151 F.3d 269, 275 n.6 (5th Cir. 1998) (en banc), *cert. denied*, 119 S. Ct. 1454 (1999)).

thoroughly tested.[144] In contrast, the concurring judge in *Moore* thought that the district judge would not have abused her discretion in admitting the excluded opinion on causation, and would "not read the majority opinion to require otherwise."[145] How the Fifth Circuit will treat this issue in future cases is not clear, but certainly a district court that admits a physician's causation testimony without a detailed exploration and explanation for doing so can expect its decision to be reversed.[146] In light of *Kumho*'s insistence on paying heed to the particular circumstances of the case, courts may be more willing to allow treating physicians' causation testimony that is based on a differential diagnosis when the etiology of the condition is understood even though no published epidemiological or toxicological studies implicate the defendant's product in causing harm.[147]

The Third Circuit's opinion on testimony by medical experts is at the opposite end of the spectrum. In *Heller v. Shaw Industries, Inc.*,[148] the plaintiff claimed that her respiratory problems were caused by volatile organic compounds (VOCs) emitted by a carpet manufactured by the defendant. After an extensive in limine hearing, the trial court excluded the testimony of the plaintiff's key expert and granted summary judgment. The appellate court, in an opinion by Judge Becker, agreed that the trial court had properly excluded the testimony of an industrial hygienist that sought to show that the carpet was the source of the VOCs in the plaintiff's home, and that consequently summary judgment was proper.[149] But the court wrote an extensive opinion on why the district judge erred in also excluding the plaintiff's medical expert.[150] Its conclusion is clearly at odds with what the Fifth Circuit said in *Moore* and *Black:*

> Assuming that Dr. Papano conducted a thorough differential diagnosis . . . and had thereby ruled out other possible causes of Heller's illness, and assuming that he had relied on a valid and strong temporal relationship between the installation of the carpet and Heller's problems . . ., we do not believe that this would be an insufficiently valid methodology for his reliably concluding that the carpet caused Heller's problems.

144. *Moore,* 151 F.3d at 281.

145. *Id.* at 279.

146. *See* Tanner v. Westbrook, 174 F.3d 542 (5th Cir. 1999), a Fifth Circuit opinion on the admissibility of causation testimony by clinical physicians, in which the appellate court reversed the trial court's judgment after finding insufficient support in the record for the expert's conclusion that birth asphyxia was more likely than not the cause of an infant's cerebral palsy. The court remanded the case, however, stating, "Whether this weakness is a by-product of the absence of exploration of the *Daubert* issues at a pretrial hearing, we do not know. Nor do we know if his opinion is supportable." *Id.* at 549.

147. *Cf.* Westberry v. Gislaved Gummi AB, 178 F.3d 257, 261–65 (4th Cir. 1999) (treating physician properly permitted to testify that breathing airborne talc aggravated plaintiff's preexisting sinus condition; no epidemiological studies, animal studies, or laboratory data supported the expert's conclusions; the opinion surveys cases in which courts have admitted testimony based on differential diagnoses).

148. 167 F.3d 146 (3d Cir. 1999).

149. *Id.* at 159–65.

150. *Id.* at 153–59.

> . . . .
>
> . . .[W]e do not believe that *Daubert* . . . require[s] a physician to rely on definitive published studies before concluding that exposure to a particular object or chemical was the most likely cause of a plaintiff's illness. Both a differential diagnosis and a temporal analysis, properly performed, would generally meet the requirements of *Daubert* . . . .[151]

Judge Becker was writing before *Kumho.* We do not know yet how much precedential weight a district court in the Third Circuit will feel impelled to accord the dictum in *Heller* in future cases and whether the decision of a district court will be reversed if it excludes testimony on causation by a treating physician because of a lack of published studies. Nor is it clear that all panels of the Fifth Circuit will follow *Black* in treating a district court's admission of testimony by a treating physician as an abuse of discretion. At this time, the possibility of an intercircuit conflict plainly exists.

V. Conclusion

In *Kumho,* the Supreme Court extended the trial judge's gatekeeping obligation concerning expert testimony that it first discussed in *Daubert.* All expert testimony, not just testimony that rests on scientific principles, is now subject to screening to ensure that it is relevant and reliable. The choice of proceedings needed to make this determination lies in the trial court's discretion.

The Court endorsed a nondoctrinaire, flexible approach that requires district courts to focus "upon the particular circumstances of the particular case at issue."[152] The Court did not develop further the technique it used in *Daubert* of pointing to particular factors that spell out reliability with regard to a particular kind of expertise. That is not to say that the factors discussed in *Daubert* are now irrelevant. They "may or may not be pertinent,"[153] even with regard to expert scientific proof, depending on the issue, the expertise in question, and the subject of the expert's testimony. The choice of factors to be used in determining reliability is also left to the trial court's discretion.

The enormous scope and open-ended nature of *Kumho* guarantee that battles over the admissibility of expert testimony will continue. Numerous issues remain unresolved, and the possibility exists that splits in the circuits will result, particularly in connection with the proof of causation in toxic tort cases, the question that engaged the Court's interest in expert testimony in the first place. It remains to be seen whether the trilogy of opinions completed by *Kumho* will constitute the Court's final statement on the subject of expert proof.

151. *Id.* at 154.

152. Kumho Tire Co. v. Carmichael, 119 S. Ct. 1167, 1175 (1999).

153. *Id.* at 1170.

Management of Expert Evidence

WILLIAM W SCHWARZER AND JOE S. CECIL

William W Schwarzer, LL.B., is a Senior U.S. District Judge for the Northern District of California, San Francisco, California, and former Director of the Federal Judicial Center, Washington, D.C.

Joe S. Cecil, Ph.D., J.D., is a Senior Research Associate at the Federal Judicial Center and director of the Center's Scientific Evidence Project.

CONTENTS

I. Introduction*

The purpose of this chapter—augmented by other parts of this manual—is to assist judges in effectively managing expert evidence that involves scientific or technical subject matter. Since the Supreme Court's decisions in *Daubert v. Merrell Dow Pharmaceuticals, Inc.*[1] and *Kumho Tire Co. v. Carmichael*,[2] management of expert evidence is now an integral part of proper case management. Under those decisions, the district judge is the gatekeeper who must pass on the sufficiency of proffered evidence to meet the test under Federal Rule of Evidence 702. The judge's performance of the gatekeeper function will be intertwined with his or her implementation of Federal Rule of Civil Procedure 16.[3] This chapter is intended to provide guidance to judges in carrying out those tasks. It focuses on pretrial management as it relates to expert evidence; matters pertaining to generic management are covered in the Federal Judicial Center's *Manual for Complex Litigation, Third* and its *Manual for Litigation Management and Cost and Delay Reduction*.[4] This chapter should be read in conjunction with Margaret A. Berger's chapter, The Supreme Court's Trilogy on the Admissibility of Expert Testimony, which discusses the Supreme Court's recent decisions on expert testimony, and the reference guides for individual areas of scientific evidence.

II. The Initial Conference

A. Assessing the Case

The court's first contact with a case usually is at the initial Rule 16 conference. To comply with Federal Rule of Civil Procedure 26(f), the attorneys should have met previously to discuss the nature and basis of their claims and defenses, develop a proposed discovery plan, and submit to the court a written report outlining the plan. Because it cannot be assumed that attorneys will always comply with that requirement, the court should ensure that they do. Conferring

* We are grateful for the assistance of Andrea Cleland, Robert Nida, Ross Jurewitz, Dean Miletich, Kristina Gill, and Tom Willging in preparing this chapter.

1. 509 U.S. 579 (1993).
2. 119 S. Ct. 1167 (1999).
3. *See* General Elec. Co. v. Joiner, 522 U.S. 136, 149 (1997) (Breyer, J., concurring):

> [J]udges have increasingly found in the Rules of Evidence and Civil Procedure ways to help them overcome the inherent difficulty of making determinations about complicated scientific or otherwise technical evidence. Among these techniques are an increased use of Rule 16's pretrial conference authority to narrow the scientific issues in dispute, pretrial hearings where potential experts are subject to examination by the court, and the appointment of special masters and specially trained law clerks.

4. *See generally* Manual for Complex Litigation, Third (Federal Judicial Center 1995) [hereinafter MCL 3d]; Litigation Management Manual (Federal Judicial Center 1992).

with each other and preparing the report will require the attorneys to focus on the issues in the case. Their report, together with the pleadings, should enable the judge to form a preliminary impression of the case and help him or her prepare for the conference. Rule 16(c)(4) specifically provides for consideration at the conference of the need for expert testimony and possible limitations on its use.[5]

Scientific evidence is increasingly used in litigation as science and technology become more pervasive in all aspects of daily life. Such evidence is integral to environmental, patent, product liability, mass tort, and much personal injury litigation, and it is also common in other types of disputes, such as trade secret, antitrust, and civil rights. Scientific evidence encompasses so-called hard sciences (such as physics, chemistry, mathematics, and biology) as well as soft sciences (such as economics, psychology, and sociology), and it may be offered by persons with scientific, technical, or other specialized knowledge whose skill, experience, training, or education may assist the trier of fact in understanding the evidence or determining a fact in issue.[6]

The initial conference should be used to determine the nature and extent of the need for judicial management of expert evidence in the case. The court should therefore use the conference to explore in depth what issues implicate expert evidence, the kinds of evidence likely to be offered and its technical and scientific subject matter, and anticipated areas of controversy. Some cases with little prospect for complexity will require little management. However, if the expert evidence promises to be protracted or controversial, or addresses novel subjects that will challenge the court's and the jury's comprehension, the court should focus on management of expert testimony as part of a coordinated case-management strategy. The court will also want to inquire into whether the science involved is novel and still in development, or whether the scientific issues have been resolved in prior litigation and whether similar issues are pending in other litigation.

5. The advisory committee's note states that the rule is intended to "clarify that in advance of trial the court may address the need for, and possible limitations on, the use of expert testimony . . . ." Fed. R. Civ. P. 16(c)(4) advisory committee's note.

6. *See* Fed. R. Evid. 702. The Judicial Conference of the United States has approved proposed amendments to Rule 702 which, if enacted, would permit expert testimony "if (1) the testimony is based upon sufficient facts or data, (2) the testimony is the product of reliable principles and methods, and (3) the witness has applied the principles and methods reliably to the facts of the case." Proposed Amendments to the Federal Rules of Evidence (visited Mar. 21, 2000) <http://www.uscourts.gov/rules/propevid.pdf>. For a breakdown of experts appearing in federal courts, see Molly Treadway Johnson et al., Problems of Expert Testimony in Federal Civil Trials (Federal Judicial Center forthcoming 2000). For a breakdown of experts appearing in state courts, see Anthony Champagne et al., *Expert Witnesses in the Courts: An Empirical Examination,* 76 Judicature 5 (1992); Samuel R. Gross, *Expert Evidence,* 1991 Wis. L. Rev. 1113.

B. Defining and Narrowing the Issues

The objective of the initial conference should be to define and narrow the issues in the litigation. Although it will generally not be possible to arrive at a definitive statement of the controverted issues at the outset, it is essential that the process begin early in the litigation. In cases presenting complex scientific and technical subject matter, the court and parties must focus on the difficult task of defining disputed issues in order to avoid unnecessarily protracting the litigation, generating confusion, and inviting wasteful expense and delay. Usually the judge will need to be educated at the outset about the science and technology involved. Because parties often underestimate the need for judicial education, the judge should raise the matter and explore available options, such as the use of tutorials, advisors, or special masters. Whatever arrangements are made for initial education, it is preferable that they be by stipulation. If an advisor is to be used, the parameters of the advisor's relationship to the judge should be defined, such as permissible ex parte communications and limits on discovery.[7] When a tutorial is arranged, it should be videotaped or transcribed so that the judge can review it as the litigation proceeds.

Although the judge will be in unfamiliar territory, that should not be a deterrent to taking charge of the issue-definition process. There is no better way to start than by asking basic questions of counsel, then exploring underlying assumptions and probing into the nature of the claims and defenses, the theories of general and specific causation, the anticipated defenses, the expert evidence expected to be offered, and the areas of disagreement among experts. The object of this exercise should be education, not argument; all participants should be given an opportunity to learn about the case. By infusing the conference with a spirit of inquiry, the court can set the tone for the litigation, encouraging clarity, candor, and civility.

The following are some additional considerations for the conduct of the Rule 16 conference.

1. Have the parties retained testifying experts?

In some cases where settlement is likely, parties may wish to defer retaining experts, thereby avoiding unnecessary expense. If the case can make progress toward resolution without early identification of experts (for example, if particular nonexpert discovery could provide a basis for settlement), the expert evidence issues can be deferred. On the other hand, deferring identification of experts until the eve of trial can be costly. In a medical malpractice case, for example, expert evidence is essential to resolve the threshold issue whether the defendant conformed to the applicable standard of practice; without such evidence, the plaintiff has no case.

7. *See infra* § VII.A.

2. When should the parties exchange experts' reports?

Federal Rule of Civil Procedure 26(a)(2) requires parties to make detailed written disclosures with respect to each expert retained to testify at trial, including a complete statement of all opinions to be expressed, the basis and reasons supporting the opinions, and the data or other information considered by the witness in forming the opinions.[8] The rule requires the disclosures to be made not less than ninety days before trial or at such other time as the judge may order. The experts' reports will obviously be helpful in identifying issues, but because their preparation is expensive, they should not be required until progress has first been made in narrowing issues to the extent possible. Thus, if the conference discloses that a particular scientific issue is not in dispute, no evidence (and no disclosure) with respect to it will be needed.

Usually the party bearing the burden at trial should make the first disclosure, and the other party should respond. There may also be reason to schedule the disclosures in accordance with the sequence in which issues are addressed. For example, in patent cases, expert disclosures relating to claims construction[9] may be called for early, whereas disclosures relating to infringement and damages are deferred. The judge should therefore consider at the conference when and in what sequence these disclosures should be made.

3. How should the court follow up on the parties' disclosures?

Once the disclosures are in hand, a follow-up Rule 16 conference may be useful to pursue further issue identification and narrowing of disputed issues. If the disclosures indicate disagreements between experts on critical points, the judge should attempt to identify the bases for their differences. Frequently differences between experts rest on tacit assumptions, such as choices among policies, selection of statistical data or databases, judgments about the level of reasonable risk, or the existence of particular facts. It may be useful to require that the experts be present at the conference to assist in the process of identifying the bases for their disagreements. Focused discovery may be helpful in resolving critical differences between experts that rest on their differing assessments or evaluations of test results.

4. Is there a need for further clarification?

Litigation will often involve arcane areas of science and technology that have a language which is foreign to the uninitiated. Although the lawyers are responsible for making the issues and the evidence comprehensible, they do not always succeed. In such cases, to arrive at informed decisions about the management of the litigation, as indicated above, the judge may need to seek assistance during

8. Fed. R. Civ. P. 26(a)(2)(B). *See also infra* § III.A.
9. *See* Markman v. Westview Instruments, Inc., 517 U.S. 370 (1996).

the pretrial phase of the litigation. Aside from using court-appointed experts,[10] the judge may arrange for a neutral expert to explain the fundamentals of the science or technology and make critical evidence comprehensible. Such experts have been used successfully to conduct tutorials for the judge and also for the jury before the presentation of evidence at trial; their utility depends on their ability to maintain objectivity and neutrality in their presentation.

C. Use of the Reference Guides

The process of defining issues should lead to the narrowing of issues. Some elements of the case may turn out not to be in dispute. For example, there may be no controversy about a plaintiff's exposure to an allegedly harmful substance, allowing that issue to be eliminated. Conversely, the plaintiff's ability to establish the requisite exposure may appear to be so questionable that it might usefully be singled out for early targeted discovery[11] and a possible motion in limine or a motion for summary judgment.[12] Unless the judge takes the lead in probing for issues that may not be in dispute, or that may lend themselves to early resolution, the case is likely to involve much unnecessary work, cost, and delay.

The conclusions of a witness offering scientific testimony will generally be the product of a multistep reasoning process. By breaking down the process, the judge may be able to narrow the dispute to a particular step in the process, and thereby facilitate its resolution. Those steps, while generally not intuitively obvious to the nonexpert, may be identified in the process of issue identification. Once the steps have been identified, it can readily be determined which ones are in dispute. As noted, the initial Rule 16 conference may be too early for the parties to be adequately prepared for this process. Nevertheless, the stage should at least be set for the narrowing of issues, though the process may continue as the litigation progresses.

The reference guides in this manual are intended to assist in the process of narrowing issues in the areas they cover.[13] By way of illustration, the Reference Guide on Survey Research facilitates narrowing a dispute over proffered evidence by dividing and breaking the inquiry into a series of questions concerning the purpose of the survey, identification of the appropriate population and sample frame, structure of the questions, recording of data, and reporting. For example, proffered survey research may be subject to a hearsay objection. Thus, it is

10. *See infra* § VII.A.

11. MCL 3d, *supra* note 4, § 21.424.

12. *See, e.g.,* Celotex Corp. v. Catrett, 477 U.S. 317 (1986). *See also* William W Schwarzer et al., The Analysis and Decision of Summary Judgment Motions: A Monograph on Rule 56 of the Federal Rules of Civil Procedure (Federal Judicial Center 1991).

13. The reference guides are not intended to be primers on substantive issues of scientific proof or normative statements on the merits of scientific proof. *See* the Preface to this manual.

critical to determine whether the purpose of the particular survey is to prove the truth of the matter asserted or only the fact of its assertion.

Each of these issues is then broken into a series of suggested questions that will enable the judge to explore the methodology and reasoning underlying the expert's opinion. For example, the questions concerning identification of the appropriate population and sample frame are as follows:

1. Was an appropriate universe or population identified?
2. Did the sampling frame approximate the population?
3. How was the sample selected to approximate the relevant characteristics of the population?
4. Was the level of nonresponse sufficient to raise questions about the representativeness of the sample?
5. What procedures were used to reduce the likelihood of a biased sample?
6. What precautions were taken to ensure that only qualified respondents were included in the survey?

The other reference guides cover additional areas in which expert evidence is frequently offered and disputed.

- The Reference Guide on Statistics identifies three issues: the design of the data-collection process, the extraction and presentation of relevant data, and the drawing of appropriate inferences.
- The Reference Guide on Multiple Regression identifies issues concerning the analysis of data bearing on the relationship of two or more variables, the presentation of such evidence, the research design, and the interpretation of the regression results.
- The Reference Guide on Estimation of Economic Losses in Damages Awards identifies issues concerning expert qualification, characterization of the harmful event, measurement of loss of earnings before trial and future loss, prejudgment interest, and related issues generally and as they arise in particular kinds of litigation.
- The Reference Guide on Epidemiology identifies issues concerning the appropriateness of the research design, the definition and selection of the research population, the measurement of exposure to the putative agent, the measurement of the association between exposure and the disease, and the assessment of the causal association between exposure and the disease.
- The Reference Guide on Toxicology identifies issues concerning the nature and strength of the research design, the expert's qualifications, the proof of association between exposure and the disease, the proof of causal relationships between exposure and the disease, the significance of the person's medical history, and the presence of other agents.

- The Reference Guide on Medical Testimony describes the various roles of physicians, the kinds of information that physicians consider, and how this information is used in reaching a diagnosis and causal attribution.
- The Reference Guide on DNA Evidence offers an overview of scientific principles that underlie DNA testing; basic methods used in such testing; characteristics of DNA samples necessary for adequate testing; laboratory standards necessary for reliable analysis; interpretation of results, including the likelihood of a coincidental match; and emerging applications of DNA testing in forensic settings.
- The Reference Guide on Engineering Practice and Methods describes the nature of engineering, including the issues that must be considered in developing a design, the evolution of subsequent design modifications, and the manner in which failure influences subsequent design.

The scope of these reference guides is necessarily limited, but their format is intended to suggest analytical approaches and opportunities that judges can use in identifying and narrowing issues presented by controversies over scientific evidence. A judge may, for example, ask counsel for both sides to exchange and provide to the court a step-by-step outline of the experts' reasoning processes (following generally the pattern of the reference guides) for use at the conference at which issue definition and narrowing is discussed. If the written statements of expert opinions required by Federal Rule of Civil Procedure 26(a)(2) have been exchanged, the judge could direct each side to identify specifically each part of the opposing expert's opinion that is disputed and to state the specific basis for the dispute. After receipt of these statements, another conference should be held to attempt to narrow the issues.

D. Limitations or Restrictions on Expert Evidence

Federal Rule of Civil Procedure 16(c)(4) contemplates that the judge will consider the "avoidance of unnecessary proof and of cumulative evidence" as well as "limitations or restrictions on the use of testimony under Rule 702 of the Federal Rules of Evidence." In the course of defining and narrowing issues, the court should address the following matters.

1. The need for expert evidence

As discussed above, the issue-narrowing process may disclose that areas otherwise appropriate for expert testimony are not disputed or not disputable, such as whether exposure to asbestos is capable of causing lung cancer and mesothelioma (i.e., general causation). Expert evidence should not be permitted on issues that are not disputed or not disputable.[14] Nor should it be permitted on issues that will not be assisted by such evidence. This would be true, for example, of expert testimony offered essentially to embellish the testimony of fact witnesses, such as testimony about the appearance of an injured party in a crash. Sometimes the line between needed and unneeded testimony is less clear. In patent cases, for example, attorneys expert in patent law may offer testimony on claims construction or patent office procedures. The court needs to balance the competing interests under Federal Rule of Civil Procedure 1, which is intended to bring about the just, speedy, and inexpensive resolution of disputes. While each party is entitled to make its best case, the court has an obligation to expedite the litigation in fairness to all parties. Accordingly, the need for particular expert testimony should be established before it is permitted.

2. *Limiting the number of experts*

Some local rules and standing orders limit parties to one expert per scientific discipline. Ordinarily it should be sufficient for each side to present, say, a single orthopedist, oncologist, or rehabilitation specialist. However, as science increases in sophistication, subspecialties develop. In addition, experts in a single specialty may be able to bring to bear a variety of experiences or perspectives relevant to the case. If a party offers testimony from more than one expert in what appears to be a distinct discipline, the party should justify the need for it and explain why a single expert will not suffice. Attorneys may try to bolster the weight of their case before the jury by cumulative expert testimony, thereby adding cost and delay. The court should not permit such cumulative evidence, even where multiple parties are represented on one or both sides.[15]

E. *Use of Magistrate Judges*

Federal Rule of Civil Procedure 16(c)(8) makes the referral of matters to a magistrate judge or a special master a subject for consideration at the initial

14. Note that courts take different positions on use of collateral estoppel to preclude relitigation of facts based on scientific evidence. *Compare* Ezagui v. Dow Chem. Corp., 598 F.2d 727 (2d Cir. 1979) (estopping litigation on the issue that vaccination package inserts inadequately apprised doctors of known hazards), *with* Hardy v. Johns-Manville Sales Corp., 681 F.2d 334 (5th Cir. 1982) (disallowing collateral estoppel to preclude relitigation of the fact that asbestos products are unreasonably dangerous and that asbestos dust causes mesothelioma). For an interesting discussion of the application of collateral estoppel, see *Bertrand v. Johns-Manville Sales Corp.*, 529 F. Supp. 539, 544 (D. Minn. 1982) (holding it is "clear" that the court should collaterally estop litigation on the specific fact that "asbestos dust can cause diseases such as asbestosis and mesothelioma [because] [t]his proposition is so firmly entrenched in the medical and legal literature that it is not subject to serious dispute" but declining to apply collateral estoppel to the more disputable use of the "state of the art" defense and the claim that asbestos is "unreasonably dangerous").

15. *In re* Factor VIII or IX Concentrate Blood Prods. Litig., 169 F.R.D. 632, 637 (N.D. Ill. 1996) (transferee court in multidistrict litigation has authority to limit the number of expert witnesses who may be called at trial).

pretrial conference. Many courts routinely refer the pretrial management of civil cases to magistrate judges. Some judges believe, however, that in complex cases, there are advantages in having pretrial management performed by the judge who will try the case; this promotes familiarity with the issues in the case and avoids the delay caused by appeals of magistrate judges' rulings.[16]

If pretrial management is nevertheless referred to a magistrate judge, he or she should keep the trial judge apprised of developments affecting the complex issues in the case. A need for decisions by the trial judge may arise during the pretrial phase; for example, the decision to appoint an expert under Federal Rule of Evidence 706 or a special master under Federal Rule of Civil Procedure 53 is one the trial judge would have to make and therefore should not be deferred until the eve of trial.

III. Discovery and Disclosure

A. Discovery Control and Management

Informed by the Rule 16 conference, the judge will be able to make the necessary decisions in managing expert discovery. The following considerations are relevant.

1. Discovery of testifying experts

Parties may depose experts who have been identified as trial witnesses under Federal Rule of Civil Procedure 26(b)(4)(A), but only after the expert disclosure required under Rule 26(a)(2)(B) has been made.[17] Although the court may relieve the parties of the obligation to exchange these disclosures, it will rarely be advisable to do so, or to permit the parties to stipulate around the obligation, for a number of reasons:

- Preparation of the expert disclosures compels parties to focus on the issues and the evidence supporting or refuting their positions. Moreover, the cost and burden of preparing disclosures forces parties to consider with care

16. MCL 3d, *supra* note 4, § 21.53.

17. Fed. R. Civ. P. 26(b)(4)(A). The report under Fed. R. Civ. P. 26(a)(2)(B) is presumptively required of any "witness who is retained or specially employed to provide expert testimony in the case or whose duties as an employee of the party regularly involve giving expert testimony." This would normally exclude a treating physician, but the rule extends to other areas of expertise. Riddick v. Washington Hosp. Ctr., 183 F.R.D. 327 (D.D.C. 1998). Courts have looked to the nature of the testimony rather than to the employment status of the witness to determine if such a report is required. Sullivan v. Glock, Inc., 175 F.R.D. 497, 500 (D. Md. 1997). The court may by order, or the parties may by stipulation, exempt a case from this requirement. Federal Rule of Civil Procedure 29 gives the parties the right to modify, without court order, the procedures or limitations governing discovery, except for stipulations that would interfere with any time set for completion of discovery, hearing of a motion, or trial.

whether to designate a particular person as an expert witness and may discourage or limit the use of excessive numbers of experts.

- Exchange of the expert disclosures, as previously noted, materially assists the court and parties in identifying and narrowing issues.[18]
- Exchange of the disclosures may lead the parties to dispense with taking the opposing experts' depositions. Some attorneys believe that depositions tend to educate the expert more than the attorney when disclosures have been made as required by the rule.
- The disclosures will inform the court's consideration of limitations and restrictions on expert evidence.[19]
- The disclosures will compel the proponent of an expert to be prepared for trial. Because the proponent must disclose all opinions to be expressed and their bases, surprise at trial will be eliminated, the opponent's trial preparation will be improved, and cross-examination will be more effective and efficient.
- The disclosures will aid in identifying evidentiary issues early so that they can be resolved in advance of trial.
- The disclosures may encourage early settlement.

It is advisable for the court to impress on counsel the seriousness of the disclosure requirement. Counsel should know that opinions and supporting facts not included in the disclosure may be excluded at trial, even if they were testified to on deposition. Also, Rule 26(a)(2)(B) requires disclosure not only of the data and materials on which the expert relied but also those that the expert "considered . . . in forming the opinions." Litigants may therefore no longer assume that materials furnished to an expert by counsel or the party will be protected from discovery.[20] Destruction of materials furnished to or produced by an expert in the course of the litigation—such as test results, correspondence, or draft memoranda—may lead to evidentiary or other sanctions.[21] In addition, under the rule, an expert's disclosure must be supplemented if it turns out that any information disclosed was, or has become, incomplete or incorrect.[22] Failure of

18. *See supra* § II.B.

19. *See supra* § II.D.

20. Fed. R. Civ. P. 26(a)(2)(B) advisory committee's note. Courts are divided on the extent to which they require disclosure of attorney work product provided to a testifying expert. *Compare* Karn v. Ingersoll-Rand Co., 168 F.R.D. 633, 639 (N.D. Ind. 1996) (holding that work-product protection does not apply to documents related to the subject matter of litigation provided by counsel to testifying experts), *with* Magee v. Paul Revere Life Ins. Co., 172 F.R.D. 627, 642 (E.D.N.Y. 1997) (holding that "data or other information" considered by the expert, which is subject to disclosure, includes only factual materials and not core attorney work product considered by the expert).

21. Schmid v. Milwaukee Elec. Tool Corp., 13 F.3d 76, 81 (3d Cir. 1994) (sanctions for spoilation of evidence arising from inspection by an expert must be commensurate with the fault and prejudice arising in the case).

22. Fed. R. Civ. P. 26(e)(1).

a party to comply with the disclosure rules may lead to exclusion of the expert's testimony at trial, unless such failure is harmless.[23]

2. Discovery of nontestifying experts

Under Federal Rule of Civil Procedure 26(b)(4)(B), the court may permit discovery by interrogatory or deposition of consulting nontestifying experts "upon a showing of exceptional circumstances under which it is impracticable for the party seeking discovery to obtain facts or opinions on the same subject by other means." Exceptional circumstances may exist where a party has conducted destructive testing, the results of which may be material, or where the opponent has retained all qualified experts. However, in the absence of such circumstances, a party should not be penalized for having sought expert assistance early in the litigation, and its opponent should not benefit from its diligence.

3. Discovery of nonretained experts

Parties may seek the opinions and expertise of persons not retained in the litigation. However, Federal Rule of Civil Procedure 45(c)(3)(B)(ii) authorizes the court to quash a subpoena requiring "disclosure of an unretained expert's opinion or information not describing specific events or occurrences in dispute and resulting from the expert's study made not at the request of any party." In ruling on such a motion to quash, the court should consider whether the party seeking discovery has shown a substantial need that cannot be otherwise met without undue hardship and will reasonably compensate the subpoenaed person, and it may impose appropriate conditions on discovery.[24]

23. *See, e.g.*, Coastal Fuels, Inc. v. Caribbean Petroleum Corp., 79 F.3d 182, 202–03 (1st Cir. 1996) (finding no abuse of discretion in district court's exclusion of expert testimony in price discrimination and monopolization case where party failed to produce expert report in accordance with the court's scheduling order); Newman v. GHS Osteopathic, Inc., 60 F.3d 153, 156 (3d Cir. 1995) (finding no abuse of discretion where district court refused to preclude expert testimony of two witnesses who were not named in Rule 26 disclosures and whose reports were not provided pursuant to Rule 26(a)(2)(B)). Appellate courts seem cautious about precluding expert testimony where such testimony is an essential element of the case. *See* Freeland v. Amigo, 103 F.3d 1271, 1276 (6th Cir. 1997) (district court abused its discretion by precluding expert testimony in a medical malpractice case as a sanction for failing to comply with a pretrial order setting the deadline for discovery where such preclusion would amount to a dismissal of the case).

24. The advisory committee's note points out that this provision was intended to protect the intellectual property of nonretained experts:

> The rule establishes the right of such persons to withhold their expertise, at least unless the party seeking it makes the kind of showing required for a conditional denial of a motion to quash . . . ; that requirement is the same as that necessary to secure work product under Rule 26(b)(3) and gives assurance of reasonable compensation.

Fed. R. Civ. P. 45(c)(3)(B)(ii) advisory committee's note. For a discussion of issues arising with a subpoena for research data from unretained scholars, see *In re American Tobacco Co.*, 880 F.2d 1520, 1527 (2d Cir. 1989); *see also* Paul D. Carrington & Traci L. Jones, *Reluctant Experts*, Law & Contemp. Probs., Summer 1996, at 51; Mark Labaton, Note, *Discovery and Testimony of Unretained Experts*, 1987

4. *Discovery of court-appointed experts*

Federal Rule of Evidence 706 contemplates that the deposition of a court-appointed expert witness may be taken by any party. Technical advisors or other nontestifying experts appointed under the inherent authority of the courts are not necessarily subject to the discovery requirements of Rule 706, permitting the court greater discretion in structuring the terms and conditions for access to such experts for discovery. The extent of discovery should be covered in the order appointing the expert.[25]

5. *Use of videotaped depositions*

Videotaping expert dispositions is particularly appropriate for several reasons: it preserves the testimony of an expert who may be unavailable for trial or whose testimony may be used in more than one trial or in different phases of a single trial; it permits demonstrations, say, of tests or of large machinery, not feasible in the courtroom; and it provides a more lively and interesting presentation than reading of a transcript at trial. Federal Rule of Civil Procedure 30(b)(2) permits a party to designate videotaping of a deposition unless otherwise ordered by the court. Where videotape is to be used, however, the ground rules should be established in advance, such as the placement and operation of the camera, off-camera breaks, lighting, procedures for objections, and review in advance of use at trial.[26]

B. *Protective Orders and Confidentiality*

Under Federal Rule of Civil Procedure 26(c), the court has broad discretion on good cause shown to issue protective orders barring disclosure or discovery or permitting it only on specified conditions. A motion for a protective order by a party or person from whom discovery is sought should be considered only after the parties have conferred and attempted in good faith to resolve the dispute. The rule specifically permits orders for the protection of trade secrets or other confidential information.[27] The court may order a deposition to be sealed and prohibit disclosure of its contents by the parties. Where the response to discovery may cause a party to incur substantial costs, the court may condition compliance on the payment of costs by the requesting parties.[28]

Protective orders are widely used in litigation involving technical and scientific subject matter, sometimes indiscriminately. Parties often stipulate to um-

Duke L.J. 140; Richard L. Marcus, *Discovery Along the Litigation/Science Interface*, 57 Brook. L. Rev. 381 (1991).

25. *See infra* § VII.A.

26. *See* William W Schwarzer et al., Civil Discovery and Mandatory Disclosure: A Guide to Efficient Practice 3-16 to 3-17, app. 2 Form 2.9 (2d ed. 1994).

27. Fed. R. Civ. P. 26(c)(7).

28. MCL 3d, *supra* note 4, § 21.433.

brella protective orders.[29] Many courts, however, will not enter protective orders without specific findings warranting their entry and will not enforce stipulated orders.[30]

Issues frequently arise concerning third-party access to protected material. Information subject to a protective order in a case may be sought by parties in other litigation, by the media, or by other interested persons or organizations. Nonparties may request the terms of a confidential settlement. State and federal laws may also define rights of access to such information. Parties should therefore be aware that issuance of a protective order will not necessarily maintain the confidentiality of the information. Where a sweeping protective order has been entered, the process of segregating protected and nonprotected information when access to it is sought may be time-consuming and expensive. Filings submitted under seal with or without stipulation will not be protected from disclosure to third parties in the absence of a proper order. The parties may bind each other to limit disclosure of such materials, but the materials are not protected against subpoena.

IV. Motion Practice

A. Motions In Limine

Objections to expert evidence relating to admissibility, qualifications of a witness, or existence of a privilege should be raised and decided in advance of trial whenever possible.[31] Exclusion of evidence may in some cases remove an essential element of a party's proof, providing the basis for summary judgment. In other cases, the ruling on an objection may permit the proponent to cure a technical deficiency before trial, such as clarifying an expert's qualifications. Motions in limine may also deal with such matters as potential prejudicial evidence or arguments at trial and the presence of witnesses in the courtroom.

After the *Daubert* and *Kumho* decisions, motions in limine under Federal Rule of Evidence 104(a) have gained new importance in implementing the court's gatekeeping role. The rule does not require the court to hold a hearing on such a motion, but where the ruling on expert evidence is likely to have a substantial effect with respect to the merits of claims or defenses, a hearing is advisable. The court has broad discretion to determine what briefing and evidentiary proceed-

29. *In re* "Agent Orange" Prod. Liab. Litig., 104 F.R.D. 559, 568–70 (E.D.N.Y. 1985), *aff'd*, 821 F.2d 139 (2d Cir.), *cert. denied*, 484 U.S. 953 (1987).

30. *See* Citizens First Nat'l Bank v. Cincinnati Ins. Co., 178 F.3d 943, 945 (7th Cir. 1999).

31. *See* Daubert v. Merrell Dow Pharms., Inc., 509 U.S. 579, 592–93 (1993) (before admitting expert testimony, the trial court must make a "preliminary assessment of whether the reasoning or methodology underlying the testimony is scientifically valid").

ings are needed for it to rule on admissibility of expert evidence.[32] When a hearing is held, it is important that its limits be well defined and its progress carefully controlled; such hearings have been known to take on a life of their own, resulting in a lengthy but unnecessary preview of the trial.

In limine motions should be scheduled sufficiently in advance of trial so that their disposition will assist the parties in preparing for trial and facilitate settlement negotiations. Resolving motions concerning damage claims may be particularly helpful in bringing about a settlement. Rulings on in limine motions should be by written order or on the record, stating specifically the effect of the ruling and the grounds for it. The court should clearly indicate whether the ruling is final or might be revisited at trial. Parties are entitled to know whether they have preserved the issue for appeal or whether an offer or objection at trial is necessary. If the court considers that the ruling might be affected by evidence received at trial, it should so indicate.[33]

B. Summary Judgment

When expert evidence offered to meet an essential element of a party's case is excluded, the ruling may be a basis for summary judgment. Summary judgment motions will therefore frequently be combined with Federal Rule of Evidence 104(a) motions in limine. The issues determinative of admissibility under Rule 104(a), however, will not necessarily be dispositive of the issues under Federal Rule of Civil Procedure 56 (i.e., the absence of a genuine issue of material fact) although they may lay the foundation for summary judgment. It is advisable for

32. There is no general requirement to hold an in limine hearing to consider the admissibility of expert testimony. Kumho Tire Co. v. Carmichael, 119 S. Ct. 1167, 1176 (1999) ("[The abuse of discretion] standard applies as much to the trial court's decisions about how to determine reliability as to its ultimate conclusion. Otherwise, the trial judge would lack the discretionary authority needed both to avoid unnecessary 'reliability' proceedings in ordinary cases where the reliability of an expert's methods is properly taken for granted, and to require appropriate proceedings in the less usual or more complex cases where cause for questioning the expert's reliability arises."); Kirstein v. Parks Corp., 159 F.3d 1065, 1067 (7th Cir. 1998) (finding an adequate basis for determining admissibility of expert evidence without a hearing).

33. *See In re* Paoli R.R. Yard PCB Litig., 916 F.2d 829, 837, 854–55 (3d Cir. 1990) (proponent of expert witness entitled to notice of grounds for exclusion and opportunity to remedy deficiency). *See also* Padillas v. Stork-Gamco, Inc., 186 F.3d 412, 418 (3d Cir. 1999) (court abused its discretion in entering summary judgment after excluding expert evidence without holding an in limine hearing to consider shortcomings of the expert's report); Hall v. Baxter Healthcare Corp., 947 F. Supp. 1387, 1392–95 (D. Or. 1996) (convening Rule 104(a) hearing to determine admissibility of evidence of harmful effects of silicone gel breast implants); Margaret A. Berger, *Procedural Paradigms for Applying the* Daubert *Test*, 78 Minn. L. Rev. 1345, 1380–81 (1994) (calling for fully developed record in challenges to scientific evidence to permit a basis for trial court ruling on summary judgment motion and for appellate court review). The Judicial Conference of the United States has approved a proposed amendment to Fed. R. Evid. 103(a) which, if enacted, would preserve a claim of error for appeal once the court makes a definitive ruling on the record admitting or excluding evidence either at or before trial without the party's renewing the objection.

the court to discuss with counsel their intentions with respect to such motions at an early Rule 16 conference and to consider whether there are likely to be grounds for a meritorious motion.[34] In the course of issue identification, issues may be found that are appropriate for summary judgment motions, where, for example, it appears that a critical element in a party's case is missing[35] or where evidence is too conclusory to raise a genuine issue of fact.[36] At the same time, the court may rule out filing of proposed motions where triable issues appear to be present; voluminous and complex motions unlikely to succeed simply delay the litigation and impose unjustified burdens on the court and parties.[37] It may be possible to focus early discovery on evidence critical to whether a motion for summary judgment can succeed. The court should also address timing of the motions; those made before the necessary discovery has been taken will be premature, whereas those delayed until the eve of trial will invite unnecessary pretrial activity.

Declarations filed in opposition to a motion for summary judgment must present specific facts that would be admissible in evidence at trial and that show the existence of a genuine issue for trial.[38] Although an expert at trial is permitted to state an opinion without first testifying to the underlying data, leaving it to cross-examination to bring out the data,[39] a declaration containing a mere conclusory statement of opinion by an expert unsupported by facts does not suffice to raise a triable issue.[40] The issue of the sufficiency of an expert's decla-

34. *See* Fed. R. Civ. P. 16(c)(5).

35. *See* Celotex Corp. v. Catrett, 477 U.S. 317 (1986).

36. Weigel v. Target Stores, 122 F.3d 461, 469 (7th Cir. 1997) ("[A] party cannot assure himself of a trial merely by trotting out in response to a motion for summary judgment his expert's naked conclusion about the ultimate issue. . . . The fact that a party opposing summary judgment has some admissible evidence does not preclude summary judgment. We and other courts have so held with specific reference to an expert's conclusional statements. . . . The Federal Rules of Evidence permit 'experts to present naked opinions,' but 'admissibility does not imply utility. . . . An expert who supplies nothing but a bottom line supplies nothing of value to the judicial process,' and his 'naked opinion' does not preclude summary judgment." (quoting American Int'l Adjustment Co. v. Galvin, 86 F.3d 1455, 1464 (7th Cir. 1996) (Posner, C.J., dissenting))). Parties must be given an adequate opportunity for discovery to develop the evidence necessary to oppose a summary judgment motion. *See Celotex*, 477 U.S. at 322 (the opponent of the motion is entitled to "adequate time for discovery" needed to oppose the motion); William W Schwarzer & Alan Hirsch, *Summary Judgment After* Eastman Kodak, 45 Hastings L.J. 1, 17 (1993). The disclosures required under Fed. R. Civ. P. 26(a)(2) should help in developing an adequate record.

37. *See generally* Berger, *supra* note 33; Edward Brunet, *The Use and Misuse of Expert Testimony in Summary Judgment*, 22 U.C. Davis L. Rev. 93 (1988).

38. *See* Fed. R. Civ. P. 56(e).

39. According to the advisory committee's note, Federal Rule of Evidence 705, as amended in 1993, permits an expert to testify "in terms of opinion or inference and [to] give reasons therefor without first testifying to the underlying facts or data, unless the court requires otherwise." The purpose of the rule is to eliminate the much criticized practice of asking experts hypothetical questions, leaving it to cross-examination at trial to bring out relevant facts. Fed. R. Evid. 705 advisory committee's note.

40. *See* Mendes-Silva v. United States, 980 F.2d 1482, 1488 (D.C. Cir. 1993); First United Fin.

ration is logically intertwined with the issue of the admissibility of the expert's testimony at trial. Thus, it makes sense, as noted above, to combine the Rule 104(a) and Rule 56 proceedings.

V. The Final Pretrial Conference

The final pretrial conference will benefit from the process of framing the issues and defining the structure of the case, begun in earlier Rule 16 conferences. The goal of the final pretrial conference is to formulate the plan for trial, including a program for facilitating the admission of evidence. Pending objections, to the extent they can be resolved prior to trial, should be ruled on, by motions in limine or otherwise.[41] Issues should at this point be defined with precision and finality. Efforts should be made to arrive at stipulations of facts and other matters to streamline the trial. To aid in this process, the court may consider a number of techniques with respect to expert evidence:

1. Direct the parties to submit statements identifying the parts of the opposing experts' reports that are in dispute and those that are not.
2. Direct the parties to have the experts submit a joint statement specifying the matters on which they disagree and the bases for each disagreement.
3. Direct the parties to have the experts attend the pretrial conference to facilitate identification of the issues remaining in dispute.
4. Clear all exhibits and demonstrations to be offered by experts at trial, such as films, videos, simulations, or models; opposing parties should have a full opportunity to review them in advance of trial and raise any objections.
5. Encourage cooperation in presenting scientific or technical evidence, such as joint use of courtroom electronics, stipulated models, charts or displays, tutorials, and a glossary of technical terms for the court and jury.
6. Encourage stipulations on relevant background facts and other noncontroverted matters.

The parties should be directed to submit a joint pretrial order, stating the legal and factual issues to be tried; the witnesses and the substance of each witness's testimony; and the exhibits to be offered, which should be marked for identifi-

Corp. v. United States Fidelity & Guar. Co., 96 F.3d 135, 140–41 (5th Cir. 1996) (expert affidavits should include some indication of the reasoning process underlying the expert's opinion); *but see* Bulthuis v. Rexall Corp., 789 F.2d 1315, 1316–17 (9th Cir. 1985) (per curiam) (holding that expert opinion is admissible and may defeat a summary judgment motion if it appears that the affiant is competent to give expert opinion and the factual basis for the opinion is stated in the affidavit, even though the underlying factual details and reasoning upon which the opinion is based are not).

41. Fed. R. Civ. P. 16(d). *See also supra* § IV.A.

cation. The order should incorporate all pretrial rulings of the court, any rulings excluding particular evidence or issues, and any other matters affecting the course of the trial. The parties should understand that the order will control the subsequent course of the action and will be modified only to prevent manifest injustice.[42]

VI. The Trial

Trials involving scientific or technical evidence present particular challenges to the judge and jurors to understand the subject matter and make informed decisions. Various techniques have been used to facilitate presentation of such cases and enhance comprehension.[43] The use of such techniques should be explored at the pretrial conference. Following is a summary of techniques that, singly or in combination, are worthy of consideration.

A. Structuring the Trial

One of the main obstacles to comprehension is a trial of excessive length. Steps should be taken to limit the trial's length by limiting the scope of the issues, the number of witnesses and the amount of evidence, and the time for each side to conduct direct examination and cross-examination. Some cases can be bifurcated, and some may be segmented by issues so that the jury retires at the conclusion of the evidence on each issue to deliberate on a special verdict.[44] Such sequential approaches to the presentation of a case to the jury may be useful for the trial of severable issues, such as punitive damages, general causation, exposure to a product, and certain affirmative defenses. The drawback of such approaches is that they make it more difficult to predict for the jurors how long the trial will last.

B. Jury Management

Steps should be taken to lighten the jurors' task, such as giving preliminary instructions that explain what the case is about and what issues the jury will have to decide; permitting jurors to take notes; and giving jurors notebooks with key exhibits, glossaries, stipulations, lists of witnesses, and time lines or chronologies. Some judges have found that permitting jurors to ask questions, usually submitted through the court, can be helpful to the attorneys by disclosing when jurors

42. Fed. R. Civ. P. 16(e).

43. *See generally* MCL 3d, *supra* note 4, §§ 21.6, 22.2–22.4; William W Schwarzer, *Reforming Jury Trials*, 1990 U. Chi. Legal F. 119.

44. *See* Fed. R. Civ. P. 42(b).

are confused. Some judges have found interim summations (or interim opening statements) helpful to juror comprehension; attorneys are allotted a certain amount of time to introduce witnesses from time to time and point out the expected significance of their testimony (e.g., "The next witness will be Dr. X, who will explain how the fracture should have been set. Pay particular attention to how he explains the proper use of screws.").

C. Expert Testimony

Some judges have found it helpful to ask a neutral expert to present a tutorial for the judge and jury before the presentation of expert evidence at trial begins, outlining the fundamentals of the relevant science or technology without touching on disputed issues. Consideration should also be given to having the parties' experts testify back-to-back at trial so that jurors can get the complete picture of a particular issue at one time rather than getting bits and pieces at various times during the trial.

D. Presentation of Evidence

Various technologies are available to facilitate presentation of exhibits. Some are computer-based and some simply facilitate projection of documents on a screen, which allows all jurors to follow testimony about a document. Where voluminous data are presented, summaries should be used; stipulated summaries of depositions in lieu of a reading of the transcript are helpful. Charts, models, pictures, videos, and demonstrations can all assist comprehension.

E. Making It Clear and Simple

Attorneys and witnesses in scientific and technological cases tend to succumb to use of the jargon of the discipline, which is a foreign language to others. From the outset the court should insist that the attorneys and the witnesses use plain English to describe the subject matter and present evidence so that it can be understood by laypersons. They will need to be reminded from time to time that they are not talking to each other, but are there to communicate with the jury and the judge.

VII. Use of Court-Appointed Experts and Special Masters

A. Court-Appointed Experts[45]

Two principal sources of authority permit a court to appoint an expert, each envisioning a somewhat different role for the appointed expert. Appointment under Federal Rule of Evidence 706 anticipates that the appointed expert will function as a testifying witness; the structure, language, and procedures of Rule 706 specifically contemplate the use of appointed experts to present evidence to the trier of fact. The rule specifies a set of procedures governing the process of appointment, the assignment of duties, the reporting of findings, testimony, and compensation of experts. The trial court has broad discretion in deciding whether to appoint a Rule 706 expert on its own motion or on the motion of a party.

Supplementing the authority of Rule 706 is the broader inherent authority of the court to appoint experts who are necessary to enable the court to carry out its duties. This includes authority to appoint a "technical advisor" to consult with the judge during the decision-making process.[46] The role of the technical advisor, as the name implies, is to give advice to the judge, not to give evidence and not to decide the case.[47] A striking exercise of this broader authority involves appointing a technical advisor to confer in chambers with the judge regarding the evidence. Although few cases deal with the inherent power of a court to appoint a technical advisor, the power to appoint remains virtually undisputed.[48] Generally, a district court has discretion to appoint a technical

45. Portions of this discussion of the use of court-appointed experts are adapted from the chapter on this topic by Joe S. Cecil and Thomas E. Willging that appeared in the first edition of this manual. The most complete treatment of the research on which this discussion is based is presented in Joe S. Cecil & Thomas E. Willging, *Accepting* Daubert's *Invitation: Defining a Role for Court-Appointed Experts in Assessing Scientific Validity*, 43 Emory L.J. 995 (1994). *See also* Ellen E. Deason, *Court-Appointed Expert Witnesses: Scientific Positivism Meets Bias and Deference*, 77 Or. L. Rev. 59 (1998); Karen Butler Reisinger, Note, *Court-Appointed Expert Panels: A Comparison of Two Models*, 32 Ind. L. Rev. 225 (1998).

46. *See generally In re* Peterson, 253 U.S. 300, 312 (1920) ("Courts have (at least in the absence of legislation to the contrary) inherent power to provide themselves with appropriate instruments required for the performance of their duties."); Reilly v. United States, 863 F.2d 149, 154 & n.4 (1st Cir. 1988) ("[S]uch power inheres generally in a district court. . . ."); Burton v. Sheheen, 793 F. Supp. 1329, 1339 (D.S.C. 1992) ("Confronted further with the unusual complexity and difficulty surrounding computer generated [legislative] redistricting plans and faced with the prospect of drawing and generating its own plan, the court appointed [name] as technical advisor to the court pursuant to the inherent discretion of the court . . . ."), *vacated on other grounds*, 508 U.S. 968 (1993).

47. *Reilly*, 863 F.2d at 157 ("Advisors . . . are not witnesses, and may not contribute evidence. Similarly, they are not judges, so they may not be allowed to usurp the judicial function."). *See also Burton*, 793 F. Supp. at 1339 n.25 ("[The advisor] was not appointed as an expert under Fed. R. Evid. 706 or [as] a special master under Fed. R. Civ. P. 53.").

48. In the words of the Advisory Committee on the Rules of Evidence, "[t]he inherent power of a trial judge to appoint an expert of his own choosing is virtually unquestioned." Fed. R. Evid. 706

advisor, but it is expected that such appointments will be "hen's-teeth rare," a "last" or "near-to-last resort."[49]

The silicone gel breast implants product liability litigation offers two examples of innovative uses of both kinds of court-appointed experts. In 1996 Chief Judge Sam Pointer, Jr., of the Northern District of Alabama, serving as transferee judge in a multidistrict litigation proceeding, appointed four scientists under authority of Rule 706 to serve on a panel of court-appointed experts.[50] Judge Pointer instructed the panel members to review the scientific literature and report whether it provided a scientific basis to conclude that silicone gel breast implants cause a number of diseases and symptoms.[51]

In a joint report in which separate chapters were authored by each of the experts, panel members concluded that the scientific literature provided no basis for such a conclusion. Following submission of their report, the panel members were subjected to discovery-type depositions and cross-examined by both sides. Then their "trial" testimony was taken in videotaped depositions over which Judge Pointer presided, and again they were cross-examined by both sides. When these cases are remanded, it is expected that these depositions will be usable—either as trial testimony or as evidence in pretrial *Daubert* hearings—in both federal district courts and state courts (as a result of cross-noticing or of conditions placed prior to ordering a remand). Having a single national panel should provide a more consistent foundation for resolving these questions, as well as eliminate the time and expense of multiple courts appointing experts.

Judge Robert E. Jones of the District of Oregon also appointed a panel of scientific experts to assist him in ruling on motions to exclude plaintiffs' expert testimony in seventy silicone gel breast implant products liability cases.[52] Judge Jones appointed these experts as "technical advisors," since they were to advise him regarding the extent to which the evidence was grounded in scientific

advisory committee's note; *see also* United States v. Green, 544 F.2d 138, 145 (3d Cir. 1976) ("[T]he inherent power of a trial judge to appoint an expert of his own choosing is clear."), *cert. denied,* 430 U.S. 910 (1977).

49. *Reilly,* 863 F.2d at 157. General factors that might justify an appointment are "problems of unusual difficulty, sophistication, and complexity, involving something well beyond the regular questions of fact and law with which judges must routinely grapple." *Id.*

50. *In re* Silicone Gel Breast Implant Prods. Liab. Litig., Order 31 (N.D. Ala. May 30, 1996) (MDL No. 926) (visited Mar. 20, 2000) <http://www.fjc.gov/BREIMLIT/ORDERS/orders.htm>. Judge Pointer's appointment of a national panel of experts grew out of actions to establish similar panels in local litigation taken by Judge Jack B. Weinstein of the Eastern District of New York and Judge Robert E. Jones of the District of Oregon. *See generally* Reisinger, *supra* note 45, at 252–55.

51. *In re* Silicone Gel Breast Implant Prods. Liab. Litig., Order 31e (N.D. Ala. Oct. 31, 1996) (MDL No. 926) (visited Mar. 20, 2000) <http://www.fjc.gov/BREIMLIT/ORDERS/orders.htm>. Judge Pointer also directed the national panel to inform the court about whether reasonable scientists might disagree with the panel's conclusions. *Id.*

52. Reisinger, *supra* note 45, at 252–55. These seventy cases were among the first remanded for trial by Judge Pointer as part of the multidistrict litigation proceeding.

methodology as part of a pretrial evidentiary proceeding.[53] After considering the reports of the experts, Judge Jones granted the defendants' motions in limine to exclude the plaintiffs' scientific evidence of a link between silicone gel breast implants and autoimmune disorders or atypical connective tissue disease, finding that the proffered evidence did not meet acceptable standards of scientific validity.[54]

To be effective, use of court-appointed experts must be grounded in a pretrial procedure that enables a judge to anticipate problems in expert testimony and to initiate the appointment process in a timely manner. The pretrial process described in this chapter, which permits narrowing of disputed issues and preliminary screening of expert evidence, should give judges an early indication of the need for court-appointed experts. Interviews with judges who have appointed experts suggest that the need for such appointments will be infrequent and will be characterized by evidence that is particularly difficult to comprehend, or by a failure of the adversarial system to provide the information necessary to sort through the conflicting claims and interpretations. Appointing an expert increases the burden on the judge, increases the expense to the parties, and raises unique problems concerning the presentation of evidence. These added costs will be worth enduring only if the information provided by the expert is critical to the resolution of the disputed issues.

The judge will most likely have to initiate the appointment process. The parties frequently will not raise this possibility on their own. One authority has suggested that identification of the need for a neutral expert should begin at a pretrial conference held pursuant to Federal Rule of Civil Procedure 16.[55] The court can initiate the appointment process on its own by entering an order to show cause why an expert witness or witnesses should not be appointed.[56]

In responding to the order, parties should address a number of issues that may prove troublesome as the appointment process proceeds. Parties should be asked

53. Hall v. Baxter Healthcare Corp., 947 F. Supp. 1387, 1392 (D. Or. 1996). In response to a plaintiff's motion following the evidentiary hearing, Judge Jones informally amended the procedure to include providing a number of procedural safeguards mentioned in Rule 706 of the Federal Rules of Evidence. Among the changes, he agreed to provide a written charge to the technical advisors, to communicate with the advisors on the record, and to allow the attorneys a limited opportunity to question the advisors regarding the contents of their reports. *Id.* at 1392–94.

54. *Id.* at 1394.

55. Jack B. Weinstein & Margaret A. Berger, Weinstein's Evidence: Commentary on Rules of Evidence for the United States Courts and Magistrates ¶ 706[02], at 706-14 to -15 (1994). Although Rule 16 of the Federal Rules of Civil Procedure does not specifically refer to court appointment of experts, subsection (c)(12) does call for consideration of "the need for adopting special procedures for managing potentially difficult . . . actions that may involve complex issues . . . or unusual proof problems." Fed. R. Civ. P. 16(c)(12).

56. Fed. R. Evid. 706(a). *See also In re* Joint E. & S. Dists. Asbestos Litig., 830 F. Supp. 686, 694 (E.D.N.Y. 1993) (parties are entitled to be notified of the court's intention to use an appointed expert and be given an opportunity to review the expert's qualifications and work in advance).

to nominate candidates for the appointment and give guidance concerning characteristics of suitable candidates. No person should be nominated who has not previously consented to it and undergone a preliminary screening for conflicts of interest. Candidates for appointment should make full disclosure of all engagements (formal or informal), publications, statements, or associations that could create an appearance of partiality. Encouraging both parties to create a list of candidates and permitting the parties to strike nominees from each other's list will increase party involvement and expand the list of acceptable candidates. Judges may also turn to academic departments and professional organizations as a source of expertise.[57]

Compensation of the expert also should be discussed with the parties during initial communications concerning the appointment. Normally public funds will not be available to compensate court-appointed experts. Unless the expert is to testify in a criminal case or a land condemnation case, the judge should inform the parties that they must compensate the appointed expert for his or her services.[58] Typically each party pays half of the expense, and the prevailing party is reimbursed by the losing party at the conclusion of the litigation. Raising this issue at the outset will indicate that the court seriously intends to pursue an appointment and may help avoid subsequent objections to compensation. Judges occasionally appoint experts over the objections of a party. If, however, difficulty in securing compensation is anticipated, the parties may be ordered to contribute a portion of the expected expense to an escrow account prior to the selection of the expert. Objections to payment should be less likely to impede the work of the expert once the appointment is made.

The court should make clear in its initial communications the anticipated procedure for interaction with the expert. If ex parte communication between the court and the expert is expected, the court should outline the specific nature of such communications, the extent to which the parties will be informed of the content of such communications, and the parties' opportunities to respond.[59]

57. The American Association for the Advancement of Science (AAAS) will aid federal judges in finding scientists and engineers suitable for appointment in specific cases. Information on the AAAS program can be found at Court-Appointed Experts: A Demonstration Project of the AAAS (visited Mar. 20, 2000) <http://www.aaas.org/spp/case/case.htm>. The Private Adjudication Center at Duke University is establishing a registry of independent scientific and technical experts who are willing to provide advice to courts or serve as court-appointed experts. Letter from Corinne A. Houpt, Registry Project Director, to Judge Rya W. Zobel, Director, Federal Judicial Center (Dec. 29, 1998) (on file with the Research Division of the Federal Judicial Center). Information on the Private Adjudication Center program can be found at Registry of Independent Scientific and Technical Advisors (visited Mar. 20, 2000) <http://www.law.duke.edu/pac/registry/index.html>.

58. Fed. R. Evid. 706(b). The Criminal Justice Act authorizes payment of experts' expenses when such assistance is needed for effective representation of indigent individuals in federal criminal proceedings. 18 U.S.C. § 3006A(e) (1988).

59. *See, e.g.*, Edgar v. K.L., 93 F.3d 256, 259 (7th Cir. 1996) (per curiam) (ordering disqualification

This initial communication may be the best opportunity to raise such considerations, entertain objections, and inform the parties of the court's expectations of the practices to be followed regarding the appointed expert.[60]

The court's appointment of an expert should be memorialized by entry of a formal order, after the parties are given an opportunity to comment on it. The following is a checklist of matters that should be addressed in connection with such an order.

1. the authority under which it is issued;
2. the name, address, and affiliation of the expert;
3. the specific tasks assigned to the expert (to submit a report, to testify at trial, to advise the court, to prepare proposed findings, etc.);
4. the subject on which the expert is to express opinions;
5. the amount or rate of compensation and the source of funds;
6. the terms for conducting discovery of the expert;
7. whether the parties may have informal access to the expert; and
8. whether the expert may have informal communications with the court, and whether they must be disclosed to the parties.

Some experts are professionals in this area; others are new to it. The court should consider providing experts with instructions describing what they can expect in court proceedings and what are permissible and impermissible contacts and relationships with litigants and other experts.[61]

B. Special Masters[62]

Special masters are appointed by courts that require particular expertise and skill to assist in some phase of litigation. The kind of person to be appointed depends on the particular expertise and skill required for the assigned task. For example, experienced attorneys, retired judges, law professors, and magistrates[63] have been appointed as special masters to supervise discovery, resolve disputes, and manage other parts of the pretrial phase of complex litigation. Persons with technical or scientific skills have been appointed as special masters to assist the court in litiga-

of a judge based on the judge's meeting ex parte with a panel of court-appointed experts to discuss the merits of the panel's conclusions).

60. For more detailed guidance with respect to the appointment and use of such experts, see Cecil & Willging, *supra* note 45.

61. *In re* Silicone Gel Breast Implant Prods. Liab. Litig., Order 31 (N.D. Ala. May 30, 1996) (visited Mar. 20, 2000) <http://www.fjc.gov/BREIMLIT/ORDERS/orders.htm>.

62. Portions of this discussion of the use of special masters are adapted from the chapter on this topic by Margaret G. Farrell that appeared in the first edition of this manual. The most complete treatment of the research on which this discussion is based is presented in Margaret G. Farrell, *Coping with Scientific Evidence: The Use of Special Masters,* 43 Emory L.J. 927 (1994).

63. 28 U.S.C. § 636(b)(2) (1988). If the parties do not consent, the appointment of a magistrate judge must meet the standards of Federal Rule of Civil Procedure 53.

tion involving difficult subject matter. When a special master is assisting with fact-finding, his or her duties must be structured so as to not intrude on the judge's authority to adjudicate the merits of the case.[64] In such instances, certain narrowly circumscribed tasks might be performed by special masters, such as assembling, collating, or analyzing information supplied by the parties.[65]

Authority for the appointment of special masters derives from two sources. Rule 53 of the Federal Rules of Civil Procedure is the most commonly cited authority.[66] Under that rule a special master may be appointed in actions to be tried by a jury only where the issues are complicated. In cases destined for bench trial, a special master may be appointed "only upon a showing that some exceptional condition requires it."[67] Calendar congestion or the judge's caseload burden will not support such a showing.[68] Courts have laid down strict limitations to preclude special masters from performing judicial functions, such as deciding substantive motions or making other dispositive rulings.[69] Alternatively, courts sometimes rely on their inherent authority when they appoint special masters to perform nonadjudicative duties that often arise in the pretrial and post-trial process, thereby avoiding the restrictions of Rule 53.[70]

Special masters have been helpful in dealing with scientific and technical evidence in a number of ways.[71] For example, special masters have been used to

64. *See* La Buy v. Howes Leather Co., 352 U.S. 249, 256–59 (1957).

65. *See* Wayne D. Brazil, *Special Masters in the Pretrial Development of Big Cases: Potential and Problems, in* Managing Complex Litigation: A Practical Guide to the Use of Special Masters 1, 6–10 (Wayne D. Brazil et al. eds., 1983).

66. Fed. R. Civ. P. 53(b). A judge may appoint a special master to try a Title VII employment discrimination case without regard to the requirements of Rule 53 if the judge is unable to hear the case within 120 days. 42 U.S.C. § 2000e-5(f)(5) (1988). The Advisory Committee on Civil Rules is currently considering a revision of Rule 53 to take such recent innovations into account. *See generally* Edward H. Cooper, *Civil Rule 53: An Enabling Act Challenge,* 76 Tex. L. Rev. 1607 (1998).

67. Fed. R. Civ. P. 53(b).

68. *La Buy,* 352 U.S. at 256–59.

69. *See, e.g.,* United States v. Microsoft Corp., 147 F.3d 935, 956 (D.C. Cir. 1998) (appointment of a special master to review government's motion for a permanent injunction was "in effect the imposition on the parties of a surrogate judge and either a clear abuse of discretion or an exercise of wholly non-existent discretion").

70. As with court-appointed experts, the inherent authority of a judge to appoint a special master to assist in performing nonadjudicatory duties in complex litigation is virtually undisputed. *See supra* notes 46–48 and accompanying text. Courts have inherent power to provide themselves with appropriate instruments for the performance of their duties; this power includes the authority to appoint persons unconnected with the court, such as special masters, auditors, examiners, and commissioners, with or without consent of the parties, to simplify and clarify issues and to make tentative findings. *In re* Peterson, 253 U.S. 300, 312–14 (1920); Reilly v. United States, 863 F.2d 149, 154–55 & n.4 (1st Cir. 1988). *See, e.g.,* Jenkins v. Missouri, 890 F.2d 65, 67–68 (8th Cir. 1989) (court relied on inherent authority to appoint a committee of special masters to monitor implementation of court's order); United States v. Connecticut, 931 F. Supp. 974, 984–85 (D. Conn. 1996) (court relied on inherent authority to appoint special master to review aspects of care and treatment of residents covered by remedial order).

71. For more specific examples of the roles of special masters, see Farrell, *supra* note 62, at 952–67, and Cooper, *supra* note 66, at 1614–15.

make preliminary assessments of technical or scientific evidence offered by the parties,[72] and to identify and supervise court-appointed experts and technical advisors who offer guidance to the court in ruling on objections to evidence.[73] Special masters are sometimes used to tutor the fact finder—judge or jury—regarding technical issues in litigation, particularly patent controversies.[74] Special masters have been used to assess claims in multiparty litigation in order to facilitate settlement, sometimes in the context of a coordinated pretrial case-management plan.[75] Special masters also have been helpful in developing statistical strategies for evaluating multiple claims on a limited recovery fund.[76]

The wide-ranging tasks assigned to special masters raise a number of issues that a judge should consider at the time of the appointment,[77] including the following.

- *Selection.* A variety of skills may be necessary to perform the particular assigned tasks. For example, the "quasi-judicial" functions of special masters make retired judges, former magistrate judges, former hearing examiners, and attorneys good candidates for selection. However, when the assigned tasks require scientific or technical expertise, judges should look for a balance of legal experience and scientific and technical expertise of candidates.
- *Appointment.* Judges generally appoint special masters with the consent, or at least the acquiescence, of the parties. The appointment should be memo-

72. *In re* Repetitive Stress Injury Cases, 142 F.R.D. 584, 586–87 (E.D.N.Y. 1992) (magistrate judges were used to facilitate sharing of scientific and medical data and experts, thereby reducing redundant discovery requests), *appeal dismissed, order vacated sub nom. In re* Repetitive Stress Injury Litig., 11 F.3d 368 (2d Cir. 1993). *See also* Wayne D. Brazil, *Special Masters in Complex Cases: Extending the Jury or Reshaping Adjudication?,* 53 U. Chi. L. Rev. 394, 410–12 (1986).

73. *See, e.g.,* Brazil, *supra* note 72, at 410–12; Hall v. Baxter Healthcare Corp., 947 F. Supp. 1387, 1392 (D. Or. 1996) (special master was used to identify candidates to serve on a panel of court-appointed experts); Fox v. Bowen, 656 F. Supp. 1236, 1253–54 (D. Conn. 1986) (master would be appointed to hire experts and conduct studies necessary to the framing of a remedial order).

74. *See, e.g., In re* Newman, 763 F.2d 407, 409 (Fed. Cir. 1985).

75. *See, e.g., In re* Joint E. & S. Dists. Asbestos Litig., 737 F. Supp. 735, 737 (E.D.N.Y. 1990) (appointment of special master to facilitate settlement); *In re* DES Cases, 789 F. Supp. 552, 559 (E.D.N.Y. 1992) (mem.) (appointment of special master to facilitate settlement), *appeal dismissed sub nom. In re* DES Litig., 7 F.3d 20 (2d Cir. 1993). *See also* Francis E. McGovern, *Toward a Functional Approach for Managing Complex Litigation,* 53 U. Chi. L. Rev. 440, 459–64 (1986) (describing strategy of special master in bringing about settlement of dispute over fishing rights). The use of a special master may be considered at a pretrial conference. Fed. R. Civ. P. 16(c)(8). Such activities are also authorized by Rule 16(c)(9), permitting federal judges to "take appropriate action, with respect to . . . settlement and the use of special procedures to assist in resolving the dispute when authorized by statute or local rule . . . ." Fed. R. Civ. P. 16(c)(9).

76. Hilao v. Estate of Marcos, 103 F.3d 767 (9th Cir. 1996); Kane v. Johns-Manville Corp., 843 F.2d 636 (2d Cir. 1988). A.H. Robins Co. v. Piccinin, 788 F.2d 994 (4th Cir.), *cert. denied,* 479 U.S. 876 (1986). *In re* A.H. Robins Co., 880 F.2d 694 (4th Cir.), *cert. denied,* 493 U.S. 959 (1989). *See also* Sol Schreiber & Laura D. Weissbach, In re Estate of Ferdinand E. Marcos Human Rights Litigation: *A Personal Account of the Role of the Special Master,* 31 Loy. L.A. L. Rev. 475 (1998).

77. For a more extensive list of issues, see Farrell, *supra* note 62.

rialized by a formal order covering the same checklist of matters addressed in orders appointing court-appointed experts.[78]

- *Conflicts of interest.* Special masters are held to a high ethical standard and are subject to the conflict-of-interest standards of the *Code of Conduct for United States Judges*, particularly when they are performing duties that are functionally equivalent to those performed by a judge.[79] When the special master takes on multiple roles, the court should be aware of the possibility of inherent conflicts among the competing roles.
- *Ex parte communication.* Ex parte contact with the parties may be improper where the special master is involved in fact-finding.[80] Ex parte communication with the judge may also be problematic if the special master is to provide an independent assessment for consideration by the court, such as a report containing proposed findings of fact.[81]
- *Compensation.* Issues regarding compensation parallel those discussed earlier with regard to court-appointed experts.[82] It is advisable to include the terms of compensation (including the rate of compensation and the source of funds) in the order of appointment.

78. *See supra* § VII.A.

79. The *Code of Conduct for United States Judges* applies in part to special masters and commissioners, as indicated in the section titled "Compliance with the Code of Conduct." Committee on Codes of Conduct, Judicial Conf. of U.S., Code of Conduct for United States Judges 19–20 (Sept. 1999). Jenkins v. Sterlacci, 849 F.2d 627, 630 n.1 (D.C. Cir. 1988) ("[I]nsofar as special masters perform duties functionally equivalent to those performed by a judge, they must be held to the same standards as judges for purposes of disqualification."); *In re* Joint E. & S. Dists. Asbestos Litig., 737 F. Supp. 735, 739 (E.D.N.Y. 1990) ("In general a special master or referee should be considered a judge for purposes of judicial ethics rules.").

80. Farrell, *supra* note 62, at 977.

81. *Id.* at 979–80.

82. *See supra* note 58 and accompanying text.

How Science Works

DAVID GOODSTEIN

David Goodstein, B.S., M.S., Ph.D., is Vice Provost, Professor of Physics and Applied Physics, and the Frank J. Gilloon Distinguished Teaching and Service Professor, California Institute of Technology, Pasadena, California.

CONTENTS

RECENT SUPREME COURT DECISIONS HAVE PUT JUDGES in the position of having to decide what is "scientific" and what is not.[1] Some judges may not feel entirely comfortable making such decisions, in spite of the guidance supplied by the Court and helpfully illuminated by learned commentators.[2] The purpose of this chapter is not to resolve the practical difficulties that judges will encounter in reaching those decisions, but, much more modestly, to demystify the business of science just a bit and to help judges understand the *Daubert* decision, at least as it appears to a scientist. In the hope of accomplishing these tasks, I take a mildly irreverent look at some formidable subjects. I hope the reader will accept this chapter in that spirit.

I. A Bit of History

Modern science can reasonably be said to have come into being during the time of Queen Elizabeth I of England and William Shakespeare. Almost immediately, it came into conflict with the law.

While Shakespeare was composing his sonnets in England, Galileo Galilei in Italy was inventing the idea that careful experiments in a laboratory could reveal universal truths about the way objects move through space. A bit later, hearing about the newly invented telescope, he made one for himself and with it made discoveries in the heavens that astonished and thrilled all of Europe. Nevertheless, in 1633, Galileo was put on trial for his scientific teachings. The trial of Galileo is usually portrayed as a conflict between science and the church, but it was, after all, a trial, with judges and lawyers, and all the other trappings of a formal legal procedure.

Another great scientist of the day, William Harvey, who discovered the circulation of the blood, worked not only at the same time as Galileo, but even at the same place—the University of Padua, in Italy, not far from Venice. If one visits the University of Padua today and gets a tour of the old campus at the heart of the city, one will be shown Galileo's *cattedra,* the wooden pulpit from which he lectured (and, curiously, one of his vertebrae in a display case just outside the rector's office—maybe the rector needs to be reminded to have a little spine). One will also be shown the lecture-theater in which Harvey dis-

1. These Supreme Court decisions are discussed in Margaret A. Berger, The Supreme Court's Trilogy on the Admissibility of Expert Testimony, §§ II–III, IV.A., in this manual. For a discussion of the difficulty in distinguishing between science and engineering, see Henry Petroski, Reference Guide on Engineering Practice and Methods, in this manual.

2. Since publication of the first edition of this manual, a number of works have been developed to assist judges and attorneys in understanding a wide range of scientific evidence. *See, e.g.*, 1 & 2 Modern Scientific Evidence: The Law and Science of Expert Testimony (David L. Faigman et al. eds., 1997); Expert Evidence: A Practitioner's Guide to Law, Science, and the FJC Manual (Bert Black & Patrick W. Lee eds., 1997).

sected cadavers while eager students peered downward from tiers of overhanging balconies. Dissecting cadavers was illegal in Harvey's time, so the floor of the theater was equipped with a mechanism to make the body disappear when a lookout gave the word that the authorities were coming. Of course, both science and the law have changed a great deal since the seventeenth century.

Another important player who lived in the same era was not a scientist at all, but a lawyer who rose to be Lord Chancellor of England in the reign of James I, Elizabeth's successor. His name was Sir Francis Bacon, and in his magnum opus, which he called *Novum Organum,* he put forth the first theory of the scientific method. In Bacon's view, the scientist should be a disinterested observer of nature, collecting observations with a mind cleansed of harmful preconceptions that might cause error to creep into the scientific record. Once enough such observations have been gathered, patterns will emerge from them, giving rise to truths about nature.

Bacon's theory has been remarkably influential down through the ages, even though in his own time there were those who knew better. "That's exactly how a Lord Chancellor *would* do science," William Harvey is said to have grumbled.

II. Theories of Science

Today, in contrast to the seventeenth century, few would deny the central importance of science to our lives, but not many would be able to give a good account of what science is. To most, the word probably brings to mind not science itself, but the fruits of science, the pervasive complex of technology that has transformed all of our lives. However, science might also be thought to include the vast body of knowledge we have accumulated about the natural world. There are still mysteries, and there always will be mysteries, but the fact is that, by and large, we understand how nature works.

A. Francis Bacon's Scientific Method

But science is even more than that. If one asks a scientist the question, What is science?, the answer will almost surely be that science is a process, a way of examining the natural world and discovering important truths about it. In short, the essence of science is the scientific method.[3]

3. The Supreme Court, in *Daubert v. Merrell Dow Pharmaceuticals, Inc.*, acknowledged the importance of defining science in terms of its methods as follows: "'Science is not an encyclopedic body of knowledge about the universe. Instead, it represents a *process* for proposing and refining theoretical explanations about the world that are subject to further testing and refinement.'" (emphasis in original). 509 U.S. 579, 590 (1993) (quoting Brief for the American Association for the Advancement of Science and the National Academy of Sciences as Amici Curiae at 7–8).

That stirring description suffers from an important shortcoming. We don't really know what the scientific method is.[4] There have been many attempts at formulating a general theory of how science works, or at least how it ought to work, starting, as we have seen, with Sir Francis Bacon's. Bacon's idea, that science proceeds through the collection of observations without prejudice, has been rejected by all serious thinkers. Everything about the way we do science—the language we use, the instruments we use, the methods we use—depends on clear presuppositions about how the world works. Modern science is full of things that cannot be observed at all, such as force fields and complex molecules. At the most fundamental level, it is impossible to observe nature without having some reason to choose what is worth observing and what is not worth observing. Once one makes that elementary choice, Bacon has been left behind.

B. Karl Popper's Falsification Theory

In this century, the ideas of the Austrian philosopher Sir Karl Popper have had a profound effect on theories of the scientific method.[5] In contrast to Bacon, Popper believed all science begins with a prejudice, or perhaps more politely, a theory or hypothesis. Nobody can say where the theory comes from. Formulating the theory is the creative part of science, and it cannot be analyzed within the realm of philosophy. However, once the theory is in hand, Popper tells us, it is the duty of the scientist to extract from it logical but unexpected predictions that, if they are shown by experiment not to be correct, will serve to render the theory invalid.

Popper was deeply influenced by the fact that a theory can never be proved right by agreement with observation, but it can be proved wrong by disagreement with observation. Because of this asymmetry, science makes progress uniquely by proving that good ideas are wrong so that they can be replaced by even better ideas. Thus, Bacon's disinterested observer of nature is replaced by Popper's skeptical theorist. The good Popperian scientist somehow comes up with a hypothesis that fits all or most of the known facts, then proceeds to attack that hypothesis at its weakest point by extracting from it predictions that can be shown to be false. This process is known as falsification.[6]

4. For a general discussion of theories of the scientific method, see Alan F. Chalmers, What Is This Thing Called Science? (1982). For a discussion of the ethical implications of the various theories, see James Woodward & David Goodstein, *Conduct, Misconduct and the Structure of Science,* 84 Am. Scientist 479 (1996).

5. *See, e.g.,* Karl R. Popper, The Logic of Scientific Discovery (Karl R. Popper, trans., 1959).

6. The Supreme Court in *Daubert* recognized Popper's conceptualization of scientific knowledge by noting that "[o]rdinarily, a key question to be answered in determining whether a theory or technique is scientific knowledge that will assist the trier of fact will be whether it can be (and has been) tested." 509 U.S. at 593. In support of this point, the Court cited as parentheticals passages from both Carl Gustav Hempel, Philosophy of Natural Science 49 (1966) ("'[T]he statements constituting a scientific

Popper's ideas have been fruitful in weaning the philosophy of science away from the Baconian view and some other earlier theories, but they fall short in a number of ways in describing correctly how science works. The first of these is the observation that, although it may be impossible to prove a theory is true by observation or experiment, it is nearly just as impossible to prove one is false by these same methods. Almost without exception, in order to extract a falsifiable prediction from a theory, it is necessary to make additional assumptions beyond the theory itself. Then, when the prediction turns out to be false, it may well be one of the other assumptions, rather than the theory itself, that is false. To take a simple example, early in the twentieth century it was found that the orbits of the outermost planets did not quite obey the predictions of Newton's laws of gravity and mechanics. Rather than take this to be a falsification of Newton's laws, astronomers concluded the orbits were being perturbed by an additional unseen body out there. They were right. That is precisely how the planet Pluto was discovered.

The apparent asymmetry between falsification and verification that lies at the heart of Popper's theory thus vanishes. But the difficulties with Popper's view go even beyond that problem. It takes a great deal of hard work to come up with a new theory that is consistent with nearly everything that is known in any area of science. Popper's notion that the scientist's duty is then to attack that theory at its most vulnerable point is fundamentally inconsistent with human nature. It would be impossible to invest the enormous amount of time and energy necessary to develop a new theory in any part of modern science if the primary purpose of all that work was to show that the theory was wrong.

This point is underlined by the fact that the behavior of the scientific community is not consistent with Popper's notion of how it should be. Credit in science is most often given for offering correct theories, not wrong ones, or for demonstrating the correctness of unexpected predictions, not for falsifying them. I know of no example of a Nobel Prize awarded to a scientist for falsifying his or her own theory.

C. Thomas Kuhn's Paradigm Shifts

Another towering figure in the twentieth century theory of science is Thomas Kuhn.[7] Kuhn was not a philosopher but a historian (more accurately, a physicist who retrained himself as a historian). It is Kuhn who popularized the word *paradigm*, which has today come to seem so inescapable.

explanation must be capable of empirical test'"), and Karl R. Popper, Conjectures and Refutations: The Growth of Scientific Knowledge 37 (5th ed. 1989) ("'[T]he criterion of the scientific status of a theory is its falsifiability, or refutability, or testability'").

7. Thomas S. Kuhn, The Structure of Scientific Revolutions (1962).

A paradigm, for Kuhn, is a sort of consensual world view within which scientists work. It comprises an agreed upon set of assumptions, methods, language, and everything else needed to do science. Within a given paradigm, scientists make steady, incremental progress, doing what Kuhn calls "normal science."

As time goes on, difficulties and contradictions arise that cannot be resolved, but one way or another, they are swept under the rug, rather than being allowed to threaten the central paradigm. However, at a certain point, enough of these difficulties have accumulated so that the situation becomes intolerable. At that point, a scientific revolution occurs, shattering the paradigm and replacing it with an entirely new one.

The new paradigm is so radically different from the old that normal discourse between the practitioners of the two paradigms becomes impossible. They view the world in different ways and speak different languages. It isn't even possible to tell which of the two paradigms is superior, because they address different sets of problems. They are incommensurate. Thus, science does not progress incrementally, as the science textbooks would have it, except during periods of normal science. Every once in a while, a scientific revolution brings about a paradigm shift, and science heads off in an entirely new direction.

Kuhn's view was formed largely on the basis of two important historical revolutions. One was the original scientific revolution that started with Nicolaus Copernicus and culminated with the new mechanics of Isaac Newton. The very word *revolution*, whether it refers to the scientific kind, the political kind, or any other kind, refers metaphorically to the revolutions in the heavens that Copernicus described in a book, *De Revolutionibus Orbium Caelestium*, which was published as he lay dying in 1543.[8] Before Copernicus, the dominant paradigm was the world view of ancient Greek philosophy, frozen in the fourth century B.C. ideas of Plato and Aristotle. After Newton, whose masterwork, *Philosophiæ Naturalis Principia Mathematica*, was published in 1687, every scientist was a Newtonian, and Aristotelianism was banished forever from the world stage. It is even possible that Sir Francis Bacon's disinterested observer was a reaction to Aristotelian authority. Look to nature, not to the ancient texts, Bacon may have been saying.

The second revolution that served as an example for Kuhn occurred early in the twentieth century. In a headlong series of events that lasted a mere twenty-five years, the Newtonian paradigm was overturned and replaced with the new physics, in the form of quantum mechanics and Einstein's relativity. The second revolution, though it happened much faster, was no less profound than the first.

The idea that science proceeds by periods of normal activity punctuated by shattering breakthroughs that make scientists rethink the whole problem is an appealing one, especially to the scientists themselves, who know from personal

8. I. Bernard Cohen, Revolution in Science (1985).

experience that it really happens that way. Kuhn's contribution is important. It gives us a new and useful structure (a paradigm, one might say) for organizing the entire history of science.

Nevertheless, Kuhn's theory does suffer from a number of shortcomings as an explanation for how science works. One of them is that it contains no measure of how big the change must be in order to count as a revolution or paradigm shift. Most scientists will say that there is a paradigm shift in their laboratory every six months or so (or at least every time it becomes necessary to write another proposal for research support). That isn't exactly what Kuhn had in mind.

Another difficulty is that even when a paradigm shift is truly profound, the paradigms it separates are not necessarily incommensurate. The new sciences of quantum mechanics and relativity, for example, did indeed show that Newton's laws of mechanics were not the most fundamental laws of nature. However, they did not show that they were wrong. Quite the contrary, they showed why Newton's laws of mechanics were right: Newton's laws arose out of new laws that were even deeper and that covered a wider range of circumstances unimagined by Newton and his followers, that is, things as small as atoms, or nearly as fast as the speed of light, or as dense as black holes. In more familiar realms of experience, Newton's laws go on working just as well as they always did. Thus, there is no ambiguity at all about which paradigm is better. The new laws of quantum mechanics and relativity subsume and enhance the older Newtonian world.

D. An Evolved Theory of Science

If neither Bacon nor Popper nor Kuhn gives us a perfect description of what science is or how it works, nevertheless all three help us to gain a much deeper understanding of it all.

Scientists are not Baconian observers of nature, but all scientists become Baconians when it comes to describing their observations. Scientists are rigorously, even passionately honest about reporting scientific results and how they were obtained, in formal publications. Scientific data are the coin of the realm in science, and they are always treated with reverence. Those rare instances in which data are found to have been fabricated or altered in some way are always traumatic scandals of the first order.[9]

Scientists are also not Popperian falsifiers of their own theories, but they don't have to be. They don't work in isolation. If a scientist has a rival with a

9. Such instances are discussed in David Goodstein, *Scientific Fraud*, 60 Am. Scholar 505 (1991). For a summary of recent investigations into scientific fraud and lesser instances of scientific misconduct, see Office of Research Integrity, Department of Health and Human Services, Scientific Misconduct Investigations: 1993–1997 (visited Nov. 21, 1999) <http://ori.dhhs.gov/PDF/scientific.pdf> (summarizing 150 scientific misconduct investigations closed by the Office of Research Integrity).

different theory of the same phenomena, the rival will be more than happy to perform the Popperian duty of attacking the scientist's theory at its weakest point. Moreover, if falsification is no more definitive than verification, and scientists prefer in any case to be right rather than wrong, they nevertheless know how to hold verification to a very high standard. If a theory makes novel and unexpected predictions, and those predictions are verified by experiments that reveal new and useful or interesting phenomena, then the chances that the theory is correct are greatly enhanced. And even if it is not correct, it has been fruitful in the sense that it has led to the discovery of previously unknown phenomena that might prove useful in themselves and that will have to be explained by the next theory that comes along.

Finally, science does not, as Kuhn seemed to think, periodically self-destruct and need to start over again, but it does undergo startling changes of perspective that lead to new and, invariably, better ways of understanding the world. Thus, science does not proceed smoothly and incrementally, but it is one of the few areas of human endeavor that is truly progressive. There is no doubt at all that twentieth century science is better than nineteenth century science, and we can be absolutely confident that what will come along in the twenty-first century will be better still. One cannot say the same about, say, art or literature.[10]

To all this, a couple of things must be added. The first is that science is, above all, an adversary process. It is an arena in which ideas do battle, with observations and data the tools of combat. The scientific debate is very different from what happens in a court of law, but just as in the law, it is crucial that every idea receive the most vigorous possible advocacy, just in case it might be right. Thus, the Popperian ideal of holding one's hypothesis in a skeptical and tentative way is not merely inconsistent with reality, it would be harmful to science if it were pursued. As I discuss shortly, not only ideas, but the scientists themselves engage in endless competition according to rules that, although they are nowhere written down, are nevertheless complex and binding.

In the competition among ideas, the institution of peer review plays a central role. Scientific articles submitted for publication and proposals for funding are

10. The law, too, can claim to be progressive. Development of legal constructs, such as due process, equal protection, and individual privacy, reflects notable progress in the betterment of mankind. *See* Laura Kalman, The Strange Career of Legal Liberalism 2–4 (1996) (recognizing the "faith" of legal liberalists in the use of law as an engine for progressive social change in favor of society's disadvantaged). Such progress is measured by a less precise form of social judgment than the consensus that develops regarding scientific progress. *See* Steven Goldberg, *The Reluctant Embrace: Law and Science in America*, 75 Geo. L.J. 1341, 1346 (1987) ("Social judgments, however imprecise, can sometimes be reached on legal outcomes. If a court's decision appears to lead to a sudden surge in the crime rate, it may be judged wrong. If it appears to lead to new opportunities for millions of citizens, it may be judged right. The law does gradually change to reflect this kind of social testing. But the process is slow, uncertain, and controversial; there is nothing in the legal community like the consensus in the scientific community on whether a particular result constitutes progress.")

often sent to anonymous experts in the field, in other words, peers of the author, for review. Peer review works superbly to separate valid science from nonsense, or, in Kuhnian terms, to ensure that the current paradigm has been respected.[11] It works less well as a means of choosing between competing valid ideas, in part because the peer doing the reviewing is often a competitor for the same resources (pages in prestigious journals, funds from government agencies) being sought by the authors. It works very poorly in catching cheating or fraud, because all scientists are socialized to believe that even their bitterest competitor is rigorously honest in the reporting of scientific results, making it easy to fool a referee with purposeful dishonesty if one wants to. Despite all of this, peer review is one of the sacred pillars of the scientific edifice.

III. Becoming a Professional Scientist

Science as a profession or career has become highly organized and structured.[12] It is not, relatively speaking, a very remunerative profession—that would be inconsistent with the Baconian ideal—but it is intensely competitive, and a certain material well-being does tend to follow in the wake of success (successful scientists, one might say, do get to bring home the Bacon).

A. The Institutions

These are the institutions of science: Research is done in the Ph.D.-granting universities, and to a lesser extent, in colleges that don't grant Ph.D.s. It is also done in national laboratories and in industrial laboratories. Before World War II, basic science was financed mostly by private foundations (Rockefeller, Carnegie), but since the war, the funding of science (except in industrial laboratories) has largely been taken over by agencies of the federal government, notably the National Science Foundation (an independent agency), the National Institutes of Health (part of the Public Health Service of the Department of

11. The Supreme Court received differing views regarding the proper role of peer review. *Compare* Brief for Amici Curiae Daryl E. Chubin et al. at 10, Daubert v. Merrell Dow Pharms., Inc., 509 U.S. 579 (1993) (No. 92-102) ("peer review referees and editors limit their assessment of submitted articles to such matters as style, plausibility, and defensibility; they do not duplicate experiments from scratch or plow through reams of computer-generated data in order to guarantee accuracy or veracity or certainty"), *with* Brief for Amici Curiae New England Journal of Medicine, Journal of the American Medical Association, and Annals of Internal Medicine in Support of Respondent, Daubert v. Merrell Dow Pharms., Inc., 509 U.S. 579 (1993) (No. 92-102) (proposing that publication in a peer-reviewed journal be the primary criterion for admitting scientific evidence in the courtroom). *See generally* Daryl E. Chubin & Edward J. Hackett, Peerless Science: Peer Review and U.S. Science Policy (1990); Arnold S. Relman & Marcia Angell, *How Good Is Peer Review?* 321 New Eng. J. Med. 827–29 (1989). As a practicing scientist and frequent peer reviewer, I can testify that Chubin's view is correct.

12. The analysis that follows is based on David Goodstein & James Woodward, *Inside Science*, 68 Am. Scholar 83 (1999).

Health and Human Services), and parts of the Department of Energy and the Department of Defense.

Scientists who work at all these organizations—universities, colleges, national and industrial laboratories, and funding agencies—belong to scientific societies that are organized mostly by discipline. There are large societies, such as the American Physical Society and the American Chemical Society; societies for subdisciplines, such as optics and spectroscopy; and even organizations of societies, such as FASEB (the Federation of American Societies of Experimental Biology).

Scientific societies are private organizations that elect their own officers, hold scientific meetings, publish journals, and finance their operations from the collection of dues and from the proceeds of their publishing and educational activities. The American Association for the Advancement of Science also holds meetings and publishes a famous journal (*Science*), but it is not restricted to any one discipline. The National Academy of Sciences holds meetings and publishes a journal, and it has an operational arm, the National Research Council, that carries out studies for various government agencies, but by far its most important activity is to elect its own members.

These are the basic institutions of American science. It should not come as news that the universities and colleges engage in a fierce but curious competition, in which no one knows who's keeping score, but everyone knows roughly what the score is. (In recent years, some national newsmagazines have found it profitable to appoint themselves scorekeepers in this competition. Academic officials dismiss these journalistic judgments, except when their own institutions come out on top.) Departments in each discipline compete with one another, as do national and industrial laboratories and even funding agencies. Competition in science is at its most refined, however, at the level of individual careers.

B. The Reward System and Authority Structure

To regulate the competition among scientists, there is a reward system and an authority structure. The fruits of the reward system are fame, glory, and immortality. The purposes of the authority structure are power and influence. The reward system and the authority structure are closely related to one another, but scientists distinguish sharply between them. When they speak of a colleague who has become president of a famous university, they will say sadly, "It's a pity—he was still capable of good work," sounding like warriors lamenting the loss of a fallen comrade. The university president is a kingpin of the authority structure, but he is a dropout from the reward system. Similar sorts of behavior can be observed in industrial and government laboratories, but a description of what goes on in universities will be enough to illustrate how the system works.

A career in academic science begins at the first step on the reward system ladder, a Ph.D., followed in many areas by one or two stints as a postdoctoral fellow. The Ph.D. and postdoctoral positions had best be at universities (or at least departments) that are high up in that fierce but invisible competition because all subsequent steps are most likely to take the individual sideways or downward on the list. The next step is a crucial one: appointment to a tenure-track junior faculty position. About two-thirds of all postdoctoral fellows in American universities believe they are going to make this step, but in fact, only about a quarter of them succeed. This step and all subsequent steps require growing fame as a scientist beyond the individual's own circle of acquaintances. Recommendations will be sought from people who know of the person because of the importance of his or her scientific accomplishments. Thus, it is essential by this time that the individual has accomplished something. The remaining steps up the reward system ladder are promotion to an academic tenured position and full professorship; various prizes, medals, and awards given out by the scientific societies; an endowed chair (the virtual equivalent of Galileo's wooden *cattedra*); election to the National Academy; the Nobel Prize; and, finally, immortality.

Positions in the authority structure are generally rewards for having achieved a certain level in the reward system. For example, starting from the junior faculty level, it is possible to step sideways temporarily or even permanently into a position as contract officer in a funding agency. Because contract officers influence the distribution of research funds, they have a role in deciding who will succeed in the climb up the reward system ladder. At successively higher levels one can become the editor of a journal; chair of a department; dean, provost, or president of a university; and even the head of a funding agency. People in these positions have stepped out of the reward system, but they have something to say about who succeeds in it.

IV. Some Myths and Facts About Science

"In matters of science," Galileo wrote, "the authority of thousands is not worth the humble reasoning of one single person."[13] Doing battle with the Aristotelian professors of his day, Galileo believed that appeal to authority was the enemy of reason. But, contrary to Galileo's famous remark, the fact is that authority is of fundamental importance to science. If a paper's author is a famous scientist, I think the paper is probably worth reading. However, an appeal from a scientific

13. I found this statement framed on the office wall of a colleague in Italy in the form, "*In questioni di scienza L'autorità di mille non vale l'umile ragionare di un singolo.*" However, I have not been able to find the famous remark in this form in Galileo's writings. An equivalent statement in different words can be found in Galileo's *Il Saggiatore* (1623). *See* Andrea Frova & Mariapiera Marenzona, *Parola di Galileo* 473 (1998).

wanna-be, asking that his great new discovery be brought to the attention of the scientific world, is almost surely not worth reading (such papers arrive in my office, on the average, about once a week). The triumph of reason over authority is just one of the many myths about science, some of which I've already discussed. Here's a brief list of others:

Myth: Scientists must have open minds, being ready to discard old ideas in favor of new ones.

Fact: Because science is an adversary process in which each idea deserves the most vigorous possible defense, it is useful for the successful progress of science that scientists tenaciously hang on to their own ideas, even in the face of contrary evidence (and they do, they do).

Myth: Science must be an open book. For example, every new experiment must be described so completely that any other scientist can reproduce it.

Fact: There is a very large component of skill in making cutting-edge experiments work. Often, the only way to import a new technique into a laboratory is to hire someone (usually a postdoctoral fellow) who has already made it work elsewhere. Nevertheless, scientists have a solemn responsibility to describe the methods they use as fully and accurately as possible. And, eventually, the skill will be acquired by enough people to make the new technique commonplace.

Myth: When a new theory comes along, the scientist's duty is to falsify it.

Fact: When a new theory comes along, the scientist's instinct is to verify it. When a theory is new, the effect of a decisive experiment that shows it to be wrong is that both the theory and the experiment are quickly forgotten. This result leads to no progress for anyone in the reward system. Only when a theory is well established and widely accepted does it pay off to prove that it's wrong.

Myth: Real science is easily distinguished from pseudoscience.

Fact: This is what philosophers call the problem of demarcation: One of Popper's principal motives in proposing his standard of falsifiability was precisely to provide a means of demarcation between real science and impostors. For example, Einstein's theory of relativity (with which Popper was deeply impressed) made clear predictions that could certainly be falsified if they were not correct. In contrast, Freud's theories of psychoanalysis (with which Popper was far less impressed) could never be proven wrong. Thus, to Popper, relativity was science but psychoanalysis was not.

As I've already shown, real scientists don't do as Popper says they should. But quite aside from that, there is another problem with Popper's criterion (or indeed any other criterion) for demarcation: Would-be scientists read books too. If it becomes widely accepted (and to some extent it has) that falsifiable predictions are the signature of real science, then pretenders to the throne of science will make falsifiable predictions, too.[14] There is no simple, mechanical criterion for distinguishing real science from something that is not real science. That certainly doesn't mean, however, that the job can't be done. As I discuss below, the Supreme Court, in the *Daubert* decision, has made a respectable stab at showing how to do it.[15]

Myth: Scientific theories are just that: theories. All scientific theories are eventually proved wrong and are replaced by other theories.

Fact: The things that science has taught us about how the world works are the most secure elements in all of human knowledge. I must distinguish here between science at the frontiers of knowledge (where by definition we don't yet understand everything and where theories are indeed vulnerable) and textbook science that is known with great confidence. Matter is made of atoms, DNA transmits the blueprints of organisms from generation to generation, light is an electromagnetic wave; these things are not likely to be proved wrong. The theory of relativity and the theory of evolution are in the same class. They are still called theories for historic reasons only. The satellite navigation system in my car routinely uses the theory of relativity to make calculations accurate enough to tell me exactly where I am and to take me to my destination with unerring precision.

It should be said here that the incorrect notion that all theories must eventually be wrong is fundamental to the work of both Popper and Kuhn, and these theorists have been crucial in helping us understand how science works. Thus, their theories, like good scientific theories at the frontiers of knowledge, can be both useful and wrong.

Myth: Scientists are people of uncompromising honesty and integrity.

Fact: They would have to be if Bacon were right about how science works, but he wasn't. Scientists are rigorously honest where honesty matters most to them: in the reporting of scientific procedures and data in peer-reviewed publications. In all else, they are ordinary mortals like all other ordinary mortals.

14. For a list of such pretenders, see Larry Laudan, Beyond Positivism and Relativism 219 (1996).

15. The Supreme Court in *Daubert* identified four nondefinitive factors that were thought to be illustrative of characteristics of scientific knowledge: testability or falsifiability, peer review, a known or potential error rate, and general acceptance within the scientific community. 509 U.S. at 590 (1993). Subsequent cases have expanded on these factors. *See, e.g., In re* TMI Litig. Cases Consol. II, 911 F. Supp. 775, 787 (M.D. Pa. 1995) (which considered the following additional factors: the relationship of the technique to methods that have been established to be reliable; the qualifications of the expert witness testifying based on the methodology; the nonjudicial uses of the method; logical or internal consistency of the hypothesis; consistency of the hypothesis with accepted theories; and precision of the hypothesis or theory). *See generally* Bert Black et al., *Science and the Law in the Wake of* Daubert: *A New Search for Scientific Knowledge,* 72 Tex. L. Rev. 715, 783–84 (1994) (discussion of expanded list of factors).

V. Comparing Science and the Law

Science and the law differ in both the language they use and the objectives they seek to accomplish.

A. Language

Someone once said that the United States and England are two nations separated by a common language. Something similar can be said of science and the law. There are any number of words that are commonly used in both disciplines, but with different meanings. Let me give just a few examples.

The word *force*, as it is used by lawyers, has connotations of violence and the domination of one person's will over another, as in phrases such as "excessive use of force" and "forced entry." In science, force is something that when applied to a body, causes its speed and direction of motion to change. Also, all forces arise from a few fundamental forces, most notably gravity and the electric force. The word carries no other baggage.

In contrast, the word *evidence* is used much more loosely in science than in the law. The law has precise rules of evidence that govern what is admissible and what isn't. In science the word merely seems to mean something less than "proof." A certain number of the papers in any issue of a scientific journal will have titles that begin with "Evidence for (or against)." What that means is, the authors weren't able to prove their point, but here are their results anyway.

The word *theory* is a particularly interesting example of a word that has different meanings in the two disciplines. A legal theory (as I understand it) is a proposal that fits the known facts and legal precedents and that favors the attorney's client. The requisite of a theory in science is that it make new predictions that can be tested by new experiments or observations and falsified or verified (as discussed above), but in any case, put to the test.

Even the word *law* has different meanings in the two disciplines. To a legal practitioner, a law is something that has been promulgated by some human authority, such as a legislature or parliament. In science, a law is a law of nature, something that humans can hope to discover and describe accurately, but that can never be changed by any human authority.

My final example is, to me, the most interesting of all. It is the word *error*. In the law, and in common usage, *error* and *mistake* are more or less synonymous. A legal decision can be overturned if it is found to be contaminated by judicial error. In science, however, *error* and *mistake* have different meanings. Anyone can make a mistake, and scientists have no obligation to report theirs in the scientific literature. They just clean up the mess and go on to the next attempt. Error, on the other hand, is intrinsic to any measurement, and far from ignoring it or covering it up or even attempting to eliminate it, authors of every paper about a scientific experiment will include a careful analysis of the errors to put limits on the uncertainty in the measured result. To make mistakes is human, one might say, but error is intrinsic to our interaction with nature, and is therefore part of science.

B. Objectives

Beyond the meanings of certain key words, science and the law differ fundamentally in their objectives. The objective of the law is justice; that of science is truth.[16] These are not at all the same thing. Justice, of course, also seeks truth, but it requires that a clear decision be made in a reasonable and limited amount of time. In the scientific search for truth there are no time limits and no point at which a final decision must be made.

And yet, in spite of all these differences, science and the law share, at the deepest possible level, the same aspirations and many of the same methods. Both disciplines seek, in structured debate, using empirical evidence, to arrive at rational conclusions that transcend the prejudices and self-interest of individuals.

VI. A Scientist's View of *Daubert*

In the 1993 *Daubert* decision, the U.S. Supreme Court took it upon itself to solve, once and for all, the knotty problem of the demarcation of science from pseudoscience. Better yet, it undertook to enable every federal judge to solve that problem in deciding the admissibility of each scientific expert witness in every case that arises. In light of all the uncertainties discussed in this chapter, it must be considered an ambitious thing to do.[17]

The presentation of scientific evidence in a court of law is a kind of shotgun marriage between the two disciplines. Both are forced to some extent to yield to the central imperatives of the other's way of doing business, and it is likely that neither will be shown in its best light. The *Daubert* decision is an attempt (not the first, of course) to regulate that encounter. Judges are asked to decide the

16. This point is made eloquently by D. Allen Bromley in Science and the Law, Address at the 1998 Annual Meeting of the American Bar Association (Aug. 2, 1998).

17. Chief Justice Rehnquist, responding to the majority opinion in *Daubert*, was the first to express his uneasiness with the task assigned to federal judges as follows: "I defer to no one in my confidence in federal judges; but I am at a loss to know what is meant when it is said that the scientific status of a theory depends on its 'falsifiability,' and I suspect some of them will be, too." 509 U.S. 579, 600 (1993) (Rehnquist, C.J., concurring in part and dissenting in part). His concern was then echoed by Judge Alex Kozinski when the case was reconsidered by the U.S. Court of Appeals for the Ninth Circuit following remand by the Supreme Court. 43 F.3d 1311, 1316 (9th Cir. 1995) ("Our responsibility, then, unless we badly misread the Supreme Court's opinion, is to resolve disputes among respected, well-credentialed scientists about matters squarely within their expertise, in areas where there is no scientific consensus as to what is and what is not 'good science,' and occasionally to reject such expert testimony because it was not 'derived by the scientific method.' Mindful of our position in the hierarchy of the federal judiciary, we take a deep breath and proceed with this heady task.")

"evidential reliability" of the intended testimony, based not on the conclusions to be offered, but on the methods used to reach those conclusions.

In particular, the methods should be judged by the following four criteria:

1. The theoretical underpinnings of the methods must yield testable predictions by means of which the theory could be falsified.
2. The methods should preferably be published in a peer-reviewed journal.
3. There should be a known rate of error that can be used in evaluating the results.
4. The methods should be generally accepted within the relevant scientific community.

In reading these four illustrative criteria mentioned by the Court, one is struck immediately by the specter of Karl Popper looming above the robed justices. (It's no mere illusion. The dependence on Popper is explicit in the written decision.) Popper alone is not enough, however, and the doctrine of falsification is supplemented by a bow to the institution of peer review, an acknowledgment of the scientific meaning of error, and a paradigm check (really, an inclusion of the earlier *Frye* standard).[18]

All in all, I would score the decision a pretty good performance.[19] The justices ventured into the treacherous crosscurrents of the philosophy of science—where even most scientists fear to tread—and emerged with at least their dignity intact. Falsifiability may not be a good way of doing science, but it's not the worst a posteriori way to judge science, and that's all that's required here. At least they managed to avoid the Popperian trap of demanding that the scientists be skeptical of their own ideas. The other considerations help lend substance and flexibility.[20] The jury is still out (so to speak) on how well this decision will work in practice, but it's certainly an impressive attempt to serve justice, if not truth. Applying it in practice will never be easy, but then that's what this manual is all about.

18. In *Frye v. United States,* 293 F. 1013, 1014 (D.C. Cir. 1923), the court stated that expert opinion based on a scientific technique is inadmissible unless the technique is "generally accepted" as reliable in the relevant scientific community.

19. For a contrary view, see Gary Edmond & David Mercer, *Recognizing* Daubert: *What Judges Should Know About Falsification,* 5 Expert Evidence 29–42 (1996).

20. *See supra* note 15.

Reference Guide on Statistics

DAVID H. KAYE AND DAVID A. FREEDMAN

David H. Kaye, M.A., J.D., is Regents' Professor, Arizona State University College of Law, and Fellow, Center for the Study of Law, Science, and Technology, Tempe, Arizona

David A. Freedman, Ph.D., is Professor of Statistics, University of California, Berkeley, California

CONTENTS

I. Introduction

Statistics, broadly defined, is the art and science of gaining information from data. For statistical purposes, data mean observations or measurements, expressed as numbers. A statistic may refer to a particular numerical value, derived from the data. Baseball statistics, for example, is the study of data about the game; a player's batting average is a statistic. The field of statistics includes methods for (1) collecting data, (2) analyzing data, and (3) drawing inferences from data.

Statistical assessments are prominent in many kinds of cases, ranging from antitrust to voting rights. Statistical reasoning can be crucial to the interpretation of psychological tests, toxicological and epidemiological studies, disparate treatment of employees, and DNA fingerprinting; this list could easily be extended.[1]

This reference guide describes the elements of statistical thinking. We hope that the explanations provided will permit judges and lawyers who deal with statistical evidence to understand the terminology, place the evidence in context, appreciate its strengths and weaknesses, and apply legal doctrine governing the use of such evidence. The reference guide is organized as follows:

- Section I provides an overview of the field, discusses the admissibility of statistical studies, and offers some suggestions about procedures that encourage the best use of statistical expertise in litigation.
- Section II addresses data collection. The design of a study is the most important determinant of its quality. The section reviews controlled experiments, observational studies, and surveys, indicating when these designs are likely to give useful data.
- Section III discusses the art of describing and summarizing data. The section considers the mean, median, and standard deviation. These are basic descriptive statistics, and most statistical analyses seen in court use them as building blocks. Section III also discusses trends and associations in data as summarized by graphs, percentages, and tables.
- Section IV describes the logic of statistical inference, emphasizing its foundations and limitations. In particular, this section explains statistical estimation, standard errors, confidence intervals, *p*-values, and hypothesis tests.
- Section V shows how relationships between two variables can be described by means of scatter diagrams, correlation coefficients, and regression lines. Statisticians often use regression techniques in an attempt to infer causation

1. *See generally* Statistics and the Law (Morris H. DeGroot et al. eds., 1986); Panel on Statistical Assessments as Evidence in the Courts, National Research Council, The Evolving Role of Statistical Assessments as Evidence in the Courts (Stephen E. Fienberg ed., 1989) [hereinafter The Evolving Role of Statistical Assessments as Evidence in the Courts]; Michael O. Finkelstein & Bruce Levin, Statistics for Lawyers (1990); 1 & 2 Joseph L. Gastwirth, Statistical Reasoning in Law and Public Policy (1988); Hans Zeisel & David Kaye, Prove It with Figures: Empirical Methods in Law and Litigation (1997).

from association; section V briefly explains the techniques and some of their limitations.

- An appendix presents certain technical details, and the glossary defines many statistical terms that might be encountered in litigation.

A. Admissibility and Weight of Statistical Studies

Statistical studies suitably designed to address a material issue generally will be admissible under the Federal Rules of Evidence. The hearsay rule rarely is a serious barrier to the presentation of statistical studies, since such studies may be offered to explain the basis for an expert's opinion or may be admissible under the learned treatise exception to the hearsay rule.[2] Likewise, since most statistical methods relied on in court are described in textbooks and journal articles and are capable of producing useful results when carefully and appropriately applied, such methods generally satisfy important aspects of the "scientific knowledge" requirement articulated in *Daubert v. Merrell Dow Pharmaceuticals, Inc.*[3] Of course, a particular study may use a method that is entirely appropriate, but so poorly executed that it should be inadmissible under Federal Rules of Evidence 403 and 702.[4] Or, the method may be inappropriate for the problem at hand and thus lacks the "fit" spoken of in *Daubert*.[5] Or, the study may rest on data of the type not reasonably relied on by statisticians or substantive experts, and hence run afoul of Federal Rule of Evidence 703. Often, however, the battle over statistical evidence concerns weight or sufficiency rather than admissibility.

B. Varieties and Limits of Statistical Expertise

For convenience, the field of statistics may be divided into three subfields: probability, theoretical statistics, and applied statistics. Theoretical statistics is the study of the mathematical properties of statistical procedures, such as error rates; probability theory plays a key role in this endeavor. Results may be used by

2. *See generally* 2 McCormick on Evidence §§ 321, 324.3 (John W. Strong ed., 5th ed. 1999). Studies published by government agencies also may be admissible as public records. *Id.* § 296. *See also* United States v. Esquivel, 88 F.3d 722, 727 (9th Cir. 1996) (taking judicial notice of 1990 census data showing the number of Hispanics eligible for jury service).

3. 509 U.S. 579, 589–90 (1993). For a discussion of the implications and scope of *Daubert* generally, see 1 Modern Scientific Evidence: The Law and Science of Expert Testimony § 1–3.0 (David L. Faigman et al. eds., 1997).

4. *See, e.g.*, Sheehan v. Daily Racing Form, Inc., 104 F.3d 940, 942 (7th Cir. 1997) ("failure to exercise the degree of care that a statistician would use in his scientific work, outside of the context of litigation" renders analysis inadmissible under *Daubert*).

5. 509 U.S. at 591; *cf.* People Who Care v. Rockford Bd. of Educ., 111 F.3d 528, 537–38 (7th Cir. 1997) ("a statistical study that fails to correct for salient explanatory variables, or even to make the most elementary comparisons, has no value as causal explanation and is therefore inadmissible in a federal court"); *Sheehan*, 104 F.3d at 942 (holding that expert's "failure to correct for any potential explanatory variables other than age" made the analyst's finding that "there was a significant correlation between age and retention" inadmissible).

applied statisticians who specialize in particular types of data collection, such as survey research, or in particular types of analysis, such as multivariate methods.

Statistical expertise is not confined to those with degrees in statistics. Because statistical reasoning underlies all empirical research, researchers in many fields are exposed to statistical ideas. Experts with advanced degrees in the physical, medical, and social sciences—and some of the humanities—may receive formal training in statistics. Such specializations as biostatistics, epidemiology, econometrics, and psychometrics are primarily statistical, with an emphasis on methods and problems most important to the related substantive discipline.

Individuals who specialize in using statistical methods—and whose professional careers demonstrate this orientation—are most likely to apply appropriate procedures and correctly interpret the results. On the other hand, forensic scientists and technicians often testify to probabilities or statistics derived from studies or databases compiled by others, even though some of these testifying experts lack the training or knowledge required to understand and apply the information. *State v. Garrison*[6] illustrates the problem. In a murder prosecution involving bite-mark evidence, a dentist was allowed to testify that "the probability factor of two sets of teeth being identical in a case similar to this is, approximately, eight in one million," even though "he was unaware of the formula utilized to arrive at that figure other than that it was 'computerized.'"[7]

At the same time, the choice of which data to examine, or how best to model a particular process, could require subject matter expertise that a statistician might lack. Statisticians often advise experts in substantive fields on the procedures for collecting data and often analyze data collected by others. As a result, cases involving statistical evidence often are (or should be) "two-expert" cases of interlocking testimony.[8] A labor economist, for example, may supply a definition of the relevant labor market from which an employer draws its employees, and the statistical expert may contrast the racial makeup of those hired to the racial composition of the labor market. Naturally, the value of the statistical analysis depends on the substantive economic knowledge that informs it.[9]

6. 585 P.2d 563 (Ariz. 1978).

7. *Id.* at 566, 568.

8. Sometimes a single witness presents both the substantive underpinnings and the statistical analysis. Ideally, such a witness has extensive expertise in both fields, although less may suffice to qualify the witness under Fed. R. Evid. 702. In deciding whether a witness who clearly is qualified in one field may testify in a related area, courts should recognize that qualifications in one field do not necessarily imply qualifications in the other.

9. In *Vuyanich v. Republic National Bank*, 505 F. Supp. 224, 319 (N.D. Tex. 1980), *vacated*, 723 F.2d 1195 (5th Cir. 1984), defendant's statistical expert criticized the plaintiffs' statistical model for an implicit, but restrictive, assumption about male and female salaries. The district court trying the case accepted the model because the plaintiffs' expert had a "very strong guess" about the assumption, and her expertise included labor economics as well as statistics. *Id.* It is doubtful, however, that economic knowledge sheds much light on the assumption, and it would have been simple to perform a less restrictive analysis. In this case, the court may have been overly impressed with a single expert who

C. Procedures that Enhance Statistical Testimony

1. Maintaining Professional Autonomy

Ideally, experts who conduct research in the context of litigation should proceed with the same objectivity that they would apply in other contexts. Thus, experts who testify (or who supply results that are used in testimony by others) should be free to do whatever analysis is required to address in a professionally responsible fashion the issues posed by the litigation.[10] Questions about the freedom of inquiry accorded to testifying experts, as well as the scope and depth of their investigations, may reveal some of the limitations to the analysis being presented.

2. Disclosing Other Analyses

Statisticians analyze data using a variety of statistical models and methods. There is much to be said for looking at the data in a variety of ways. To permit a fair evaluation of the analysis that the statistician does settle on, however, the testifying expert may explain the history behind the development of the final statistical approach.[11] Indeed, some commentators have urged that counsel who know of other data sets or analyses that do not support the client's position should reveal this fact to the court, rather than attempt to mislead the court by presenting only favorable results.[12]

combined substantive and statistical expertise. Once the issue is defined by legal and substantive knowledge, some aspects of the statistical analysis will turn on statistical considerations alone, and expertise in another subject will not be pertinent.

10. *See* The Evolving Role of Statistical Assessments as Evidence in the Courts, *supra* note 1, at 164 (recommending that the expert be free to consult with colleagues who have not been retained by any party to the litigation and that the expert receive a letter of engagement providing for these and other safeguards).

11. *See, e.g.*, Mikel Aickin, *Issues and Methods in Discrimination Statistics, in* Statistical Methods in Discrimination Litigation 159 (David H. Kaye & Mikel Aickin eds., 1986).

12. The Evolving Role of Statistical Assessments as Evidence in the Courts, *supra* note 1, at 167; *cf.* William W Schwarzer, *In Defense of "Automatic Disclosure in Discovery,"* 27 Ga. L. Rev. 655, 658–59 (1993) ("[T]he lawyer owes a duty to the court to make disclosure of core information."). The Panel on Statistical Assessments as Evidence in the Courts also recommends that "if a party gives statistical data to different experts for competing analyses, that fact be disclosed to the testifying expert, if any." The Evolving Role of Statistical Assessments as Evidence in the Courts, *supra* note 1, at 167. Whether and under what circumstances a particular statistical analysis might be so imbued with counsel's thoughts and theories of the case that it should receive protection as the attorney's work product is an issue beyond the scope of this reference guide.

3. Disclosing Data and Analytical Methods Before Trial

The collection of data often is expensive, and data sets typically contain at least some minor errors or omissions. Careful exploration of alternative modes of analysis also can be expensive and time consuming. To minimize the occurrence of distracting debates at trial over the accuracy of data and the choice of analytical techniques, and to permit informed expert discussions of method, pretrial procedures should be used, particularly with respect to the accuracy and scope of the data, and to discover the methods of analysis. Suggested procedures along these lines are available elsewhere.[13]

4. Presenting Expert Statistical Testimony

The most common format for the presentation of evidence at trial is sequential. The plaintiff's witnesses are called first, one by one, without interruption except for cross-examination, and testimony is in response to specific questions rather than by an extended narration. Although traditional, this structure is not compelled by the Federal Rules of Evidence.[14] Some alternatives have been proposed that might be more effective in cases involving substantial statistical testimony. For example, when the reports of witnesses go together, the judge might allow their presentations to be combined and the witnesses to be questioned as a panel rather than sequentially. More narrative testimony might be allowed, and the expert might be permitted to give a brief tutorial on statistics as a preliminary to some testimony. Instead of allowing the parties to present their experts in the midst of all the other evidence, the judge might call for the experts for opposing sides to testify at about the same time. Some courts, particularly in bench trials, may have both experts placed under oath and, in effect, permit them to engage in a dialogue. In such a format, experts are able to say whether they agree or disagree on specific issues. The judge and counsel can interject questions. Such practices may improve the judge's understanding and reduce the tensions associated with the experts' adversarial role.[15]

13. *See* The Special Comm. on Empirical Data in Legal Decision Making, Recommendations on Pretrial Proceedings in Cases with Voluminous Data, *reprinted in* The Evolving Role of Statistical Assessments as Evidence in the Courts, *supra* note 1, app. F. *See also* David H. Kaye, *Improving Legal Statistics*, 24 L. & Soc'y Rev. 1255 (1990).

14. *See* Fed. R. Evid. 611.

15. The Evolving Role of Statistical Assessments as Evidence in the Courts, *supra* note 1, at 174.

II. How Have the Data Been Collected?

An analysis is only as good as the data on which it rests.[16] To a large extent, the design of a study determines the quality of the data. Therefore, the proper interpretation of data and their implications begins with an understanding of study design, and different designs help answer different questions. In many cases, statistics are introduced to show causation. Would additional information in a securities prospectus disclosure have caused potential investors to behave in some other way? Does capital punishment deter crime? Do food additives cause cancer? The design of studies intended to prove causation is the first and perhaps the most important topic of this section.

Another issue is the use of sample data to characterize a population: the population is the whole class of units that are of interest; the sample is a set of units chosen for detailed study. Inferences from the part to the whole are justified only when the sample is representative, and that is the second topic of this section.

Finally, it is important to verify the accuracy of the data collection. Errors can arise in the process of making and recording measurements on individual units. This aspect of data quality is the third topic in this section.

A. Is the Study Properly Designed to Investigate Causation?

1. Types of Studies

When causation is at issue, advocates have relied on three major types of information: anecdotal evidence, observational studies, and controlled experiments.[17] As we shall see, anecdotal reports can provide some information, but they are

16. For introductory treatments of data collection, see, e.g., David Freedman et al., Statistics (3d ed. 1998); Darrell Huff, How to Lie with Statistics (1954); David S. Moore, Statistics: Concepts and Controversies (3d ed. 1991); Hans Zeisel, Say It with Figures (6th ed. 1985); and Zeisel & Kaye, *supra* note 1.

17. When relevant studies exist before the commencement of the litigation, it becomes the task of the lawyer and appropriate experts to explain this research to the court. Examples of such "off-the-shelf" research are experiments pinpointing conditions under which eyewitnesses tend to err in identifying criminals and studies of how sex stereotyping affects perceptions of women in the workplace. *See, e.g.*, State v. Chapple, 660 P.2d 1208, 1223–24 (Ariz. 1983) (reversing a conviction for excluding expert testimony about scientific research on eyewitness accuracy); Price Waterhouse v. Hopkins, 490 U.S. 228, 235 (1989). Some psychologists have questioned the applicability of these experiments to litigation. *See, e.g.*, Gerald V. Barrett & Scott B. Morris, *The American Psychological Association's Amicus Curiae Brief in* Price Waterhouse v. Hopkins*: The Values of Science Versus the Values of the Law*, 17 Law & Hum. Behav. 201 (1993). For a rejoinder, see Susan T. Fiske et al., *What Constitutes a Scientific Review?: A Majority Retort to Barrett and Morris*, 17 Law & Hum. Behav. 217 (1993).

If no preexisting studies are available, a case-specific one may be devised. *E.g.*, United States v. Youritan Constr. Co., 370 F. Supp. 643, 647 (N.D. Cal. 1973) (investigating racial discrimination in the rental-housing market by using "testers"—who should differ only in their race—to rent a property), more useful as a stimulus for further inquiry than as a basis for establishing association. Observational studies can establish that one factor is associated with another, but considerable analysis may be necessary to bridge the gap from association to causation.[18] Controlled experiments are ideal for ascertaining causation, but they can be difficult to undertake.

"Anecdotal evidence" means reports of one kind of event following another. Typically, the reports are obtained haphazardly or selectively, and the logic of "post hoc, ergo propter hoc" does not suffice to demonstrate that the first event causes the second. Consequently, while anecdotal evidence can be suggestive,[19] it can also be quite misleading.[20] For instance, some children who live near power lines develop leukemia; but does exposure to electrical and magnetic fields cause this disease? The anecdotal evidence is not compelling because leukemia also occurs among children who have minimal exposure to such fields.[21] It is necessary to compare disease rates among those who are exposed and those who are not. If exposure causes the disease, the rate should be higher among the exposed, lower among the unexposed. Of course, the two groups may differ in crucial ways other than the exposure. For example, children who live near power

aff'd in part, 509 F.2d 623 (9th Cir. 1975). For a critical review of studies using testers, see James J. Heckman & Peter Siegelman, *The Urban Institute Audit Studies: Their Methods and Findings*, *in* Clear and Convincing Evidence: Measurement of Discrimination in America 187 (Michael Fix & Raymond J. Struyk eds., 1993) (including commentary).

18. For example, smokers have higher rates of lung cancer than nonsmokers; thus smoking and lung cancer are associated.

19. In medicine, evidence from clinical practice is often the starting point for the demonstration of a causal effect. One famous example involves exposure of mothers to German measles during pregnancy, followed by blindness in their babies. N. McAlister Gregg, *Congenital Cataract Following German Measles in the Mother*, 3 Transactions Ophthalmological Soc'y Austl. 35 (1941), *reprinted in* The Challenge of Epidemiology 426 (Carol Buck et al. eds., 1988).

20. Indeed, some courts have suggested that attempts to infer causation from anecdotal reports are inadmissible as unsound methodology under *Daubert v. Merrell Dow Pharmaceuticals, Inc.*, 509 U.S. 579 (1993). *See, e.g.*, Haggerty v. Upjohn Co., 950 F. Supp. 1160, 1163–64 (S.D. Fla. 1996) (holding that reports to the Food and Drug Administration of "adverse medical events" involving the drug Halcion and "anecdotal case reports appearing in medical literature . . . can be used to generate hypotheses about causation, but not causation conclusions" because "scientifically valid cause and effect determinations depend on controlled clinical trials and epidemiological studies"); Cartwright v. Home Depot U.S.A., Inc., 936 F. Supp. 900, 905 (M.D. Fla. 1996) (excluding an expert's opinion that latex paint caused plaintiff's asthma, in part because "case reports . . . are no substitute for a scientifically designed and conducted inquiry").

21. *See* Committee on the Possible Effects of Electromagnetic Fields on Biologic Sys., National Research Council, Possible Health Effects of Exposure to Residential Electric and Magnetic Fields (1997); Zeisel & Kaye, *supra* note 1, at 66–67. There are serious problems in measuring exposure to electromagnetic fields, and results are somewhat inconsistent from one study to another. For such reasons, the epidemiologic evidence for an effect on health is quite inconclusive. *Id.*; Martha S. Linet et al., *Residential Exposure to Magnetic Fields and Acute Lymphoblastic Leukemia in Children*, 337 New Eng. J. Med. 1 (1997); Edward W. Campion, *Power Lines, Cancer, and Fear*, 337 New Eng. J. Med. 44 (1997) (editorial); Gary Taubes, *Magnetic Field-Cancer Link: Will It Rest in Peace?*, 277 Science 29 (1997) (quoting various epidemiologists).

lines could come from poorer families and be exposed to other environmental hazards. These differences could create the appearance of a cause-and-effect relationship, or they can mask a real relationship. Cause-and-effect relationships often are quite subtle, and carefully designed studies are needed to draw valid conclusions.[22]

Typically, a well-designed study will compare outcomes for subjects who are exposed to some factor—the treatment group—and other subjects who are not so exposed—the control group. A distinction must then be made between controlled experiments and observational studies. In a controlled experiment, the investigators decide which subjects are exposed to the factor of interest and which subjects go into the control group. In most observational studies, the subjects themselves choose their exposures. Because of this self-selection, the treatment and control groups are likely to differ with respect to important factors other than the one of primary interest.[23] (These other factors are called confounding variables or lurking variables.[24]) With studies on the health effects of power lines, family background is a possible confounder; so is exposure to other hazards.[25]

22. Here is a classic example from epidemiology. At one time, it was thought that lung cancer was caused by fumes from tarring the roads, because many lung cancer patients lived near roads that had recently been paved. This is anecdotal evidence. But the logic is quite incomplete, because many people without lung cancer were exposed to asphalt fumes. A comparison of rates is needed. Careful study showed that lung cancer patients had similar rates of exposure to tar fumes as other people; the real difference was in exposure to cigarette smoke. Richard Doll & A. Bradford Hill, *A Study of the Aetiology of Carcinoma of the Lung*, 2 Brit. Med. J. 1271 (1952).

23. For present purposes, a variable is a numerical characteristic of units in a study. For instance, in a survey of people, the unit of analysis is the person, and variables might include income (in dollars per year) and educational level (years of schooling completed). In a study of school districts, the unit of analysis is the district, and variables might include average family income of residents and average test scores of students. When investigating a possible cause-and-effect relationship, the variable that characterizes the effect is called the dependent variable, since it may depend on the causes; dependent variables also are called response variables. In contrast, the variables that represent the causes are called independent variables; independent variables also are called factors or explanatory variables.

24. A confounding variable is correlated with the independent variables and with the dependent variable. If the units being studied differ on the independent variables, they are also likely to differ on the confounder. Therefore, the confounder—not the independent variables—could be responsible for differences seen on the dependent variable.

25. Confounding is a problem even in careful epidemiologic studies. For example, women with herpes are more likely to develop cervical cancer than women who have not been exposed to the virus. It was concluded that herpes caused cancer; in other words, the association was thought to be causal. Later research suggests that herpes is only a marker of sexual activity. Women who have had multiple sexual partners are more likely to be exposed not only to herpes but also to human papilloma virus. Certain strains of papilloma virus seem to cause cervical cancer, while herpes does not. Apparently, the association between herpes and cervical cancer is not causal but is due to the effect of other variables. *See* Viral Etiology of Cervical Cancer (Richard Peto & Harald zur Hausen eds., 1986); The Epidemiology of Cervical Cancer and Human Papillomavirus (N. Muñoz et al. eds. 1992). For additional examples and discussion, see Freedman et al., *supra* note 16, at 12–27, 150–52; David Freedman, *From Association to Causation: Some Remarks on the History of Statistics,* 14 Stat. Sci. 243 (1999).

2. *Randomized Controlled Experiments*

In randomized controlled experiments, investigators assign subjects to treatment or control groups at random. The groups are therefore likely to be quite comparable—except for the treatment. Choosing at random tends to balance the groups with respect to possible confounders, and the effect of remaining imbalances can be assessed by statistical techniques.[26] Consequently, inferences based on well-executed randomized experiments are more secure than inferences based on observational studies.[27]

The following illustration brings together the points made thus far. Many doctors think that taking aspirin helps prevent heart attacks, but there is some controversy. Most people who take aspirin do not have heart attacks; this is anecdotal evidence for the protective effect, but proves very little. After all, most people do not suffer heart attacks—whether or not they take aspirin regularly. A careful study must compare heart attack rates for two groups: persons who take aspirin (the treatment group) and persons who do not (the controls). An observational study would be easy to do, but then the aspirin-takers are likely to be different from the controls. If, for instance, the controls are healthier to begin with, the study would be biased against the drug. Randomized experiments with aspirin are harder to do, but they provide much better evidence. It is the experiments that demonstrate a protective effect.

To summarize: First, outcome figures from a treatment group without a control group generally reveal very little and can be misleading. Comparisons are essential. Second, if the control group was obtained through random assignment before treatment, a difference in the outcomes between treatment and control groups may be accepted, within the limits of statistical error, as the true measure of the treatment effect.[28] However, if the control group was created in any

26. *See infra* § IV.

27. Experiments, however, are often impractical, as in the power-line example. Even when randomized controlled experiments are feasible, true randomization can be difficult to achieve. *See, e.g.*, Kenneth F. Schulz, *Subverting Randomization in Controlled Trials*, 274 JAMA 1456 (1995); Rachel Nowak, *Problems in Clinical Trials Go Far Beyond Misconduct*, 264 Science 1538 (1994). For statistical purposes, randomization should be accomplished using some definite, objective method (like a random number generator on a computer); haphazard assignment may not be sufficient.

28. Of course, the possibility that the two groups will not be comparable in some unrecognized way can never be eliminated. Random assignment, however, allows the researcher to compute the probability of seeing a large difference in the outcomes when the treatment actually has no effect. When this probability is small, the difference in the response is said to be "statistically significant." *See infra* § IV.B.2. Randomization of subjects to treatment or control groups puts statistical tests of significance on a secure footing. Freedman et al., *supra* note 16, at 503–24, 547–78.

Even more important, randomization also ensures that the assignment of subjects to treatment and control groups is free from conscious or unconscious manipulation by investigators or subjects. Randomization may not be the only way to ensure such protection, but "it is the simplest and best understood way to certify that one has done so." Philip W. Lavori et al., *Designs for Experiments—Parallel Comparisons of Treatment*, *in* Medical Uses of Statistics 61, 66 (John C. Bailar III & Frederick Mosteller other way, differences in the groups that existed before treatment may contribute to differences in the outcomes, or mask differences that otherwise would be observed. Thus, observational studies succeed to the extent that their treatment and control groups are comparable—apart from the treatment.

3. Observational Studies

The bulk of the statistical studies seen in court are observational, not experimental. Take the question of whether capital punishment deters murder. To do a randomized controlled experiment, people would have to be assigned randomly to a control group and a treatment group. The controls would know that they could not receive the death penalty for murder, while those in the treatment group would know they could be executed. The rate of subsequent murders by the subjects in these groups would be observed. Such an experiment is unacceptable—politically, ethically, and legally.[29]

Nevertheless, many studies of the deterrent effect of the death penalty have been conducted, all observational, and some have attracted judicial attention.[30] Researchers have catalogued differences in the incidence of murder in states with and without the death penalty, and they have analyzed changes in homicide rates and execution rates over the years. In such observational studies, investigators may speak of control groups (such as the states without capital punishment) and of controlling for potentially confounding variables (e.g., worsening economic conditions).[31] However, association is not causation, and the causal inferences that can be drawn from such analyses rest on a less secure foundation than that provided by a randomized controlled experiment.[32]

eds., 2d ed. 1992). To avoid ambiguity, the researcher should be explicit "about how the randomization was done (e.g., table of random numbers) and executed (e.g., by sealed envelopes prepared in advance)." *Id. See also* Colin Begg et al., *Improving the Quality of Reporting of Randomized Controlled Trials: The CONSORT Statement*, 276 JAMA 637 (1996).

29. *Cf.* Experimentation in the Law: Report of the Federal Judicial Center Advisory Committee on Experimentation in the Law (Federal Judicial Center 1981) [hereinafter Experimentation in the Law] (study of ethical issues raised by controlled experimentation in the evaluation of innovations in the justice system).

30. *See generally* Hans Zeisel, *The Deterrent Effect of the Death Penalty: Facts v. Faith*, 1976 Sup. Ct. Rev. 317.

31. A procedure often used to control for confounding in observational studies is regression analysis. The underlying logic is described *infra* § V.D and in Daniel L. Rubinfeld, Reference Guide on Multiple Regression, § II, in this manual. The early enthusiasm for using multiple regression analysis to study the death penalty was not shared by reviewers. *Compare* Isaac Ehrlich, *The Deterrent Effect of Capital Punishment: A Question of Life and Death*, 65 Am. Econ. Rev. 397 (1975), *with, e.g.*, Lawrence R. Klein et al., *The Deterrent Effect of Capital Punishment: An Assessment of the Estimates, in* Panel on Research on Deterrent and Incapacitative Effects, National Research Council, Deterrence and Incapacitation: Estimating the Effects of Criminal Sanctions on Crime Rates 336 (Alfred Blumstein et al. eds., 1978); Edward Leamer, *Let's Take the Con Out of Econometrics*, 73 Am. Econ. Rev. 31 (1983).

32. *See, e.g.*, Experimentation in the Law, *supra* note 29, at 18:

> [G]roups selected without randomization will [almost] always differ in some systematic way other than exposure to the experimental program. Statistical techniques can eliminate chance as a feasible explanation for the

Of course, observational studies can be very useful. The evidence that smoking causes lung cancer in humans, although largely observational, is compelling. In general, observational studies provide powerful evidence in the following circumstances:

- The association is seen in studies of different types among different groups. This reduces the chance that the observed association is due to a defect in one type of study or a peculiarity in one group of subjects.
- The association holds when the effects of plausible confounding variables are taken into account by appropriate statistical techniques, such as comparing smaller groups that are relatively homogeneous with respect to the factor.[33]
- There is a plausible explanation for the effect of the independent variables; thus, the causal link does not depend on the observed association alone. Other explanations linking the response to confounding variables should be less plausible.[34]

When these criteria are not fulfilled, observational studies may produce legitimate disagreement among experts, and there is no mechanical procedure for ascertaining who is correct. In the end, deciding whether associations are causal is not a matter of statistics, but a matter of good scientific judgment, and the questions that should be asked with respect to data offered on the question of causation can be summarized as follows:

- Was there a control group? If not, the study has little to say about causation.
- If there was a control group, how were subjects assigned to treatment or control: through a process under the control of the investigator (a controlled experiment) or a process outside the control of the investigator (an observational study)?

differences, . . . [b]ut without randomization there are no certain methods for determining that observed differences between groups are not related to the preexisting, systematic difference. . . . [C]omparison between systematically different groups will yield ambiguous implications whenever the systematic difference affords a plausible explanation for apparent effects of the experimental program.

33. The idea is to control for the influence of a confounder by making comparisons separately within groups for which the confounding variable is nearly constant and therefore has little influence over the variables of primary interest. For example, smokers are more likely to get lung cancer than nonsmokers. Age, gender, social class, and region of residence are all confounders, but controlling for such variables does not really change the relationship between smoking and cancer rates. Furthermore, many different studies—of different types and on different populations—confirm the causal link. That is why most experts believe that smoking causes lung cancer and many other diseases. For a review of the literature, see 38 International Agency for Research on Cancer (IARC), World Health Org., IARC Monographs on the Evaluation of the Carcinogenic Risk of Chemicals to Humans: Tobacco Smoking (1986).

34. A. Bradford Hill, *The Environment and Disease: Association or Causation?*, 58 Proc. Royal Soc'y Med. 295 (1965); Alfred S. Evans, Causation and Disease: A Chronological Journey 187 (1993).

- If the study was a controlled experiment, was the assignment made using a chance mechanism (randomization), or did it depend on the judgment of the investigator?
- If the data came from an observational study or a nonrandomized controlled experiment, how did the subjects come to be in treatment or in control groups? Are the groups comparable? What factors are confounded with treatment? What adjustments were made to take care of confounding? Were they sensible?[35]

4. Can the Results Be Generalized?

Any study must be conducted on a certain group of subjects, at certain times and places, using certain treatments. With respect to these subjects, the study may be persuasive. There may be adequate control over confounding variables, and there may be an unequivocally large difference between the treatment and control groups. If so, the study's internal validity will not be disputed: for the subjects in the study, the treatment had an effect. But an issue of external validity remains. To extrapolate from the conditions of a study to more general circumstances always raises questions. For example, studies suggest that definitions of insanity given to jurors influence decisions in cases of incest;[36] would the definitions have a similar effect in cases of murder? Other studies indicate that recidivism rates for ex-convicts are not affected by temporary financial support after release.[37] Would the same results be obtained with different conditions in the labor market?

Confidence in the appropriateness of an extrapolation cannot come from the experiment itself.[38] It must come from knowledge about which outside factors

35. These questions are adapted from Freedman et al., *supra* note 16, at 28. For discussions of the admissibility or weight of studies that overlook obvious possible confounders, see *People Who Care v. Rockford Board of Education*, 111 F.3d 528, 537–38 (7th Cir. 1997) ("The social scientific literature on educational achievement identifies a number of other variables besides poverty and discrimination that explain differences in scholastic achievement, such as the educational attainments of the student's parents and the extent of their involvement in their children's schooling. . . . These variables cannot be assumed to be either randomly distributed across the different racial and ethnic groups in Rockford or perfectly correlated with poverty. . . ."); cases cited *supra* note 5 and *infra* note 230.

36. *See* Rita James Simon, The Jury and the Defense of Insanity 58–59 (1967).

37. For an experiment on income support and recidivism, see Peter H. Rossi et al., Money, Work, and Crime: Experimental Evidence (1980). The interpretation of the data has proved controversial. *See* Hans Zeisel, *Disagreement over the Evaluation of a Controlled Experiment*, 88 Am. J. Soc. 378 (1982) (with commentary).

38. Suppose an epidemiologic study is conducted on the relationship between a toxic substance and a disease. The rate of occurrence of the disease in a group of persons exposed to the substance is compared to the rate in a control group, and the rate in the exposed group turns out to be more than double the rate in the control group. (More technically, the relative risk exceeds two.) Do these data imply that a plaintiff who was exposed to the toxic substance and contracted the disease probably would not have contracted the disease but for the exposure? If we assume that the substance causes the disease and all confounding has been properly accounted for (a judgment that might not be easy to defend),

would or would not affect the outcome.[39] Sometimes, several experiments or other studies, each having different limitations, all point in the same direction. This is the case, for example, with eight studies indicating that jurors who approve of the death penalty are more likely to convict in a capital case.[40] Such convergent results strongly suggest the validity of the generalization.

then we can conclude that over half the cases of disease in the exposed group would not be there but for the exposure. Applying this arithmetic to a specific person, however, is problematic. For instance, the relative risk is an average over all the subjects included in the study. The exposures and susceptibilities almost certainly are not uniform, and the plaintiff's exposure and susceptibility cannot be known from the study. Nevertheless, several courts and commentators have stated that a relative risk of more than two demonstrates specific causation, or, conversely, that a relative risk of two or less precludes a finding of specific causation. *E.g.*, DeLuca v. Merrell Dow Pharms., Inc., 911 F.2d 941, 958–59 (3d Cir. 1990); Marder v. G.D. Searle & Co., 630 F. Supp. 1087, 1092 (D. Md. 1986) ("a two-fold increased risk is . . . the equivalent of the required legal burden of proof—a showing of causation by the preponderance of the evidence or, in other words, a probability of greater than 50%"), *aff'd sub nom.* Wheelahan v. G.D. Searle & Co., 814 F.2d 655 (4th Cir. 1987); Bert Black & David E. Lilienfeld, *Epidemiologic Proof in Toxic Tort Litigation*, 52 Fordham L. Rev. 732, 769 (1984); Michael D. Green et al., Reference Guide on Epidemiology, § VII, in this manual. A few commentators have sharply criticized this reasoning. Steven E. Fienberg et al., *Understanding and Evaluating Statistical Evidence in Litigation*, 36 Jurimetrics J. 1, 9 (1995); Diana B. Petitti, *Reference Guide on Epidemiology*, 36 Jurimetrics J. 159, 168 (1996) (review essay); D.A. Freedman & Philip B. Stark, *The Swine Flu Vaccine and Guillain-Barré Syndrome: A Case Study in Relative Risk and Specific Causation*, 23 Evaluation Rev. 619 (1999); James Robins & Sander Greenland, *The Probability of Causation Under a Stochastic Model for Individual Risk*, 45 Biometrics 1125, 1126 (1989); Melissa Moore Thompson, Comment, *Causal Inference in Epidemiology: Implications for Toxic Tort Litigation*, 71 N.C. L. Rev. 247 (1992).

39. Such judgments are easiest in the physical and life sciences, but even here, there are problems. For example, it may be difficult to infer human reactions to substances that affect animals. First, there are often inconsistencies across test species: A chemical may be carcinogenic in mice but not in rats. Extrapolation from rodents to humans is even more problematic. Second, to get measurable effects in animal experiments, chemicals are administered at very high doses. Results are extrapolated—using mathematical models—to the very low doses of concern in humans. However, there are many dose-response models to use and few grounds for choosing among them. Generally, different models produce radically different estimates of the "virtually safe dose" in humans. David A. Freedman & Hans Zeisel, *From Mouse to Man: The Quantitative Assessment of Cancer Risks*, 3 Stat. Sci. 3 (1988). For these reasons, many experts—and some courts in toxic tort cases—have concluded that evidence from animal experiments is generally insufficient by itself to establish causation. *See generally* Bruce N. Ames et al., *The Causes and Prevention of Cancer*, 92 Proc. Nat'l Acad. Sci. USA 5258 (1995); Susan R. Poulter, *Science and Toxic Torts: Is There a Rational Solution to the Problem of Causation?*, 7 High Tech. L.J. 189 (1993) (epidemiological evidence on humans is needed). *See also* Committee on Comparative Toxicity of Naturally Occurring Carcinogens, National Research Council, Carcinogens and Anticarcinogens in the Human Diet: A Comparison of Naturally Occurring and Synthetic Substances (1996); Committee on Risk Assessment of Hazardous Air Pollutants, National Research Council, Science and Judgment in Risk Assessment 59 (1994) ("There are reasons based on both biologic principles and empirical observations to support the hypothesis that many forms of biologic responses, including toxic responses, can be extrapolated across mammalian species, including *Homo sapiens*, but the scientific basis of such extrapolation is not established with sufficient rigor to allow broad and definitive generalizations to be made.").

40. Phoebe C. Ellsworth, *Some Steps Between Attitudes and Verdicts*, *in* Inside the Juror 42, 46 (Reid Hastie ed., 1993). Nevertheless, in *Lockhart v. McCree*, 476 U.S. 162 (1986), the Supreme Court held that the exclusion of opponents of the death penalty in the guilt phase of a capital trial does not violate the constitutional requirement of an impartial jury.

B. Descriptive Surveys and Censuses

Having discussed the statistical logic of studies to investigate causation, we now turn to a second topic—sampling, that is, choosing units for study. A census tries to measure some characteristic of every unit in a population of individuals or objects. A survey, alternatively, measures characteristics only in part of a population. The accuracy of the information collected in a census or survey depends on how the units are selected, which units are actually measured, and how the measurements are made.[41]

1. What Method Is Used to Select the Units?

By definition, a census seeks to measure some characteristic of every unit in a whole population. It may fall short of this goal, in which case the question must be asked whether the missing data are likely to differ in some systematic way from the data that are collected. The U.S. Bureau of the Census estimates that the past six censuses failed to count everyone, and there is evidence that the undercount is greater in certain subgroups of the population.[42] Supplemental studies may enable statisticians to adjust for such omissions, but the adjustments may rest on uncertain assumptions.[43]

The methodological framework of a scientific survey is more complicated than that of a census. In surveys that use probability sampling methods, a sampling frame (that is, an explicit list of units in the population) is created. Individual units then are selected by a kind of lottery procedure, and measurements are made on these sampled units. For example, a defendant charged with a notorious crime who seeks a change of venue may commission an opinion poll to show that popular opinion is so adverse and deep-rooted that it will be difficult

41. For more extended treatment of these issues, see Shari Seidman Diamond, Reference Guide on Survey Research, § III, in this manual.

42. *See generally* Harvey M. Choldin, Looking for the Last Percent: The Controversy Over Census Undercounts 42–43 (1994).

43. For conflicting views on proposed adjustments to the 1990 census, see the exchanges of papers at 9 Stat. Sci. 458 (1994), 18 Surv. Methodology No. 1 (1992), 88 J. Am. Stat. Ass'n 1044 (1993), and 34 Jurimetrics J. 65 (1993). In *Wisconsin v. City of New York*, 517 U.S. 1 (1996), the Supreme Court resolved the conflict among the circuits over the legal standard governing claims that adjustment is compelled by statute or the Constitution. The Court unanimously determined that the exacting requirements of the equal protection clause, as explicated in congressional redistricting and state reapportionment cases, do not "translate into a requirement that the Federal Government conduct a census that is as accurate as possible" and do not provide any basis for "preferring numerical accuracy to distributive accuracy." *Id.* at 17, 18. The Court therefore applied a much less demanding standard to the Secretary's decision. Concluding that the government had shown "a reasonable relationship" between the decision not to make post hoc adjustments and "the accomplishment of an actual enumeration of the population, keeping in mind the constitutional purpose of the census . . . to determine the apportionment of the Representatives among the States," the Court held that the decision satisfied the Constitution. Indeed, having rejected the argument that the Constitution compelled statistical adjustment, the Court noted that the Constitution might prohibit such adjustment. *Id.* at 19 n.9, 20.

to impanel an unbiased jury. The population consists of all persons in the jurisdiction who might be called for jury duty. A sampling frame here could be the list of these persons as maintained by appropriate officials.[44] In this case, the fit between the sampling frame and the population would be excellent.[45]

In other situations, the sampling frame may cover less of the population. In an obscenity case, for example, the defendant's opinion poll about community standards[46] should identify the population as all adults in the legally relevant community, but obtaining a full list of all such people may not be possible. If names from a telephone directory are used, people with unlisted numbers are excluded from the sampling frame. If these people, as a group, hold different opinions from those included in the sampling frame, the poll will not reflect this difference, no matter how many individuals are polled and no matter how well their opinions are elicited.[47] The poll's measurement of community opinion will be biased, although the magnitude of this bias may not be great.

44. If the jury list is not compiled properly from appropriate sources, it might be subject to challenge. *See* David Kairys et al., *Jury Representativeness: A Mandate for Multiple Source Lists*, 65 Cal. L. Rev. 776 (1977).

45. Likewise, in drug investigations the sampling frame for testing the contents of vials, bags, or packets seized by police easily can be devised to match the population of all the items seized in a single case. Because testing each and every item can be quite time-consuming and expensive, chemists often draw a probability sample, analyze the material that is sampled, and use the percentage of illicit drugs found in the sample to determine the total quantity of illicit drugs in all the items seized. *E.g.*, United States v. Shonubi, 895 F. Supp. 460, 470 (E.D.N.Y. 1995) (citing cases), *rev'd on other grounds*, 103 F.3d 1085 (2d Cir. 1997). For discussions of statistical estimation in such cases, see C.G.G. Aitken et al., *Estimation of Quantities of Drugs Handled and the Burden of Proof*, 160 J. Royal Stat. Soc'y 333 (1997); Dov Tzidony & Mark Ravreby, *A Statistical Approach to Drug Sampling: A Case Study*, 37 J. Forensic Sci. 1541 (1992); Johan Bring & Colin Aitken, *Burden of Proof and Estimation of Drug Quantities Under the Federal Sentencing Guidelines*, 18 Cardozo L. Rev. 1987 (1997).

46. On the admissibility of such polls, compare *Saliba v. State*, 475 N.E.2d 1181, 1187 (Ind. Ct. App. 1985) ("Although the poll did not . . . [ask] the interviewees . . . whether the particular film was obscene, the poll was relevant to an application of community standards"), with *United States v. Pryba*, 900 F.2d 748, 757 (4th Cir. 1990) ("Asking a person in a telephone interview as to whether one is offended by nudity, is a far cry from showing the materials . . . and then asking if they are offensive," so exclusion of the survey results was proper).

47. A classic example of selection bias is the 1936 *Literary Digest* poll. After successfully predicting the winner of every U.S. presidential election since 1916, the *Digest* used the replies from 2.4 million respondents to predict that Alf Landon would win 57% to 43%. In fact, Franklin Roosevelt won by a landslide vote of 62% to 38%. *See* Freedman et al., *supra* note 16, at 334–35. The *Digest* was so far off, in part, because it chose names from telephone books, rosters of clubs and associations, city directories, lists of registered voters, and mail order listings. *Id.* at 335, A-20 n.6. In 1936, when only one household in four had a telephone, the people whose names appeared on such lists tended to be more affluent. Lists that overrepresented the affluent had worked well in earlier elections, when rich and poor voted along similar lines, but the bias in the sampling frame proved fatal when the Great Depression made economics a salient consideration for voters. *See* Judith M. Tanur, *Samples and Surveys*, *in* Perspectives on Contemporary Statistics 55, 57 (David C. Hoaglin & David S. Moore eds., 1992). Today, survey organizations conduct polls by telephone, but most voters have telephones, and these organizations select the numbers to call at random rather than sampling names from telephone books.

Not all surveys use random selection. In some commercial disputes involving trademarks or advertising, the population of all potential purchasers of the products is difficult to identify. Some surveyors may resort to an easily accessible subgroup of the population, such as shoppers in a mall.[48] Such convenience samples may be biased by the interviewer's discretion in deciding whom to interview—a form of selection bias—and the refusal of some of those approached to participate—nonresponse bias.[49] Selection bias is acute when constituents write their representatives, listeners call into radio talk shows, interest groups collect information from their members,[50] or attorneys choose cases for trial.[51] Selection bias also affects data from jury-reporting services that gather information from readily available sources.

Various procedures are available to cope with selection bias. In quota sampling, the interviewer is instructed to interview so many women, so many older men, so many ethnic minorities, or the like. But quotas alone still leave too much discretion to the interviewers in selecting among the members of each category, and therefore do not solve the problem of selection bias.

Probability sampling methods, in contrast, ideally are suited to avoid selection bias. Once the conceptual population is reduced to a tangible sampling frame, the units to be measured are selected by some kind of lottery that gives each unit in the sampling frame a known, nonzero probability of being chosen. Selection according to a table of random digits or the like[52] leaves no room for selection bias. These procedures are used routinely to select individuals for jury

48. *E.g.*, R.J. Reynolds Tobacco Co. v. Loew's Theatres, Inc., 511 F. Supp. 867, 876 (S.D.N.Y. 1980) (questioning the propriety of basing a "nationally projectable statistical percentage" on a suburban mall intercept study).

49. Nonresponse bias is discussed *infra* § II.B.2.

50. *E.g.*, Pittsburgh Press Club v. United States, 579 F.2d 751, 759 (3d Cir. 1978) (tax-exempt club's mail survey of its members to show little sponsorship of income-producing uses of facilities was held to be inadmissible hearsay because it "was neither objective, scientific, nor impartial"), *rev'd on other grounds*, 615 F.2d 600 (3d Cir. 1980).

51. *See In re* Chevron U.S.A., Inc., 109 F.3d 1016 (5th Cir. 1997). In that case, the district court decided to try 30 cases to resolve common issues or to ascertain damages in 3,000 claims arising from Chevron's allegedly improper disposal of hazardous substances. The court asked the opposing parties to select 15 cases each. Selecting 30 extreme cases, however, is quite different from drawing a random sample of 30 cases. Thus, the court of appeals wrote that although random sampling would have been acceptable, the trial court could not use the results in the 30 extreme cases to resolve issues of fact or ascertain damages in the untried cases. *Id.* at 1020. Those cases, it warned, were "not cases calculated to represent the group of 3,000 claimants." *Id.*

52. In simple random sampling, units are drawn at random without replacement. In particular, each unit has the same probability of being chosen for the sample. More complicated methods, such as stratified sampling and cluster sampling, have advantages in certain applications. In systematic sampling, every fifth, tenth, or hundredth (in mathematical jargon, every *n*th) unit in the sampling frame is selected. If the starting point is selected at random and the units are not in any special order, then this procedure is comparable to simple random sampling.

duty;[53] they also have been used to choose "bellwether" cases for representative trials to resolve issues in all similar cases.[54]

2. *Of the Units Selected, Which Are Measured?*

Although probability sampling ensures that, within the limits of chance, the sample will be representative of the sampling frame, the question remains as to which units actually get measured. When objects like receipts are sampled for an audit, or vegetation is sampled for a study of the ecology of a region, all the selected units can be examined. Human beings are more troublesome. Some may refuse to respond, and the survey should report the nonresponse rate. A large nonresponse rate warns of bias,[55] although supplemental study may establish that the nonrespondents do not differ systematically from the respondents with respect to the characteristics of interest[56] or may permit the missing data to

53. Before 1968, most federal districts used the "key man" system for compiling lists of eligible jurors. Individuals believed to have extensive contacts in the community would suggest names of prospective jurors, and the qualified jury wheel would be made up from those names. To reduce the risk of discrimination associated with this system, the Jury Selection and Service Act of 1968, 28 U.S.C. §§ 1861–1878 (1988), substituted the principle of "random selection of juror names from the voter lists of the district or division in which court is held." S. Rep. No. 891, 90th Cong., 1st Sess. 10 (1967), *reprinted in* 1968 U.S.C.C.A.N. 1792, 1793.

54. Hilao v. Estate of Marcos, 103 F.3d 767 (9th Cir. 1996); Cimino v. Raymark Indus., Inc., 751 F. Supp. 649 (E.D. Tex. 1990); *cf. In re* Chevron U.S.A., Inc., 109 F.3d 1016 (5th Cir. 1997) (discussed *supra* note 51). Although trials in a suitable random sample of cases can produce reasonable estimates of average damages, the propriety of precluding individual trials has been debated. *Compare* Michael J. Saks & Peter David Blanck, *Justice Improved: The Unrecognized Benefits of Aggregation and Sampling in the Trial of Mass Torts*, 44 Stan. L. Rev. 815 (1992), *with Chevron*, 109 F.3d at 1021 (Jones, J., concurring); Robert G. Bone, *Statistical Adjudication: Rights, Justice, and Utility in a World of Process Scarcity*, 46 Vand. L. Rev. 561 (1993).

55. The 1936 *Literary Digest* election poll (see *supra* note 47) illustrates the danger. Only 24% of the 10 million people who received questionnaires returned them. Most of the respondents probably had strong views on the candidates, and most of them probably objected to President Roosevelt's economic program. This self-selection is likely to have biased the poll. Maurice C. Bryson, *The* Literary Digest *Poll: Making of a Statistical Myth*, 30 Am. Statistician 184 (1976); Freedman et al., *supra* note 16, at 335–36.

In *United States v. Gometz*, 730 F.2d 475, 478 (7th Cir. 1984) (en banc), the Seventh Circuit recognized that "a low rate of response to juror questionnaires could lead to the underrepresentation of a group that is entitled to be represented on the qualified jury wheel." Nevertheless, the court held that under the Jury Selection and Service Act of 1968, 28 U.S.C. §§ 1861–1878 (1988), the clerk did not abuse his discretion by failing to take steps to increase a response rate of 30%. According to the court, "Congress wanted to make it possible for all qualified persons to serve on juries, which is different from forcing all qualified persons to be available for jury service." *Gometz*, 730 F.2d at 480. Although it might "be a good thing to follow up on persons who do not respond to a jury questionnaire," the court concluded that Congress "was not concerned with anything so esoteric as nonresponse bias." *Id.* at 479, 482.

56. Even when demographic characteristics of the sample match those of the population, however, caution still is indicated. In the 1980s, a behavioral researcher sent out 100,000 questionnaires to explore how women viewed their relationships with men. Shere Hite, Women and Love: A Cultural Revolution in Progress (1987). She amassed a huge collection of anonymous letters from thousands of women disillusioned with love and marriage, and she wrote that these responses established that the

be imputed.[57]

In short, a good survey defines an appropriate population, uses an unbiased method for selecting the sample, has a high response rate, and gathers accurate information on the sample units. When these goals are met, the sample tends to be representative of the population: the measurements within the sample describe fairly the characteristics in the population. It remains possible, however, that despite every precaution, the sample, being less than exhaustive, is not representative; proper statistical analysis helps address the magnitude of this risk, at least for probability samples.[58] Of course, surveys may be useful even if they fail to meet all of the criteria given above; but then, additional arguments are needed to justify the inferences.

C. Individual Measurements

1. Is the Measurement Process Reliable?

There are two main aspects to the accuracy of measurements—reliability and validity. In science, "reliability" refers to reproducibility of results.[59] A reliable measuring instrument returns consistent measurements of the same quantity. A scale, for example, is reliable if it reports the same weight for the same object time and again. It may not be accurate—it may always report a weight that is too high or one that is too low—but the perfectly reliable scale always reports the

"outcry" of feminists "against the many injustices of marriage—exploitation of women financially, physically, sexually, and emotionally" is "just and accurate." *Id.* at 344. The outcry may indeed be justified, but this research does little to prove the point. About 95% of the 100,000 inquiries did not produce responses. The nonrespondents may have had less distressing experiences with men and therefore did not see the need to write autobiographical letters. Furthermore, this systematic difference would be expected within every demographic and occupational class. Therefore, the argument that the sample responses are representative because "those participating according to age, occupation, religion, and other variables known for the U.S. population at large in most cases quite closely mirrors that of the U.S. female population" is far from convincing. *Id.* at 777. In fact, the results of this nonrandom sample differ dramatically from those of polls with better response rates. *See* Chamont Wang, Sense and Nonsense of Statistical Inference: Controversy, Misuse, and Subtlety 174–76 (1993). For further criticism of this study, see David Streitfeld, *Shere Hite and the Trouble with Numbers*, 1 Chance 26 (1988).

57. Methods for "imputing" missing data are discussed in, e.g., Tanur, *supra* note 47, at 66 and Howard Wainer, *Eelworms, Bullet Holes, and Geraldine Ferraro: Some Problems with Statistical Adjustment and Some Solutions*, 14 J. Educ. Stat. 121 (1989) (with commentary). The easy case is one in which the response rate is so high that even if all nonrespondents had responded in a way adverse to the proponent of the survey, the substantive conclusion would be unaltered. Otherwise, imputation can be problematic.

58. *See infra* § IV.

59. Courts often use "reliable" to mean "that which can be relied on" for some purpose, such as establishing probable cause or crediting a hearsay statement when the declarant is not produced for confrontation. *Daubert v. Merrell Dow Pharmaceuticals, Inc.*, 509 U.S. 579, 590 n.9 (1993), for instance, distinguishes "evidentiary reliability" from reliability in the technical sense of giving consistent results. We use "reliability" to denote the latter.

same weight for the same object. Its errors, if any, are systematic; they always point in the same direction.

Reliability can be ascertained by measuring the same quantity several times. For instance, one method of DNA identification requires a laboratory to determine the lengths of fragments of DNA. By making duplicate measurements of DNA fragments, a laboratory can determine the likelihood that two measurements will differ by specified amounts.[60] Such results are needed when deciding whether an observed discrepancy between a crime sample and a suspect sample is sufficient to exclude the suspect.[61]

In many studies, descriptive information is obtained on the subjects. For statistical purposes, the information may have to be reduced to numbers, a process called "coding." The reliability of the coding process should be considered. For instance, in a study of death sentencing in Georgia, legally trained evaluators examined short summaries of cases and ranked them according to the defendant's culpability.[62] Two different aspects of reliability are worth considering. First, the "within-observer" variability of judgments should be small—the same evaluator should rate essentially identical cases the same way. Second, the "between-observer" variability should be small—different evaluators should rate the same cases the same way.

2. *Is the Measurement Process Valid?*

Reliability is necessary, but not sufficient, to ensure accuracy. In addition to reliability, "validity" is needed. A valid measuring instrument measures what it is supposed to. Thus, a polygraph measures certain physiological responses to stimuli. It may accomplish this task reliably. Nevertheless, it is not valid as a lie detector unless increases in pulse rate, blood pressure, and the like are well correlated with conscious deception. Another example involves the MMPI (Minnesota Multiphasic Personality Inventory), a pencil and paper test that, many psychologists agree, measures aspects of personality or psychological functioning. Its reliability can be quantified. But this does not make it a valid test of sexual deviancy.[63]

When an independent and reasonably accurate way of measuring the variable of interest is available, it may be used to validate the measuring system in ques-

60. *See* Committee on DNA Forensic Science: An Update, National Research Council, The Evaluation of Forensic DNA Evidence 139–41 (1996).

61. *Id.*; Committee on DNA Tech. in Forensic Science, National Research Council, DNA Technology in Forensic Science 61–62 (1992); David H. Kaye & George F. Sensabaugh, Jr., Reference Guide on DNA Evidence, § VII, in this manual.

62. David C. Baldus et al., Equal Justice and the Death Penalty: A Legal and Empirical Analysis 49–50 (1990).

63. *See* People v. John W., 229 Cal. Rptr. 783, 785 (Ct. App. 1986) (holding that because the use of the MMPI to diagnose sexual deviancy was not shown to be generally accepted as valid in the scientific community, a diagnosis based in part on the MMPI was inadmissible).

tion. Breathalyzer readings may be validated against alcohol levels found in blood samples. Employment test scores may be validated against job performance. A common measure of validity is the correlation coefficient between the criterion (job performance) and the predictor (the test score).[64]

3. Are the Measurements Recorded Correctly?

Judging the adequacy of data collection may involve examining the process by which measurements are recorded and preserved. Are responses to interviews coded and logged correctly? Are all the responses to a survey included? If gaps or mistakes are present, do they distort the results?[65]

III. How Have the Data Been Presented?

After data have been collected, they should be presented in a way that makes them intelligible. Data can be summarized with a few numbers or with graphical displays. However, the wrong summary can mislead.[66] Section III.A discusses rates or percentages, and gives some cautionary examples of misleading summaries, indicating the sorts of questions that might be considered when numerical summaries are presented in court. Percentages are often used to demonstrate statistical association, which is the topic of section III.B. Section III.C

64. *E.g.*, Washington v. Davis, 426 U.S. 229, 252 (1976); Albemarle Paper Co. v. Moody, 422 U.S. 405, 430–32 (1975). As the discussion of the correlation coefficient indicates, *infra* § V.B, the closer the coefficient is to 1, the greater the validity. Various statistics are used to characterize the reliability of laboratory instruments, psychological tests, or human judgments. These include the standard deviation as well as the correlation coefficient. *See infra* §§ III, V.

65. *See, e.g.*, McCleskey v. Kemp, 753 F.2d 877, 914–15 (11th Cir. 1985) (district court was unpersuaded by a statistical analysis of capital sentencing, in part because of various imperfections in the study, including discrepancies in the data and missing data; concurring and dissenting opinion concludes that the district court's findings on missing and misrecorded data were clearly erroneous because the possible errors were not large enough to affect the overall results; for an exposition of the study and response to such criticisms, see Baldus et al., *supra* note 62), *aff'd*, 481 U.S. 279 (1987); G. Heileman Brewing Co. v. Anheuser-Busch, Inc., 676 F. Supp. 1436, 1486 (E.D. Wis. 1987) ("many coding errors . . . affected the results of the survey"); EEOC v. Sears, Roebuck & Co., 628 F. Supp. 1264, 1304, 1305 (N.D. Ill. 1986) ("[E]rrors in EEOC's mechanical coding of information from applications in its hired and nonhired samples also make EEOC's statistical analysis based on this data less reliable." The EEOC "consistently coded prior experience in such a way that less experienced women are considered to have the same experience as more experienced men" and "has made so many general coding errors that its data base does not fairly reflect the characteristics of applicants for commission sales positions at Sears."), *aff'd*, 839 F.2d 302 (7th Cir. 1988); Dalley v. Michigan Blue Cross-Blue Shield, Inc., 612 F. Supp. 1444, 1456 (E.D. Mich. 1985) ("although plaintiffs show that there were some mistakes in coding, plaintiffs still fail to demonstrate that these errors were so generalized and so pervasive that the entire study is invalid").

66. *See generally* Freedman et al., *supra* note 16; Huff, *supra* note 16; Moore, *supra* note 16; Zeisel, *supra* note 16.

considers graphical summaries of data, while sections III.D and III.E discuss some of the basic descriptive statistics that are likely to be encountered in litigation, including the mean, median and standard deviation.

A. Are Rates or Percentages Properly Interpreted?

1. Have Appropriate Benchmarks Been Provided?

Selective presentation of numerical information is like quoting someone out of context. A television commercial for the Investment Company Institute (the mutual fund trade association) said that a $10,000 investment made in 1950 in an average common stock mutual fund would have increased to $113,500 by the end of 1972. On the other hand, according to the *Wall Street Journal,* the same investment spread over all the stocks making up the New York Stock Exchange Composite Index would have grown to $151,427. Mutual funds performed worse than the stock market as a whole.[67] In this example, and in many other situations, it is helpful to look beyond a single number to some benchmark that places the isolated figure into perspective.

2. Have the Data-Collection Procedures Changed?

Changes in the process of collecting data can create problems of interpretation. Statistics on crime provide many examples. The number of petty larcenies reported in Chicago more than doubled between 1959 and 1960—not because of an abrupt crime wave, but because a new police commissioner introduced an improved reporting system.[68] During the 1970s, police officials in Washington, D.C., "demonstrated" the success of President Nixon's law-and-order campaign by valuing stolen goods at $49, just below the $50 threshold for inclusion in the Federal Bureau of Investigation's (FBI) Uniform Crime Reports.[69]

Changes in data-collection procedures are by no means limited to crime statistics.[70] Indeed, almost all series of numbers that cover many years are affected by changes in definitions and collection methods. When a study includes such time series data, it is useful to inquire about changes and to look for any sudden jumps, which may signal such changes.[71]

67. Moore, *supra* note 16, at 161.

68. *Id.* at 162.

69. James P. Levine et al., Criminal Justice in America: Law in Action 99 (1986).

70. For example, improved survival rates for cancer patients may result from improvements in therapy. Or, the change may simply mean that cancers now are detected earlier, due to improvements in diagnostic techniques, so that patients with these cancers merely appear to live longer. *See* Richard Doll & Richard Peto, The Causes of Cancer: Quantitative Estimates of Avoidable Risks of Cancer in the United States Today app. C at 1278–79 (1981).

71. Moore, *supra* note 16, at 162.

3. Are the Categories Appropriate?

Misleading summaries also can be produced by choice of categories for comparison. In *Philip Morris, Inc. v. Loew's Theatres, Inc.*,[72] and *R.J. Reynolds Tobacco Co. v. Loew's Theatres, Inc.*,[73] Philip Morris and R.J. Reynolds sought an injunction to stop the maker of Triumph low-tar cigarettes from running advertisements claiming that participants in a national taste test preferred Triumph to other brands. Plaintiffs alleged that claims that Triumph was a "national taste test winner" or Triumph "beats" other brands were false and misleading. An exhibit introduced by the defendant contained the data shown in Table 1.[74]

Table 1. Data used by defendant to refute plaintiffs' false advertising claim

	Triumph much better than Merit	Triumph somewhat better than Merit	Triumph about the same as Merit	Triumph somewhat worse than Merit	Triumph much worse than Merit
Number	45	73	77	93	36
Percentage	14%	22%	24%	29%	11%

Only 14% + 22% = 36% of the sample preferred Triumph to Merit, while 29% + 11% = 40% preferred Merit to Triumph.[75] By selectively combining categories, however, defendant attempted to create a different impression. Since 24% found the brands about the same, and 36% preferred Triumph, defendant claimed that a clear majority (36% + 24% = 60%) found Triumph "as good or better than Merit."[76] The court correctly resisted this chicanery, finding that defendant's test results did not support the advertising claims.[77]

There was a similar distortion in claims for the accuracy of a home pregnancy test.[78] The manufacturer advertised the test as 99.5% accurate under laboratory conditions. The data underlying this claim are summarized in Table 2.

Table 2. Home pregnancy test results

	Actually pregnant	Actually not pregnant
Test says pregnant	197	0
Test says not pregnant	1	2
Total	198	2

72. 511 F. Supp. 855 (S.D.N.Y. 1980).
73. 511 F. Supp. 867 (S.D.N.Y. 1980).
74. 511 F. Supp. at 866.
75. *Id.* at 856.
76. *Id.* at 866.
77. *Id.* at 856–57. The statistical issues in these cases are discussed more fully in 2 Gastwirth, *supra* note 1, at 633–39.
78. This incident is reported in Arnold Barnett, *How Numbers Can Trick You*, Tech. Rev., Oct. 1994, at 38, 44–45.

Table 2 does indicate only one error in 200 assessments, or 99.5% overall accuracy. But the table also shows that the test can make two types of errors—it can tell a pregnant woman that she is not pregnant (a false negative), and it can tell a woman who is not pregnant that she is (a false positive). The reported 99.5% accuracy rate conceals a crucial fact—the company had virtually no data with which to measure the rate of false positives.[79]

4. How Big Is the Base of a Percentage?

Rates and percentages often provide effective summaries of data, but these statistics can be misinterpreted. A percentage makes a comparison between two numbers: one number is the base, and the other number is compared to that base. When the base is small, actual numbers may be more revealing than percentages. Media accounts in 1982 of a crime wave by the elderly give an example. The annual Uniform Crime Reports showed a near tripling of the crime rate by older people since 1964, while crimes by younger people only doubled. But people over 65 years of age account for less than 1% of all arrests. In 1980, for instance, there were only 151 arrests of the elderly for robbery out of 139,476 total robbery arrests.[80]

5. What Comparisons Are Made?

Finally, there is the issue of which numbers to compare. Researchers sometimes choose among alternative comparisons. It may be worthwhile to ask why they chose the one they did. Would another comparison give a different view? A government agency, for example, may want to compare the amount of service now being given with that of earlier years—but what earlier year ought to be the baseline? If the first year of operation is used, a large percentage increase should be expected because of start-up problems.[81] If last year is used as the base, was it also part of the trend, or was it an unusually poor year? If the base year is not representative of other years, then the percentage may not portray the trend fairly.[82] No single question can be formulated to detect such distortions, but it may help to ask for the numbers from which the percentages were obtained;

79. Only two women in the sample were not pregnant; the test gave correct results for both of them. Although a false-positive rate of zero is ideal, an estimate based on a sample of only two women is not.

80. Mark H. Maier, The Data Game: Controversies in Social Science Statistics 83 (1991). *See also* Alfred Blumstein & Jacqueline Cohen, *Characterizing Criminal Careers*, 237 Science 985 (1987).

81. *Cf.* Michael J. Saks, *Do We Really Know Anything About the Behavior of the Tort Litigation System—And Why Not?*, 140 U. Pa. L. Rev. 1147, 1203 (1992) (using 1974 as the base year for computing the growth of federal product liability filings exaggerates growth because "1974 was the first year that product liability cases had their own separate listing on the cover sheets. . . . The count for 1974 is almost certainly an understatement . . . .").

82. Jeffrey Katzer et al., Evaluating Information: A Guide for Users of Social Science Research 106 (2d ed. 1982).

asking about the base can also be helpful. Ultimately, however, recognizing which numbers are related to which issues requires a species of clear thinking not easily reducible to a checklist.[83]

B. Is an Appropriate Measure of Association Used?

Many cases involve statistical association. Does a test for employee promotion have an exclusionary effect that depends on race or gender? Does the incidence of murder vary with the rate of executions for convicted murderers? Do consumer purchases of a product depend on the presence or absence of a product warning? This section discusses tables and percentage-based statistics that are frequently presented to answer such questions.[84]

Percentages often are used to describe the association between two variables. Suppose that a university alleged to discriminate against women in admitting students consists of only two colleges, engineering and business. The university admits 350 out of 800 male applicants; by comparison, it admits only 200 out of 600 female applicants. Such data commonly are displayed as in Table 3.[85]

Table 3. Admissions by gender

Decision	Male	Female	Total
Admit	350	200	550
Deny	450	400	850
Total	800	600	1,400

As Table 3 indicates, 350/800 = 44% of the males are admitted, compared with only 200/600 = 33% of the females. One way to express the disparity is to subtract the two percentages: 44% – 33% = 11 percentage points. Although such subtraction is commonly seen in jury discrimination cases,[86] the difference is inevitably small when the two percentages are both close to zero. If the selection rate for males is 5% and that for females is 1%, the difference is only 4 percentage points. Yet, females have only 1/5 the chance of males of being admitted, and that may be of real concern.[87]

83. For assistance in coping with percentages, see Zeisel, *supra* note 16, at 1–24.

84. Correlation and regression are discussed *infra* § V.

85. A table of this sort is called a "cross-tab" or a "contingency table." Table 3 is "two-by-two" because it has two rows and two columns, not counting rows or columns containing totals.

86. *See, e.g.*, D.H. Kaye, *Statistical Evidence of Discrimination in Jury Selection*, *in* Statistical Methods in Discrimination Litigation, *supra* note 11, at 13.

87. *Cf.* United States v. Jackman, 46 F.3d 1240, 1246–47 (2d Cir. 1995) (holding that the small percentage of minorities in the population makes it "inappropriate" to use an "absolute numbers" or "absolute impact" approach for measuring underrepresentation of these minorities in the list of potential jurors).

For Table 3, the selection ratio (used by the Equal Employment Opportunity Commission (EEOC) in its "80% rule")[88] is 33/44 = 75%, meaning that, on average, women have 75% the chance of admission that men have.[89] However, the selection ratio has its own problems. In the last example, if the selection rates are 5% and 1%, then the exclusion rates are 95% and 99%. The corresponding ratio is 99/95 = 104%, meaning that females have, on average, 104% the risk of males of being rejected. The underlying facts are the same, of course, but this formulation sounds much less disturbing.[90]

The odds ratio is more symmetric. If 5% of male applicants are admitted, the odds on a man being admitted are 5/95 = 1/19; the odds on a woman being admitted are 1/99. The odds ratio is (1/99)/(1/19) = 19/99. The odds ratio for rejection instead of acceptance is the same, except that the order is reversed.[91] Although the odds ratio has desirable mathematical properties, its meaning may be less clear than that of the selection ratio or the simple difference.

Data showing disparate impact are generally obtained by aggregating—putting together—statistics from a variety of sources. Unless the source material is fairly homogenous, aggregation can distort patterns in the data. We illustrate the problem with the hypothetical admission data in Table 3. Applicants can be classified not only by gender and admission but also by the college to which they applied, as in Table 4:

Table 4. Admissions by gender and college

	Engineering		Business	
Decision	Male	Female	Male	Female
Admit	300	100	50	100
Deny	300	100	150	300

The entries in Table 4 add up to the entries in Table 3; said more technically, Table 3 is obtained by aggregating the data in Table 4. Yet, there is no association between gender and admission in either college; men and women are ad-

88. The EEOC generally regards any procedure that selects candidates from the least successful group at a rate less than 80% of the rate for the most successful group as having an adverse impact. EEOC Uniform Guidelines on Employee Selection Procedures, 29 C.F.R. § 1607.4(D) (1993). The rule is designed to help spot instances of substantially discriminatory practices, and the commission usually asks employers to justify any procedures that produce selection ratios of 80% or less.

89. The analogous statistic used in epidemiology is called the relative risk. *See supra* note 38; Michael D. Green et al., Reference Guide on Epidemiology, § III.A, in this manual. Relative risks are usually quoted as decimals rather than percentages; for instance, a selection ratio of 75% corresponds to a relative risk of 0.75. A variation on this idea is the relative difference in the proportions, which expresses the proportion by which the probability of selection is reduced. Kairys et al., *supra* note 44, at 776, 789–90; *cf.* David C. Baldus & James W.L. Cole, Statistical Proof of Discrimination § 5.1, at 153 (1980 & Supp. 1987) (listing various ratios that can be used to measure disparities).

90. The Illinois Department of Employment Security tried to exploit this feature of the selection

mitted at identical rates. Combining two colleges with no association produces a university in which gender is associated strongly with admission. The explanation for this paradox: the business college, to which most of the women applied, admits relatively few applicants; the engineering college, to which most of the men applied, is easier to get into. This example illustrates a common issue: association can result from combining heterogeneous statistical material.[92]

C. Does a Graph Portray Data Fairly?

Graphs are useful for revealing key characteristics of a batch of numbers, trends over time, and the relationships among variables.[93]

1. How Are Trends Displayed?

Graphs that plot values over time are useful for seeing trends. However, the scales on the axes matter. In Figure 1, the federal debt appears to skyrocket during the Reagan and Bush administrations; in Figure 2, the federal debt appears to grow slowly.[94] The moral is simple: Pay attention to the markings on the axes to determine whether the scale is appropriate.

ratio in *Council 31, Am. Fed'n of State, County and Mun. Employees v. Ward*, 978 F.2d 373 (7th Cir. 1992). In January 1985, the department laid off 8.6% of the blacks on its staff in comparison with 3.0% of the whites. *Id.* at 375. Recognizing that these layoffs ran afoul of the 80% rule (since 3.0/8.6 = 35%, which is far less than 80%), the department instead presented the selection ratio for retention. *Id.* at 375–76. Since black employees were retained at 91.4/97.0 = 94% of the white rate, the retention rates showed no adverse impact under the 80% rule. *Id.* at 376. When a subsequent wave of layoffs was challenged as discriminatory, the department argued "that its retention rate analysis is the right approach to this case and . . . shows conclusively that the layoffs did not have a disparate impact." *Id.* at 379. The Seventh Circuit disagreed and, in reversing an order granting summary judgment to defendants on other grounds, left it to the district court on remand "to decide what method of proof is most appropriate." *Id.*

91. For women, the odds on rejection are 99 to 1; for men, 19 to 1. The ratio of these odds is 99/19. Likewise, the odds ratio for an admitted applicant being a man as opposed to a denied applicant being man is also 99/19.

92. Tables 3 and 4 are hypothetical, but closely patterned on a real example. *See* P.J. Bickel et al., *Sex Bias in Graduate Admissions: Data from Berkeley*, 187 Science 398 (1975). *See also* Freedman et al., *supra* note 16, at 17–20; Moore, *supra* note 16, at 246–47. The tables are an instance of "Simpson's Paradox." *See generally* Myra L. Samuels, *Simpson's Paradox and Related Phenomena*, 88 J. Am. Stat. Ass'n 81 (1993). Another perspective on Table 3 may be helpful. The college to which a student applies is a confounder. *See supra* § II.A.1. In the present context, confounders often are called "omitted variables." For opinions discussing the legal implications of omitted variables, see cases cited *supra* note 5 and *infra* note 230.

93. *See generally* William S. Cleveland, The Elements of Graphing Data (1985); David S. Moore & George P. McCabe, Introduction to the Practice of Statistics 3–20 (2d ed. 1993). Graphs showing relationships among variables are discussed *infra* § V.

94. *See* Howard Wainer, *Graphs in the Presidential Campaign*, Chance, Winter 1993, at 48, 50.

Figure 1. The federal debt skyrockets under Reagan–Bush.

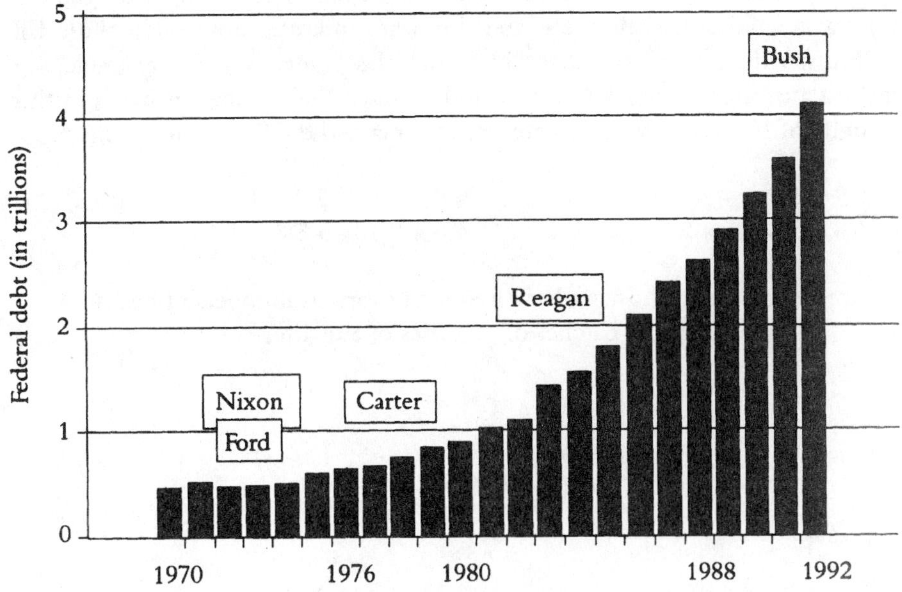

Figure 2. The federal debt grows steadily under Reagan–Bush.

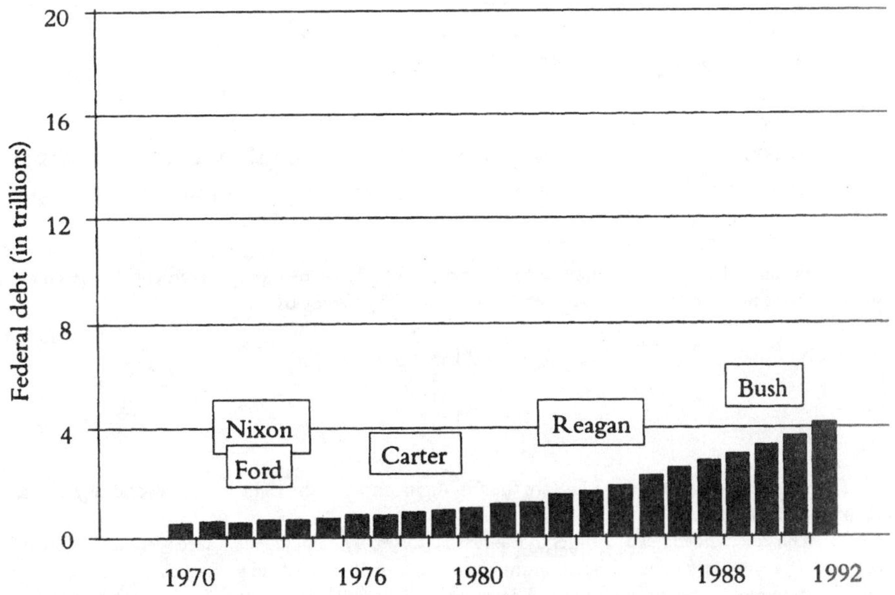

2. How Are Distributions Displayed?

A graph commonly used to display the distribution of data is the histogram.[95] One axis denotes the numbers, and the other indicates how often those fall within specified intervals (called "bins" or "class intervals"). For example, we flipped a quarter 10 times in a row and counted the number of heads in this "batch" of 10 tosses. With 50 batches, we obtained the following counts:[96]

7 7 5 6 8	4 2 3 6 5	4 3 4 7 4	6 8 4 7 4	7 4 5 4 3
4 4 2 5 3	5 4 2 4 4	5 7 2 3 5	4 6 4 9 10	5 5 6 6 4

Figure 3. Histogram showing how frequently various numbers of heads appeared in 50 batches of 10 tosses of a quarter.

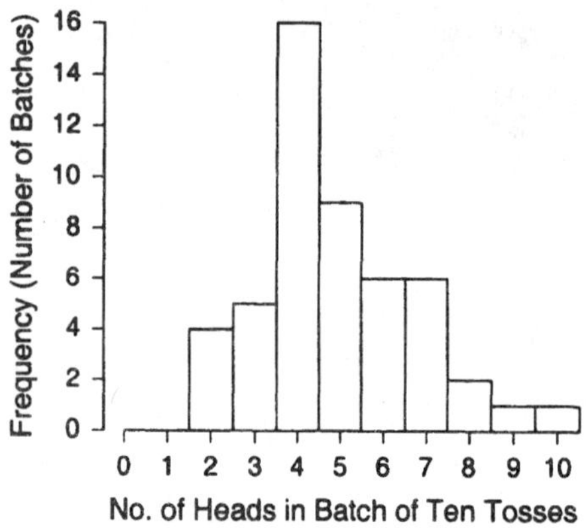

The histogram is shown in Figure 3.[97] A histogram shows how the data are distributed over the range of possible values. The spread can be made to appear

95. For small batches of numbers, a "stem-and-leaf plot" may be more convenient. For instance, a stem-and-leaf plot for 11, 12, 23, 23, 23, 23, 33, 45, 69 is given below:

1	1 2
2	3 3 3 3
3	3
4	5
5	
6	9

The numbers to the left of the line are the first digits; those to the right are the second digits. Thus, "2 | 3 3 3 3" stands for "23, 23, 23, 23."

96. The coin landed heads 7 times in the first 10 tosses; by coincidence, there were also 7 heads in the next 10 tosses; there were 5 heads in the third batch of 10 tosses; and so forth.

97. In Figure 3, the bin width is 1. There were no 0's or 1's in the data, so the bars over 0 and 1 disappear. There is a bin from 1.5 to 2.5; the four 2's in the data fall into this bin, so the bar over the

larger or smaller, however, by changing the scale of the horizontal axis. Likewise, the shape can be altered somewhat by changing the size of the bins.[98] It may be worth inquiring how the analyst chose the bin widths.

D. Is an Appropriate Measure Used for the Center of a Distribution?

Perhaps the most familiar descriptive statistic is the mean (or "arithmetic mean"). The mean can be found by adding up all the numbers and dividing by how many there are. By comparison, the median is defined so that half the numbers are bigger than the median, and half are smaller.[99] Yet a third statistic is the mode, which is the most common number in the data set. These statistics are different, although they are not always clearly distinguished.[100] The mean takes account of all the data—it involves the total of all the numbers; however, particularly with small data sets, a few unusually large or small observations may have too much influence on the mean. The median is resistant to such outliers.

To illustrate the distinction between the mean and the median, consider a report that the "average" award in malpractice cases skyrocketed from $220,000

interval from 1.5 to 2.5 has height four. There is another bin from 2.5 to 3.5, which catches five 3's; the height of the corresponding bar is five. And so forth.

All the bins in Figure 3 have the same width, so this histogram is just like a bar graph. However, data are often published in tables with unequal intervals. The resulting histograms will have unequal bin widths; bar heights should be calculated so that the areas (height × width) are proportional to the frequencies. In general, a histogram differs from a bar graph in that it represents frequencies by area, not height. *See* Freedman et al., *supra* note 16, at 31–41.

98. As the width of the bins decreases, the graph becomes more detailed. But the appearance becomes more ragged until finally the graph is effectively a plot of each datum. The optimal bin width "depends on the subject matter and the goal of the analysis." Cleveland, *supra* note 93, at 125.

99. Technically, at least half the numbers are at the median or larger; at least half are at the median or smaller. When the distribution is symmetric, the mean equals the median. The values diverge, however, when the distribution is asymmetric, or skewed. The distinction between the mean and the median is critical to the interpretation of the Railroad Revitalization and Regulatory Reform Act, 49 U.S.C. § 11503 (1988), which forbids the taxation of railroad property at a higher rate than other commercial and industrial property. To compare the rates, tax authorities often use the mean, whereas railroads prefer the median. The choice has important financial consequences, and much litigation has resulted. *See* David A. Freedman, *The Mean Versus the Median: A Case Study in 4-R Act Litigation*, 3 J. Bus. & Econ. Stat. 1 (1985).

100. In ordinary language, the arithmetic mean, the median, and the mode seem to be referred to interchangeably as "the average." In statistical parlance, the average is the arithmetic mean. The distinctions are brought out by the following question: How big an error would be made if every number in a batch were replaced by the "center" of the batch? The mode minimizes the number of errors; all errors count the same, no matter what their size. Similar distributions can have very different modes, and the mode is rarely used by statisticians. The median minimizes a different measure of error—the sum of all the differences between the center and the data points; signs are not taken into account when computing this sum, so positive and negative differences are treated the same way. The mean minimizes the sum of the squared differences.

in 1975 to more than $1 million in 1985.[101] The median award almost certainly was far less than $1 million,[102] and the apparently explosive growth may result from a few very large awards. Still, if the issue is whether insurers were experiencing more costs from jury verdicts, the mean is the more appropriate statistic: The total of the awards is directly related to the mean, not to the median.[103]

E. Is an Appropriate Measure of Variability Used?

The location of the center of a batch of numbers reveals nothing about the variations exhibited by these numbers.[104] Statistical measures of variability include the range, the interquartile range, and the standard deviation. The range is the difference between the largest number in the batch and the smallest. The range seems natural, and it indicates the maximum spread in the numbers, but it is generally the most unstable because it depends entirely on the most extreme values.[105] The interquartile range is the difference between the 25th and 75th percentiles.[106] The interquartile range contains 50% of the numbers and is resistant to changes in extreme values. The standard deviation is a sort of mean deviation from the mean.[107]

101. Kenneth Jost, *Still Warring Over Medical Malpractice: Time for Something Better*, A.B.A. J., May 1993, at 68, 70–71.

102. A study of cases in North Carolina reported an "average" (mean) award of about $368,000, and a median award of only $36,000. *Id.* at 71. In *TXO Production Corp. v. Alliance Resources Corp.*, 509 U.S. 443 (1993), briefs portraying the punitive damage system as out of control reported mean punitive awards, some ten times larger than the median awards described in briefs defending the current system of punitive damages. *See* Michael Rustad & Thomas Koenig, *The Supreme Court and Junk Social Science: Selective Distortion in Amicus Briefs*, 72 N.C. L. Rev. 91, 145–47 (1993). The mean differs so dramatically from the median because the mean takes into account (indeed, is heavily influenced by) the magnitudes of the few very large awards; the median screens these out. Of course, representative data on verdicts and awards are hard to find. For a study using a probability sample of cases, see Carol J. DeFrances et al., *Civil Jury Cases and Verdicts in Large Counties*, Bureau Just. Stats. Special Rep., July 1995, at 1.

103. To get the total award, just multiply the mean by the number of awards; by contrast, the total cannot be computed from the median. (The more pertinent figure for the insurance industry is not the total of jury awards, but actual claims experience including settlements; of course, even the risk of large punitive damage awards may have considerable impact.) These and related statistical issues are pursued further in, e.g., Theodore Eisenberg & Thomas A. Henderson, Jr., *Inside the Quiet Revolution in Products Liability*, 39 UCLA L. Rev. 731, 764–72 (1992); Scott Harrington & Robert E. Litan, *Causes of the Liability Insurance Crisis*, 239 Science 737, 740–41 (1988); Saks, *supra* note 81, at 1147, 1248–54.

104. The numbers 1, 2, 5, 8, 9 have 5 as their mean and median. So do the numbers 5, 5, 5, 5, 5. In the first batch, the numbers vary considerably about their mean; in the second, the numbers do not vary at all.

105. Typically, the range increases with the size of the sample, i.e., the number of units chosen for the sample.

106. By definition, 25% of the data fall below the 25th percentile, 90% fall below the 90th percentile, and so on. The median is the 50th percentile.

107. As discussed in the Appendix, when the distribution follows the normal curve, about 68% of the data will be within one standard deviation of the mean, and about 95% will be within two standard deviations of the mean. For other distributions, the proportions of the data within specified numbers of standard deviations will be different.

There are no hard and fast rules as to which statistic is the best. In general, the bigger these measures of spread are, the more the numbers are dispersed. Particularly in small data sets, the standard deviation can be influenced heavily by a few outlying values. To remove this influence, the mean and the standard deviation can be recomputed with the outliers discarded. Beyond this, any of the statistics can be supplemented with a figure that displays much of the data.[108]

IV. What Inferences Can Be Drawn from the Data?

The inferences that may be drawn from a study depend on the quality of the data and the design of the study. As discussed in section II, the data might not address the issue of interest, might be systematically in error, or might be difficult to interpret due to confounding. We turn now to an additional concern—random error.[109] Are patterns in the data the result of chance? Would a pattern wash out if more data were collected?

The laws of probability are central to analyzing random error. By applying these laws, the statistician can assess the likely impact of chance error, using "standard errors," "confidence intervals," "significance probabilities," "hypothesis tests," or "posterior probability distributions." The following example illustrates the ideas. An employer plans to use a standardized examination to select trainees from a pool of 5,000 male and 5,000 female applicants. This total pool of 10,000 applicants is the statistical "population." Under Title VII of the Civil

Technically, the standard deviation is the square root of the variance; the variance is the mean square deviation from the mean. For instance, if the mean is 100, the datum 120 deviates from the mean by 20, and the square of 20 is $20^2 = 400$. If the variance (i.e., the mean of all the squared deviations) is 900, then the standard deviation is the square root of 900, that is, $\sqrt{900} = 30$. Among other things, taking the square root corrects for the fact that the variance is on a different scale than the measurements themselves. For example, if the measurements are of length in inches, the variance is in square inches; taking the square root changes back to inches.

To compare distributions on different scales, the coefficient of variation may be used: this statistic is the standard deviation, expressed as a percentage of the mean. For instance, consider the batch of numbers 1,4,4,7,9. The mean is $25/5 = 5$, the variance is $(16 + 1 + 1 + 4 + 16)/5 = 7.6$, and the standard deviation is $\sqrt{7.6} = 2.8$. The coefficient of variation is $2.8/5 = 56\%$.

108. For instance, the "five-number summary" lists the smallest value, the 25th percentile, the median, the 75th percentile, and the largest value. The five-number summary may be presented as a box plot. If the five numbers were 10, 25, 40, 65 and 90, the box plot would look like the following:

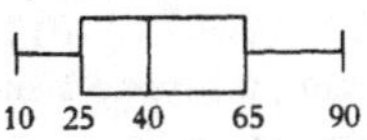

There are many variations on this idea in which the boundaries of the box, or the "whiskers" extending from it, represent slightly different points in the distribution of numbers.

109. Random error is also called sampling error, chance error, or statistical error. Econometricians use the parallel concept of random disturbance terms.

Rights Act, if the proposed examination excludes a disproportionate number of women, the employer needs to show that the exam is job related.[110]

To see whether there is disparate impact, the employer administers the exam to a sample of 50 men and 50 women drawn at random from the population of job applicants. In the sample, 29 of the men but only 19 of the women pass; the sample pass rates are therefore 29/50 = 58% and 19/50 = 38%. The employer announces that it will use the exam anyway, and several applicants bring an action under Title VII. Disparate impact seems clear. The difference in sample pass rates is 20 percentage points: 58% − 38% = 20 percentage points. The employer argues, however, that the disparity could just reflect random error. After all, only a small number of people took the test, and the sample could have included disproportionate numbers of high-scoring men and low-scoring women. Clearly, even if there were no overall difference in pass rates for male and female applicants, in some samples the men will outscore the women. More generally, a sample is unlikely to be a perfect microcosm of the population; statisticians call differences between the sample and the population, just due to the luck of the draw in choosing the sample, "random error" or "sampling error."

When assessing the impact of random error, a statistician might consider the following topics:

- *Estimation*. Plaintiffs use the difference of 20 percentage points between the sample men and women to estimate the disparity between all male and female applicants. How good is this estimate? Precision can be expressed using the "standard error" or a "confidence interval."
- *Statistical significance*. Suppose the defendant is right, and there is no disparate impact: in the population of all 5,000 male and 5,000 female applicants, pass rates are equal. How likely is it that a random sample of 50 men and 50 women will produce a disparity of 20 percentage points or more? This chance is known as a *p*-value. Statistical significance is determined by reference to the *p*-value, and "hypothesis testing" is the technique for computing *p*-values or determining statistical significance.[111]
- *Posterior probability*. Given the observed disparity of 20 percentage points in the sample, what is the probability that—in the population as a whole—men and women have equal pass rates? This question is of direct interest to the courts. For a subjectivist statistician, posterior probabilities may be com-

110. The seminal case is *Griggs v. Duke Power Co.*, 401 U.S. 424, 431 (1971). The requirements and procedures for the validation of tests can go beyond a simple showing of job relatedness. *See, e.g.*, Richard R. Reilly, *Validating Employee Selection Procedures*, *in* Statistical Methods in Discrimination Litigation, *supra* note 11, at 133; Michael Rothschild & Gregory J. Werden, *Title VII and the Use of Employment Tests: An Illustration of the Limits of the Judicial Process*, 11 J. Legal Stud. 261 (1982).

111. "Hypothesis testing" is also called "significance testing." For details on the example, see *infra* Appendix, especially note 245.

puted using "Bayes' rule." Within the framework of classical statistical theory, however, such a posterior probability has no meaning.[112]

- *Applicability of statistical models.* Statistical inference—whether done with confidence intervals or significance probabilities, by objective methods or subjective—depends on the validity of statistical models for the data. If the data are collected on the basis of a probability sample or a randomized experiment, there will be statistical models that fit the situation very well, and inferences based on these models will be quite secure. Otherwise, calculations are generally based on analogy: this group of people is like a random sample, that observational study is like a randomized experiment. The fit between the statistical model and the data may then require examination: how good is the analogy?

A. Estimation

1. What Estimator Should Be Used?

An estimator is a statistic computed from sample data and used to estimate a numerical characteristic of the population. For example, we used the difference in pass rates for a sample of men and women to estimate the corresponding disparity in the population of all applicants. In our sample, the pass rates were 58% and 38%; the difference in pass rates for the whole population was estimated as 20 percentage points: 58% − 38% = 20 percentage points. In more complex problems, statisticians may have to choose among several estimators. Generally, estimators that tend to make smaller errors are preferred. However, this idea can be made precise in more than one way,[113] leaving room for judgment in selecting an estimator.

2. What Is the Standard Error? The Confidence Interval?

An estimate based on a sample is likely to be off the mark, at least by a little, due to random error. The standard error gives the likely magnitude of this random error.[114] Whenever possible, an estimate should be accompanied by its standard

112. This classical framework is also called "objectivist" or "frequentist," by contrast with the "subjectivist" or "Bayesian" framework. In brief, objectivist statisticians view probabilities as objective properties of the system being studied. Subjectivists view probabilities as measuring subjective degrees of belief. Section IV.B.1 explains why posterior probabilities are excluded from the classical calculus, and section IV.C briefly discusses the subjectivist position. The procedure for computing posterior probabilities is presented *infra* Appendix. For more discussion, see David Freedman, *Some Issues in the Foundation of Statistics*, 1 Found. Sci. 19 (1995), *reprinted in* Topics in the Foundation of Statistics 19 (Bas C. van Fraasen ed., 1997).

113. Furthermore, reducing error in one context may increase error in other contexts; there may also be a trade-off between accuracy and simplicity.

114. "Standard errors" are also called "standard deviations," and courts seem to prefer the latter term, as do many authors.

error.[115] In our example, the standard error is about 10 percentage points: the estimate of 20 percentage points is likely to be off by something like 10 percentage points or so, in either direction.[116] Since the pass rates for all 5,000 men and 5,000 women are unknown, we cannot say exactly how far off the estimate is going to be, but 10 percentage points gauges the likely magnitude of the error.

Confidence intervals make the idea more precise. Statisticians who say that population differences fall within plus-or-minus 1 standard error of the sample differences will be correct about 68% of the time. To write this more compactly, we can abbreviate "standard error" as "SE." A 68% confidence interval is the range

$$\text{estimate} - 1\ \text{SE to estimate} + 1\ \text{SE}.$$

In our example, the 68% confidence interval goes from 10 to 30 percentage points. If a higher confidence level is wanted, the interval must be widened. The 95% confidence interval is about

$$\text{estimate} - 2\ \text{SE to estimate} + 2\ \text{SE}.$$

This runs from 0 to 40 percentage points.[117] Although 95% confidence intervals are used commonly, there is nothing special about 95%. For example, a 99.7% confidence interval is about

$$\text{estimate} - 3\ \text{SE to estimate} + 3\ \text{SE}.$$

This stretches from –10 to 50 percentage points.

The main point is that an estimate based on a sample will differ from the exact population value, due to random error; the standard error measures the likely size of the random error. If the standard error is small, the estimate probably is close to the truth. If the standard error is large, the estimate may be seriously wrong. Confidence intervals are a technical refinement, and

115. The standard error can also be used to measure reproducibility of estimates from one random sample to another. *See infra* note 237.

116. The standard error depends on the pass rates of men and women in the sample, and the size of the sample. With larger samples, chance error will be smaller, so the standard error goes down as sample size goes up. ("Sample size" is the number of subjects in the sample.) The Appendix gives the formula for computing the standard error of a difference in rates based on random samples. Generally, the formula for the standard error must take into account the method used to draw the sample and the nature of the estimator. Statistical expertise is needed to choose the right formula.

117. Confidence levels are usually read off the normal curve (*see infra* Appendix). Technically, the area under the normal curve between –2 and +2 is closer to 95.4% than 95.0%; thus, statisticians often use ±1.96 SEs for a 95% confidence interval. However, the normal curve only gives an approximation to the relevant chances, and the error in that approximation will often be larger than the difference between 95.4% and 95.0%. For simplicity, we use ±2 SEs for 95% confidence. Likewise, we use ±1 SE for 68% confidence, although the area under the curve between –1 and +1 is closer to 68.3%. The normal curve gives good approximations when the sample size is reasonably large; for small samples, other techniques should be used.

"confidence" is a term of art.[118] For a given confidence level, a narrower interval indicates a more precise estimate. For a given sample size, increased confidence can be attained only by widening the interval. A high confidence level alone means very little,[119] but a high confidence level for a small interval is impressive,[120] indicating that the random error in the sample estimate is low.

Standard errors and confidence intervals are derived using statistical models of the process that generated the data.[121] If the data come from a probability

118. In the standard frequentist theory of statistics, one cannot make probability statements about population characteristics. *See, e.g.*, Freedman et al., *supra* note 16, at 383–86; *infra* § IV.B.1. Consequently, it is imprecise to suggest that "[a] 95% confidence interval means that there is a 95% probability that the 'true' relative risk falls within the interval." DeLuca v. Merrell Dow Pharms., Inc., 791 F. Supp. 1042, 1046 (D.N.J. 1992), *aff'd*, 6 F.3d 778 (3d Cir. 1993). Because of the limited technical meaning of "confidence," it has been argued that the term is misleading and should be replaced by a more neutral one, such as "frequency coefficient," in courtroom presentations. David H. Kaye, *Is Proof of Statistical Significance Relevant?*, 61 Wash. L. Rev. 1333, 1354 (1986).

Another misconception is that the confidence level gives the chance that repeated estimates fall into the confidence interval. *E.g.*, Turpin v. Merrell Dow Pharms., Inc., 959 F.2d 1349, 1353 (6th Cir. 1992) ("a confidence interval of '95 percent between 0.8 and 3.10' . . . means that random repetition of the study should produce, 95 percent of the time, a relative risk somewhere between 0.8 and 3.10"); United States *ex rel.* Free v. Peters, 806 F. Supp. 705, 713 n.6 (N.D. Ill. 1992) ("A 99% confidence interval, for instance, is an indication that if we repeated our measurement 100 times under identical conditions, 99 times out of 100 the point estimate derived from the repeated experimentation will fall within the initial interval estimate . . . ."), *rev'd in part*, 12 F.3d 700 (7th Cir. 1993). However, the confidence level does not give the percentage of the time that repeated estimates fall in the interval; instead, it gives the percentage of the time that intervals from repeated samples cover the true value.

119. Statements about the confidence in a sample without any mention of the interval estimate are practically meaningless. In *Hilao v. Estate of Marcos*, 103 F.3d 767 (9th Cir. 1996), for instance, "an expert on statistics . . . testified that . . . a random sample of 137 claims would achieve 'a 95% statistical probability that the same percentage determined to be valid among the examined claims would be applicable to the totality of [9,541 facially valid] claims filed.'" *Id.* at 782. Unfortunately, there is no 95% "statistical probability" that a percentage computed from a sample will be "applicable" to a population. One can compute a confidence interval from a random sample and be 95% confident that the interval covers some parameter. That can be done for a sample of virtually any size, with larger samples giving smaller intervals. What is missing from the opinion is a discussion of the widths of the relevant intervals.

120. Conversely, a broad interval signals that random error is substantial. In *Cimino v. Raymark Industries, Inc.*, 751 F. Supp. 649 (E.D. Tex. 1990), the district court drew certain random samples from more than 6,000 pending asbestos cases, tried these cases, and used the results to estimate the total award to be given to all plaintiffs in the pending cases. The court then held a hearing to determine whether the samples were large enough to provide accurate estimates. The court's expert, an educational psychologist, testified that the estimates were accurate because the samples matched the population on such characteristics as race and the percentage of plaintiffs still alive. *Id.* at 664. However, the matches occurred only in the sense that population characteristics fell within very broad 99% confidence intervals computed from the samples. The court thought that matches within the 99% confidence intervals proved more than matches within 95% intervals. *Id.* Unfortunately, this is backwards. To be correct in a few instances with a 99% confidence interval is not very impressive—by definition, such intervals are broad enough to ensure coverage 99% of the time. *Cf.* Saks & Blanck, *supra* note 54.

121. Generally, statistical models enable the analyst to compute the chances of the various possible outcomes. For instance, the model may contain parameters, that is, numerical constants describing the population from which samples were drawn. *See infra* § V. That is the case for our example, where one

sample or a randomized controlled experiment,[122] the statistical model may be connected tightly to the actual data-collection process. In other situations, using the model may be tantamount to assuming that a sample of convenience is like a random sample, or that an observational study is like a randomized experiment.

Our example was based on a random sample, and that justified the statistical calculations.[123] In many contexts, the choice of an appropriate statistical model is not obvious.[124] When a model does not fit the data-collection process so well,

parameter is the pass rate of the 5,000 male applicants, and another parameter is the pass rate of the 5,000 female applicants. As explained in the Appendix, these parameters can be used to compute the chance of getting any particular sample difference. Using a model with known parameters to find the probability of an observed outcome (or one like it) is common in cases alleging discrimination in the selection of jurors. *E.g.*, Castaneda v. Partida, 430 U.S. 482, 496 (1977); Kaye, *supra* note 86, at 13; *cf.* Hazelwood Sch. Dist. v. United States, 433 U.S. 299, 311 n.17 (1977) (computing probabilities of selecting black teachers). But when the values of the parameters are not known, the statistician must work backwards, using the sample data to estimate the unknown population parameters. That is the kind of statistical inference described in this section.

122. *See supra* § II.A–B.

123. As discussed in the Appendix, large random samples give rise to certain normally distributed statistics. Partly because the Supreme Court used such a model in *Hazelwood* and *Castaneda*, courts and attorneys sometimes are skeptical of analyses that produce other types of random variables. *See, e.g.*, EEOC v. Western Elec. Co., 713 F.2d 1011 (4th Cir. 1983), *discussed in* David H. Kaye, *Ruminations on Jurimetrics: Hypergeometric Confusion in the Fourth Circuit*, 26 Jurimetrics J. 215 (1986). *But see* Branion v. Gramly, 855 F.2d 1256 (7th Cir. 1988) (questioning an apparently arbitrary assumption of normality), *discussed in* David H. Kaye, *Statistics for Lawyers and Law for Statistics*, 89 Mich. L. Rev. 1520 (1991) (defending the use of the normal approximation); Michael O. Finkelstein & Bruce Levin, *Reference Guide on Statistics: Non Lasciare Esperanza*, 36 Jurimetrics J. 201, 205 (1996) (review essay) ("The court was right to reject the normal distribution . . . ."). Whether a given variable is normally distributed is an empirical or statistical question, not a matter of law.

124. *See infra* § V. For examples of legal interest, see, e.g., Mary W. Gray, *Can Statistics Tell Us What We Do Not Want to Hear?: The Case of Complex Salary Structures*, 8 Stat. Sci. 144 (1993); Arthur P. Dempster, *Employment Discrimination and Statistical Science*, 3 Stat. Sci. 149 (1988). As one statistician describes the issue:

> [A] given data set can be viewed from more than one perspective, can be represented by a model in more than one way. Quite commonly, no unique model stands out as "true" or correct; justifying so strong a conclusion might require a depth of knowledge that is simply lacking. So it is not unusual for a given data set to be analyzed in several apparently reasonable ways. If conclusions are qualitatively concordant, that is regarded as grounds for placing additional trust in them. But more often, only a single model is applied, and the data are analyzed in accordance with it. . . .
>
> Desirable features in a model include (i) tractability, (ii) parsimony, and (iii) realism. That there is some tension among these is not surprising.
>
> *Tractability.* A model that is easy to understand and to explain is tractable in one sense. Computational tractability can also be an advantage, though with cheap computing available not too much weight can be given to it.
>
> *Parsimony.* Simplicity, like tractability, has a direct appeal, not wisely ignored—but not wisely over-valued either. If several models are plausible and more than one of them fits adequately with the data, then in choosing among them, one criterion is to prefer a model that is simpler than the other models.
>
> *Realism.* . . . First, does the model reflect well the actual [process that generated the data]? This question is really a host of questions, some about the distributions of the random errors, others about the mathematical relations among the [variables and] parameters. The second aspect of realism is sometimes called robustness.

estimates and standard errors will be less probative.[125]

Standard errors and confidence intervals generally ignore systematic errors such as selection bias or non-response bias; in other words, these biases are assumed to be negligible.[126] For example, one court—reviewing studies of whether a particular drug causes birth defects—observed that mothers of children with birth defects may be more likely to remember taking a drug during pregnancy than women with normal children.[127] This selective recall would bias comparisons between samples from the two groups of women. The standard error for the estimated difference in drug usage between the two groups ignores this bias; so does the confidence interval.[128] Likewise, the standard error does not address problems inherent in using convenience samples rather than random samples.[129]

B. Significance Levels and Hypothesis Tests

1. What Is the p-value?

In our example, 50 men and 50 women were drawn at random from 5,000 male and 5,000 female applicants. An exam was administered to this sample, and in the sample, the pass rates for the men and women were 58% and 38%, respectively. The sample difference in pass rates was 58% − 38% = 20 percentage points. The *p*-value answers the following question: If the pass rates among all 5,000 male applicants and 5,000 female applicants were identical, how probable would it be to find a discrepancy as big as or bigger than the 20 percentage point difference observed in our sample? The question is delicate, because the pass rates in the population are unknown—that is why a sample was taken in the first place.

> If the model is *false* in certain respects, how badly does that affect estimates, significance test results, etc., that are based on the flawed model?

Lincoln E. Moses, *The Reasoning of Statistical Inference*, *in* Perspectives on Contemporary Statistics, *supra* note 47, at 107, 117–18.

125. It still may be helpful to consider the standard error, perhaps as a minimal estimate for statistical uncertainty in the quantity being estimated.

126. For a discussion of such systematic errors, see *supra* § II.B.

127. Brock v. Merrell Dow Pharms., Inc., 874 F.2d 307, 311–12 (5th Cir.), *modified*, 884 F.2d 166 (5th Cir. 1989).

128. In *Brock*, the court stated that the confidence interval took account of bias (in the form of selective recall) as well as random error. 874 F.2d at 311–12. With respect, we disagree. Even if sampling error were nonexistent—which would be the case if one could interview every woman who had a child in the period that the drug was available—selective recall would produce a difference in the percentages of reported drug exposure between mothers of children with birth defects and those with normal children. In this hypothetical situation, the standard error would vanish. Therefore, the standard error could disclose nothing about the impact of selective recall. The same conclusion holds even in the presence of sampling error.

129. *See supra* § II.B.1.

The assertion that the pass rates in the population are the same is called the null hypothesis. The null hypothesis asserts that there is no difference between men and women in the whole population—differences in the sample are due to the luck of the draw. The *p*-value is the probability of getting data as extreme as, or more extreme than, the actual data, given that the null hypothesis is true:

$$p = \text{Probability}(\text{extreme data} \mid \text{null hypothesis in model})$$

In our example, $p = 5\%$. If the null hypothesis is true, there is only a 5% chance of getting a difference in the pass rates of 20 percentage points or more.[130] The *p*-value for the observed discrepancy is 5%, or .05.

In such cases, small *p*-values are evidence of disparate impact, while large *p*-values are evidence against disparate impact. Regrettably, multiple negatives are involved here. A statistical test is essentially an argument by contradiction. The "null hypothesis" asserts no difference in the population—that is, no disparate impact. Small *p*-values speak against the null hypothesis—there is disparate impact, because the observed difference is hard to explain by chance alone. Conversely, large *p*-values indicate that the data are compatible with the null hypothesis: the observed difference is easy to explain by chance. In this context, small *p*-values argue for the plaintiffs, while large *p*-values argue for the defense.[131]

Since *p* is calculated by assuming that the null hypothesis is correct (no real difference in pass rates), the *p*-value cannot give the chance that this hypothesis is true. The *p*-value merely gives the chance of getting evidence against the null hypothesis as strong or stronger than the evidence at hand—assuming the null hypothesis to be correct. No matter how many samples are obtained, the null hypothesis is either always right or always wrong. Chance affects the data, not the hypothesis. With the frequency interpretation of chance, there is no meaningful way to assign a numerical probability to the null hypothesis.[132]

130. *See infra* Appendix.

131. Of course, sample size must also be considered, among other factors. *See infra* § IV.C.

132. *See, e.g.*, The Evolving Role of Statistical Assessments as Evidence in the Courts, *supra* note 1, at 196–98; David H. Kaye, *Statistical Significance and the Burden of Persuasion*, Law & Contemp. Probs., Autumn 1983, at 13. Some opinions suggest a contrary view. *E.g.*, Vasquez v. Hillery, 474 U.S. 254, 259 n.3 (1986) ("the District Court . . . ultimately accepted . . . a probability of 2 in 1,000 that the phenomenon was attributable to chance"); EEOC v. Olson's Dairy Queens, Inc., 989 F.2d 165, 167 (5th Cir. 1993) ("Dr. Straszheim concluded that the likelihood that [the] observed hiring patterns resulted from truly race-neutral hiring practices was less than one chance in ten thousand"); Capaci v. Katz & Besthoff, Inc., 711 F.2d 647, 652 (5th Cir. 1983) ("the highest probability of unbiased hiring was 5.367×10^{-20}"). Such statements confuse the probability of the kind of outcome observed, which is computed under some model of chance, with the probability that chance is the explanation for the outcome.

In scientific notation, 10^{20} is 1 followed by 20 zeros, and 10^{-20} is the reciprocal of that number. The proverbial "one-in-a-million" is more dryly expressed as 1×10^{-6}.

Computing *p*-values requires statistical expertise. Many methods are available, but only some will fit the occasion. Sometimes standard errors will be part of the analysis, while other times they will not be. Sometimes a difference of 2 standard errors will imply a *p*-value of about .05, other times it will not. In general, the *p*-value depends on the model and its parameters, the size of the sample, and the sample statistics.[133]

Because the *p*-value is affected by sample size, it does not measure the extent or importance of a difference.[134] Suppose, for instance, that the 5,000 male and 5,000 female job applicants would differ in their pass rates, but only by a single percentage point. This difference might not be enough to make a case of disparate impact, but by including enough men and women in the sample, the data could be made to have an impressively small *p*-value. This *p*-value would confirm that the 5,000 men and 5,000 women have different pass rates, but it would not show the difference is substantial.[135] In short, the *p*-value does not measure the strength or importance of an association.

2. *Is a Difference Statistically Significant?*

Statistical significance is determined by comparing a *p*-value to a preestablished value, the significance level.[136] If an observed difference is in the middle of the distribution that would be expected under the null hypothesis, there is no surprise. The sample data are of the type that often would be seen when the null hypothesis is true: the difference is not significant, and the null hypothesis cannot be rejected. On the other hand, if the sample difference is far from the expected value—according to the null hypothesis—then the sample is unusual: the difference is "significant," and the null hypothesis is rejected. In our example, the 20 percentage point difference in pass rates for the men and women in the sample, whose *p*-value was about .05, might be considered significant at

133. In this context, a parameter is an unknown numerical constant that is part of the statistical model. *See supra* note 121.

134. Some opinions seem to equate small *p*-values with "gross" or "substantial" disparities. *E.g.*, Craik v. Minnesota St. Univ. Bd., 731 F.2d 465, 479 (8th Cir. 1984). Other courts have emphasized the need to decide whether the underlying sample statistics reveal that a disparity is large. *E.g.*, McCleskey v. Kemp, 753 F.2d 877, 892–94 (11th Cir. 1985), *aff'd*, 481 U.S. 279 (1987).

135. *Cf.* Frazier v. Garrison Indep. Sch. Dist., 980 F.2d 1514, 1526 (5th Cir. 1993) (rejecting claims of intentional discrimination in the use of a teacher competency examination that resulted in retention rates exceeding 95% for all groups).

136. Statisticians use the Greek letter alpha (α) to denote the significance level; α gives the chance of getting a "significant" result, assuming that the null hypothesis is true. Thus, α represents the chance of what is variously termed a "false rejection" of the null hypothesis or a "Type I error" (also called a "false positive" or a "false alarm"). For example, suppose $\alpha = 5\%$. If investigators do many studies, and the null hypothesis happens to be true in each case, then about 5% of the time they would obtain significant results—and falsely reject the null hypothesis.

the .05 level. If the threshold were set lower, say at .01, the result would not be significant.[137]

In practice, statistical analysts often use certain preset significance levels—typically .05 or .01.[138] The .05 level is the most common in social science, and an analyst who speaks of "significant" results without specifying the threshold probably is using this figure.[139] An unexplained reference to "highly significant" results probably means that p is less than .01.[140]

Since the term "significant" is merely a label for certain kinds of p-values, it is subject to the same limitations as are p-values themselves. Analysts may refer to a difference as "significant," meaning only that the p-value is below some threshold value. Significance depends not only on the magnitude of the effect, but also on the sample size (among other things). Thus, significant differences are evidence that something besides random error is at work, but they are not evidence that this "something" is legally or practically important. Statisticians distinguish between "statistical" and "practical" significance to make the point. When practical significance is lacking—when the size of a disparity or correlation is negligible—there is no reason to worry about statistical significance.[141]

As noted above, it is easy to mistake the p-value for the probability that there is no difference. Likewise, if results are significant at the .05 level, it is tempting to conclude that the null hypothesis has only a 5% chance of being correct.[142]

137. For another example of the relationship between a test statistic and significance, see *infra* § V.D.2.

138. The Supreme Court implicitly referred to this practice in *Castaneda v. Partida*, 430 U.S. 482, 496 n.17 (1977), and *Hazelwood School District v. United States*, 433 U.S. 299, 311 n.17 (1977). In these footnotes, the Court described the null hypothesis as "suspect to a social scientist" when a statistic from "large samples" falls more than "two or three standard deviations" from its expected value under the null hypothesis. Although the Court did not say so, these differences produce p-values of about .05 and .01 when the statistic is normally distributed. The Court's "standard deviation" is our "standard error."

139. Some have suggested that data not "significant" at the .05 level should be disregarded. *E.g.*, Paul Meier et al., *What Happened in* Hazelwood: *Statistics, Employment Discrimination, and the 80% Rule*, 1984 Am. B. Found. Res. J. 139, 152, *reprinted in* Statistics and the Law, *supra* note 1, at 1, 13. This view is challenged in, e.g., Kaye, *supra* note 118, at 1344 & n.56, 1345.

140. Merely labeling results as "significant" or "not significant" without providing the underlying information that goes into this conclusion is of limited value. *See, e.g.*, John C. Bailar III & Frederick Mosteller, *Guidelines for Statistical Reporting in Articles for Medical Journals: Amplifications and Explanations*, *in* Medical Uses of Statistics, *supra* note 28, at 313, 316.

141. *E.g.*, Waisome v. Port Auth., 948 F.2d 1370, 1376 (2d Cir. 1991) ("though the disparity was found to be statistically significant, it was of limited magnitude"); *cf.* Thornburg v. Gingles, 478 U.S. 30, 53–54 (1986) (repeating the district court's explanation of why "the correlation between the race of the voter and the voter's choice of certain candidates was [not only] statistically significant," but also "so marked as to be substantively significant, in the sense that the results of the individual election would have been different depending upon whether it had been held among only the white voters or only the black voters").

142. *E.g.*, *Waisome*, 948 F.2d at 1376 ("Social scientists consider a finding of two standard deviations significant, meaning there is about one chance in 20 that the explanation for a deviation could be random . . . ."); Rivera v. City of Wichita Falls, 665 F.2d 531, 545 n.22 (5th Cir. 1982) ("A variation

This temptation should be resisted. From the frequentist perspective, statistical hypotheses are either true or false; probabilities govern the samples, not the models and hypotheses. The significance level tells us what is likely to happen when the null hypothesis is correct; it cannot tell us the probability that the hypothesis is true. Significance comes no closer to expressing the probability that the null hypothesis is true than does the underlying *p*-value.[143]

C. Evaluating Hypothesis Tests

1. What Is the Power of the Test?

When a *p*-value is high, findings are not significant, and the null hypothesis is not rejected. This could happen for at least two reasons:

1. there is no difference in the population—the null hypothesis is true; or
2. there is some difference in the population—the null hypothesis is false—but, by chance, the data happened to be of the kind expected under the null hypothesis.

If the "power" of a statistical study is low, the second explanation may be plausible. Power is the chance that a statistical test will declare an effect when there is an effect to declare.[144] This chance depends on the size of the effect and

of two standard deviations would indicate that the probability of the observed outcome occurring purely by chance would be approximately five out of 100; that is, it could be said with a 95% certainty that the outcome was not merely a fluke."); Vuyanich v. Republic Nat'l Bank, 505 F. Supp. 224, 272 (N.D. Tex. 1980) ("[I]f a 5% level of significance is used, a sufficiently large *t*-statistic for the coefficient indicates that the chances are less than one in 20 that the true coefficient is actually zero."), *vacated*, 723 F.2d 1195 (5th Cir. 1984); Sheehan v. Daily Racing Form, Inc., 104 F.3d 940, 941 (7th Cir. 1997) ("An affidavit by a statistician . . . states that the probability that the retentions . . . are uncorrelated with age is less than 5 percent.").

143. For more discussion, see Kaye, *supra* note 118; *cf. infra* note 167.

144. More precisely, power is the probability of rejecting the null hypothesis when the alternative hypothesis is right. (On the meaning of "alternative hypothesis," see *infra* § IV.C.5.) Typically, this probability will depend on the values of unknown parameters, as well as the pre-set significance level α. Therefore, no single number gives the power of the test. One can specify particular values for the parameters and significance level and compute the power of the test accordingly. *See infra* Appendix for an example. Power may be denoted by the Greek letter beta (β).

Accepting the null hypothesis when the alternative is true is known as a "false acceptance" of the null hypothesis or a "Type II error" (also called a "false negative" or a "missed signal"). The chance of a false negative may be computed from the power, as $1 - \beta$. Frequentist hypothesis testing keeps the risk of a false positive to a specified level (such as $\alpha = .05$) and then tries to minimize the chance of a false negative ($1 - \beta$) for that value of α. Regrettably, the notation is in some degree of flux; many authors use β to denote the chance of a false negative; then, it is β that should be minimized.

Some commentators have claimed that the cutoff for significance should be chosen to equalize the chance of a false positive and a false negative, on the ground that this criterion corresponds to the "more-probable-than-not" burden of proof. Unfortunately, the argument is fallacious, because α and β do not give the probabilities of the null and alternative hypotheses; *see supra* § IV.B.2; *infra* note 167. *See* D.H. Kaye, *Hypothesis Testing in the Courtroom*, *in* Contributions to the Theory and Application of Statistics: A Volume in Honor of Herbert Solomon 331, 341–43 (Alan E. Gelfand ed., 1987); *supra* § IV.B.1; *infra* note 165.

the size of the sample. Discerning subtle differences in the population requires large samples; even so, small samples may detect truly substantial differences.[145]

When a study with low power fails to show a significant effect, the results are more fairly described as inconclusive than as negative: the proof is weak because power is low.[146] On the other hand, when studies have a good chance of detecting a meaningful association, failure to obtain significance can be persuasive evidence that there is no effect to be found.[147]

2. One- or Two-tailed Tests?

In many cases, a statistical test can be done either one-tailed or two-tailed. The second method will produce a p-value twice as big as the first method. Since

145. For simplicity, the numerical examples of statistical inference in this reference guide presuppose large samples. Some courts have expressed uneasiness about estimates or analyses based on small samples; indeed, a few courts have refused even to consider such studies or formal statistical procedures for handling small samples. *See, e.g.*, Bunch v. Bullard, 795 F.2d 384, 395 n.12 (5th Cir. 1986) (that 12 of 15 whites and only 3 of 13 blacks passed a police promotion test created a prima facie case of disparate impact; however, "[t]he district court did not perform, nor do we attempt, the application of probability theories to a sample size as small as this" because "[a]dvanced statistical analysis may be of little help in determining the significance of such disparities"); United States v. Lansdowne Swim Club, 713 F. Supp. 785, 809–10 (E.D. Pa. 1989) (collecting cases). Other courts have been more venturesome. *E.g.*, Bazemore v. Friday, 751 F.2d 662, 673 & n.9 (4th Cir. 1984) (court of appeals applied its own t-test rather than the normal curve to quartile rankings in an attempt to account for a sample size of nine), *rev'd on other grounds*, 478 U.S. 385 (1986).

Analyzing data from small samples may require more stringent assumptions, but there is no fundamental difference in the meaning of confidence intervals and p-values. If the assumptions underlying the statistical analysis are justified—and this can be more difficult to demonstrate with small samples—then confidence intervals and test statistics are no less trustworthy than those for large samples. Aside from the problem of choosing the correct analytical technique, the concern with small samples is not that they are beyond the ken of statistical theory, but that (1) the statistical tests involving small samples might lack power, and (2) the underlying assumptions may be hard to validate.

146. In our example, with $\alpha = .05$, power to detect a difference of 10 percentage points between the male and female job applicants is only about 1/6. *See infra* Appendix. Not seeing a "significant" difference therefore provides only weak proof that the difference between men and women is smaller than 10 percentage points. We prefer estimates accompanied by standard errors to tests because the former seem to make the state of the statistical evidence clearer: The estimated difference is 20 ± 10 percentage points, indicating that a difference of 10 percentage points is quite compatible with the data.

147. Some formal procedures are available to aggregate results across studies. *See In re* Paoli R.R. Yard PCB Litig., 916 F.2d 829 (3d Cir. 1990). In principle, the power of the collective results will be greater than the power of each study. *See, e.g.*, The Handbook of Research Synthesis 226–27 (Harris Cooper & Larry V. Hedges eds., 1993); Larry V. Hedges & Ingram Olkin, Statistical Methods for Meta-Analysis (1985); Jerome P. Kassirer, *Clinical Trials and Meta-Analysis: What Do They Do for Us?*, 327 New Eng. J. Med. 273, 274 (1992) ("[C]umulative meta-analysis represents one promising approach."); National Reseach Council, Combining Information: Statistical Issues and Opportunities for Research (1992); Symposium, *Meta-Analysis of Observational Studies*, 140 Am. J. Epidemiology 771 (1994). Unfortunately, the procedures have their own limitations. *E.g.*, Diana B. Petitti, Meta-Analysis, Decision Analysis, and Cost-Effectiveness Analysis Methods for Quantitative Synthesis in Medicine (2d ed. 2000); Michael Oakes, Statistical Inference: A Commentary for the Social and Behavioural Sciences 157 (1986) ("a retrograde development"); John C. Bailar III, *The Promise and Problems of Meta-Analysis*, 337 New Eng. J. Med. 559 (1997) (editorial); Charles Mann, *Meta-Analysis in the Breech*, 249 Science 476 (1990).

small *p*-values are evidence against the null hypothesis, a one-tailed test seems to produce stronger evidence than a two-tailed test. However, this difference is largely illusory.[148]

Some courts have expressed a preference for two-tailed tests,[149] but a rigid rule is not required if *p*-values and significance levels are used as clues rather than as mechanical rules for statistical proof. One-tailed tests make it easier to reach a threshold like .05, but if .05 is not used as a magic line, then the choice between one tail and two is less important—as long as the choice and its effect on the *p*-value are made explicit.[150]

3. How Many Tests Have Been Performed?

Repeated testing complicates the interpretation of significance levels. If enough comparisons are made, random error almost guarantees that some will yield "significant" findings, even when there is no real effect. Consider the problem of deciding whether a coin is biased. The probability that a fair coin will produce ten heads when tossed ten times is $(1/2)^{10} = 1/1{,}024$. Observing ten heads in the first ten tosses, therefore, would be strong evidence that the coin is biased. Nevertheless, if a fair coin is tossed a few thousand times, it is likely that at least one string of ten consecutive heads will appear. The test—looking for a run of ten heads—can be repeated far too often.

148. In our pass rate example, the *p*-value of the test is approximated by a certain area under the normal curve. The one-tailed procedure uses the "tail area" under the curve to the right of 2, giving $p = .025$ (approximately). The two-tailed procedure contemplates the area to the left of -2, as well as the area to the right of 2. Now there are two tails, and $p = .05$. *See infra* Appendix (figure 13); Freedman et al., *supra* note 16, at 549–52.

According to formal statistical theory, the choice between one tail or two can sometimes be made by considering the exact form of the "alternative hypothesis." *See infra* § IV.C.5. In our example, the null hypothesis is that pass rates are equal for men and women in the whole population of applicants. The alternative hypothesis may exclude a priori the possibility that women have a higher pass rate, and hold that more men will pass than women. This asymmetric alternative suggests a one-tailed test. On the other hand, the alternative hypothesis may simply be that pass rates for men and women in the whole population are unequal. This symmetric alternative admits the possibility that women may score higher than men, and points to a two-tailed test. *See, e.g.*, Freedman et al., *supra* note 16, at 551. Some experts think that the choice between one-tailed and two-tailed tests can often be made by considering the exact form of the null and alternative hypothesis.

149. *See, e.g.*, Baldus & Cole, *supra* note 89, § 9.1, at 308 n.35a; The Evolving Role of Statistical Assessments as Evidence in the Courts, *supra* note 1, at 38–40 (citing EEOC v. Federal Reserve Bank, 698 F.2d 633 (4th Cir. 1983), *rev'd on other grounds sub nom.* Cooper v. Federal Reserve Bank, 467 U.S. 867 (1984)); Kaye, *supra* note 118, at 1358 n.113; David H. Kaye, *The Numbers Game: Statistical Inference in Discrimination Cases*, 80 Mich. L. Rev. 833 (1982) (citing Hazelwood Sch. Dist. v. United States, 433 U.S. 299 (1977)). Arguments for one-tailed tests are discussed in Finkelstein & Levin, *supra* note 1, at 125–26; Richard Goldstein, *Two Types of Statistical Errors in Employment Discrimination Cases*, 26 Jurimetrics J. 32 (1985); Kaye, *supra* at 841.

150. One-tailed tests at the .05 level are viewed as weak evidence—no weaker standard is commonly used in the technical literature.

Such artifacts are commonplace. Since research that fails to uncover significance is not usually published, reviews of the literature may produce an unduly large number of studies finding statistical significance.[151] Even a single researcher may search for so many different relationships that a few will achieve statistical significance by mere happenstance. Almost any large data set—even pages from a table of random digits—will contain some unusual pattern that can be uncovered by a diligent search. Having detected the pattern, the analyst can perform a statistical test for it, blandly ignoring the search effort. Statistical significance is bound to follow. Ten heads in the first ten tosses means one thing; a run of ten heads somewhere along the way in a few thousand tosses of a coin means quite another.

There are statistical methods for coping with multiple looks at the data, which permit the calculation of meaningful *p*-values in certain cases.[152] However, no general solution is available, and the existing methods would be of little help in the typical case where analysts have tested and rejected a variety of regression models before arriving at the one considered the most satisfactory. In these situations, courts should not be overly impressed with claims that estimates are significant. Instead, they should be asking how analysts developed their models.[153]

4. *Tests or Interval Estimates?*

Statistical significance depends on the *p*-value, and *p*-values depend on sample size. Therefore, a "significant" effect could be small. Conversely, an effect that is "not significant" could be large.[154] By inquiring into the magnitude of an effect, courts can avoid being misled by *p*-values. To focus attention where it belongs—on the actual size of an effect and the reliability of the statistical analysis—interval estimates may be valuable.[155] Seeing a plausible range of values for the quantity of interest helps describe the statistical uncertainty in the estimate.

In our example, the 95% confidence interval for the difference in the pass rates of men and women ranged from 0 to 40 percentage points. Our best

151. *E.g.*, Stuart J. Pocock et al., *Statistical Problems in the Reporting of Clinical Trials: A Survey of Three Medical Journals*, 317 New Eng. J. Med. 426 (1987).

152. *See, e.g.*, Rupert G. Miller, Jr., Simultaneous Statistical Inference (2d ed. 1981).

153. *See, e.g.*, On Model Uncertainty and Its Statistical Implications: Lecture Notes in Econometric and Mathematical Systems (Theo K. Dijkstra ed., 1988); Frank T. Denton, *Data Mining As an Industry*, 67 Rev. Econ. & Stat. 124 (1985). Intuition may suggest that the more variables included in the model, the better. However, this idea often seems to be wrong. Complex models may reflect only accidental features of the data. Standard statistical tests offer little protection against this possibility when the analyst has tried a variety of models before settling on the final specification.

154. *See supra* § IV.B.1.

155. An interval estimate may be composed of a point estimate—like the sample mean used to estimate the population mean—together with its standard error; or the point estimate and standard error can be combined in a confidence interval.

estimate is that the pass rate for men is 20 percentage points higher than for women; and the difference may plausibly be as little as 0 or as much as 40 percentage points. The *p*-value does not yield this information. The confidence interval contains the information provided by a significance test—and more.[156] For instance, significance at the .05 level can be read off the 95% confidence interval.[157] In our example, zero is at the extreme edge of the 95% confidence interval, so we have "significant" evidence that the true difference in pass rates between male and female applicants is not zero. But there are values very close to zero inside the interval.

On the other hand, suppose a significance test fails to reject the null hypothesis. The confidence interval may prevent the mistake of thinking there is positive proof for the null hypothesis. To illustrate, let us change our example slightly: say that 29 men and 20 women passed the test. The 95% confidence interval goes from -2 to 38 percentage points. Because a difference of zero falls within the 95% confidence interval, the null hypothesis—that the true difference is zero—cannot be rejected at the .05 level. But the interval extends to 38 percentage points, indicating that the population difference could be substantial. Lack of significance does not exclude this possibility.[158]

5. *What Are the Rival Hypotheses?*

The *p*-value of a statistical test is computed on the basis of a model for the data—the null hypothesis. Usually, the test is made in order to argue for the alternative hypothesis—another model. However, on closer examination, both models may prove to be unreasonable.[159] A small *p*-value means something is going on, besides random error; the alternative hypothesis should be viewed as one possible explanation—out of many—for the data.[160]

156. Accordingly, it has been argued that courts should demand confidence intervals (whenever they can be computed) to the exclusion of explicit significance tests and *p*-values. Kaye, *supra* note 118, at 1349 n.78; *cf.* Bailar & Mosteller, *supra* note 140, at 317.

157. Instead of referring to significance at the .05 level, some writers refer to "the 95 percent confidence level that is often used by scientists to reject the possibility that chance alone accounted for observed differences." Carnegie Comm'n on Science, Tech. & Gov't, Science and Technology in Judicial Decision Making: Creating Opportunities and Meeting Challenges 28 (1993).

158. We have used two-sided intervals, corresponding to two-tailed tests. One-sided intervals, corresponding to one-tailed tests, also are available.

159. Often, the null and alternative hypotheses are statements about possible ranges of values for parameters in a common statistical model. *See, e.g., supra* note 148. Computations of standard errors, *p*-values, and power all take place within the confines of this basic model. The statistical analysis looks at the relative plausibility for competing values of the parameters, but makes no global assessment of the reasonableness of the basic model.

160. *See, e.g.*, Paul Meier & Sandy Zabell, *Benjamin Peirce and the Howland Will*, 75 J. Am. Stat. Ass'n 497 (1980) (competing explanations in a forgery case). Outside the legal realm there are many intriguing examples of the tendency to think that a small *p*-value is definitive proof of an alternative hypothesis, even though there are other plausible explanations for the data. *See, e.g.*, Freedman et al., *supra* note 16, at 562–63; C.E.M. Hansel, ESP: A Scientific Evaluation (1966).

In *Mapes Casino, Inc. v. Maryland Casualty Co.*,[161] for example, the court recognized the importance of explanations that the proponent of the statistical evidence had failed to consider. In this action to collect on an insurance policy, Mapes Casino sought to quantify the amount of its loss due to employee defalcation. The casino argued that certain employees were using an intermediary to cash in chips at other casinos. It established that over an 18-month period, the win percentage at its craps tables was 6%, compared to an expected value of 20%. The court recognized that the statistics were probative of the fact that *something* was wrong at the craps tables—the discrepancy was too big to explain as the mere product of random chance. But it was not convinced by plaintiff's alternative hypothesis. The court pointed to other possible explanations (Runyonesque activities like "skimming," "scamming," and "crossroading") that might have accounted for the discrepancy without implicating the suspect employees.[162] In short, rejection of the null hypothesis does not leave the proffered alternative hypothesis as the only viable explanation for the data.[163]

In many studies, the validity of the model is secured by the procedures used to collect the data. There are formulas for standard errors and confidence intervals that hold when random samples are used. *See supra* §§ II.B, IV.A.2. There are statistical tests for comparing two random samples, or evaluating the results of a randomized experiment. *See supra* §§ II.A, IV.B.2. In such examples, the statistical procedures flow from the sampling method and the design of the study. On the other hand, if samples of convenience are used, or subjects are not randomized, the validity of the statistical procedures can be contested. *See* Freedman et al., *supra* note 16, at 387–88, 424, 557–65.

161. 290 F. Supp. 186 (D. Nev. 1968).

162. *Id.* at 193. "Skimming" consists of "taking off the top before counting the drop," "scamming" is "cheating by collusion between dealer and player," and "crossroading" involves "professional cheaters among the players." *Id.* In plainer language, the court seems to have ruled that the casino itself might be cheating, or there could have been cheaters other than the particular employees identified in the case. At the least, plaintiff's statistical evidence did not rule out such possibilities.

163. *Compare* EEOC v. Sears, Roebuck & Co., 839 F.2d 302, 312 & n.9, 313 (7th Cir. 1988) (EEOC's regression studies showing significant differences did not establish liability because surveys and testimony supported the rival hypothesis that women generally had less interest in commission sales positions), *with* EEOC v. General Tel. Co., 885 F.2d 575 (9th Cir. 1989) (unsubstantiated rival hypothesis of "lack of interest" in "non-traditional" jobs insufficient to rebut prima facie case of gender discrimination); *cf. supra* § II.A (problem of confounding); *infra* note 230 (effect of omitting important variables from a regression model).

D. Posterior Probabilities

Standard errors, *p*-values, and significance tests are common techniques for assessing random error. These procedures rely on the sample data, and are justified in terms of the "operating characteristics" of the statistical procedures.[164] However, this frequentist approach does not permit the statistician to compute the probability that a particular hypothesis is correct, given the data.[165] For instance, a frequentist may postulate that a coin is fair: it has a 50–50 chance of landing heads, and successive tosses are independent; this is viewed as an empirical statement—potentially falsifiable—about the coin. On this basis, it is easy to calculate the chance that the coin will turn up heads in the next ten tosses:[166] the answer is 1/1,024. Therefore, observing ten heads in a row brings into serious question the initial hypothesis of fairness. Rejecting the hypothesis of fairness when there are ten heads in ten tosses gives the wrong result—when the coin is fair—only one time in 1,024. That is an example of an operating characteristic of a statistical procedure.

But what of the converse probability: if a coin lands heads ten times in a row, what is the chance that it is fair?[167] To compute such converse probabilities, it is necessary to postulate initial probabilities that the coin is fair, as well as probabilities of unfairness to various degrees.[168] And that is beyond the scope of frequentist statistics.[169]

164. "Operating characteristics" are the expected value and standard error of estimators, probabilities of error for statistical tests, and related quantities.

165. *See supra* § IV.B.1; *infra* Appendix. Consequently, quantities such as *p*-values or confidence levels cannot be compared directly to numbers like .95 or .50 that might be thought to quantify the burden of persuasion in criminal or civil cases. *See* Kaye, *supra* note 144; D.H. Kaye, *Apples and Oranges: Confidence Coefficients and the Burden of Persuasion*, 73 Cornell L. Rev. 54 (1987).

166. Stated slightly more formally, if the coin is fair and each outcome is independent (the hypothesis), then the probability of observing ten heads (the data) is $\Pr(\text{data} \mid H_0) = (1/2)^{10} = 1/1{,}024$, where H_0 stands for the hypothesis that the coin is fair.

167. We call this a "converse probability" because it is of the form $\Pr(H_0 \mid \text{data})$ rather than $\Pr(\text{data} \mid H_0)$; an equivalent phrase, "inverse probability," also is used. The tendency to think of $\Pr(\text{data} \mid H_0)$ as if it were the converse probability $\Pr(H_0 \mid \text{data})$ is the "transposition fallacy." For instance, most United States senators are men, but very few men are senators. Consequently, there is a high probability that an individual who is a senator is a man, but the probability that an individual who is a man is a senator is practically zero. For examples of the transposition fallacy in court opinions, see cases cited *supra* note 142. *See also* Committee on DNA Forensic Science: An Update, *supra* note 60, at 133 (describing the fallacy in cases involving DNA identification evidence as the "prosecutor's fallacy"). The frequentist *p*-value, $\Pr(\text{data} \mid H_0)$, is generally not a good approximation to the Bayesian $\Pr(H_0 \mid \text{data})$; the latter includes considerations of power and base rates.

168. *See infra* Appendix.

169. In some situations, the probability of an event on which a case depends can be computed with objective methods. However, these events are measurable outcomes (like the number of heads in a series of tosses of a coin) rather than hypotheses about the process that generated the data (like the claim that the coin is fair). For example, in *United States v. Shonubi*, 895 F. Supp. 460 (E.D.N.Y. 1995), *rev'd*,

In the Bayesian or subjectivist approach, probabilities represent subjective degrees of belief rather than objective facts. The observer's confidence in the hypothesis that a coin is fair, for example, is expressed as a number between zero and one;[170] likewise, the observer must quantify beliefs about the chance that the coin is unfair to various degrees—all in advance of seeing the data.[171] These subjective probabilities, like the probabilities governing the tosses of the coin, are set up to obey the axioms of probability theory. The probabilities for the various hypotheses about the coin, specified before data collection, are called prior probabilities.

These prior probabilities can then be updated, using "Bayes' rule," given data on how the coin actually falls.[172] In short, Bayesian statisticians can compute posterior probabilities for various hypotheses about the coin, given the data.[173] Although such posterior probabilities can pertain directly to hypotheses of legal interest, they are necessarily subjective, for they reflect not just the data but also

103 F.3d 1085 (2d Cir. 1997), a government expert estimated for sentencing purposes the total quantity of heroin that a Nigerian defendant living in New Jersey had smuggled (by swallowing heroin-filled balloons) in the course of eight trips to and from Nigeria. He applied a method known as "resampling" or "bootstrapping." Specifically, he drew 100,000 independent simple random samples of size seven from a population of weights distributed as in customs data on 117 other balloon swallowers caught in the same airport during the same time period; he discovered that for 99% of these samples, the total weight was at least 2090.2 grams. 895 F. Supp. at 504. Thus, the researcher reported that "there is a 99% chance that Shonubi carried at least 2090.2 grams of heroin on the seven [prior] trips . . . ." *Id.* However, the Second Circuit reversed this finding for want of "specific evidence of what Shonubi had done." 103 F.3d at 1090. Although the logical basis for this "specific evidence" requirement is unclear, a difficulty with the expert's analysis is apparent. Statistical inference generally involves an extrapolation from the units sampled to the population of all units. Thus, the sample needs to be representative. In *Shonubi*, the government used a sample of weights, one for each courier on the trip at which that courier was caught. It sought to extrapolate from these data to many trips taken by a single courier—trips on which that other courier was not caught.

170. Here "confidence" has the meaning ordinarily ascribed to it rather than the technical interpretation applicable to a frequentist "confidence interval." Consequently, it can be related to the burden of persuasion. *See* Kaye, *supra* note 165.

171. For instance, let p be the unknown probability that coin lands heads: What is the chance that p exceeds .6? The Bayesian statistician must be prepared to answer all such questions. Bayesian procedures are sometimes defended on the ground that the beliefs of any rational observer must conform to the Bayesian rules. However, the definition of "rational" is purely formal. *See* Peter C. Fishburn, *The Axioms of Subjective Probability*, 1 Stat. Sci. 335 (1986); David Kaye, *The Laws of Probability and the Law of the Land*, 47 U. Chi. L. Rev. 34 (1979).

172. *See infra* Appendix.

173. *See generally* George E.P. Box & George C. Tiao, Bayesian Inference in Statistical Analysis (Wiley Classics Library ed., John Wiley & Sons, Inc. 1992) (1973). For applications to legal issues, see, e.g., Aitken et al., *supra* note 45, at 337–48; David H. Kaye, *DNA Evidence: Probability, Population Genetics, and the Courts*, 7 Harv. J.L. & Tech. 101 (1993).

the subjective prior probabilities—that is, the degrees of belief about the various hypotheses concerning the coin specified prior to obtaining the data.[174]

Such analyses have rarely been used in court,[175] and the question of their forensic value has been aired primarily in the academic literature.[176] Some statisticians favor Bayesian methods,[177] and some legal commentators have proposed their use in certain kinds of cases in certain circumstances.[178]

V. Correlation and Regression

Regression models are often used to infer causation from association; for example, such models are frequently introduced to prove disparate treatment in discrimination cases, or to estimate damages in antitrust actions. Section V.D explains the ideas and some of the pitfalls. Sections V.A–C cover some preliminary material, showing how scatter diagrams, correlation coefficients, and regression lines can be used to summarize relationships between variables.

174. In this framework, the question arises of whose beliefs to use—the statistician's or the factfinder's. *See, e.g.*, Michael O. Finkelstein & William B. Fairley, *A Bayesian Approach to Identification Evidence*, 83 Harv. L. Rev. 489 (1970) (proposing that experts give posterior probabilities for a wide range of prior probabilities, to allow jurors to use their own prior probabilities or just to judge the impact of the data on possible values of the prior probabilities). *But see* Laurence H. Tribe, *Trial by Mathematics: Precision and Ritual in the Legal Process*, 84 Harv. L. Rev. 1329 (1971) (arguing that efforts to describe the impact of evidence on a juror's subjective probabilities would unduly impress jurors and undermine the presumption of innocence and other legal values).

175. The exception is paternity litigation; when genetic tests are indicative of paternity, testimony as to a posterior "probability of paternity" is common. *See, e.g.*, 1 Modern Scientific Evidence: The Law and Science of Expert Testimony, *supra* note 3, § 19–2.5.

176. *See, e.g.*, Probability and Inference in the Law of Evidence: The Uses and Limits of Bayesianism (Peter Tillers & Eric D. Green eds., 1988); Symposium, *Decision and Inference in Litigation*, 13 Cardozo L. Rev. 253 (1991). The Bayesian framework probably has received more acceptance in explicating legal concepts such as the relevance of evidence, the nature of prejudicial evidence, probative value, and burdens of persuasion. *See, e.g.*, Richard D. Friedman, *Assessing Evidence*, 94 Mich. L. Rev. 1810 (1996) (book review); Richard O. Lempert, *Modeling Relevance*, 75 Mich. L. Rev. 1021 (1977); D.H. Kaye, *Clarifying the Burden of Persuasion: What Bayesian Decision Rules Do and Do Not Do*, 3 Int'l J. Evidence & Proof 1 (1999).

177. *E.g.*, Donald A. Berry, *Inferences Using DNA Profiling in Forensic Identification and Paternity Cases*, 6 Stat. Sci. 175, 180 (1991); Stephen E. Fienberg & Mark J. Schervish, *The Relevance of Bayesian Inference for the Presentation of Statistical Evidence and for Legal Decisionmaking*, 66 B.U. L. Rev. 771 (1986). Nevertheless, many statisticians question the general applicability of Bayesian techniques: The results of the analysis may be substantially influenced by the prior probabilities, which in turn may be quite arbitrary. *See, e.g.*, Freedman, *supra* note 112.

178. *E.g.*, Joseph C. Bright, Jr. et al., *Statistical Sampling in Tax Audits*, 13 L. & Soc. Inquiry 305 (1988); Ira Mark Ellman & David Kaye, *Probabilities and Proof: Can HLA and Blood Group Testing Prove Paternity?*, 54 N.Y.U. L. Rev. 1131 (1979); Finkelstein & Fairley, *supra* note 174; Kaye, *supra* note 173.

A. Scatter Diagrams

The relationship between two variables can be graphed in a scatter diagram.[179] Data on income and education for a sample of 350 men, ages 25 to 29, residing in Texas[180] provide an example. Each person in the sample corresponds to one dot in the diagram. As indicated in Figure 4, the horizontal axis shows the person's education, and the vertical axis shows his income. Person A completed 8 years of schooling (grade school) and had an income of $19,000. Person B completed 16 years of schooling (college) and had an income of $38,000.

Figure 4. Plotting a scatter diagram. The horizontal axis shows educational level and the vertical axis shows income.

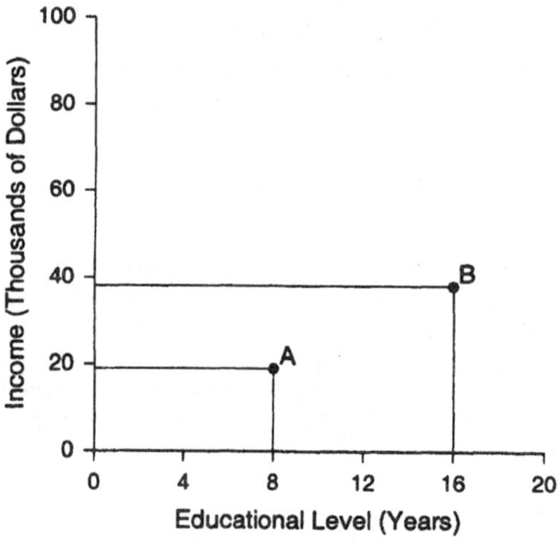

Figure 5 is the scatter diagram for the Texas data. The diagram confirms an obvious point. There is a "positive association" between income and education: in general, persons with a higher educational level have higher incomes. However, there are many exceptions to this rule, and the association is not as strong as one might expect.

179. These diagrams are also referred to as scatterplots or scattergrams.

180. These data are from a public-use data tape, Bureau of the Census, U.S. Dep't of Commerce, for the March 1988 Current Population Survey. Income and education (years of schooling completed) are self-reported. Income is truncated at $100,000 and education at 18 years.

Figure 5. Scatter diagram for income and education: men age 25 to 29 in Texas.[181]

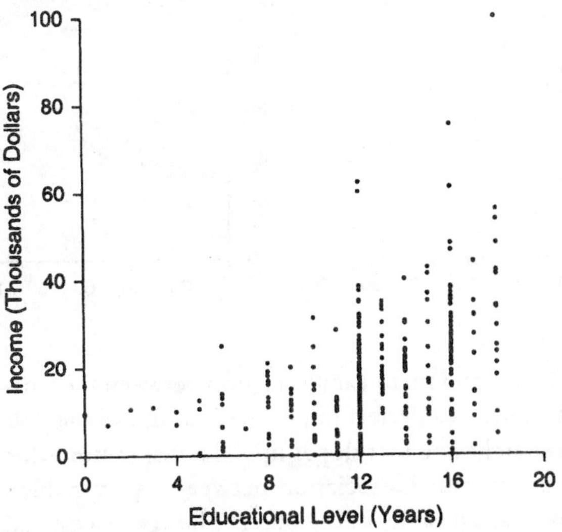

B. Correlation Coefficients

Two variables are positively correlated when their values tend to go up or down together.[182] Income and education in Figure 5 provides an example. The correlation coefficient (usually denoted by the letter *r*) is a single number that reflects the strength of an association. Figure 6 shows the values of *r* for three scatter diagrams.

181. Education may be compulsory, but the Current Population Survey generally finds a small percentage of respondents who report very little schooling. Such respondents will be found at the lower left corner of the scatter diagram.

182. Many statistics and displays are available to investigate association. The most common are the correlation coefficient and the scatter diagram.

Figure 6. The correlation coefficient measures the strength of linear association.

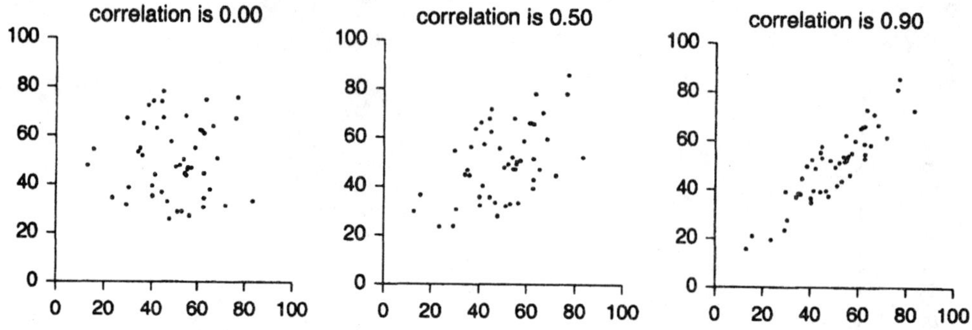

A correlation coefficient of 0 indicates no linear association between the variables, while a coefficient of +1 indicates a perfect linear relationship: all the dots in the scatter diagram fall on a straight line that slopes up. The maximum value for *r* is +1. Sometimes, there is a negative association between two variables: large values of one tend to go with small values of the other. The age of a car and its fuel economy in miles per gallon provide an example. Negative association is indicated by negative values for *r*. The extreme case is an *r* of −1, indicating that all the points in the scatter diagram lie on a straight line which slopes down.

Moderate associations are the general rule in the social sciences; correlations larger than, say, 0.7 are quite unusual in many fields. For example, the correlation between college grades and first-year law school grades is under 0.3 at most law schools, while the correlation between LSAT scores and first-year law grades is generally about 0.4.[183] The correlation between heights of fraternal twins is about 0.5, while the correlation between heights of identical twins is about 0.95. In Figure 5, the correlation between income and education was 0.43. The correlation coefficient cannot capture all the underlying information. Several issues may arise in this regard, and we consider them in turn.

183. Linda F. Wightman, Predictive Validity of the LSAT: A National Summary of the 1990–1992 Correlation Studies 10 (1993); *cf.* Linda F. Wightman & David G. Muller, An Analysis of Differential Validity and Differential Prediction for Black, Mexican-American, Hispanic, and White Law School Students 11–13 (1990). A combination of LSAT and undergraduate grade point average has a higher correlation with first-year law school grades than either item alone. The multiple correlation coefficient is typically about 0.5. Wightman, *supra*, at 10.

1. Is the Association Linear?

The correlation coefficient is designed to measure linear association. Figure 7 shows a strong nonlinear pattern with a correlation close to zero. When the scatter diagram reveals a strong nonlinear pattern, the correlation coefficient may not be a useful summary statistic.

Figure 7. The correlation coefficient only measures linear association. The scatter diagram shows a strong nonlinear association with a correlation coefficient close to zero.

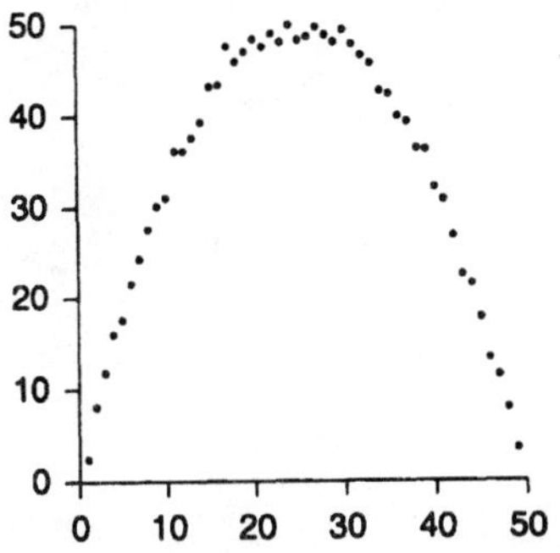

2. Do Outliers Influence the Correlation Coefficient?

The correlation coefficient can be distorted by outliers—a few points that are far removed from the bulk of the data. The left hand panel in Figure 8 shows that one outlier (lower right hand corner) can reduce a perfect correlation to nearly nothing. Conversely, the right hand panel shows that one outlier (upper right hand corner) can raise a correlation of zero to nearly one.

Figure 8. The correlation coefficient can be distorted by outliers. The left hand panel shows an outlier (in the lower right hand corner) that destroys a nearly perfect correlation. The right hand panel shows an outlier (in the upper right hand corner) that changes the correlation from zero to nearly one.

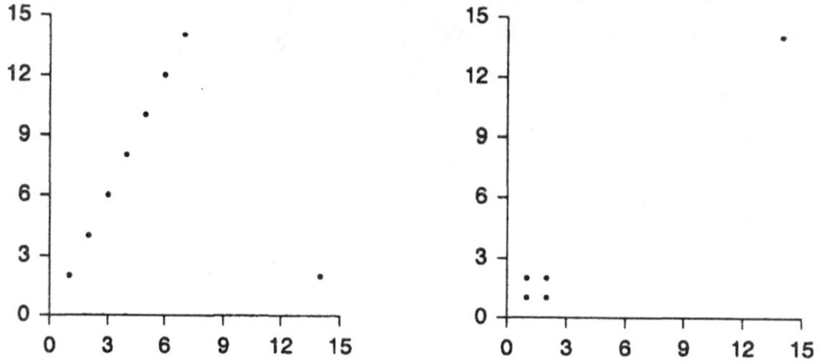

3. Does a Confounding Variable Influence the Coefficient?

The correlation coefficient measures the association between two variables. Investigators—and the courts—are usually more interested in causation. Association is not necessarily the same as causation. As noted in section II.A, the association between two variables may be driven largely by a "third variable" that has been omitted from the analysis. For an easy example, among school children, there is an association between shoe size and vocabulary. However, learning more words does not cause feet to get bigger, and swollen feet do not make children more articulate. In this case, the third variable is easy to spot—age. In more realistic examples, the driving variable may be harder to identify.

Technically, third variables are called confounders or confounding variables.[184] The basic methods of dealing with confounding variables involve controlled experiments[185] or the application, typically though a technique called "multiple regression,"[186] of "statistical controls."[187] In many examples, association really does reflect causation, but a large correlation coefficient is not enough to warrant such a conclusion. A large value of *r* only means that the dependent variable

184. *See supra* § II.A.1.

185. *See supra* § II.A.2.

186. Multiple regression analysis is discussed *infra* § V.D and again in Daniel L. Rubinfeld, Reference Guide on Multiple Regression, § II, in this manual.

187. For the reasons stated *supra* § II.A, efforts to control confounding in observational studies are generally less convincing than randomized controlled experiments.

marches in step with the independent one—for any number of possible reasons, ranging from causation to confounding.[188]

C. Regression Lines

The regression line can be used to describe a linear trend in the data. The regression line for income on education in the Texas sample is shown in Figure 9. The height of the line estimates the average income for a given educational level. For example, the average income for people with eight years of education is estimated at $9,600, indicated by the height of the line at eight years; the average income for people with sixteen years of education is estimated at about $23,200.

Figure 10 repeats the scatter diagram for income and education (see Figure 5); the regression line is plotted too. In a general way, the line shows the average trend of income as education increases. Thus, the regression line indicates the extent to which a change in one variable (income) is associated with a change in another variable (education).

Figure 9. The regression line for income on education, and its estimates.

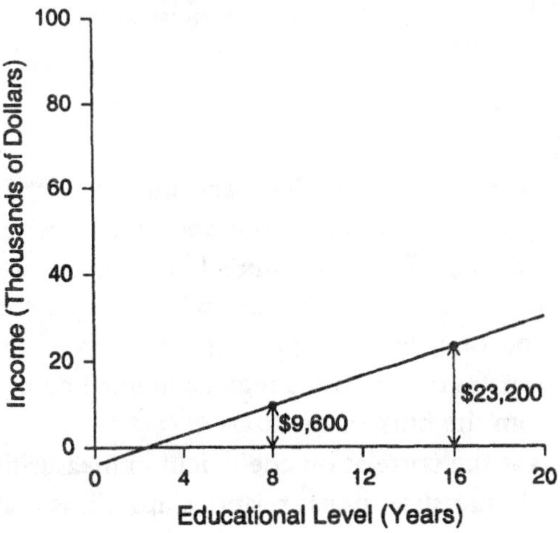

188. The square of the correlation coefficient, r^2, is sometimes called the proportion of variance "explained." However, "explained" is meant in a purely technical sense, and large values of r^2 need not point to a causal explanation.

Figure 10. Scatter diagram for income and education, with the regression line indicating the trend.

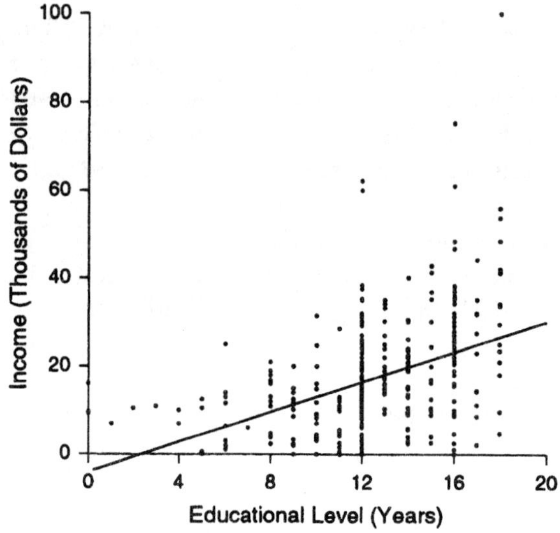

1. *What Are the Slope and Intercept?*

The regression line can be described in terms of its slope and intercept.[189] In Figure 10, the slope is $1,700 per year. On average, each additional year of education is associated with an additional $1,700 of income. The intercept is –$4,000. This is an estimate of the average income for persons with zero years of education. The estimate is not a good one, for such persons are far from the center of the diagram. In general, estimates based on the regression line become less trustworthy as we move away from the bulk of the data.

The slope has the same limitations as the correlation coefficient in measuring the degree of association:[190] (1) It only measures linear relationships; (2) it may

189. The regression line, like any straight line, has an equation of the form $y = mx + b$. Here, m is the slope, that is, the change in y per unit change in x. The slope is the same anywhere along the line. Mathematically, that is what distinguishes straight lines from curves. The intercept b is the value of y when x is zero. The slope of a line is akin to the grade of a road; the intercept gives the starting elevation. In Figure 9, the regression line estimates an average income of $23,200 for people with 16 years of education. This may be computed from the slope and intercept as follows:

($1,700 per year) × 16 years – $4,000 = $27,200 – $4,000 = $23,200

190. In fact, the correlation coefficient is the slope of the regression line if the variables are "standardized," that is, measured in terms of standard deviations away from the mean.

be influenced by outliers; and (3) it does not control for the effect of other variables. With respect to (1), the slope of $1,700 per year presents each additional year of education as having the same value, but some years of schooling surely are worth more and others less. With respect to (3), the association between education and income graphed in Figure 10 is partly causal, but there are other factors to consider, including the family backgrounds of the people in the sample. For instance, people with college degrees probably come from richer and better educated families than those who drop out after grade school. College graduates have other advantages besides the extra education. Factors like these must have some effect on income. That is why statisticians use the qualified language of "on average" and "associated with."[191]

2. *What Is the Unit of Analysis?*

If association between the characteristics of individuals is of interest, these characteristics should be measured on individuals. Sometimes the individual data are not available, but rates or averages are; correlations computed from rates or averages are termed "ecological." However, ecological correlations generally overstate the strength of an association. An example makes the point. The average income and average education can be determined for the men living in each state. The correlation coefficient for these 50 pairs of averages turns out to be 0.66. However, states do not go to school and do not earn incomes. People do. The correlation for income and education for all men in the United States is only about 0.44.[192] The correlation for state averages overstates the correlation for individuals—a common tendency for such ecological correlations.[193]

Ecological correlations are often used in cases claiming a dilution in the voting strength of a racial minority. In this type of voting rights case plaintiffs must prove three things: (1) the minority group constitutes a majority in at least one district of a proposed plan; (2) the minority group is politically cohesive, that is, votes fairly solidly for its preferred candidate; and (3) the majority group votes sufficiently as a bloc to defeat the minority-preferred candidate.[194] The first test is called compactness. The second and third tests deal with racially polarized voting.

191. Many investigators would use multiple regression to isolate the effects of one variable on another—for instance, the independent effect of education on income. Such efforts may run into problems. *See generally supra* § II.A, *infra* § V.D.

192. Correlations are computed from a public-use data tape, Bureau of the Census, Dep't of Commerce, for the March 1993 Current Population Survey.

193. The ecological correlation uses only the average figures, but within each state there is a lot of spread about the average. The ecological correlation overlooks this individual variation.

194. *See* Thornburg v. Gingles, 478 U.S. 30, 50–51 (1986) ("First, the minority group must be able to demonstrate that it is sufficiently large and geographically compact to constitute a majority in a single-member district. . . . Second, the minority group must be able to show that it is politically

Of course, the secrecy of the ballot box means that racially polarized voting cannot be directly observed.[195] Instead, plaintiffs in these voting rights cases rely on scatter diagrams and regression lines to estimate voting behavior by racial or ethnic groups. The unit of analysis is typically the precinct; hence, the technique is called "ecological regression." For each precinct, public records may suffice to determine the percentage of registrants in each racial or ethnic group, as well as the percentage of the total vote for each candidate—by voters from all demographic groups combined. The statistical issue, then, is to estimate how each demographic subgroup voted.

Figure 11 provides an example. Each point in the scatter diagram shows data for a precinct in the 1982 Democratic primary election for auditor in Lee County, South Carolina. The horizontal axis shows the percentage of registrants who are white. The vertical axis shows the "turnout rate" for the white candidate.[196] The regression line is plotted too. In this sort of diagram, the slope is often interpreted as the difference between the white turnout rate and the black turnout rate for the white candidate; the intercept would be interpreted as the black turnout rate for the white candidate.[197] However, the validity of such estimates is contested in statistical literature.[198]

cohesive. . . . Third, the minority must be able to demonstrate that the white majority votes sufficiently as a bloc to enable it . . . usually to defeat the minority's preferred candidate."). In subsequent cases, the Court has emphasized that these factors are not sufficient to make out a violation of section 2 of the Voting Rights Act. *E.g.*, Johnson v. De Grandy, 512 U.S. 997, 1011 (1994) ("*Gingles* . . . clearly declined to hold [these factors] sufficient in combination, either in the sense that a court's examination of relevant circumstances was complete once the three factors were found to exist, or in the sense that the three in combination necessarily and in all circumstances demonstrated dilution.").

195. Some information could be obtained from exit polls. *E.g.*, Aldasoro v. Kennerson, 922 F. Supp. 339, 344 (S.D. Cal. 1995).

196. By definition, the turnout rate equals the number of votes for the candidate, divided by the number of registrants; the rate is computed separately for each precinct.

197. Figure 11 contemplates only one white candidate; more complicated techniques could be used if there were several candidates of each race. The intercept of the line is 4% and the slope is .52. Plaintiffs would conclude that only 4% of the black registrants voted for the white candidate, while 4% + 52% = 56% of the white registrants voted for the white candidate, which demonstrates polarization.

198. For further discussion of the problem of ecological regression in this context, see Stephen P. Klein & David A. Freedman, *Ecological Regression in Voting Rights Cases*, Chance, Summer 1993, at 38; Bernard Grofman & Chandler Davidson, Controversies in Minority Voting: The Voting Rights Act in Perspective (1992). The use of ecological regression increased considerably after the Supreme Court noted in *Thornburg v. Gingles*, 478 U.S. 30, 53 n.20 (1986), that "[t]he District Court found both methods [extreme case analysis and bivariate ecological regression analysis] standard in the literature for the analysis of racially polarized voting." *See, e.g.*, Teague v. Attala County, 92 F.3d 283, 285 (5th Cir. 1996) (one of "two standard methods for analyzing electoral data"); Houston v. Lafayette County, 56 F.3d 606, 612 (5th Cir. 1995) (holding that district court erred in ignoring ecological regression results). Nevertheless, courts have cautioned against "overreliance on bivariate ecological regression" in light of the inherent limitations of the technique (Lewis v. Alamance County, 99 F.3d 600, 604 n.3 (4th Cir. 1996)), and some courts have found ecological regressions unconvincing. *E.g.*, Aldasoro v. Kennerson,

Figure 11. Turnout rate for the white candidate plotted against the percentage of registrants who are white. Precinct-level data, 1982 Democratic Primary for Auditor, Lee County, South Carolina.[199]

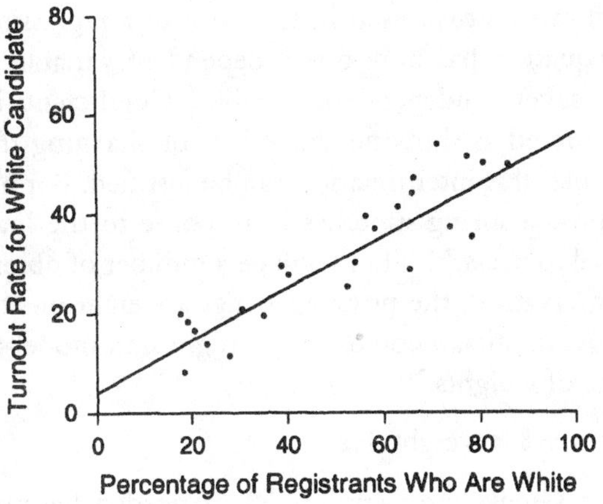

D. Statistical Models

Statistical models are widely used in the social sciences and in litigation.[200] For example, the census suffers an undercount, more severe in certain places than others; if some statistical models are to be believed, the undercount can be corrected—moving seats in Congress and millions of dollars a year in entitlement funds.[201] Other models purport to lift the veil of secrecy from the ballot

922 F. Supp. 339 (S.D. Cal. 1995); Romero v. City of Pomona, 665 F. Supp. 853, 860 (C.D. Cal. 1987), *aff'd*, 883 F.2d 1418 (9th Cir. 1989); *cf.* Johnson v. Miller, 864 F. Supp. 1354, 1390 (S.D. Ga. 1994) ("mind-numbing and contradictory statistical data," including bivariate ecological regression, established "that some degree of vote polarization exists, but not in alarming quantities. Exact levels are unknowable."), *aff'd*, 515 U.S. 900 (1995).

Redistricting plans based predominantly on racial considerations are unconstitutional unless narrowly tailored to meet a compelling state interest. Shaw v. Reno, 509 U.S. 630 (1993). Whether compliance with the Voting Rights Act can be considered a compelling interest is an open question, but efforts to sustain racially motived redistricting on this basis have not fared well before the Supreme Court. *See* Abrams v. Johnson, 521 U.S. 74 (1997); Shaw v. Hunt, 517 U.S. 899 (1996); Bush v. Vera, 517 U.S. 952 (1996).

199. Data from James W. Loewen & Bernard Grofman, *Recent Developments in Methods Used in Vote Dilution Litigation*, 21 Urb. Law. 589, 591 tbl.1 (1989).

200. The frequency with which regression models are used is no guarantee that they are the best choice for a particular problem. *See, e.g.*, David W. Peterson, *Reference Guide on Multiple Regression*, 36 Jurimetrics J. 213, 214–15 (1996) (review essay). On the factors that might justify the choice of a particular model, see Moses, *supra* note 124.

201. *See supra* note 43.

box, enabling the experts to determine how racial or ethnic groups have voted—a crucial step in litigation to enforce minority voting rights.[202] This section discusses the statistical logic of regression models.[203]

A regression model attempts to combine the values of certain variables (the independent variables) in order to get expected values for another variable (the dependent variable). The model can be expressed in the form of a regression equation. A simple regression equation has only one independent variable; a multiple regression equation has several independent variables. Coefficients in the equation will often be interpreted as showing the effects of changing the corresponding variables. Sometimes, this interpretation can be justified. For instance, Hooke's law describes how a spring stretches in response to the load hung from it: strain is proportional to stress.[204] There will be a number of observations on a spring. For each observation, the physicist hangs a weight on the spring, and measures its length. A statistician could apply a regression model to these data: for quite a large range of weights,[205]

$$\text{length} = a + b \times \text{weight} + \varepsilon. \qquad (1)$$

The error term, denoted by the Greek letter epsilon (ε), is needed because measured length will not be exactly equal to $a + b \times$ weight. If nothing else, measurement error must be reckoned with. We model ε as a draw made at random with replacement from a box of tickets. Each ticket shows a potential error, which will be realized if that ticket is drawn. The average of all the potential errors in the box is assumed to be zero. In more standard statistical terminology, the εs for different observations are assumed to be "independent and identically distributed, with mean zero."[206]

In equation (1), a and b are parameters, unknown constants of nature that characterize the spring: a is the length of the spring under no load, and b is elasticity, the increase in length per unit increase in weight.[207] These parameters

202. *See supra* § V.C.2.

203. For a more detailed treatment, see Daniel L. Rubinfeld, Reference Guide on Multiple Regression at app., in this manual.

204. This law is named after Robert Hooke (England, 1653–1703).

205. The dependent or response variable in equation (1) is the length of the spring, on the left hand side of the equation. There is one independent or explanatory variable on the right hand side—weight. Since there is only one explanatory variable, equation (1) is a simple regression equation.

Hooke's law is only an approximation, although it is a very good one. With large enough weights, a quadratic term will be needed in equation (1). Moreover, beyond some point, the spring exceeds its elastic limit and snaps.

206. For some purposes, it is also necessary to assume that the errors follow the normal distribution.

207. *Cf. supra* note 121 (defining the term "parameter").

are not observable,[208] but they can be estimated by "the method of least squares."[209] In statistical notation, estimates are often denoted by hats; thus, $\hat{a}$ is the estimate for a, and $\hat{b}$ is the estimate for b.[210] Basically, the values of $\hat{a}$ and $\hat{b}$ are chosen to minimize the sum of the squared "prediction errors."[211] These errors are also called "residuals": they measure the difference between the actual length and the predicted length, the latter being $\hat{a} + \hat{b} \times$ weight.[212]

$$\text{residual} = \text{actual length} - \hat{a} - \hat{b} \times \text{weight} \qquad (2)$$

Of course, no one really imagines there to be a box of tickets hidden in the spring. However, the variability of physical measurements (under many but by no means all circumstances) does seem to be remarkably like the variability in draws from a box.[213] In short, the statistical model corresponds rather closely to the empirical phenomenon.

1. A Social Science Example

We turn now to social science applications of the kind that might be seen in litigation. A case study would take us too far afield, but a stylized example of regression analysis used to demonstrate sex discrimination in salaries may give the idea.[214] We use a regression model to predict salaries (dollars per year) of employees in a firm using three explanatory variables: education (years of schooling completed), experience (years with the firm), and a dummy variable for

208. It might seem that a is observable; after all, one can measure the length of the spring with no load. However, the measurement is subject to error, so one observes not a but $a + \varepsilon$. *See* equation (1). The parameters a and b can be estimated, even estimated very well, but they cannot be observed directly.

209. The method was developed by Adrien-Marie Legendre (France, 1752–1833) and Carl Friedrich Gauss (Germany, 1777–1855) to fit astronomical orbits.

210. Another convention is use Greek letters for the parameters and English letters for the estimates.

211. Given trial values for a and b, one computes residuals as in equation (2), and then the sum of the squares of these residuals. The "least squares" estimates $\hat{a}$ and $\hat{b}$ are the values of a and b that minimize this sum of squares. These least squares values can be computed from the data by a mathematical formula. They are the intercept and slope of the regression line. *See supra* § V.C.1; Freedman et al., *supra* note 16, at 208–10.

212. The residual is observable, but because the estimates $\hat{a}$ and $\hat{b}$ are only approximations to the parameters a and b, the residual is only an approximation to the error term in equation (1). The term "predicted value" is used in a specialized sense, because the actual values are available too; statisticians often refer to "fitted value" rather than "predicted value," to avoid possible misinterpretations.

213. This is Gauss's model for measurement error. *See* Freedman et al., *supra* note 16, at 450–52.

214. For a more extended treatment of the concepts, see Daniel L. Rubinfeld, Reference Guide on Multiple Regression, at app., in this manual.

gender, taking the value 1 for men and 0 for women.[215] The equation is[216]

$$\text{salary} = a + b \times \text{education} + c \times \text{experience} + d \times \text{gender} + \varepsilon \qquad (3)$$

Equation (3) is a statistical model for the data, with unknown parameters *a, b, c,* and *d*; here, *a* is the intercept and the others are regression coefficients; ε is an unobservable error term. This is a formal analog of Hooke's law, shown as equation (1); the same assumptions are made about the errors. In other words, an employee's salary is determined as if by computing

$$a + b \times \text{education} + c \times \text{experience} + d \times \text{gender} \qquad (4)$$

then adding an error drawn at random from a box of tickets. The expression (4) is the expected value for salary given the explanatory variables (education, experience, gender); the error term in equation (3) represents deviations from the expected.

The parameters in equation (3) are estimated from the data using least squares. If the estimated coefficient for the dummy variable turns out to be positive and statistically significant (by a *t*-test[217]), that would be taken as evidence of disparate impact: men earn more than women, even after adjusting for differences in background factors that might affect productivity. Education and experience are entered into equation (3) as statistical controls, precisely in order to claim that adjustment has been made for differences in backgrounds.

Suppose the estimated equation turns out as follows:

$$\text{predicted salary} = \$7{,}100 + \$1{,}300 \times \text{education} + \$2{,}200 \times \text{experience} + \$700 \times \text{gender} \qquad (5)$$

That is, $\hat{a} = \$7{,}100$, $\hat{b} = \$1{,}300$, and so forth. According to equation (5), every extra year of education is worth on average \$1,300; similarly, every extra year of experience is worth on average \$2,200; and, most important, the company gives men a salary premium of \$700 over women with the same education and expe-

215. A dummy variable takes only two values (e.g., 0 and 1) and serves to identify two mutually exclusive and exhaustive categories.

216. In equation (3), the variable on the left hand side, salary, is the response variable. On the right hand side are the explanatory variables—education, experience, and the dummy variable for gender. Because there are several explanatory variables, this is a multiple regression equation rather than a simple regression equation; *cf. supra* note 205.

Equations like (3) are suggested, somewhat loosely, by "human capital theory." However, there remains considerable uncertainty about which variables to put into the equation, what functional form to assume, and how error terms are supposed to behave. Adding more variables is no panacea. *See* Peterson, *supra* note 200, at 214–15.

217. *See infra* § V.D.2.

rience, on average. For example, a male employee with 12 years of education (high school) and 10 years of experience would have a predicted salary of

$$\begin{aligned}&\$7{,}100 + \$1{,}300 \times 12 + \$2{,}200 \times 10 + \$700 \times 1 \\ &\quad = \$7{,}100 + \$15{,}600 + \$22{,}000 + \$700 = \$45{,}400 \qquad (6)\end{aligned}$$

A similarly situated female employee has a predicted salary of only

$$\begin{aligned}&\$7{,}100 + \$1{,}300 \times 12 + \$2{,}200 \times 10 + \$700 \times 0 \\ &\quad = \$7{,}100 + \$15{,}600 + \$22{,}000 + \$0 = \$44{,}700 \qquad (7)\end{aligned}$$

Notice the impact of the dummy variable: $700 is added to equation (6), but not to equation (7).

A major step in proving discrimination is establishing that the estimated coefficient of the dummy variable—$700 in our numerical illustration—is statistically significant. This depends on the statistical assumptions built into the model. For instance, each extra year of education is assumed to be worth the same (on average) across all levels of experience, both for men and women. Similarly, each extra year of experience is worth the same across all levels of education, both for men and women. Furthermore, the premium paid to men does not depend systematically on education or experience. Ability, quality of education, or quality of experience are assumed not to make any systematic difference to the predictions of the model.[218]

The assumptions about the error term—that the errors are independent and identically distributed from person to person in the data set—turn out to be critical for computing *p*-values and demonstrating statistical significance. Regression modeling that does not produce statistically significant coefficients is unlikely to establish discrimination, and statistical significance cannot be established unless stylized assumptions are made about unobservable error terms.[219]

The typical regression model is based on a host of such assumptions; without them, inferences cannot be drawn from the model. With Hooke's law—equation (1)—the model rests on assumptions that are relatively easy to validate experimentally. For the salary discrimination model—equation (3)—validation seems more difficult.[220] Court or counsel may well inquire: What are the assumptions behind the model, and why do they apply to the case at bar? In this regard, it is important to distinguish between situations where (1) the nature of the relationship between the variables is known and regression is being used to make quantitative estimates, and (2) where the nature of the relationship is largely unknown and regression is being used to determine the nature of the relation-

218. Technically, these omitted variables are assumed to be uncorrelated with the error term in the equation.

219. *See supra* note 124.

220. Some of the material in this section is taken from Freedman, *supra* note 112, at 29–35.

ship—or indeed whether any relationship exists at all. The statistical basis for regression theory was developed to handle situations of the first type, with Hooke's law being an example. The basis for the second type of application is analogical, and the tightness of the analogy is a critical issue.

2. *Standard Errors, t-statistics, and Statistical Significance*

Statistical proof of discrimination depends on the significance of $\hat{d}$ (the estimated coefficient for gender); significance is determined by the *t*-test, using the standard error of $\hat{d}$. The standard error of $\hat{d}$ measures the likely difference between $\hat{d}$ and d, the difference being due to the action of the error term in equation (3). The *t*-statistic is $\hat{d}$ divided by its standard error. For example, in equation (5), $\hat{d} = \$700$. If the standard error of $\hat{d}$ is \$325, then $t = \$700/\$325 = 2.15$. This is significant, that is, hard to explain as the mere product of random chance. Under the null hypothesis that $d = 0$, there is only about a 5% chance that the absolute value of t (denoted $|t|$) is greater than 2. A value of t greater than 2 would therefore demonstrate statistical significance.[221] On the other hand, if the standard error is \$1,400, then $t = \$700/\$1{,}400 = 0.5$, and the discrepancy could easily result from chance. Of course, the parameter d is only a construct in a model. If the model is wrong, the standard error, *t*-statistic, and significance level are rather difficult to interpret.

Even if the model is granted, there is a further issue: the 5% is a probability for the data given the model, namely, $P(|t| > 2 \mid d = 0)$. However, the 5% is often misinterpreted as $P(d = 0 \mid \text{data})$. This misinterpretation is commonplace in the social science literature, and it appears in some opinions describing expert testimony.[222] For an objectivist statistician, $P(d = 0 \mid \text{data})$ makes no sense: parameters do not exhibit chance variation. For a subjectivist statistician, $P(d = 0 \mid \text{data})$ makes good sense, but its computation via the *t*-test could be seriously in error, because the prior probability that $d = 0$ has not been taken into account.[223]

3. *Summary*

The main ideas of regression modeling can be captured in a hypothetical exchange between a plaintiff seeking to prove salary discrimination and a company denying that allegation. Such a dialog might proceed as follows:

1. Plaintiff argues that the defendant company pays male employees more than females, which establishes prima facie case of discrimination.[224]

221. The cutoff at 2 applies to large samples. Small samples require higher thresholds.

222. *See supra* § IV.B and notes 142, 167.

223. For an objectivist, the vertical bar "$|$" in $P(|t| > 2 \mid d = 0)$ means "computed on the assumption that." For a subjectivist, the bar would signify a conditional probability. *See supra* § IV.B.1, C; *infra* Appendix.

224. The conditions under which a simple disparity between two groups amounts to a prima facie case that shifts the burden of proof to the defendant in Title VII and other discrimination cases have yet

2. The company responds that the men are paid more because they are better educated and have more experience.
3. Plaintiff tries to refute the company's theory by fitting a regression equation like equation (5). Even after adjusting for differences in education and experience, men earn $700 a year more than women, on average. This remaining difference in pay shows discrimination.
4. The company argues that a small difference like $700 could be the result of chance, not discrimination.
5. Plaintiff replies that the coefficient of "gender" in equation (5) is statistically significant, so chance is not a good explanation for the data.

Statistical significance is determined by reference to the observed significance level, which is usually abbreviated to *p*.[225] The *p*-value depends not only on the $700 difference in salary levels, but also on the sample size, among other things.[226] The bigger the sample, other things being equal, the smaller is *p*—and the tighter is plaintiff's argument that the disparity cannot be explained by chance. Often, a cutoff at 5% is used; if *p* is less than 5%, the difference is "statistically significant."[227]

In some cases, the *p*-value has been interpreted as the probability that defendants are innocent of discrimination. However, such an interpretation is wrong: *p* merely represents the probability of getting a large test statistic, given that the model is correct and the true coefficient of "gender" is zero.[228] Therefore, even if the model is undisputed, a *p*-value less than 50% does not necessarily demonstrate a "preponderance of the evidence" against the null hypothesis. Indeed, a *p*-value less than 5% or 1% might not meet the preponderance standard.

In employment discrimination cases, and other contexts too, a wide variety of models are used. This is perhaps not surprising, for specific equations are not dictated by the science. Thus, in a strongly contested case, our dialog would be likely to continue with an exchange about which model is better. Although

to be articulated clearly and comprehensively. *Compare* EEOC v. Olson's Dairy Queens, Inc., 989 F.2d 165, 168 (5th Cir. 1993) (reversing district court for failing to find a prima facie case from the EEOC's statistics on the proportion of African-Americans in defendant's workforce as compared to the proportion of food preparation and service workers in the Houston Standard Metropolitan Statistical Area), *with* Wilkins v. University of Houston, 654 F.2d 388 (5th Cir. 1981) (holding that the district court correctly found that plaintiffs' proof of simple disparities in faculty salaries of men and women did not constitute a prima facie case), *vacated and remanded on other grounds*, 459 U.S. 809 (1982), *aff'd on remand*, 695 F.2d 134 (5th Cir. 1983). *See generally*, D.H. Kaye, *Statistical Evidence: How to Avoid the "Diderot Effect" of Getting Stumped*, Inside Litig., Apr. 1988, at 21. Richard Lempert, *Befuddled Judges: Statistical Evidence in Title VII Cases, in* Controversies in Civil Rights (Bernard Grofman ed., forthcoming 2000).

225. *See supra* § IV.B.1.

226. The *p*-value depends on the estimated value of the coefficient and its standard error. These quantities can be computed from (1) the sample size, (2) the means and SDs of the variables, and (3) the correlations between pairs of variables. The computation is rather intricate.

227. *See supra* § IV.B.2.

228. *See supra* §§ IV.B, V.D.2.

statistical assumptions[229] are challenged in court from time to time, arguments more commonly revolve around the choice of variables. One model may be questioned because it omits variables that should be included—for instance, skill levels or prior evaluations;[230] another model may be challenged because it includes "tainted" variables reflecting past discriminatory behavior by the firm.[231] Frequently, each side will have its own equations and its own team of experts; the court then must decide which model—if either—fits the occasion.[232]

229. *See generally supra* § V.D.1 (discussion following equation (7)); Finkelstein & Levin, *supra* note 1, at 397–403; Daniel L. Rubinfeld, Reference Guide on Multiple Regression, in this manual. One example of a statistical assumption is the independence from subject to subject of the error term in equation (3); another example is that the errors have mean zero and constant variance.

230. *E.g.*, Smith v. Virginia Commonwealth Univ., 84 F.3d 672 (4th Cir. 1996) (dispute over omitted variables precludes summary judgment). *Compare* Bazemore v. Friday, 478 U.S. 385 (1986), *on remand*, 848 F.2d 476 (4th Cir. 1988) *and* Sobel v. Yeshiva Univ., 839 F.2d 18, 34 (2d Cir. 1988) (failure to include variables for scholarly productivity did not vitiate plaintiffs' regression study of salary differences because "Yeshiva's experts . . . [offered] no reason, in evidence or analysis, for concluding that they correlated with sex"), *with* Penk v. Oregon State Bd. of Higher Educ., 816 F.2d 458, 465 (9th Cir. 1987) ("Missing parts of the plaintiffs' interpretation of the board's decision-making equation included such highly determinative quality and productivity factors as teaching quality, community and institutional service, and quality of research and scholarship . . . that . . . must have had a significant influence on salary and advancement decisions.") *and* Chang v. University of R.I., 606 F. Supp. 1161, 1207 (D.R.I. 1985) (plaintiff's regression not entitled to substantial weight because the analyst "excluded salient variables even though he knew of their importance").

The same issue arises, of course, with simpler statistical models, such as those used to assess the difference between two proportions. *See, e.g.*, Sheehan v. Daily Racing Form, Inc., 104 F.3d 940, 942 (7th Cir. 1997) ("Completely ignored was the more than remote possibility that age was correlated with a legitimate job-related qualification, such as familiarity with computers. Everyone knows that younger people are on average more comfortable with computers than older people are, just as older people are on average more comfortable with manual-shift cars than younger people are.").

231. Michael O. Finkelstein, *The Judicial Reception of Multiple Regression Studies in Race and Sex Discrimination Cases*, 80 Colum. L. Rev. 737 (1980).

232. *E.g.*, *Chang*, 606 F. Supp. at 1207 ("it is plain to the court that [defendant's] model comprises a better, more useful, more reliable tool than [plaintiff's] counterpart"); Presseisen v. Swarthmore College, 442 F. Supp. 593, 619 (E.D. Pa. 1977) ("[E]ach side has done a superior job in challenging the other's regression analysis, but only a mediocre job in supporting their own . . . and the Court is . . . left with nothing."), *aff'd*, 582 F.2d 1275 (3d Cir. 1978).

Appendix

A. Probability and Statistical Inference

The mathematical theory of probability consists of theorems derived from axioms and definitions. The mathematical reasoning is not controversial, but there is some disagreement as to how the theory should be applied; that is, statisticians may differ on the proper interpretation of probabilities in specific applications. There are two main interpretations. For a subjectivist statistician, probabilities represent degrees of belief, on a scale between 0 and 1. An impossible event has probability 0, an event that is sure to happen has probability 1. For an objectivist statistician, probabilities are not beliefs; rather, they are inherent properties of an experiment. If the experiment can be repeated, then in the long run, the relative frequency of an event tends to its probability. For instance, if a fair coin is tossed, the probability of heads is 1/2; if the experiment is repeated, the coin will land heads about one-half the time. If a fair die is rolled, the probability of getting an ace (one spot) is 1/6; if the die is rolled many times, an ace will turn up about one-sixth of the time.[233] (Objectivist statisticians are also called frequentists, while subjectivists are Bayesians, after the Reverend Thomas Bayes, England, c.1701–1761.)

Statisticians also use conditional probability, that is, the probability of one event given that another has occurred. For instance, suppose a coin is tossed twice. One event is that the coin will land HH. Another event is that at least one H will be seen. Before the coin is tossed, there are four possible, equally likely, outcomes: HH, HT, TH, TT. So the probability of HH is 1/4. However, if we know that at least one head has been obtained, then we can rule out two tails TT. In other words, given that at least one H has been obtained, the conditional probability of TT is 0, and the first three outcomes have conditional probability 1/3 each. In particular, the conditional probability of HH is 1/3. This is usually written as P(HH | at least one H) = 1/3. More generally, the probability of any event B is denoted as P(B); the conditional probability of B given A is written as P(B | A).

Two events A and B are independent if the conditional probability of B given that A occurs is equal to the conditional probability of B given that A does not occur. Statisticians often use "$\sim A$" to denote the event that A does not occur, so A and B are independent if $P(B \mid A) = P(B \mid \sim A)$. If A and B are inde-

233. Probabilities may be estimated from relative frequencies, but probability itself is a subtler idea. For instance, suppose a computer prints out a sequence of ten letters H and T (for heads and tails), which alternate between the two possibilities H and T as follows: H T H T H T H T H T. The relative frequency of heads is 5/10 or 50%, but it is not at all obvious that the chance of an H at the next position is 50%.

pendent, then the probability that both occur is equal to the product of the probabilities:

$$P(A \text{ and } B) = P(A) \times P(B) \quad (1)$$

This is the multiplication rule (or product rule) for independent events. If events are dependent, then conditional probabilities must be used:

$$P(A \text{ and } B) = P(A) \times P(B \mid A) \quad (2)$$

This is the multiplication rule for dependent events.

Assessing probabilities, conditional probabilities, and independence is not entirely straightforward. Inquiry into the basis for expert judgment may be useful, and casual assumptions about independence should be questioned.[234]

Bayesian statisticians assign probabilities to hypotheses as well as to events; indeed, for them, the distinction between hypotheses and events may not be a sharp one. If H_0 and H_1 are two hypotheses[235] which govern the probability of an event A, a Bayesian statistician might use the multiplication rule (2) to find that

$$P(A \text{ and } H_0) = P(A \mid H_0)\, P(H_0) \quad (3a)$$

and

$$P(A \text{ and } H_1) = P(A \mid H_1)\, P(H_1) \quad (3b)$$

Reasoning further that $P(A) = P(A \text{ and } H_0) + P(A \text{ and } H_1)$, the statistician would conclude that

$$P(H_0 \mid A) = \frac{P(A \mid H_0)P(H_0)}{P(A \mid H_0)P(H_0) + P(A \mid H_1)P(H_1)} \quad (4)$$

This is a special case of Bayes' rule, which yields the conditional probability of hypothesis H_0 given that event A has occurred. For example, H_0 might be the hypothesis that blood found at the scene of a crime came from a person unrelated to the defendant; H_1 might deny H_0 and assert that the blood came from the defendant; and A could be the event that blood from both the crime scene and the defendant is type A. Then $P(H_0)$ is the prior probability of H_0, based on subjective judgment, while $P(H_0 \mid A)$ is the posterior probability—the prior probability updated using the data. Here, we have observed a match in type A blood,

234. For problematic assumptions of independence in litigation, see, e.g., *Branion v. Gramly*, 855 F.2d 1256 (7th Cir. 1988); *People v. Collins*, 438 P.2d 33 (Cal. 1968); D.H. Kaye, *The Admissibility of "Probability Evidence" in Criminal Trials* (pts. 1 & 2), 26 Jurimetrics J. 343 (1986), 27 Jurimetrics J. 160 (1987).

235. H_0 is read "H-sub-zero," while H_1 is "H-sub-one."

which occurs in about 42% of the population, so $P(A \mid H_0) = 0.42$.[236] Because the defendant has type A blood, the match probability given that the blood came from him is $P(A \mid H_1) = 1$. If the prior probabilities were, say, $P(H_0) = P(H_1) = 0.5$, then according to (4), the posterior probability would be

$$P(H_0 \mid A) = \frac{0.42 \times 0.5}{0.42 \times 0.5 + 1 \times 0.5} = 0.30 \tag{5}$$

Conversely, the posterior probability that the blood is from the defendant would be

$$P(H_1 \mid A) = 1 - P(H_0 \mid A) = 0.70 \tag{6}$$

Thus, the data make it more probable that the blood is the defendant's: the probability rises from the prior value of $P(H_1) = 0.50$ to the posterior value of $P(H_1 \mid A) = 0.70$.

A frequentist statistician would be hesitant to quantify the probability of hypotheses like H_0 and H_1. Such a statistician would merely report that if H_0 is true, then the probability of type A blood is 42%, whereas if H_1 is true, the probability is 100%.

More generally, H_0 could refer to parameters in a statistical model. For example, H_0 might specify equal selection rates for a population of male and female applicants; H_1 might deny H_0 and assert that the selection rates are not equal; and A could be the event that a test statistic exceeds 2 in absolute value. In such situations, the frequentist statistician would compute $P(A \mid H_0)$ and reject H_0 if this probability fell below a figure such as 0.05.

B. Technical Details on the Standard Error, the Normal Curve, and Significance Levels

This section of the Appendix describes several calculations for the pass rate example of section IV. In that example, the population consisted of all 5,000 men and 5,000 women in the applicant pool. Suppose by way of illustration that the pass rates for these men and women were 60% and 35%, respectively; so the "population difference" is 60% – 35% = 25 percentage points. We chose 50 men at random from the population, and 50 women. In our sample, the pass rate for the men was 58% and the pass rate for the women was 38%, so the sample difference was 58% – 38% = 20 percentage points. Another sample might have pass rates of 62% and 36%, for a sample difference of 62% – 36% = 26 percentage points. And so forth.

236. Not all statisticians would accept the identification of a population frequency with $P(A \mid H_0)$; indeed, H_0 has been translated into a hypothesis that the true donor has been randomly selected from the population, which is a major step needing justification.

In principle, we can consider the set of all possible samples from the population, and make a list of the corresponding differences. This is a long list. Indeed, the number of distinct samples of 50 men and 50 women that can be formed is immense—nearly 5×10^{240}, or 5 followed by 240 zeros. Our sample difference was chosen at random from this list. Statistical theory enables us to make some precise statements about the list, and hence about the chances in the sampling procedure.

- The average of the list—that is, the average of the differences over the 5×10^{240} possible samples—equals the difference between the pass rates of all 5,000 men and 5,000 women. In more technical language, the expected value of the sample difference equals the population difference. Even more tersely, the sample difference is an unbiased estimate of the population difference.
- The standard deviation (SD) of the list—that is, the standard deviation of the differences over the 5×10^{240} possible samples—is equal to[237]

$$\sqrt{\frac{5{,}000 - 50}{5{,}000 - 1}} \times \sqrt{\frac{P_{men}(1 - P_{men})}{50} + \frac{P_{women}(1 - P_{women})}{50}} \qquad (7)$$

In expression (7), P_{men} stands for the proportion of the 5,000 male applicants who would pass the exam, and P_{women} stands for the corresponding proportion of women. With the 60% and 35% figures we have postulated, the standard deviation of the sample differences would be 9.6 percentage points:

$$\sqrt{\frac{5{,}000 - 50}{5{,}000 - 1}} \times \sqrt{\frac{.60\,(1 - .60)}{50} + \frac{.35\,(1 - .35)}{50}} = .096 \qquad (8)$$

Figure 12 shows the histogram for the sample differences.[238] The graph is drawn so the area between two values gives the relative frequency of sample

237. *See, e.g.*, Freedman et al., *supra* note 16, at 414, 503–04; Moore & McCabe, *supra* note 93, at 590–91. The standard error for the sample difference equals the standard deviation of the list of all possible sample differences, making the connection between standard error and standard deviation. If we drew two samples at random, the difference between them would be on the order of $\sqrt{2} \approx 1.4$ times this standard deviation. The standard error can therefore be used to measure reproducibility of sample data. On the standard deviation, see *supra* § III.E; Freedman et al., *supra* note 16, at 67–72.

238. The "probability histogram" in Figure 12 shows the "distribution" of the sample differences, indicating the relative likelihoods of the various ranges of possible values; likelihood is represented by

differences falling in that range, among all 5×10^{240} possible samples. For instance, take the range from 20 to 30 percentage points. About half the area under the histogram falls into this range. Therefore, given our assumptions, there is about a 50% chance that for a sample of 50 men and 50 women chosen at random, the difference between the pass rates for the sample men and women will be in the range from 20 to 30 percentage points. The "central limit theorem" establishes that the histogram for the sample differences follows the normal curve, at least to a good approximation. Figure 12 shows this curve for comparison.[239] The main point is that chances for the sample difference can be approximated by areas under the normal curve.

Generally, we do not know the pass rates P_{men} and P_{women} in the population. We chose 60% and 35% just by way of illustration. Statisticians would use the pass rates in the sample—58% and 38%—to estimate the pass rates in the population. Substituting the sample pass rates into expression (7) yields

$$\sqrt{\frac{5{,}000 - 50}{5{,}000 - 1}} \times \sqrt{\frac{.58\,(1 - .58)}{50} + \frac{.38\,(1 - .38)}{50}} = .097 \qquad (9)$$

That is about 10 percentage points—the standard error reported in section IV.A.2.[240]

area. The lower horizontal scale shows "standard units," that is, deviations from the expected value relative to the standard error. In our example, the expected value is 25 percentage points and the standard error is 9.6 percentage points. Thus, 35 percentage points would be expressed as (35 – 25)/9.6 = 1.04 standard units. The vertical scale in the figure shows probability per standard unit. Probability is measured on a percentage scale, with 100% representing certainty; the maximum shown on the vertical scale in the figure is 50, i.e., 50% per standard unit. *See* Freedman et al., *supra* note 16, at 80, 315.

239. The normal curve is the famous bell-shaped curve of statistics, whose equation is

$$y = \frac{100\%}{\sqrt{2\pi}} e^{-x^2/2}$$

240. There is little difference between (8) and (9)—the standard error does not depend very strongly on the pass rates.

Figure 12. The distribution of the sample difference in pass rates when P_{men} = 60% and P_{women} = 35%

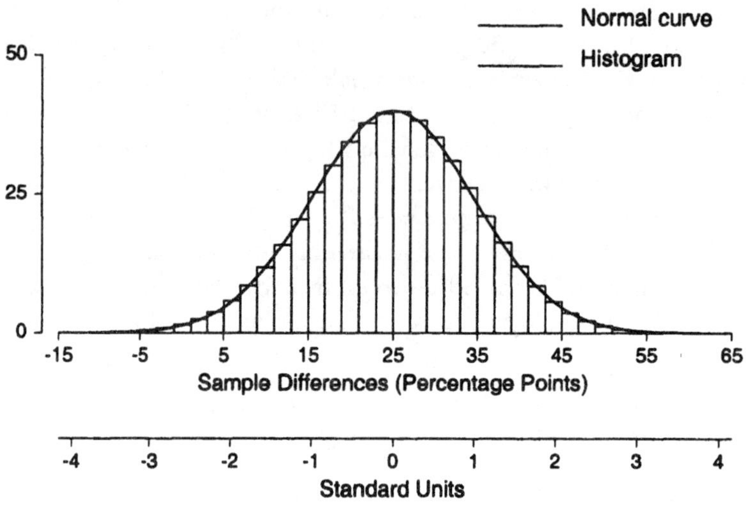

To sum up, the histogram for the sample differences follows the normal curve, centered at the population difference. The spread is given by the standard error. That is why confidence levels can be based on the standard error, with confidence levels read off the normal curve: 68% of the area under the curve is between −1 and 1, while 95% is between −2 and 2, and 99.7% is between −3 and 3, approximately.

We turn to *p*-values.[241] Consider the null hypothesis that the men and women in the population have the same overall pass rates. In that case, the sample differences are centered at zero, because $P_{men} - P_{women} = 0$. Since the overall pass rate in the sample is 48%, we use this value to estimate both P_{men} and P_{women} in expression (7):

$$\sqrt{\frac{5{,}000 - 50}{5{,}000 - 1}} \times \sqrt{\frac{.48\,(1 - .48)}{50} + \frac{.48\,(1 - .48)}{50}} = .099 \qquad (10)$$

Again, the standard error (SE) is about 10 percentage points. The observed difference of 20 percentage points is 20/10 = 2.0 SEs. As shown in Figure 13, differences of that magnitude or larger have about a 5% chance of occurring:

241. *See supra* § IV.B.1.

About 5% of the area under the normal curve lies beyond ±2. (In Figure 13, this tail area is shaded.) The *p*-value is about 5%.[242]

Figure 13. *p*-value for observed difference of 20 percentage points, computed using the null hypothesis. The chance of getting a sample difference of 20 points in magnitude (or more) is about equal to the area under the normal curve beyond ±2. That shaded area is about 5%.

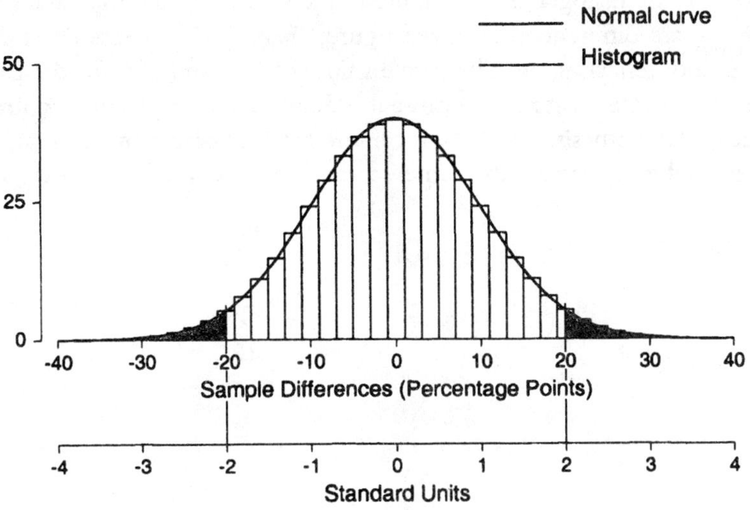

Finally, we calculate power.[243] We are making a two-tailed test at the .05 level. Instead of the null hypothesis, we assume an alternative: In the applicant pool, 55% of the men would pass, and 45% of the women. So there is a difference of 10 percentage points between the pass rates. The distribution of sample differences would now be centered at 10 percentage points (see Figure 14). Again, the sample differences follow the normal curve. The true SE is about 10

242. Technically, the *p*-value is the chance of getting data as extreme as, or more extreme than, the data at hand. *See supra* § IV.B.1. That is the chance of getting a difference of 20 percentage points or more on the right, together with the chance of getting –20 or less on the left. This chance equals the area under the histogram to the right of 19, together with the area to the left of –19. (The rectangle whose area represents the chance of getting a difference of 20 is included, and likewise for the rectangle above –20.) The area under the histogram may in turn be approximated by the area under the normal curve beyond ± 1.9, which is 5.7%. *See, e.g.*, Freedman et al., *supra* note 16, at 318. Keeping track of the edges of the rectangles is called the "continuity correction." *Id.* The histogram is computed assuming pass rates of 48% for the men and the women. Other values could be dealt with in a similar way. *See infra* note 245.

243. *See supra* note 144.

percentage points by equation (1), and the SE estimated from the sample will be about the same. On that basis, only sample differences larger than 20 percentage points or smaller than –20 points will be declared significant.[244] About 1/6 of the area under the normal curve in Figure 14 lies in this region.[245] Therefore, the power of the test against the specified alternative is only about 1/6. In the figure, it is the shaded area that corresponds to power.

Figures 12, 13, and 14 have the same shape: the central limit theorem is at work. However, the histograms are centered differently, because the values of P_{men} and P_{women} are different in all three figures. Figure 12 is centered at 25 percentage points, reflecting our illustrative values of 60% and 35% for the pass rates. Figure 13 is centered at zero, because it is drawn according to the requirements of the null hypothesis. Figure 14 is centered at 10, because the alternative hypothesis is used to determine the center, rather than the null hypothesis.

244. The null hypothesis asserts a difference of zero. In Figure 13, 20 percentage points is 2 SEs to the right of the value expected under the null hypothesis; likewise, –20 is 2 SEs to the left. However, Figure 14 takes the alternative hypothesis to be true; on that basis, the expected value is 10 instead of zero, so 20 is 1 SE to the right of the expected value, while –20 is 3 SEs to the left.

245. Let t = sample difference/SE, where the SE is estimated from the data, as in expression (10). One formal version of our test rejects the null hypothesis if $|t| \geq 2$. To find the power, we replace the estimated SE by the true SE, computed as in expression (7); and we replace the probability histogram by the normal curve. These approximations are quite good. The size can be approximated in a similar way, given a common value for the two population pass rates. Of course, more exact calculations are possible. *See supra* note 242.

Figure 14. Power when P_{men} = 55% and P_{women} = 45%. The chance of getting a significant difference (at the 5% level, two-tailed) is about equal to the area under the normal curve, to the right of +1 or to the left of −3. That shaded area is about 1/6. Power is about 1/6, or 17%.

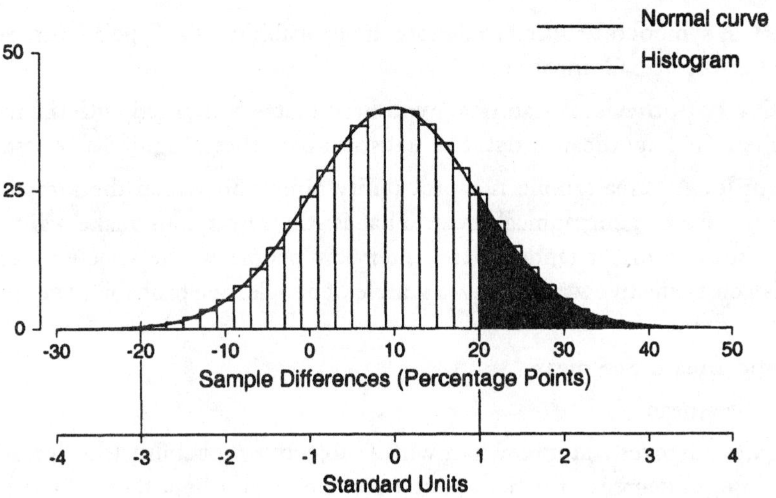

Glossary of Terms

The following terms and definitions are adapted from a variety of sources, including Michael O. Finkelstein & Bruce Levin, Statistics for Lawyers (1990), and David A. Freedman et al., Statistics (3d ed. 1998).

adjust for. See control for.

alpha (α). A symbol often used to denote the probability of a Type I error. See Type I error; size. Compare beta.

alternative hypothesis. A statistical hypothesis that is contrasted with the null hypothesis in a significance test. See statistical hypothesis; significance test.

area sample. An area sample is a probability sample in which the sampling frame is a list of geographical areas. That is, the researchers make a list of areas, choose some at random, and interview people in the selected areas. This is a cost-effective way to draw a sample of people. See probability sample; sampling frame.

arithmetic mean. See mean.

average. See mean.

Bayes' rule. An investigator may start with a subjective probability (the "prior") that expresses degrees of belief about a parameter or a hypothesis. Data are collected according to some statistical model, at least in the investigator's opinion. Bayes' rule gives a procedure for combining the prior with the data to compute the "posterior" probability, which expresses the investigator's belief about the parameter or hypothesis given the data. See Appendix.

beta (β). A symbol sometimes used to denote power, and sometimes to denote the probability of a Type II error. See Type II error; power. Compare alpha.

bias. A systematic tendency for an estimate to be too high or too low. An estimate is "unbiased" if the bias is zero. (Does not mean prejudice, partiality, or discriminatory intent.) See non-sampling error. Compare sampling error.

bin. A class interval in a histogram. See class interval; histogram.

binary variable. A variable that has only two possible values (e.g., gender). Also called a "dummy variable."

binomial distribution. A distribution for the number of occurrences in repeated, independent "trials" where the probabilities are fixed. For example, the number of heads in 100 tosses of a coin follows a binomial distribution. When the probability is not too close to zero or one and the number of trials is large, the binomial distribution has about the same shape as the normal distribution. See normal distribution; Poisson distribution.

blind. See double-blind experiment.

bootstrap. Also called resampling; Monte Carlo method. A procedure for estimating sampling error by constructing a simulated population on the basis of the sample, then repeatedly drawing samples from this simulated population.

categorical data; categorical variable. See qualitative variable. Compare quantitative variable.

central limit theorem. Shows that under suitable conditions, the probability histogram for a sum (or average or rate) will follow the normal curve.

chance error. See random error; sampling error.

chi-squared (χ^2). The chi-squared statistic measures the distance between the data and expected values computed from a statistical model. If χ^2 is too large to explain by chance, the data contradict the model. The definition of "large" depends on the context. See statistical hypothesis; significance test.

class interval. Also, bin. The base of a rectangle in a histogram; the area of the rectangle shows the percentage of observations in the class interval. See histogram.

cluster sample. A type of random sample. For example, one might take households at random, then interview all people in the selected households. This is a cluster sample of people: a cluster consists of all the people in a selected household. Generally, clustering reduces the cost of interviewing. See multistage cluster sample.

coefficient of determination. A statistic (more commonly known as R^2) that describes how well a regression equation fits the data. See R-squared.

coefficient of variation. A statistic that measures spread relative to the mean: SD/mean, or SE/expected value. See expected value; mean; standard deviation; standard error.

collinearity. See multicollinearity.

conditional probability. The probability that one event will occur given that another has occurred.

confidence coefficient. See confidence interval.

confidence interval. An estimate, expressed as a range, for a quantity in a population. If an estimate from a large sample is unbiased, a 95% "confidence interval" is the range from about two standard errors below to two standard errors above the estimate. Intervals obtained this way cover the true value about 95% of the time, and 95% is the "confidence level" or the "confidence coefficient." See unbiased estimator; standard error. Compare bias.

confidence level. See confidence interval.

confounding. See confounding variable; observational study.

confounding variable; confounder. A variable that is correlated with the independent variables and the dependent variable. An association between the dependent and independent variables in an observational study may not be causal, but may instead be due to confounding. See controlled experiment; observational study.

consistency; consistent. See consistent estimator.

consistent estimator. An estimator that tends to become more and more accurate as the sample size grows. Inconsistent estimators, which do not become more accurate as the sample gets large, are seldom used by statisticians.

content validity. The extent to which a skills test is appropriate to its intended purpose, as evidenced by a set of questions that adequately reflect the domain being tested.

continuous variable. A variable that has arbitrarily fine gradations, such as a person's height. Compare discrete variable.

control for. Statisticians may "control for" the effects of confounding variables in nonexperimental data by making comparisons for smaller and more homogeneous groups of subjects, or by entering the confounders as explanatory variables in a regression model. To "adjust for" is perhaps a better phrase in the regression context, because in an observational study the confounding factors are not under experimental control; statistical adjustments are an imperfect substitute. See regression model.

control group. See controlled experiment.

controlled experiment. An experiment where the investigators determine which subjects are put into the "treatment group" and which are put into the "control group." Subjects in the treatment group are exposed by the investigators to some influence—the "treatment"; those in the control group are not so exposed. For instance, in an experiment to evaluate a new drug, subjects in the treatment group are given the drug, subjects in the control group are given some other therapy; the outcomes in the two groups are compared to see whether the new drug works.

"Randomization"—that is, randomly assigning subjects to each group—is usually the best way to assure that any observed difference between the two groups comes from the treatment rather than pre-existing differences. Of course, in many situations, a randomized controlled experiment is impractical, and investigators must then rely on observational studies. Compare observational study.

convenience sample. A non-random sample of units, also called a "grab sample." Such samples are easy to take, but may suffer from serious bias. Mall samples are convenience samples.

correlation coefficient. A number between −1 and 1 that indicates the extent of the linear association between two variables. Often, the correlation coefficient is abbreviated as "*r*."

covariance. A quantity that describes the statistical interrelationship of two variables. Compare correlation coefficient; standard error; variance.

covariate. A variable that is related to other variables of primary interest in a study; a measured confounder; a statistical control in a regression equation.

criterion. The variable against which an examination or other selection procedure is validated. See predictive validity.

data. Observations or measurements, usually of units in a sample taken from a larger population.

dependent variable. See independent variable.

descriptive statistics. Like the mean or standard deviation, used to summarize data.

differential validity. Differences in the correlation between skills test scores and outcome measures across different subgroups of test-takers.

discrete variable. A variable that has only a finite number of possible values, such as the number of automobiles owned by a household. Compare continuous variable.

distribution. See frequency distribution; probability distribution; sampling distribution.

disturbance term. A synonym for error term.

double-blind experiment. An experiment with human subjects in which neither the diagnosticians nor the subjects know who is in the treatment group or the control group. This is accomplished by giving a placebo treatment to patients in the control group. In a *single-blind experiment*, the patients do not know whether they are in treatment or control; however, the diagnosticians have this information.

dummy variable. Generally, a dummy variable takes only the values 0 or 1, and distinguishes one group of interest from another. See binary variable; regression model.

econometrics. Statistical study of economic issues.

epidemiology. Statistical study of disease or injury in human populations.

error term. The part of a statistical model that describes random error, i.e., the impact of chance factors unrelated to variables in the model. In econometric models, the error term is called a "disturbance term."

estimator. A sample statistic used to estimate the value of a population parameter. For instance, the sample mean commonly is used to estimate the population mean. The term "estimator" connotes a statistical procedure, while an "estimate" connotes a particular numerical result.

expected value. See random variable.

experiment. See controlled experiment; randomized controlled experiment. Compare observational study.

explanatory variable. See independent variable, regression model.

factors. See independent variable.

Fisher's exact test. When comparing two sample proportions, for instance the proportions of whites and blacks getting a promotion, an investigator may wish to test the null hypothesis that promotion does not depend on race. Fisher's exact test is one way to arrive at a *p*-value. The calculation is based on the hypergeometric distribution. For more details, see Michael O. Finkelstein & Bruce Levin, Statistics for Lawyers 156–59 (1990). See hypergeometric distribution; *p*-value; significance test; statistical hypothesis.

fitted value. See residual.

fixed significance level. Also alpha; size. A pre-set level, such as 0.05 or 0.01; if the *p*-value of a test falls below this level, the result is deemed "statistically significant." See significance test. Compare observed significance level; *p*-value.

frequency distribution. Shows how often specified values occur in a data set.

Gaussian distribution. A synonym for the normal distribution. See normal distribution.

general linear model. Expresses the dependent variable as a linear combination of the independent variables plus an error term whose components may be dependent and have differing variances. See error term; linear combination; variance. Compare regression model.

grab sample. See convenience sample.

heteroscedastic. See scatter diagram.

histogram. A plot showing how observed values fall within specified intervals, called "bins" or "class intervals." Generally, matters are arranged so the area under the histogram, but over a class interval, gives the frequency or relative frequency of data in that interval. With a probability histogram, the area gives the chance of observing a value that falls in the corresponding interval.

homoscedastic. See scatter diagram.

hypergeometric distribution. Suppose a sample is drawn at random without replacement, from a finite population. How many times will items of a certain type come into the sample? The hypergeometric distribution gives the probabilities. For more details, see 1 William Feller, An Introduction to Probability Theory and its Applications 41–42 (2d ed. 1957). Compare Fisher's exact test.

hypothesis. See alternative hypothesis; null hypothesis; one-sided hypothesis; significance test; statistical hypothesis; two-sided hypothesis.

hypothesis test. See significance test.

independence. Events are independent when the probability of one is unaffected by the occurrence or non-occurrence of the other. Compare conditional probability.

independent variable. Independent variables (also called explanatory variables or factors) are used in a regression model to predict the dependent variable. For instance, the unemployment rate has been used as the independent variable in a model for predicting the crime rate; the unemployment rate is the independent variable in this model, and the crime rate is the dependent variable. See regression model. Compare dependent variable.

indicator variable. See dummy variable.

interquartile range. Difference between 25th and 75th percentile. See percentile.

interval estimate. A "confidence interval," or an estimate coupled with a standard error. See confidence interval; standard error. Compare point estimate.

least squares. See least squares estimator; regression model.

least squares estimator. An estimator that is computed by minimizing the sum of the squared residuals. See residual.

level. The level of a significance test is denoted alpha (α). See alpha; fixed significance level; observed significance level; *p*-value; significance test.

linear combination. To obtain a linear combination of two variables, multiply the first variable by some constant, multiply the second variable by another constant, and add the two products. For instance, $2u + 3v$ is a linear combination of u and v.

loss function. Statisticians may evaluate estimators according to a mathematical formula involving the errors, i.e., differences between actual values and estimated values. The "loss" may be the total of the squared errors, or the total of the absolute errors, etc. Loss functions seldom quantify real losses, but may be useful summary statistics and may prompt the construction of useful statistical procedures. Compare risk.

lurking variable. See confounding variable.

mean. Also, the average; the expected value of a random variable. The mean is one way to find the center of a batch of numbers: add up the numbers, and divide by how many there are. Weights may be employed, as in "weighted mean" or "weighted average." See random variable. Compare median; mode.

median. The median is another way to find the center of a batch of numbers. The median is the 50th percentile. Half the numbers are larger, and half are smaller. (To be very precise: at least half the numbers are greater than or equal to the median; at least half the numbers are less than or equal to the median; for small data sets, the median may not be uniquely defined.) Compare mean; mode; percentile.

meta-analysis. Attempts to combine information from all studies on a certain topic. For example, in the epidemiologic context, a meta-analysis may attempt to provide a summary odds ratio and confidence interval for the effect of a certain exposure on a certain disease.

mode. The most commonly observed value. Compare mean; median.

model. See probability model; regression model; statistical model.

multicollinearity. Also, collinearity. The existence of correlations among the "independent variables" in a regression model. See independent variable; regression model.

multiple comparison. Making several statistical tests on the same data set. Multiple comparisons complicate the interpretation of a *p*-value. For example, if 20 divisions of a company are examined, and one division is found to have a disparity "significant" at the 0.05 level, the result is not surprising; indeed, it should be expected under the null hypothesis. Compare *p*-value; significance test; statistical hypothesis.

multiple correlation coefficient. A number that indicates the extent to which one variable can be predicted as a linear combination of other variables. Its magnitude is the square root of R^2. See linear combination; *R*-squared; regression model. Compare correlation coefficient.

multiple regression. A regression equation that includes two or more independent variables. See regression model. Compare simple regression.

multivariate methods. Methods for fitting models with multiple variables, especially, multiple response variables; occasionally, multiple explanatory variables. See regression model.

multi-stage cluster sample. A probability sample drawn in stages, usually after stratification; the last stage will involve drawing a cluster. See cluster sample; probability sample; stratified random sample.

natural experiment. An observational study in which treatment and control groups have been formed by some natural development; however, the assignment of subjects to groups is judged akin to randomization. See observational study. Compare controlled experiment.

nonresponse bias. Systematic error created by differences between respondents and nonrespondents. If the nonresponse rate is high, this bias may be severe.

non-sampling error. A catch-all term for sources of error in a survey, other than sampling error. Non-sampling errors cause bias. One example is selection bias: the sample is drawn in a way that tends to exclude certain subgroups in the population. A second example is non-response bias: people who do not respond to a survey are usually different from respondents. A final example: response bias arises, for instance, if the interviewer uses a loaded question.

normal distribution. Also, Gaussian distribution. The density for this distribution is the famous "bell-shaped" curve. Statistical terminology notwithstanding, there need be nothing wrong with a distribution that differs from the normal.

null hypothesis. For example, a hypothesis that there is no difference between two groups from which samples are drawn. See significance test; statistical hypothesis. Compare alternative hypothesis.

observational study. A study in which subjects select themselves into groups; investigators then compare the outcomes for the different groups. For example, studies of smoking are generally observational. Subjects decide whether or not to smoke; the investigators compare the death rate for smokers to the death rate for non-smokers. In an observational study, the groups may differ in important ways that the investigators do not notice; controlled experiments minimize this problem. The critical distinction is that in a controlled experiment, the investigators intervene to manipulate the circumstances of the subjects; in an observational study, the investigators are passive observers. (Of course, running a good observational study is hard work, and may be quite useful.) Compare confounding variable; controlled experiment.

observed significance level. A synonym for *p*-value. See significance test. Compare fixed significance level.

odds. The probability that an event will occur divided by the probability that it will not. For example, if the chance of rain tomorrow is 2/3, then the odds on rain are (2/3)/(1/3) = 2/1, or 2 to 1; the odds against rain are 1 to 2.

odds ratio. A measure of association, often used in epidemiology. For instance, if 10% of all people exposed to a chemical develop a disease, compared to 5% of people who are not exposed, then the odds of the disease in the exposed group are 10/90 = 1/9, compared to 5/95 = 1/19 in the unexposed group. The odds ratio is 19/9 = 2.1. An odds ratio of 1 indicates no association. Compare relative risk.

one-sided hypothesis. Excludes the possibility that a parameter could be, e.g., less than the value asserted in the null hypothesis. A one-sided hypothesis leads to a one-tailed test. See significance test; statistical hypothesis; compare two-sided hypothesis.

one-tailed test. See significance test.

outlier. An observation that is far removed from the bulk of the data. Outliers may indicate faulty measurements and they may exert undue influence on summary statistics, such as the mean or the correlation coefficient.

***p*-value.** The output of a statistical test. The probability of getting, just by chance, a test statistic as large as or larger than the observed value. Large *p*-values are consistent with the null hypothesis; small *p*-values undermine this hypothesis. However, *p* itself does not give the probability that the null hypothesis is true. If *p* is smaller than 5%, the result is said to be "statistically significant." If *p* is smaller than 1%, the result is "highly significant." The *p*-value is also called "the observed significance level." See significance test; statistical hypothesis.

parameter. A numerical characteristic of a population or a model. See probability model.

percentile. To get the percentiles of a data set, array the data from the smallest value to the largest. Take the 90th percentile by way of example: 90% of the values fall below the 90th percentile, and 10% are above. (To be very precise: at least 90% of the data are at the 90th percentile or below; at least 10% of the data are at the 90th percentile or above.) The 50th percentile is the median: 50% of the values fall below the median, and 50% are above. When the LSAT first was scored on a 10–50 scale in 1982, a score of 32 placed a test taker at the 50th percentile; a score of 40 was at the 90th percentile (approximately). Compare mean; median; quartile.

placebo. See double-blind experiment.

point estimate. An estimate of the value of a quantity expressed as a single number. See estimator. Compare confidence interval; interval estimate.

Poisson distribution. The Poisson distribution is a limiting case of the binomial distribution, when the number of trials is large and the common probability is small. The "parameter" of the approximating Poisson distribution is the number of "trials" times the common probability, which is the "expected" number of events. When this number is large, the Poisson distribution may be approximated by a normal distribution.

population. Also, universe. All the units of interest to the researcher. Compare sample; sampling frame.

posterior probability. See Bayes' rule.

power. The probability that a statistical test will reject the null hypothesis. To compute power, one has to fix the size of the test and specify parameter values outside the range given in the null hypothesis. A powerful test has a good chance of detecting an effect, when there is an effect to be detected. See beta; significance test. Compare alpha; size; *p*-value.

practical significance. Substantive importance. Statistical significance does not necessarily establish practical significance. With large samples, small differences can be statistically significant. See significance test.

predicted value. See residual.

predictive validity. A skills test has predictive validity to the extent that test scores are well correlated with later performance, or more generally with outcomes that the test is intended to predict.

prior probability. See Bayes' rule.

probability. Chance, on a scale from 0 to 1. Impossibility is represented by 0, certainty by 1. Equivalently, chances may be quoted in percent; 100% corresponds to 1, while 5% corresponds to .05, and so forth.

probability density. Describes the probability distribution of a random variable. The chance that the random variable falls in an interval equals the area below the density and above the interval. (However, not all random variables have densities.) See probability distribution; random variable.

probability distribution. Gives probabilities for possible values or ranges of values of a random variable. Often, the distribution is described in terms of a density. See probability density.

probability histogram. See histogram.

probability model. Relates probabilities of outcomes to parameters; also, statistical model. The latter connotes unknown parameters.

probability sample. A sample drawn from a sampling frame by some objective chance mechanism; each unit has a known probability of being sampled. Such samples minimize selection bias, but can be expensive to draw.

psychometrics. The study of psychological measurement and testing.

qualitative variable; quantitative variable. A "qualitative" or "categorical" variable describes qualitative features of subjects in a study (e.g., marital status—never-married, married, widowed, divorced, separated). A "quantitative" variable describes numerical features of the subjects (e.g., height, weight, income). This is not a hard-and-fast distinction, because qualitative features may be given numerical codes, as in a "dummy variable." Quantitative variables may be classified as "discrete" or "continuous." Concepts like the mean and the standard deviation apply only to quantitative variables. Compare continuous variable; discrete variable; dummy variable. See variable.

quartile. The 25th or 75th percentile. See percentile. Compare median.

***R*-squared (R^2).** Measures how well a regression equation fits the data. R^2 varies between zero (no fit) and one (perfect fit). R^2 does not measure the validity of underlying assumptions. See regression model. Compare multiple correlation coefficient; standard error of regression.

random error. Sources of error that are haphazard in their effect. These are reflected in the "error term" of a statistical model. Some authors refer to "random error" as "chance error" or "sampling error." See regression model.

random variable. A variable whose possible values occur according to some probability mechanism. For example, if a pair of dice are thrown, the total number of spots is a random variable. The chance of two spots is 1/36, the chance of three spots is 2/36, and so forth; the most likely number is 7, with chance 6/36.

The "expected value" of a random variable is the weighted average of the possible values; the weights are the probabilities. In our example, the expected value is

$$\frac{1}{36} \times 2 + \frac{2}{36} \times 3 + \frac{3}{36} \times 4 + \frac{4}{36} \times 5 + \frac{5}{36} \times 6 + \frac{6}{36} \times 7$$

$$+ \frac{5}{36} \times 8 + \frac{4}{36} \times 9 + \frac{3}{36} \times 10 + \frac{2}{36} \times 11 + \frac{1}{36} \times 12 = 7$$

In many problems, the weighted average is computed with respect to the density; then sums must be replaced by integrals. The expected value need not be a possible value for the random variable.

Generally, a random variable will be somewhere around its expected value, but will be off (in either direction) by something like a standard error (SE) or so. If the random variable has a more or less normal distribution, there is about a 68% chance for it to fall in the range "expected value – SE" to "expected value + SE." See normal curve; standard error.

randomization. See controlled experiment; randomized controlled experiment.

randomized controlled experiment. A controlled experiment in which subjects are placed into the treatment and control groups at random—as if by lot, that is, by randomization. See controlled experiment. Compare observational study.

range. The difference between the biggest and the smallest values in a batch of numbers.

regression coefficient. A constant in a regression equation. See regression model.

regression diagnostics. Procedures intended to check whether the assumptions of a regression model are appropriate.

regression equation. See regression model.

regression line. The graph of a (simple) regression equation.

regression model. A "regression model" attempts to combine the values of certain variables (the "independent" or "explanatory" variables) in order to get expected values for another variable (the "dependent" variable). Sometimes, "regression model" refers to a probability model for the data; if no qualifications are made, the model will generally be linear, and errors will be assumed independent across observations, with common variance; the coefficients in the linear combination are called "regression coefficients"; these are parameters. At times, "regression model" refers to an equation (the "regression equation") estimated from data, typically by least squares.

For example, in a regression study of salary differences between men and women in a firm, the analyst may include a "dummy variable" for gender, as well as "statistical controls" like education and experience to adjust for productivity differences between men and women. The dummy variable would be defined as 1 for the men, 0 for the women. Salary would be the dependent variable; education, experience, and the dummy would be the independent variables. See least squares; multiple regression; random error; variance. Compare general linear model.

relative risk. A measure of association used in epidemiology. For instance, if 10% of all people exposed to a chemical develop a disease, compared to 5% of people who are not exposed, then the disease occurs twice as frequently among the exposed people: the relative risk is 10%/5% = 2. A relative risk of 1 indicates no association. For more details, see Abraham M. Lilienfeld & David E. Lilienfeld, Foundations of Epidemiology 209 (2d ed. 1980). Compare odds ratio.

reliability. The extent to which a measuring instrument gives the same results on repeated measurement of the same thing. Compare validity.

resampling. See bootstrap.

residual. The difference between an actual and a "predicted" value. The predicted value comes typically from a regression equation, and is also called the "fitted value." See regression model; independent variable.

response variable. See independent variable.

risk. Expected loss. "Expected" means on average, over the various data sets that could be generated by the statistical model under examination. Usually, risk cannot be computed exactly but has to be estimated, because the parameters in the statistical model are unknown and must be estimated. See loss function; random variable.

robust. A statistic or procedure that does not change much when data or assumptions are modified slightly.

sample. A set of units collected for study. Compare population.

sample size. The number of units in a sample.

sampling distribution. The distribution of the values of a statistic, over all possible samples from a population. For example, suppose a random sample is drawn. Some values of the sample mean are more likely, others are less likely. The "sampling distribution" specifies the chance that the sample mean will fall in one interval rather than another.

sampling error. A sample is part of a population. When a sample is used to estimate a numerical characteristic of the population, the estimate is likely to differ from the population value because the sample is not a perfect microcosm of the whole. If the estimate is unbiased, the difference between the estimate and the exact value is "sampling error." More generally,

$$\text{estimate} = \text{true value} + \text{bias} + \text{sampling error}.$$

Sampling error is also called "chance error" or "random error." See standard error. Compare bias; non-sampling error.

sampling frame. A list of units designed to represent the entire population as completely as possible. The sample is drawn from the frame.

scatter diagram. Also, scatterplot; scatter diagram. A graph showing the relationship between two variables in a study. Each dot represents one subject. One variable is plotted along the horizontal axis, the other variable is plotted along the vertical axis. A scatter diagram is "homoscedastic" when the spread is more or less the same inside any vertical strip. If the spread changes from one strip to another, the diagram is "heteroscedastic."

selection bias. Systematic error due to non-random selection of subjects for study.

sensitivity. In clinical medicine, the probability that a test for a disease will give a positive result given that the patient has the disease. Sensitivity is analogous to the power of a statistical test. Compare specificity.

sensitivity analysis. Analyzing data in different ways to see how results depend on methods or assumptions.

significance level. See fixed significance level; p-value.

significance test. Also, statistical test; hypothesis test; test of significance. A significance test involves formulating a statistical hypothesis and a test statistic, computing a p-value, and comparing p to some pre-established value ("alpha") to decide if the test statistic is "significant." The idea is to see whether the data conform to the predictions of the null hypothesis. Generally, a large test statistic goes with a small *p*-value; and small *p*-values would undermine the null hypothesis.

For instance, suppose that a random sample of male and female employees were given a skills test and the mean scores of the men and women were different—in the sample. To judge whether the difference is due to sampling error, a statistician might consider the implications of competing hypotheses about the difference in the population. The "null hypothesis" would say that on average, in the population, men and women have the same scores: the difference observed in the data is then just due to sampling error. A "one-sided alternative hypothesis" would be that on average, in the population, men score higher than women. The "one-tailed" test would reject the null hypothesis if the sample men score substantially higher than the women—so much so that the difference is hard to explain on the basis of sampling error.

In contrast, the null hypothesis could be tested against the "two-sided alternative" that on average, in the population, men score differently than women—higher or lower. The corresponding "two-tailed" test would reject the null hypothesis if the sample men score substantially higher or substantially lower than the women.

The one-tailed and two-tailed tests would both be based on the same data, and use the same *t*-statistic. However, if the men in the sample score higher than the women, the one-tailed test would give a *p*-value only half as large as the two-tailed test, that is, the one-tailed test would appear to give stronger evidence against the null hypothesis. See *p*-value; statistical hypothesis; *t*-statistic.

significant. See *p*-value; practical significance; significance test.

simple random sample. A random sample in which each unit in the sampling frame has the same chance of being sampled. One takes a unit at random (as if by lottery), sets it aside, takes another at random from what is left, and so forth.

simple regression. A regression equation that includes only one independent variable. Compare multiple regression.

size. A synonym for alpha (α).

specificity. In clinical medicine, the probability that a test for a disease will give a negative result given that the patient does not have the disease. Specificity is analogous to $1 - \alpha$, where α is the significance level of a statistical test. Compare sensitivity.

spurious correlation. When two variables are correlated, one is not necessarily the cause of the other. The vocabulary and shoe size of children in elementary school, for instance, are correlated—but learning more words will not make the feet grow. Such non-causal correlations are said to be "spurious." (Originally, the term seems to have been applied to the correlation between two rates with the same denominator: even if the numerators are unrelated, the common denominator will create some association.) Compare confounding variable.

standard deviation (SD). The SD indicates how far a typical element deviates from the average. For instance, in round numbers, the average height of women age 18 and over in the United States is 5 feet 4 inches. However, few women are exactly average; most will deviate from average, at least by a little. The SD is sort of an average deviation from average. For the height distribution, the SD is 3 inches. The height of a typical woman is around 5 feet 4 inches, but is off that average value by something like 3 inches.

For distributions that follow the normal curve, about 68% of the elements are in the range "mean – SD" to "mean + SD." Thus, about 68% of women have heights in the range 5 feet 1 inch to 5 feet 7 inches. Deviations from the average that exceed three or four SDs are extremely unusual. Many authors use "standard deviation" to also mean standard error. See standard error.

standard error (SE). Indicates the likely size of the sampling error in an estimate. Many authors use the term "standard deviation" instead of standard error. Compare expected value; standard deviation.

standard error of regression. Indicates how actual values differ (in some average sense) from the fitted values in a regression model. See regression model; residual. Compare *R*-squared.

standardization. See standardized variable.

standardized variable. Transformed to have mean zero and variance one. This involves two steps: (1) subtract the mean, (2) divide by the standard deviation.

statistic. A number that summarizes data. A "statistic" refers to a sample; a "parameter" or a "true value" refers to a population or a probability model.

statistical controls. Procedures that try to filter out the effects of confounding variables on non-experimental data, for instance, by "adjusting" through statistical procedures (like multiple regression). Variables in a multiple regression equation. See multiple regression; confounding variable; observational study. Compare controlled experiment.

statistical hypothesis. Data may be governed by a probability model; "parameters" are numerical characteristics describing features of the model. Generally, a "statistical hypothesis" is a statement about the parameters in a probability model. The "null hypothesis" may assert that certain parameters have specified values or fall in specified ranges; the alternative hypothesis would specify other values or ranges. The null hypothesis is "tested" against the data with a "test statistic"; the null hypothesis may be "rejected" if there is a "statistically significant" difference between the data and the predictions of the null hypothesis.

Typically, the investigator seeks to demonstrate the alternative hypothesis; the null hypothesis would explain the findings as a result of mere chance, and the investigator uses a significance test to rule out this explanation. See significance test.

statistical model. See probability model.

statistical test. See significance test.

statistical significance. See *p*-value.

stratified random sample. A type of probability sample. One divides the population up into relatively homogeneous groups called "strata," and draws a random sample separately from each stratum.

systematic sampling. The elements of the population are numbered consecutively as 1, 2, 3 . . . . Then, every *k*th element is chosen. If $k = 10$, for instance, the sample would consist of items 1, 11, 21 . . . . Sometimes the starting point is chosen at random from 1 to *k*.

***t*-statistic.** A test statistic, used to make the "*t*-test." The *t*-statistic indicates how far away an estimate is from its expected value, relative to the standard error. The expected value is computed using the null hypothesis that is being tested. Some authors refer to the *t*-statistic, others to the "*z*-statistic," especially when the sample is large. In such cases, a *t*-statistic larger than 2 or 3 in absolute value makes the null hypothesis rather unlikely—the estimate is too many standard errors away from its expected value. See statistical hypothesis; significance test; *t*-test.

***t*-test.** A statistical test based on the *t*-statistic. Large *t*-statistics are beyond the usual range of sampling error. For example, if *t* is bigger than 2, or smaller than −2, then the estimate is "statistically significant" at the 5% level: such values of *t* are hard to explain on the basis of sampling error. The scale for *t*-statistics is tied to areas under the normal curve. For instance, a *t*-statistic of 1.5 is not very striking, because 13% = 13/100 of the area under the normal curve is outside the range from −1.5 to 1.5. On the other hand, $t = 3$ is remarkable: only 3/1,000 of the area lies outside the range from −3 to 3. This discussion is predicated on having a reasonably large sample; in that context, many authors refer to the "*z*-test" rather than the *t*-test.

For small samples drawn at random from a population known to be normal, the *t*-statistic follows "Student's *t*-distribution" (when the null hypothesis holds) rather than the normal curve; larger values of *t* are required to achieve "significance." A *t*-test is not appropriate for small samples drawn from a population that is not normal. See *p*-value; significance test; statistical hypothesis.

test statistic. A statistic used to judge whether data conform to the null hypothesis. The parameters of a probability model determine expected values for the data; differences between expected values and observed values are measured by a "test statistic." Such test statistics include the chi-squared statistic (χ^2) and the *t*-statistic. Generally, small values of the test statistic are consistent with the null hypothesis; large values lead to rejection. See *p*-value; statistical hypothesis; *t*-statistic.

time series. A series of data collected over time, for instance, the Gross National Product of the United States from 1940 to 1990.

treatment group. See controlled experiment.

two-sided hypothesis. An alternative hypothesis asserting that the values of a parameter are different from—either greater than or less than—the value asserted in the null hypothesis. A two-sided alternative hypothesis suggests a two-tailed test. See statistical hypothesis; significance test. Compare one-sided hypothesis.

two-tailed test. See significance test.

Type I error. A statistical test makes a "Type I error" when (1) the null hypothesis is true and (2) the test rejects the null hypothesis, i.e., there is a false positive. For instance, a study of two groups may show some difference between samples from each group, even when there is no difference in the population. When a statistical test deems the difference to be "significant" in this situation, it makes a Type I error. See significance test; statistical hypothesis. Compare alpha; Type II error.

Type II error. A statistical test makes a "Type II error" when (1) the null hypothesis is false and (2) the test fails to reject the null hypothesis, i.e., there is a false negative. For instance, there may not be a "significant" difference between samples from two groups when, in fact, the groups are different. See significance test; statistical hypothesis. Compare beta; Type I error.

unbiased estimator. An estimator that is correct on average, over the possible data sets. The estimates have no systematic tendency to be high or low. Compare bias.

uniform distribution. For example, a whole number picked at random from 1 to 100 has the uniform distribution: all values are equally likely. Similarly, a uniform distribution is obtained by picking a real number at random between 0.75 and 3.25: the chance of landing in an interval is proportional to the length of the interval.

validity. The extent to which an instrument measures what it is supposed to, rather than something else. The validity of a standardized test is often indicated (in part) by the correlation coefficient between the test scores and some outcome measure.

variable. A property of units in a study, which varies from one unit to another. For example, in a study of households, household income; in a study of people, employment status (employed, unemployed, not in labor force).

variance. The square of the standard deviation. Compare standard error; covariance.

***z*-statistic.** See *t*-statistic.

***z*-test.** See *t*-test.

References on Statistics

General Surveys

David Freedman et al., Statistics (3d ed. 1998).

Darrell Huff, How to Lie with Statistics (1954).

Gregory A. Kimble, How to Use (and Misuse) Statistics (1978).

David S. Moore, Statistics: Concepts and Controversies (3d ed. 1991).

David S. Moore & George P. McCabe, Introduction to the Practice of Statistics (2d ed. 1993).

Michael Oakes, Statistical Inference: A Commentary for the Social and Behavioral Sciences (1986).

Perspectives on Contemporary Statistics (David G. Hoaglin & David S. Moore eds., 1992).

Statistics: A Guide to the Unknown (Judith M. Tanur et al. eds., 2d ed. 1978).

Hans Zeisel, Say It with Figures (6th ed. 1985).

Reference Works for Lawyers and Judges

David C. Baldus & James W.L. Cole, Statistical Proof of Discrimination (1980 & Supp. 1987).

David W. Barnes & John M. Conley, Statistical Evidence in Litigation: Methodology, Procedure, and Practice (1986).

James Brooks, A Lawyer's Guide to Probability and Statistics (1990).

Michael O. Finkelstein & Bruce Levin, Statistics for Lawyers (1990).

1 & 2 Modern Scientific Evidence: The Law and Science of Expert Testimony (David L. Faigman et al. eds., 1997)

Ramona Paetzold & Steven L. Willborn, The Statistics of Discrimination: Using Statistical Evidence in Discrimination Cases (1994)

Panel on Statistical Assessments as Evidence in the Courts, National Research Council, The Evolving Role of Statistical Assessments as Evidence in the Courts (Stephen E. Fienberg ed., 1989).

Statistical Methods in Discrimination Litigation (David H. Kaye & Mikel Aickin eds., 1986).

Hans Zeisel & David Kaye, Prove It with Figures: Empirical Methods in Law and Litigation (1997)

General Reference

International Encyclopedia of Statistics (William H. Kruskal & Judith M. Tanur eds., 1978).

Reference Guide on Multiple Regression

DANIEL L. RUBINFELD

Daniel L. Rubinfeld, Ph.D., is Robert L. Bridges Professor of Law and Professor of Economics at the University of California, Berkeley, California.

CONTENTS

I. Introduction

Multiple regression analysis is a statistical tool for understanding the relationship between two or more variables.[1] Multiple regression involves a variable to be explained—called the dependent variable—and additional explanatory variables that are thought to produce or be associated with changes in the dependent variable.[2] For example, a multiple regression analysis might estimate the effect of the number of years of work on salary. Salary would be the dependent variable to be explained; years of experience would be the explanatory variable.

Multiple regression analysis is sometimes well suited to the analysis of data about competing theories in which there are several possible explanations for the relationship among a number of explanatory variables.[3] Multiple regression typically uses a single dependent variable and several explanatory variables to assess the statistical data pertinent to these theories. In a case alleging sex discrimination in salaries, for example, a multiple regression analysis would examine not only sex, but also other explanatory variables of interest, such as education and experience.[4] The employer–defendant might use multiple regression to argue that salary is a function of the employee's education and experience, and the employee–plaintiff might argue that salary is also a function of the individual's sex.

Multiple regression also may be useful (1) in determining whether a particular effect is present; (2) in measuring the magnitude of a particular effect; and (3) in forecasting what a particular effect would be, but for an intervening event. In a patent infringement case, for example, a multiple regression analysis could be

1. A variable is anything that can take on two or more values (for example, the daily temperature in Chicago or the salaries of workers at a factory).

2. Explanatory variables in the context of a statistical study are also called independent variables. *See* David H. Kaye & David A. Freedman, Reference Guide on Statistics, § II.A.1, in this manual. That guide also offers a brief discussion of multiple regression analysis. *Id.* § V.

3. Multiple regression is one type of statistical analysis involving several variables. Other types include matching analysis, stratification, analysis of variance, probit analysis, logit analysis, discriminant analysis, and factor analysis.

4. Thus, in *Ottaviani v. State University of New York*, 875 F.2d 365, 367 (2d Cir. 1989) (citations omitted), *cert. denied*, 493 U.S. 1021 (1990), the court stated:

> In disparate treatment cases involving claims of gender discrimination, plaintiffs typically use multiple regression analysis to isolate the influence of gender on employment decisions relating to a particular job or job benefit, such as salary.
>
> The first step in such a regression analysis is to specify all of the possible "legitimate" (i.e., nondiscriminatory) factors that are likely to significantly affect the dependent variable and which could account for disparities in the treatment of male and female employees. By identifying those legitimate criteria that affect the decision-making process, individual plaintiffs can make predictions about what job or job benefits similarly situated employees should ideally receive, and then can measure the difference between the predicted treatment and the actual treatment of those employees. If there is a disparity between the predicted and actual outcomes for female employees, plaintiffs in a disparate treatment case can argue that the net "residual" difference represents the unlawful effect of discriminatory animus on the allocation of jobs or job benefits.

used to determine (1) whether the behavior of the alleged infringer affected the price of the patented product; (2) the size of the effect; and (3) what the price of the product would have been had the alleged infringement not occurred.

Over the past several decades the use of multiple regression analysis in court has grown widely. Although regression analysis has been used most frequently in cases of sex and race discrimination[5] and antitrust violation,[6] other applications include census undercounts,[7] voting rights,[8] the study of the deterrent

5. Discrimination cases using multiple regression analysis are legion. *See, e.g.*, Bazemore v. Friday, 478 U.S. 385 (1986), *on remand*, 848 F.2d 476 (4th Cir. 1988); King v. General Elec. Co., 960 F.2d 617 (7th Cir. 1992); Diehl v. Xerox Corp., 933 F. Supp. 1157 (W.D.N.Y. 1996) (age and sex discrimination); Csicseri v. Bowsher, 862 F. Supp. 547 (D.D.C. 1994) (age discrimination), *aff'd*, 67 F.3d 972 (D.C. Cir. 1995); Tennes v. Massachusetts Dep't of Revenue, No. 88-C3304, 1989 WL 157477 (N.D. Ill. Dec. 20, 1989) (age discrimination); EEOC v. General Tel. Co. of N.W., 885 F.2d 575 (9th Cir. 1989), *cert. denied*, 498 U.S. 950 (1990); Churchill v. IBM, Inc., 759 F. Supp. 1089 (D.N.J. 1991); Denny v. Westfield State College, 880 F.2d 1465 (1st Cir. 1989) (sex discrimination); Black Law Enforcement Officers Ass'n v. City of Akron, 920 F.2d 932 (6th Cir. 1990); Bridgeport Guardians, Inc. v. City of Bridgeport, 735 F. Supp. 1126 (D. Conn. 1990), *aff'd*, 933 F.2d 1140 (2d Cir.), *cert. denied*, 502 U.S. 924 (1991); Dicker v. Allstate Life Ins. Co., No. 89-C-4982, 1993 WL 62385 (N.D. Ill. Mar. 5, 1993) (race discrimination). *See also* Keith N. Hylton & Vincent D. Rougeau, *Lending Discrimination: Economic Theory, Econometric Evidence, and the Community Reinvestment Act*, 85 Geo. L.J. 237, 238 (1996) ("regression analysis is probably the best empirical tool for uncovering discrimination").

6. *E.g.*, United States v. Brown Univ., 805 F. Supp. 288 (E.D. Pa. 1992) (price-fixing of college scholarships), *rev'd*, 5 F.3d 658 (3d Cir. 1993); Petruzzi IGA Supermarkets, Inc. v. Darling-Delaware Co., 998 F.2d 1224 (3d Cir.), *cert. denied*, 510 U.S. 994 (1993); Ohio v. Louis Trauth Dairy, Inc., 925 F. Supp. 1247 (S.D. Ohio 1996); *In re* Chicken Antitrust Litig., 560 F. Supp. 963, 993 (N.D. Ga. 1980); New York v. Kraft Gen. Foods, Inc., 926 F. Supp. 321 (S.D.N.Y. 1995). *See also* Jerry Hausman et al., *Competitive Analysis with Differenciated Products*, 34 Annales D'Economie et de Statistique 159 (1994); Gregory J. Werden, *Simulating the Effects of Differentiated Products Mergers: A Practical Alternative to Structural Merger Policy*, 5 Geo. Mason L. Rev. 363 (1997).

7. *See, e.g.*, City of New York v. United States Dep't of Commerce, 822 F. Supp. 906 (E.D.N.Y. 1993) (decision of Secretary of Commerce not to adjust the 1990 census was not arbitrary and capricious), *vacated*, 34 F.3d 1114 (2d Cir. 1994) (applying heightened scrutiny), *rev'd sub nom.* Wisconsin v. City of New York, 517 U.S. 565 (1996); Cuomo v. Baldrige, 674 F. Supp. 1089 (S.D.N.Y. 1987); Carey v. Klutznick, 508 F. Supp. 420, 432–33 (S.D.N.Y. 1980) (use of reasonable and scientifically valid statistical survey or sampling procedures to adjust census figures for the differential undercount is constitutionally permissible), *stay granted*, 449 U.S. 1068 (1980), *rev'd on other grounds*, 653 F.2d 732 (2d Cir. 1981), *cert. denied*, 455 U.S. 999 (1982); Young v. Klutznick, 497 F. Supp. 1318, 1331 (E.D. Mich. 1980), *rev'd on other grounds*, 652 F.2d 617 (6th Cir. 1981), *cert. denied*, 455 U.S. 939 (1982).

8. Multiple regression analysis was used in suits charging that at-large area-wide voting was instituted to neutralize black voting strength, in violation of section 2 of the Voting Rights Act, 42 U.S.C. § 1973 (1988). Multiple regression demonstrated that the race of the candidates and that of the electorate were determinants of voting. *See, e.g.*, Williams v. Brown, 446 U.S. 236 (1980); Bolden v. City of Mobile, 423 F. Supp. 384, 388 (S.D. Ala. 1976), *aff'd*, 571 F.2d 238 (5th Cir. 1978), *stay denied*, 436 U.S. 902 (1978), *rev'd*, 446 U.S. 55 (1980); Jeffers v. Clinton, 730 F. Supp. 196, 208–09 (E.D. Ark. 1989), *aff'd*, 498 U.S. 1019 (1991); League of United Latin Am. Citizens, Council No. 4434 v. Clements, 986 F.2d 728, 774–87 (5th Cir.), *reh'g en banc*, 999 F.2d 831 (5th Cir. 1993), *cert. denied*, 498 U.S. 1060 (1994). For commentary on statistical issues in voting rights cases, see, e.g., Symposium, *Statistical and Demographic Issues Underlying Voting Rights Cases*, 15 Evaluation Rev. 659 (1991); Stephen P. Klein et al., *Ecological Regression versus the Secret Ballot*, 31 Jurimetrics J. 393 (1991); James W. Loewen & Bernard

effect of the death penalty,[9] rate regulation,[10] and intellectual property.[11]

Multiple regression analysis can be a source of valuable scientific testimony in litigation. However, when inappropriately used, regression analysis can confuse important issues while having little, if any, probative value. In *EEOC v. Sears, Roebuck & Co.*,[12] in which Sears was charged with discrimination against women in hiring practices, the Seventh Circuit acknowledged that "[m]ultiple regression analyses, designed to determine the effect of several independent variables on a dependent variable, which in this case is hiring, are an accepted and common method of proving disparate treatment claims."[13] However, the court affirmed the district court's findings that the "E.E.O.C's regression analyses did not 'accurately reflect Sears' complex, nondiscriminatory decision-making processes'" and that the "'E.E.O.C.'s statistical analyses [were] so flawed that they lack[ed] any persuasive value.'"[14] Serious questions also have been raised about the use of multiple regression analysis in census undercount cases and in death penalty cases.[15]

Moreover, in interpreting the results of a multiple regression analysis, it is important to distinguish between correlation and causality. Two variables are correlated when the events associated with the variables occur more frequently

Grofman, *Recent Developments in Methods Used in Vote Dilution Litigation,* 21 Urb. Law. 589 (1989); Arthur Lupia & Kenneth McCue, *Why the 1980s Measures of Racially Polarized Voting Are Inadequate for the 1990s,* 12 Law & Pol'y 353 (1990).

9. *See, e.g.*, Gregg v. Georgia, 428 U.S. 153, 184–86 (1976). For critiques of the validity of the deterrence analysis, see National Research Council, Deterrence and Incapacitation: Estimating the Effects of Criminal Sanctions on Crime Rates (Alfred Blumstein et al. eds., 1978); Edward Leamer, *Let's Take the Con Out of Econometrics,* 73 Am. Econ. Rev. 31 (1983); Richard O. Lempert, *Desert and Deterrence: An Assessment of the Moral Bases of the Case for Capital Punishment,* 79 Mich. L. Rev. 1177 (1981); Hans Zeisel, *The Deterrent Effect of the Death Penalty: Facts v. Faith,* 1976 Sup. Ct. Rev. 317.

10. *See, e.g.*, Time Warner Entertainment Co. v. FCC, 56 F.3d 151 (D.C. Cir. 1995) (challenge to FCC's application of multiple regression analysis to set cable rates), *cert. denied,* 516 U.S. 1112 (1996).

11. *See* Polaroid Corp. v. Eastman Kodak Co., No. 76-1634-MA, 1990 WL 324105, at *29, *62–*63 (D. Mass. Oct. 12, 1990) (damages awarded because of patent infringement), *amended by* No. 76-1634-MA, 1991 WL 4087 (D. Mass. Jan. 11, 1991); Estate of Vane v. The Fair, Inc., 849 F.2d 186, 188 (5th Cir. 1988) (lost profits were due to copyright infringement), *cert. denied,* 488 U.S. 1008 (1989). The use of multiple regression analysis to estimate damages has been contemplated in a wide variety of contexts. *See, e.g.*, David Baldus et al., *Improving Judicial Oversight of Jury Damages Assessments: A Proposal for the Comparative Additur/Remittitur Review of Awards for Nonpecuniary Harms and Punitive Damages,* 80 Iowa L. Rev. 1109 (1995); Talcott J. Franklin, *Calculating Damages for Loss of Parental Nurture Through Multiple Regression Analysis,* 52 Wash. & Lee L. Rev. 271 (1997); Roger D. Blair & Amanda Kay Esquibel, *Yardstick Damages in Lost Profit Cases: An Econometric Approach,* 72 Denv. U. L. Rev. 113 (1994).

12. 839 F.2d 302 (7th Cir. 1988).

13. *Id.* at 324 n.22.

14. *Id.* at 348, 351 (quoting EEOC v. Sears, Roebuck & Co., 628 F. Supp. 1264, 1342, 1352 (N.D. Ill. 1986)). The district court commented specifically on the "severe limits of regression analysis in evaluating complex decision-making processes." 628 F. Supp. at 1350.

15. *See* David H. Kaye & David A. Freedman, Reference Guide on Statistics, § II.A.e, B.1, in this manual.

together than one would expect by chance. For example, if higher salaries are associated with a greater number of years of work experience, and lower salaries are associated with fewer years of experience, there is a positive correlation between salary and number of years of work experience. However, if higher salaries are associated with less experience, and lower salaries are associated with more experience, there is a negative correlation between the two variables.

A correlation between two variables does not imply that one event causes the second. Therefore, in making causal inferences, it is important to avoid spurious correlation.[16] Spurious correlation arises when two variables are closely related but bear no causal relationship because they are both caused by a third, unexamined variable. For example, there might be a negative correlation between the age of certain skilled employees of a computer company and their salaries. One should not conclude from this correlation that the employer has necessarily discriminated against the employees on the basis of their age. A third, unexamined variable, such as the level of the employees' technological skills, could explain differences in productivity and, consequently, differences in salary.[17] Or, consider a patent infringement case in which increased sales of an allegedly infringing product are associated with a lower price of the patented product. This correlation would be spurious if the two products have their own noncompetitive market niches and the lower price is due to a decline in the production costs of the patented product.

Pointing to the possibility of a spurious correlation should not be enough to dispose of a statistical argument, however. It may be appropriate to give little weight to such an argument absent a showing that the alleged spurious correlation is either qualitatively or quantitatively substantial. For example, a statistical showing of a relationship between technological skills and worker productivity might be required in the age discrimination example above.[18]

Causality cannot be inferred by data analysis alone; rather, one must infer that a causal relationship exists on the basis of an underlying causal theory that explains the relationship between the two variables. Even when an appropriate

16. *See* David H. Kaye & David A. Freedman, Reference Guide on Statistics, § V.B.3, in this manual.

17. *See, e.g.*, Sheehan v. Daily Racing Form Inc., 104 F.3d 940, 942 (7th Cir.) (rejecting plaintiff's age discrimination claim because statistical study showing correlation between age and retention ignored the "more than remote possibility that age was correlated with a legitimate job-related qualification"), *cert. denied*, 521 U.S. 1104 (1997).

18. *See, e.g.*, Allen v. Seidman, 881 F.2d 375 (7th Cir. 1989) (Judicial skepticism was raised when the defendant did not submit a logistic regression incorporating an omitted variable—the possession of a higher degree or special education; defendant's attack on statistical comparisons must also include an analysis that demonstrates that comparisons are flawed.). The appropriate requirements for the defendant's showing of spurious correlation could, in general, depend on the discovery process. *See, e.g.*, Boykin v. Georgia Pac. Co., 706 F.2d 1384 (1983) (criticism of a plaintiff's analysis for not including omitted factors, when plaintiff considered all information on an application form, was inadequate).

theory has been identified, causality can never be inferred directly. One must also look for empirical evidence that there is a causal relationship. Conversely, the fact that two variables are correlated does not guarantee the existence of a relationship; it could be that the model—a characterization of the underlying causal theory—does not reflect the correct interplay among the explanatory variables. In fact, the absence of correlation does not guarantee that a causal relationship does not exist. Lack of correlation could occur if (1) there are insufficient data; (2) the data are measured inaccurately; (3) the data do not allow multiple causal relationships to be sorted out; or (4) the model is specified wrongly because of the omission of a variable or variables that are related to the variable of interest.

There is a tension between any attempt to reach conclusions with near certainty and the inherently probabilistic nature of multiple regression analysis. In general, statistical analysis involves the formal expression of uncertainty in terms of probabilities. The reality that statistical analysis generates probabilities that there are relationships should not be seen in itself as an argument against the use of statistical evidence. The only alternative might be to use less reliable anecdotal evidence.

This reference guide addresses a number of procedural and methodological issues that are relevant in considering the admissibility of, and weight to be accorded to, the findings of multiple regression analyses. It also suggests some standards of reporting and analysis that an expert presenting multiple regression analyses might be expected to meet. Section II discusses research design—how the multiple regression framework can be used to sort out alternative theories about a case. Section III concentrates on the interpretation of the multiple regression results, from both a statistical and practical point of view. Section IV briefly discusses the qualifications of experts. Section V emphasizes procedural aspects associated with use of the data underlying regression analyses. Finally, the Appendix delves into the multiple regression framework in further detail; it also contains a number of specific examples that illustrate the application of the technique.

II. Research Design: Model Specification

Multiple regression allows the testifying economist or other expert to choose among alternative theories or hypotheses and assists the expert in distinguishing correlations between variables that are plainly spurious from those that may reflect valid relationships.

A. What Is the Specific Question That Is Under Investigation by the Expert?

Research begins with a clear formulation of a research question. The data to be collected and analyzed must relate directly to this question; otherwise, appropriate inferences cannot be drawn from the statistical analysis. For example, if the question at issue in a patent infringement case is what price the plaintiff's product would have been but for the sale of the defendant's infringing product, sufficient data must be available to allow the expert to account statistically for the important factors that determine the price of the product.

B. What Model Should Be Used to Evaluate the Question at Issue?

Model specification involves several steps, each of which is fundamental to the success of the research effort. Ideally, a multiple regression analysis builds on a theory that describes the variables to be included in the study. For example, the theory of labor markets might lead one to expect salaries in an industry to be related to workers' experience and the productivity of workers' jobs. A belief that there is job discrimination would lead one to add a variable or variables reflecting discrimination.

Models are often characterized in terms of parameters—numerical characteristics of the model. In the labor market example, one parameter might reflect the increase in salary associated with each additional year of job experience. Multiple regression uses a sample, or a selection of data, from the population (all the units of interest) to obtain estimates of the values of the parameters of the model. An estimate associated with a particular explanatory variable is an estimated regression coefficient.

Failure to develop the proper theory, failure to choose the appropriate variables, or failure to choose the correct form of the model can bias substantially the statistical results, that is, create a systematic tendency for an estimate of a model parameter to be too high or too low.

1. Choosing the Dependent Variable

The variable to be explained, the dependent variable, should be the appropriate variable for analyzing the question at issue.[19] Suppose, for example, that pay

19. In multiple regression analysis, the dependent variable is usually a continuous variable that takes on a range of numerical values. When the dependent variable is categorical, taking on only two or three values, modified forms of multiple regression, such as probit analysis or logit analysis, are appropriate. For an example of the use of the latter, see *EEOC v. Sears, Roebuck & Co.*, 839 F.2d 302, 325 (7th Cir. 1988) (EEOC used logit analysis to measure the impact of variables, such as age, education, job-type experience, and product-line experience, on the female percentage of commission hires). *See also* David H. Kaye & David A. Freedman, Reference Guide on Statistics § V, in this manual.

discrimination among hourly workers is a concern. One choice for the dependent variable is the hourly wage rate of the employees; another choice is the annual salary. The distinction is important, because annual salary differences may be due in part to differences in hours worked. If the number of hours worked is the product of worker preferences and not discrimination, the hourly wage is a good choice. If the number of hours is related to the alleged discrimination, annual salary is the more appropriate dependent variable to choose.[20]

2. Choosing the Explanatory Variable That Is Relevant to the Question at Issue

The explanatory variable that allows the evaluation of alternative hypotheses must be chosen appropriately. Thus, in a discrimination case, the variable of interest may be the race or sex of the individual. In an antitrust case, it may be a variable that takes on the value 1 to reflect the presence of the alleged anticompetitive behavior and the value 0 otherwise.[21]

3. Choosing the Additional Explanatory Variables

An attempt should be made to identify additional known or hypothesized explanatory variables, some of which are measurable and may support alternative substantive hypotheses that can be accounted for by the regression analysis. Thus, in a discrimination case, a measure of the skills of the workers may provide an alternative explanation—lower salaries may have been the result of inadequate skills.[22]

20. In job systems in which annual salaries are tied to grade or step levels, the annual salary corresponding to the job position could be more appropriate.

21. Explanatory variables may vary by type, which will affect the interpretation of the regression results. Thus, some variables may be continuous and others may be categorical.

22. In *Ottaviani v. State University of New York*, 679 F. Supp. 288, 306–08 (S.D.N.Y. 1988), *aff'd*, 875 F.2d 365 (2d Cir. 1989), *cert. denied*, 493 U.S. 1021 (1990), the court ruled (in the liability phase of the trial) that the university showed there was no discrimination in either placement into initial rank or promotions between ranks, so rank was a proper variable in multiple regression analysis to determine whether women faculty members were treated differently from men.

However, in *Trout v. Garrett*, 780 F. Supp. 1396, 1414 (D.D.C. 1991), the court ruled (in the damage phase of the trial) that the extent of civilian employees' prehire work experience was not an appropriate variable in a regression analysis to compute back pay in employment discrimination. According to the court, including the prehire level would have resulted in a finding of no sex discrimination, despite a contrary conclusion in the liability phase of the action. *Id. See also* Stuart v. Roache, 951 F.2d 446 (1st Cir. 1991) (allowing only three years of seniority to be considered as the result of prior discrimination), *cert. denied*, 504 U.S. 913 (1992). Whether a particular variable reflects "legitimate" considerations or itself reflects or incorporates illegitimate biases is a recurring theme in discrimination cases. *See, e.g.*, Smith v. Virginia Commonwealth Univ., 84 F.3d 672, 677 (4th Cir. 1996) (en banc) (suggesting that whether "performance factors" should have been included in a regression analysis was a question of material fact); *id.* at 681–82 (Luttig, J., concurring in part) (suggesting that the regression analysis' failure to include "performance factors" rendered it so incomplete as to be inadmissible); *id.* at 690–91 (Michael, J., dissenting) (suggesting that the regression analysis properly excluded "performance factors"); *see also* Diehl v. Xerox Corp., 933 F. Supp. 1157, 1168 (W.D.N.Y. 1996).

Not all possible variables that might influence the dependent variable can be included if the analysis is to be successful; some cannot be measured, and others may make little difference.[23] If a preliminary analysis shows the unexplained portion of the multiple regression to be unacceptably high, the expert may seek to discover whether some previously undetected variable is missing from the analysis.[24]

Failure to include a major explanatory variable that is correlated with the variable of interest in a regression model may cause an included variable to be credited with an effect that actually is caused by the excluded variable.[25] In general, omitted variables that are correlated with the dependent variable reduce the probative value of the regression analysis.[26] This may lead to inferences made from regression analyses that do not assist the trier of fact.[27]

Omitting variables that are not correlated with the variable of interest is, in general, less of a concern, since the parameter that measures the effect of the variable of interest on the dependent variable is estimated without bias. Sup-

23. The summary effect of the excluded variables shows up as a random error term in the regression model, as does any modeling error. *See infra* the Appendix for details. *But see* David W. Peterson, *Reference Guide on Multiple Regression*, 36 Jurimetrics J. 213, 214 n.2 (1996) (review essay) (asserting that "the presumption that the combined effect of the explanatory variables omitted from the model are uncorrelated with the included explanatory variables" is "a knife-edge condition . . . not likely to occur").

24. A very low *R*-square (R^2) is one indication of an unexplained portion of the multiple regression model that is unacceptably high. However, the inference that one makes from a particular value of R^2 will depend, of necessity, on the context of the particular issues under study and the particular data set that is being analyzed. For reasons discussed in the Appendix, a low R^2 does not necessarily imply a poor model (and vice versa).

25. Technically, the omission of explanatory variables that are correlated with the variable of interest can cause biased estimates of regression parameters.

26. The importance of the effect depends on the strength of the relationship between the omitted variable and the dependent variable, and the strength of the correlation between the omitted variable and the explanatory variables of interest.

27. *See* Bazemore v. Friday, 751 F.2d 662, 671–72 (4th Cir. 1984) (upholding the district court's refusal to accept a multiple regression analysis as proof of discrimination by a preponderance of the evidence, the court of appeals stated that, although the regression used four variable factors (race, education, tenure, and job title), the failure to use other factors, including pay increases which varied by county, precluded their introduction into evidence), *aff'd in part, vacated in part*, 478 U.S. 385 (1986).

Note, however, that in *Sobel v. Yeshiva University*, 839 F.2d 18, 33, 34 (2d Cir. 1988), *cert. denied*, 490 U.S. 1105 (1989), the court made clear that "a [Title VII] defendant challenging the validity of a multiple regression analysis [has] to make a showing that the factors it contends ought to have been included would weaken the showing of salary disparity made by the analysis," by making a specific attack and "a showing of relevance for each particular variable it contends . . . ought to [be] includ[ed]" in the analysis, rather than by simply attacking the results of the plaintiffs' proof as inadequate for lack of a given variable. *See also* Smith v. Virginia Commonwealth Univ., 84 F.3d 672 (4th Cir. 1996) (en banc) (finding that whether certain variables should have been included in a regression analysis is a question of fact that precludes summary judgment).

Also, in *Bazemore v. Friday*, the Court, declaring that the Fourth Circuit's view of the evidentiary value of the regression analyses was plainly incorrect, stated that "[n]ormally, failure to include variables pose, for example, that the effect of a policy introduced by the courts to encourage husbands' payments of child support has been tested by randomly choosing some cases to be handled according to current court policies and other cases to be handled according to a new, more stringent policy. The effect of the new policy might be measured by a multiple regression using payment success as the dependent variable and a 0 or 1 explanatory variable (1 if the new program was applied; 0 if it was not). Failure to include an explanatory variable that reflected the age of the husbands involved in the program would not affect the court's evaluation of the new policy, since men of any given age are as likely to be affected by the old policy as they are the new policy. Randomly choosing the court's policy to be applied to each case has ensured that the omitted age variable is not correlated with the policy variable.

Bias caused by the omission of an important variable that is related to the included variables of interest can be a serious problem.[28] Nevertheless, it is possible for the expert to account for bias qualitatively if the expert has knowledge (even if not quantifiable) about the relationship between the omitted variable and the explanatory variable. Suppose, for example, that the plaintiff's expert in a sex discrimination pay case is unable to obtain quantifiable data that reflect the skills necessary for a job, and that, on average, women are more skillful than men. Suppose also that a regression analysis of the wage rate of employees (the dependent variable) on years of experience and a variable reflecting the sex of each employee (the explanatory variable) suggests that men are paid substantially more than women with the same experience. Because differences in skill levels have not been taken into account, the expert may conclude reasonably that the wage difference measured by the regression is a conservative estimate of the true discriminatory wage difference.

The precision of the measure of the effect of a variable of interest on the dependent variable is also important.[29] In general, the more complete the explained relationship between the included explanatory variables and the dependent variable, the more precise the results. Note, however, that the inclusion of explanatory variables that are irrelevant (i.e., not correlated with the dependent variable) reduces the precision of the regression results. This can be a source of concern when the sample size is small, but it is not likely to be of great consequence when the sample size is large.

will affect the analysis' probativeness, not its admissibility. Importantly, it is clear that a regression analysis that includes less than 'all measurable variables' may serve to prove a plaintiff's case." 478 U.S. 385, 400 (1986) (footnote omitted).

28. *See also* David H. Kaye & David A. Freedman, Reference Guide on Statistics § V.B.3, in this manual.

29. A more precise estimate of a parameter is an estimate with a smaller standard error. See *infra* the Appendix for details.

4. Choosing the Functional Form of the Multiple Regression Model

Choosing the proper set of variables to be included in the multiple regression model does not complete the modeling exercise. The expert must also choose the proper form of the regression model. The most frequently selected form is the linear regression model (described in the Appendix). In this model, the magnitude of the change in the dependent variable associated with the change in any of the explanatory variables is the same no matter what the level of the explanatory variables. For example, one additional year of experience might add $5,000 to salary, irrespective of the previous experience of the employee.

In some instances, however, there may be reason to believe that changes in explanatory variables will have differential effects on the dependent variable as the values of the explanatory variables change. In these instances, the expert should consider the use of a nonlinear model. Failure to account for nonlinearities can lead to either overstatement or understatement of the effect of a change in the value of an explanatory variable on the dependent variable.

One particular type of nonlinearity involves the interaction among several variables. An interaction variable is the product of two other variables that are included in the multiple regression model. The interaction variable allows the expert to take into account the possibility that the effect of a change in one variable on the dependent variable may change as the level of another explanatory variable changes. For example, in a salary discrimination case, the inclusion of a term that interacts a variable measuring experience with a variable representing the sex of the employee (1 if a female employee, 0 if a male employee) allows the expert to test whether the sex differential varies with the level of experience. A significant negative estimate of the parameter associated with the sex variable suggests that inexperienced women are discriminated against, whereas a significant negative estimate of the interaction parameter suggests that the extent of discrimination increases with experience.[30]

Note that insignificant coefficients in a model with interactions may suggest a lack of discrimination, whereas a model without interactions may suggest the contrary. It is especially important to account for the interactive nature of the discrimination; failure to do so may lead to false conclusions concerning discrimination.

30. For further details concerning interactions, see *infra* the Appendix. Note that in *Ottaviani v. State University of New York*, 875 F.2d 365, 367 (2d Cir. 1989), *cert. denied*, 493 U.S. 1021 (1990), the defendant relied on a regression model in which a dummy variable reflecting gender appeared as an explanatory variable. The female plaintiff, however, used an alternative approach in which a regression model was developed for men only (the alleged protected group). The salaries of women predicted by this equation were then compared with the actual salaries; a positive difference would, according to the plaintiff, provide evidence of discrimination. For an evaluation of the methodological advantages and disadvantages of this approach, see Joseph L. Gastwirth, *A Clarification of Some Statistical Issues in* Watson v. Fort Worth Bank and Trust, 29 Jurimetrics J. 267 (1989).

5. Choosing Multiple Regression as a Method of Analysis

There are many multivariate statistical techniques other than multiple regression that are useful in legal proceedings. Some statistical methods are appropriate when nonlinearities are important.[31] Others apply to models in which the dependent variable is discrete, rather than continuous.[32] Still others have been applied predominantly to respond to methodological concerns arising in the context of discrimination litigation.[33]

It is essential that a valid statistical method be applied to assist with the analysis in each legal proceeding. Therefore, the expert should be prepared to explain why any chosen method, including multiple regression, was more suitable than the alternatives.

III. Interpreting Multiple Regression Results

Multiple regression results can be interpreted in purely statistical terms, through the use of significance tests, or they can be interpreted in a more practical, nonstatistical manner. Although an evaluation of the practical significance of regression results is almost always relevant in the courtroom, tests of statistical significance are appropriate only in particular circumstances.

A. What Is the Practical, as Opposed to the Statistical, Significance of Regression Results?

Practical significance means that the magnitude of the effect being studied is not de minimis—it is sufficiently important substantively for the court to be concerned. For example, if the average wage rate is $10.00 per hour, a wage differential between men and women of $0.10 per hour is likely to be deemed practically insignificant because the differential represents only 1% ($0.10/$10.00) of

31. These techniques include, but are not limited to, piecewise linear regression, polynomial regression, maximum likelihood estimation of models with nonlinear functional relationships, and autoregressive and moving average time-series models. *See, e.g.*, Robert S. Pindyck & Daniel L. Rubinfeld, Econometric Models and Economic Forecasts 117–21, 136–37, 273–84, 463–601 (4th ed. 1998).

32. For a discussion of probit analysis and logit analysis, techniques that are useful in the analysis of qualitative choice, see *id.* at 248–81.

33. The correct model for use in salary discrimination suits is a subject of debate among labor economists. As a result, some have begun to evaluate alternative approaches, including urn models (Bruce Levin & Herbert Robbins, *Urn Models for Regression Analysis, with Applications to Employment Discrimination Studies*, Law & Contemp. Probs., Autumn 1983, at 247) and, as a means of correcting for measurement errors, reverse regression (Delores A. Conway & Harry V. Roberts, *Reverse Regression, Fairness, and Employment Discrimination*, 1 J. Bus. & Econ. Stat. 75 (1983)). *But see* Arthur S. Goldberger, *Redirecting Reverse Regressions*, 2 J. Bus. & Econ. Stat. 114 (1984); Arlene S. Ash, *The Perverse Logic of Reverse Regression*, *in* Statistical Methods in Discrimination Litigation 85 (D.H. Kaye & Mikel Aickin eds., 1986).

the average wage rate.[34] That same difference could be statistically significant, however, if a sufficiently large sample of men and women was studied.[35] The reason is that statistical significance is determined, in part, by the number of observations in the data set.

Other things being equal, the statistical significance of a regression coefficient increases as the sample size increases. Thus, a $1 per hour wage differential between men and women that was determined to be insignificantly different from zero with a sample of 20 men and women could be highly significant if the sample were increased to 200.

Often, results that are practically significant are also statistically significant.[36] However, it is possible with a large data set to find statistically significant coefficients that are practically insignificant. Similarly, it is also possible (especially when the sample size is small) to obtain results that are practically significant but statistically insignificant. Suppose, for example, that an expert undertakes a damages study in a patent infringement case and predicts "but-for sales"—what sales would have been had the infringement not occurred—using data that predate the period of alleged infringement. If data limitations are such that only three or four years of preinfringement sales are known, the difference between but-for sales and actual sales during the period of alleged infringement could be practically significant but statistically insignificant.

1. When Should Statistical Tests Be Used?

A test of a specific contention, a hypothesis test, often assists the court in determining whether a violation of the law has occurred in areas in which direct evidence is inaccessible or inconclusive. For example, an expert might use hypothesis tests in race and sex discrimination cases to determine the presence of a discriminatory effect.

34. There is no specific percentage threshold above which a result is practically significant. Practical significance must be evaluated in the context of a particular legal issue. *See also* David H. Kaye & David A. Freedman, Reference Guide on Statistics § IV.B.2, in this manual.

35. Practical significance also can apply to the overall credibility of the regression results. Thus, in *McCleskey v. Kemp,* 481 U.S. 279 (1987), coefficients on race variables were statistically significant, but the Court declined to find them legally or constitutionally significant.

36. In *Melani v. Board of Higher Education,* 561 F. Supp. 769, 774 (S.D.N.Y. 1983), a Title VII suit was brought against the City University of New York (CUNY) for allegedly discriminating against female instructional staff in the payment of salaries. One approach of the plaintiff's expert was to use multiple regression analysis. The coefficient on the variable that reflected the sex of the employee was approximately $1,800 when all years of data were included. Practically (in terms of average wages at the time) and statistically (in terms of a 5% significance test), this result was significant. Thus, the court stated that "[p]laintiffs have produced statistically *significant* evidence that women hired as CUNY instructional staff since 1972 received *substantially* lower salaries than similarly qualified men." *Id.* at 781 (emphasis added). For a related analysis involving multiple comparison, see *Csicseri v. Bowsher,* 862 F. Supp. 547, 572 (D.D.C. 1994) (noting that plaintiff's expert found "statistically significant instances of

Statistical evidence alone never can prove with absolute certainty the worth of any substantive theory. However, by providing evidence contrary to the view that a particular form of discrimination has not occurred, for example, the multiple regression approach can aid the trier of fact in assessing the likelihood that discrimination has occurred.[37]

Tests of hypotheses are appropriate in a cross-section analysis, in which the data underlying the regression study have been chosen as a sample of a population at a particular point in time, and in a time-series analysis, in which the data being evaluated cover a number of time periods. In either analysis, the expert may want to evaluate a specific hypothesis, usually relating to a question of liability or to the determination of whether there is measurable impact of an alleged violation. Thus, in a sex discrimination case, an expert may want to evaluate a null hypothesis of no discrimination against the alternative hypothesis that discrimination takes a particular form.[38] Alternatively, in an antitrust damages proceeding, the expert may want to test a null hypothesis of no legal impact against the alternative hypothesis that there was an impact. In either type of case, it is important to realize that rejection of the null hypothesis does not in itself prove legal liability. It is possible to reject the null hypothesis and believe that an alternative explanation other than one involving legal liability accounts for the results.[39]

Often, the null hypothesis is stated in terms of a particular regression coefficient being equal to 0. For example, in a wage discrimination case, the null hypothesis would be that there is no wage difference between sexes. If a negative difference is observed (meaning that women are found to earn less than men, after the expert has controlled statistically for legitimate alternative explanations), the difference is evaluated as to its statistical significance using the *t*-test.[40] The *t*-test uses the *t*-statistic to evaluate the hypothesis that a model parameter takes on a particular value, usually 0.

discrimination" in 2 of 37 statistical comparisons, but suggesting that "2 of 37 amounts to roughly 5% and is hardly indicative of a pattern of discrimination"), *aff'd*, 67 F.3d 972 (D.C. Cir. 1995).

37. *See* International Bhd. of Teamsters v. United States, 431 U.S. 324 (1977) (the Court inferred discrimination from overwhelming statistical evidence by a preponderance of the evidence).

38. Tests are also appropriate when comparing the outcomes of a set of employer decisions with those that would have been obtained had the employer chosen differently from among the available options.

39. *See* David H. Kaye & David A. Freedman, Reference Guide on Statistics § IV.C.5, in this manual.

40. The *t*-test is strictly valid only if a number of important assumptions hold. However, for many regression models, the test is approximately valid if the sample size is sufficiently large. See *infra* the Appendix for a more complete discussion of the assumptions underlying multiple regression.

2. *What Is the Appropriate Level of Statistical Significance?*

In most scientific work, the level of statistical significance required to reject the null hypothesis (i.e., to obtain a statistically significant result) is set conventionally at .05, or 5%.[41] The significance level measures the probability that the null hypothesis will be rejected incorrectly, assuming that the null hypothesis is true. In general, the lower the percentage required for statistical significance, the more difficult it is to reject the null hypothesis; therefore, the lower the probability that one will err in doing so. Although the 5% criterion is typical, reporting of more stringent 1% significance tests or less stringent 10% tests can also provide useful information.

In doing a statistical test, it is useful to compute an observed significance level, or *p*-value. The *p*-value associated with the null hypothesis that a regression coefficient is 0 is the probability that a coefficient of this magnitude or larger could have occurred by chance if the null hypothesis were true. If the *p*-value were less than or equal to 5%, the expert would reject the null hypothesis in favor of the alternative hypothesis; if the *p*-value were greater than 5%, the expert would fail to reject the null hypothesis.[42]

3. *Should Statistical Tests Be One-Tailed or Two-Tailed?*

When the expert evaluates the null hypothesis that a variable of interest has no association with a dependent variable against the alternative hypothesis that there is an association, a two-tailed test, which allows for the effect to be either positive or negative, is usually appropriate. A one-tailed test would usually be applied when the expert believes, perhaps on the basis of other direct evidence presented at trial, that the alternative hypothesis is either positive or negative, but not both. For example, an expert might use a one-tailed test in a patent infringement case if he or she strongly believes that the effect of the alleged infringement on the price of the infringed product was either zero or negative. (The sales of the infringing product competed with the sales of the infringed product, thereby lowering the price.)

41. *See, e.g.*, Palmer v. Shultz, 815 F.2d 84, 92 (D.C. Cir. 1987) ("'the .05 level of significance . . . [is] certainly sufficient to support an inference of discrimination'" (quoting Segar v. Smith, 738 F.2d 1249, 1283 (D.C. Cir. 1984), *cert. denied*, 471 U.S. 1115 (1985))).

42. The use of 1%, 5%, and, sometimes, 10% levels for determining statistical significance remains a subject of debate. One might argue, for example, that when regression analysis is used in a price-fixing antitrust case to test a relatively specific alternative to the null hypothesis (e.g., price-fixing), a somewhat lower level of confidence (a higher level of significance, such as 10%) might be appropriate. Otherwise, when the alternative to the null hypothesis is less specific, such as the rather vague alternative of "effect" (e.g., the price increase is caused by the increased cost of production, increased demand, a sharp increase in advertising, or price-fixing), a high level of confidence (associated with a low significance level, such as 1%) may be appropriate. *See, e.g.*, Vuyanich v. Republic Nat'l Bank, 505 F. Supp. 224, 272 (N.D. Tex. 1980) (noting the "arbitrary nature of the adoption of the 5% level of [statistical] significance" to be required in a legal context).

Because using a one-tailed test produces *p*-values that are one-half the size of *p*-values using a two-tailed test, the choice of a one-tailed test makes it easier for the expert to reject a null hypothesis. Correspondingly, the choice of a two-tailed test makes null hypothesis rejection less likely. Since there is some arbitrariness involved in the choice of an alternative hypothesis, courts should avoid relying solely on sharply defined statistical tests.[43] Reporting the *p*-value or a confidence interval should be encouraged, since it conveys useful information to the court, whether or not a null hypothesis is rejected.

B. Are the Regression Results Robust?

The issue of robustness—whether regression results are sensitive to slight modifications in assumptions (e.g., that the data are measured accurately)—is of vital importance. If the assumptions of the regression model are valid, standard statistical tests can be applied. However, when the assumptions of the model are violated, standard tests can overstate or understate the significance of the results.

The violation of an assumption does not necessarily invalidate a regression analysis, however. In some instances in which the assumptions of multiple regression analysis fail, there are other statistical methods that are appropriate. Consequently, experts should be encouraged to provide additional information that goes to the issue of whether regression assumptions are valid, and if they are not valid, the extent to which the regression results are robust. The following questions highlight some of the more important assumptions of regression analysis.

1. What Evidence Exists That the Explanatory Variable Causes Changes in the Dependent Variable?

In the multiple regression framework, the expert often assumes that changes in explanatory variables affect the dependent variable, but changes in the dependent variable do not affect the explanatory variables—that is, there is no feedback.[44] In making this assumption, the expert draws the conclusion that a correlation between an explanatory variable and the dependent variable is due to the effect of the former on the latter and not vice versa. Were the assumption not valid, spurious correlation might cause the expert and the trier of fact to reach the wrong conclusion.[45]

43. Courts have shown a preference for two-tailed tests. *See, e.g.*, Palmer v. Shultz, 815 F.2d 84, 95–96 (D.C. Cir. 1987) (rejecting the use of one-tailed tests, the court found that because some appellants were claiming overselection for certain jobs, a two-tailed test was more appropriate in Title VII cases). *See also* David H. Kaye & David A. Freedman, Reference Guide on Statistics § IV.C.2, in this manual; Csicseri v. Bowsher, 862 F. Supp. 547, 565 (D.D.C. 1994) (finding that although a one-tailed test is "not without merit," a two-tailed test is preferable).

44. When both effects occur at the same time, this is described as "simultaneity."

45. The assumption of no feedback is especially important in litigation, because it is possible for the defendant (if responsible, for example, for price-fixing or discrimination) to affect the values of the explanatory variables and thus to bias the usual statistical tests that are used in multiple regression.

Figure 1 illustrates this point. In Figure 1(a), the dependent variable, Price, is explained through a multiple regression framework by three explanatory variables, Demand, Cost, and Advertising, with no feedback. In Figure 1(b), there is feedback, since Price affects Demand, and Demand, Cost, and Advertising affect Price. Cost and Advertising, however, are not affected by Price. As a general rule, there is no direct statistical test for determining the direction of causality; rather, the expert, when asked, should be prepared to defend his or her assumption based on an understanding of the underlying behavior of the firms or individuals involved.

Figure 1. Feedback

1(a). No Feedback

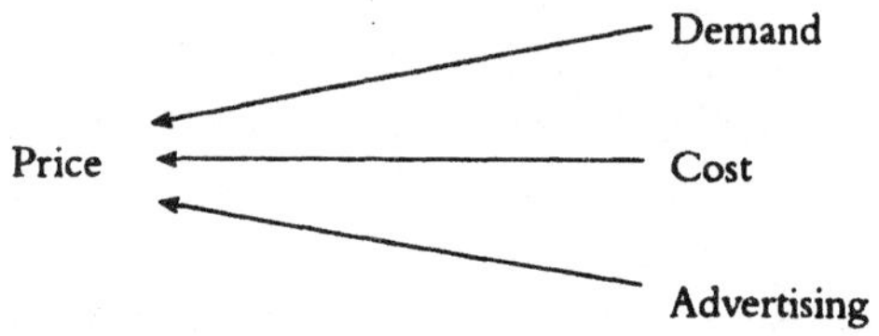

1(b). Feedback

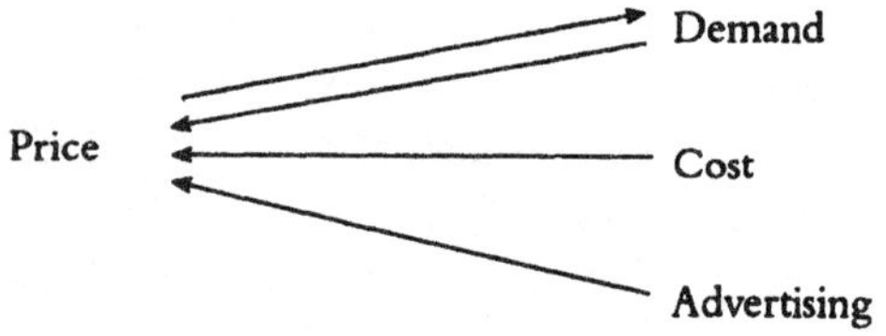

Although there is no single approach that is entirely suitable for estimating models when the dependent variable affects one or more explanatory variables, one possibility is for the expert to drop the questionable variable from the regression to determine whether the variable's exclusion makes a difference. If it does not, the issue becomes moot. Another approach is for the expert to expand the multiple regression model by adding one or more equations that explain the relationship between the explanatory variable in question and the dependent variable.

Suppose, for example, that in a salary-based sex discrimination suit the defendant's expert considers employer-evaluated test scores to be an appropriate explanatory variable for the dependent variable, salary. If the plaintiff were to provide information that the employer adjusted the test scores in a manner that penalized women, the assumption that salaries were determined by test scores and not that test scores were affected by salaries might be invalid. If it is clearly inappropriate, the test-score variable should be removed from consideration. Alternatively, the information about the employer's use of the test scores could be translated into a second equation in which a new dependent variable, test score, is related to workers' salary and sex. A test of the hypothesis that salary and sex affect test scores would provide a suitable test of the absence of feedback.

2. *To What Extent Are the Explanatory Variables Correlated with Each Other?*

It is essential in multiple regression analysis that the explanatory variable of interest not be correlated perfectly with one or more of the other explanatory variables. If there were perfect correlation between two variables, the expert could not separate out the effect of the variable of interest on the dependent variable from the effect of the other variable. Suppose, for example, that in a sex discrimination suit a particular form of job experience is determined to be a valid source of high wages. If all men had the requisite job experience and all women did not, it would be impossible to tell whether wage differentials between men and women were due to sex discrimination or differences in experience.

When two or more explanatory variables are correlated perfectly—that is, when there is perfect collinearity—one cannot estimate the regression parameters. When two or more variables are highly, but not perfectly, correlated—that is, when there is multicollinearity—the regression can be estimated, but some concerns remain. The greater the multicollinearity between two variables, the less precise are the estimates of individual regression parameters (even though there is no problem in estimating the joint influence of the two variables and all other regression parameters).

Fortunately, the reported regression statistics take into account any multicollinearity that might be present.[46] It is important to note as a corollary, however, that a failure to find a strong relationship between a variable of interest and a dependent variable need not imply that there is no relationship.[47] A relatively

46. *See* Denny v. Westfield State College, 669 F. Supp. 1146, 1149 (D. Mass. 1987) (The court accepted the testimony of one expert that "the presence of multicollinearity would merely tend to *overestimate* the amount of error associated with the estimate . . . . In other words, *p*-values will be artificially higher than they would be if there were no multicollinearity present.") (emphasis added).

47. If an explanatory variable of concern and another explanatory variable are highly correlated, dropping the second variable from the regression can be instructive. If the coefficient on the explanatory variable of concern becomes significant, a relationship between the dependent variable and the explanatory variable of concern is suggested.

small sample, or even a large sample with substantial multicollinearity, may not provide sufficient information for the expert to determine whether there is a relationship.

3. To What Extent Are Individual Errors in the Regression Model Independent?

If the expert calculated the parameters of a multiple regression model using as data the entire population, the estimates might still measure the model's population parameters with error. Errors can arise for a number of reasons, including (1) the failure of the model to include the appropriate explanatory variables; (2) the failure of the model to reflect any nonlinearities that might be present; and (3) the inclusion of inappropriate variables in the model. (Of course, further sources of error will arise if a sample, or subset, of the population is used to estimate the regression parameters.)

It is useful to view the cumulative effect of all of these sources of modeling error as being represented by an additional variable, the error term, in the multiple regression model. An important assumption in multiple regression analysis is that the error term and each of the explanatory variables are independent of each other. (If the error term and an explanatory variable are independent, they are not correlated with each other.) To the extent this is true, the expert can estimate the parameters of the model without bias; the magnitude of the error term will affect the precision with which a model parameter is estimated, but will not cause that estimate to be consistently too high or too low.

The assumption of independence may be inappropriate in a number of circumstances. In some instances, failure of the assumption makes multiple regression analysis an unsuitable statistical technique; in other instances, modifications or adjustments within the regression framework can be made to accommodate the failure.

The independence assumption may fail, for example, in a study of individual behavior over time, in which an unusually high error value in one time period is likely to lead to an unusually high value in the next time period. For example, if an economic forecaster underpredicted this year's Gross National Product, he or she is likely to underpredict next year's as well; the factor that caused the prediction error (e.g., an incorrect assumption about Federal Reserve policy) is likely to be a source of error in the future.

Alternatively, the assumption of independence may fail in a study of a group of firms at a particular point in time, in which error terms for large firms are systematically higher than error terms for small firms. For example, an analysis of the profitability of firms may not accurately account for the importance of advertising as a source of increased sales and profits. To the extent that large firms advertise more than small firms, the regression errors would be large for the large firms and small for the small firms.

In some instances, there are statistical tests that are appropriate for evaluating the independence assumption.[48] If the assumption has failed, the expert should ask first whether the source of the lack of independence is the omission of an important explanatory variable from the regression. If so, that variable should be included when possible, or the potential effect of its omission should be estimated when inclusion is not possible. If there is no important missing explanatory variable, the expert should apply one or more procedures that modify the standard multiple regression technique to allow for more accurate estimates of the regression parameters.[49]

4. To What Extent Are the Regression Results Sensitive to Individual Data Points?

Estimated regression coefficients can be highly sensitive to particular data points. Suppose, for example, that one data point deviates greatly from its expected value, as indicated by the regression equation, whereas the remaining data points show little deviation. It would not be unusual in this situation for the coefficients in a multiple regression to change substantially if the data point in question were removed from the sample.

Evaluating the robustness of multiple regression results is a complex endeavor. Consequently, there is no agreed-on set of tests for robustness which analysts should apply. In general, it is important to explore the reasons for unusual data points. If the source is an error in recording data, the appropriate corrections can be made. If all the unusual data points have certain characteristics in common (e.g., they all are associated with a supervisor who consistently gives high ratings in an equal-pay case), the regression model should be modified appropriately.

One generally useful diagnostic technique is to determine to what extent the estimated parameter changes as each data point in the regression analysis is dropped from the sample. An influential data point—a point that causes the estimated parameter to change substantially—should be studied further to determine whether mistakes were made in the use of the data or whether important explanatory variables were omitted.[50]

48. In a time-series analysis, the correlation of error values over time, the serial correlation, can be tested (in most instances) using a Durbin-Watson test. The possibility that some error terms are consistently high in magnitude and others are systematically low, heteroscedasticity, can also be tested in a number of ways. *See, e.g.*, Pindyck & Rubinfeld, *supra* note 31, at 146–59.

49. When serial correlation is present, a number of closely related statistical methods are appropriate, including generalized differencing (a type of generalized least-squares) and maximum-likelihood estimation. When heteroscedasticity is the problem, weighted least-squares and maximum-likelihood estimation are appropriate. *See, e.g.*, *id.* All these techniques are readily available in a number of statistical computer packages. They also allow one to perform the appropriate statistical tests of the significance of the regression coefficients.

50. A more complete and formal treatment of the robustness issue appears in David A. Belsley et al., Regression Diagnostics: Identifying Influential Data and Sources of Collinearity 229–44 (1980). For a

5. To What Extent Are the Data Subject to Measurement Error?

In multiple regression analysis it is assumed that variables are measured accurately.[51] If there are measurement errors in the dependent variable, estimates of regression parameters will be less accurate, though they will not necessarily be biased. However, if one or more independent variables are measured with error, the corresponding parameter estimates are likely to be biased, typically toward zero.[52]

To understand why, suppose that the dependent variable, salary, is measured without error, and the explanatory variable, experience, is subject to measurement error. (Seniority or years of experience should be accurate, but the type of experience is subject to error, since applicants may overstate previous job responsibilities.) As the measurement error increases, the estimated parameter associated with the experience variable will tend toward 0, that is, eventually, there will be no relationship between salary and experience.

It is important for any source of measurement error to be carefully evaluated. In some circumstances, little can be done to correct the measurement-error problem; the regression results must be interpreted in that light. In other circumstances, however, the expert can correct measurement error by finding a new, more reliable data source. Finally, alternative estimation techniques (using related variables that are measured without error) can be applied to remedy the measurement-error problem in some situations.[53]

IV. The Expert

Multiple regression analysis is taught to students in extremely diverse fields, including statistics, economics, political science, sociology, psychology, anthropology, public health, and history. Consequently, any individual with substantial training in and experience with multiple regression and other statistical methods may be qualified as an expert.[54] A doctoral degree in a discipline that teaches theoretical or applied statistics, such as economics, history, and psychology, usu-

useful discussion of the detection of outliers and the evaluation of influential data points, see R.D. Cook & S. Weisberg, *Residuals and Influence in Regression, in* Monographs on Statistics and Applied Probability (1982).

51. Inaccuracy can occur not only in the precision with which a particular variable is measured, but also in the precision with which the variable to be measured corresponds to the appropriate theoretical construct specified by the regression model.

52. Other coefficient estimates are likely to be biased as well.

53. *See, e.g.*, Pindyck & Rubinfeld, *supra* note 31, at 178–98 (discussion of instrumental variables estimation).

54. A proposed expert whose only statistical tool is regression analysis may not be able to judge when a statistical analysis should be based on an approach other than regression analysis.

ally signifies to other scientists that the proposed expert meets this preliminary test of the qualification process.

The decision to qualify an expert in regression analysis rests with the court. Clearly, the proposed expert should be able to demonstrate an understanding of the discipline. Publications relating to regression analysis in peer-reviewed journals, active memberships in related professional organizations, courses taught on regression methods, and practical experience with regression analysis can indicate a professional's expertise. However, the expert's background and experience with the specific issues and tools that are applicable to a particular case should also be considered during the qualification process.

V. Presentation of Statistical Evidence

The costs of evaluating statistical evidence can be reduced and the precision of that evidence increased if the discovery process is used effectively. In evaluating the admissibility of statistical evidence, courts should consider the following issues:[55]

1. Has the expert provided sufficient information to replicate the multiple regression analysis?
2. Are the methodological choices that the expert made reasonable, or are they arbitrary and unjustified?

A. What Disagreements Exist Regarding Data on Which the Analysis Is Based?

In general, a clear and comprehensive statement of the underlying research methodology is a requisite part of the discovery process. The expert should be encouraged to reveal both the nature of the experimentation carried out and the sensitivity of the results to the data and to the methodology. The following suggestions are useful requirements that can substantially improve the discovery process.

1. To the extent possible, the parties should be encouraged to agree to use a common database. Even if disagreement about the significance of the data remains, early agreement on a common database can help focus the discovery process on the important issues in the case.
2. A party that offers data to be used in statistical work, including multiple regression analysis, should be encouraged to provide the following to the other parties: (a) a hard copy of the data when available and manageable in size, along with the underlying sources; (b) computer disks or tapes on

55. *See also* David H. Kaye & David A. Freedman, Reference Guide on Statistics § I.C, in this manual.

which the data are recorded; (c) complete documentation of the disks or tapes; (d) computer programs that were used to generate the data (in hard copy, on a computer disk or tape, or both); and (e) documentation of such computer programs.

3. A party offering data should make available the personnel involved in the compilation of such data to answer the other parties' technical questions concerning the data and the methods of collection or compilation.
4. A party proposing to offer an expert's regression analysis at trial should ask the expert to fully disclose: (a) the database and its sources;[56] (b) the method of collecting the data; and (c) the methods of analysis. When possible, this disclosure should be made sufficiently in advance of trial so that the opposing party can consult its experts and prepare cross-examination. The court must decide on a case-by-case basis where to draw the disclosure line.
5. An opposing party should be given the opportunity to object to a database or to a proposed method of analysis of the database to be offered at trial. Objections may be to simple clerical errors or to more complex issues relating to the selection of data, the construction of variables, and, on occasion, the particular form of statistical analysis to be used. Whenever possible, these objections should be resolved before trial.
6. The parties should be encouraged to resolve differences as to the appropriateness and precision of the data to the extent possible by informal conference. The court should make an effort to resolve differences before trial.

B. *What Database Information and Analytical Procedures Will Aid in Resolving Disputes over Statistical Studies?*[57]

The following are suggested guidelines that experts should follow in presenting database information and analytical procedures. Following these guidelines can be helpful in resolving disputes over statistical studies.

1. The expert should state clearly the objectives of the study, as well as the time frame to which it applies and the statistical population to which the results are being projected.
2. The expert should report the units of observation (e.g., consumers, businesses, or employees).

56. These sources would include all variables used in the statistical analyses conducted by the expert, not simply those variables used in a final analysis on which the expert expects to rely.

57. For a more complete discussion of these requirements, see The Evolving Role of Statistical Assessments as Evidence in the Courts app. F at 256 (Stephen E. Fienberg ed., 1989) (Recommended Standards on Disclosure of Procedures Used for Statistical Studies to Collect Data Submitted in Evidence in Legal Cases).

3. The expert should clearly define each variable.
4. The expert should clearly identify the sample for which data are being studied,[58] as well as the method by which the sample was obtained.
5. The expert should reveal if there are missing data, whether caused by a lack of availability (e.g., in business data) or nonresponse (e.g., in survey data), and the method used to handle the missing data (e.g., deletion of observations).
6. The expert should report investigations that were made into errors associated with the choice of variables and assumptions underlying the regression model.
7. If samples were chosen randomly from a population (i.e., probability sampling procedures were used),[59] the expert should make a good-faith effort to provide an estimate of a sampling error, the measure of the difference between the sample estimate of a parameter (such as the mean of a dependent variable under study) and the (unknown) population parameter (the population mean of the variable).[60]
8. If probability sampling procedures were not used, the expert should report the set of procedures that were used to minimize sampling errors.

58. The sample information is important because it allows the expert to make inferences about the underlying population.

59. In probability sampling, each representative of the population has a known probability of being in the sample. Probability sampling is ideal because it is highly structured, and in principle, it can be replicated by others. Nonprobability sampling is less desirable because it is often subjective, relying to a large extent on the judgment of the expert.

60. Sampling error is often reported in terms of standard errors or confidence intervals. See *infra* the Appendix for details.

Appendix: The Basics of Multiple Regression

I. Introduction

This appendix illustrates, through examples, the basics of multiple regression analysis in legal proceedings. Often, visual displays are used to describe the relationship between variables that are used in multiple regression analysis. Figure 2 is a scatterplot that relates scores on a job aptitude test (shown on the x-axis) and job performance ratings (shown on the y-axis). Each point on the scatterplot shows where a particular individual scored on the job aptitude test and how his or her job performance was rated. For example, the individual represented by Point A in Figure 2 scored 49 on the job aptitude test and had a job performance rating of 62.

Figure 2. Scatterplot

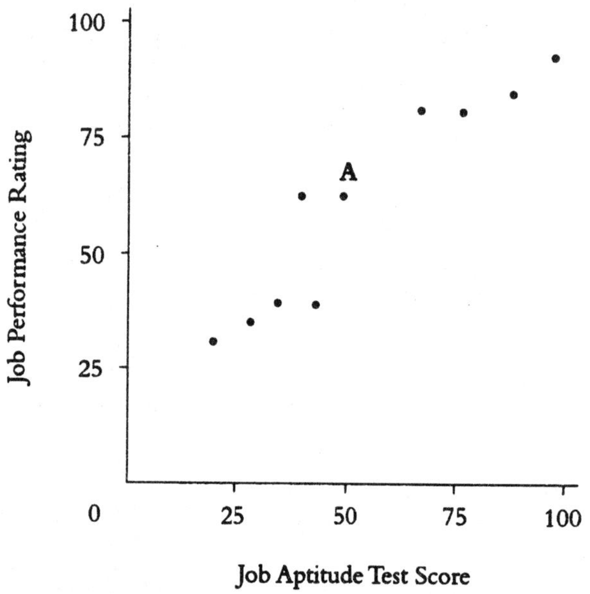

The relationship between two variables can be summarized by a correlation coefficient, which ranges in value from −1 (a perfect negative relationship) to +1 (a perfect positive relationship). Figure 3 depicts three possible relationships between the job aptitude variable and the job performance variable. In Figure 3(a), there is a positive correlation: In general, higher job performance ratings are associated with higher aptitude test scores, and lower job performance ratings are associated with lower aptitude test scores. In Figure 3(b), the correlation is negative: Higher job performance ratings are associated with lower aptitude test scores, and lower job performance ratings are associated with higher aptitude test scores. Positive and negative correlations can be relatively strong or relatively weak. If the relationship is sufficiently weak, there is effectively no correlation, as is illustrated in Figure 3(c).

Figure 3. Correlation

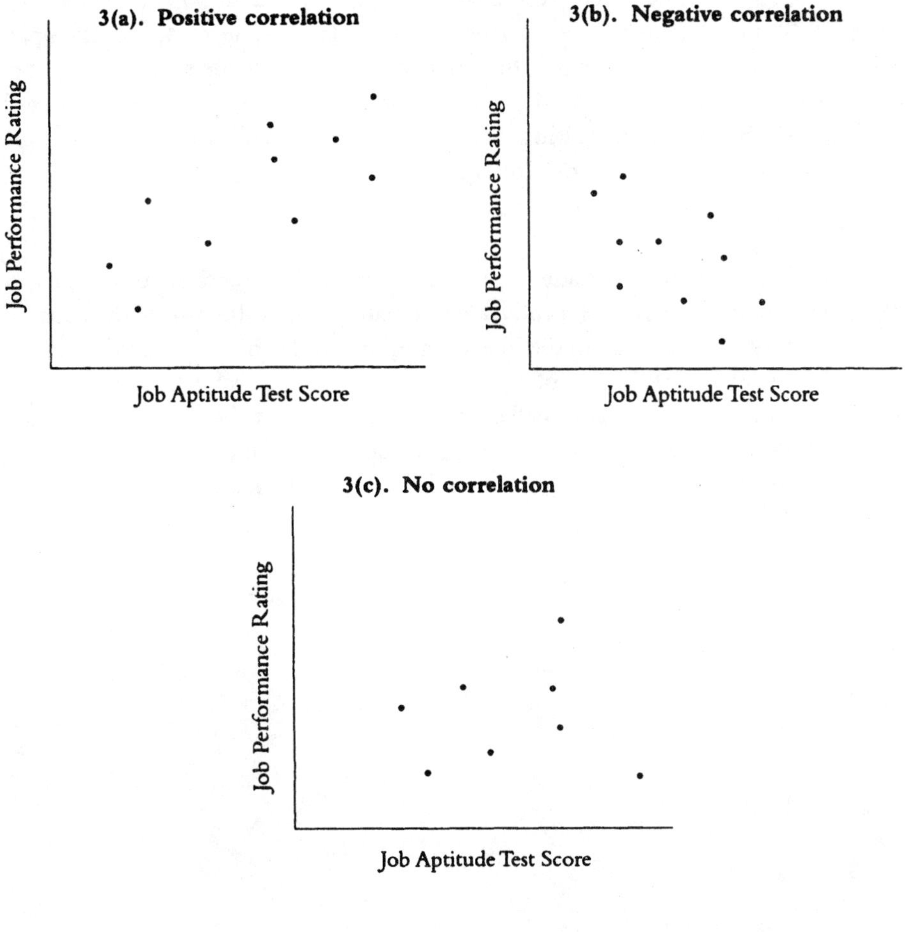

Multiple regression analysis goes beyond the calculation of correlations; it is a method in which a regression line is used to relate the average of one variable—the dependent variable—to the values of other explanatory variables. As a result, regression analysis can be used to predict the values of one variable using the values of others. For example, if average job performance ratings depend on aptitude test scores, regression analysis can use information about test scores to predict job performance.

A regression line is the best-fitting straight line through a set of points in a scatterplot. If there is only one explanatory variable, the straight line is defined by the equation

$$Y = a + bX \tag{1}$$

In the equation above, *a* is the intercept of the line with the *y*-axis when *X* equals 0, and *b* is the slope—the change in the dependent variable associated with a 1-unit change in the explanatory variable. In Figure 4, for example, when the aptitude test score is 0, the predicted (average) value of the job performance rating is the intercept, 18.4. Also, for each additional point on the test score, the job performance rating increases .73 units, which is given by the slope .73. Thus, the estimated regression line is

$$Y = 18.4 + .73X \tag{2}$$

The regression line typically is estimated using the standard method of least-squares, where the values of *a* and *b* are calculated so that the sum of the squared deviations of the points from the line are minimized. In this way, positive deviations and negative deviations of equal size are counted equally, and large deviations are counted more than small deviations. In Figure 4 the deviation lines are vertical because the equation is predicting job performance ratings from aptitude test scores, not aptitude test scores from job performance ratings.

Figure 4. Regression Line

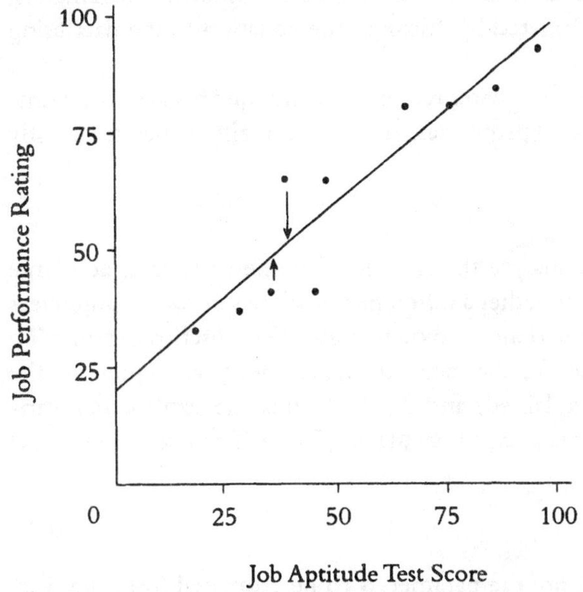

The important variables that systematically might influence the dependent variable, and for which data can be obtained, typically should be included explicitly in a statistical model. All remaining influences, which should be small individually, but can be substantial in the aggregate, are included in an additional random error term.[61] Multiple regression is a procedure that separates the systematic effects (associated with the explanatory variables) from the random effects (associated with the error term) and also offers a method of assessing the success of the process.

II. Linear Regression Model

When there is an arbitrary number of explanatory variables, the linear regression model takes the following form:

$$Y = \beta_0 + \beta_1 X_1 + \beta_2 X_2 + \ldots + \beta_k X_k + \varepsilon \qquad (3)$$

where Y represents the dependent variable, such as the salary of an employee, and $X_1 \ldots X_k$ represent the explanatory variables (e.g., the experience of each

61. It is clearly advantageous for the random component of the regression relationship to be small relative to the variation in the dependent variable.

employee and his or her sex, coded as a 1 or 0, respectively). The error term, ε, represents the collective unobservable influence of any omitted variables. In a linear regression, each of the terms being added involves unknown parameters, $\beta_0, \beta_1, \ldots \beta_k$,[62] which are estimated by "fitting" the equation to the data using least-squares.

Most statisticians use the least-squares regression technique because of its simplicity and its desirable statistical properties. As a result, it also is used frequently in legal proceedings.

A. An Example

Suppose an expert wants to analyze the salaries of women and men at a large publishing house to discover whether a difference in salaries between employees with similar years of work experience provides evidence of discrimination.[63] To begin with the simplest case, Y, the salary in dollars per year, represents the dependent variable to be explained, and X_1 represents the explanatory variable—the number of years of experience of the employee. The regression model would be written

$$Y = \beta_0 + \beta_1 X_1 + \varepsilon \qquad (4)$$

In equation (4), β_0 and β_1 are the parameters to be estimated from the data, and ε is the random error term. The parameter β_0 is the average salary of all employees with no experience. The parameter β_1 measures the average effect of an additional year of experience on the average salary of employees.

B. Regression Line

Once the parameters in a regression equation, such as equation (3), have been estimated, the fitted values for the dependent variable can be calculated. If we denote the estimated regression parameters, or regression coefficients, for the model in equation (3) by $b_0, b_1, \ldots b_k$, the fitted values for Y, denoted $\hat{Y}$, are given by

$$\hat{Y} = b_0 + b_1 X_1 + b_2 X_2 + \ldots b_k X_k \qquad (5)$$

62. The variables themselves can appear in many different forms. For example, Y might represent the logarithm of an employee's salary, and X_1 might represent the logarithm of the employee's years of experience. The logarithmic representation is appropriate when Y increases exponentially as X increases—for each unit increase in X, the corresponding increase in Y becomes larger and larger. For example, if an expert were to graph the growth of the U.S. population (Y) over time (t), an equation of the form $\log(Y) = \beta_0 + \beta_1 \log(t)$ might be appropriate.

63. The regression results used in this example are based on data for 1,715 men and women, which were used by the defense in a sex discrimination case against the *New York Times* that was settled in 1978. Professor Orley Ashenfelter, of the Department of Economics, Princeton University, provided the data.

Figure 5 illustrates this for the example involving a single explanatory variable. The data are shown as a scatter of points; salary is on the vertical axis, and years of experience is on the horizontal axis. The estimated regression line is drawn through the data points. It is given by

$$\hat{Y} = \$15{,}000 + \$2{,}000X_1 \quad (6)$$

Thus, the fitted value for the salary associated with an individual's years of experience X_{1i} is given by

$$\hat{Y}_i = b_0 + b_1X_{1i} \text{ (at Point B).} \quad (7)$$

The intercept of the straight line is the average value of the dependent variable when the explanatory variable or variables are equal to 0; the intercept b_0 is shown on the vertical axis in Figure 5. Similarly, the slope of the line measures the (average) change in the dependent variable associated with a unit increase in an explanatory variable; the slope b_1 also is shown. In equation (6), the intercept \$15,000 indicates that employees with no experience earn \$15,000 per year. The slope parameter implies that each year of experience adds \$2,000 to an "average" employee's salary.

Figure 5. Goodness-of-Fit

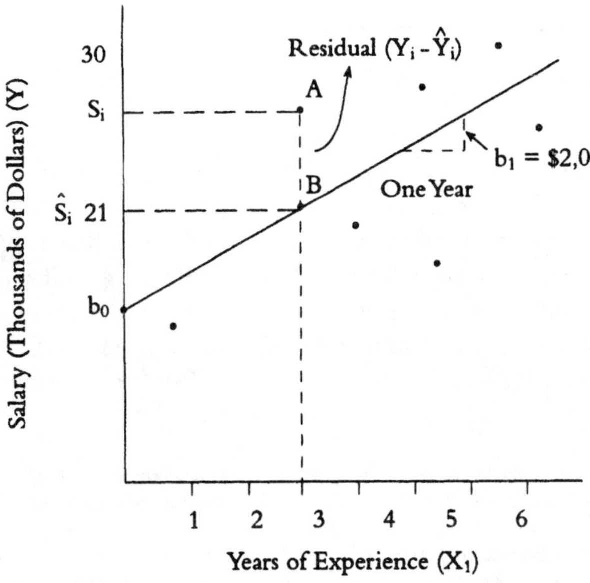

Now, suppose that the salary variable is related simply to the sex of the employee. The relevant indicator variable, often called a dummy variable, is X_2, which is equal to 1 if the employee is male, and 0 if the employee is female. Suppose the regression of salary Y on X_2 yields the following result: Y = \$30,449 + \$10,979X_2. The coefficient \$10,979 measures the difference between the average salary of men and the average salary of women.[64]

1. Regression Residuals

For each data point, the regression residual is the difference between the actual values and fitted values of the dependent variable. Suppose, for example, that we are studying an individual with three years of experience and a salary of \$27,000. According to the regression line in Figure 5, the average salary of an individual with three years of experience is \$21,000. Since the individual's salary is \$6,000 higher than the average salary, the residual (the individual's salary minus the average salary) is \$6,000. In general, the residual *e* associated with a data point, such as Point A in Figure 5, is given by $e = Y_i - \hat{Y}_i$. Each data point in the figure has a residual, which is the error made by the least-squares regression method for that individual.

2. Nonlinearities

Nonlinear models account for the possibility that the effect of an explanatory variable on the dependent variable may vary in magnitude as the level of the explanatory variable changes. One useful nonlinear model uses interactions among variables to produce this effect. For example, suppose that

$$S = \beta_1 + \beta_2\text{SEX} + \beta_3\text{EXP} + \beta_4(\text{EXP})(\text{SEX}) + \varepsilon \qquad (8)$$

where *S* is annual salary, SEX is equal to 1 for women and 0 for men, EXP represents years of job experience, and ε is a random error term. The coefficient β_2 measures the difference in average salary (across all experience levels) between men and women for employees with no experience. The coefficient β_3 measures the effect of experience on salary for men (when SEX = 0), and the coefficient β_4 measures the difference in the effect of experience on salary between men and women. It follows, for example, that the effect of one year of experience on salary for men is β_3, whereas the comparable effect for women is $\beta_3 + \beta_4$.[65]

64. To understand why, note that when X_2 equals 0, the average salary for women is \$30,449 + \$10,979 × 0 = \$30,449. Correspondingly, when X_2 equals 1, the average salary for men is \$30,449 + \$10,979 × 1 = \$41,428. The difference, \$41,428 – \$30,449, is \$10,979.

65. Estimating a regression in which there are interaction terms for all explanatory variables, as in equation (8), is essentially the same as estimating two separate regressions, one for men and one for women.

III. Interpreting Regression Results

To explain how regression results are interpreted, we can expand the earlier example associated with Figure 5 to consider the possibility of an additional explanatory variable—the square of the number of years of experience, X_3. The X_3 variable is designed to capture the fact that for most individuals, salaries increase with experience, but eventually salaries tend to level off. The estimated regression line using the third additional explanatory variable, as well as the first explanatory variable for years of experience (X_1) and the dummy variable for sex (X_2), is

$$\hat{Y} = \$14{,}085 + \$2{,}323X_1 + \$1{,}675X_2 - \$36X_3 \qquad (9)$$

The importance of including relevant explanatory variables in a regression model is illustrated by the change in the regression results after the X_3 and X_1 variables are added. The coefficient on the variable X_2 measures the difference in the salaries of men and women while holding the effect of experience constant. The differential of \$1,675 is substantially lower than the previously measured differential of \$10,979. Clearly, failure to control for job experience in this example leads to an overstatement of the difference in salaries between men and women.

Now consider the interpretation of the explanatory variables for experience, X_1 and X_3. The positive sign on the X_1 coefficient shows that salary increases with experience. The negative sign on the X_3 coefficient indicates that the rate of salary increase decreases with experience. To determine the combined effect of the variables X_1 and X_3, some simple calculations can be made. For example, consider how the average salary of women ($X_2 = 0$) changes with the level of experience. As experience increases from 0 to 1 year, the average salary increases by \$2,251, from \$14,085 to \$16,336. However, women with 2 years of experience earn only \$2,179 more than women with 1 year of experience, and women with 3 years of experience earn only \$2,127 more than women with 2 years. Furthermore, women with 7 years of experience earn \$28,582 per year, which is only \$1,855 more than the \$26,727 earned by women with 6 years of experience.[66] Figure 6 illustrates the results; the regression line shown is for women's salaries; the corresponding line for men's salaries would be parallel and \$1,675 higher.

66. These numbers can be calculated by substituting different values of X_1 and X_3 in equation (9).

Figure 6. Regression Slope

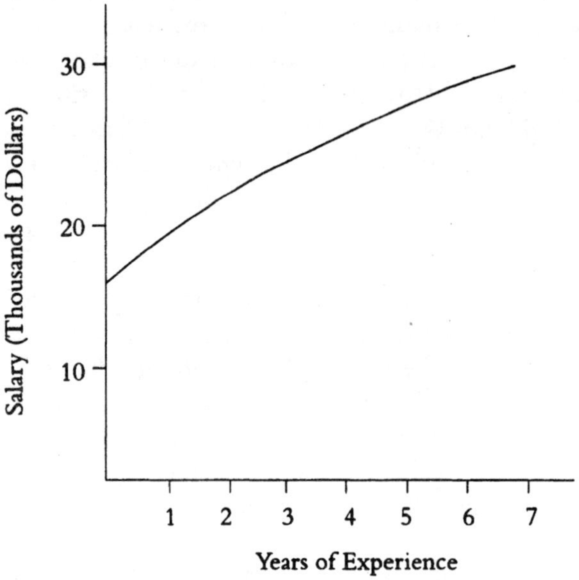

IV. Determining the Precision of the Regression Results

Least-squares regression provides not only parameter estimates that indicate the direction and magnitude of the effect of a change in the explanatory variable on the dependent variable, but also an estimate of the reliability of the parameter estimates and a measure of the overall goodness-of-fit of the regression model. Each of these factors is considered in turn.

A. Standard Errors of the Coefficients and t-*Statistics*

Estimates of the true but unknown parameters of a regression model are numbers that depend on the particular sample of observations under study. If a different sample were used, a different estimate would be calculated.[67] If the expert continued to collect more and more samples and generated additional estimates, as might happen when new data became available over time, the estimates of each parameter would follow a probability distribution (i.e., the expert could determine the percentage or frequency of the time that each estimate occurs). This probability distribution can be summarized by a mean and a measure of

67. The least-squares formula that generates the estimates is called the least-squares estimator, and its values vary from sample to sample.

dispersion around the mean, a standard deviation, which usually is referred to as the standard error of the coefficient, or the standard error (SE).[68]

Suppose, for example, that an expert is interested in estimating the average price paid for a gallon of unleaded gasoline by consumers in a particular geographic area of the United States at a particular point in time. The mean price for a sample of ten gas stations might be $1.25, while the mean for another sample might be $1.29, and the mean for a third, $1.21. On this basis, the expert also could calculate the overall mean price of gasoline to be $1.25 and the standard deviation to be $0.04.

Least-squares regression generalizes this result, by calculating means whose values depend on one or more explanatory variables. The standard error of a regression coefficient tells the expert how much parameter estimates are likely to vary from sample to sample. The greater the variation in parameter estimates from sample to sample, the larger the standard error and consequently the less reliable the regression results. Small standard errors imply results that are likely to be similar from sample to sample, whereas results with large standard errors show more variability.

Under appropriate assumptions, the least-squares estimators provide "best" determinations of the true underlying parameters.[69] In fact, least-squares has several desirable properties. First, least-squares estimators are unbiased. Intuitively, this means that if the regression were calculated over and over again with different samples, the average of the many estimates obtained for each coefficient would be the true parameter. Second, least-squares estimators are consistent; if the sample were very large, the estimates obtained would come close to the true parameters. Third, least-squares is efficient, in that its estimators have the smallest variance among all (linear) unbiased estimators.

If the further assumption is made that the probability distribution of each of the error terms is known, statistical statements can be made about the precision of the coefficient estimates. For relatively large samples (often, thirty or more data points will be sufficient for regressions with a small number of explanatory variables), the probability that the estimate of a parameter lies within an interval of 2 standard errors around the true parameter is approximately .95, or 95%. A frequent, although not always appropriate, assumption in statistical work is that the error term follows a normal distribution, from which it follows that the estimated parameters are normally distributed. The normal distribution has the

68. *See* David H. Kaye & David A. Freedman, Reference Guide on Statistics § IV.A, in this manual.

69. The necessary assumptions of the regression model include (a) the model is specified correctly; (b) errors associated with each observation are drawn randomly from the same probability distribution and are independent of each other; (c) errors associated with each observation are independent of the corresponding observations for each of the explanatory variables in the model; and (d) no explanatory variable is correlated perfectly with a combination of other variables.

property that the area within 1.96 standard errors of the mean is equal to 95% of the total area. Note that the normality assumption is not necessary for least-squares to be used, since most of the properties of least-squares apply regardless of normality.

In general, for any parameter estimate b, the expert can construct an interval around b such that there is a 95% probability that the interval covers the true parameter. This 95% confidence interval[70] is given by

$$b \pm 1.96 \times (\text{SE of } b) \qquad (10)^{71}$$

The expert can test the hypothesis that a parameter is actually equal to 0 (often stated as testing the null hypothesis) by looking at its t-statistic, which is defined as

$$t = \frac{b}{\text{SE}(b)} \qquad (11)$$

If the t-statistic is less than 1.96 in magnitude, the 95% confidence interval around b must include 0.[72] Because this means that the expert cannot reject the hypothesis that β equals 0, the estimate, whatever it may be, is said to be not statistically significant. Conversely, if the t-statistic is greater than 1.96 in absolute value, the expert concludes that the true value of β is unlikely to be 0 (intuitively, b is "too far" from 0 to be consistent with the true value of β being 0). In this case, the expert rejects the hypothesis that β equals 0 and calls the estimate statistically significant. If the null hypothesis β equals 0 is true, using a 95% confidence level will cause the expert to falsely reject the null hypothesis 5% of the time. Consequently, results often are said to be significant at the 5% level.[73]

As an example, consider a more complete set of regression results associated with the salary regression described in equation (9):

$$\begin{array}{lllll} \hat{Y} = & \$14{,}085 + & \$2{,}323X_1 + & \$1{,}675X_2 - & \$36X_3 \\ & (1{,}577) & (140) & (1{,}435) & (3.4) \\ t = & 8.9 & 16.5 & 1.2 & -10.8 \end{array} \qquad (12)$$

The standard error of each estimated parameter is given in parentheses directly

70. Confidence intervals are used commonly in statistical analyses because the expert can never be certain that a parameter estimate is equal to the true population parameter.

71. If the number of data points in the sample is small, the standard error must be multiplied by a number larger than 1.96.

72. The t-statistic applies to any sample size. As the sample gets large, the underlying distribution, which is the source of the t-statistic (the student's t distribution), approximates the normal distribution.

73. A t-statistic of 2.57 in magnitude or greater is associated with a 99% confidence level, or a 1% level of significance, that includes a band of 2.57 standard deviations on either side of the estimated coefficient.

below the parameter, and the corresponding *t*-statistics appear below the standard error values.

Consider the coefficient on the dummy variable X_2. It indicates that $1,675 is the best estimate of the mean salary difference between men and women. However, the standard error of $1,435 is large in relation to its coefficient $1,675. Because the standard error is relatively large, the range of possible values for measuring the true salary difference, the true parameter, is great. In fact, a 95% confidence interval is given by

$$\$1{,}675 \pm 1{,}435 \times 1.96 = \$1{,}675 \pm \$2{,}813 \qquad (13)$$

In other words, the expert can have 95% confidence that the true value of the coefficient lies between –$1,138 and $4,488. Because this range includes 0, the effect of sex on salary is said to be insignificantly different from 0 at the 5% level. The *t* value of 1.2 is equal to $1,675 divided by $1,435. Because this *t*-statistic is less than 1.96 in magnitude (a condition equivalent to the inclusion of a 0 in the above confidence interval), the sex variable again is said to be an insignificant determinant of salary at the 5% level of significance.

Note also that experience is a highly significant determinant of salary, since both the X_1 and the X_3 variables have *t*-statistics substantially greater than 1.96 in magnitude. More experience has a significant positive effect on salary, but the size of this effect diminishes significantly with experience.

B. Goodness-of-Fit

Reported regression results usually contain not only the point estimates of the parameters and their standard errors or *t*-statistics, but also other information that tells how closely the regression line fits the data. One statistic, the standard error of the regression (SER), is an estimate of the overall size of the regression residuals.[74] An SER of 0 would occur only when all data points lie exactly on the regression line—an extremely unlikely possibility. Other things being equal, the larger the SER, the poorer the fit of the data to the model.

For a normally distributed error term, the expert would expect approximately 95% of the data points to lie within 2 SERs of the estimated regression line, as shown in Figure 7 (in Figure 7, the SER is approximately $5,000).

R-square (R^2) is a statistic that measures the percentage of variation in the dependent variable that is accounted for by all the explanatory variables.[75] Thus, R^2 provides a measure of the overall goodness-of-fit of the multiple regression equation.[76] Its value ranges from 0 to 1. An R^2 of 0 means that the explanatory

74. More specifically, it is a measure of the standard deviation of the regression error *e*. It sometimes is called the root mean square error of the regression line.

75. The variation is the square of the difference between each Y value and the average Y value, summed over all the Y values.

76. R^2 and SER provide similar information, because R^2 is approximately equal to $1 - SER^2$/Variance of Y.

variables explain none of the variation of the dependent variable; an R^2 of 1 means that the explanatory variables explain all of the variation. The R^2 associated with equation (12) is .56. This implies that the three explanatory variables explain 56% of the variation in salaries.

Figure 7. Standard Error of the Regression

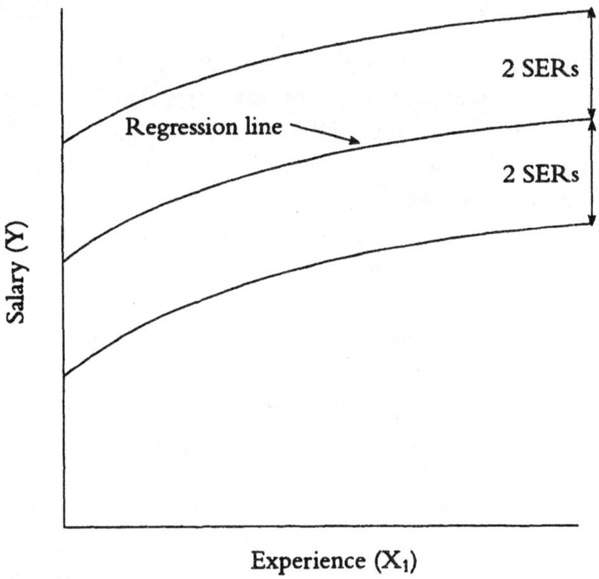

What level of R^2, if any, should lead to a conclusion that the model is satisfactory? Unfortunately, there is no clear-cut answer to this question, since the magnitude of R^2 depends on the characteristics of the data being studied and, in particular, whether the data vary over time or over individuals. Typically, an R^2 is low in cross-section studies in which differences in individual behavior are explained. It is likely that these individual differences are caused by many factors that cannot be measured. As a result, the expert cannot hope to explain most of the variation. In time-series studies, in contrast, the expert is explaining the movement of aggregates over time. Since most aggregate time series have substantial growth, or trend, in common, it will not be difficult to "explain" one time series using another time series, simply because both are moving together. It follows as a corollary that a high R^2 does not by itself mean that the variables included in the model are the appropriate ones.

As a general rule, courts should be reluctant to rely solely on a statistic such as

R^2 to choose one model over another. Alternative procedures and tests are available.[77]

C. Sensitivity of Least-Squares Regression Results

The least-squares regression line can be sensitive to extreme data points. This sensitivity can be seen most easily in Figure 8. Assume initially that there are only three data points, A, B, and C, relating information about X_1 to the variable Y. The least-squares line describing the best-fitting relationship between Points A, B, and C is represented by Line 1. Point D is called an outlier because it lies far from the regression line that fits the remaining points. When a new, best-fitting least-squares line is reestimated to include Point D, Line 2 is obtained. Figure 8 shows that the outlier Point D is an influential data point, since it has a dominant effect on the slope and intercept of the least-squares line. Because least squares attempts to minimize the sum of squared deviations, the sensitivity of the line to individual points sometimes can be substantial.[78]

Figure 8. Least-Squares Regression

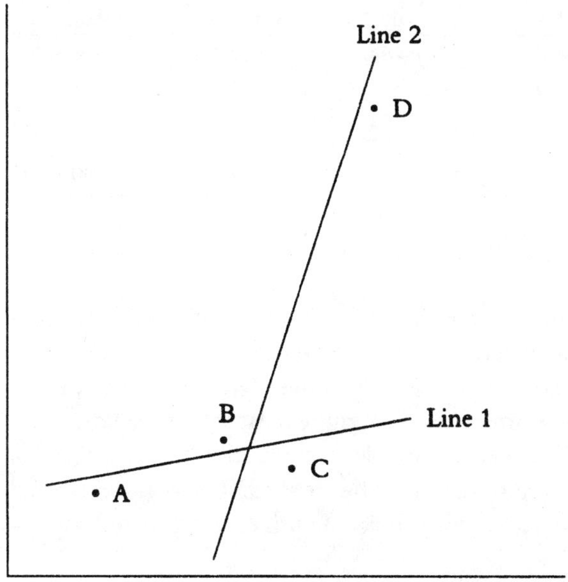

77. These include *F*-tests and specification error tests. *See* Pindyck & Rubinfeld, *supra* note 31, at 88–95, 128–36, 194–98.

78. This sensitivity is not always undesirable. In some instances it may be much more important to predict Point D when a big change occurs than to measure the effects of small changes accurately.

What makes the influential data problem even more difficult is that the effect of an outlier may not be seen readily if deviations are measured from the final regression line. The reason is that the influence of Point D on Line 2 is so substantial that its deviation from the regression line is not necessarily larger than the deviation of any of the remaining points from the regression line.[79] Although they are not as popular as least-squares, alternative estimation techniques that are less sensitive to outliers, such as robust estimation, are available.

V. Reading Multiple Regression Computer Output

Statistical computer packages that report multiple regression analyses vary to some extent in the information they provide and the form that the information takes. Table 1 contains a sample of the basic computer output that is associated with equation (9).

Table 1. Regression Output

Dependent Variable: Y		SSE DFE MSE	62346266124 561 111134164	*F* Test Prob > *F* R^2	174.71 0.0001 0.556
Variable	DF	Parameter Estimate	Standard Error	*t*-stat	Prob > |*t*|
Intercept	1	14084.89	1577.484	8.9287	.0001
X_1	1	2323.17	140.70	16.5115	.0001
X_2	1	1675.11	1435.422	1.1670	.2437
X_3	1	-36.71	3.41	-10.7573	.0001

Note: SSE = sum of squared errors; DFE = degrees of freedom associated with the error term; MSE = mean square error; DF = degrees of freedom; *t*-stat = *t*-statistic; Prob = probability.

In the lower portion of Table 1, note that the parameter estimates, the standard errors, and the *t*-statistics match the values given in equation (12).[80] The variable "Intercept" refers to the constant term b_0 in the regression. The column "DF" represents degrees of freedom. The "1" signifies that when the computer calculates the parameter estimates, each variable that is added to the linear regression adds an additional constraint that must be satisfied. The column labeled "Prob > |*t*|" lists the two-tailed *p*-values associated with each estimated param-

79. The importance of an outlier also depends on its location in the data set. Outliers associated with relatively extreme values of explanatory variables are likely to be especially influential. *See, e.g.*, Fisher v. Vassar College, 70 F.3d 1420, 1436 (2d Cir. 1995) (court required to include assessment of "service in academic community," since concept was too amorphous and not a significant factor in tenure review), *rev'd on other grounds*, 114 F.3d 1332 (2d Cir. 1997) (en banc).

80. Computer programs give results to more decimal places than are meaningful. This added detail should not be seen as evidence that the regression results are exact.

eter; the *p*-value measures the observed significance level—the probability of getting a test statistic as extreme or more extreme than the observed number if the model parameter is in fact 0. The very low *p*-values on the variables X_1 and X_3 imply that each variable is statistically significant at less than the 1% level—both highly significant results. In contrast, the X_2 coefficient is only significant at the 24% level, implying that it is insignificant at the traditional 5% level. Thus, the expert cannot reject with confidence the null hypothesis that salaries do not differ by sex after the expert has accounted for the effect of experience.

The top portion of Table 1 provides data that relate to the goodness-of-fit of the regression equation. The sum of squared errors (SSE) measures the sum of the squares of the regression residuals—the sum that is minimized by the least-squares procedure. The degrees of freedom associated with the error term (DFE) is given by the number of observations minus the number of parameters that were estimated. The mean square error (MSE) measures the variance of the error term (the square of the standard error of the regression). MSE is equal to SSE divided by DFE.

The R^2 of 0.556 indicates that 55.6% of the variation in salaries is explained by the regression variables, X_1, X_2, and X_3. Finally, the *F*-test is a test of the null hypothesis that all regression coefficients (except the intercept) are jointly equal to 0—that there is no association between the dependent variable and any of the explanatory variables. This is equivalent to the null hypothesis that R^2 is equal to 0. In this case, the *F*-ratio of 174.71 is sufficiently high that the expert can reject the null hypothesis with a very high degree of confidence (i.e., with a 1% level of significance).

VI. Forecasting

In general, a forecast is a prediction made about the values of the dependent variable using information about the explanatory variables. Often, ex ante forecasts are performed; in this situation, values of the dependent variable are predicted beyond the sample (e.g., beyond the time period in which the model has been estimated). However, ex post forecasts are frequently used in damage analyses.[81] An ex post forecast has a forecast period such that all values of the dependent and explanatory variables are known; ex post forecasts can be checked against existing data and provide a direct means of evaluation.

For example, to calculate the forecast for the salary regression discussed above, the expert uses the estimated salary equation

$$\hat{Y} = \$14{,}085 + \$2{,}323X_1 + \$1{,}675X_2 - \$36X_3 \qquad (14)$$

81. Frequently, in cases involving damages, the question arises, what the world would have been like had a certain event not taken place. For example, in a price-fixing antitrust case, the expert can ask

To predict the salary of a man with two years' experience, the expert calculates

$$\hat{Y}(2) = \$14{,}085 + (\$2{,}323 \times 2) + \$1{,}675 - (\$36 \times 2^2) = \$20{,}262 \qquad (15)$$

The degree of accuracy of both ex ante and ex post forecasts can be calculated provided that the model specification is correct and the errors are normally distributed and independent. The statistic is known as the standard error of forecast (SEF). The SEF measures the standard deviation of the forecast error that is made within a sample in which the explanatory variables are known with certainty.[82] The SEF can be used to determine how accurate a given forecast is. In equation (15), the SEF associated with the forecast of $20,262 is approximately $5,000. If a large sample size is used, the probability is roughly 95% that the predicted salary will be within 1.96 standard errors of the forecasted value. In this case, the appropriate 95% interval for the prediction is $10,822 to $30,422. Because the estimated model does not explain salaries effectively, the SEF is large, as is the 95% interval. A more complete model with additional explanatory variables would result in a lower SEF and a smaller 95% interval for the prediction.

There is a danger when using the SEF, which applies to the standard errors of the estimated coefficients as well. The SEF is calculated on the assumption that the model includes the correct set of explanatory variables and the correct functional form. If the choice of variables or the functional form is wrong, the estimated forecast error may be misleading. In some instances, it may be smaller, perhaps substantially smaller, than the true SEF; in other instances, it may be larger, for example, if the wrong variables happen to capture the effects of the correct variables.

The difference between the SEF and the SER is shown in Figure 9. The SER measures deviations within the sample. The SEF is more general, since it calculates deviations within or without the sample period. In general, the difference between the SEF and the SER increases as the values of the explanatory variables increase in distance from the mean values. Figure 9 shows the 95% prediction interval created by the measurement of 2 SEFs about the regression line.

what the price of a product would have been had a certain event associated with the price-fixing agreement not occurred. If prices would have been lower, the evidence suggests impact. If the expert can predict how much lower they would have been, the data can help the expert develop a numerical estimate of the amount of damages.

82. There are actually two sources of error implicit in the SEF. The first source arises because the estimated parameters of the regression model may not be exactly equal to the true regression parameters. The second source is the error term itself; when forecasting, the expert typically sets the error equal to 0 when a turn of events not taken into account in the regression model may make it appropriate to make the error positive or negative.

Figure 9. Standard Error of Forecast

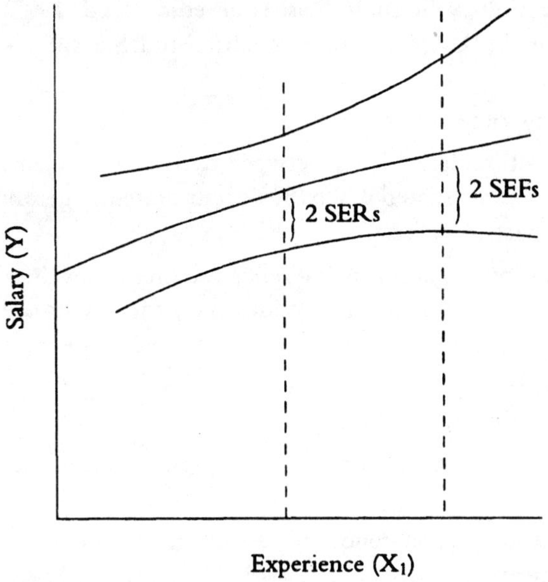

Glossary of Terms

The following terms and definitions are adapted from a variety of sources, including A Dictionary of Epidemiology (John M. Last et al. eds., 3d ed. 1995) and Robert S. Pindyck & Daniel L. Rubinfeld, Econometric Models and Economic Forecasts (4th ed. 1998).

alternative hypothesis. See hypothesis test.

association. The degree of statistical dependence between two or more events or variables. Events are said to be associated when they occur more frequently together than one would expect by chance.

bias. Any effect at any stage of investigation or inference tending to produce results that depart systematically from the true values (i.e., the results are either too high or too low). A biased estimator of a parameter differs on average from the true parameter.

coefficient. An estimated regression parameter.

confidence interval. An interval that contains a true regression parameter with a given degree of confidence.

consistent estimator. An estimator that tends to become more and more accurate as the sample size grows.

correlation. A statistical means of measuring the association between variables. Two variables are correlated positively if, on average, they move in the same direction; two variables are correlated negatively if, on average, they move in opposite directions.

cross-section analysis. A type of multiple regression analysis in which each data point is associated with a different unit of observation (e.g., an individual or a firm) measured at a particular point in time.

degrees of freedom (DF). The number of observations in a sample minus the number of estimated parameters in a regression model. A useful statistic in hypothesis testing.

dependent variable. The variable to be explained or predicted in a multiple regression model.

dummy variable. A variable that takes on only two values, usually 0 and 1, with one value indicating the presence of a characteristic, attribute, or effect (1) and the other value indicating its absence (0).

efficient estimator. An estimator of a parameter that produces the greatest precision possible.

error term. A variable in a multiple regression model that represents the cumulative effect of a number of sources of modeling error.

estimate. The calculated value of a parameter based on the use of a particular sample.

estimator. The sample statistic that estimates the value of a population parameter (e.g., a regression parameter); its values vary from sample to sample.

ex ante forecast. A prediction about the values of the dependent variable that go beyond the sample; consequently, the forecast must be based on predictions for the values of the explanatory variables in the regression model.

explanatory variable. A variable that is associated with changes in a dependent variable.

ex post forecast. A prediction about the values of the dependent variable made during a period in which all the values of the explanatory and dependent variables are known. Ex post forecasts provide a useful means of evaluating the fit of a regression model.

***F*-test.** A statistical test (based on an *F*-ratio) of the null hypothesis that a group of explanatory variables are jointly equal to 0. When applied to all the explanatory variables in a multiple regression model, the *F*-test becomes a test of the null hypothesis that R^2 equals 0.

feedback. When changes in an explanatory variable affect the values of the dependent variable, and changes in the dependent variable also affect the explanatory variable. When both effects occur at the same time, the two variables are described as being determined simultaneously.

fitted value. The estimated value for the dependent variable; in a linear regression this value is calculated as the intercept plus a weighted average of the values of the explanatory variables, with the estimated parameters used as weights.

heteroscedasticity. When the error associated with a multiple regression model has a nonconstant variance; that is, the error values associated with some observations are typically high, whereas the values associated with other observations are typically low.

hypothesis test. A statement about the parameters in a multiple regression model. The null hypothesis may assert that certain parameters have specified values or ranges; the alternative hypothesis would specify other values or ranges.

independence. When two variables are not correlated with each other (in the population).

independent variable. An explanatory variable that affects the dependent variable but is not affected by the dependent variable.

influential data point. A data point whose deletion from a regression sample causes one or more estimated regression parameters to change substantially.

interaction variable. The product of two explanatory variables in a regression model. Used in a particular form of nonlinear model.

intercept. The value of the dependent variable when each of the explanatory variables takes on the value of 0 in a regression equation.

least-squares. A common method for estimating regression parameters. Least-squares minimizes the sum of the squared differences between the actual values of the dependent variable and the values predicted by the regression equation.

linear regression model. A regression model in which the effect of a change in each of the explanatory variables on the dependent variable is the same, no matter what the values of those explanatory variables.

mean (sample). An average of the outcomes associated with a probability distribution, where the outcomes are weighted by the probability that each will occur.

mean square error (MSE). The estimated variance of the regression error, calculated as the average of the sum of the squares of the regression residuals.

model. A representation of an actual situation.

multicollinearity. When two or more variables are highly correlated in a multiple regression analysis. Substantial multicollinearity can cause regression parameters to be estimated imprecisely, as reflected in relatively high standard errors.

multiple regression analysis. A statistical tool for understanding the relationship between two or more variables.

nonlinear regression model. A model having the property that changes in explanatory variables will have differential effects on the dependent variable as the values of the explanatory variables change.

normal distribution. A bell-shaped probability distribution having the property that about 95% of the distribution lies within two standard deviations of the mean.

null hypothesis. In regression analysis the null hypothesis states that the results observed in a study with respect to a particular variable are no different from what might have occurred by chance, independent of the effect of that variable. See hypothesis test.

one-tailed test. A hypothesis test in which the alternative to the null hypothesis that a parameter is equal to 0 is for the parameter to be either positive or negative, but not both.

outlier. A data point that is more than some appropriate distance from a regression line that is estimated using all the other data points in the sample.

***p*-value.** The significance level in a statistical test; the probability of getting a test statistic as extreme or more extreme than the observed value. The larger the *p*-value, the more likely the null hypothesis is true.

parameter. A numerical characteristic of a population or a model.

perfect collinearity. When two or more explanatory variables are correlated perfectly.

population. All the units of interest to the researcher; also, universe.

practical significance. Substantive importance. Statistical significance does not ensure practical significance, since, with large samples, small differences can be statistically significant.

probability distribution. The process that generates the values of a random variable. A probability distribution lists all possible outcomes and the probability that each will occur.

probability sampling. A process by which a sample of a population is chosen so that each unit of observation has a known probability of being selected.

random error term. A term in a regression model that reflects random error (sampling error) that is due to chance. As a consequence, the result obtained in the sample differs from the result that would be obtained if the entire population were studied.

regression coefficient. Also, regression parameter. The estimate of a population parameter obtained from a regression equation that is based on a particular sample.

regression residual. The difference between the actual value of a dependent variable and the value predicted by the regression equation.

robust estimation. An alternative to least-squares estimation that is less sensitive to outliers.

robustness. A statistic or procedure that does not change much when data or assumptions are slightly modified is robust.

***R*-square (R^2).** A statistic that measures the percentage of the variation in the dependent variable that is accounted for by all of the explanatory variables in a regression model. *R*-square is the most commonly used measure of goodness-of-fit of a regression model.

sample. A selection of data chosen for a study; a subset of a population.

sampling error. A measure of the difference between the sample estimate of a parameter and the population parameter.

scatterplot. A graph showing the relationship between two variables in a study; each dot represents one subject. One variable is plotted along the horizontal axis; the other variable is plotted along the vertical axis.

serial correlation. The correlation of the values of regression errors over time.

slope. The change in the dependent variable associated with a 1-unit change in an explanatory variable.

spurious correlation. When two variables are correlated, but one is not the cause of the other.

standard deviation. The square root of the variance of a random variable. The variance is a measure of the spread of a probability distribution about its mean; it is calculated as a weighted average of the squares of the deviations of the outcomes of a random variable from its mean.

standard error of the coefficient; standard error (SE). A measure of the variation of a parameter estimate or coefficient about the true parameter. The standard error is a standard deviation that is calculated from the probability distribution of estimated parameters.

standard error of forecast (SEF). An estimate of the standard deviation of the forecast error; it is based on forecasts made within a sample in which the values of the explanatory variables are known with certainty.

standard error of the regression (SER). An estimate of the standard deviation of the regression error; it is calculated as an average of the squares of the residuals associated with a particular multiple regression analysis.

statistical significance. A test used to evaluate the degree of association between a dependent variable and one or more explanatory variables. If the calculated *p*-value is smaller than 5%, the result is said to be statistically significant (at the 5% level). If *p* is greater than 5%, the result is statistically insignificant (at the 5% level).

***t*-statistic.** A test statistic that describes how far an estimate of a parameter is from its hypothesized value (i.e., given a null hypothesis). If a *t*-statistic is sufficiently large (in absolute magnitude), an expert can reject the null hypothesis.

***t*-test.** A test of the null hypothesis that a regression parameter takes on a particular value, usually 0. The test is based on the *t*-statistic.

time-series analysis. A type of multiple regression analysis in which each data point is associated with a particular unit of observation (e.g., an individual or a firm) measured at different points in time.

two-tailed test. A hypothesis test in which the alternative to the null hypothesis that a parameter is equal to 0 is for the parameter to be either positive or negative, or both.

variable. Any attribute, phenomenon, condition, or event that can have two or more values.

variable of interest. The explanatory variable that is the focal point of a particular study or legal issue.

References on Multiple Regression

Jonathan A. Baker & Daniel L. Rubinfeld, *Empirical Methods in Antitrust: Review and Critique,* 1 Am. L. & Econ. Rev. 386 (1999).

Thomas J. Campbell, *Regression Analysis in Title VII Cases: Minimum Standards, Comparable Worth, and Other Issues Where Law and Statistics Meet,* 36 Stan. L. Rev. 1299 (1984).

Arthur P. Dempster, *Employment Discrimination and Statistical Science,* 3 Stat. Sci. 149 (1988).

The Evolving Role of Statistical Assessments as Evidence in the Courts (Stephen E. Fienberg ed., 1989).

Michael O. Finkelstein, *The Judicial Reception of Multiple Regression Studies in Race and Sex Discrimination Cases,* 80 Colum. L. Rev. 737 (1980).

Michael O. Finkelstein & Hans Levenbach, *Regression Estimates of Damages in Price-Fixing Cases,* Law & Contemp. Probs., Autumn 1983, at 145.

Franklin M. Fisher, *Statisticians, Econometricians, and Adversary Proceedings,* 81 J. Am. Stat. Ass'n 277 (1986).

Franklin M. Fisher, *Multiple Regression in Legal Proceedings,* 80 Colum. L. Rev. 702 (1980).

Joseph L. Gastwirth, *Methods for Assessing the Sensitivity of Statistical Comparisons Used in Title VII Cases to Omitted Variables,* 33 Jurimetrics J. 19 (1992).

Note, *Beyond the Prima Facie Case in Employment Discrimination Law: Statistical Proof and Rebuttal,* 89 Harv. L. Rev. 387 (1975).

Daniel L. Rubinfeld, *Econometrics in the Courtroom,* 85 Colum. L. Rev. 1048 (1985).

Daniel L. Rubinfeld & Peter O. Steiner, *Quantitative Methods in Antitrust Litigation,* Law & Contemp. Probs., Autumn 1983, at 69.

Symposium, *Statistical and Demographic Issues Underlying Voting Rights Cases,* 15 Evaluation Rev. 659 (1991).

Reference Guide on Survey Research

SHARI SEIDMAN DIAMOND

Shari Seidman Diamond, J.D., Ph.D., is Professor of Law and Psychology, Northwestern University, Evanston, Illinois, and Senior Research Fellow, American Bar Foundation, Chicago, Illinois.

CONTENTS

I. Introduction

Surveys are used to describe or enumerate objects or the beliefs, attitudes, or behavior of persons or other social units.[1] Surveys typically are offered in legal proceedings to establish or refute claims about the characteristics of those objects, individuals, or social units. Although surveys may count or measure every member of the relevant population (e.g., all plaintiffs eligible to join in a suit, all employees currently working for a corporation, all trees in a forest), sample surveys count or measure only a portion of the objects, individuals, or social units that the survey is intended to describe.[2]

Some statistical and sampling experts apply the phrase "sample survey" only to a survey in which probability sampling techniques are used to select the sample.[3] Although probability sampling offers important advantages over nonprobability sampling,[4] experts in some fields (e.g., marketing) regularly rely on various forms of nonprobability sampling when conducting surveys. Consistent with Federal Rule of Evidence 703, courts generally have accepted such evidence.[5] Thus, in this reference guide, both the probability sample and the nonprobability sample are discussed. The strengths of probability sampling and the weaknesses of various types of nonprobability sampling are described so that the trier of fact can consider these features in deciding what weight to give to a particular sample survey.

As a method of data collection, surveys have several crucial potential advantages over less systematic approaches.[6] When properly designed, executed, and

1. Social scientists describe surveys as "conducted for the purpose of collecting data from individuals about themselves, about their households, or about other larger social units." Peter H. Rossi et al., *Sample Surveys: History, Current Practice, and Future Prospects*, *in* Handbook of Survey Research 1, 2 (Peter H. Rossi et al. eds., 1983). Used in its broader sense, however, the term *survey* applies to any description or enumeration, whether or not a person is the source of this information. Thus, a report on the number of trees destroyed in a forest fire might require a survey of the trees and stumps in the damaged area.

2. In *J.H. Miles & Co. v. Brown*, 910 F. Supp. 1138 (E.D. Va. 1995), clam processors and fishing vessel owners sued the Secretary of Commerce for failing to use the unexpectedly high results from 1994 survey data on the size of the clam population to determine clam fishing quotas for 1995. The estimate of clam abundance is obtained from surveys of the amount of fishing time the research survey vessels require to collect a specified yield of clams in major fishing areas over a period of several weeks. *Id.* at 1144–45.

3. *E.g.*, Leslie Kish, Survey Sampling 26 (1965).

4. *See infra* § III.C.

5. Fed. R. Evid. 703 recognizes facts or data "of a type reasonably relied upon by experts in the particular field . . . ."

6. This does not mean that surveys can be relied on to address all types of questions. For example, some respondents may not be able to predict accurately whether they would volunteer for military service if Washington, D.C., were to be bombed. Their inaccuracy may arise not because they are unwilling to answer the question or to say they don't know, but because they believe they can predict accurately, and they are simply wrong. Thus, the availability of a "don't know" option cannot cure the inaccuracy. Although such a survey is suitable for assessing their predictions, it may not provide a very accurate estimate of what their actual responses would be.

described, surveys (1) economically present the characteristics of a large group of objects or respondents and (2) permit an assessment of the extent to which the measured objects or respondents are likely to adequately represent a relevant group of objects, individuals, or social units.[7] All questions asked of respondents and all other measuring devices used can be examined by the court and the opposing party for objectivity, clarity, and relevance, and all answers or other measures obtained can be analyzed for completeness and consistency. To make it possible for the court and the opposing party to closely scrutinize the survey so that its relevance, objectivity, and representativeness can be evaluated, the party proposing to offer the survey as evidence should describe in detail the design and execution of the survey.

The questions listed in this reference guide are intended to assist judges in identifying, narrowing, and addressing issues bearing on the adequacy of surveys either offered as evidence or proposed as a method for developing information.[8] These questions can be (1) raised from the bench during a pretrial proceeding to determine the admissibility of the survey evidence; (2) presented to the contending experts before trial for their joint identification of disputed and undisputed issues; (3) presented to counsel with the expectation that the issues will be addressed during the examination of the experts at trial; or (4) raised in bench trials when a motion for a preliminary injunction is made to help the judge evaluate what weight, if any, the survey should be given.[9] These questions are intended to improve the utility of cross-examination by counsel, where appropriate, not to replace it.

All sample surveys, whether they measure objects, individuals, or other social units, should address the issues concerning purpose and design (section II), population definition and sampling (section III), accuracy of data entry (section VI), and disclosure and reporting (section VII). Questionnaire and interview surveys raise methodological issues involving survey questions and structure (section IV) and confidentiality (section VII.C), and interview surveys introduce additional issues (e.g., interviewer training and qualifications) (section V). The sections of this reference guide are labeled to direct the reader to those topics that are relevant to the type of survey being considered. The scope of this reference guide is necessarily limited, and additional issues might arise in particular cases.

7. The ability to quantitatively assess the limits of the likely margin of error is unique to probability sample surveys.

8. *See infra* text accompanying note 27.

9. Lanham Act cases involving trademark infringement or deceptive advertising frequently require expedited hearings that request injunctive relief, so judges may need to be more familiar with survey methodology when considering the weight to accord a survey in these cases than when presiding over cases being submitted to a jury. Even in a case being decided by a jury, however, the court must be prepared to evaluate the methodology of the survey evidence in order to rule on admissibility. *See* Daubert v. Merrell Dow Pharms., Inc., 509 U.S. 579, 589 (1993).

A. Use of Surveys in Court

Forty years ago the question whether surveys constituted acceptable evidence still was unsettled.[10] Early doubts about the admissibility of surveys centered on their use of sampling techniques[11] and their status as hearsay evidence.[12] Federal Rule of Evidence 703 settled both matters for surveys by redirecting attention to the "validity of the techniques employed."[13] The inquiry under Rule 703 focuses on whether facts or data are "of a type reasonably relied upon by experts in the particular field in forming opinions or inferences upon the subject."[14] For a survey, the question becomes, "Was the poll or survey conducted in accordance with generally accepted survey principles, and were the results used in a

10. Hans Zeisel, *The Uniqueness of Survey Evidence*, 45 Cornell L.Q. 322, 345 (1960).

11. In an early use of sampling, Sears, Roebuck & Co. claimed a tax refund based on sales made to individuals living outside city limits. Sears randomly sampled 33 of the 826 working days in the relevant working period, computed the proportion of sales to out-of-city individuals during those days, and projected the sample result to the entire period. The court refused to accept the estimate based on the sample. When a complete audit was made, the result was almost identical to that obtained from the sample. *Sears, Roebuck & Co. v. City of Inglewood*, tried in Los Angeles Superior Court in 1955, is described in R. Clay Sprowls, *The Admissibility of Sample Data into a Court of Law: A Case History*, 4 UCLA L. Rev. 222, 226–29 (1956–1957).

12. Judge Wilfred Feinberg's thoughtful analysis in *Zippo Manufacturing Co. v. Rogers Imports, Inc.*, 216 F. Supp. 670, 682–83 (S.D.N.Y. 1963), provides two alternative grounds for admitting opinion surveys: (1) surveys are not hearsay because they are not offered in evidence to prove the truth of the matter asserted; and (2) even if they are hearsay, they fall under one of the exceptions as a "present sense impression." In *Schering Corp. v. Pfizer Inc.*, 189 F.3d 218 (2d Cir. 1999), the Second Circuit distinguished between perception surveys designed to reflect the present sense impressions of respondents and "memory" surveys designed to collect information about a past occurrence based on the recollections of the survey respondents. The court in *Schering* suggested that if a survey is offered to prove the existence of a specific idea in the public mind, then the survey does constitute hearsay evidence. As the court observed, Federal Rule of Evidence 803(3), creating "an exception to the hearsay rule for such statements [i.e., state of mind expressions] rather than excluding the statements from the definition of hearsay, makes sense only in this light." *Id.* at 230 n.3.

Two additional exceptions to the hearsay exclusion can be applied to surveys. First, surveys may constitute a hearsay exception if the survey data were collected in the normal course of a regularly conducted business activity, unless "the source of information or the method or circumstances of preparation indicate lack of trustworthiness." Fed. R. Evid. 803(6); *see also* Ortho Pharm. Corp. v. Cosprophar, Inc., 828 F. Supp. 1114, 1119–20 (S.D.N.Y. 1993) (marketing surveys prepared in the course of business were properly excluded due to lack of foundation from a person who saw the original data or knew what steps were taken in preparing the report), *aff'd*, 32 F.3d 690 (2d Cir. 1994). In addition, if a survey shows guarantees of trustworthiness equivalent to those in other hearsay exceptions, it can be admitted if the court determines that the statement is offered as evidence of a material fact, it is more probative on the point for which it is offered than any other evidence which the proponent can procure through reasonable efforts, and admissibility serves the interests of justice. Fed. R. Evid. 807; *e.g.*, Keith v. Volpe, 618 F. Supp. 1132 (C.D. Cal. 1985); *Schering*, 189 F.3d at 232. Admissibility as an exception to the hearsay exclusion thus depends on the trustworthiness of the survey.

13. Fed. R. Evid. 703 advisory committee's note.

14. Fed. R. Evid. 703.

statistically correct way?"[15] This focus on the adequacy of the methodology used in conducting and analyzing results from a survey is also consistent with the Supreme Court's discussion of admissible scientific evidence in *Daubert v. Merrell Dow Pharmaceuticals, Inc.*[16]

Because the survey method provides an economical and systematic way to gather information about a large number of individuals or social units, surveys are used widely in business, government, and, increasingly, administrative settings and judicial proceedings. Both federal and state courts have accepted survey evidence on a variety of issues. In a case involving allegations of discrimination in jury panel composition, the defense team surveyed prospective jurors to obtain age, race, education, ethnicity, and income distribution.[17] Surveys of employees or prospective employees are used to support or refute claims of employment discrimination.[18] In ruling on the admissibility of scientific claims, courts have examined surveys of scientific experts to assess the extent to which the theory or technique has received widespread acceptance.[19] Some courts have admitted surveys in obscenity cases to provide evidence about community standards.[20] Requests for a change of venue on grounds of jury pool bias often are backed by evidence from a survey of jury-eligible respondents in the area of the original venue.[21] The plaintiff in an antitrust suit conducted a survey to assess what characteristics, including price, affected consumers' preferences. The sur-

15. Manual for Complex Litigation § 2.712 (1982). Survey research also is addressed in the Manual for Complex Litigation, Second § 21.484 (1985) [hereinafter MCL 2d] and the Manual for Complex Litigation, Third § 21.493 (1995) [hereinafter MCL 3d]. Note, however, that experts who collect survey data, along with the professions that rely on those surveys, may differ in some of their methodological standards and principles. An assessment of the precision of sample estimates and an evaluation of the sources and magnitude of likely bias are required to distinguish methods that are acceptable from methods that are not.

16. 509 U.S. 579 (1993). *See also* General Elec. Co. v. Joiner, 522 U.S. 136, 147 (1997).

17. People v. Harris, 679 P.2d 433 (Cal.), *cert. denied*, 469 U.S. 965 (1984).

18. EEOC v. Sears, Roebuck & Co., 628 F. Supp. 1264, 1308 (N.D. Ill. 1986), *aff'd*, 839 F.2d 302 (7th Cir. 1988); Stender v. Lucky Stores, Inc., 803 F. Supp. 259, 326 (N.D. Cal. 1992); Richardson v. Quik Trip Corp., 591 F. Supp. 1151, 1153 (S.D. Iowa 1984).

19. United States v. Scheffer, 523 U.S. 303, 309 (1998); Meyers v. Arcudi, 947 F. Supp. 581, 588 (D. Conn. 1996); United States v. Varoudakis, No. 97-10158, 1998 WL 151238 (D. Mass. Mar. 27, 1998); United States v. Bishop, 64 F. Supp. 2d 1149 (D. Utah 1999); United States v. Orians, 9 F. Supp. 2d 1168, 1174 (D. Ariz. 1998) (all cases in which courts determined, based on the inconsistent reactions revealed in several surveys, that the polygraph test has failed to achieve general acceptance in the scientific community).

20. *E.g.*, People v. Page Books, Inc., 601 N.E.2d 273, 279–80 (Ill. App. Ct. 1992); People v. Nelson, 410 N.E.2d 476, 477–79 (Ill. App. Ct. 1980); State v. Williams, 598 N.E.2d 1250, 1256–58 (Ohio Ct. App. 1991).

21. *E.g.*, United States v. Eagle, 586 F.2d 1193, 1195 (8th Cir. 1978); United States v. Tokars, 839 F. Supp. 1578, 1583 (D. Ga. 1993), *aff'd*, 95 F.3d 1520 (11th Cir. 1996); Powell v. Superior Court, 283 Cal. Rptr. 777, 783 (Ct. App. 1991).

vey was offered as one way to estimate damages.[22] A routine use of surveys in federal courts occurs in Lanham Act[23] cases, where the plaintiff alleges trademark infringement[24] or claims that false advertising[25] has confused or deceived consumers. The pivotal legal question in such cases virtually demands survey research because it centers on consumer perception and memory (i.e., is the consumer likely to be confused about the source of a product, or does the advertisement imply an inaccurate message?).[26] In addition, survey methodology has been used creatively to assist federal courts in managing mass torts litigation. Faced with the prospect of conducting discovery concerning 10,000 plaintiffs, the plaintiffs and defendants in *Wilhoite v. Olin Corp.*[27] jointly drafted a discovery survey that was administered in person by neutral third parties, thus replacing interrogatories and depositions. It resulted in substantial savings in both time and cost.

B. A Comparison of Survey Evidence and Individual Testimony

To illustrate the value of a survey, it is useful to compare the information that can be obtained from a competently done survey with the information obtained

22. Dolphin Tours, Inc. v. Pacifico Creative Servs., Inc., 773 F.2d 1506, 1508 (9th Cir. 1985). *See also* SMS Sys. Maintenance Servs., Inc. v. Digital Equip. Corp., 188 F.3d 11 (1st Cir. 1999); Benjamin F. King, *Statistics in Antitrust Litigation*, *in* Statistics and the Law 49 (Morris H. DeGroot et al. eds., 1986). Surveys also are used in litigation to help define relevant markets. In *United States v. E.I. DuPont de Nemours & Co.*, 118 F. Supp. 41, 60 (D. Del. 1953), *aff'd*, 351 U.S. 377 (1956), a survey was used to develop the "market setting" for the sale of cellophane. In *Mukand, Ltd. v. United States*, 937 F. Supp. 910 (Ct. Int'l Trade 1996), a survey of purchasers of stainless steel wire rods was conducted to support a determination of competition and fungibility between domestic and Indian wire rod.

23. Lanham Act § 43(a), 15 U.S.C. § 1125(a) (1946) (amended 1992).

24. *E.g.*, Union Carbide Corp. v. Ever-Ready, Inc., 531 F.2d 366 (7th Cir.), *cert. denied*, 429 U.S. 830 (1976); Qualitex Co. v. Jacobson Prods. Co., No. CIV-90-1183HLH, 1991 U.S. Dist. LEXIS 21172 (C.D. Cal. Sept. 3, 1991), *aff'd in part & rev'd on other grounds*, 13 F.3d 1297 (9th. Cir. 1994), *rev'd on other grounds*, 514 U.S. 159 (1995). According to Neal Miller, *Facts, Expert Facts, and Statistics: Descriptive and Experimental Research Methods in Litigation*, 40 Rutgers L. Rev. 101, 137 (1987), trademark law has relied on the institutionalized use of statistical evidence more than any other area of the law.

25. *E.g.*, Southland Sod Farms v. Stover Seed Co., 108 F.3d 1134, 1142–43 (9th Cir. 1997); American Home Prods. Corp. v. Johnson & Johnson, 577 F.2d 160 (2d Cir. 1978).

26. Courts have observed that "the court's reaction is at best not determinative and at worst irrelevant. The question in such cases is, what does the person to whom the advertisement is addressed find to be the message?" American Brands, Inc. v. R.J. Reynolds Tobacco Co., 413 F. Supp. 1352, 1357 (S.D.N.Y. 1976). The wide use of surveys in recent years was foreshadowed in *Triangle Publications, Inc. v. Rohrlich*, 167 F.2d 969, 974 (2d Cir. 1948) (Frank, J., dissenting). Called on to determine whether a manufacturer of girdles labeled "Miss Seventeen" infringed the trademark of the magazine *Seventeen*, Judge Frank suggested that, in the absence of a test of the reactions of "numerous girls and women," the trial court judge's finding as to what was likely to confuse was "nothing but a surmise, a conjecture, a guess," noting that "neither the trial judge nor any member of this court is (or resembles) a teen-age girl or the mother or sister of such a girl." *Id.* at 976–77.

27. No. CV-83-C-5021-NE (N.D. Ala. filed Jan. 11, 1983). The case ultimately settled before trial. *See* Francis E. McGovern & E. Allan Lind, *The Discovery Survey*, Law & Contemp. Probs., Autumn 1988, at 41.

by other means. A survey is presented by a survey expert who testifies about the responses of a substantial number of individuals who have been selected according to an explicit sampling plan and asked the same set of questions by interviewers who were not told who sponsored the survey or what answers were predicted or preferred. Although parties presumably are not obliged to present a survey conducted in anticipation of litigation by a nontestifying expert if it produced unfavorable results,[28] the court can and should scrutinize the method of respondent selection for any survey that is presented.

A party using a nonsurvey method generally identifies several witnesses who testify about their own characteristics, experiences, or impressions. While the party has no obligation to select these witnesses in any particular way or to report on how they were chosen, the party is not likely to select witnesses whose attributes conflict with the party's interests. The witnesses who testify are aware of the parties involved in the case and have discussed the case before testifying.

Although surveys are not the only means of demonstrating particular facts, presenting the results of a well-done survey through the testimony of an expert is an efficient way to inform the trier of fact about a large and representative group of potential witnesses. In some cases, courts have described surveys as the most direct form of evidence that can be offered.[29] Indeed, several courts have drawn negative inferences from the absence of a survey, taking the position that failure to undertake a survey may strongly suggest that a properly done survey would not support the plaintiff's position.[30]

II. Purpose and Design of the Survey

A. Was the Survey Designed to Address Relevant Questions?

The report describing the results of a survey should include a statement describing the purpose or purposes of the survey. One indication that a survey offers probative evidence is that it was designed to collect information relevant to the legal controversy (e.g., to estimate damages in an antitrust suit or to assess con-

28. Loctite Corp. v. National Starch & Chem. Corp., 516 F. Supp. 190, 205 (S.D.N.Y. 1981) (distinguishing between surveys conducted in anticipation of litigation and surveys conducted for nonlitigation purposes which cannot be reproduced because of the passage of time, concluding that parties should not be compelled to introduce the former at trial, but may be required to provide the latter).

29. *E.g.*, Charles Jacquin et Cie, Inc. v. Destileria Serralles, Inc., 921 F.2d 467, 475 (3d Cir. 1990). *See also* Brunswick Corp. v. Spinit Reel Co., 832 F.2d 513, 522 (10th Cir. 1987).

30. E.S. Originals, Inc. v. Stride Rite Corp., 656 F. Supp. 484, 490 (S.D.N.Y. 1987); *see also* Ortho Pharm. Corp. v. Cosprophar, Inc., 32 F.3d 690, 695 (2d Cir. 1994); Henri's Food Prods. Co. v. Kraft, Inc., 717 F.2d 352, 357 (7th Cir. 1983); Information Clearing House, Inc. v. Find Magazine, 492 F. Supp. 147, 160 (S.D.N.Y. 1980).

sumer confusion in a trademark case). Surveys not conducted specifically in preparation for, or in response to, litigation may provide important information,[31] but they frequently ask irrelevant questions[32] or select inappropriate samples of respondents for study.[33] Nonetheless, surveys do not always achieve their stated goals. Thus, the content and execution of a survey must be scrutinized even if the survey was designed to provide relevant data on the issue before the court. Moreover, if a survey was not designed for purposes of litigation, one source of bias is less likely: The party presenting the survey is less likely to have designed and constructed the survey to prove its side of the issue in controversy.

B. Was Participation in the Design, Administration, and Interpretation of the Survey Appropriately Controlled to Ensure the Objectivity of the Survey?

An early handbook for judges recommended that survey interviews be "conducted independently of the attorneys in the case."[34] Some courts have interpreted this to mean that any evidence of attorney participation is objectionable.[35] A better interpretation is that the attorney should have no part in carrying out the survey.[36] However, some attorney involvement in the survey design is

31. *See, e.g.*, Wright v. Jeep Corp., 547 F. Supp. 871, 874 (E.D. Mich. 1982). Indeed, as courts increasingly have been faced with scientific issues, parties have requested in a number of recent cases that the courts compel production of research data and testimony by unretained experts. The circumstances under which an unretained expert can be compelled to testify or to disclose research data and opinions, as well as the extent of disclosure that can be required when the research conducted by the expert has a bearing on the issues in the case, are the subject of considerable current debate. *See, e.g.*, Richard L. Marcus, *Discovery Along the Litigation/Science Interface*, 57 Brook. L. Rev. 381, 393–428 (1991); Joe S. Cecil, *Judicially Compelled Disclosure of Research Data*, 1 Cts. Health Sci. & L. 434 (1991); *see also* Symposium, *Court-Ordered Disclosure of Academic Research: A Clash of Values of Science and Law*, Law & Contemp. Probs., Summer 1996, at 1.

32. Loctite Corp. v. National Starch & Chem. Corp., 516 F. Supp. 190, 206 (S.D.N.Y. 1981) (marketing surveys conducted before litigation were designed to test for brand awareness, whereas the "single issue at hand . . . [was] whether consumers understood the term 'Super Glue' to designate glue from a single source").

33. In *Craig v. Boren*, 429 U.S. 190 (1976), the state unsuccessfully attempted to use its annual roadside survey of the blood alcohol level, drinking habits, and preferences of drivers to justify prohibiting the sale of 3.2% beer to males under the age of 21 and to females under the age of 18. The data were biased because it was likely that the male would be driving if both the male and female occupants of the car had been drinking. As pointed out in 2 Joseph L. Gastwirth, Statistical Reasoning in Law and Public Policy: Tort Law, Evidence, and Health 527 (1988), the roadside survey would have provided more relevant data if all occupants of the cars had been included in the survey (and if the type and amount of alcohol most recently consumed had been requested so that the consumption of 3.2% beer could have been isolated).

34. Judicial Conference of the U.S., Handbook of Recommended Procedures for the Trial of Protracted Cases 75 (1960).

35. *E.g.*, Boehringer Ingelheim G.m.b.H. v. Pharmadyne Lab., 532 F. Supp. 1040, 1058 (D.N.J. 1980).

36. Upjohn Co. v. American Home Prods. Corp., No. 1-95-CV-237, 1996 U.S. Dist. LEXIS 8049, at *42 (W.D. Mich. Apr. 5, 1996) (objection that "counsel reviewed the design of the survey

necessary to ensure that relevant questions are directed to a relevant population.[37] The trier of fact evaluates the objectivity and relevance of the questions on the survey and the appropriateness of the definition of the population used to guide sample selection. These aspects of the survey are visible to the trier of fact and can be judged on their quality, irrespective of who suggested them. In contrast, the interviews themselves are not directly visible, and any potential bias is minimized by having interviewers and respondents blind to the purpose and sponsorship of the survey and by excluding attorneys from any part in conducting interviews and tabulating results.

C. Are the Experts Who Designed, Conducted, or Analyzed the Survey Appropriately Skilled and Experienced?

Experts prepared to design, conduct, and analyze a survey generally should have graduate training in psychology (especially social, cognitive, or consumer psychology), sociology, marketing, communication sciences, statistics, or a related discipline; that training should include courses in survey research methods, sampling, measurement, interviewing, and statistics. In some cases, professional experience in conducting and publishing survey research may provide the requisite background. In all cases, the expert must demonstrate an understanding of survey methodology, including sampling,[38] instrument design (questionnaire and interview construction), and statistical analysis.[39] Publication in peer-reviewed journals, authored books, membership in professional organizations, faculty appointments, consulting experience, research grants, and membership on scientific advisory panels for government agencies or private foundations are indications of a professional's area and level of expertise. In addition, if the survey involves highly technical subject matter (e.g., the particular preferences of electrical engineers for various pieces of electrical equipment and the bases for those preferences) or involves a special population (e.g., developmentally disabled adults with limited cognitive skills), the survey expert also should be able to demonstrate sufficient familiarity with the topic or population (or assistance from an individual on the research team with suitable expertise) to design a survey instrument that will communicate clearly with relevant respondents.

carries little force with this Court because [opposing party] has not identified any flaw in the survey that might be attributed to counsel's assistance").

37. 3 J. Thomas McCarthy, McCarthy on Trademarks and Unfair Competition § 32:166 (4th ed. 1996).

38. The one exception is that sampling expertise is unnecessary if the survey is administered to all members of the relevant population. *See, e.g.*, McGovern & Lind, *supra* note 27.

39. If survey expertise is being provided by several experts, a single expert may have general familiarity but not special expertise in all these areas.

D. *Are the Experts Who Will Testify About Surveys Conducted by Others Appropriately Skilled and Experienced?*

Parties often call on an expert to testify about a survey conducted by someone else. The secondary expert's role is to offer support for a survey commissioned by the party who calls the expert, to critique a survey presented by the opposing party, or to introduce findings or conclusions from a survey not conducted in preparation for litigation or by any of the parties to the litigation. The trial court should take into account the exact issue that the expert seeks to testify about and the nature of the expert's field of expertise.[40] The secondary expert who gives an opinion about the adequacy and interpretation of a survey not only should have general skills and experience with surveys and be familiar with all of the issues addressed in this reference guide, but also should demonstrate familiarity with the following properties of the survey being discussed:

1. the purpose of the survey;
2. the survey methodology, including
   a. the target population,
   b. the sampling design used in conducting the survey,
   c. the survey instrument (questionnaire or interview schedule), and
   d. (for interview surveys) interviewer training and instruction;
3. the results, including rates and patterns of missing data; and
4. the statistical analyses used to interpret the results.

III. Population Definition and Sampling

A. *Was an Appropriate Universe or Population Identified?*

One of the first steps in designing a survey or in deciding whether an existing survey is relevant is to identify the target population (or universe).[41] The target population consists of all elements (i.e., objects, individuals, or other social units) whose characteristics or perceptions the survey is intended to represent. Thus, in trademark litigation, the relevant population in some disputes may include all prospective and actual purchasers of the plaintiff's goods or services and all prospective and actual purchasers of the defendant's goods or services. Similarly, the population for a discovery survey may include all potential plaintiffs or all em-

40. Margaret A. Berger, The Supreme Court's Triology on the Admissibility of Expert Testimony § IV.C, in this manual.

41. Identification of the proper universe is recognized uniformly as a key element in the development of a survey. *See, e.g.*, Judicial Conference of the U.S., *supra* note 34; MCL 3d, *supra* note 15, § 21.493. *See also* 3 McCarthy, *supra* note 37, § 32:166; Council of Am. Survey Res. Orgs., Code of Standards and Ethics for Survey Research § III.B.4 (1997).

ployees who worked for Company A between two specific dates. In a community survey designed to provide evidence for a motion for a change of venue, the relevant population consists of all jury-eligible citizens in the community in which the trial is to take place.[42] The definition of the relevant population is crucial because there may be systematic differences in the responses of members of the population and nonmembers. (For example, consumers who are prospective purchasers may know more about the product category than consumers who are not considering making a purchase.)

The universe must be defined carefully. For example, a commercial for a toy or breakfast cereal may be aimed at children, who in turn influence their parents' purchases. If a survey assessing the commercial's tendency to mislead were conducted based on the universe of prospective and actual adult purchasers, it would exclude a crucial group of eligible respondents. Thus, the appropriate population in this instance would include children as well as parents.[43]

B. Did the Sampling Frame Approximate the Population?

The target population consists of all the individuals or units that the researcher would like to study. The sampling frame is the source (or sources) from which the sample actually is drawn. The surveyor's job generally is easier if a complete list of every eligible member of the population is available (e.g., all plaintiffs in a discovery survey), so that the sampling frame lists the identity of all members of the target population. Frequently, however, the target population includes members who are inaccessible or who cannot be identified in advance. As a result, compromises are sometimes required in developing the sampling frame. The survey report should contain a description of the target population, a description of the survey population actually sampled, a discussion of the difference between the two populations, and an evaluation of the likely consequences of that difference.

42. A second relevant population may consist of jury-eligible citizens in the community where the party would like to see the trial moved. By questioning citizens in both communities, the survey can test whether moving the trial is likely to reduce the level of animosity toward the party requesting the change of venue. *See* United States v. Haldeman, 559 F.2d 31, 140, 151, app. A at 176–79 (D.C. Cir. 1976) (court denied change of venue over the strong objection of Judge MacKinnon, who cited survey evidence that Washington, D.C., residents were substantially more likely to conclude, before trial, that the defendants were guilty), *cert. denied*, 431 U.S. 933 (1977); *see also* People v. Venegas, 31 Cal. Rptr. 2d 114, 117 (Ct. App. 1994) (change of venue denied because defendant failed to show that the defendant would face a less hostile jury in a different court).

43. Children and some other populations create special challenges for researchers. For example, very young children should not be asked about sponsorship or licensing, concepts that are foreign to them. Concepts, as well as wording, should be age-appropriate.

A survey that provides information about a wholly irrelevant universe of respondents is itself irrelevant.[44] Courts are likely to exclude the survey or accord it little weight. Thus, when the plaintiff submitted the results of a survey to prove that the green color of its fishing rod had acquired a secondary meaning, the court gave the survey little weight in part because the survey solicited the views of fishing rod dealers rather than consumers.[45] More commonly, however, the sampling frame is either underinclusive or overinclusive relative to the target population. If it is underinclusive, the survey's value depends on the extent to which the excluded population is likely to react differently from the included population. Thus, a survey of spectators and participants at running events would be sampling a sophisticated subset of those likely to purchase running shoes. Because this subset probably would consist of the consumers most knowledgeable about the trade dress used by companies that sell running shoes, a survey based on this population would be likely to substantially overrepresent the strength of a particular design as a trademark, and the extent of that overrepresentation would be unknown and not susceptible to any reasonable estimation.[46]

Similarly, in a survey designed to project demand for cellular phones, the assumption that businesses would be the primary users of cellular service led surveyors to exclude potential nonbusiness users from the survey. The Federal Communications Commission (FCC) found the assumption unwarranted and concluded that the research was flawed, in part because of this underinclusive universe.[47]

44. A survey aimed at assessing how persons in the trade respond to an advertisement should be conducted on a sample of persons in the trade and not on a sample of consumers. Home Box Office v. Showtime/The Movie Channel, 665 F. Supp. 1079, 1083 (S.D.N.Y.), *aff'd in part & vacated in part*, 832 F.2d 1311 (2d Cir. 1987). *But see* Lon Tai Shing Co. v. Koch + Lowy, No. 90-C4464, 1990 U.S. Dist. LEXIS 19123, at *50 (S.D.N.Y. Dec. 14, 1990), in which the judge was willing to find likelihood of consumer confusion from a survey of lighting store salespersons questioned by a survey researcher posing as a customer. The court was persuaded that the salespersons who were misstating the source of the lamp, whether consciously or not, must have believed reasonably that the consuming public would be misled by the salespersons' inaccurate statements about the name of the company that manufactured the lamp they were selling.

45. R.L. Winston Rod Co. v. Sage Mfg. Co., 838 F. Supp. 1396, 1401-02 (D. Mont. 1993).

46. Brooks Shoe Mfg. Co. v. Suave Shoe Corp., 533 F. Supp. 75, 80 (S.D. Fla. 1981), *aff'd*, 716 F.2d 854 (11th Cir. 1983). *See also* Winning Ways, Inc. v. Holloway Sportswear, Inc., 913 F. Supp. 1454, 1467 (D. Kan. 1996) (survey flawed in failing to include sporting goods customers who constituted a major portion of customers). *But see* Thomas & Betts Corp. v. Panduit Corp., 138 F.3d 277, 294–95 (7th Cir. 1998) (survey of store personnel admissible because relevant market included both distributors and ultimate purchasers).

47. Gencom, Inc., 56 Rad. Reg. 2d (P&F) 1597, 1604 (1984). This position was affirmed on appeal. *See* Gencom, Inc. v. FCC, 832 F.2d 171, 186 (D.C. Cir. 1987).

In some cases, it is difficult to determine whether an underinclusive universe distorts the results of the survey and, if so, the extent and likely direction of the bias. For example, a trademark survey was designed to test the likelihood of confusing an analgesic currently on the market with a new product that was similar in appearance.[48] The plaintiff's survey included only respondents who had used the plaintiff's analgesic, and the court found that the universe should have included users of other analgesics, "so that the full range of potential customers for whom plaintiff and defendants would compete could be studied."[49] In this instance, it is unclear whether users of the plaintiff's product would be more or less likely to be confused than users of the defendant's product or users of a third analgesic.[50]

An overinclusive universe generally presents less of a problem in interpretation than does an underinclusive universe. If the survey expert can demonstrate that a sufficiently large (and representative) subset of respondents in the survey was drawn from the appropriate universe, the responses obtained from that subset can be examined, and inferences about the relevant universe can be drawn based on that subset.[51] If the relevant subset cannot be identified, however, an overbroad universe will reduce the value of the survey.[52] If the sample is drawn from an underinclusive universe, there is generally no way to know how the unrepresented members would have responded.[53]

C. How Was the Sample Selected to Approximate the Relevant Characteristics of the Population?

Identification of a survey population must be followed by selection of a sample that accurately represents that population.[54] The use of probability sampling techniques maximizes both the representativeness of the survey results and the ability to assess the accuracy of estimates obtained from the survey.

Probability samples range from simple random samples to complex multi-stage sampling designs that use stratification, clustering of population elements into various groupings, or both. In simple random sampling, the most basic type

48. American Home Prods. Corp. v. Barr Lab., Inc., 656 F. Supp. 1058 (D.N.J.), *aff'd*, 834 F.2d 368 (3d Cir. 1987).

49. *Id.* at 1070.

50. *See also* Craig v. Boren, 429 U.S. 190 (1976).

51. This occurred in *National Football League Properties, Inc. v. Wichita Falls Sportswear, Inc.*, 532 F. Supp. 651, 657–58 (W.D. Wash. 1982).

52. Schieffelin & Co. v. Jack Co. of Boca, 850 F. Supp. 232, 246 (S.D.N.Y. 1994).

53. *See, e.g.*, Amstar Corp. v. Domino's Pizza, Inc., 615 F.2d 252, 263–64 (5th Cir.) (court found both plaintiff's and defendant's surveys substantially defective for a systematic failure to include parts of the relevant population), *cert. denied*, 449 U.S. 899 (1980).

54. MCL 3d, *supra* note 15, § 21.493. *See also* David H. Kaye & David A. Freedman, Reference Guide on Statistics § II.B, in this manual.

of probability sampling, every element in the population has a known, equal probability of being included in the sample, and all possible samples of a given size are equally likely to be selected.[55] In all forms of probability sampling, each element in the relevant population has a known, nonzero probability of being included in the sample.[56]

Probability sampling offers two important advantages over other types of sampling. First, the sample can provide an unbiased estimate of the responses of all persons in the population from which the sample was drawn; that is, the expected value of the sample estimate is the population value being estimated. Second, the researcher can calculate a confidence interval that describes explicitly how reliable the sample estimate of the population is likely to be. Thus, suppose a survey tested a sample of 400 dentists randomly selected from the population of all dentists licensed to practice in the United States and found that 80, or 20%, of them mistakenly believed that a new toothpaste, Goldgate, was manufactured by the makers of Colgate. A survey expert could properly compute a confidence interval around the 20% estimate obtained from this sample. If the survey was repeated a large number of times, and a 95% confidence interval was computed each time, 95% of the confidence intervals would include the actual percentage of dentists in the entire population who would believe that Goldgate was manufactured by the makers of Colgate.[57] In this example, the confidence interval, or margin of error, is the estimate (20%) plus or minus 4%, or the distance between 16% and 24%.

All sample surveys produce estimates of population values, not exact measures of those values. Strictly speaking, the margin of sampling error associated with the sample estimate assumes probability sampling. Assuming a probability sample, a confidence interval describes how stable the mean response in the sample is likely to be. The width of the confidence interval depends on three characteristics:

55. Systematic sampling, in which every *n*th unit in the population is sampled and the starting point is selected randomly, fulfills the first of these conditions. It does not fulfill the second, because no systematic sample can include elements adjacent to one another on the list of population members from which the sample is drawn. Except in very unusual situations when periodicities occur, systematic samples and simple random samples generally produce the same results. Seymour Sudman, *Applied Sampling*, *in* Handbook of Survey Research, *supra* note 1, at 145, 169.

56. Other probability sampling techniques include (1) stratified random sampling, in which the researcher subdivides the population into mutually exclusive and exhaustive subpopulations, or strata, and then randomly selects samples from within these strata; and (2) cluster sampling, in which elements are sampled in groups or clusters, rather than on an individual basis. Martin Frankel, *Sampling Theory*, *in* Handbook of Survey Research, *supra* note 1, at 21, 37, 47.

57. Actually, since survey interviewers would be unable to locate some dentists and some dentists would be unwilling to participate in the survey, technically the population to which this sample would be projectable would be all dentists with current addresses who would be willing to participate in the survey if they were asked.

1. the size of the sample (the larger the sample, the narrower the interval);
2. the variability of the response being measured; and
3. the confidence level the researcher wants to have.

Traditionally, scientists adopt the 95% level of confidence, which means that if 100 samples of the same size were drawn, the confidence interval expected for at least 95 of the samples would be expected to include the true population value.[58]

Although probability sample surveys often are conducted in organizational settings and are the recommended sampling approach in academic and government publications on surveys, probability sample surveys can be expensive when in-person interviews are required, the target population is dispersed widely, or qualified respondents are scarce. A majority of the consumer surveys conducted for Lanham Act litigation present results from nonprobability convenience samples.[59] They are admitted into evidence based on the argument that nonprobability sampling is used widely in marketing research and that "results of these studies are used by major American companies in making decisions of considerable consequence."[60] Nonetheless, when respondents are not selected randomly from the relevant population, the expert should be prepared to justify the method used to select respondents. Special precautions are required to reduce the likelihood of biased samples.[61] In addition, quantitative values computed from such samples (e.g., percentage of respondents indicating confusion) should be viewed as rough indicators rather than as precise quantitative estimates. Confidence intervals should not be computed.

58. To increase the likelihood that the confidence interval contains the actual population value (e.g., from 95% to 99%), the width of the confidence interval can be expanded. An increase in the confidence interval brings an increase in the confidence level. For further discussion of confidence intervals, see David H. Kaye & David A. Freedman, Reference Guide on Statistics § IV.A, in this manual.

59. Jacob Jacoby & Amy H. Handlin, *Non-Probability Sampling Designs for Litigation Surveys*, 81 Trademark Rep. 169, 173 (1991). For probability surveys conducted in trademark cases, see *National Football League Properties, Inc. v. Wichita Falls Sportswear, Inc.*, 532 F. Supp. 651 (W.D. Wash. 1982); James Burrough, Ltd. v. Sign of Beefeater, Inc., 540 F.2d 266 (7th Cir. 1976).

60. National Football League Properties, Inc. v. New Jersey Giants, Inc., 637 F. Supp. 507, 515 (D.N.J. 1986). A survey of members of the Council of American Survey Research Organizations, the national trade association for commercial survey research firms in the United States, revealed that 95% of the in-person independent contacts in studies done in 1985 took place in malls or shopping centers. Jacoby & Handlin, *supra* note 59, at 172–73, 176.

D. *Was the Level of Nonresponse Sufficient to Raise Questions About the Representativeness of the Sample? If So, What Is the Evidence That Nonresponse Did Not Bias the Results of the Survey?*

Even when a sample is drawn randomly from a complete list of elements in the target population, responses or measures may be obtained on only part of the selected sample. If this lack of response were distributed randomly, valid inferences about the population could be drawn from the characteristics of the available elements in the sample. The difficulty is that nonresponse often is not random, so that, for example, persons who are single typically have three times the "not at home" rate in U.S. Census Bureau surveys as do family members.[62] Efforts to increase response rates include making several attempts to contact potential respondents and providing financial incentives for participating in the survey.

One suggested formula for quantifying a tolerable level of nonresponse in a probability sample is based on the guidelines for statistical surveys issued by the former U.S. Office of Statistical Standards.[63] According to these guidelines, response rates of 90% or more are reliable and generally can be treated as random samples of the overall population. Response rates between 75% and 90% usually yield reliable results, but the researcher should conduct some check on the representativeness of the sample. Potential bias should receive greater scrutiny when the response rate drops below 75%. If the response rate drops below 50%, the survey should be regarded with significant caution as a basis for precise quantitative statements about the population from which the sample was drawn.[64]

Determining whether the level of nonresponse in a survey is critical generally requires an analysis of the determinants of nonresponse. For example, even a survey with a high response rate may seriously underrepresent some portions of the population, such as the unemployed or the poor. If a general population sample was used to chart changes in the proportion of the population that knows someone with HIV, the survey would underestimate the population value if some groups more likely to know someone with HIV (e.g., intravenous drug users) were underrepresented in the sample. The survey expert should be prepared to provide evidence on the potential impact of nonresponse on the survey results.

61. *See infra* § III.E.

62. 2 Gastwirth, *supra* note 33, at 501. This volume contains a useful discussion of sampling, along with a set of examples. *Id.* at 467.

63. This standard is cited with approval by Gastwirth. *Id.* at 502.

64. For thoughtful examples of judges closely scrutinizing potential sample bias when response rates were below 75%, see *Vuyanich v. Republic National Bank*, 505 F. Supp. 224 (N.D. Tex. 1980); Rosado v. Wyman, 322 F. Supp. 1173 (E.D.N.Y.), *aff'd*, 437 F.2d 619 (2d Cir. 1970), *aff'd*, 402 U.S. 991 (1971).

In surveys that include sensitive or difficult questions, particularly surveys that are self-administered, some respondents may refuse to provide answers or may provide incomplete answers. To assess the impact of nonresponse to a particular question, the survey expert should analyze the differences between those who answered and those who did not answer. Procedures to address the problem of missing data include recontacting respondents to obtain the missing answers and using the respondent's other answers to predict the missing response.[65]

E. *What Procedures Were Used to Reduce the Likelihood of a Biased Sample?*

If it is impractical for a survey researcher to sample randomly from the entire target population, the researcher still can apply probability sampling to some aspects of respondent selection to reduce the likelihood of biased selection. For example, in many studies the target population consists of all consumers or purchasers of a product. Because it is impractical to randomly sample from that population, research is conducted in shopping malls where some members of the target population may not shop. Mall locations, however, can be sampled randomly from a list of possible mall sites. By administering the survey at several different malls, the expert can test for and report on any differences observed across sites. To the extent that similar results are obtained in different locations using different on-site interview operations, it is less likely that idiosyncrasies of sample selection or administration can account for the results.[66] Similarly, since the characteristics of persons visiting a shopping center vary by day of the week and time of day, bias in sampling can be reduced if the survey design calls for sampling time segments as well as mall locations.[67]

In mall intercept surveys, the organization that manages the on-site interview facility generally employs recruiters who approach potential survey respondents in the mall and ascertain if they are qualified and willing to participate in the survey. If a potential respondent agrees to answer the questions and meets the specified criteria, he or she is escorted to the facility where the survey interview takes place. If recruiters are free to approach potential respondents without controls on how an individual is to be selected for screening, shoppers who spend more time in the mall are more likely to be approached than shoppers who visit the mall only briefly. Moreover, recruiters naturally prefer to approach friendly-

65. Andy B. Anderson et al., *Missing Data: A Review of the Literature*, *in* Handbook of Survey Research, *supra* note 1, at 415.

66. Note, however, that differences in results across sites may be due to genuine differences in respondents across geographic locations or to a failure to administer the survey consistently across sites.

67. Seymour Sudman, *Improving the Quality of Shopping Center Sampling*, 17 J. Marketing Res. 423 (1980).

looking potential respondents, so that it is more likely that certain types of individuals will be selected. These potential biases in selection can be reduced by providing appropriate selection instructions and training recruiters effectively. Training that reduces the interviewer's discretion in selecting a potential respondent is likely to reduce bias in selection, as are instructions to approach every *n*th person entering the facility through a particular door.[68]

F. What Precautions Were Taken to Ensure That Only Qualified Respondents Were Included in the Survey?

In a carefully executed survey, each potential respondent is questioned or measured on the attributes that determine his or her eligibility to participate in the survey. Thus, the initial questions screen potential respondents to determine if they are within the target population of the survey (e.g., Is she at least fourteen years old? Does she own a dog? Does she live within ten miles?). The screening questions must be drafted so that they do not convey information that will influence the respondent's answers on the main survey. For example, if respondents must be prospective and recent purchasers of Sunshine orange juice in a trademark survey designed to assess consumer confusion with Sun Time orange juice, potential respondents might be asked to name the brands of orange juice they have purchased recently or expect to purchase in the next six months. They should not be asked specifically if they recently have purchased, or expect to purchase, Sunshine orange juice, because this may affect their responses on the survey either by implying who is conducting the survey or by supplying them with a brand name that otherwise would not occur to them.

The content of a screening questionnaire (or screener) can also set the context for the questions that follow. In *Pfizer, Inc. v. Astra Pharmaceutical Products, Inc.*,[69] physicians were asked a screening question to determine whether they prescribed particular drugs. The court found that the screener conditioned the physicians to respond with the name of a drug rather than a condition.[70]

The criteria for determining whether to include a potential respondent in the survey should be objective and clearly conveyed, preferably using written instructions addressed to those who administer the screening questions. These instructions and the completed screening questionnaire should be made avail-

68. In the end, even if malls are randomly sampled and shoppers are randomly selected within malls, results from mall surveys technically can be used to generalize only to the population of mall shoppers. The ability of the mall sample to describe the likely response pattern of the broader relevant population will depend on the extent to which a substantial segment of the relevant population (1) is not found in malls and (2) would respond differently to the interview.

69. 858 F. Supp. 1305, 1321 & n.13 (S.D.N.Y. 1994).

70. *Id.* at 1321.

able to the court and the opposing party along with the interview form for each respondent.

IV. Survey Questions and Structure

A. Were Questions on the Survey Framed to Be Clear, Precise, and Unbiased?

Although it seems obvious that questions on a survey should be clear and precise, phrasing questions to reach that goal is often difficult. Even questions that appear clear can convey unexpected meanings and ambiguities to potential respondents. For example, the question "What is the average number of days each week you have butter?" appears to be straightforward. Yet some respondents wondered whether margarine counted as butter, and when the question was revised to include the introductory phrase "not including margarine," the reported frequency of butter use dropped dramatically.[71]

When unclear questions are included in a survey, they may threaten the validity of the survey by systematically distorting responses if respondents are misled in a particular direction, or by inflating random error if respondents guess because they do not understand the question.[72] If the crucial question is sufficiently ambiguous or unclear, it may be the basis for rejecting the survey. For example, a survey was designed to assess community sentiment that would warrant a change of venue in trying a case for damages sustained when a hotel skywalk collapsed.[73] The court found that the question "Based on what you have heard, read or seen, do you believe that in the current compensatory damage trials, the defendants, such as the contractors, designers, owners, and operators of the Hyatt Hotel, should be punished?" could neither be correctly understood nor easily answered.[74] The court noted that the phrase "compensatory damages," although well-defined for attorneys, was unlikely to be meaningful for laypersons.[75]

Texts on survey research generally recommend pretests as a way to increase the likelihood that questions are clear and unambiguous,[76] and some courts have

71. Floyd J. Fowler, Jr., *How Unclear Terms Affect Survey Data*, 56 Pub. Opinion Q. 218, 225–26 (1992).

72. *Id.* at 219.

73. Firestone v. Crown Ctr. Redevelopment Corp., 693 S.W.2d 99 (Mo. 1985) (en banc).

74. *Id.* at 102, 103.

75. *Id.* at 103. When there is any question about whether some respondent will understand a particular term or phrase, the term or phrase should be defined explicitly.

76. For a thorough treatment of pretesting methods, see Jean M. Converse & Stanley Presser, Survey Questions: Handcrafting the Standardized Questionnaire 51 (1986). *See also* Fred W. Morgan, *Judicial Standards for Survey Research: An Update and Guidelines*, 54 J. Marketing 59, 64 (1990).

recognized the value of pretests.[77] In a pretest or pilot test,[78] the proposed survey is administered to a small sample (usually between twenty-five and seventy-five)[79] of the same type of respondents who would be eligible to participate in the full-scale survey. The interviewers observe the respondents for any difficulties they may have with the questions and probe for the source of any such difficulties so that the questions can be rephrased if confusion or other difficulties arise. Attorneys who commission surveys for litigation sometimes are reluctant to approve pilot work or to reveal that pilot work has taken place because they are concerned that if a pretest leads to revised wording of the questions, the trier of fact may believe that the survey has been manipulated and is biased or unfair. A more appropriate reaction is to recognize that pilot work can improve the quality of a survey and to anticipate that it often results in word changes that increase clarity and correct misunderstandings. Thus, changes may indicate informed survey construction rather than flawed survey design.[80]

B. Were Filter Questions Provided to Reduce Guessing?

Some survey respondents may have no opinion on an issue under investigation, either because they have never thought about it before or because the question mistakenly assumes a familiarity with the issue. For example, survey respondents may not have noticed that the commercial they are being questioned about guaranteed the quality of the product being advertised and thus they may have no opinion on the kind of guarantee it indicated. Likewise, in an employee survey, respondents may not be familiar with the parental leave policy at their company and thus may have no opinion on whether they would consider taking advantage of the parental leave policy if they became parents. The following three alternative question structures will affect how those respondents answer and how their responses are counted.

First, the survey can ask all respondents to answer the question (e.g., "Did you understand the guarantee offered by Clover to be a one-year guarantee, a sixty-day guarantee, or a thirty-day guarantee?"). Faced with a direct question, particularly one that provides response alternatives, the respondent obligingly may supply an answer even if (in this example) the respondent did not notice the guarantee (or is unfamiliar with the parental leave policy). Such answers will

77. *E.g.*, Zippo Mfg. Co. v. Rogers Imports, Inc., 216 F. Supp. 670 (S.D.N.Y. 1963).

78. The terms *pretest* and *pilot test* are sometimes used interchangeably to describe pilot work done in the planning stages of research. When they are distinguished, the difference is that a pretest tests the questionnaire, whereas a pilot test generally tests proposed collection procedures as well.

79. Converse & Presser, *supra* note 76, at 69. Converse and Presser suggest that a pretest with twenty-five respondents is appropriate when the survey uses professional interviewers.

80. *See infra* § VII.B for a discussion of obligations to disclose pilot work.

reflect only what the respondent can glean from the question, or they may reflect pure guessing. The imprecision introduced by this approach will increase with the proportion of respondents who are unfamiliar with the topic at issue.

Second, the survey can use a quasi-filter question to reduce guessing by providing "don't know" or "no opinion" options as part of the question (e.g., "Did you understand the guarantee offered by Clover to be for more than a year, a year, or less than a year, or don't you have an opinion?").[81] By signaling to the respondent that it is appropriate not to have an opinion, the question reduces the demand for an answer and, as a result, the inclination to hazard a guess just to comply. Respondents are more likely to choose a "no opinion" option if it is mentioned explicitly by the interviewer than if it is merely accepted when the respondent spontaneously offers it as a response. The consequence of this change in format is substantial. Studies indicate that, although the relative distribution of the respondents selecting the *listed* choices is unlikely to change dramatically, presentation of an explicit "don't know" or "no opinion" alternative commonly leads to a 20%–25% increase in the proportion of respondents selecting that response.[82]

Finally, the survey can include full-filter questions, that is, questions that lay the groundwork for the substantive question by first asking the respondent if he or she has an opinion about the issue or happened to notice the feature that the interviewer is preparing to ask about (e.g., "Based on the commercial you just saw, do you have an opinion about how long Clover stated or implied that its guarantee lasts?"). The interviewer then asks the substantive question only of those respondents who have indicated that they have an opinion on the issue.

Which of these three approaches is used and the way it is used can affect the rate of "no opinion" responses that the substantive question will evoke.[83] Respondents are more likely to say they do not have an opinion on an issue if a full filter is used than if a quasi-filter is used.[84] However, in maximizing respondent expressions of "no opinion," full filters may produce an underreporting of opinions. There is some evidence that full-filter questions discourage respondents who actually have opinions from offering them by conveying the implicit suggestion that respondents can avoid difficult follow-up questions by saying that they have no opinion.[85]

81. Norbert Schwarz & Hans-Jürgen Hippler, *Response Alternatives: The Impact of Their Choice and Presentation Order*, *in* Measurement Errors in Surveys 41, 45–46 (Paul P. Biemer et al. eds., 1991).

82. Howard Schuman & Stanley Presser, Questions and Answers in Attitude Surveys: Experiments on Question Form, Wording and Context 113–46 (1981).

83. Considerable research has been conducted on the effects of filters. For a review, see George F. Bishop et al., *Effects of Filter Questions in Public Opinion Surveys*, 47 Pub. Opinion Q. 528 (1983).

84. Schwarz & Hippler, *supra* note 81, at 45–46.

85. *Id.* at 46.

In general, then, a survey that uses full filters tends to provide a conservative estimate of the number of respondents holding an opinion, whereas a survey that uses neither full filters nor quasi-filters tends to overestimate the number of respondents with opinions, because some respondents offering opinions are guessing. The strategy of including a "no opinion" or "don't know" response as a quasi-filter avoids both of these extremes. Thus, rather than asking, "Based on the commercial, do you believe that the two products are made in the same way, or are they made differently?"[86] or prefacing the question with a preliminary, "Do you have an opinion, based on the commercial, concerning the way that the two products are made?" the question could be phrased, "Based on the commercial, do you believe that the two products are made in the same way, or that they are made differently, or don't you have an opinion about the way they are made?"

C. *Did the Survey Use Open-Ended or Closed-Ended Questions? How Was the Choice in Each Instance Justified?*

The questions that make up a survey instrument may be open-ended, closed-ended, or a combination of both. Open-ended questions require the respondent to formulate and express an answer in his or her own words (e.g., "What was the main point of the commercial?" "Where did you catch the fish you caught in these waters?"[87]). Closed-ended questions provide the respondent with an explicit set of responses from which to choose; the choices may be as simple as yes or no (e.g., "Is Colby College coeducational?"[88]) or as complex as a range of alternatives (e.g., "The two pain relievers have (1) the same likelihood of causing gastric ulcers; (2) about the same likelihood of causing gastric ulcers; (3) a somewhat different likelihood of causing gastric ulcers; (4) a very different likelihood of causing gastric ulcers; or (5) none of the above."[89]).

Open-ended and closed-ended questions may elicit very different responses.[90]

86. The question in the example without the "no opinion" alternative was based on a question rejected by the court in *Coors Brewing Co. v. Anheuser-Busch Cos.*, 802 F. Supp. 965, 972–73 (S.D.N.Y. 1992).

87. A relevant example from *Wilhoite v. Olin Corp.* is described in McGovern & Lind, *supra* note 27, at 76.

88. Presidents & Trustees of Colby College v. Colby College–N.H., 508 F.2d 804, 809 (1st Cir. 1975).

89. This question is based on one asked in *American Home Products Corp. v. Johnson & Johnson*, 654 F. Supp. 568, 581 (S.D.N.Y. 1987), that was found to be a leading question by the court, primarily because the choices suggested that the respondent had learned about aspirin's and ibuprofen's relative likelihood of causing gastric ulcers. In contrast, in *McNeilab, Inc. v. American Home Products Corp.*, 501 F. Supp. 517, 525 (S.D.N.Y. 1980), the court accepted as nonleading the question, "Based only on what the commercial said, would Maximum Strength Anacin contain more pain reliever, the same amount of pain reliever, or less pain reliever than the brand you, yourself, currently use most often?"

90. Howard Schuman & Stanley Presser, *Question Wording as an Independent Variable in Survey Analysis*,

Most responses are less likely to be volunteered by respondents who are asked an open-ended question than they are to be chosen by respondents who are presented with a closed-ended question. The response alternatives in a closed-ended question may remind respondents of options that they would not otherwise consider or which simply do not come to mind as easily.[91]

The advantage of open-ended questions is that they give the respondent fewer hints about the answer that is expected or preferred. Precoded responses on a closed-ended question, in addition to reminding respondents of options that they might not otherwise consider,[92] may direct the respondent away from or toward a particular response. For example, a commercial reported that in shampoo tests with more than 900 women, the sponsor's product received higher ratings than other brands.[93] According to a competitor, the commercial deceptively implied that each woman in the test rated more than one shampoo, when in fact each woman rated only one. To test consumer impressions, a survey might have shown the commercial and asked an open-ended question: "How many different brands mentioned in the commercial did each of the 900 women try?"[94] Instead, the survey asked a closed-ended question; respondents were given the choice of "one," "two," "three," "four," or "five or more." The fact that four of the five choices in the closed-ended question provided a response that was greater than one implied that the correct answer was probably more than one.[95] Note, however, that the open-ended question also may suggest that the answer is more than one. By asking "how many different brands," the question suggests (1) that the viewer should have received some message from the commercial about the number of brands each woman tried and (2) that different brands were tried. Thus, the wording of a question, open-ended or closed-ended, can be leading, and the degree of suggestiveness of each question must be considered in evaluating the objectivity of a survey.

6 Soc. Methods & Res. 151 (1977); Schuman & Presser, *supra* note 82, at 79–112; Converse & Presser, *supra* note 76, at 33.

91. For example, when respondents in one survey were asked, "What is the most important thing for children to learn to prepare them for life?", 62% picked "to think for themselves" from a list of five options, but only 5% spontaneously offered that answer when the question was open-ended. Schuman & Presser, *supra* note 82, at 104–07. An open-ended question presents the respondent with a free-recall task, whereas a closed-ended question is a recognition task. Recognition tasks in general reveal higher performance levels than recall tasks. Mary M. Smyth et al., Cognition in Action 25 (1987). In addition, there is evidence that respondents answering open-ended questions may be less likely to report some information that they would reveal in response to a closed-ended question when that information seems self-evident or irrelevant.

92. Schwarz & Hippler, *supra* note 81, at 43.

93. *See* Vidal Sassoon, Inc. v. Bristol-Myers Co., 661 F.2d 272, 273 (2d Cir. 1981).

94. This was the wording of the stem of the closed-ended question in the survey discussed in *Vidal Sassoon*, 661 F.2d at 275–76.

95. Ninety-five percent of the respondents who answered the closed-ended question in the plaintiff's survey said that each woman had tried two or more brands. The open-ended question was never asked.

Closed-ended questions have some additional potential weaknesses that arise if the choices are not constructed properly. If the respondent is asked to choose one response from among several choices, the response chosen will be meaningful only if the list of choices is exhaustive, that is, if the choices cover all possible answers a respondent might give to the question. If the list of possible choices is incomplete, a respondent may be forced to choose one that does not express his or her opinion.[96] Moreover, if respondents are told explicitly that they are not limited to the choices presented, most respondents nevertheless will select an answer from among the listed ones.[97]

Although many courts prefer open-ended questions on the grounds that they tend to be less leading, the value of any open-ended or closed-ended question depends on the information it is intended to elicit. Open-ended questions are more appropriate when the survey is attempting to gauge what comes first to a respondent's mind, but closed-ended questions are more suitable for assessing choices between well-identified options or obtaining ratings on a clear set of alternatives.

D. If Probes Were Used to Clarify Ambiguous or Incomplete Answers, What Steps Were Taken to Ensure That the Probes Were Not Leading and Were Administered in a Consistent Fashion?

When questions allow respondents to express their opinions in their own words, some of the respondents may give ambiguous or incomplete answers. In such instances, interviewers may be instructed to record any answer that the respondent gives and move on to the next question, or they may be instructed to probe to obtain a more complete response or clarify the meaning of the ambiguous response. In either situation, interviewers should record verbatim both what the respondent says and what the interviewer says in the attempt to get clarification. Failure to record every part of the exchange in the order in which it occurs raises questions about the reliability of the survey, because neither the court nor the opposing party can evaluate whether the probe affected the views expressed by the respondent.

Vidal Sassoon, 661 F.2d at 276. Norbert Schwarz, *Assessing Frequency Reports of Mundane Behaviors: Contributions of Cognitive Psychology to Questionnaire Construction*, *in* Research Methods in Personality and Social Psychology 98 (Clyde Hendrick & Margaret S. Clark eds., 1990), suggests that respondents often rely on the range of response alternatives as a frame of reference when they are asked for frequency judgments. *See, e.g.*, Roger Tourangeau & Tom W. Smith, *Asking Sensitive Questions: The Impact of Data Collection Mode, Question Format, and Question Context*, 60 Pub. Opinion Q. 275, 292 (1996).

96. *See, e.g.*, American Home Prods. Corp. v. Johnson & Johnson, 654 F. Supp. 568, 581 (S.D.N.Y. 1987).

97. *See* Howard Schuman, *Ordinary Questions, Survey Questions, and Policy Questions*, 50 Pub. Opinion Q. 432, 435–36 (1986).

If the survey is designed to allow for probes, interviewers must be given explicit instructions on when they should probe and what they should say in probing. Standard probes used to draw out all that the respondent has to say (e.g., "Any further thoughts?" "Anything else?" "Can you explain that a little more?") are relatively innocuous and noncontroversial in content, but persistent continued requests for further responses to the same or nearly identical questions may convey the idea to the respondent that he or she has not yet produced the "right" answer.[98] Interviewers should be trained in delivering probes to maintain a professional and neutral relationship with the respondent (as they should during the rest of the interview), which minimizes any sense of passing judgment on the content of the answers offered. Moreover, interviewers should be given explicit instructions on when to probe, so that probes are administered consistently.

A more difficult type of probe to construct and deliver reliably is one that requires a substantive question tailored to the answer given by the respondent. The survey designer must provide sufficient instruction to interviewers so that they avoid giving directive probes that suggest one answer over another. Those instructions, along with all other aspects of interviewer training, should be made available for evaluation by the court and the opposing party.

E. What Approach Was Used to Avoid or Measure Potential Order or Context Effects?

The order in which questions are asked on a survey and the order in which response alternatives are provided in a closed-ended question can influence the answers.[99] Thus, although asking a general question before a more specific question on the same topic is unlikely to affect the response to the specific question, reversing the order of the questions may influence responses to the general question. As a rule, then, surveys are less likely to be subject to order effects if

98. *See, e.g.*, Johnson & Johnson-Merck Consumer Pharms. Co. v. Rhone-Poulenc Rorer Pharms., Inc., 19 F.3d 125, 135 (3d Cir. 1994); American Home Prods. Corp. v. Procter & Gamble Co., 871 F. Supp. 739, 748 (D.N.J. 1994).

99. *See* Schuman & Presser, *supra* note 82, at 23, 56–74; Norman M. Bradburn, *Response Effects, in* Handbook of Survey Research, *supra* note 1, at 289, 302. In *R.J. Reynolds Tobacco Co. v. Loew's Theatres, Inc.*, 511 F. Supp. 867, 875 (S.D.N.Y. 1980), the court recognized the biased structure of a survey which disclosed the tar content of the cigarettes being compared before questioning respondents about their cigarette preferences. Not surprisingly, respondents expressed a preference for the lower tar product. *See also* E. & J. Gallo Winery v. Pasatiempos Gallo, S.A., 905 F. Supp. 1403, 1409–10 (E.D. Cal. 1994) (court recognized that earlier questions referring to playing cards, board or table games, or party supplies, such as confetti, increased the likelihood that respondents would include these items in answers to the questions that followed).

the questions go from the general (e.g., "What do you recall being discussed in the advertisement?") to the specific (e.g., "Based on your reading of the advertisement, what companies do you think the ad is referring to when it talks about rental trucks that average five miles per gallon?").[100]

The mode of questioning can influence the form that an order effect takes. In mail surveys, respondents are more likely to select the first choice offered (a primacy effect); in telephone surveys, respondents are more likely to choose the last choice offered (a recency effect). Although these effects are typically small, no general formula is available that can adjust values to correct for order effects, because the size and even the direction of the order effects may depend on the nature of the question being asked and the choices being offered. Moreover, it may be unclear which order is most appropriate. For example, if the respondent is asked to choose between two different products, and there is a tendency for respondents to choose the first product mentioned,[101] which order of presentation will produce the more accurate response?[102]

To control for order effects, the order of the questions and the order of the response choices in a survey should be rotated,[103] so that, for example, one-third of the respondents have Product A listed first, one-third of the respondents have Product B listed first, and one-third of the respondents have Product C listed first. If the three different orders[104] are distributed randomly among respondents, no response alternative will have an inflated chance of being selected because of its position, and the average of the three will provide a reasonable estimate of response level.[105]

100. This question was accepted by the court in *U-Haul International, Inc. v. Jartran, Inc.*, 522 F. Supp. 1238, 1249 (D. Ariz. 1981), *aff'd*, 681 F.2d 1159 (9th Cir. 1982).

101. Similarly, candidates in the first position on the ballot tend to attract extra votes when the candidates are not well known. Henry M. Bain & Donald S. Hecock, Ballot Position and Voter's Choice: The Arrangement of Names on the Ballot and Its Effect on the Voter (1973).

102. *See* Rust Env't & Infrastructure, Inc. v. Teunissen, 131 F.3d 1210, 1218 (7th Cir. 1997) (survey did not pass muster in part because of failure to incorporate random rotation of corporate names that were the subject of a trademark dispute).

103. *See, e.g.*, Stouffer Foods Corp., 118 F.T.C. 746, No. 9250, 1994 FTC LEXIS 196, at *24–25 (Sept. 26, 1994); *cf.* Winning Ways, Inc. v. Holloway Sportswear, Inc., 913 F. Supp. 1454, 1465–67 (D. Kan. 1996) (failure to rotate the order in which the jackets were shown to the consumers led to reduced weight for the survey).

104. Actually, there are six possible orders of the three alternatives: ABC, ACB, BAC, BCA, CAB, and CBA. Thus, the optimal survey design would allocate equal numbers of respondents to each of the six possible orders.

105. Although rotation is desirable, many surveys are conducted with no attention to this potential bias. Since it is impossible to know in the abstract whether a particular question suffers much, little, or not at all from an order bias, lack of rotation should not preclude reliance on the answer to the question, but it should reduce the weight given to that answer.

F. If the Survey Was Designed to Test a Causal Proposition, Did the Survey Include an Appropriate Control Group or Question?

Most surveys that are designed to provide evidence of trademark infringement or deceptive advertising are not conducted to describe consumer beliefs. Instead, they are intended to show how a trademark or the content of a commercial influences respondents' perceptions or understanding of a product or commercial. Thus, the question is whether the commercial misleads the consumer into thinking that Product A is a superior pain reliever, not whether consumers hold inaccurate beliefs about the product. Yet if consumers already believe, before viewing the commercial, that Product A is a superior pain reliever, a survey that records consumers' impressions after they view the commercial may reflect those preexisting beliefs rather than impressions produced by the commercial.

Surveys that record consumer impressions have a limited ability to answer questions about the origins of those impressions. The difficulty is that the consumer's response to any question on the survey may be the result of information or misinformation from sources other than the trademark the respondent is being shown or the commercial he or she has just watched. In a trademark survey attempting to show secondary meaning, for example, respondents were shown a picture of the stripes used on Mennen stick deodorant and asked, "[W]hich [brand] would you say uses these stripes on their package?"[106] The court recognized that the high percentage of respondents selecting "Mennen" from an array of brand names may have represented "merely a playback of brand share"[107]; that is, respondents asked to give a brand name may guess the one that is most familiar, generally the brand with the largest market share.[108]

Some surveys attempt to reduce the impact of preexisting impressions on respondents' answers by instructing respondents to focus solely on the stimulus as a basis for their answers. Thus, the survey includes a preface (e.g., "based on the commercial you just saw") or directs the respondent's attention to the mark at issue (e.g., "these stripes on the package"). Such efforts are likely to be only partially successful. It is often difficult for respondents to identify accurately the source of their impressions.[109] The more routine the idea being examined in the survey (e.g., that the advertised pain reliever is more effective than others on the

106. Mennen Co. v. Gillette Co., 565 F. Supp. 648, 652 (S.D.N.Y. 1983), *aff'd*, 742 F.2d 1437 (2d Cir. 1984). To demonstrate secondary meaning, "the [c]ourt must determine whether the mark has been so associated in the mind of consumers with the entity that it identifies that the goods sold by that entity are distinguished by the mark or symbol from goods sold by others." *Id.*

107. *Id.*

108. *See also* Upjohn Co. v. American Home Prods. Corp., No. 1-95-CV-237, 1996 U.S. Dist. LEXIS 8049, at *42-44 (W.D. Mich. Apr. 5, 1996).

109. *See* Richard E. Nisbett & Timothy D. Wilson, *Telling More Than We Can Know: Verbal Reports on Mental Processes*, 84 Psychol. Rev. 231 (1977).

market; that the mark belongs to the brand with the largest market share), the more likely it is that the respondent's answer is influenced by preexisting impressions, by expectations about what commercials generally say (e.g., the product being advertised is better than its competitors), or by guessing, rather than by the actual content of the commercial message or trademark being evaluated.

It is possible to adjust many survey designs so that causal inferences about the effect of a trademark or an allegedly deceptive commercial become clear and unambiguous. By adding an appropriate control group, the survey expert can test directly the influence of the stimulus.[110] In the simplest version of a survey experiment, respondents are assigned randomly to one of two conditions.[111] For example, respondents assigned to the experimental condition view an allegedly deceptive commercial, and respondents assigned to the control condition either view a commercial that does not contain the allegedly deceptive material or do not view any commercial.[112] Respondents in both the experimental and control groups answer the same set of questions. The effect of the allegedly deceptive message is evaluated by comparing the responses made by the experimental group members with those of the control group members. If 40% of the respondents in the experimental group responded with the deceptive message (e.g., the advertised product has fewer calories than its competitor), whereas only 8% of the respondents in the control group gave that response, the difference between 40% and 8% (within the limits of sampling error[113]) can be attributed only to the allegedly deceptive commercial. Without the control group, it is not possible to determine how much of the 40% is due to respondents' preexisting beliefs or other background noise (e.g., respondents who misunderstand the question or misstate their responses). Both preexisting beliefs and other background noise should have produced similar response levels in the experimental

110. *See* Shari S. Diamond, *Using Psychology to Control Law: From Deceptive Advertising to Criminal Sentencing*, 13 Law & Hum. Behav. 239, 244–46 (1989); Shari S. Diamond & Linda Dimitropoulos, Deception and Puffery in Advertising: Behavioral Science Implications for Regulation (American Bar Found. Working Paper Series No. 9105, 1994); Jacob Jacoby & Constance Small, *Applied Marketing: The FDA Approach to Defining Misleading Advertising*, 39 J. Marketing 65, 68 (1975). For a more general discussion of the role of control groups, see David H. Kaye & David A. Freedman, Reference Guide on Statistics, § II.A, in this manual.

111. Random assignment should not be confused with random selection. When respondents are assigned randomly to different treatment groups (e.g., respondents in each group watch a different commercial), the procedure ensures that within the limits of sampling error the two groups of respondents will be equivalent except for the different treatments they receive. Respondents selected for a mall intercept study, and not from a probability sample, may be assigned randomly to different treatment groups. Random selection, in contrast, describes the method of selecting a sample of respondents in a probability sample. *See supra* § III.C.

112. This alternative commercial could be a "tombstone" advertisement that includes only the name of the product or a more elaborate commercial that does not include the claim at issue.

113. For a discussion of sampling error, see David H. Kaye & David A. Freedman, Reference Guide on Statistics, § IV, in this manual.

and control groups. In addition, if respondents who viewed the allegedly deceptive commercial respond differently than respondents who viewed the control commercial, the difference cannot be the result of a leading question, because both groups answered the same question. The ability to evaluate the effect of the wording of a particular question makes the control group design particularly useful in assessing responses to closed-ended questions,[114] which may encourage guessing or particular responses. Thus, the focus on the response level in a control group design is not on the absolute response level, but on the difference between the response level of the experimental group and that of the control group.

In designing a control group study, the expert should select a stimulus for the control group that shares as many characteristics with the experimental stimulus as possible, with the key exception of the characteristic whose influence is being assessed. A survey with an imperfect control group generally provides better information than a survey with no control group at all, but the choice of the specific control group requires some care and should influence the weight that the survey receives. For example, a control stimulus should not be less attractive than the experimental stimulus if the survey is designed to measure how familiar the experimental stimulus is to respondents, since attractiveness may affect perceived familiarity.[115] Nor should the control stimulus share with the experimental stimulus the feature whose impact is being assessed. If, for example, the control stimulus in a case of alleged trademark infringement is itself a likely source of consumer confusion, reactions to the experimental and control stimuli may not differ because both cause respondents to express the same level of confusion.[116]

Explicit attention to the value of control groups in trademark and deceptive-advertising litigation is a recent phenomenon, but it is becoming more common.[117] A LEXIS search using *Lanham Act* and *control group* revealed fourteen

114. The Federal Trade Commission has long recognized the need for some kind of control for closed-ended questions, although it has not specified the type of control that is necessary. Stouffer Foods Corp., 118 F.T.C. 746, No. 9250, 1994 FTC LEXIS 196, at *31 (Sept. 26, 1994).

115. *See, e.g.*, Indianapolis Colts, Inc. v. Metropolitan Baltimore Football Club Ltd. Partnership, 34 F.3d 410, 415–16 (7th Cir. 1994) (The court recognized that the name "Baltimore Horses" was less attractive for a sports team than the name "Baltimore Colts."). *See also* Reed-Union Corp. v. Turtle Wax, Inc., 77 F.3d 909, 912 (7th Cir. 1996) (court noted that one expert's choice of a control brand with a well-known corporate source was less appropriate than the opposing expert's choice of a control brand whose name did not indicate a specific corporate source).

116. *See, e.g.*, Western Publ'g Co. v. Publications Int'l, Ltd., No. 94-C-6803, 1995 U.S. Dist. LEXIS 5917, at *45 (N.D. Ill. May 2, 1995) (court noted that the control product was "arguably more infringing than" the defendant's product) (emphasis omitted).

117. *See, e.g.*, American Home Prods. Corp. v. Procter & Gamble Co., 871 F. Supp. 739, 749 (D.N.J. 1994) (discounting survey results based on failure to control for participants' preconceived notions); ConAgra, Inc. v. Geo. A. Hormel & Co., 784 F. Supp. 700, 728 (D. Neb. 1992) ("Since no control was used, the . . . study, standing alone, must be significantly discounted."), *aff'd*, 990 F.2d 368 (8th Cir. 1993).

district court cases in the six years since the first edition of this manual in 1994,[118] five district court cases in the seven years from 1987 to 1993,[119] and only one case before 1987[120] in which surveys with control groups were discussed. Other cases, however, have described or considered surveys using control group designs without labeling the comparison group a control group.[121] Indeed, one reason why cases involving surveys with control groups may be underrepresented in reported cases is that a survey with a control group produces less ambiguous findings, which may lead to a resolution before a preliminary injunction hearing or trial occurs.[122]

Another more common use of control methodology is a control question. Rather than administering a control stimulus to a separate group of respondents,

118. National Football League Properties, Inc. v. Prostyle, Inc., 57 F. Supp. 2d 665 (E.D. Wis. 1999); Nabisco, Inc. v. PF Brands, Inc., 50 F. Supp. 2d 188 (S.D.N.Y. 1999); Proctor & Gamble Co. v. Colgate-Palmolive Co., No. 96 Civ. 9123, 1998 U.S. Dist. LEXIS 17773 (S.D.N.Y. Nov. 5, 1998); Mattel, Inc. v. MCA Records, Inc., 28 F. Supp. 2d 1120 (C.D. Cal. 1998); Westchester Media Co. v. PRL USA Holdings, No. H-97-3278, 1998 U.S. Dist. LEXIS 11737 (S.D. Tex. July 2, 1998); Time Inc. v. Petersen Publ'g Co., 976 F. Supp. 263 (S.D.N.Y. 1997), *aff'd*, 173 F.3d 113 (2d Cir. 1999); Adjusters Int'l, Inc. v. Public Adjusters Int'l, Inc., No. 92-CV-1426, 1996 U.S. Dist. LEXIS 12604 (N.D.N.Y. Aug. 27, 1996); Upjohn Co. v. American Home Prods. Corp., No. 1-95-CV-237, 1996 U.S. Dist. LEXIS 8049 (W.D. Mich. Apr. 5, 1996); Copy Cop, Inc. v. Task Printing, Inc., 908 F. Supp. 37 (D. Mass. 1995); Volkswagen Aktiengesellschaft v. Uptown Motors, No. 91-CIV-3447, 1995 U.S. Dist. LEXIS 13869 (S.D.N.Y. July 13, 1995); Western Publ'g Co. v. Publications Int'l, Ltd., No. 94-C-6803, 1995 U.S. Dist. LEXIS 5917 (N.D. Ill. May 2, 1995); Dogloo, Inc. v. Doskocil Mfg. Co., 893 F. Supp. 911 (C.D. Cal. 1995); Reed-Union Corp. v. Turtle Wax, Inc., 869 F. Supp. 1304 (N.D. Ill. 1994), *aff'd*, 77 F.3d 909 (7th Cir. 1996); Pfizer, Inc. v. Miles, Inc., 868 F. Supp. 437 (D. Conn. 1994).

119. ConAgra, Inc. v. Geo. A. Hormel & Co., 784 F. Supp. 700 (D. Neb. 1992), *aff'd*, 990 F.2d 368 (8th Cir. 1993); Johnson & Johnson-Merck Consumer Pharms. Co. v. Smithkline Beecham Corp., No. 91 Civ. 0960, 1991 U.S. Dist. LEXIS 13689 (S.D.N.Y. Sept. 30, 1991), *aff'd*, 960 F.2d 294 (2d Cir. 1992); Goya Foods, Inc. v. Condal Distribs., Inc., 732 F. Supp. 453 (S.D.N.Y. 1990); Sturm, Ruger & Co. v. Arcadia Mach. & Tool, Inc., No. 85-8459, 1988 U.S. Dist. LEXIS 16451 (C.D. Cal. Nov. 7, 1988); Frisch's Restaurant, Inc. v. Elby's Big Boy, Inc., 661 F. Supp. 971 (S.D. Ohio 1987), *aff'd*, 849 F.2d 1012 (6th Cir. 1988).

120. American Basketball Ass'n v. AMF Voit, Inc., 358 F. Supp. 981 (S.D.N.Y.), *aff'd*, 487 F.2d 1393 (2d Cir. 1973).

121. Indianapolis Colts, Inc. v. Metropolitan Baltimore Football Club Ltd. Partnership, No. 94-727-C, 1994 U.S. Dist. LEXIS 19277, at *10–11 (S.D. Ind. June 27, 1994), *aff'd*, 34 F.3d 410 (7th Cir. 1994). In *Indianapolis Colts*, the district court described a survey conducted by the plaintiff's expert in which half of the interviewees were shown a shirt with the name "Baltimore CFL Colts" on it and half were shown a shirt on which the word "Horses" had been substituted for the word "Colts." *Id.* The court noted that the comparison of reactions to the horse and colt versions of the shirt made it possible "to determine the impact from the use of the word 'Colts.'" *Id.* at *11. *See also* Quality Inns Int'l, Inc. v. McDonald's Corp., 695 F. Supp. 198, 218 (D. Md. 1988) (survey revealed confusion between McDonald's and McSleep, but control survey revealed no confusion between McDonald's and McTavish).

122. The relatively infrequent mention of control groups in surveys discussed in federal cases is not confined to Lanham Act litigation. A LEXIS search using *survey* and *control group* revealed thirty district court cases in the six years from 1994 in which *control group* was used to refer to a methodological feature: the fourteen Lanham Act cases cited *supra* note 118; nine that referred to medical, physiological, or pharmacological experiments; and seven others.

the survey asks all respondents one or more control questions along with the question about the product or service. In a trademark dispute, for example, a survey indicated that 7.2% of respondents believed that "The Mart" and "K-Mart" were owned by the same individuals. The court found no likelihood of confusion based on survey evidence that 5.7% of the respondents also thought that "The Mart" and "King's Department Store" were owned by the same source.[123]

Similarly, a standard technique used to evaluate whether a brand name is generic is to present survey respondents with a series of product or service names and ask them to indicate in each instance whether they believe the name is a brand name or a common name. By showing that 68% of respondents considered Teflon a brand name (a proportion similar to the 75% of respondents who recognized the acknowledged trademark Jell-O as a brand name, and markedly different from the 13% who thought aspirin was a brand name), the makers of Teflon retained their trademark.[124]

Every measure of opinion or belief in a survey reflects some degree of error. Control groups and control questions are the most reliable means for assessing response levels against the baseline level of error associated with a particular question.

G. What Limitations Are Associated with the Mode of Data Collection Used in the Survey?

Three primary methods are used to collect survey data: (1) in-person interviews, (2) telephone surveys, and (3) mail surveys.[125] The choice of a data collection method for a survey should be justified by its strengths and weaknesses.

1. In-person interviews

Although costly, in-person interviews generally are the preferred method of data collection, especially when visual materials must be shown to the respondent under controlled conditions.[126] When the questions are complex and the interviewers are skilled, in-person interviewing provides the maximum oppor-

123. S.S. Kresge Co. v. United Factory Outlet, Inc., 598 F.2d 694, 697 (1st Cir. 1979). Note that the aggregate percentages reported here do not reveal how many of the same respondents were confused by both names, an issue that may be relevant in some situations. *See* Joseph L. Gastwirth, *Reference Guide on Survey Research*, 36 Jurimetrics J. 181, 187–88 (1996) (review essay).

124. E.I. DuPont de Nemours & Co. v. Yoshida Int'l, Inc., 393 F. Supp. 502, 526-27 & n.54 (E.D.N.Y. 1975).

125. Methods also may be combined, as when the telephone is used to "screen" for eligible respondents, who then are invited to participate in an in-person interview.

126. A mail survey also can include limited visual materials but cannot exercise control over when and how the respondent views them.

tunity to clarify or probe. Unlike a mail survey, both in-person and telephone interviews have the capability to implement complex skip sequences (in which the respondent's answer determines which question will be asked next) and the power to control the order in which the respondent answers the questions. As described in section V.A, appropriate interviewer training is necessary if these potential benefits are to be realized. Objections to the use of in-person interviews arise primarily from their high cost or, on occasion, from evidence of inept or biased interviewers.

2. *Telephone surveys*

Telephone surveys offer a comparatively fast and low-cost alternative to in-person surveys and are particularly useful when the population is large and geographically dispersed. Telephone interviews (unless supplemented with mailed materials) can be used only when it is unnecessary to show the respondent any visual materials. Thus, an attorney may present the results of a telephone survey of jury-eligible citizens in a motion for a change of venue in order to provide evidence that community prejudice raises a reasonable suspicion of potential jury bias.[127] Similarly, potential confusion between a restaurant called McBagel's and the McDonald's fast-food chain was established in a telephone survey. Over objections from defendant McBagel's that the survey did not show respondents the defendant's print advertisements, the court found likelihood of confusion based on the survey, noting that "by soliciting audio responses [, the telephone survey] was closely related to the radio advertising involved in the case."[128] In contrast, when words are not sufficient because, for example, the survey is assessing reactions to the trade dress or packaging of a product that is alleged to promote confusion, a telephone survey alone does not offer a suitable vehicle for questioning respondents.[129]

In evaluating the sampling used in a telephone survey, the trier of fact should consider

- (when prospective respondents are not business personnel) whether some form of random-digit dialing[130] was used instead of or to supplement tele-

127. United States v. Partin, 320 F. Supp. 275, 279-80 (E.D. La. 1970). For a discussion of surveys used in motions for change of venue, see Neal Miller, *Facts, Expert Facts, and Statistics: Descriptive and Experimental Research Methods in Litigation, Part II*, 40 Rutgers L. Rev. 467, 470–74 (1988); National Jury Project, Jurywork: Systematic Techniques (Elissa Krauss & Beth Bonora eds., 2d ed. 1983).

128. McDonald's Corp. v. McBagel's, Inc., 649 F. Supp. 1268, 1278 (S.D.N.Y. 1986).

129. Thompson Med. Co. v. Pfizer Inc., 753 F.2d 208 (2d Cir. 1985); Incorporated Publ'g Corp. v. Manhattan Magazine, Inc., 616 F. Supp. 370 (S.D.N.Y. 1985), *aff'd without op.*, 788 F.2d 3 (2d Cir. 1986).

130. Random digit dialing provides coverage of households with both listed and unlisted telephone numbers by generating numbers at random from the frame of all possible telephone numbers. James M. Lepkowski, *Telephone Sampling Methods in the United States*, *in* Telephone Survey Methodology 81–91 (Robert M. Groves et al. eds., 1988).

phone numbers obtained from telephone directories, because up to 65% of all residential telephone numbers in some areas may be unlisted;[131]

- whether the sampling procedures required the interviewer to sample within the household or business, instead of allowing the interviewer to administer the survey to any qualified individual who answered the telephone;[132] and
- whether interviewers were required to call back at several different times of the day and on different days to increase the likelihood of contacting individuals or businesses with different schedules.

Telephone surveys that do not include these procedures may, like other nonprobability sampling approaches, be adequate for providing rough approximations. The vulnerability of the survey depends on the information being gathered. More elaborate procedures for achieving a representative sample of respondents are advisable if the survey instrument requests information that is likely to differ for individuals with listed telephone numbers and individuals with unlisted telephone numbers, or individuals rarely at home and those usually at home.

The report submitted by a survey expert who conducts a telephone survey should specify

1. the procedures that were used to identify potential respondents;
2. the number of telephone numbers for which no contact was made; and
3. the number of contacted potential respondents who refused to participate in the survey.

Computer-assisted telephone interviewing, or CATI, is increasingly used in the administration and data entry of large-scale surveys.[133] A computer protocol may be used to generate telephone numbers and dial them as well as to guide the interviewer. The interviewer conducting a computer-assisted interview (CAI), whether by telephone or in a face-to-face setting, follows the script for the interview generated by the computer program and types in the respondent's answers as the interview proceeds. A primary advantage of CATI and other CAI procedures is that skip patterns can be built into the program so that, for example, if the respondent is asked whether she has ever been the victim of a burglary and she says yes, the computer will generate further questions about

131. In 1992, the percentage of households with unlisted numbers reached 65% in Las Vegas and 62% in Los Angeles. Survey Sampling, Inc., The Frame 2 (March 1993). Studies comparing listed and unlisted household characteristics show some important differences. Lepkowski, *supra* note 130, at 76.

132. This is a consideration only if the survey is sampling individuals. If the survey is seeking information on the household, more than one individual may be able to answer questions on behalf of the household.

133. William L. Nicholls II & R.M. Groves, *The Status of Computer-Assisted Telephone Interviewing*, 2 J. Official Stat. 93 (1986); Mary A. Spaeth, *CATI Facilities at Academic Research Organizations*, 21 Surv. Res. 11 (1990); William E. Saris, Computer-Assisted Interviewing (1991).

the burglary, but if she says no, the program will automatically skip the follow-up burglary questions. Interviewer errors in following the skip patterns are therefore avoided, making CAI procedures particularly valuable when the survey involves complex branching and skip patterns.[134] CAI procedures can also be used to control for order effects by having the program rotate the order in which questions or choices are presented.[135] CAI procedures, however, require additional planning to take advantage of the potential for improvements in data quality. When a CAI protocol is used in a survey presented in litigation, the party offering the survey should supply for inspection the computer program that was used to generate the interviews. Moreover, CAI procedures do not eliminate the need for close monitoring of interviews to ensure that interviewers are accurately reading the questions in the interview protocol and accurately entering the answers that the respondent is giving to those questions.

3. Mail surveys

In general, mail surveys tend to be substantially less costly than both in-person and telephone surveys.[136] Although response rates for mail surveys are often low, researchers have obtained 70% response rates in some general public surveys and response rates of over 90% with certain specialized populations.[137] Procedures that encourage high response rates include multiple mailings, highly personalized communications, prepaid return envelopes and incentives or gratuities, assurances of confidentiality, and first-class outgoing postage.[138]

A mail survey will not produce a high rate of return unless it begins with an accurate and up-to-date list of names and addresses for the target population. Even if the sampling frame is adequate, the sample may be unrepresentative if some individuals are more likely to respond than others. For example, if a survey targets a population that includes individuals with literacy problems, these individuals will tend to be underrepresented. Open-ended questions are generally of limited value on a mail survey because they depend entirely on the respondent to answer fully and do not provide the opportunity to probe or clarify

134. Saris, *supra* note 133, at 20, 27.

135. *See, e.g.*, Intel Corp. v. Advanced Micro Devices, Inc., 756 F. Supp. 1292, 1296–97 (N.D. Cal. 1991) (survey designed to test whether the term *386* as applied to a microprocessor was generic used a CATI protocol that tested reactions to five terms presented in rotated order).

136. Don A. Dillman, *Mail and Other Self-Administered Questionnaires*, *in* Handbook of Survey Research, *supra* note 1, at 359, 373.

137. *Id.* at 360.

138. *See, e.g.*, Richard J. Fox et al., *Mail Survey Response Rate: A Meta-Analysis of Selected Techniques for Inducing Response*, 52 Pub. Opinion Q. 467, 482 (1988); Eleanor Singer et al., *Confidentiality Assurances and Response: A Quantitative Review of the Experimental Literature*, 59 Pub. Opinion Q. 66, 71 (1995); Kenneth D. Hopkins & Arlen R. Gullickson, *Response Rates in Survey Research: A Meta-Analysis of the Effects of Monetary Gratuities*, 61 J. Experimental Educ. 52, 54–57, 59 (1992).

unclear answers. Similarly, if eligibility to answer some questions depends on the respondent's answers to previous questions, such skip sequences may be difficult for some respondents to follow. Finally, because respondents complete mail surveys without supervision, survey personnel are unable to prevent respondents from discussing the questions and answers with others before completing the survey and to control the order in which respondents answer the questions. If it is crucial to have respondents answer questions in a particular order, a mail survey cannot be depended on to provide adequate data.[139]

4. *Internet surveys*

A more recent innovation in survey technology is the Internet survey in which potential respondents are contacted and their responses are collected over the Internet. Internet surveys can substantially reduce the cost of reaching potential respondents and offer some of the advantages of in-person interviews by allowing the computer to show the respondent pictures or lists of response choices in the course of asking the respondent questions. The key limitation is that the respondents accessible over the Internet must fairly represent the relevant population whose responses the survey was designed to measure. Thus, a litigant presenting the results of a web-based survey should be prepared to provide evidence on the potential bias in sampling that the web-based survey is likely to introduce. If the target population consists of computer users, the bias may be minimal. If the target population consists of owners of television sets, significant bias is likely.

V. Surveys Involving Interviewers

A. *Were the Interviewers Appropriately Selected and Trained?*

A properly defined population or universe, a representative sample, and clear and precise questions can be depended on to produce trustworthy survey results only if "sound interview procedures were followed by competent interviewers."[140] Properly trained interviewers receive detailed written instructions on everything they are to say to respondents, any stimulus materials they are to use in the survey, and how they are to complete the interview form. These instructions should be made available to the opposing party and to the trier of fact. Thus, interviewers should be told, and the interview form on which answers are recorded should indicate, which responses, if any, are to be read to the respondent. Interviewers also should be instructed to record verbatim the respondent's

139. Dillman, *supra* note 136, at 368–70.

140. Toys "R" Us, Inc. v. Canarsie Kiddie Shop, Inc., 559 F. Supp. 1189, 1205 (E.D.N.Y. 1983).

answers, to indicate explicitly whenever they repeat a question to the respondent, and to record any statements they make to or supplementary questions they ask the respondent.

Interviewers require training to ensure that they are able to follow directions in administering the survey questions. Some training in general interviewing techniques is required for most interviews (e.g., practice in pausing to give the respondent enough time to answer and practice in resisting invitations to express the interviewer's beliefs or opinions). Although procedures vary, one treatise recommends at least five hours of training in general interviewing skills and techniques for new interviewers.[141]

The more complicated the survey instrument is, the more training and experience the interviewers require. Thus, if the interview includes a skip pattern (where, e.g., Questions 4–6 are asked only if the respondent says yes to Question 3, and Questions 8–10 are asked only if the respondent says no to Question 3), interviewers must be trained to follow the pattern. Similarly, if the questions require specific probes to clarify ambiguous responses, interviewers must receive instruction on when to use the probes and what to say. In some surveys, the interviewer is responsible for last-stage sampling (i.e., selecting the particular respondents to be interviewed), and training is especially crucial to avoid interviewer bias in selecting respondents who are easiest to approach or easiest to find.

Training and instruction of interviewers should include directions on the circumstances under which interviews are to take place (e.g., question only one respondent at a time out of the hearing of any other respondent). The trustworthiness of a survey is questionable if there is evidence that some interviews were conducted in a setting in which respondents were likely to have been distracted or in which others were present and could overhear. Such evidence of careless administration of the survey was one ground used by a court to reject as inadmissible a survey that purported to demonstrate consumer confusion.[142]

Some compromises may be accepted when surveys must be conducted swiftly. In trademark and deceptive advertising cases, the plaintiff's usual request is for a preliminary injunction, because a delay means irreparable harm. Nonetheless, careful instruction and training of interviewers who administer the survey and complete disclosure of the methods used for instruction and training are crucial elements that, if compromised, seriously undermine the trustworthiness of any survey.

141. Eve Weinberg, *Data Collection: Planning and Management*, *in* Handbook of Survey Research, *supra* note 1, at 329, 332.

142. *Toys "R" Us*, 559 F. Supp. at 1204 (some interviews apparently were conducted in a bowling alley; some interviewees waiting to be interviewed overheard the substance of the interview while they were waiting).

B. *What Did the Interviewers Know About the Survey and Its Sponsorship?*

One way to protect the objectivity of survey administration is to avoid telling interviewers who is sponsoring the survey. Interviewers who know the identity of the survey's sponsor may affect results inadvertently by communicating to respondents their expectations or what they believe are the preferred responses of the survey's sponsor. To ensure objectivity in the administration of the survey, it is standard interview practice to conduct double-blind research whenever possible: both the interviewer and the respondent are blind to the sponsor of the survey and its purpose. Thus, the survey instrument should provide no explicit clues (e.g., a sponsor's letterhead appearing on the survey) and no implicit clues (e.g., reversing the usual order of the yes and no response boxes on the interviewer's form next to a crucial question, thereby potentially increasing the likelihood that *no* will be checked[143]) about the sponsorship of the survey or the expected responses.

Nonetheless, in some surveys (e.g., some government surveys), disclosure of the survey's sponsor to respondents (and thus to interviewers) is required. Such surveys call for an evaluation of the likely biases introduced by interviewer or respondent awareness of the survey's sponsorship. In evaluating the consequences of sponsorship awareness, it is important to consider (1) whether the sponsor has views and expectations that are apparent and (2) whether awareness is confined to the interviewers or involves the respondents. For example, if a survey concerning attitudes toward gun control is sponsored by the National Rifle Association, it is clear that responses opposing gun control are likely to be preferred. In contrast, if the survey on gun control attitudes is sponsored by the Department of Justice, the identity of the sponsor may not suggest the kind of responses the sponsor expects or would find acceptable.[144] When interviewers are well trained, their awareness of sponsorship may be a less serious threat than respondents' awareness. The empirical evidence for the effects of interviewers' prior expectations on respondents' answers generally reveals modest effects when the interviewers are well trained.[145]

143. Centaur Communications, Ltd. v. A/S/M Communications, Inc., 652 F. Supp. 1105, 1111 n.3 (S.D.N.Y.) (pointing out that reversing the usual order of response choices, yes or no, to no or yes may confuse interviewers as well as introduce bias), *aff'd*, 830 F.2d 1217 (2d Cir. 1987).

144. *See, e.g.*, Stanley Presser et al., *Survey Sponsorship, Response Rates, and Response Effects*, 73 Soc. Sci. Q. 699, 701 (1992) (different responses to a university-sponsored telephone survey and a newspaper-sponsored survey for questions concerning attitudes toward the mayoral primary, an issue on which the newspaper had taken a position).

145. *See, e.g.*, Seymour Sudman et al., *Modest Expectations: The Effects of Interviewers' Prior Expectations on Responses*, 6 Soc. Methods & Res. 171, 181 (1977).

C. What Procedures Were Used to Ensure and Determine That the Survey Was Administered to Minimize Error and Bias?

Three methods are used to ensure that the survey instrument was implemented in an unbiased fashion and according to instructions. The first, monitoring the interviews as they occur, is done most easily when telephone surveys are used. A supervisor listens to a sample of interviews for each interviewer. Field settings make monitoring more difficult, but evidence that monitoring has occurred provides an additional indication that the survey has been reliably implemented.

Second, validation of interviews occurs when respondents in a sample are recontacted to ask whether the initial interviews took place and to determine whether the respondents were qualified to participate in the survey. The standard procedure for validation of in-person interviews is to telephone a random sample of about 10% to 15% of the respondents.[146] Some attempts to reach the respondent will be unsuccessful, and occasionally a respondent will deny that the interview took place even though it did. Because the information checked is limited to whether the interview took place and whether the respondent was qualified, this validation procedure does not determine whether the initial interview as a whole was conducted properly. Nonetheless, this standard validation technique warns interviewers that their work is being checked and can detect gross failures in the administration of the survey.

A third way to verify that the interviews were conducted properly is to compare the work done by each individual interviewer. By reviewing the interviews and individual responses recorded by each interviewer, researchers can identify any response patterns or inconsistencies for further investigation.

When a survey is conducted at the request of a party for litigation rather than in the normal course of business, a heightened standard for validation checks may be appropriate. Thus, independent validation of at least 50% of interviews by a third party rather than by the field service that conducted the interviews increases the trustworthiness of the survey results.[147]

146. *See, e.g.*, National Football League Properties, Inc. v. New Jersey Giants, Inc., 637 F. Supp. 507, 515 (D.N.J. 1986); Davis v. Southern Bell Tel. & Tel. Co., No. 89-2839, 1994 U.S. Dist. LEXIS 13257, at *16 (S.D. Fla. Feb. 1, 1994).

147. In *Rust Environment & Infrastructure, Inc. v. Teunissen*, 131 F.3d 1210, 1218 (7th Cir. 1997), the court criticized a survey in part because it "did not comport with accepted practice for independent validation of the results."

VI. Data Entry and Grouping of Responses

A. What Was Done to Ensure That the Data Were Recorded Accurately?

Analyzing the results of a survey requires that the data obtained on each sampled element be recorded, edited, and often coded before the results can be tabulated and processed. Procedures for data entry should include checks for completeness, checks for reliability and accuracy, and rules for resolving inconsistencies. Accurate data entry is maximized when responses are verified by duplicate entry and comparison, and when data entry personnel are unaware of the purposes of the survey.

B. What Was Done to Ensure That the Grouped Data Were Classified Consistently and Accurately?

Coding of answers to open-ended questions requires a detailed set of instructions so that decision standards are clear and responses can be scored consistently and accurately. Two trained coders should independently score the same responses to check for the level of consistency in classifying responses. When the criteria used to categorize verbatim responses are controversial or allegedly inappropriate, those criteria should be sufficiently clear to reveal the source of disagreements. In all cases, the verbatim responses should be available so that they can be recoded using alternative criteria.[148]

148. *See, e.g.*, Coca-Cola Co. v. Tropicana Prods., Inc., 538 F. Supp. 1091, 1094–96 (S.D.N.Y.) (plaintiff's expert stated that respondents' answers to the several open-ended questions revealed that 43% of respondents thought Tropicana was portrayed as fresh squeezed; the court's own tabulation found no more than 15% believed this was true), *rev'd on other grounds*, 690 F.2d 312 (2d Cir. 1982). *See also* McNeilab, Inc. v. American Home Prods. Corp., 501 F. Supp. 517 (S.D.N.Y. 1980); Rock v. Zimmerman, 959 F.2d 1237, 1253 n.9 (3d Cir. 1992) (court found that responses on a change of venue survey incorrectly categorized respondents who believed the defendant was insane as believing he was guilty); Revlon Consumer Prods. Corp. v. Jennifer Leather Broadway, Inc., 858 F. Supp. 1268, 1276 (S.D.N.Y. 1994) (inconsistent scoring and subjective coding led court to find survey so unreliable that it was entitled to no weight), *aff'd*, 57 F.3d 1062 (2d Cir. 1995).

VII. Disclosure and Reporting

A. When Was Information About the Survey Methodology and Results Disclosed?

Objections to the definition of the relevant population, the method of selecting the sample, and the wording of questions generally are raised for the first time when the results of the survey are presented. By that time it is too late to correct methodological deficiencies that could have been addressed in the planning stages of the survey. The plaintiff in a trademark case[149] submitted a set of proposed survey questions to the trial judge, who ruled that the survey results would be admissible at trial while reserving the question of the weight the evidence would be given.[150] The court of appeals called this approach a commendable procedure and suggested that it would have been even more desirable if the parties had "attempt[ed] in good faith to agree upon the questions to be in such a survey."[151]

The *Manual for Complex Litigation, Second,* recommended that parties be required, "before conducting any poll, to provide other parties with an outline of the proposed form and methodology, including the particular questions that will be asked, the introductory statements or instructions that will be given, and other controls to be used in the interrogation process."[152] The parties then were encouraged to attempt to resolve any methodological disagreements before the survey was conducted.[153] Although this passage in the second edition of the manual has been cited with apparent approval,[154] the prior agreement the manual recommends has occurred rarely and the *Manual for Complex Litigation, Third,* recommends, but does not advocate requiring, prior disclosure and discussion of survey plans.[155]

Rule 26 of the Federal Rules of Civil Procedure requires extensive disclosure of the basis of opinions offered by testifying experts. However, these provisions may not produce disclosure of all survey materials, because parties are not obli-

149. Union Carbide Corp. v. Ever-Ready, Inc., 392 F. Supp. 280 (N.D. Ill. 1975), *rev'd,* 531 F.2d 366 (7th Cir.), *cert. denied,* 429 U.S. 830 (1976).

150. Before trial, the presiding judge was appointed to the court of appeals, so the case was tried by another district court judge.

151. *Union Carbide,* 531 F.2d at 386. More recently, the Seventh Circuit recommended the filing of a motion *in limine,* asking the district court to determine the admissibility of a survey based on an examination of the survey questions and the results of a preliminary survey before the party undertakes the expense of conducting the actual survey. Piper Aircraft Corp. v. Wag-Aero, Inc., 741 F.2d 925, 929 (7th Cir. 1984).

152. MCL 2d, *supra* note 15, § 21.484.

153. *Id.*

154. *E.g.,* National Football League Properties, Inc. v. New Jersey Giants, Inc., 637 F. Supp. 507, 514 n.3 (D.N.J. 1986).

155. MCL 3d, *supra* note 15, § 21.493.

gated to disclose information about nontestifying experts. Parties considering whether to commission or use a survey for litigation are not obligated to present a survey that produces unfavorable results. Prior disclosure of a proposed survey instrument places the party that ultimately would prefer not to present the survey in the position of presenting damaging results or leaving the impression that the results are not being presented because they were unfavorable. Anticipating such a situation, parties do not decide whether an expert will testify until after the results of the survey are available.

Nonetheless, courts are in a position to encourage early disclosure and discussion even if they do not lead to agreement between the parties. In *McNeilab, Inc. v. American Home Products Corp.*,[156] Judge William C. Conner encouraged the parties to submit their survey plans for court approval to ensure their evidentiary value; the plaintiff did so and altered its research plan based on Judge Conner's recommendations. Parties can anticipate that changes consistent with a judicial suggestion are likely to increase the weight given to, or at least the prospects of admissibility of, the survey.[157]

B. Does the Survey Report Include Complete and Detailed Information on All Relevant Characteristics?

The completeness of the survey report is one indicator of the trustworthiness of the survey and the professionalism of the expert who is presenting the results of the survey. A survey report generally should provide in detail

1. the purpose of the survey;
2. a definition of the target population and a description of the population that was actually sampled;
3. a description of the sample design, including the method of selecting respondents, the method of interview, the number of callbacks, respondent eligibility or screening criteria, and other pertinent information;
4. a description of the results of sample implementation, including (a) the number of potential respondents contacted, (b) the number not reached, (c) the number of refusals, (d) the number of incomplete interviews or terminations, (e) the number of noneligibles, and (f) the number of completed interviews;
5. the exact wording of the questions used, including a copy of each version of the actual questionnaire, interviewer instructions, and visual exhibits;
6. a description of any special scoring (e.g., grouping of verbatim responses into broader categories);

156. 848 F.2d 34, 36 (2d Cir. 1988) (discussing with approval the actions of the district court).

157. Larry C. Jones, *Developing and Using Survey Evidence in Trademark Litigation*, 19 Memphis St. U. L. Rev. 471, 481 (1989).

7. estimates of the sampling error, where appropriate (i.e., in probability samples);
8. statistical tables clearly labeled and identified as to source of data, including the number of raw cases forming the base for each table, row, or column; and
9. copies of interviewer instructions, validation results, and code books.[158]

A description of the procedures and results of pilot testing is not included on this list. Survey professionals generally do not describe pilot testing in their reports. The Federal Rules of Civil Procedure, however, may require that a testifying expert disclose pilot work that serves as a basis for the expert's opinion. The situation is more complicated when a nontestifying expert conducts the pilot work and the testifying expert learns about the pilot testing only indirectly through the attorney's advice about the relevant issues in the case. Some commentators suggest that attorneys are obligated to disclose such pilot work.[159]

C. In Surveys of Individuals, What Measures Were Taken to Protect the Identities of Individual Respondents?

The respondents questioned in a survey generally do not testify in legal proceedings and are unavailable for cross-examination. Indeed, one of the advantages of a survey is that it avoids a repetitious and unrepresentative parade of witnesses. To verify that interviews occurred with qualified respondents, standard survey practice includes validation procedures,[160] the results of which should be included in the survey report.

Conflicts may arise when an opposing party asks for survey respondents' names and addresses in order to reinterview some respondents. The party introducing the survey or the survey organization that conducted the research generally resists supplying such information.[161] Professional surveyors as a rule guarantee

158. These criteria were adapted from the Council of Am. Survey Res. Orgs., *supra* note 41, § III. B. Failure to supply this information substantially impairs a court's ability to evaluate a survey. *In re* Prudential Ins. Co. of Am. Sales Practices Litig., 962 F. Supp. 450, 532 (D.N.J. 1997) (citing the first edition of this manual). *But see Florida Bar v. Went for It, Inc.*, 515 U.S. 618, 626–28 (1995), in which a majority of the Supreme Court relied on a summary of results prepared by the Florida Bar from a consumer survey purporting to show consumer objections to attorney solicitation by mail. In a strong dissent, Justice Kennedy, joined by three of his colleagues, found the survey inadequate based on the document available to the court, pointing out that the summary included "no actual surveys, few indications of sample size or selection procedures, no explanations of methodology, and no discussion of excluded results . . . no description of the statistical universe or scientific framework that permits any productive use of the information the so-called Summary of Record contains." *Id.* at 640.

159. Yvonne C. Schroeder, *Pretesting Survey Questions*, 11 Am. J. Trial Advoc. 195, 197–201 (1987).

160. *See supra* § V.C.

161. *See, e.g.*, Alpo Petfoods, Inc. v. Ralston Purina Co., 720 F. Supp. 194 (D.D.C. 1989), *aff'd in part & vacated in part*, 913 F.2d 958 (D.C. Cir. 1990).

confidentiality in an effort to increase participation rates and to encourage candid responses. Because failure to extend confidentiality may bias both the willingness of potential respondents to participate in a survey and their responses, the professional standards for survey researchers generally prohibit disclosure of respondents' identities. "The use of survey results in a legal proceeding does not relieve the Survey Research Organization of its ethical obligation to maintain in confidence all Respondent-identifiable information or lessen the importance of Respondent anonymity."[162] Although no surveyor–respondent privilege currently is recognized, the need for surveys and the availability of other means to examine and ensure their trustworthiness argue for deference to legitimate claims for confidentiality in order to avoid seriously compromising the ability of surveys to produce accurate information.[163]

Copies of all questionnaires should be made available upon request so that the opposing party has an opportunity to evaluate the raw data. All identifying information, such as the respondent's name, address, and telephone number, should be removed to ensure respondent confidentiality.

162. Council of Am. Survey Res. Orgs., *supra* note 41, § I.A.3.f. Similar provisions are contained in the By-Laws of the American Association for Public Opinion Research.

163. Litton Indus., Inc., No. 9123, 1979 FTC LEXIS 311, at *13 & n.12 (June 19, 1979) (Order Concerning the Identification of Individual Survey-Respondents with Their Questionnaires) (citing Frederick H. Boness & John F. Cordes, Note, *The Researcher–Subject Relationship: The Need for Protection and a Model Statute*, 62 Geo. L.J. 243, 253 (1973)). *See also* Lampshire v. Procter & Gamble Co., 94 F.R.D. 58, 60 (N.D. Ga. 1982) (defendant denied access to personal identifying information about women involved in studies by the Centers for Disease Control based on Fed. R. Civ. P. 26(c) giving court the authority to enter "any order which justice requires to protect a party or persons from annoyance, embarrassment, oppression, or undue burden or expense.") (citation omitted).

Glossary of Terms

The following terms and definitions were adapted from a variety of sources, including Handbook of Survey Research (Peter H. Rossi et al. eds., 1983); 1 Environmental Protection Agency, Survey Management Handbook (1983); Measurement Errors in Surveys (Paul P. Biemer et al. eds., 1991); William E. Saris, Computer-Assisted Interviewing (1991); Seymour Sudman, Applied Sampling (1976).

branching. A questionnaire structure that uses the answers to earlier questions to determine which set of additional questions should be asked (e.g., citizens who report having served as jurors on a criminal case are asked different questions about their experiences than citizens who report having served as jurors on a civil case).

CAI (computer-assisted interviewing). A method of conducting interviews in which an interviewer asks questions and records the respondent's answer by following a computer-generated protocol.

CATI (computer-assisted telephone interviewing). A method of conducting telephone interviews in which an interviewer asks questions and records the respondent's answer by following a computer-generated protocol.

closed-ended question. A question that provides the respondent with a list of choices and asks the respondent to choose from among them.

cluster sampling. A sampling technique allowing for the selection of sample elements in groups or clusters, rather than on an individual basis; it may significantly reduce field costs and may increase sampling error if elements in the same cluster are more similar to one another than are elements in different clusters.

confidence interval. An indication of the probable range of error associated with a sample value obtained from a probability sample. Also, margin of error.

convenience sample. A sample of elements selected because they were readily available.

double-blind research. Research in which the respondent and the interviewer are not given information that will alert them to the anticipated or preferred pattern of response.

error score. The degree of measurement error in an observed score (see true score).

full-filter question. A question asked of respondents to screen out those who do not have an opinion on the issue under investigation before asking them the question proper.

mall intercept survey. A survey conducted in a mall or shopping center in which potential respondents are approached by a recruiter (intercepted) and invited to participate in the survey.

multistage sampling design. A sampling design in which sampling takes place in several stages, beginning with larger units (e.g., cities) and then proceeding with smaller units (e.g., households or individuals within these units).

nonprobability sample. Any sample that does not qualify as a probability sample.

open-ended question. A question that requires the respondent to formulate his or her own response.

order effect. A tendency of respondents to choose an item based in part on the order in which it appears in the question, questionnaire, or interview (see primacy effect and recency effect); also referred to as a context effect because the context of the question influences the way the respondent perceives and answers it.

parameter. A summary measure of a characteristic of a population (e.g., average age, proportion of households in an area owning a computer). Statistics are estimates of parameters.

pilot test. A small field test replicating the field procedures planned for the full-scale survey; although the terms *pilot test* and *pretest* are sometimes used interchangeably, a pretest tests the questionnaire, whereas a pilot test generally tests proposed collection procedures as well.

population. The totality of elements (objects, individuals, or other social units) that have some common property of interest; the target population is the collection of elements that the researcher would like to study; the survey population is the population that is actually sampled and for which data may be obtained. Also, universe.

population value, population parameter. The actual value of some characteristic in the population (e.g., the average age); the population value is estimated by taking a random sample from the population and computing the corresponding sample value.

pretest. A small preliminary test of a survey questionnaire. See pilot test.

primacy effect. A tendency of respondents to choose early items from a list of choices; the opposite of a recency effect.

probability sample. A type of sample selected so that every element in the population has a known nonzero probability of being included in the sample; a simple random sample is a probability sample.

probe. A follow-up question that an interviewer asks to obtain a more complete answer from a respondent (e.g., "Anything else?" "What kind of medical problem do you mean?").

quasi-filter question. A question that offers a "don't know" or "no opinion" option to respondents as part of a set of response alternatives; used to screen out respondents who may not have an opinion on the issue under investigation.

random sample. See simple random sample.

recency effect. A tendency of respondents to choose later items from a list of choices; the opposite of a primacy effect.

sample. A subset of a population or universe selected so as to yield information about the population as a whole.

sampling error. The estimated size of the difference between the result obtained from a sample study and the result that would be obtained by attempting a complete study of all units in the sampling frame from which the sample was selected in the same manner and with the same care.

sampling frame. The source or sources from which the objects, individuals, or other social units in a sample are drawn.

secondary meaning. A descriptive term that becomes protectable as a trademark if it signifies to the purchasing public that the product comes from a single producer or source.

simple random sample. The most basic type of probability sample; each unit in the population has an equal probability of being in the sample, and all possible samples of a given size are equally likely to be selected.

skip pattern, skip sequence. A sequence of questions in which some should not be asked (should be skipped) based on the respondent's answer to a previous question (e.g., if the respondent indicates that he does not own a car, he should not be asked what brand of car he owns).

stratified sampling. A sampling technique that permits the researcher to subdivide the population into mutually exclusive and exhaustive subpopulations, or strata; within these strata, separate samples are selected; results can be combined to form overall population estimates or used to report separate within-stratum estimates.

survey population. See population.

systematic sampling. A sampling technique that consists of a random starting point and the selection of every *n*th member of the population; it generally produces the same results as simple random sampling.

target population. See population.

trade dress. A distinctive and nonfunctional design of a package or product protected under state unfair competition law and the federal Lanham Act §43(a), 15 U.S.C. §1125(a) (1946) (amended 1992).

true score. The underlying true value, which is unobservable because there is always some error in measurement; the observed score = true score + error score.

universe. See population.

References on Survey Research

William G. Cochran, Sampling Techniques (3d ed. 1977).

Jean M. Converse & Stanley Presser, Survey Questions: Handcrafting the Standardized Questionnaire (1986).

Thomas D. Cook & Donald T. Campbell, Quasi-Experimentation: Design and Analysis Issues for Field Settings (1979).

Shari S. Diamond, *Methods for the Empirical Study of Law, in* Law and the Social Sciences (Leon Lipson & Stanton Wheeler eds., 1986).

Floyd J. Fowler, Survey Research Methods (2d ed. 1984).

Robert M. Groves & Robert L. Kahn, Surveys by Telephone: A National Comparison with Personal Interviews (1979).

Handbook of Survey Research (Peter H. Rossi et al. eds., 1983).

Leslie Kish, Survey Sampling (1965).

Measurement Errors in Surveys (Paul P. Biemer et al. eds., 1991).

Questions About Questions: Inquiries into the Cognitive Bases of Surveys (Judith M. Tanur ed., 1992).

Howard Schuman & Stanley Presser, Questions and Answers in Attitude Surveys: Experiments on Question Form, Wording and Context (1981).

Seymour Sudman, Applied Sampling (1976).

Seymour Sudman & Norman M. Bradburn, Response Effects in Surveys: A Review and Synthesis (1974).

Telephone Survey Methodology (Robert M. Groves et al. eds., 1988).

Reference Guide on Estimation of Economic Losses in Damages Awards

ROBERT E. HALL AND VICTORIA A. LAZEAR

Robert E. Hall, Ph.D., is the McNeil Joint Professor, Department of Economics, and Senior Fellow, Hoover Institution, Stanford University, Stanford, California.

Victoria A. Lazear, M.S., is Partner, Applied Economics Partners, Menlo Park, California.

CONTENTS

I. Introduction

This reference guide identifies areas of dispute that will likely arise when economic losses are at issue. Although this material differs from other topics presented in this manual, it is included because expert testimony is commonly offered on these matters. This reference guide discusses the application of economic analysis within the established legal framework for damages. It is not a commentary on the legal framework. It does not lay out a comprehensive theory of damages measurement, nor does it describe the applicable law. We provide citations to cases to illustrate the principles and techniques discussed in the text.

This reference guide has three major sections. Section II discusses the qualifications required of experts who quantify damages. Section III considers issues common to most studies of economic damages (the harmful event, pretrial earnings and mitigation, prejudgment interest, future earnings and losses, subsequent events, consideration of taxes, and apportionment). Section IV considers the major subject areas of economic loss measurement (personal lost earnings, intellectual property losses, antitrust losses, securities losses, and liquidated damages).

Our discussion follows the structure of the standard damages study, as shown in Figure 1. We assume that the defendant has been found liable for damages for a harmful event committed sometime in the past. The plaintiff is entitled to recover monetary damages for losses occurring before and possibly after the time of the trial. The top line of Figure 1 measures the losses before trial; the bottom line measures the losses after trial.[1]

The defendant's harmful act has reduced the plaintiff's earnings, or stream of economic value. The stream of economic value may take the form of compensation received by a worker, the profit earned by a business, or one-time receipts, such as the proceeds from the sale of property. They are measured net of any associated costs.

The essential features of a study of losses are the quantification of the reduction in earnings, the calculation of interest on past losses, and the application of financial discounting to future losses. The losses are measured as the difference between the earnings the plaintiff would have received if the harmful event had not occurred and the earnings the plaintiff has or will receive, given the harmful event. The plaintiff may be entitled to interest for losses occurring before the trial. Losses occurring after trial will normally be discounted. The majority of damages studies fit this format, so we have used such a format as the basic model for this reference guide.[2]

1. Our scope here is limited to losses of actual dollar income. However, economists sometimes have a role in the measurement of nondollar damages, including pain and suffering and the hedonic value of life. *See generally* W. Kip Viscusi, Reforming Products Liability (1991).

2. In the Appendix, we give an example of a complete damages study in the spreadsheet format

We use numerous brief examples to explain the disputes that can arise. These examples are not full case descriptions; they are deliberately stylized. They attempt to capture the types of disagreements about damages that arise in practical experience, though they are purely hypothetical. In many examples, the dispute involves factual as well as legal issues. We do not try to resolve the disputes in these examples. We hope that the examples will help clarify the legal and factual disputes that need to be resolved before or at trial.

Each area of potential dispute is introduced with a question. It is our hope that the majority of disputes over economic damages can be identified by asking each of these questions to the parties. Of course, some questions, especially in section IV, are only relevant in their specific subject areas. Most of the questions in section III, however, should help sort out areas of contention that may well arise in any dispute involving economic losses.

Figure 1. Standard Format for a Damages Study

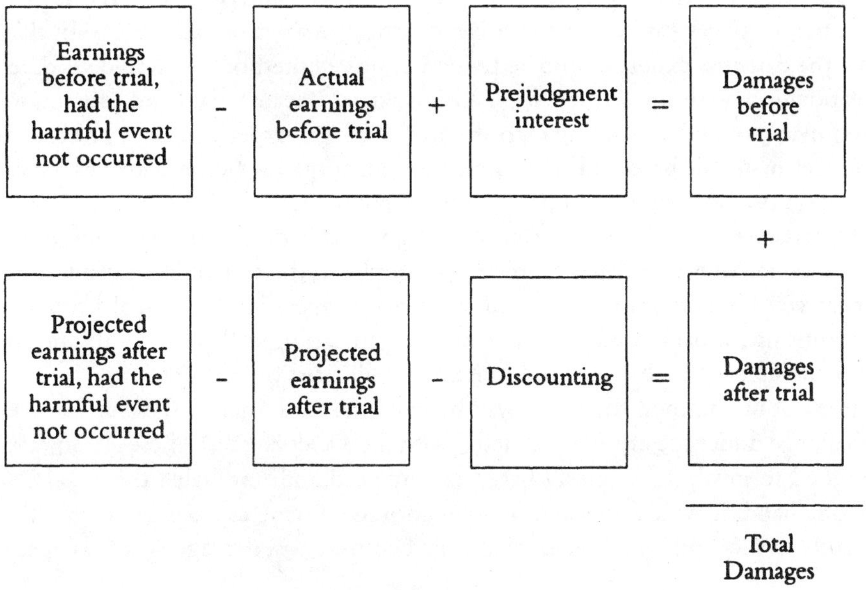

often presented by damages experts. Readers who prefer learning from an example may want to read the Appendix before the body of this reference guide.

II. Experts' Qualifications

Experts who quantify damages come from a variety of backgrounds. Whatever his or her background, however, a damages expert should be trained and experienced in quantitative analysis. For economists, the standard qualification is the Ph.D. Damages experts with business or accounting backgrounds often have MBA degrees or CPA credentials, or both. The specific areas of specialization needed by the expert are dictated by the method used and the substance of the damages claim. In some cases, participation in original research and the authorship of professional publications may add to the qualifications of an expert. The relevant research and publications are less likely to be in damages measurement per se than in topics and methods encountered in damages analysis. For example, a damages expert may need to restate prices and quantities in a market with more sellers than are actually present. Direct participation in research on the relation between market structure and performance would be helpful for an expert undertaking that task.

Statistical regression analysis is sometimes used to make inferences in damages studies.[3] Specific training is required to apply regression analysis. As another example, damages studies may involve statistical surveys of customers.[4] In this case, the damages expert should be trained in survey methods or should work in collaboration with a qualified survey statistician. Because damages estimation often makes use of accounting records, most damages experts need to be able to interpret materials prepared by professional accountants. Some damages issues may require assistance from a professional accountant.

Experts benefit from professional training and experience in areas relevant to the substance of the damages claim. For example, in the case of lost earnings, an expert will benefit from training in labor economics; in intellectual property and antitrust, a background in industrial organization will be helpful; and in securities damages, a background in finance will assist the expert.

It is not uncommon for an analysis by even the most qualified expert to face a challenge under the criteria associated with the *Daubert* case.[5] These criteria are intended to prevent testimony based on untested and unreliable theories. On the one hand, it would appear that an economist serving as a damages expert is unlikely to succumb to a *Daubert* challenge because most damages analyses oper-

3. For a discussion of regression analysis, see generally Daniel L. Rubinfeld, Reference Guide on Multiple Regression, in this manual.

4. For a discussion of survey methods, see generally Shari Seidman Diamond, Reference Guide on Survey Research, in this manual.

5. Daubert v. Merrell Dow Pharms., Inc., 509 U.S. 579 (1993). For a discussion of emerging standards of scientific evidence, see Margaret A. Berger, The Supreme Court's Trilogy on the Admissibility of Expert Testimony, § IV, in this manual.

ate in the familiar territory of restating economic flows using a combination of professional judgment and standard tools. The parts of economics that might be accused of verging on junk science are rarely used in damages work. But the circumstances of each damages analysis are unique, and a party may raise a *Daubert* challenge based on the proposition that the tools have never before been applied to these circumstances. Even if a *Daubert* challenge fails, it is an effective way for the opposing party to probe the damages analysis prior to trial. Using a *Daubert* challenge to try to disable a damages analysis is relatively new, and it remains to be seen if it is a successful way to disqualify an expert.

III. Issues Common to Most Damages Studies

Throughout our discussion, we assume that the plaintiff is entitled to compensation for losses sustained from a harmful act of the defendant. The harmful act may be an act whose occurrence itself is wrongful, as in a tort, or it may be a failure to fulfill a promise, as in a breach of contract. In the first instance, damages have traditionally been calculated under the principle that compensation should place the plaintiff in a position economically equivalent to the plaintiff's position absent the harmful event. In applications of this principle, either restitution damages or reliance damages are calculated. These two terms are essentially synonyms with respect to their economic content. The term restitution is used when the harmful act is an injury or theft and the defendant is unjustly enriched at the expense of the plaintiff, and reliance is used when the harmful act is fraud and the intent of damages is to place the plaintiff in as good a position as if no promises had been made. In the second instance, breach of contract, damages are generally calculated under the expectation principle, where the compensation is intended to replace what the plaintiff would have received if the promise or bargain had been fulfilled. These types of damages are called expectation damages.

In this section, we review the elements of the standard loss measurement in the format of Figure 1. For each element, there are several areas of potential dispute. The sequence of questions posed in section III should identify most if not all of the areas of disagreement between the damages analyses of opposing parties.

A. Characterization of the Harmful Event

1. How was the plaintiff harmed and what legal principles govern compensation for the harm?

The first step in a damages study is the translation of the legal theory of the harmful event into an analysis of the economic impact of that event. In most cases, the analysis considers the difference between the plaintiff's economic position if the harmful event had not occurred and the plaintiff's actual economic position. The damages study restates the plaintiff's position "but for" the harmful event; this part is often called the but-for analysis. Damages are the difference between the but-for value and the actual value.

In cases where damages are calculated under the restitution–reliance principle, the but-for analysis[6] posits that the harmful event did not occur. In many cases—such as injuries resulting from accidents—the but-for analysis presumes no contact at all between the parties. Damages are the difference between the value the plaintiff would have received had there been no contact with the defendant and the value actually received.

Expectation damages[7] generally arise from the breach of a contract. The harmful event is the defendant's failure to perform. Damages are the difference between the value the plaintiff would have received had the defendant performed its obligations and the value the plaintiff actually obtained. However, when one party has only partly performed under the contract, then damages may be calculated under the reliance-restitution principle.

Example: Agent contracts with Owner for Agent to sell Owner's farm. The asking price is $1,000,000 and the agreed fee is 6%. Agent incurs costs of $1,000 in listing the property. A potential buyer offers the asking price, but Owner withdraws the listing. Plaintiff calculates damages as $60,000, the agreed fee for selling the property. The defendant calculates damages as $1,000, the amount that Agent spent to advertise the property.

6. *See, e.g.*, May v. Secretary of Health & Human Servs., No. 91-1057V, 1997 WL 402412, at *2 (Fed. Cl. June 27, 1997) (holding correct analysis for plaintiff's personal injury claim is the but-for test where the appropriate question is but for the injury, would the expenditure have been made); Rite-Hite Corp. v. Kelley Co., Inc., 56 F.3d 1538 (Fed. Cir.) (holding that under patent statute but-for analysis is not the sole test for damages since judicial relief cannot redress all conceivable harm that can be traced to the but-for cause; thus, the but-for analysis may be coupled with the question of whether the alleged injury may be compensated), *cert. denied*, 516 U.S. 867 (1995).

7. *See* John R. Trentacosta, *Damages in Breach of Contract Cases*, 76 Mich. B.J. 1068, 1068 (1997) (describing expectation damages as damages that place the injured party in the same position as if the breaching party completely performed the contract); Bausch & Lomb, Inc. v. Bressler, 977 F.2d 720, 728–29 (2d Cir. 1992) (defining expectation damages as damages that put the injured party in the same economic position the party would have enjoyed if the contract had been performed).

Comment: Under the expectation remedy, Agent is entitled to $60,000, the fee for selling the property. However, the Agent has only partly performed under the contract, thus it may be appropriate to limit damages to $1,000. Some states limit recovery in this situation by law to the $1,000, the reliance measure of damages, unless the property is actually sold.

When the harmful event is misrepresentation by the defendant, resulting in an economically detrimental relationship between the defendant and the plaintiff, the but-for analysis may consider the value the plaintiff would have received in the absence of that relationship. In this case, the but-for analysis for fraud will adopt the premise that the plaintiff would have entered into a valuable relationship with an entity other than the defendant. For example, if the defendant's misrepresentations have caused the plaintiff to purchase property unsuited to the plaintiff's planned use, the but-for analysis might consider the value that the plaintiff would have received by purchasing a suitable property from another seller.

Even though cases of intentional misrepresentation or fraud are torts, courts today more commonly award expectation damages. In cases where the court interprets the fraudulent statement as an actual warranty, then the appropriate remedy is expectation damages. Courts, though, have awarded expectation damages even when the fraudulent statement is not interpreted as an actual warranty. Some of these cases may be situations where a contract exists but is legally unenforceable for technical reasons. Nonetheless, in the majority of jurisdictions, courts award expectation damages for fraud, but there appears to be no consistent explanation as to why some courts award expectation damages and others, reliance damages.[8]

Plaintiffs cannot normally seek punitive damages under an expectation remedy for breach, but may seek them under a reliance-restitution theory.

In other situations, the plaintiff may have a choice of remedies under different legal theories. For example, fraud, where there is a contract, may be considered under tort law for deceit or under contract law for breach in determining compensatory damages.

Example: Buyer purchases a condominium from Owner for $90,000. However, the condominium is known by the Owner to be worth only $80,000 at the time of sale because of defects. Buyer chooses to compute damages under the expectation measure of damages as $10,000 and to retain the condominium. Owner computes dam-

8. Prosser and Keeton on the Law of Torts § 110, at 767–69 (W. Page Keeton ed., 5th ed. 1984).

ages under the reliance measure as $90,000 together with the return of the condominium, which is now worth $120,000.

Comment: Defendant's application of the reliance remedy is incomplete. Absent the fraud, Buyer would have purchased another condominium and enjoyed the general appreciation in the market. Thus, correctly applied, the two measures may be similar.

The characterization of the harmful event begins with a clear statement of what it entailed. It must also include:

- a statement about the economic situation absent the wrongdoing;
- a characterization of the causal link between the wrongdoing and the harm the plaintiff suffered; and
- a description of the defendant's proper behavior.

In addition, the characterization will resolve such questions as whether to measure damages before or after taxes and the appropriate measure of costs. Many conflicts between the damages experts for the plaintiff and the defendant arise from different characterizations of the harmful event and its effects.

A comparison of the parties' statements about the harmful event and what would have happened in its absence will likely reveal differences in legal theories that can result in large differences in damages claims.

Example: Client is the victim of unsuitable investment advice by Broker (all of Client's investments made by Broker are the result of Broker's negligence). Client's damages study measures the sum of the losses of the investments made by Broker, including only the investments that incurred losses. Broker's damages study measures the net loss by including an offset for those investments that achieved gains.

Comment: Client is considering the harmful event to be the recommendation of investments that resulted in losses, whereas Broker is considering the harmful event to be the entire body of investment advice. Under Client's theory, Client would not have made the unsuccessful investments but would have made the successful ones, absent the unsuitable advice. Under Broker's theory, Client would not have made any investments based on Broker's advice.

A clear statement about the plaintiff's situation but for the harmful event is also helpful in avoiding double counting that can arise if a damages study confuses or combines reliance[9] and expectation damages.

9. *See* Trentacosta, *supra* note 7, at 1068. Reliance damages are distinguished from expectation damages. Reliance damages are defined as damages that do not place the injured party in as good a position as if the contract had been fully performed (expectation damages) but in the same position as if

Example: Marketer is the victim of defective products made by Manufacturer; Marketer's business fails as a result. Marketer's damages study adds together the out-of-pocket costs of creating the business in the first place and the projected profits of the business had there been no defects. Manufacturer's damages study measures the difference between the profit margin Marketer would have made absent the defects and the profit margin he actually made.

Comment: Marketer has mistakenly added together damages from the reliance principle and the expectation principle.[10] Under the reliance principle, Marketer is entitled to be put back to where he would have been had he not started the business in the first place. Damages are his total outlays less the revenue he actually received. Under the expectation principle, applied in Manufacturer's damages study, Marketer is entitled to the profit on the extra sales he would have received had there been no product defects. Out-of-pocket expenses of starting the business would have no effect on expectation damages because they would be present in both the actual and the but-for cases, and would offset each other in the comparison of actual and but-for value.

2. *Are the parties disputing differences in the plaintiff's economic environment absent the harmful event?*

The analysis of some types of harmful events requires consideration of effects, such as price erosion,[11] that involve changes in the economic environment caused by the harmful event. For a business, the main elements of the economic environment that may be affected by the harmful event are the prices charged by rivals, the demand facing the seller, and the prices of inputs. Misappropriation of intellectual property can cause lower prices because products produced with the misappropriated intellectual property compete with products sold by the owner of the intellectual property. In contrast, some harmful events do not change the

promises were never made. Reliance damages reimburse the injured party for expenses incurred in reliance of promises made. *See, e.g.*, Satellite Broad. Cable, Inc. v. Telefonica de Espana, S.A., 807 F. Supp. 218 (D.P.R. 1992) (holding that under Puerto Rican law an injured party is entitled to reliance but not expectation damages due to the wrongdoer's willful and malicious termination or withdrawal from precontractual negotiations).

10. *See* Trentacosta, *supra* note 7, at 1068. The injured party cannot recover both reliance and expectation damages.

11. *See, e.g.*, General Am. Transp. Corp. v. Cryo-Trans, Inc., 897 F. Supp. 1121, 1123–24 (N.D. Ill. 1995), *modified*, 93 F.3d 766 (Fed. Cir. 1996); Rawlplug Co., Inc. v. Illinois Tool Works Inc., No. 91 Civ. 1781, 1994 WL 202600, at *2 (S.D.N.Y. May 23, 1994); Micro Motion, Inc. v. Exac Corp., 761 F. Supp. 1420, 1430–31 (N.D. Cal. 1991) (holding in all three cases that patentee is entitled to recover lost profits due to past price erosion caused by the wrongdoer's infringement).

plaintiff's economic environment. For example, the theft of some of the plaintiff's products would not change the market price of those products, nor would an injury to a worker change the general level of wages in the labor market. A damages study need not analyze changes in broader markets when the harmful act plainly has minuscule effects in those markets.

For example, the plaintiff may assert that, absent the defendant's wrongdoing, a higher price could have been charged; the defendant's harmful act has eroded the market price. The defendant may reply that the higher price would lower the quantity sold. The parties may then dispute by how much the quantity would fall as a result of higher prices.

Example: Valve Maker infringes patent of Rival. Rival calculates lost profits as the profits actually made by Valve Maker plus a price-erosion effect. The amount of price erosion is the difference between the higher price that Rival would have been able to charge absent Valve Maker's presence in the market and the actual price. The price-erosion effect is the price difference multiplied by the combined sales volume of the Valve Maker and Rival. Defendant Valve Maker counters that the volume would have been lower had the price been higher. Defendant measures damages taking account of lower volume.

Comment: Wrongful competition is likely to cause some price erosion[12] and, correspondingly, some enlargement of the total market because of the lower price. The more elastic the demand the lower the volume would have been with a higher price. The actual magnitude of the price-erosion effect could be determined by economic analysis.

We consider price erosion in more detail in section IV.B, in connection with intellectual property damages. However, price erosion may be an issue in many other commercial disputes. For example, a plaintiff may argue that the disparagement of its product in false advertising has eroded its price.[13]

In more complicated situations, the damages analysis may need to focus on how an entire industry would be affected by the defendant's wrongdoing. For

12. *See, e.g.*, Micro Motion, 761 F. Supp. at 1430 (citing *Yale Lock Mfg. Co. v. Sargent*, 117 U.S. 536, 553 (1886), the court stated that "in most price erosion cases, a patent owner has reduced the actual price of its patented product in response to an infringer's competition").

13. *See, e.g.*, BASF Corp. v. Old World Trading Co., Inc., Nos. 92-3928, 92-3645, 92-3486, 92-3471, 1994 WL 617918 (7th Cir. Nov. 9, 1994) (finding that the plaintiff's damages only consisted of lost profits before consideration of price erosion, prejudgment interest, and costs despite plaintiff's argument that it was entitled to price erosion damages as a result of the defendant's false advertising—the court determined there were other competitors who would keep prices low).

example, one federal appeals court held that a damages analysis for exclusionary conduct must consider that other firms beside the plaintiff would have enjoyed the benefits of the absence of that conduct, so prices would have been lower and the plaintiff's profits correspondingly less than those posited in the plaintiff's damages analysis.[14]

Example: Photographic Film Maker has used unlawful means to exclude rival film manufacturers. Rival calculates damages on the assumption that it would have been the only additional seller in the market absent the exclusionary conduct, and that Rival would have been able to sell its film at the same price actually charged by Film Maker. Film Maker counters that other sellers would have entered the market and driven the price down, so Rival has overstated damages.

Comment: Increased competition lowers price in all but the most unusual situation. Again, determination of the number of entrants attracted by the elimination of exclusionary conduct and their effect on the price probably requires a full economic analysis.

3. Is there disagreement about the causal effect of the injury?

The plaintiff might argue that the injury has dramatically reduced earnings for many years. The defendant might reply that most of the reduction in earnings that occurred up to the time of trial is the result of influences other than the injury and that the effects of the injury will disappear completely soon after the trial. Alternatively, the defendant may agree that earnings have been dramatically reduced but argue that the reduction in earnings is the result of other causes.

Example: Worker is the victim of a disease caused either by exposure to xerxium or by smoking. Worker makes leather jackets tanned with xerxium. The Worker sues the producer of the xerxium, Xerxium Mine, and calculates damages as all lost wages. Defendant Xerxium Mine, in contrast, attributes most of the losses to smoking and calculates damages as only a fraction of lost wages.

Comment: The resolution of this dispute will turn on the legal question of comparative or contributory fault. If the law permits the division of damages into parts attributable to exposure to xerxium and smoking, then medical evidence on the likelihood of cause may be needed to make that division.

14. *See* Dolphin Tours, Inc. v. Pacifico Creative Servs., Inc., 773 F.2d 1506, 1512 (9th Cir. 1985).

Example: Real Estate Agent is wrongfully denied affiliation with Broker. Plaintiff Agent's damages study projects past earnings into the future at the rate of growth of the previous three years. Broker's study projects that earnings would have declined even without the breach because the real estate market has turned downward.

Comment: The difference between a damages study based on extrapolation from the past, here used by Agent, and a study based on actual data after the harmful act, here used by Broker, is one of the most common sources of disagreement in damages. This is a factual dispute that hinges on the relationship between real estate market conditions and the earnings of agents.

Frequently, the defendant will calculate damages on the premise that the harmful act had little, if any, causal relationship to the plaintiff's losses.

Example: Defendants conspired to rig bids in a construction deal. Plaintiff seeks damages for subsequent higher prices. Defendants' damages calculation is zero because they assert that the only effect of the bid rigging was to determine the winner of the contract and that prices were not affected.

Comment: This is a factual dispute about how much effect bid rigging has on the ultimate price. The analysis must go beyond the mechanics of the bid-rigging system to consider how the bids would be different had there been no collaboration among the bidders.

The defendant may also argue that the plaintiff has overstated the scope of the injury. Here the legal character of the harmful act may be critical; the law may limit the scope to proximate effects if the harmful act was negligence, but require a broader scope if the harmful act was intentional.[15]

Example: Plaintiff Drugstore Network experiences losses because defendant Superstore priced its products predatorily. Drugstore Network reduced prices in all its stores because it has a policy of uniform national pricing. Drugstore Network's damages study considers the entire effect of national price cuts on profits. Defendant Superstore argues that Network should have lowered prices only on the West Coast and its price reductions elsewhere should not be included in damages.

15. *See generally* Prosser and Keeton on the Law of Torts, *supra* note 8, § 65, at 462. Dean Prosser stated that simple negligence and intentional wrongdoing differ "not merely in degree but in the kind of fault . . . and in the social condemnation attached to it." *Id.*

Comment: It is a factual question whether adherence to a policy of national pricing is the reasonable response to predatory pricing in only part of the market.

4. *Is there disagreement about how the nonharmful conduct of the defendant should be defined in projecting the plaintiff's earnings but for the harmful event?*

One party's damages analysis may hypothesize the absence of any act of the defendant that influenced the plaintiff, whereas the other's damages analysis may hypothesize an alternative, legal act. This type of disagreement is particularly common in antitrust and intellectual property disputes. Although, generally, disagreement over the alternative scenario in a damages study is a legal question, opposing experts may have been given different legal guidance and therefore made different economic assumptions, resulting in major differences in their damages estimates.

Example: Defendant Copier Service's long-term contracts with customers are found to be unlawful because they create a barrier to entry that maintains Copier Service's monopoly power. Rival's damages study hypothesizes no contracts between Copier Service and its customers, so Rival would face no contractual barrier to bidding those customers away from Copier Service. Copier Service's damages study hypothesizes medium-term contracts with its customers and argues that these would not have been found to be unlawful. Under Copier Service's assumption, Rival would have been much less successful in bidding away Copier Service's customers, and damages are correspondingly lower.

Comment: Assessment of damages will depend greatly on the substantive law governing the injury. The proper characterization of Copier Service's permissible conduct usually is an economic issue. However, sometimes the expert must also have legal guidance as to the proper legal framework for damages. Counsel for plaintiff may prescribe a different legal framework from that of counsel for the defendant.

5. *Are losses measured before or after the plaintiff's income taxes?*

A damages award compensates the plaintiff for lost economic value. In principle, the calculation of compensation should measure the plaintiff's loss after taxes and then calculate the magnitude of the pretax award needed to compensate the plaintiff fully, once taxation of the award is considered. In practice, the tax rates applied to the original loss and to the compensation are frequently the same. When the rates are the same, the two tax adjustments are a wash. In that case, the appropriate pretax compensation is simply the pretax loss, and the damages calculation may be simplified by the omission of tax considerations.[16]

In some damages analyses, explicit consideration of taxes is essential, and disagreements between the parties may arise about these tax issues. If the plaintiff's lost income would have been taxed as a capital gain (at a preferential rate), but the damages award will be taxed as ordinary income, the plaintiff can be expected to include an explicit calculation of the extra compensation needed to make up for the loss of the tax advantage. Sometimes tax considerations are paramount in damages calculations.[17]

Example: Trustee wrongfully sells Beneficiary's property, at full market value. Beneficiary would have owned the property until death and avoided all capital gains tax.

Comment: Damages are the amount of the capital gains tax, even though the property fetched its full value upon sale.

In some cases, the law requires different tax treatment of loss and compensatory award. Again, the tax adjustments do not offset each other, and consideration of taxes may be a source of dispute.

Example: Driver injures Victim in a truck accident. A state law provides that awards for personal injury are not taxable, even though the income lost as a result of the injury is taxable. Victim calculates damages as lost pretax earnings, but Driver calculates damages as lost earnings after tax.[18] Driver argues that the nontaxable award would exceed actual economic loss if it were not adjusted for the taxation of the lost income.

Comment: Under the principle that damages are to restore the plaintiff to the economic equivalent of the plaintiff's position absent the harmful act, it may be recognized that the income to be replaced by the award would have been taxed. However, case law in a particular

16. There is a separate issue about the effect of taxes on the interest rate for prejudgment interest and discounting. *See* discussion *infra* §§ III.C, III.E.

17. *See generally* John H. Derrick, Annotation, *Damages for Breach of Contract as Affected by Income Tax Considerations*, 50 A.L.R. 4th 452 (1987) (discussing a variety of state and federal cases in which courts ruled on the propriety of tax considerations in damage calculations; courts have often been reluctant to award difference in taxes as damages because it is calling for too much speculation).

18. *See generally* Brian C. Brush & Charles H. Breedon, *A Taxonomy for the Treatment of Taxes in Cases Involving Lost Earnings*, 6 J. Legal Econ. 1 (1996) (discussing four general approaches for treating tax consequences in cases involving lost future earnings or earning capacity based on the economic objective and the tax treatment of the lump sum award). *See, e.g.*, Myers v. Griffin-Alexander Drilling Co., 910 F.2d 1252 (5th Cir. 1990) (holding loss of past earnings between the time of the accident and the trial could not be based on pretax earnings).

jurisdiction may not allow a jury instruction on the taxability of an award.[19]

Example: Worker is wrongfully deprived of tax-free fringe benefits by Employer. Under applicable law, the award is taxable. Worker's damages estimate includes a factor so that the amount of the award, after tax, is sufficient to replace the lost tax-free value.

Comment: Again, to achieve the goal of restoring plaintiff to a position economically equivalent absent the harmful act, an adjustment of this type is appropriate. The adjustment is often called "grossing up" damages.[20] To accomplish grossing up, divide the lost tax-free value by one minus the tax rate. For example, if the loss is $100,000 of tax-free income, and the income tax rate is 25%, the award should be $100,000 divided by 0.75, or $133,333.

6. *Is there disagreement about the costs that the plaintiff would have incurred but for the harmful event?*

Where the injury takes the form of lost volume of sales, the plaintiff's lost value is the lost present value of profit. Lost profit is lost revenue less the costs avoided by selling a lower volume. Calculation of these costs is a common area of disagreement about damages.

Conceptually, avoided cost is the difference between the cost that would have been incurred at the higher volume of sales but for the harmful event and the cost actually incurred at the lower volume of sales achieved. In the format of Figure 1, the avoided-cost calculation is done each year. The following are some of the issues that arise in calculating avoided cost:

- For a firm operating at capacity, expansion of sales is cheaper in the longer run than in the short run; whereas, if there is unused capacity, expansion may be cheaper in the short run.
- The costs that can be avoided if sales fall abruptly are smaller in the short run than in the longer run.

19. *See generally* John E. Theuman, Annotation, *Propriety of Taking Income Tax into Consideration in Fixing Damages in Personal Injury or Death Action*, 16 A.L.R. 4th 589 (1981) (discussing a variety of state and federal cases in which the propriety of jury instructions regarding tax consequences is at issue). *See, e.g.*, Bussell v. DeWalt Prods. Corp., 519 A.2d 1379 (N.J. 1987) (holding that trial court hearing a personal injury case must instruct jury, upon request, that personal injury damages are not subject to state and federal income taxes); Gorham v. Farmington Motor Inn, Inc., 271 A.2d 94 (Conn. 1970) (holding court did not err in refusing to instruct jury that personal injury damages were tax-free).

20. *See* Cecil D. Quillen, Jr., *Income, Cash, and Lost Profits Damages Awards in Patent Infringement Cases*, 2 Fed. Circuit B.J. 201, 207 (1992) (discussing the importance of taking tax consequences and cash flows into account when estimating damages).

- Avoided costs may include marketing, selling, and administrative costs as well as the cost of manufacturing.
- Some costs are fixed, at least in the shorter run, and are not avoided as a result of the reduced volume of sales caused by the harmful act.

Sometimes it is useful to put cost into just two categories, that which varies in proportion to sales (variable cost) and that which does not vary with sales (fixed cost). This breakdown is rough, however, and does not do justice to important aspects of avoided costs. In particular, costs that are fixed in the short run may be variable in the longer run. Disputes frequently arise over whether particular costs are fixed or variable. One side may argue that most costs are fixed and were not avoided by losing sales volume, while the other side will argue that many costs are variable.

Certain accounting concepts are related to the calculation of avoided cost. Profit and loss statements frequently report the "cost of goods sold."[21] Costs in this category are frequently, but not uniformly, avoided when sales volume is lower. But costs in other categories, called "operating costs" or "overhead costs," also may be avoided, especially in the longer run. One approach to the measurement of avoided cost is based on an examination of all of a firm's cost categories. The expert determines how much of each category of cost was avoided.

An alternative approach uses regression analysis or some other statistical method to determine how costs vary with sales as a general matter within the firm or across similar firms. The results of such an analysis can be used to measure the costs avoided by the decline in sales volume caused by the harmful act.

7. *Is there a dispute about the costs of stock options?*

In some firms, employee stock options are a significant part of total compensation. The parties may dispute whether the value of options should be included in the costs avoided by the plaintiff as a result of lost sales volume. The defendant might argue that stock options should be included, because their issuance is costly to the existing shareholders. The defendant might place a value on newly issued options and amortize this value over the period from issuance to vesting. The plaintiff, in contrast, might exclude options costs on the grounds that the options cost the firm nothing, even though they impose costs on the firm's shareholders.

21. *See, e.g.*, United States v. Arnous, 122 F.3d 321, 323 (6th Cir. 1997) (holding that district court erred when it relied on government's theory of loss because the theory ignored the cost of goods sold).

B. Mitigation and Earnings Before Trial

We use the term *earnings* for almost any dollar receipts that a plaintiff should have received. Earnings could include:

- wages, salary, commissions, bonuses, or other compensation;
- profits of a business;
- cash flow;
- royalties;
- proceeds from sales of property; and
- purchases and sales of securities.

Note that earnings in some of these categories, such as cash flow or purchases of securities, could be negative in some years.

1. *Is there a dispute about mitigation?*

Normally, the actual earnings of the plaintiff before trial are not an important source of disagreement. Sometimes, however, the defendant will argue that the plaintiff has failed to meet its duty to mitigate.[22] In a factual dispute about mitigation, the burden of proof rests with the defendant to show that the plaintiff failed to make a reasonable effort to mitigate or failed to mitigate in good faith. The defendant will propose that the proper offset is the earnings the plaintiff should have achieved, under proper mitigation, rather than actual earnings. In some cases the defendant may presume the ability of the plaintiff to mitigate in certain ways unless the defendant has specific knowledge otherwise at the time of a breach. For example, unless the defendant could reasonably foresee otherwise, the defendant may presume that the plaintiff could mitigate by locating another source of supply in the event of a breach of a supply agreement. Damages are limited to the difference between the contract price and the current market price in that situation.

For personal injuries, the issue of mitigation often arises because the defendant believes that the plaintiff's failure to work after the injury is a withdrawal from the labor force or retirement rather than the result of the injury. For commercial torts, mitigation issues can be more subtle. Where the plaintiff believes that the harmful act destroyed a company, the defendant may argue that the company could have been put back together and earned profit, possibly in a different line of business. The defendant will then treat the hypothetical profits as an offset to damages.

Alternatively, where the plaintiff continues to operate the business after the harmful act, and includes subsequent losses in damages, the defendant may argue that the proper mitigation was to shut down after the harmful act.

22. *See, e.g.*, Thibodaux v. Guilbeau Marine, Inc., No. Civ. A. 96-3389, 1998 WL 66130, at *8 (E.D. La. Feb. 18, 1998) (addressing defendant's claim that plaintiff failed in his duty to mitigate damages).

Example: Franchisee Soil Tester starts up a business based on Franchiser's proprietary technology, which Franchiser represents as meeting government standards. During the start-up phase, Franchiser notifies Soil Tester that the technology has failed. Soil Tester continues to develop the business but sues Franchiser for profits it would have made from successful technology. Franchiser calculates much lower damages on the theory that Soil Tester should have mitigated by terminating start-up.

Comment: This is primarily a factual dispute about mitigation. Presumably Soil Tester believes it has a good case, that it was appropriate to continue to develop the business despite notification of the failure of the technology.

Disagreements about mitigation may be hidden within the frameworks of the plaintiff's and the defendant's damages studies.

Example: Defendant Board Maker has been found to have breached an agreement to supply circuit boards. Plaintiff Computer Maker's damages study is based on the loss of profits on the computers to be made from the circuit boards. Board Maker's damages study is based on the difference between the contract price for the boards and the market price at the time of the breach.

Comment: There is an implicit disagreement about Computer Maker's duty to mitigate by locating alternative sources for the boards not supplied by the defendant. The Uniform Commercial Code spells out the principles for resolving these legal issues under the contracts it governs.[23]

23. *See, e.g.*, Aircraft Guaranty Corp. v. Strato-Lift, Inc., 991 F. Supp. 735, 738–39 (E.D. Pa. 1998) (mem.) (Both defendant-seller and plaintiff-buyer turned to the Uniform Commercial Code to support their respective positions that the plaintiff-buyer had a duty to mitigate damages when the defendant-seller breached its contract and that the plaintiff-buyer did not have a duty to mitigate when the defendant-seller breached its contract. Court held that according to the UCC, plaintiff-buyer did have a duty to mitigate if the duty was reasonable in light of all the facts and circumstances; however, failure to mitigate does not preclude recovery.); S.J. Groves & Sons Co. v. Warner Co., 576 F.2d 524 (3d Cir. 1978) (holding that the duty to mitigate is a tool to lessen plaintiff's recovery and is a question of fact); Thomas Creek Lumber & Log Co. v. United States, 36 Fed. Cl. 220 (1996) (holding that U.S. government has a duty to mitigate in breach of contract cases but it is not required to make an extraordinary effort; however, federal common law rather than UCC applies in cases involving nationwide federal programs).

C. Prejudgment Interest

1. Do the parties agree about how to calculate prejudgment interest?[24]

The law may specify how to calculate interest for past losses (prejudgment interest). State law may exclude prejudgment interest, limit prejudgment interest to a statutory rate, or exclude compounding. Table 1 illustrates these alternatives. With simple uncompounded interest, losses from five years before trial earn five times the specified interest, so compensation for a $100 loss from five years ago is exactly $135 at 7% interest. With compound interest, the plaintiff earns interest on past interest. Compensation is about $140 for a loss of $100 five years before trial. The difference between simple and compound interest becomes much larger if the time from loss to trial is greater or if the interest rate is higher. Because, in practice, interest receipts do earn further interest, economic analysis would generally support the use of compound interest.

Table 1. Calculation of Prejudgment Interest (in Dollars)

Years Before Trial	Loss Without Interest	Loss with Compound Interest at 7%	Loss with Simple Uncompounded Interest at 7%
10	100	197	170
9	100	184	163
8	100	172	156
7	100	161	149
6	100	150	142
5	100	140	135
4	100	131	128
3	100	123	121
2	100	114	114
1	100	107	107
0	100	100	100
Total	1,100	1,579	1,485

24. *See generally* Michael S. Knoll, *A Primer on Prejudgment Interest*, 75 Tex. L. Rev. 293 (1996) (discussing prejudgment interest extensively). *See, e.g.*, Ford v. Rigidply Rafters, Inc., 984 F. Supp. 386, 391–92 (D. Md. 1997) (deciding appropriate method of calculating prejudgment interest in an employment discrimination case to ensure plaintiff is fairly compensated rather than given a windfall); Acron/Pacific Ltd. v. Coit, No. C-81-4264-VRW, 1997 WL 578673, at *2 (N.D. Cal. Sept. 8, 1997) (reviewing supplemental interest calculations and applying California state law to determine the appropriate amount of prejudgment interest to be awarded); Prestige Cas. Co. v. Michigan Mut. Ins. Co., 969 F. Supp. 1029 (E.D. Mich. 1997) (analyzing Michigan state law to determine the appropriate prejudgment interest award).

Where the law does not prescribe the form of interest for past losses, the experts will normally apply a reasonable interest rate to bring those losses forward. The parties may disagree on whether the interest rate should be measured before or after tax. The before-tax interest rate is the normally quoted rate. To calculate the corresponding after-tax rate, one subtracts the amount of income tax the recipient would have to pay on the interest. Thus, the after-tax rate depends on the tax situation of the plaintiff. The format for calculation of the after-tax interest rate is shown in the following example:

(1) Interest rate before tax: 9%

(2) Tax rate: 30%

(3) Tax on interest (line (1) times line (2)): 2.7%

(4) After-tax interest rate (line (1) less line (3)): 6.3%

Even where damages are calculated on a pretax basis, economic considerations suggest that the prejudgment interest rate should be on an after-tax basis: Had the plaintiff actually received the lost earnings in the past and invested the earnings at the assumed rate, income tax would have been due on the interest. The plaintiff's accumulated value would be the amount calculated by compounding past losses at the after-tax interest rate.

Where there is economic disparity between the parties, there may be a disagreement about whose interest rate should be used—the borrowing rate of the defendant or the lending rate of the plaintiff, or some other rate. There may also be disagreements about adjustment for risk.[25]

Example: Insurance company disputes payment of insurance to Farmer. Farmer calculates damages as payment due plus the large amount of interest charged by a personal finance company; no bank was willing to lend to him, given his precarious financial condition. Crop Insurer calculates damages as a lower payment plus the interest on the late payment at the normal bank loan rate.

Comment: The law may limit claims for prejudgment interest to a specified interest rate, and a court may hold that this situation falls within the limit. Economic analysis does support the idea that delays in payments are more costly to people with higher borrowing rates and that the actual rate incurred may be considered damages.

25. *See generally* James M. Patell et al., *Accumulating Damages in Litigation: The Roles of Uncertainty and Interest Rates*, 11 J. Legal Stud. 341 (1982) (extensive discussion of interest rates in damages calculations).

D. Projections of Future Earnings

1. Is there disagreement about the projection of profitability but for the harmful event?

A common source of disagreement about the likely profitability of a business is the absence of a track record of earlier profitability. Whenever the plaintiff is a start-up business, the issue will arise of reconstructing the value of a business with no historical benchmark.

Example: Plaintiff Xterm is a failed start-up. Defendant VenFund has been found to have breached a venture-capital financing agreement. Xterm's damages study projects the profits it would have made under its business plan. VenFund's damages estimate, which is much lower, is based on the value of the start-up revealed by sales of Xterm equity made just before the breach.

Comment: Both sides confront factual issues to validate their damages estimates. Xterm needs to show that its business plan was still a reasonable forecast as of the time of the breach. VenFund needs to show that the sale of equity places a reasonable value on the firm; that is, that the equity sale was at arm's length and was not subject to discounts. This dispute can also be characterized as whether the plaintiff is entitled to expectation damages or must settle for reliance damages. The specific jurisdiction may specify damages for firms with no track record.

2. Is there disagreement about the plaintiff's actual earnings after the harmful event?

When the plaintiff has mitigated the adverse effects of the harmful act by making an investment that has not yet paid off at the time of trial, disagreement may arise about the value that the plaintiff has actually achieved.

Example: Manufacturer breaches agreement with Distributor. Distributor starts a new business that shows no accounting profit as of the time of trial. Distributor's damages study makes no deduction for actual earnings during the period from breach to trial. Manufacturer's damages study places a value on the new business as of the time of trial and deducts that value from damages.

Comment: Some offset for economic value created by Distributor's mitigation efforts may be appropriate. Note that if Distributor made a good-faith effort to create a new business, but was unsuccessful because of adverse events outside its control, the issue of the treatment of unexpected subsequent events will arise. (See section III.G.1.)

3. *Do the parties use constant dollars[26] for future losses, or is there escalation for inflation?*

Persistent inflation in the U.S. economy complicates projections of future losses. Although inflation rates in the 1990s have been only in the range of 3% per year, the cumulative effect of inflation has a pronounced effect on future dollar quantities. At 3% annual inflation, a dollar today buys what $4.38 will buy 50 years from now. Under inflation, the unit of measurement of economic values becomes smaller each year, and this shrinkage must be considered if future losses are measured in the smaller dollars of the future. We refer to the calculations of this process as embodying escalation. Dollar losses grow into the future because of the use of the shrinking unit of measurement. For example, an expert might project that revenues will rise at 5% per year for the next 10 years—3% because of general inflation and 2% more because of the growth of a firm.

Alternatively, the expert may project future losses in constant dollars without escalation for future inflation.[27] The use of constant dollars avoids the problems of dealing with a shrinking unit of measurement and often results in more intuitive damages calculations. In the example just given, the expert might project that revenues will rise at 2% per year in constant dollars. Constant dollars must be stated with respect to a base year. Thus a calculation in constant 1999 dollars means that the unit for future measurement is the purchasing power of the dollar in 1999.

E. Discounting Future Losses

For future losses, a damages study calculates the amount of compensation needed at the time of trial to replace expected future lost income. The result is discounted future losses;[28] it is also sometimes referred to as the present discounted value of the future losses.[29] Discounting is conceptually separate from the adjustment for inflation considered in the previous section. Discounting is typically carried out in the format shown in Table 2.

26. *See, e.g.*, Eastern Minerals Int'l, Inc. v. United States, 39 Fed. Cl. 621, 627 n.5 (1997) (stating both expert witnesses used constant dollars for damage analysis); *In re* California Micro Devices Sec. Litig., 965 F. Supp. 1327, 1333–37 (N.D. Cal. 1997) (discussing whether constant-dollar method should be used in the proposed plan of damage allocation).

27. *See, e.g.*, Willamette Indus., Inc. v. Commissioner, 64 T.C.M. (CCH) 202 (1992) (holding expert witness erred in failing to take inflation escalation into account).

28. *See generally* Michael A. Rosenhouse, Annotation, *Effect of Anticipated Inflation on Damages for Future Losses—Modern Cases*, 21 A.L.R. 4th 21 (1981) (discussing discounted future losses extensively).

29. *See generally* George A. Schieren, *Is There an Advantage in Using Time-Series to Forecast Lost Earnings?*, 4 J. Legal Econ. 43 (1994) (discussing effects of different forecasting methods on present discounted value of future losses). *See, e.g.*, Wingad v. John Deere & Co., 523 N.W.2d 274, 277–79 (Wis. Ct. App. 1994) (calculating present discounted value of future losses).

Table 2. Calculation of Discounted Loss at 5% Interest

Years in Future	Loss	Discount Factor	Discounted Loss*
0	$100.0 0	1.000	$100.00
1	125.00	0.952	119.00
2	130.00	0.907	118.00
Total			$337.00

*"Discounted Loss" equals "Loss" times "Discount Factor."

"Loss" is the estimated future loss, in either escalated or constant-dollar form. "Discount Factor" is a factor that calculates the number of dollars needed at the time of trial to compensate for a lost dollar in the future year. The discount factor is calculated by applying compound interest forward from the base year to the future year, and then taking the reciprocal. For example, in Table 2, the interest rate is 5%. The discount factor for the next year is calculated as the reciprocal of 1.05. The discount factor for two years in the future is calculated as the reciprocal of 1.05 times 1.05. Future discounts would be obtained by multiplying by 1.05 a suitably larger number of times and then taking the reciprocal. The discounted loss is the loss multiplied by the discount factor for that year. The number of dollars at time of trial that compensates for the loss is the sum of the discounted losses, $337 in this example.

The interest rate used in discounting future losses is often called the discount rate.

1. *Are the parties using a discount rate properly matched to the projection in constant dollars or escalated terms?*

To discount a future loss projected in escalated terms, one should use an ordinary interest rate. For example, in Table 2, if the losses of $125 and $130 are in dollars of those years, and not in constant dollars of the initial year, then the use of a 5% discount rate is appropriate if 5% represents an accurate measure of the time value of money.

To discount a future loss projected in constant dollars, one should use a real interest rate as the discount rate. A real interest rate is an ordinary interest rate less an assumed rate of future inflation. The deduction of the inflation rate from the discount rate is the counterpart of the omission of escalation for inflation from the projection of future losses. In Table 2, the use of a 5% discount rate for discounting constant-dollar losses would be appropriate if the ordinary interest rate was 8% and the rate of inflation was 3%. Then the real interest rate would be 8% minus 3%, or 5%.

The ordinary interest rate is often called the nominal interest rate to distinguish it from the real interest rate.

2. Is one of the parties assuming that discounting and earnings growth offset each other?

An expert might make the assumption that future growth of losses will occur at the same rate as the appropriate discount rate. Table 3 illustrates the standard format for this method of calculating discounted loss.

Table 3. Calculation of Discounted Loss when Growth and Discounting Offset Each Other

Years in Future	Loss	Discount Factor	Discounted Loss*
0	$100.00	1.000	$100.00
1	105.00	0.952	100.00
2	110.30	0.907	100.00
Total			$300.00

*"Discounted Loss" equals "Loss" times "Discount Factor."

When growth and discounting exactly offset each other, the present discounted value is the number of years of lost future earnings multiplied by the current amount of lost earnings.[30] In Table 3, the loss of $300 is exactly three times the base year's loss of $100. Thus the discounted value of future losses can be calculated by a shortcut in this special case. The explicit projection of future losses and the discounting back to the time of trial are unnecessary. However, the parties may dispute whether the assumption that growth and discounting are exactly offsetting is realistic in view of projected rates of growth of losses and market interest rates at the time of trial.

In *Jones & Laughlin Steel Corp. v. Pfeifer*,[31] the Supreme Court considered the issue of escalated dollars with nominal discounting against constant dollars with real discounting. It found both acceptable, though the Court seemed to express a preference for the second format. In general, the Court appeared to favor discount rates in the range of 1% to 3% per year in excess of the growth of earnings.

30. Certain state courts have, in the past, required that the offset rule be used so as to avoid speculation about future earnings growth. In *Beaulieu v. Elliott*, 434 P.2d 665, 671–72 (Alaska 1967), the court ruled that discounting was exactly offset by wage growth. In *Kaczkowki v. Bolubasz*, 421 A.2d 1027, 1036–38 (Pa. 1980), the Pennsylvania Supreme Court ruled that no evidence on price inflation was to be introduced and deemed that inflation was exactly offset by discounting.

31. 462 U.S. 523 (1983).

3. Is there disagreement about the interest rate used to discount future lost value?

Discount calculations should use a reasonable interest rate drawn from current data at the time of trial. The interest rate might be obtained from the rates that could be earned in the bond market from a bond of maturity comparable to the lost stream of receipts. As in the case of prejudgment interest, there is an issue as to whether the interest rate should be on a before- or after-tax basis. The parties may also disagree about adjusting the interest rate for risk. A common approach for determining lost business profit is to use the Capital Asset Pricing Model (CAPM)[32] to calculate the risk-adjusted discount rate. The CAPM is the standard method in financial economics to analyze the relation between risk and discounting. In the CAPM method, the expert first measures the firm's "beta"—the amount of variation in one firm's value per percentage point of variation in the value of all businesses. Then the risk-adjusted discount rate is the risk-free rate from a U.S. Treasury security plus the beta multiplied by the historical average risk premium for the stock market.[33] For example, the calculation may be presented in the following format:

(1) Risk-free interest rate: 4.0%
(2) Beta for this firm: 1.2%
(3) Market equity premium: 8.0%
(4) Equity premium for this firm [(2) times (3)]: 9.6%
(5) Discount rate for this firm [(1) plus (4)]: 13.6%

4. Is one of the parties using a capitalization factor?

Another approach to discounting a stream of losses uses a market capitalization factor. A capitalization factor[34] is the ratio of the value of a future stream of income to the current amount of the stream; for example, if a firm is worth $1 million and its current earnings are $100,000, its capitalization factor is ten.

The capitalization factor is generally obtained from the market values of comparable assets or businesses. For example, the expert might locate a comparable

32. *See, e.g.*, Cede & Co. v. Technicolor, Inc., No. CIV.A.7129, 1990 WL 161084 (Del. Ch. Oct. 19, 1990) (mem.) (explaining CAPM and propriety of using CAPM to determine the discount rate); Gilbert v. MPM Enters., Inc., No. 14416, 1997 WL 633298, at *8 (Del. Ch. Oct. 9, 1997) (holding that petitioner's expert witnesses' use of CAPM is appropriate).

33. Richard A. Brealey & Stewart C. Myers, Principles of Corporate Finance 141–228 (5th ed. 1996).

34. *See, e.g.*, United States v. 22.80 Acres of Land, 839 F.2d 1362 (9th Cir. 1988) (holding that landowners' market data were not fatally flawed because of failure to use a capitalization factor); Maureen S. Duggan, Annotation, *Proper Measure and Elements of Recovery for Insider Short-Swing Transaction*, 86 A.L.R. Fed. 16 (1988) (mentioning use of capitalization factor to derive price of purchased stock).

business traded in the stock market and compute the capitalization factor as the ratio of stock market value to operating income. In addition to capitalization factors derived from markets, experts sometimes use rule-of-thumb capitalization factors. For example, the value of a dental practice might be taken as one year's gross revenue (the capitalization factor for revenue is one). Often the parties dispute whether there is reliable evidence that the capitalization factor accurately measures value for the specific asset or business.

Once the capitalization factor is determined, the calculation of the discounted value of the loss is straightforward: It is the current annual loss in operating profit multiplied by the capitalization factor. A capitalization-factor approach to valuing future losses may be formatted in the following way:

(1) Ratio of market value to current annual earnings in comparable publicly traded firms: 13

(2) Plaintiff's lost earnings over past year: $200

(3) Value of future lost earnings [(1) times (2)]: $2,600

The capitalization-factor approach might also be applied to revenue, cash flow, accounting profit, or other measures. The expert might adjust market values for any differences between the valuation principles relevant for damages and those that the market applies. For example, the value in the stock market may be considered the value placed on a business for a minority interest, whereas the plaintiff's loss relates to a controlling interest. The parties may dispute almost every element of the capitalization calculation.

Example: Lender is responsible for failure of Auto Dealer. Plaintiff Auto Dealer's damages study projects rapid growth of future profits based on current year's profit but for Lender's misconduct. The study uses a discount rate calculated as the after-tax interest rate on Treasury bills. The application of the discount rate to the future stream of earnings implies a capitalization rate of 12 times the current pretax profit. The resulting estimate of lost value is $10 million. Defendant Lender's damages study uses data on the actual sale prices of similar dealerships in various parts of the country. The data show that the typical sales price of a dealership is six times its five-year average annual pretax profit. Lender's damages study multiplies the capitalization factor of six by the five-year average annual pretax profit of Auto Dealer of $500,000 to estimate lost value as $3 million.

Comment: Part of the difference comes from the higher implied capitalization factor used by Auto Dealer. Another reason may be that the five-year average pretax profit is less than the current year profit.

5. *Is one party using the appraisal approach to valuation and the other, the discounted-income approach?*

The appraisal approach places a value on a stream of earnings by determining the value of a similar stream in a similar market. For example, to place a value on the stream of earnings from a rental property, the appraisal approach would look at the market values of similar properties. The appraisal approach is suitable for many kinds of real property and some kinds of businesses.

Example: Oil Company deprives Gas Station Operator of the benefits of Operator's business. Operator's damages study projects future profits and discounts them to the time of trial, to place a value of $5 million on the lost business. Oil Company's damages study takes the average market prices of five nearby gas station businesses with comparable gasoline volume, to place a value of $500,000 on the lost business.

Comment: This large a difference probably results from a fundamental difference in assumptions. Operator's damages study is probably assuming that profits are likely to grow, while Oil Company's damages study may be assuming that there is a high risk that the neighborhood will deteriorate and the business will shrink.

F. *Damages with Multiple Challenged Acts: Disaggregation*

It is common for a plaintiff to challenge a number of the defendant's acts and to offer an estimate of the combined effect of those acts. If the fact finder determines that only some of the challenged acts are illegal, the damages analysis needs to be adjusted to consider only those acts. This issue seems to arise most often in antitrust cases, but can arise in any type of case. Ideally the damages testimony would equip the fact finder to determine damages for any combination of the challenged acts, but that may be tedious. If there are, say, 10 challenged acts, it would take 1,023 separate studies to determine damages for every possible combination of findings about illegality of the acts.

There have been several cases where the jury has found partially for the plaintiff but the jury lacked assistance from the damages experts on how the damages should be calculated for the combination of acts the jury found to be illegal. Even though the jury has attempted to resolve the issue, damages have been remanded upon appeal.[35]

35. *See* Litton Sys. Inc. v. Honeywell Inc., 1996 U.S. Dist. LEXIS 14662 (C.D. Cal. July 26, 1996) (order granting new trial on damages only—"Because there is no rational basis on which the jury could have reduced Litton's 'lump sum' damage estimate to account for Litton's losses attributable to conduct

One solution to this problem is to make the determination of the illegal acts before damages testimony is heard. The damages experts can adjust their testimony to consider only the acts found to be illegal.

In some situations, damages are the sum of separate damages for the various illegal acts. For example, there may be one injury in New York and another in Oregon. Then the damages testimony may consider the acts separately.

When the challenged acts have effects that interact, it is not possible to consider damages separately and add up their effects. This is an area of great confusion. When the harmful acts substitute for each other, the damages attributable to each separately sum to *less* than their combined effect. As an example, suppose that the defendant has used exclusionary contracts and illegal acquisitions to ruin the plaintiff's business. Either one would have ruined the business. Damages for the combination of acts are the value of the business, which would have thrived absent both the contracts and the acquisitions. Now consider damages if only the contracts but not the acquisitions are illegal. In the but-for analysis, the acquisitions are hypothesized to occur, because they are not illegal. But plaintiff's business cannot function in that but-for situation, because of the acquisitions. Hence damages—the difference in value of the plaintiff's business in the but-for and actual situations—are zero. The same would be true for a separate damages measurement for the acquisitions, with the contracts taken to be legal.

When the effects of the challenged conduct are complementary, the damages estimates for separate types of conduct will add to *more* than the combined damages. For example, suppose there is a challenge to the penalty provisions and to the duration of contracts for their combined exclusionary effect. The actual amount of the penalty would cause little exclusion if the duration were brief but substantial exclusion were the duration long. Similarly, the actual duration of the contracts would cause little exclusion if the penalty were small but substantial exclusion were the penalty large. A damages analysis for the penalty provision in isolation compares but-for—without the penalty provision but with long duration—to actual, where both provisions are in effect. Damages are large. Similarly, a damages estimate for the duration in isolation gives large damages. The sum of the two estimates is nearly double the damages from the combined use of both provisions.

excluded from the jury's consideration, the conclusion is inescapable that the jury's verdict was based on speculation. For these reasons, the Court orders a new trial limited to the issue of the amount of damages sustained by Litton that is attributable to unlawful Honeywell conduct."); Image Technical Servs., Inc. v. Eastman Kodak Co., 125 F.3d 1195, 1224 (9th Cir. 1997), *cert. denied*, 118 S. Ct. 1560 (1998) (plaintiffs "must segregate damages attributable to lawful competition from damages attributable to Kodak's monopolizing conduct").

Thus, a request that the damages expert disaggregate damages across the challenged acts is far more than a request that the total damages estimate be broken down into components that add up to the damages attributable to the combination of all the challenged acts. In principle, a separate damages analysis—with its own carefully specified but-for scenario and analysis—needs to be done for every possible combination of illegal acts.

Example: Hospital challenges Glove Maker for illegally obtaining market power through the use of long-term contracts and the use of a discount program that gives discounts to consortiums of hospitals if they purchase exclusively from Glove Maker. The jury finds that Defendant has attempted to monopolize the market with its discount programs, but that the long-term contracts were legal because of efficiencies. Hospital argues that damages are unchanged because either act was sufficient to achieve the observed level of market power. Defendant argues that damages are zero because the long-term contracts would have been enough to allow it to dominate the market.

Comment: The appropriate damages analysis is based on a careful new comparison of the market with and without the discount program. The but-for analysis should include the presence of the long-term contracts since they were found to be legal.

Apportionment or disaggregation sometimes arises in a different setting. A damages measure may be challenged as encompassing more than the harm caused by the defendant's harmful act. The expert may be asked to disaggregate damages between those caused by the defendant and those caused by other factors not caused by the defendant. We believe that this use of terms is confusing and should be avoided. If a damages analysis includes the effects not caused by the defendant, it is a defective analysis. It has not followed the standard format for damages, which, by its nature, isolates the effects of the harmful act on the plaintiff. The proper response is not to tell the expert to disaggregate, but rather to carry out a valid damages analysis that includes only damages, and not the effects of other events.

In the standard format, the but-for analysis differs from the actual environment only by hypothesizing the absence of the harmful act committed by the defendant. The comparison of but-for to actual automatically isolates the causal effects of the harmful act on the plaintiff. No disaggregation of damages caused by the harmful act is needed once the standard format is applied.

G. Other Issues Arising in General in Damages Measurement

1. *Is there disagreement about the role of subsequent unexpected events?*

Random events occurring after the harmful event can affect the plaintiff's actual loss. The effect might be either to amplify the economic loss from what might have been expected at the time of the harmful event or to reduce the loss.

Example: Housepainter uses faulty paint, which begins to peel a month after the paint job. Owner measures damages as the cost of repainting. Painter disputes on the grounds that a hurricane that actually occurred three months after the paint job would have ruined a proper paint job anyway.

Comment: This dispute will need to be resolved on legal rather than economic grounds. Both sides can argue that their approach to damages will, on the average over many applications, result in the right incentives for proper house painting.

The issue of subsequent random events should be distinguished from the legal principle of supervening events.[36] The subsequent events occur after the harmful act; there is no ambiguity about who caused the damage, only an issue of quantification of damages. Under the theory of a supervening event, there is precisely a dispute about who caused an injury. In the example above, there would be an issue of the role of a supervening event if the paint did not begin to peel until after the hurricane.

Disagreements about the role of subsequent random events are particularly likely when the harmful event is fraud.

Example: Seller of property misstates condition of property. Buyer shows that he would not have purchased the property absent the misstatement. Property values in general decline sharply between the fraud and the trial. Buyer measures damages as the difference between the market value of the property at the time of trial and the purchase price. Seller measures damages as the difference between the purchase price and the market value at the time of purchase, assuming full disclosure.

36. *See, e.g.*, Derdiarian v. Felix Contracting Corp., 414 N.E.2d 666 (N.Y. 1980) (holding jury could find that, although third person's negligence is a supervening event, defendant is ultimately liable to plaintiff for negligence); Lavin v. Emery Air Freight Corp., 980 F. Supp. 93 (D. Conn. 1997) (holding that under Connecticut law, a party seeking to be excused from a promised performance as a result of a supervening event must show the performance was made impracticable, nonoccurrence was an assumption at the time the contract was made, impracticability did not arise from the party's actions, and the party seeking to be excused did not assume a greater liability than the law imposed).

Comment: Buyer may be able to argue that retaining the property was the reasonable course of action after uncovering the fraud; in other words, there may be no issue of mitigation here. In that sense, Seller's fraud caused not only an immediate loss, as measured by Seller's damages analysis, but also a subsequent loss. Seller, however, did not cause the decline in property values. The dispute needs to be resolved as a matter of law.

As a general matter, it is preferable to exclude the effects of random subsequent effects, especially if the effects are large in relation to the original loss.[37] The reason is that plaintiffs choose which cases to bring and that may influence the approach to damages. If random subsequent events are always included in damages, then plaintiffs will bring the cases that happen to have amplified damages and will not pursue those where damages, including the random later event, are negative. The effect of the selection of cases will be to overcompensate plaintiffs. Similarly, if plaintiffs can choose whether or not to include the effects of random subsequent events, plaintiffs will choose to include those effects when they are positive and exclude them when they are negative. Again, the result will be to overcompensate plaintiffs as a general matter.[38]

2. *How should damages be apportioned among the various stakeholders?*

Usually the plaintiff need not distinguish between the defendant and the beneficiaries of the wrongdoing. In some cases, the law unambiguously determines who should pay for losses. For example, if a corporation increases its own profit through an antitrust violation, the defendant is the corporation and the shareholders are the recipients of the illegal profits. In general, the corporation is sued and current shareholder profits are reduced by the amount of the damages award. A current shareholder who may have purchased shares after the wrongdoing ceased will pay for the plaintiff's injury even though the shareholder did not share in the illegal profits. The shareholder's only recourse is to sue the firm and its officers.

A related issue can arise when a public utility is sued.

Example: Electric Utility infringes a patent. Patent Owner seeks compensation for lost royalties. Utility argues that the royalty would have been part of its rate base, and it would have been allowed higher

37. *See* Franklin M. Fisher & R. Craig Romaine, *Janis Joplin's Yearbook and the Theory of Damages, in* Industrial Organization, Economics, and the Law 392, 399–402 (John Monz ed., 1991); Fishman v. Estate of Wirtz, 807 F.2d 520, 563 (7th Cir. 1986) (Easterbrook, J., dissenting in part).

38. *See* William B. Tye et al., *How to Value a Lost Opportunity: Defining and Measuring Damages from Market Foreclosure*, 17 Res. L. & Econ. 83 (1995).

prices so as to achieve its allowed rate of return had it paid a royalty. It, therefore, did not profit from its infringement. Instead, the ratepayers benefited. Patent Owner argues that Utility stands in for all stakeholders.

Comment: In addition to the legal issue of whether Utility does stand in for ratepayers, there are two factual issues: Would a royalty actually have been passed on to ratepayers? Will the award be passed on to ratepayers?

Similar issues can arise in employment law.

Example: Plaintiff Sales Representative sues for wrongful denial of a commission. Sales Representative has subcontracted with another individual to do the actual selling and pays a portion of any commission to that individual as compensation. The subcontractor is not a party to the suit. Defendant Manufacturer argues that damages should be Sales Representative's lost profit measured as the commission less costs, including the payout to the subcontractor. Sales Representative argues that she is entitled to the entire commission.

Comment: Given that the subcontractor is not a plaintiff, and Sales Representative avoided the subcontractor's commission, the literal application of standard damages-measurement principles would appear to call for the lost-profit measure. The subcontractor, however, may be able to claim its share of the damages award. In that case, restitution would call for damages equal to the entire lost commission, so that, after paying off the subcontractor, Sales Representative receives exactly what she would have received absent the breach. Note that the second approach would place the subcontractor in exactly the same position as the Internal Revenue Service in our discussion of adjustments for taxes in section III.A.5.[39]

The issue also arises acutely in the calculation of damages on behalf of a nonprofit corporation. When the corporation is entitled to damages for lost profits, the defendant may argue that the corporation intentionally operates its business without profit. The actual losers in such a case are the people who would have enjoyed the benefits from the nonprofit that would have been financed from the profits at issue.

39. This example provoked vehement reactions from our reviewers. All believed the resolution was obvious, but some thought the plaintiff should receive only its anticipated profit, and others thought the plaintiff should receive the entire commission.

3. *Structured settlements*

Sometimes, particularly in personal injury cases, the damages award will be paid over time. Many of the issues that arise in section III.E, Discounting Future Losses, arise in determining how damages should be structured. Damages should first be measured at the time of trial. The different payouts need to be discounted before summing to insure that the plaintiff is properly compensated. Thus, the same issues in determining the proper discount rate for losses are applicable in determining the proper discount rate for payouts. In addition, the structured settlement should consider the chance that not all payments may be made, either because the plaintiff may not be alive (unless payments are to continue after death of the plaintiff) or because the defendant is not alive or ceases business.

IV. Subject Areas of Economic Loss Measurement

A. Personal Lost Earnings

A claim for loss of personal earnings occurs as the result of wrongful termination, discrimination, injury, or death. The earnings usually come from employment, but essentially the same issues arise if self-employment or partnership earnings are lost. Most damages studies for personal lost earnings fit the model of Figure 1 quite closely.

1. *Is there a dispute about projected earnings but for the harmful event?*

The plaintiff seeking compensation for lost earnings will normally include wages or salary; other cash compensation, such as commissions, overtime, and bonuses; and the value of fringe benefits. Disputes about wages and salary before trial are the least likely, especially if there are employees in similar jobs whose earnings were not interrupted. Even so, the plaintiff may make the case that a promotion would have occurred after the time of the termination or injury. The more variable elements of cash compensation are more likely to be in dispute. One side may measure bonuses and overtime during a period when these parts of compensation were unusually high, and the other side may choose a longer period, during which the average is lower.

2. *What benefits are part of damages?*

Loss of benefits may be an important part of lost personal earnings damages. A frequent source of dispute is the proper measurement of vacation and sick pay. Here the strict adherence to the format of Figure 1 can help resolve these disputes. Vacation and sick pay[40] are part of the earnings the plaintiff would have received but for the harmful event. It would be double counting[41] to include vacation and sick pay in benefits when they have already been included in cash earnings.

The valuation of fringe benefits is frequently a source of important disputes. When benefits take a form other than immediate cash, there are two basic approaches to valuation: (1) the cost to the employer, and (2) the value to the worker. Disputes may arise because of differences between these two approaches or in the application of either one.

Example: Employee is terminated in breach of an employment agreement. Employee's damages analysis includes the value of Employee's coverage under Employer's company medical plan, estimated by the cost of obtaining similar coverage as an individual. Employee's damages analysis also includes Employer's contribution to Social Security. Employer's opposing study values the medical benefits at the cost of the company plan, which is much less than an individual plan. Employer places a value of zero on Social Security contributions, on the grounds that the Social Security benefit formula would give the same benefits to Employee whether or not the additional employer contributions had been made.

Comment: Although the valuation of benefits from Employer's point of view has theoretical merit, the obstacles are obvious from these two examples. On the value of the medical benefits, if Employee actually has purchased equivalent coverage as an individual, there is a case for using that cost. The valuation of prospective Social Security benefits is forbiddingly complex, and most experts settle for measuring the value as the employer's contribution.[42]

3. *Is there a dispute about mitigation?*

Actual earnings before trial, although known, may be subject to dispute if the defendant argues that the plaintiff took too long to find a job or the job taken was not sufficiently remunerative. Even more problematic may be the situation where the plaintiff continues to be unemployed.

40. *See, e.g.*, Ross v. Buckeye Cellulose Corp., 764 F. Supp. 1543 (M.D. Ga. 1991) (holding vacation and sick pay are components of back pay awards), *modified*, 980 F.2d 648 (11th Cir. 1993).

41. *See, e.g.*, James B. Smith, Jr. & Jack A. Taylor, *Injuries and Loss of Earnings*, 57 Ala. Law. 176, 177 (1996) (stating need to avoid double counting when taking fringe benefits such as vacation and sick pay into account when calculating lost earnings).

42. *See, e.g.*, *id.* (stating employer's contribution to employee's Social Security may be taken into consideration when calculating lost earnings to avoid double counting); Rupp v. Purolator Courier Corp., Nos. 93-3276, 93-3288, 1994 WL 730892, at *2 (10th Cir. Dec. 20, 1994) (holding damage award should not include employer's contribution to employee's Social Security taxes).

Parties disputing the length of a job search frequently offer testimony from job placement experts. Testimony from a psychologist also may be offered if the plaintiff has suffered emotional trauma as a result of the defendant's actions. Recovery from temporarily disabling injuries may be the subject of testimony by experts in vocational rehabilitation. Also, data about displaced workers, which can be obtained from the U.S. Bureau of Labor Statistics, provide information about how long others have taken to find jobs.

The defendant may argue that the plaintiff—for reason of illness, injury, or vacation, not related to the liability issues in the case—has chosen not to undertake a serious job search and therefore failed to meet the duty to mitigate. A damages study based on that conclusion will impute earnings to replace the actual earnings (if any) in the box labeled "Actual earnings before trial" in Figure 1.

Example: Plumber loses two years of work as a result of slipping on ice. His damages claim is for two years of earnings as a plumber. Defendant Hotel Owner calculates damages as the difference between those earnings and one year of earnings as a bartender, on the grounds that Plumber was capable of working as a bartender during the second year of his recovery.

Comment: Employment law may limit the type of alternative job that the plaintiff is obligated to consider.[43]

Resolution of the mitigation issue can also be complicated if the plaintiff has taken a less remunerative job in anticipation of subsequent increases. For example, the plaintiff may have gone back to school to qualify for a better-paying job in the future. Or, the plaintiff may have taken a lower-paying job in which the career path offers more advancement. A common occurrence, particularly for more experienced workers with the appropriate skills, is to become a self-employed businessperson. The problem becomes how to value the plaintiff's activities during the development period of the business. On the one hand, the plaintiff may have made a reasonable choice of mitigating action by starting a business. On the other hand, the defendant is entitled to an offset to damages for the value of the plaintiff's investment in the development of the business.

When damages are computed over the entire remaining work life of the plaintiff, the timing of earnings on the mitigation side is less critical. The economic criterion for judging the adequacy of mitigation is that the present value of the stream of earnings over the plaintiff's work life in the chosen career exceeds the present value of the stream of earnings from alternative careers. In

43. *See, e.g.*, Shore v. Federal Express Corp., 42 F.3d 373, 376 (6th Cir. 1994) (rejecting defendant's claim that plaintiff failed to mitigate damages because the alternative jobs available to plaintiff were not comparable to the job from which she was wrongfully discharged).

other words, it is appropriate that the defendant should be charged with replacing the entire amount of but-for earnings during a period of schooling or other investment if the defendant is being relieved of even more responsibility in future years as the investment pays off. If, however, the plaintiff appears to have chosen a lower-paying career for noneconomic reasons, then the defendant may argue that the amounts corresponding to the boxes labeled "Actual earnings before trial" and "Projected earnings after trial" in Figure 1 should be based on the plaintiff's highest-paying alternative. The defendant may also argue along these lines if damages are computed over a period shorter than the plaintiff's work life.

4. *Is there disagreement about how the plaintiff's career path should be projected?*

The issues that arise in projecting but-for and actual earnings after trial are similar to the issues that arise in measuring damages before trial. In addition, the parties are likely to disagree regarding the plaintiff's future increases in compensation. A damages analysis should be internally consistent. For example, the compensation path for both but-for and actual earnings paths should be based on consistent assumptions about general economic conditions, about conditions in the local labor market for the plaintiff's type of work, and about the plaintiff's likely increases in skills and earning capacity. The analysis probably should project a less successful career on the mitigation side if it is projecting a slow earnings growth absent the harm. Similarly, if the plaintiff is projected as president of the company in ten years absent the harm, the study should probably project similar success in the mitigating career, unless the injury limits his or her potential in the mitigating career.

Example: Executive suffers wrongful termination. His damages study projects rapid growth in salary, bonus, and options, thanks to a series of likely promotions had he not been terminated. After termination, he looked for work unsuccessfully for a year and then started up a consulting business. Earnings from the consulting business rise, but never reach the level of his projected compensation but for the termination. Damages are estimated at $3.6 million. His former employer's opposing damages study is based on the hypothesis that he would have been able to find a similar job within nine months if he had searched diligently. Damages are estimated at $275,000.

Comment: This example illustrates the type of factual disputes that are typical of executive termination damages. Note that there may be an issue of random subsequent events both in the duration of Executive's job search and in the success of his consulting business.

5. *Is there disagreement about how earnings should be discounted to present value?*

Because personal lost earnings damages may accrue over the remainder of a plaintiff's working life, the issues of predicting future inflation and discounting earnings to present value are particularly likely to generate quantitatively important disagreements. As we noted in section III.D, projections of future compensation can be done in constant dollars or escalated terms. In the first case, the interest rate used to discount future constant-dollar losses should be a real interest rate—the difference between the ordinary interest rate and the projected future rate of inflation. All else being the same, the two approaches will give identical calculations of damages. Under some conditions, future wage growth may be about equal to the interest rate, so that discounted future losses are the same in each future year. Damages after trial are then just the appropriate multiple of the current year's loss. Equivalently, the calculation can be done by projected future wage growth in escalating dollars and discounting by an ordinary interest rate. Of course, the projected wage growth must be consistent with the expert's conclusion about inflation.

Substantial disagreements can arise about the rate of interest. Even when the parties agree that the interest rate should approximate what the plaintiff can actually earn by investing the award prudently, the parties may dispute the type of investment the plaintiff is likely to make. The plaintiff may argue that the real rate of interest[44] should correspond to the real rate of interest for a money market fund, while the defendant may argue that the plaintiff would be expected to invest in instruments, such as the stock market, with higher expected returns. There may also be a disagreement about whether the discount rate should be calculated before or after taxes.[45]

6. *Is there disagreement about subsequent unexpected events?*

Disagreements about subsequent unexpected events are likely in cases involving personal earnings, as we discussed in general in section III.F. For example, the plaintiff may have suffered a debilitating illness that would have compelled the resignation from a job a year later even if the termination or injury had not occurred. Or the plaintiff would have been laid off as a result of employer hardship one year after the termination. The defendant may argue that damages should be limited to one year. The plaintiff might respond that the bad times

44. *See, e.g.*, Clark v. Secretary of Dep't of Health & Human Servs., No. 88-44-V, 1989 WL 250075, at *2 (Cl. Ct. July 28, 1989) (defining real rate of interest as the difference between the rate of return and the rate of inflation).

45. *See, e.g.*, McCarthy v. United States, 870 F.2d 1499, 1502–03 (9th Cir. 1989) (determining the appropriate real rate of interest).

were unexpected at the time of the termination and so should be excluded from consideration in the calculation of damages. Plaintiff, therefore, argues that damages should be calculated without consideration of these events.

7. *Is there disagreement about retirement and mortality?*

For damages after trial, there is another issue related to the issue of unexpected events before trial: How should future damages reflect the probability that the plaintiff will die or decide to retire? Sometimes an expert will assume a work-life expectancy and terminate damages at the end of that period. Tables of work-life expectancy incorporate the probability of both retirement and death. Another approach is to multiply each year's lost earnings by the probability that the plaintiff will be alive and working in that year. That probability declines gradually with age; it can be inferred from data on labor-force participation and mortality by age.

Within either approach, there may be disagreements about how much information to use about the individual. For example, if the plaintiff is known to smoke, should his survival rates be those of a smoker? Similarly, if the plaintiff is a woman executive, should her retirement probability be inferred from data on women in general, or would it be more reasonable to look at data on executives, who are mostly men?

B. *Intellectual Property Damages*

Intellectual property damages are calculated under federal law for patents, trademarks, and copyrights,[46] and calculated under state law for trade secrets and sometimes for trademarks if there are violations of state law and not federal law. Damages may be a combination of the value lost by the intellectual property owner and the value gained by the infringer[47] with adjustment to avoid double counting. The value lost by the intellectual property owner is lost profits, calculated as in other types of damages analysis. Under patent law, the lost profit includes a reasonable royalty the infringer should have paid the patent owner for

46. *See* 28 U.S.C. § 1338(a) (1988) ("The district courts shall have original jurisdiction of any civil action arising under any Act of Congress relating to patents, plant variety protection, copyrights and trade-marks. Such jurisdiction shall be exclusive of the courts of the states in patent, plant variety protection and copyright cases."). *See, e.g.*, David Hricik, *Remedies of the Infringer: The Use by the Infringer of Implied and Common Law Federal Rights, State Law Claims, and Contract to Shift Liability for Infringement of Patents, Copyrights, and Trademarks*, 28 Tex. Tech. L. Rev. 1027, 1068–69 (1997) (discussing use of federal common law by patent, trademark, and copyright infringers to shift liability to third parties).

47. *See, e.g.*, Walker v. Forbes, Inc., 28 F.3d 409, 412 (4th Cir. 1994) (explaining that 17 U.S.C. § 504(b) regarding copyright infringement indicates "an injured party is awarded not only an amount to compensate for the injury that results from the infringement, but also the amount of the infringer's profit that is found to derive from the infringement, avoiding double counting").

the use of the patented invention. The reasonable royalty[48] is generally defined as the amount the defendant would have paid the patent owner as the result of a license negotiation occurring at the time the infringement began or the patent issued. Patent law does not provide for recovery of value gained by the infringer, except through the reasonable royalty.[49]

Under copyright law, the plaintiff is entitled to the revenue received by the infringer as a result of selling the copyrighted work, but the defendant is entitled to deduct the costs of reproducing the infringing work as an offset to damages (the plaintiff's damages case need not include the offset; the defendant typically raises this issue later). Under the Uniform Trade Secrets Law,[50] the standard is disgorgement of defendant's gain. However, the measurement of defendant's gain can be any reasonable way of calculating the value of the trade secret, including the cost to create, the value to the plaintiff, or the value to the defendant.

Damages for trademark infringement can be similar to those for copyright and patent infringement claims, but not always. Where a trademark is licensed in connection with the sale of marked goods on a royalty basis, then damages can be calculated based on a reasonable royalty. However, trademarks often are not licensed and thus a plaintiff in a trademark infringement case cannot always use the reasonable royalty measure.

In such cases involving a nonlicensed trademark, the trademark infringement plaintiff must prove one or more elements of special damage. First, the plaintiff may claim lost sales due to the infringement. Lost sales, however, can be difficult

48. *See, e.g.*, Faulkner v. Gibbs, 199 F.2d 635, 639 (9th Cir. 1952) (defining reasonable royalty as "an amount which a person, desiring to use a patented article, as a business proposition, would be willing to pay as a royalty and yet be able to use the patented article at a reasonable profit. The primary inquiry, often complicated by secondary ones, is what the parties would have agreed upon, if both were reasonably trying to reach an agreement."); Vermont Microsystems, Inc. v. Autodesk, Inc., 138 F.3d 449, 450 (2d Cir. 1998) (explaining reasonable royalty, in terms of trade secrets, as "royalty that the plaintiff and defendant would have agreed to for the use of the trade secret made by the defendant may be one measure of the approximate portion of the defendant's profits attributable to the use").

49. *See, e.g.*, Gargoyles, Inc. v. United States, 113 F.3d 1572, 1580 (Fed. Cir. 1997) (upholding district court's decision that lost profits were not appropriate in the patent case and that the appropriate damages were reasonable royalties); Vermont Microsystems, 138 F.3d at 450 (2d Cir. 1998) (stating reasonable royalty is a common award in patent cases).

50. *See, e.g.*, Vermont Microsystems, Inc. v. Autodesk, Inc., 138 F.3d 449 (2d Cir. 1998); Reingold v. Swiftships, Inc., 126 F.3d 645 (5th Cir. 1997); Duncan v. Stuetzle, 76 F.3d 1480 (9th Cir. 1996); Kovarik v. American Family Ins. Group, 108 F.3d 962 (8th Cir. 1997). In all of these cases, the state has adopted the Uniform Trade Secrets Act (UTSA). Consequently, the courts use the UTSA definition of trade secrets, which states trade secrets derive independent economic value, actual or potential, from disclosure or use.

to identify where a competitor has used an infringing mark. Proof of trademark infringement plus a general decline in sales will be insufficient to establish damages based on lost sales unless the plaintiff can also show that factors other than the infringement did not cause the decline. *Exact* proof of such losses, however, is neither possible nor required.

The plaintiff may also claim damages based on a loss of reputation in his or her business. Plaintiff may recover, for example, the costs expended to minimize any loss of reputation, such as corrective advertising or a name change.

Finally, the trademark infringement plaintiff may claim damages based on the profits of the infringer. Such profits may be recovered to prevent unjust enrichment, or they may be considered as an indication of the plaintiff's losses. Care must be taken, however, to ensure that the infringer is actually a competitor of the plaintiff; otherwise the defendant's profits would not represent an accurate measurement of the plaintiff's losses. As under copyright law, the plaintiff may recover damages based on the gross receipts from the sale of the infringing items. The defendant, however, can seek to offset such damages by deducting for the expense of producing the infringing goods or by apportioning the profits attributable to the infringing mark and those attributable to the intrinsic merit of his or her product. To recover damages based on the defendant's lost profits, the plaintiff must usually prove either a willful infringement or that he or she put the defendant on notice of the infringement, depending on the jurisdiction.

1. *Is there disagreement about what fraction of the defendant's sales would have gone to the plaintiff?*

Patent law now makes it easier for a patent owner to argue that it would have received a share of the infringer's actual sale.[51] Previously, the presence of a noninfringing product in the market required a lost-profit analysis to show, directly, which sales were lost to the defendant rather than to other noninfringing alternatives. This often required documents that showed that both parties, and only those parties, were contending for a sale. Damages were limited to those sales that could be documented. The damages analysis may now use some type of market-share model to show that the plaintiff lost sales in relation to its market share. For example, if the plaintiff had one-third of the market, the defendant also had one-third of the market, and the noninfringing alternative had one-third of the market, then the plaintiff could argue that it would have made one-half of defendant's sales absent the infringement. This is an example of the

51. State Indus., Inc. v. Mor-Flo Indus., Inc., 639 F. Supp. 937 (E.D. Tenn. 1986), *aff'd without op.*, 818 F.2d 875 (Fed. Cir.), *cert. denied*, 484 U.S. 845 (1987).

simplest model. This model would consider the total market to have a given volume of sales, S. If the market shares of the plaintiff and the defendant are P and D, respectively, this model would predict that the plaintiff's market share, absent the defendant's sales, would be:

$$\frac{P}{1 - D}$$

This formula corresponds to the assumption that the defendant's sales would have been distributed evenly across the other sellers, including the plaintiff. Then the plaintiff's sales, absent the presence of the infringer in the market, would be:

$$\frac{P}{1 - D} S$$

But this model is likely to be disputed. The issues are how large the market would have been, absent the defendant's infringing product, and what share of that market the plaintiff would have enjoyed. The defendant may argue that it enlarged the total market. Its product may appeal to customers who would not buy from any of the other sellers; for example, some of the infringing sales may be to affiliates of the infringer. With respect to the plaintiff's market share but for the infringement, the defendant may demonstrate that the rivals for the defendant's sales rarely included the plaintiff. Either the plaintiff or the defendant may argue that there are actually several different markets, each to be analyzed according to some type of market-share model.

2. *Is there disagreement about the effect of infringement or misappropriation on prices as well as quantities (price erosion)?*[52]

The plaintiff may measure price erosion directly, by comparing prices before and after infringement, or indirectly, through an economic analysis of the market. The defendant may dispute direct measures of price erosion on the grounds that the drop in prices would have occurred despite the infringement as a result of normal trends or events occurring at the same time, unrelated to the infringement.

The parties may also dispute the relation between the size of the total market and prices. When a plaintiff's analysis projects that prices would have been higher

52. *See, e.g.*, General Am. Transp. Corp. v. Cryo-Trans, Inc., 897 F. Supp. 1121, 1123–24 (N.D. Ill. 1995); Rawlplug Co., Inc. v. Illinois Tool Works Inc., No. 91 Civ. 1781, 1994 WL 202600, at *2 (S.D.N.Y. May 23, 1994); Micro Motion, Inc. v. Exac Corp., 761 F. Supp. 1420, 1430–31 (N.D. Cal. 1991) (holding in all three cases that patentee is entitled to recover lost profits due to past price erosion caused by the wrongdoer's infringement).

absent infringement, the defendant may point out that higher prices would reduce the volume of total sales and thus reduce the plaintiff's sales. Disagreements about the measurement of lost profit are most likely to be resolved if both parties make their lost-profit calculations in the same format. The preferred format is:

Lost profit = [price but for infringement] × [quantity sold but for infringement] - [actual revenue] - [extra cost of producing the extra quantity]

This format avoids the danger of double counting that arises when the plaintiff makes separate claims for lost sales and price erosion.

3. Is there a dispute about whether the lost-profit calculation includes contributions from noninfringing features of the work or product (apportionment)?[53]

Where the protected work or technology is not the only feature or selling point of the defendant's product, there may be disagreement about apportionment. One approach to quantitative apportionment of damages is to hypothesize that the defendant would have sold a different, noninfringing product containing the other features or selling points. The damages study then measures the plaintiff's losses from the defendant's selling of the actual product rather than the alternative, hypothetical, noninfringing product.

Example: Camera Maker sells a camera that competes directly with Rival's similar camera. A court has determined that this is an infringement of Rival's autofocus patent. Rival's damages study hypothesizes the absence of Camera Maker's product from the market. Camera Maker's damages study hypothesizes that it would have sold the same camera with a different, noninfringing autofocus system. Camera Maker has apportioned lost sales to take account of the other selling points of the camera, whereas Rival is considering all of the lost sales. Rival argues that its approach is correct because the camera would not have been put on the market absent the infringing autofocus system.

Comment: Note that the issue of apportionment here is, in essence, a special

53. *See, e.g.*, 15 U.S.C.A. § 1117 (1997). "Owner of trademark can recover profits acquired by infringer from infringing sales, and impossibility of apportionment between profits from infringement and those due to intrinsic merit excuses owner of trademark from showing what part of infringer's profits were attributable to the use of the infringing mark." (citing Hamilton-Brown Shoe Co. v. Wolf Bros. & Co., 240 U.S. 251 (1916)). "Seller of video game cartridges was not entitled to apportionment of damages for trademark infringement on grounds that not all games on cartridges were infringing, where seller failed to present evidence on workable distinction for identifying infringing and noninfringing elements." (citing Nintendo of Am., Inc. v. Dragon Pac. Int'l, 40 F.3d 1007 (9th Cir. 1994), *cert. denied*, 515 U.S. 1107 (1995)).

case of the more general issue discussed in section III.A—disagreements about the alternative nonharmful conduct of the defendant. Here the alternative is what type of noninfringing product Camera Maker can hypothesize it would have sold absent infringement.[54]

4. *Do the parties disagree about whether the defendant could have designed around the plaintiff's patent?*

Under patent law, part of the plaintiff's lost profit from infringement is measured as the reasonable royalty the defendant would have paid for a license under the patent. The conceptual basis for the reasonable royalty is the outcome of a hypothetical negotiation occurring at the time the infringement began. Validity of the patent and the defendant's use of the protected technology are presumed in the hypothetical negotiation.

An important source of disagreement about the basis for the reasonable royalty and corresponding quantum of damages is the defendant's ability to design around the patent. A defendant may argue that any but a modest royalty would have caused it to reject the license and choose not to use the technology but to design around it instead.

5. *Is there disagreement about how much of the defendant's advantage actually came from infringement (apportionment)?*

Under patent law, apportionment is implicit in the reasonable-royalty framework; a defendant would not pay more for a patent license than its contribution to profit. Under copyright law, where damages include the defendant's gain measured as its revenue or profit, apportionment may be a major source of disagreement.

Example: Recording Company's compact disk contains one infringing song among twelve. Defendant's damages study is based on one-twelfth of the profit from the sales of the disk. Rock Composer argues that the infringing song is the main selling point of the disk and seeks all of Defendant's profit.

Comment: This is a factual dispute. The parties may use survey evidence on consumers' reasons for purchasing the disk.

54. In *Computer Associates International v. Altai, Inc.*, 982 F.2d 693 (2d Cir. 1992), the appeals court determined that defendant could hypothesize that sales of its noninfringing earlier version of a software package would partially replace the actual sales of its infringing package, thus limiting the extra sales that plaintiff would have enjoyed absent the infringement.

6. *Is there disagreement about how to combine the plaintiff's loss and the defendant's gain in a way that avoids double counting?*[55]

Calculating such a damages figure normally involves finding the profit from the defendant's sales that are not considered the plaintiff's lost sales. For example, if the defendant has sold 100 units and in the process has taken 60 units of sales away from the plaintiff, the damages would consist of the plaintiff's lost profits on the 60 units and the defendant's revenue or profit on the remaining 40 units that were incremental sales not taken from the plaintiff.

Disputes can arise about the elimination of double counting when the plaintiff and the defendant sell their products in different ways. For example, the plaintiff may bundle its product with related products, while the defendant sells a component to be bundled[56] by others.

C. Antitrust Damages

Where the plaintiff is the customer of the defendant or purchases goods in a market where the defendant's monopolistic misconduct has raised prices, damages are the amount of the overcharge. This amount may exceed the lost profit of the plaintiff, if it is a business, because the plaintiff may pass along part of the effect of the price increase to its own customers.[57] Where the plaintiff is a rival of the defendant, injured by exclusionary or predatory conduct, damages are the lost profits from the misconduct.

1. *Is there disagreement about the scope of the damages?*

The plaintiff might calculate damages affecting all of its business activities, whereas the defendant might calculate damages only in markets where there is a likelihood of adverse impact from the defendant's conduct.

Example: Trucker's exclusionary conduct has monopolized certain routes, but only modestly raised its market share on many other nonmonopolized routes. Shippers seek damages for elevated prices in all af-

55. *See supra* note 49; Dolori Fabrics, Inc. v. The Limited, Inc., 662 F. Supp. 1347 (S.D.N.Y. 1987) (holding award of actual damages and profits of infringers to copyright-holder did not constitute double counting because the copyright-holder did not compete for and could not have made the same sales as the infringer made).

56. *See, e.g.*, Deltak, Inc. v. Advanced Sys., Inc., 767 F.2d 357, 363 (7th Cir. 1985) (determining the market value of the infringed product by reviewing the list price of plaintiff's book and video kit, without the infringed product, which was not bundled in a package with other products).

57. Hanover Shoe v. United Shoe Mach. Corp., 392 U.S. 481, 499 (1968); Illinois Brick Co. v. Illinois, 431 U.S. 720 (1977) (establishing the principle under the federal antitrust laws that, generally, a business plaintiff should not lower its damages claim on account of passing on overcharges to its customers, but rather the plaintiff should stand in for the downstream victims of overcharges).

fected markets, but Trucker's damages study considers only the routes where monopolization has occurred.

Comment: Here is a mixture of legal and economic issues. The law may set limits on the reach of antitrust damages even if economic analysis could quantify price elevation in all of the markets. The analysis here is similar to the more general analysis in section III.A.3 about the causal effect of the injury.

2. *Is there a dispute about the causal link between the misconduct and the measured damages?*

Experts face a particular challenge in making a complete analysis of the economic impact of antitrust misconduct on the relevant market. To overcome the analytical challenge, experts sometimes compare market conditions in a period affected by the misconduct with conditions in another period, during which the misconduct is known to be absent. The plaintiff might take the increase in price from the benchmark period to the affected period as a measure of the price elevation caused by the misconduct. The defendant may argue that the misconduct is not the only difference between the periods—prices rose, for example, because of cost increases or rising demand and not just because of a conspiracy or other misconduct.

Example: The price of plywood rises soon after a meeting of Plywood Producers. Plywood Purchasers attribute all of the price increase to a price-fixing conspiracy. Plywood Producers argue that increases in timber prices would have compelled increases in plywood prices even without a price-fixing agreement; their damages study attributes only part of the price increase to the conspiracy.

Comment: Economic analysis is capable, in principle, of inferring how much of a price increase is caused by a cost increase. Plywood Purchasers' damages analysis could be strengthened in this example by direct evidence on the amount of the price increase determined by the conspirators. In more sophisticated measurements of damages through comparisons of periods with and without the misconduct, experts may use regression analysis to adjust for influences other than the misconduct. Explanatory variables may include general economic indicators such as the national price level and Gross Domestic Product, along with variables specific to the industry.[58]

58. *See* Daniel L. Rubinfeld, Reference Guide on Multiple Regression § II.B.3, in this manual.

3. Is there a dispute about how conditions would differ absent the challenged misconduct?

The plaintiff may calculate damages for exclusionary conduct on the basis that prices in the market would have been the same but for that conduct. The defendant may argue that the activities of the plaintiff and other firms, absent exclusion, would have driven prices down, and thus that the plaintiff has overstated the profit it lost from exclusion.

Example: Concert Promoter is the victim of exclusion by Incumbent through Incumbent's unlawful contracts with a ticket agency. Promoter's damages study hypothesizes that Promoter would be the only additional seller in the industry absent the contracts. Incumbent's damages study hypothesizes numerous additional sellers and price reductions sufficient to eliminate almost all profit. Incumbent's estimate of damages is a small fraction of Promoter's.

Comment: The elimination of one barrier to entry in the market—the unlawful contracts—will increase the profit available to potential rivals. On this account, some new rivals to the Concert Promoter might enter the market and share the benefits flowing from the elimination of the unlawful contracts. This is a limiting factor for Concert Promoter's damages. But there may be other barriers to the entry of rivals. For example, it may take an extended period for a new promoter to attract major performers. The plaintiff, already established in the business, might expect to make added profits from the elimination of the unlawful contracts, even though some new competitors would enter. See *supra* note 14 and accompanying text.

When the harmful act is a tied sale, the issue of different conditions absent the harmful act is particularly critical. Tying arrangements are attempts by a business to extend its monopoly in one market into a related market. A purchaser who wants the "tying" good must also purchase the "tied" good.[59] The plaintiff, if a purchaser, may calculate damages as the price paid for the purchase of the tied product, on the theory that the purchase was unwanted and would not have occurred absent the tie. If the plaintiff is a rival in the market for the tied good, the plaintiff may calculate damages on the theory that it would have enjoyed higher sales absent the tie. In both cases, the defendant may respond that, absent the tie, the price for the tying good would have been higher and the price for

59. For further explanation, see Stephen H. Knowlton et al., *Antitrust, in* Litigation Services Handbook: The Role of the Accountant as Expert Witness 208–09 (Peter B. Frank et al. eds., 1990).

the tied good would have been lower. Damages are then lower than those calculated by the purchaser plaintiff based on the higher price for the tying good. Damages are lower than those calculated by the rival plaintiff because the lost sales would occur at a lower price.

Example: Dominant Film Seller has required that purchasers of film also buy processing. Film and processing Purchasers calculate damages on the theory that they could have bought film at the stated price from Dominant Seller but could have bought processing from a cheaper rival, absent the tie. Dominant Seller counters that it would have charged more for film absent the tie. In addition, Independent Processor calculates damages based on the theory that it would have picked up part of Dominant Seller's processing business, which would have enabled it to charge the same price charged by Dominant Seller. Defendant Dominant Seller responds that it would have charged less for processing and more for film, absent the tie, so Independent Processor would be forced to charge a lower price.

Comment: When there is a strict tie between two products, the economist will be careful in interpreting the separate stated prices for the two products. In this example, all that matters to the customer is the combined price of film and processing. A full factual analysis is needed to restate pricing absent a tie. Eliminating a tie may stimulate entry into the market for the tied product (indeed, there was an upsurge of competition in the independent film processing market when tying was eliminated). Economists sometimes disagree why dominant firms use ties rather than simply extract all of the available monopoly profit from the product in which they are dominant.

D. Securities Damages

Where the harmful act takes the form of a failure to disclose adverse information about a firm whose securities are publicly traded, damages are typically sought by investors who bought the securities after the information should have been disclosed and before it was actually disclosed. Their losses are the excess value they paid for the securities, provided they did not sell before the adverse information affected the market. The damages study typically measures the excess price by the decline in the price that occurred when the information reached the market. Finance theory provides the framework generally used for this purpose.[60] The effect of the adverse information on the price of the securities is the

60. *See generally* Brealey & Myers, *supra* note 33.

part of the total price change not predicted by finance theory, considering what happened in similar securities markets at the time the information affected the market.

1. *Is there disagreement about when the adverse information affected the market?*

The plaintiff might argue that the adverse information reached the market in a number of steps, and thus measure damages as the excess decline in value over a period including all of the steps. Defendant might reply that only one of those steps involved the actual disclosure, and measure damages as the excess decline only on the day of that disclosure. The length and timing of the "window" for measuring the excess decline is probably the most important source of disagreement in securities damages.

2. *Is there disagreement about how to take proper account of turnover of the securities?*

Frequently, securities damages must be measured before the victims are individually identified. The victims are those who purchased the securities after the time when a disclosure should have been made and still owned them when the disclosure was actually made. In order to estimate the volume of securities for which damages accrued, the pattern of turnover in ownership must be determined. Generally, data on total daily purchases of the securities will be available. These data provide an upper bound on the volume for damages. However, the actual volume will be lower because some of the securities will change hands more than once during the period between proper and actual disclosure. A detailed study of turnover patterns is needed for this purpose. The representatives of the plaintiff class might argue that few shares turned over more than once, while the defendant might reply that the observed transactions were largely the same shares turning over repeatedly.

E. Liquidated Damages

1. *Is there a dispute about the proper application of a provision for liquidated damages?*

After parties have entered into a contract with liquidated damages, they may dispute whether the liquidated-damages provision actually should apply to a subsequent harmful event. The parties may disagree on whether the event falls within the class intended by the contract provision, or they may disagree on whether the liquidated damages bear a reasonable relation to actual damages, in the sense required by applicable law. In particular, the defendant may attack the amount of liquidated damages as a penalty that exaggerates the plaintiff's actual loss.

Changes in economic conditions may be an important source of disagreement about the reasonableness of a liquidated-damages provision. One party may seek to overturn a liquidated-damages provision on the grounds that new conditions make it unreasonable.

Example: Scrap Iron Supplier breaches supply agreement and pays liquidated damages. Buyer seeks to set aside the liquidated-damages provision because the price of scrap iron has risen, and the liquidated damages are a small fraction of actual damages under the expectation principle.

Comment: There may be conflict between the date for judging the reasonableness of a liquidated-damages provision and the date for measurement of expectation damages, as in this example. Generally, the date for evaluating the reasonableness of liquidated damages is the date the contract is made. In contrast, the date for expectation damages is the date of the breach. The result is a conundrum for which the economist needs guidance from the law. Enforcement of the liquidated-damages provision in this example will induce inefficient breach.

Appendix: Example of a Damages Study

Plaintiff SBM makes telephone switchboards. Defendant TPC is a telephone company. By denying SBM technical information and by informing SBM's potential customers that SBM's switchboards are incompatible with TPC's network, TPC has imposed economic losses on SBM. TPC's misconduct began in 1996. SBM's damages study presented at trial at the end of 1998 proceeds as follows (see Table 4):

1. Damages theory is compensation for lost profit from TPC's exclusionary conduct.
2. SBM would have sold more units and achieved a higher price per unit had SBM had access to complete technical information and had SBM not faced disparagement from TPC.
3. SBM would have earned profits before tax in 1996–1998 in millions of dollars as shown in column 2 of Table 4, based on an analysis of lost business and avoided costs.
4. SBM's actual profits before tax are shown in column 3. Column 4 shows lost earnings. Column 5 shows the factor for the time value of money prescribed by law, with 7% annual simple interest without compounding. Column 6 shows the loss including prejudgment interest.
5. For the years 1999 through 2003, column 2 shows projected earnings but for TPC's misconduct.
6. For the same years, column 3 shows projected actual earnings.
7. Column 4 shows SBM's future earnings losses. Column 5 shows the discount factor based on a 4% annual after-tax interest rate, obtained by applying SBM's corporate tax rate to TPC's medium-term borrowing rate. TPC has an AA bond rating. Column 6 shows the discounted future loss. At the bottom of the table is the total loss of economic value, according to SBM's damages study, of $1.237 billion.

Table 4. SBM's Damages Analysis (in Millions of Dollars)

(1) Year	(2) Earnings but for Misconduct	(3) Actual Earnings	(4) Loss	(5) Discount Factor	(6) Discounted Loss
1996	$187	$34	$153	$1.21	$185
1997	200	56	144	1.14	164
1998	213	45	168	1.07	180
1999	227	87	140	1.00	140
2000	242	96	147	0.96	141
2001	259	105	153	0.92	142
2002	276	116	160	0.89	142
2003	294	127	167	0.85	143
Total					1,237

Table 5. TPC's Damages Analysis (in Millions of Dollars)

(1) Year	(2) Earnings but for Misconduct	(3) Mitigation with Earnings	(4) Loss	(5) Discount Factor	(6) Discounted Loss
1996	$101	$79	$22	$1.21	$27
1997	108	85	23	1.14	26
1998	115	81	34	1.07	36
1999	123	98	25	1.00	25
2000	131	108	23	0.87	20
2001	140	119	21	0.76	16
2002	149	130	19	0.66	12
2003	159	143	16	0.57	9
Total					171

Defendant TPC presents an alternative damages study in the same format (see Table 5). TPC argues that SBM's earnings but for the misconduct, before and after trial, are the numbers in column 2 of Table 5. TPC believes that the number of units sold would be lower, the price would be lower, and costs of production higher than in SBM's damages study. TPC further argues that SBM failed to mitigate the effects of TPC's misconduct—SBM could have obtained the technical information it needed from other sources, and SBM could have counteracted TPC's disparagement with vigorous marketing. Column 3 displays the earnings that TPC believes SBM could have achieved with proper mitigation. TPC argues that future losses should be discounted at a 14% rate determined from SBM's cost of equity and debt; SBM is a small, risky corporation with a high cost of funds. According to TPC's damages study, total lost value is only $171 million.

Glossary of Terms

appraisal. A method of determining the value of the plaintiff's claim on an earnings stream by reference to the market values of comparable earnings streams. For example, if the plaintiff has been deprived of the use of a piece of property, the appraised value of the property might be used to determine damages.

avoided cost. Cost that the plaintiff did not incur as a result of the harmful act. Usually it is the cost that a business would have incurred in order to make the higher level of sales the business would have enjoyed but for the harmful act.

but-for analysis. Restatement of the plaintiff's economic situation but for the defendant's harmful act. Damages are generally measured as but-for value less actual value received by the plaintiff.

capitalization factor. Factor used to convert a stream of revenue or profit into its capital or property value. A capitalization factor of 10 for profit means that a firm with $1 million in annual profit is worth $10 million.

compound interest. Interest calculation giving effect to interest earned on past interest. As a result of compound interest at rate r, it takes

$$(1 + r)(1 + r) = 1 + 2r + r^2$$

dollars to make up for a lost dollar of earnings two years earlier.

constant dollars. Dollars adjusted for inflation. When calculations are done in constant 1999 dollars, it means that future dollar amounts are reduced in proportion to increases in the cost of living expected to occur after 1999.

discount rate. Rate of interest used to discount future losses.

discounting. Calculation of today's equivalent to a future dollar to reflect the time value of money. If the interest rate is r, the discount applicable to one year in the future is:

$$\frac{1}{1 + r}$$

The discount for two years is this amount squared, for three years is this amount to the third power, and so on for longer periods. The result of the calculation is to give effect to compound interest.

earnings. Economic value received by the plaintiff. Earnings could be salary and benefits from a job, profit from a business, royalties from licensing intellectual property, or the proceeds from a one-time or recurring sale of property. Earnings are measured net of costs. Thus, lost earnings are lost receipts less costs avoided.

escalation. Consideration of future inflation in projecting earnings or other dollar flows. The alternative is to make projections in constant dollars.

expectation damages. Damages measured on the principle that the plaintiff is entitled to the benefit of the bargain originally made with the defendant.

fixed cost. Cost that does not change with a change in the amount of products or services sold.

mitigation. Action taken by the plaintiff to minimize the economic effect of the harmful act. Also often refers to the actual level of earnings achieved by the plaintiff after the harmful act.

nominal interest rate. Interest rate quoted in ordinary dollars, without adjustment for inflation. Interest rates quoted in markets and reported in the financial press are always nominal interest rates.

prejudgment interest. Interest on losses occurring before trial.

present value. Value today of money due in the past (with interest) or in the future (with discounting).

price erosion. Effect of the harmful act on the price charged by the plaintiff. When the harmful act is wrongful competition, as in intellectual property infringement, price erosion is one of the ways that the plaintiff's earnings have been harmed.

real interest rate. Interest rate adjusted for inflation. The real interest rate is the nominal interest rate less the annual rate of inflation.

regression analysis. Statistical technique for inferring stable relationships among quantities. For example, regression analysis may be used to determine how costs typically vary when sales rise or fall.

reliance damages. Damages designed to reimburse a party for expenses incurred from reliance upon the promises of the other party.

restitution damages. Damages measured on the principle of restoring the economic equivalent of lost property or value.

variable cost. Component of a business's cost that would have been higher if the business had enjoyed higher sales. See also avoided cost.

References on Damages Awards

Richard A. Brealey & Stewart C. Myers, Principles of Corporate Finance (5th ed. 1996).

Industrial Organization, Economics and the Law: Collected Papers of Franklin M. Fisher (John Monz ed., 1991).

Litigation Services Handbook: The Role of the Accountant as Expert Witness (Peter B. Frank et al. eds., 1990).

A. Mitchell Polinsky, An Introduction to Law and Economics (2d ed. 1989).

W. Kip Viscusi, Reforming Products Liability (1991).

Reference Guide on Epidemiology

MICHAEL D. GREEN, D. MICHAL FREEDMAN, AND LEON GORDIS

Michael D. Green, B.S., J.D., is Bess & Walter Williams Chair in Law, Wake Forest University School of Law, Winston-Salem, North Carolina.

D. Michal Freedman, J.D., Ph.D., M.P.H., is Epidemiologist, Division of Cancer Epidemiology and Genetics, National Cancer Institute, Bethesda, Maryland.

Leon Gordis, M.D., Dr.P.H., is Professor of Epidemiology, Johns Hopkins School of Public Health, and Professor of Pediatrics, Johns Hopkins School of Medicine, Baltimore, Maryland.

CONTENTS

I. Introduction

Epidemiology is the field of public health and medicine that studies the incidence, distribution, and etiology of disease in human populations. The purpose of epidemiology is to better understand disease causation and to prevent disease in groups of individuals. Epidemiology assumes that disease is not distributed randomly in a group of individuals and that identifiable subgroups, including those exposed to certain agents, are at increased risk of contracting particular diseases.[1]

Judges and juries increasingly are presented with epidemiologic evidence as the basis of an expert's opinion on causation.[2] In the courtroom, epidemiologic research findings[3] are offered to establish or dispute whether exposure to an agent[4] caused a harmful effect or disease.[5] Epidemiologic evidence identifies

1. Although epidemiologists may conduct studies of beneficial agents that prevent or cure disease or other medical conditions, this reference guide refers exclusively to outcomes as diseases, because they are the relevant outcomes in most judicial proceedings in which epidemiology is involved.

2. Epidemiologic studies have been well received by courts trying mass tort suits. Well-conducted studies are uniformly admitted. 2 Modern Scientific Evidence: The Law and Science of Expert Testimony § 28-1.1, at 302–03 (David L. Faigman et al. eds., 1997) [hereinafter Modern Scientific Evidence]. It is important to note that often the expert testifying before the court is not the scientist who conducted the study or series of studies. *See, e.g.*, DeLuca v. Merrell Dow Pharms., Inc., 911 F.2d 941, 953 (3d Cir. 1990) (pediatric pharmacologist expert's credentials sufficient pursuant to Fed. R. Evid. 702 to interpret epidemiologic studies and render an opinion based thereon); *cf.* Landrigan v. Celotex Corp., 605 A.2d 1079, 1088 (N.J. 1992) (epidemiologist permitted to testify to both general causation and specific causation); Loudermill v. Dow Chem. Co., 863 F.2d 566, 569 (8th Cir. 1988) (toxicologist permitted to testify that chemical caused decedent's death).

3. An epidemiologic study, which often is published in a medical journal or other scientific journal, is hearsay. An epidemiologic study that is performed by the government, such as one performed by the Centers for Disease Control (CDC), may be admissible based on the hearsay exception for government records contained in Fed. R. Evid. 803(8)(C). *See* Ellis v. International Playtex, Inc., 745 F.2d 292, 300–01 (4th Cir. 1984); Kehm v. Procter & Gamble Co., 580 F. Supp. 890, 899 (N.D. Iowa 1982), *aff'd sub nom.* Kehm v. Procter & Gamble Mfg. Co., 724 F.2d 613 (8th Cir. 1983). A study that is not conducted by the government might qualify for the learned treatise exception to the hearsay rule, Fed. R. Evid. 803(18), or possibly the catchall exceptions, Fed. R. Evid. 803(24) & 804(5). *See Ellis*, 745 F.2d at 305, 306 & n.18.

In any case, an epidemiologic study might be part of the basis of an expert's opinion and need not be independently admissible pursuant to Fed. R. Evid. 703. *See In re* "Agent Orange" Prod. Liab. Litig., 611 F. Supp. 1223, 1240 (E.D.N.Y. 1985), *aff'd*, 818 F.2d 187 (2d Cir. 1987), *cert. denied*, 487 U.S. 1234 (1988); *cf.* Grassis v. Johns-Manville Corp., 591 A.2d 671, 676 (N.J. Super. Ct. App. Div. 1991) (epidemiologic study offered in evidence to support expert's opinion under New Jersey evidentiary rule equivalent to Fed. R. Evid. 703).

4. We use *agent* to refer to any substance external to the human body that potentially causes disease or other health effects. Thus, drugs, devices, chemicals, radiation, and minerals (e.g., asbestos) are all agents whose toxicity an epidemiologist might explore. A single agent or a number of independent agents may cause disease, or the combined presence of two or more agents may be necessary for the development of the disease. Epidemiologists also conduct studies of individual characteristics, such as blood pressure and diet, which might pose risks, but those studies are rarely of interest in judicial proceedings. Epidemiologists may also conduct studies of drugs and other pharmaceutical products to assess their efficacy and safety.

5. DeLuca v. Merrell Dow Pharms., Inc., 911 F.2d 941, 945–48, 953–59 (3d Cir. 1990) (litigation

agents that are associated with an increased risk of disease in groups of individuals, quantifies the amount of excess disease that is associated with an agent, and provides a profile of the type of individual who is likely to contract a disease after being exposed to an agent. Epidemiology focuses on the question of general causation (i.e., is the agent capable of causing disease?) rather than that of specific causation (i.e., did it cause disease in a particular individual?).[6] For example, in the 1950s Doll and Hill and others published articles about the increased risk of lung cancer in cigarette smokers. Doll and Hill's studies showed that smokers who smoked ten to twenty cigarettes a day had a lung cancer mortality rate that was about ten times higher than that for nonsmokers.[7] These studies identified an association between smoking cigarettes and death from lung cancer, which contributed to the determination that smoking causes lung cancer.

However, it should be emphasized that *an association is not equivalent to causation.*[8] An association identified in an epidemiologic study may or may not be causal.[9] Assessing whether an association is causal requires an understanding of

over morning sickness drug, Bendectin); Cook v. United States, 545 F. Supp. 306, 307–16 (N.D. Cal. 1982) (swine flu vaccine alleged to have caused plaintiff's Guillain-Barré disease); Allen v. United States, 588 F. Supp. 247, 416–25 (D. Utah 1984) (residents near atomic test site claimed exposure to radiation caused leukemia and other cancers), *rev'd on other grounds*, 816 F.2d 1417 (10th Cir. 1987), *cert. denied*, 484 U.S. 1004 (1988); *In re* "Agent Orange" Prod. Liab. Litig., 597 F. Supp. 740, 780–90 (E.D.N.Y. 1984) (Vietnam veterans exposed to Agent Orange and dioxin contaminant brought suit for various diseases and birth defects in their offspring), *aff'd*, 818 F.2d 145 (2d Cir. 1987); Christophersen v. Allied-Signal Corp., 939 F.2d 1106, 1115 (5th Cir. 1991) (cancer alleged to have resulted from exposure to nickel-cadmium fumes), *cert. denied*, 503 U.S. 912 (1992); Kehm v. Procter & Gamble Co., 580 F. Supp. 890, 898–902 (N.D. Iowa 1982) (toxic shock syndrome alleged to result from use of Rely tampons), *aff'd sub nom.* Kehm v. Procter & Gamble Mfg. Co., 724 F.2d 613 (8th Cir. 1983).

6. This terminology and the distinction between general causation and specific causation is widely recognized in court opinions. *See, e.g.*, Kelley v. American Heyer-Schulte Corp., 957 F. Supp. 873, 875–76 (W.D. Tex. 1997) (recognizing the different concepts of general causation and specific causation), *appeal dismissed*, 139 F.3d 899 (5th Cir. 1998); Cavallo v. Star Enter., 892 F. Supp. 756, 771 n.34 (E.D. Va. 1995), *aff'd in part and rev'd in part*, 100 F.3d 1150 (4th Cir. 1996), *cert. denied*, 522 U.S. 1044 (1998); Casey v. Ohio Med. Prods., 877 F. Supp. 1380, 1382 (N.D. Cal. 1995). For a discussion of specific causation, see *infra* § VII.

7. Richard Doll & A. Bradford Hill, *Lung Cancer and Other Causes of Death in Relation to Smoking*, 2 Brit. Med. J. 1071 (1956).

8. *See* Kelley v. American Heyer-Schulte Corp., 957 F. Supp 873, 878 (W.D. Tex. 1997), *appeal dismissed*, 139 F.3d 899 (5th Cir. 1998). Association is more fully discussed *infra* § III. The term is used to describe the relationship between two events (e.g., exposure to a chemical agent and development of disease) that occur more frequently together than one would expect by chance. Association does not necessarily imply a causal effect. Causation is used to describe the association between two events when one event is a necessary link in a chain of events that results in the effect. Of course, alternative causal chains may exist that do not include the agent but that result in the same effect. Epidemiologic methods cannot deductively prove causation; indeed, all empirically based science cannot affirmatively prove a causal relation. *See, e.g.*, Stephan F. Lanes, *The Logic of Causal Inference in Medicine*, *in* Causal Inference 59 (Kenneth J. Rothman ed., 1988). However, epidemiologic evidence can justify an inference that an agent causes a disease. *See infra* § V.

9. *See infra* § IV.

the strengths and weaknesses of the study's design and implementation, as well as a judgment about how the study findings fit with other scientific knowledge. It is important to emphasize that most studies have flaws.[10] Some flaws are inevitable given the limits of technology and resources. In evaluating epidemiologic evidence, the key questions, then, are the extent to which a study's flaws compromise its findings and whether the effect of the flaws can be assessed and taken into account in making inferences.

A final caveat is that employing the results of group-based studies of risk to make a causal determination for an individual plaintiff is beyond the limits of epidemiology. Nevertheless, a substantial body of legal precedent has developed that addresses the use of epidemiologic evidence to prove causation for an individual litigant through probabilistic means, and these cases are discussed later in this reference guide.[11]

The following sections of this reference guide address a number of critical issues that arise in considering the admissibility of, and weight to be accorded to, epidemiologic research findings. Over the past couple of decades, courts frequently have confronted the use of epidemiologic studies as evidence and recognized their utility in proving causation. As the Third Circuit observed in *DeLuca v. Merrell Dow Pharmaceuticals, Inc.*: "The reliability of expert testimony founded on reasoning from epidemiological data is generally a fit subject for judicial notice; epidemiology is a well-established branch of science and medicine, and epidemiological evidence has been accepted in numerous cases."[12]

Three basic issues arise when epidemiology is used in legal disputes and the methodological soundness of a study and its implications for resolution of the question of causation must be assessed:

1. Do the results of an epidemiologic study reveal an association between an agent and disease?
2. What sources of error in the study may have contributed to an inaccurate result?
3. If the agent is associated with disease, is the relationship causal?

Section II explains the different kinds of epidemiologic studies, and section III addresses the meaning of their outcomes. Section IV examines concerns about the methodological validity of a study, including the problem of sampling er-

10. *See In re* Orthopedic Bone Screw Prods. Liab. Litig., MDL No. 1014, 1997 U.S. Dist. LEXIS 6441, at *26–*27 (E.D. Pa. May 5, 1997) (holding that despite potential for several biases in a study that "may . . . render its conclusions inaccurate," the study was sufficiently reliable to be admissible); Joseph L. Gastwirth, *Reference Guide on Survey Research*, 36 Jurimetrics J. 181, 185 (1996) (review essay) ("One can always point to a potential flaw in a statistical analysis.").

11. *See infra* § VII.

12. 911 F.2d 941, 954 (3d Cir. 1990); *see also* Smith v. Ortho Pharm. Corp., 770 F. Supp. 1561, 1571 (N.D. Ga. 1991) (explaining increased reliance of courts on epidemiologic evidence in toxic substances litigation).

ror.[13] Section V discusses general causation, considering whether an agent is capable of causing disease. Section VI deals with methods for combining the results of multiple epidemiologic studies, and the difficulties entailed in extracting a single global measure of risk from multiple studies. Additional legal questions that arise in most toxic substances cases are whether population-based epidemiologic evidence can be used to infer specific causation, and if so, how. Section VII examines issues of specific causation, considering whether an agent caused an individual's disease.

II. What Different Kinds of Epidemiologic Studies Exist?

A. Experimental and Observational Studies of Suspected Toxic Agents

To determine whether an agent is related to the risk of developing a certain disease or an adverse health outcome, we might ideally want to conduct an experimental study in which the subjects would be randomly assigned to one of two groups: one group exposed to the agent of interest and the other not exposed. After a period of time, the study participants in both groups would be evaluated for development of the disease. This type of study, called a randomized trial, clinical trial, or true experiment, is considered the gold standard for determining the relationship of an agent to a disease or health outcome. Such a study design is often used to evaluate new drugs or medical treatments and is the best way to ensure that any observed difference between the two groups in outcome is likely to be the result of exposure to the drug or medical treatment.

Randomization minimizes the likelihood that there are differences in relevant characteristics between those exposed to the agent and those not exposed. Researchers conducting clinical trials attempt to use study designs that are placebo controlled, which means that the group not receiving the agent or treatment is given a placebo, and that use double blinding, which means that neither the participants nor those conducting the study know which group is receiving the agent or treatment and which group is given the placebo. However, ethical and practical constraints limit the use of such experimental methodologies to assessing the value of agents that are thought to be beneficial to human beings.

13. For a more in-depth discussion of the statistical basis of epidemiology, see David H. Kaye & David A. Freedman, Reference Guide on Statistics § II.A, in this manual, and two case studies: Joseph Sanders, *The Bendectin Litigation: A Case Study in the Life Cycle of Mass Torts*, 43 Hastings L.J. 301 (1992); Devra L. Davis et al., *Assessing the Power and Quality of Epidemiologic Studies of Asbestos-Exposed Populations*, 1 Toxicological & Indus. Health 93 (1985). *See also* References on Epidemiology and References on Law and Epidemiology at the end of this reference guide.

When an agent's effects are suspected to be harmful, we cannot knowingly expose people to the agent.[14] Instead of the investigator controlling who is exposed to the agent and who is not, most epidemiologic studies are observational—that is, they "observe" a group of individuals who have been exposed to an agent of interest, such as cigarette smoking or an industrial chemical, and compare them with another group of individuals who have not been so exposed. Thus, the investigator identifies a group of subjects who have been knowingly or unknowingly exposed and compares their rate of disease or death with that of an unexposed group. In contrast to clinical studies, in which potential risk factors can be controlled, epidemiologic investigations generally focus on individuals living in the community, for whom characteristics other than the one of interest, such as diet, exercise, exposure to other environmental agents, and genetic background, may contribute to the risk of developing the disease in question. Since these characteristics cannot be controlled directly by the investigator, the investigator addresses their possible role in the relationship being studied by considering them in the design of the study and in the analysis and interpretation of the study results (see *infra* section IV).

B. The Types of Observational Study Design

Several different types of observational epidemiologic studies can be conducted.[15] Study designs may be chosen because of suitability for investigating the question of interest, timing constraints, resource limitations, or other considerations. An important question that might be asked initially about a given epidemiologic study is whether the study design used was appropriate to the research question.

Most observational studies collect data about both exposure and health outcome in every individual in the study. The two main types of observational studies are cohort studies and case-control studies. A third type of observational study is a cross-sectional study, although cross-sectional studies are rarely useful in identifying toxic agents.[16] A final type of observational study, one in which data about individuals is not gathered, but rather population data about expo-

14. Experimental studies in which human beings are exposed to agents known or thought to be toxic are ethically proscribed. *See* Ethyl Corp. v. United States Envtl. Protection Agency, 541 F.2d 1, 26 (D.C. Cir.), *cert. denied*, 426 U.S. 941 (1976). Experimental studies can be used where the agent under investigation is believed to be beneficial, as is the case in the development and testing of new pharmaceutical drugs. *See, e.g.*, E.R. Squibb & Sons, Inc. v. Stuart Pharms., No. 90-1178, 1990 U.S. Dist. LEXIS 15788 (D.N.J. Oct. 16, 1990); Gordon H. Guyatt, *Using Randomized Trials in Pharmacoepidemiology*, *in* Drug Epidemiology and Post-Marketing Surveillance 59 (Brian L. Strom & Giampaolo Velo eds., 1992). Experimental studies may also be conducted that entail discontinuation of exposure to a harmful agent, such as studies in which smokers are randomly assigned to a variety of smoking-cessation programs or no cessation.

15. Other epidemiologic studies collect data about the group as a whole, rather than about each individual in the group. These group studies are discussed *infra* § II.B.4.

16. *See infra* § II.B.3.

sure and disease are used, is an ecological study.

The difference between cohort studies and case-control studies is that cohort studies measure and compare the incidence of disease in the exposed and unexposed ("control") groups, while case-control studies measure and compare the frequency of exposure in the group with the disease (the "cases") and the group without the disease (the "controls"). Thus, a cohort study takes the exposed status of participants (the independent variable) and examines its effect on incidence of disease (the dependent variable). A case-control study takes the disease status as the independent variable and examines its relationship with exposure, which is the dependent variable. In a case-control study, the rates of exposure in the cases and the rates in the controls are compared, and the odds of having the disease when exposed to a suspected agent can be compared with the odds when not exposed. The critical difference between cohort studies and case-control studies is that cohort studies begin with exposed people and unexposed people, while case-control studies begin with individuals who are selected based on whether they have the disease or do not have the disease and their exposure to the agent in question is measured. The goal of both types of studies is to determine if there is an association between exposure to an agent and a disease, and the strength (magnitude) of that association.

1. Cohort studies

In cohort studies[17] the researcher identifies two groups of individuals: (1) individuals who have been exposed to a substance that is considered a possible cause of a disease and (2) individuals who have not been exposed (see Figure 1).[18] Both groups are followed for a specified length of time, and the proportions of individuals in each group who develop the disease are compared.[19] Thus, as illustrated in Table 1, a researcher would compare the proportion of unexposed individuals (controls) with the disease ($b/(a + b)$) with the proportion of exposed individuals (cohort) with the disease ($d/(c + d)$). If the exposure causes

17. Cohort studies also are referred to as prospective studies and follow-up studies.

18. In some studies, there may be several groups, each with a different magnitude of exposure to the agent being studied. Thus, a study of cigarette smokers might include heavy smokers (> 3 packs a day), moderate smokers (1–2 packs a day), and light smokers (< 1 pack a day). *See, e.g.*, Robert A. Rinsky et al., *Benzene and Leukemia: An Epidemiologic Risk Assessment,* 316 New Eng. J. Med. 1044 (1987).

19. Sometimes retrospective cohort studies are conducted, in which the researcher gathers historical data about exposure and disease outcome of the exposed cohort. Harold A. Kahn, An Introduction to Epidemiologic Methods 39–41 (1983). Irving Selikoff, in his seminal study of asbestotic disease in insulation workers, included several hundred workers who had died before he began the study. Selikoff was able to obtain information about exposure from union records and information about disease from hospital and autopsy records. Irving J. Selikoff et al., *The Occurrence of Asbestosis Among Insulation Workers in the United States,* 132 Annals N.Y. Acad. Sci. 139, 143 (1965).

the disease, the researcher would expect a greater proportion of the exposed individuals than of the unexposed individuals to develop the disease.[20]

Figure 1. Design of a Cohort Study

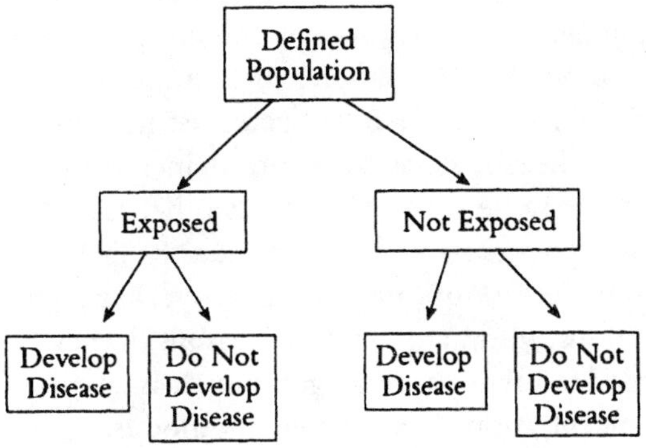

Table 1. Cross-Tabulation of Exposure by Disease Status

	No Disease	Disease
Not Exposed	a	b
Exposed	c	d

One advantage of the cohort study design is that the temporal relationship between exposure and disease can often be established more readily. By tracking the exposed and unexposed groups over time, the researcher can determine the time of disease onset. This temporal relationship is critical to the question of causation, since exposure must precede disease onset if exposure caused the disease.

As an example, in 1950 a cohort study was begun to determine whether uranium miners exposed to radon were at increased risk for lung cancer as compared with nonminers. The study group (also referred to as the exposed cohort) consisted of 3,400 white, underground miners. The control group (which need not be the same size as the exposed cohort) comprised white nonminers from the same geographic area. Members of the exposed cohort were examined ev-

20. Researchers often examine the rate of disease or death in the exposed and control groups. The rate of disease or death entails consideration of the number within a time period. All smokers and nonsmokers will, if followed for 100 years, die. Smokers will die at a greater rate than nonsmokers.

ery three years, and the degree of this cohort's exposure to radon was measured from samples taken in the mines. Ongoing testing for radioactivity and periodic medical monitoring of lungs permitted the researchers to examine whether disease was linked to prior work exposure to radiation and allowed them to discern the relationship between exposure to radiation and disease. Exposure to radiation was associated with the development of lung cancer in uranium miners.[21]

The cohort design is often used in occupational studies such as the one just cited. Since the design is not experimental, and the investigator has no control over what other exposures a subject in the study may have had, an increased risk of disease among the exposed group may be caused by agents other than the exposure of interest. A cohort study of workers in a certain industry that pays below-average wages might find a higher risk of cancer in those workers. This may be because they work in that industry, or, among other reasons, it may be because low-wage groups are exposed to other harmful agents, such as environmental toxins present in higher concentrations in their neighborhoods. In the study design, the researcher must attempt to identify factors other than the exposure that may be responsible for the increased risk of disease. If data are gathered on other possible etiologic factors, the researcher generally uses statistical methods[22] to assess whether a true association exists between working in the industry and cancer. Evaluating whether the association is causal involves additional analysis, as discussed in section V.

2. Case-control studies

In case-control studies,[23] the researcher begins with a group of individuals who have a disease (cases) and then selects a group of individuals who do not have the disease (controls). The researcher then compares the groups in terms of past exposures. If a certain exposure is associated with or caused the disease, a higher proportion of past exposure among the cases than among the controls would be expected (see Figure 2).

Thus, for example, in the late 1960s, doctors in Boston were confronted with an unusual incidence of vaginal adenocarcinoma in young female patients. Those patients became the "cases" in a case-control study (because they had the disease in question) and were matched with "controls," who did not have the disease. Controls were selected based on their being born in the same hospitals and at the same time as the cases. The cases and controls were compared for exposure

21. This example is based on a study description in Abraham M. Lilienfeld & David E. Lilienfeld, Foundations of Epidemiology 237–39 (2d ed. 1980). The original study is Joseph K. Wagoner et al., *Radiation as the Cause of Lung Cancer Among Uranium Miners*, 273 New Eng. J. Med. 181 (1965).

22. *See* Daniel L. Rubinfeld, Reference Guide on Multiple Regression § II.B, in this manual.

23. Case-control studies are also referred to as retrospective studies, because researchers gather historical information about rates of exposure to an agent in the case and control groups.

to agents that might be responsible, and researchers found maternal ingestion of DES (diethylstilbestrol) in all but one of the cases but none of the controls.[24]

Figure 2. Design of a Case-Control Study

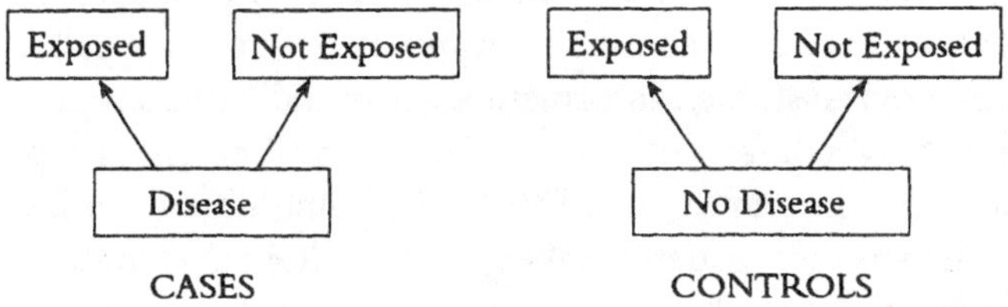

An advantage of the case-control study is that it usually can be completed in less time and with less expense than a cohort study. Case-control studies are also particularly useful in the study of rare diseases, because if a cohort study were conducted, an extremely large group would have to be studied in order to observe the development of a sufficient number of cases for analysis.[25] A number of potential problems with case-control studies are discussed in section IV.B.

3. Cross-sectional studies

A third type of observational study is a cross-sectional study. In this type of study, individuals are interviewed or examined, and the presence of both the exposure of interest and the disease of interest is determined in each individual at a single point in time. Cross-sectional studies determine the presence (prevalence) of both exposure and disease in the subjects and do not determine the development of disease or risk of disease (incidence). Moreover, since both exposure and disease are determined in an individual at the same point in time, it is not possible to establish the temporal relation between exposure and disease—that is, that the exposure preceded the disease, which would be necessary for drawing any causal inference. Thus, a researcher may use a cross-sectional study to determine the connection between a personal characteristic that does not change over time, such as blood type, and existence of a disease, such as aplastic anemia, by examining individuals and determining their blood types and whether they suffer from aplastic anemia. Cross-sectional studies are infrequently used when the exposure of interest is an environmental toxic agent (current smoking status is a poor measure of an individual's history of smoking),

24. *See* Arthur L. Herbst et al., *Adenocarcinoma of the Vagina: Association of Maternal Stilbestrol Therapy with Tumor Appearance*, 284 New Eng. J. Med. 878 (1971).

25. Thus, for example, to detect a doubling of disease caused by exposure to an agent where the incidence of disease is 1 in 100 in the unexposed population would require sample sizes of 3,100 each for a cohort study, but only 177 each for a case-control study. Harold A. Kahn & Christopher T. Sempos, Statistical Methods in Epidemiology 66 (1989).

but these studies can provide valuable leads to further directions for research.[26]

4. *Ecological studies*

Up to now, we have discussed studies in which data on both exposure and health outcome are obtained for each individual included in the study.[27] In contrast, studies that collect data only about the group as a whole are called ecological studies.[28] In ecological studies, information about individuals is generally not gathered; instead, overall rates of disease or death for different groups are obtained and compared. The objective is to identify some difference between the two groups, such as diet, genetic makeup, or alcohol consumption, that might explain differences in the risk of disease observed in the two groups.[29] Such studies may be useful for identifying associations, but they rarely provide definitive causal answers. The difficulty is illustrated below with an ecological study of the relationship between dietary fat and cancer.

If a researcher were interested in determining whether a high dietary fat intake is associated with breast cancer, he or she could compare different countries in terms of their average fat intakes and their average rates of breast cancer. If a country with a high average fat intake also tends to have a high rate of breast cancer, the finding would suggest an association between dietary fat and breast cancer. However, such a finding would be far from conclusive, because it lacks particularized information about an individual's exposure and disease status (i.e., whether an individual with high fat intake is more likely to have breast cancer).[30] In addition to the lack of information about an individual's intake of fat, the researcher does not know about the individual's exposures to other agents (or other factors, such as a mother's age at first birth) that may also be responsible for the increased risk of breast cancer. This lack of information about each individual's exposure to an agent and disease status detracts from the usefulness of the study and can lead to an erroneous inference about the relationship between fat intake and breast cancer, a problem known as an ecological fallacy. The fallacy is assuming that, on average, the individuals in the study who have

26. For more information (and references) about cross-sectional studies, see Leon Gordis, Epidemiology 137–39 (1996).

27. Some individual studies may be conducted in which all members of a group or community are treated as exposed to an agent of interest (e.g., a contaminated water system) and disease status is determined individually. These studies should be distinguished from ecological studies.

28. In *Renaud v. Martin Marietta Corp.*, 749 F. Supp. 1545, 1551 (D. Colo. 1990), *aff'd*, 972 F.2d 304 (10th Cir. 1992), the plaintiffs attempted to rely on an excess incidence of cancers in their neighborhood to prove causation. Unfortunately, the court confused the role of epidemiology in proving causation with the issue of the plaintiffs' exposure to the alleged carcinogen and never addressed the evidentiary value of the plaintiffs' evidence of a disease cluster (i.e., an unusually high incidence of a particular disease in a neighborhood or community). *Id.* at 1554.

29. David E. Lilienfeld & Paul D. Stolley, Foundations of Epidemiology 12 (3d ed. 1994).

30. For a discussion of the data on this question and what they might mean, see David Freedman et al., Statistics (3d ed. 1998).

suffered from breast cancer consumed more dietary fat than those who have not suffered from the disease. This assumption may not be true. Nevertheless, the study is useful in that it identifies an area for further research: the fat intake of individuals who have breast cancer as compared with the fat intake of those who do not. Researchers who identify a difference in disease or death in a demographic study may follow up with a study based on gathering data about individuals.

Another epidemiologic approach is to compare disease rates over time and focus on disease rates before and after a point in time when some event of interest took place.[31] For example, thalidomide's teratogenicity (capacity to cause birth defects) was discovered after Dr. Widukind Lenz found a dramatic increase in the incidence of limb reduction birth defects in Germany beginning in 1960. Yet other than with such powerful agents as thalidomide, which increased the incidence of limb reduction defects by several orders of magnitude, these secular-trend studies (also known as time-line studies) are less reliable and less able to detect modest causal effects than the observational studies described above. Other factors that affect the measurement or existence of the disease, such as improved diagnostic techniques and changes in lifestyle or age demographics, may change over time. If those factors can be identified and measured, it may be possible to control for them with statistical methods. Of course, unknown factors cannot be controlled for in these or any other kind of epidemiologic studies.

C. Epidemiologic and Toxicologic Studies

In addition to observational epidemiology, toxicology models based on animal studies (in vivo) may be used to determine toxicity in humans.[32] Animal studies have a number of advantages. They can be conducted as true experiments, and researchers control all aspects of the animals' lives. Thus, they can avoid the problem of confounding,[33] which epidemiology often confronts. Exposure can be carefully controlled and measured. Refusals to participate in a study are not an issue, and loss to follow-up very often is minimal. Ethical limitations are diminished, and animals can be sacrificed and their tissues examined, which may improve the accuracy of disease assessment. Animal studies often provide useful

31. In *Wilson v. Merrell Dow Pharmaceuticals, Inc.*, 893 F.2d 1149, 1152–53 (10th Cir. 1990), the defendant introduced evidence showing total sales of Bendectin and the incidence of birth defects during the 1970–1984 period. In 1983, Bendectin was removed from the market, but the rate of birth defects did not change. The Tenth Circuit affirmed the lower court's ruling that the time-line data were admissible and that the defendant's expert witnesses could rely on them in rendering their opinions.

32. For an in-depth discussion of toxicology, see Bernard D. Goldstein & Mary Sue Henifin, Reference Guide on Toxicology, in this manual.

33. *See infra* § IV.C.

information about pathological mechanisms and play a complementary role to epidemiology by assisting researchers in framing hypotheses and in developing study designs for epidemiologic studies.

Animal studies have two significant disadvantages, however. First, animal study results must be extrapolated to another species—human beings—and differences in absorption, metabolism, and other factors may result in interspecies variation in responses. For example, one powerful human teratogen, thalidomide, does not cause birth defects in most rodent species.[34] Similarly, some known teratogens in animals are not believed to be human teratogens. In general, it is often difficult to confirm that an agent known to be toxic in animals is safe for human beings.[35] The second difficulty with inferring human causation from animal studies is that the high doses customarily used in animal studies require consideration of the dose–response relationship and whether a threshold no-effect dose exists.[36] Those matters are almost always fraught with considerable, and currently unresolvable, uncertainty.[37]

Toxicologists also use in vitro methods, in which human or animal tissue or cells are grown in laboratories and exposed to certain substances. The problem with this approach is also extrapolation—whether one can generalize the findings from the artificial setting of tissues in laboratories to whole human beings.[38]

Often toxicologic studies are the only or best available evidence of toxicity. Epidemiologic studies are difficult, time-consuming, and expensive, and consequently they do not exist for a large array of environmental agents. Where both animal toxicology and epidemiologic studies are available, no universal rules exist for how to interpret or reconcile them.[39] Careful assessment of the meth-

34. Phillip Knightley et al., Suffer the Children: The Story of Thalidomide 271–72 (1979).

35. *See* Ian C.T. Nesbit & Nathan J. Karch, Chemical Hazards to Human Reproduction 98–106 (1983); International Agency for Research on Cancer (IARC), Interpretation of Negative Epidemiological Evidence for Carcinogenicity (N.J. Wald & R. Doll eds., 1985).

36. *See infra* § V.C & note 119.

37. *See* General Elec. Co. v. Joiner, 522 U.S. 136, 143–45 (1997) (holding that the district court did not abuse its discretion in excluding expert testimony on causation based on expert's failure to explain how animal studies supported expert's opinion that agent caused disease in humans).

38. For a further discussion of these issues, see Bernard D. Goldstein & Mary Sue Henifin, Reference Guide on Toxicology § III.A, in this manual.

39. *See* IARC, *supra* note 35 (identifying a number of substances and comparing animal toxicology evidence with epidemiologic evidence).

A number of courts have grappled with the role of animal studies in proving causation in a toxic substance case. One line of cases takes a very dim view of their probative value. For example, in *Brock v. Merrell Dow Pharmaceuticals, Inc.*, 874 F.2d 307, 313 (5th Cir. 1989), *cert. denied*, 494 U.S. 1046 (1990), the court noted the "very limited usefulness of animal studies when confronted with questions of toxicity." A similar view is reflected in *Richardson v. Richardson-Merrell, Inc.*, 857 F.2d 823, 830 (D.C. Cir. 1988), *cert. denied*, 493 U.S. 882 (1989); *Bell v. Swift Adhesives, Inc.*, 804 F. Supp. 1577, 1579–80 (S.D. Ga. 1992); and *Cadarian v. Merrell Dow Pharmaceuticals, Inc.*, 745 F. Supp. 409, 412 (E.D. Mich. 1989). Other courts have been more amenable to the use of animal toxicology in proving causation.

odological validity and power[40] of the epidemiologic evidence must be undertaken, and the quality of the toxicologic studies and the questions of interspecies extrapolation and dose–response relationship must be considered.[41]

Thus, in *Marder v. G.D. Searle & Co.*, 630 F. Supp. 1087, 1094 (D. Md. 1986), *aff'd sub nom.* Wheelahan v. G.D. Searle & Co., 814 F.2d 655 (4th Cir. 1987), the court observed: "There is a range of scientific methods for investigating questions of causation—for example, toxicology and animal studies, clinical research, and epidemiology—which all have distinct advantages and disadvantages." *See also* Villari v. Terminix Int'l, Inc., 692 F. Supp. 568, 571 (E.D. Pa. 1988); Peterson v. Sealed Air Corp., Nos. 86-C3498, 88-C9859 Consol., 1991 U.S. Dist. LEXIS 5333, at *27–*29 (N.D. Ill. Apr. 23, 1991); *cf. In re* Paoli R.R. Yard PCB Litig., 916 F.2d 829, 853–54 (3d Cir. 1990) (questioning the exclusion of animal studies by the lower court), *cert. denied*, 499 U.S. 961 (1991). The Third Circuit in a subsequent opinion in *Paoli* observed:

> [I]n order for animal studies to be admissible to prove causation in humans, there must be good grounds to extrapolate from animals to humans, just as the methodology of the studies must constitute good grounds to reach conclusions about the animals themselves. Thus, the requirement of reliability, or "good grounds," extends to each step in an expert's analysis all the way through the step that connects the work of the expert to the particular case.

In re Paoli R.R. Yard PCB Litig., 35 F.3d 717, 743 (3d Cir. 1994), *cert. denied*, 513 U.S. 1190 (1995); *see also* Cavallo v. Star Enter., 892 F. Supp. 756, 761–63 (E.D. Va. 1995) (courts must examine each of the steps that lead to an expert's opinion), *aff'd in part and rev'd in part*, 100 F.3d 1150 (4th Cir. 1996), *cert. denied*, 522 U.S. 1044 (1998).

One explanation for these conflicting lines of cases may be that when there is a substantial body of epidemiologic evidence that addresses the causal issue, animal toxicology has much less probative value. That was the case, for example, in the Bendectin cases of *Richardson*, *Brock*, and *Cadarian*. Where epidemiologic evidence is not available, animal toxicology may be thought to play a more prominent role in resolving a causal dispute. *See* Michael D. Green, *Expert Witnesses and Sufficiency of Evidence in Toxic Substances Litigation: The Legacy of Agent Orange and Bendectin Litigation*, 86 Nw. U. L. Rev. 643, 680–82 (1992) (arguing that plaintiffs should be required to prove causation by a preponderance of the available evidence); Turpin v. Merrell Dow Pharms., Inc., 959 F.2d 1349, 1359 (6th Cir.), *cert. denied*, 506 U.S. 826 (1992); *In re* Paoli R.R. Yard PCB Litig., No. 86-2229, 1992 U.S. Dist. LEXIS 16287, at *16 (E.D. Pa. Oct. 21, 1992). For another explanation of these cases, see Gerald W. Boston, *A Mass-Exposure Model of Toxic Causation: The Control of Scientific Proof and the Regulatory Experience*, 18 Colum. J. Envtl. L. 181 (1993) (arguing that epidemiologic evidence should be required in mass-exposure cases but not in isolated-exposure cases). *See also* IARC, *supra* note 35; Bernard D. Goldstein & Mary Sue Henifin, Reference Guide on Toxicology § I.F, in this manual. The Supreme Court, in *General Electric Co. v. Joiner*, 522 U.S. 136, 144–45 (1997), suggested that there is not a categorical rule for toxicologic studies, observing, "[W]hether animal studies can ever be a proper foundation for an expert's opinion [is] not the issue. . . . The [animal] studies were so dissimilar to the facts presented in this litigation that it was not an abuse of discretion for the District Court to have rejected the experts' reliance on them."

40. *See infra* § IV.A.3.

41. *See* Ellen F. Heineman & Shelia Hoar Zahm, *The Role of Epidemiology in Hazard Evaluation*, 9 Toxic Substances J. 255, 258–62 (1989).

III. How Should Results of an Epidemiologic Study Be Interpreted?

Epidemiologists are ultimately interested in whether a causal relationship exists between an agent and a disease. However, the first question an epidemiologist addresses is whether an association exists between exposure to the agent and disease. An association between exposure to an agent and disease exists when they occur together more frequently than one would expect by chance.[42] Although a causal relationship is one possible explanation for an observed association between an exposure and a disease, an association does not necessarily mean that there is a cause–effect relationship. Interpreting the meaning of an observed association is discussed below.

This section begins by describing the ways of expressing the existence and strength of an association between exposure and disease. It reviews ways in which an incorrect result can be produced because of the sampling methods used in all observational epidemiologic studies and then examines statistical methods for evaluating whether an association is real or due to sampling error.

The strength of an association between exposure and disease can be stated as a relative risk, an odds ratio, or an attributable risk (often abbreviated as "RR," "OR," and "AR," respectively). Each of these measurements of association examines the degree to which the risk of disease increases when individuals are exposed to an agent.

A. Relative Risk

A commonly used approach for expressing the association between an agent and disease is relative risk (RR). It is defined as the ratio of the incidence rate (often referred to as incidence) of disease in exposed individuals to the incidence rate in unexposed individuals:

$$\text{Relative Risk (RR)} = \frac{\text{Incidence rate in the exposed}}{\text{Incidence rate in the unexposed}}$$

The incidence rate of disease reflects the number of cases of disease that develop during a specified period of time divided by the number of persons in the cohort under study.[43] Thus, the incidence rate expresses the risk that a

42. A negative association implies that the agent has a protective or curative effect. Because the concern in toxic substances litigation is whether an agent caused disease, this reference guide focuses on positive associations.

43. Epidemiologists also use the concept of prevalence, which measures the existence of disease in a population at a given point in time, regardless of when the disease developed. Prevalence is expressed as the proportion of the population with the disease at the chosen time. *See* Gordis, *supra* note 26, at 32–34.

member of the population will develop the disease within a specified period of time.

For example, a researcher studies 100 individuals who are exposed to an agent and 200 who are not exposed. After one year, 40 of the exposed individuals are diagnosed as having a disease, and 20 of the unexposed individuals also are diagnosed as having the disease. The relative risk of contracting the disease is calculated as follows:

- The incidence rate of disease in the exposed individuals is 40 cases per year per 100 persons (40/100), or 0.4.
- The incidence rate of disease in the unexposed individuals is 20 cases per year per 200 persons (20/200), or 0.1.
- The relative risk is calculated as the incidence rate in the exposed group (0.4) divided by the incidence rate in the unexposed group (0.1), or 4.0.

A relative risk of 4.0 indicates that the risk of disease in the exposed group is four times as high as the risk of disease in the unexposed group.[44]

In general, the relative risk can be interpreted as follows:

- If the relative risk equals 1.0, the risk in exposed individuals is the same as the risk in unexposed individuals. There is no association between exposure to the agent and disease.
- If the relative risk is greater than 1.0, the risk in exposed individuals is greater than the risk in unexposed individuals. There is a positive association between exposure to the agent and the disease, which could be causal.
- If the relative risk is less than 1.0, the risk in exposed individuals is less than the risk in unexposed individuals. There is a negative association, which could reflect a protective or curative effect of the agent on risk of disease. For example, immunizations lower the risk of disease. The results suggest that immunization is associated with a decrease in disease and may have a protective effect on the risk of disease.

Although relative risk is a straightforward concept, care must be taken in interpreting it. Researchers should scrutinize their results for error. Error in the design of a study could yield an incorrect relative risk. Sources of bias and confounding should be examined.[45] Whenever an association is uncovered, further analysis should be conducted to determine if the association is real or due to an error or bias. Similarly, a study that does not find an association between an agent and disease may be erroneous because of bias or random error.

44. *See* DeLuca v. Merrell Dow Pharms., Inc., 911 F.2d 941, 947 (3d Cir. 1990); Gaul v. United States, 582 F. Supp. 1122, 1125 n.9 (D. Del. 1984).

45. *See infra* § IV.B–C.

B. Odds Ratio

The odds ratio (OR) is similar to a relative risk in that it expresses in quantitative terms the association between exposure to an agent and a disease.[46] In a case-control study, the odds ratio is the ratio of the odds that a case (one with the disease) was exposed to the odds that a control (one without the disease) was exposed. In a cohort study, the odds ratio is the ratio of the odds of developing a disease when exposed to a suspected agent to the odds of developing the disease when not exposed. The odds ratio approximates the relative risk when the disease is rare.[47]

Consider a case-control study, with results as shown schematically in a 2 x 2 table (Table 2):

Table 2. Cross-Tabulation of Cases and Controls by Exposure Status

	Cases	Controls
Exposed	a	b
Not Exposed	c	d

In a case-control study

$$\text{Odds Ratio (OR)} = \frac{\text{the odds that a case was exposed}}{\text{the odds that a control was exposed}}$$

Looking at the above 2 x 2 table, this ratio can be calculated as

$$\frac{a/c}{b/d}$$

This works out to ad/bc. Since we are multiplying two diagonal cells in the table and dividing by the product of the other two diagonal cells, the odds ratio is also called the cross-products ratio.

Consider the following hypothetical study: A researcher identifies 100 individuals with a disease who serve as "cases" and 100 people without the disease who serve as "controls" for her case-control study. Forty of the 100 cases were exposed to the agent and 60 were not. Among the control group, 20 people were exposed and 80 were not. The data can be presented in a 2 x 2 table (Table 3):

46. A relative risk cannot be calculated for a case-control study, because a case-control study begins by examining a group of persons who already have the disease. That aspect of the study design prevents a researcher from determining the rate at which individuals develop the disease. Without a rate or incidence of disease, a researcher cannot calculate a relative risk.

47. *See* Marcello Pagano & Kimberlee Gauvreau, Principles of Biostatistics 320–22 (1993). For further detail about the odds ratio and its calculation, see Kahn & Sempos, *supra* note 25, at 47–56.

Table 3. Case-Control Study Outcome

	Cases (with disease)	Controls (no disease)
Exposed	40	20
Not Exposed	60	80
Total	100	100

The calculation of the odds ratio would be

$$OR = \frac{40/60}{20/80} = 2.67$$

If the disease is relatively rare in the general population (about 5% or less), the odds ratio is a good approximation of the relative risk, which means that there is almost a tripling of the disease in those exposed to the agent.[48]

C. Attributable Risk

A frequently used measurement of risk is the attributable risk (AR). The attributable risk represents the amount of disease among exposed individuals that can be attributed to the exposure. It can also be expressed as the proportion of the disease among exposed individuals that is associated with the exposure (also called the "attributable proportion of risk," the "etiologic fraction" or "attributable risk percent"). The attributable risk reflects the maximum proportion of the disease that can be attributed to exposure to an agent and consequently the maximum proportion of disease that could be potentially prevented by blocking the effect of the exposure or by eliminating the exposure.[49] In other words, if the association is causal, the attributable risk is the proportion of disease in an exposed population that might be caused by the agent and that might be prevented by eliminating exposure to that agent (see Figure 3).[50]

48. The odds ratio is usually marginally greater than the relative risk. As the disease in question becomes more common, the difference between the odds ratio and the relative risk grows.

49. Kenneth J. Rothman & Sander Greenland, Modern Epidemiology 53–55 (2d ed. 1998). *See also* Landrigan v. Celotex Corp., 605 A.2d 1079, 1086 (N.J. 1992) (illustrating that a relative risk of 1.55 conforms to an attributable risk of 35%, i.e., (1.55 - 1.0)/1.55 = .35 or 35%).

50. Risk is not zero for the control group (those not exposed) when there are other causal chains that cause the disease which do not require exposure to the agent. For example, some birth defects are the result of genetic sources, which do not require the presence of any environmental agent. Also, some degree of risk in the control group may be the result of background exposure to the agent being studied. For example, nonsmokers in a control group may have been exposed to passive cigarette smoke, which is responsible for some cases of lung cancer and other diseases. *See also* Ethyl Corp. v. United States Envtl. Protection Agency, 541 F.2d 1, 25 (D.C. Cir.), *cert. denied*, 426 U.S. 941 (1976). There are some diseases that do not occur without exposure to an agent; these are known as signature diseases. *See infra* note 128.

Figure 3. Risks in Exposed and Unexposed Groups

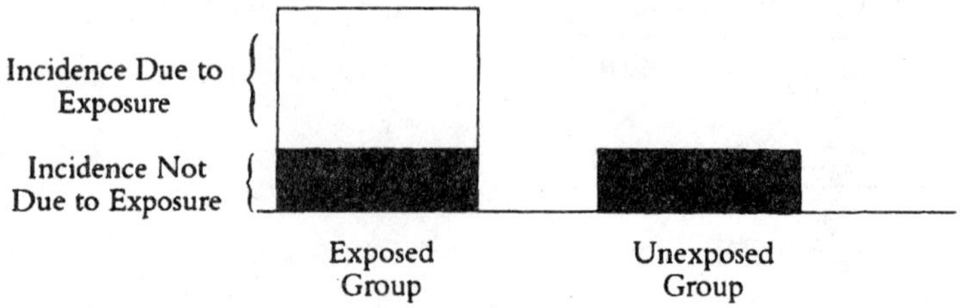

To determine the proportion of a disease that is attributable to an exposure, a researcher would need to know the incidence of the disease in the exposed group and the incidence of disease in the unexposed group. The attributable risk is

$$AR = \frac{\text{(incidence in the exposed) - (incidence in the unexposed)}}{\text{incidence in the exposed}}$$

The attributable risk can be calculated using the example described in section III.A. Suppose a researcher studies 100 individuals who are exposed to a substance and 200 who are not exposed. After one year, 40 of the exposed individuals are diagnosed as having a disease, and 20 of the unexposed individuals are also diagnosed as having the disease.

- The incidence of disease in the exposed group is 40 persons out of 100 who contract the disease in a year.
- The incidence of disease in the unexposed group is 20 persons out of 200 (or 10 out of 100) who contract the disease in a year.
- The proportion of disease that is attributable to the exposure is 30 persons out of 40, or 75%.

This means that 75% of the disease in the exposed group is attributable to the exposure. We should emphasize here that "attributable" does not necessarily mean "caused by." Up to this point we have only addressed associations. Inferring causation from an association is addressed in section V.

D. Adjustment for Study Groups That Are Not Comparable

Populations often differ in characteristics that relate to disease risk, such as age, sex, and race. Florida has a much higher death rate than Alaska.[51] Is sunshine dangerous? Perhaps, but the Florida population is much older than the Alaska population, and some adjustment must be made for the different age demo-

51. *See* Lilienfeld & Stolley, *supra* note 29, at 68–70 (mortality rate in Florida approximately three times what it is in Alaska).

graphics. The technique used to accomplish this is called adjustment, and two types of adjustment are used—direct and indirect.

In direct age adjustment, a standard population is used in order to eliminate the effects of any age differences between two study populations. Thus, in comparing two populations, A and B, the age-specific mortality rates for Population A are applied to each age group of the standard reference population, and the numbers of deaths expected in each age group of the standard population are calculated. These expected numbers of deaths are then totaled to yield the number of deaths expected in the standard population if it experienced the mortality risk of Population A. The same procedure is then carried out for Population B. Using these expected numbers of deaths, mortality rates are calculated for the standard population on the basis of the number of deaths expected if it had the mortality experience of Population A and the number of deaths expected if it had the mortality experience of Population B. We can then compare these rates, called age-adjusted rates, knowing that any difference between these rates cannot be attributed to differences in age, since both age-adjusted rates were generated using the same standard population.

A second approach, indirect age adjustment, is often used, for example, in studying mortality in an occupationally exposed population, such as miners or construction workers. To answer the question whether a population of miners has a higher mortality rate than we would expect in a similar population not engaged in mining, we must apply the age-specific rates for a known population, such as all men of the same age, to each age group in the population of interest. This will yield the number of deaths expected in each age group in the population of interest if this population had had the mortality experience of the known population. The number of deaths expected is thus calculated for each age group and totaled; the numbers of deaths that were actually observed in that population are counted. The ratio of the total number of deaths actually observed to the total number of deaths that would be expected if the population of interest actually had the mortality experience of the known population is then calculated. This ratio is called the standardized mortality ratio (SMR). When the outcome of interest is disease rather than death, it is called the standardized morbidity ratio.[52] If the ratio equals 1.0, the observed number of deaths equals the expected number of deaths, and the mortality experience of the population of interest is no different from that of the known population. If the SMR is greater than 1.0, the population of interest has a higher mortality risk than that of the known population, and if the SMR is less than 1.0, the population of interest has a lower mortality risk than that of the known population.

52. *See In re* Joint E. & S. Dist. Asbestos Litig., 52 F.3d 1124, 1128 (2d Cir. 1995) (using SMR to describe relative risk of an agent in causing disease). For an example of adjustment used to calculate an SMR for workers exposed to benzene, see Robert A. Rinsky et al., *Benzene and Leukemia: An Epidemiologic Risk Assessment*, 316 New Eng. J. Med. 1044 (1987).

Thus, age adjustment provides a way to compare populations while in effect holding age constant. Adjustment is used not only for comparing mortality rates in different populations but also for comparing rates in different groups of subjects selected for study in epidemiologic investigations. Although this discussion has focused on adjusting for age, it is also possible to adjust for any number of other variables, such as gender, race, occupation, and socioeconomic status. It is also possible to adjust for several factors simultaneously.[53]

IV. What Sources of Error Might Have Produced a False Result?

Incorrect study results occur in a variety of ways. A study may find a positive association (relative risk greater than 1.0) when there is no association. Or a study may erroneously conclude that there is no association when in reality there is. A study may also find an association when one truly exists, but the association found may be greater or less than the real association.

There are three explanations why an association found in a study may be erroneous: chance, bias, and confounding. Before any inferences about causation are drawn from a study, the possibility of these phenomena must be examined.[54]

The findings of a study may be the result of chance (or sampling error) because virtually all epidemiologic studies are based on sampling a small proportion of the relevant population. During the design of a study, the size of the sample can be increased to reduce (but not eliminate) the likelihood of sampling error. Once a study has been completed, statistical methods (discussed in the next subsection) permit an assessment of whether the results of a study are likely to represent a true association or random error.

The two main techniques for assessing random error are statistical significance and confidence intervals. A study that is statistically significant has results that are unlikely to be the result of random error, although the level of significance used entails a somewhat arbitrary determination.[55] A confidence interval

53. For further elaboration on adjustment, see Rothman & Greenland, *supra* note 49, at 234–35; Gordis, *supra* note 26, at 49–52; Philip Cole, *Causality in Epidemiology, Health Policy, and Law*, [1997] 27 Envtl. L. Rep. (Envtl. L. Inst.) 10279, 10281 (June 1997).

54. *See* Cole, *supra* note 53, at 10285. In *DeLuca v. Merrell Dow Pharmaceuticals, Inc.*, 911 F.2d 941, 955 (3d Cir. 1990), the court recognized and discussed random sampling error. It then went on to refer to other errors (i.e., systematic bias) that create as much or more error in the outcome of a study. For a similar description of error in study procedure and random sampling, see David H. Kaye & David A. Freedman, Reference Guide on Statistics § IV, in this manual.

55. Describing a study result as "statistically significant" does not mean that the result—the relative risk—is of a significant or substantial magnitude. *Statistical significance does not address the magnitude of the*

provides both the relative risk found in the study and a range (interval) within which the true relative risk resides with some (arbitrarily chosen) level of confidence. Both of these techniques are explained in subsection IV.A.

Bias (or systematic error) also can produce error in the outcome of a study. Epidemiologists attempt to minimize the existence of bias through their study design, which is developed before they begin gathering data. However, even the best designed and conducted studies can have biases, which may be subtle. Consequently, after a study is completed it should be evaluated for potential sources of bias. Sometimes, after bias is identified, the epidemiologist can determine whether the bias would tend to inflate or dilute any association that may exist. Identification of the bias may permit the epidemiologist to make an assessment of whether the study's conclusions are valid. Epidemiologists may reanalyze a study's data to correct for a bias identified in a completed study or to validate the analytic methods used.[56] Common biases and how they may produce invalid results are described in subsection IV.B.

Finally, a study may reach incorrect conclusions about causation because, although the agent and disease are associated, the agent is not a true causal factor. Rather, the agent may be associated with another agent that is the true causal factor, and this factor confounds the relationship being examined in the study. Confounding is explained in subsection IV.C.

A. What Statistical Methods Exist to Evaluate the Possibility of Sampling Error?[57]

Before detailing the statistical methods used to assess random error (which we use as synonymous with sampling error), we explain two concepts that are central to epidemiology and statistical analysis. Understanding these concepts should facilitate comprehension of the statistical methods.

Epidemiologists often refer to the true association (also called "real association"), which is the association that really exists between an agent and a disease and that might be found by a perfect (but nonexistent) study. The true association is a concept that is used in evaluating the results of a given study even though its value is unknown. By contrast, a study's outcome will produce an observed association, which is known.

relative risk found in a study, only the likelihood that it would have resulted from random error if there is no real association between the agent and disease.

56. *E.g.*, Richard A. Kronmal et al., *The Intrauterine Device and Pelvic Inflammatory Disease: The Women's Health Study Reanalyzed*, 44 J. Clinical Epidemiology 109 (1991) (reanalysis of a study that found an association between use of IUDs and pelvic inflammatory disease concluded that IUDs do not increase the risk of pelvic inflammatory disease).

57. For a bibliography on the role of statistical significance in legal proceedings, see Sanders, *supra* note 13, at 329 n.138.

Scientists, including epidemiologists, generally begin an empirical study with a hypothesis that they seek to disprove,[58] called the null hypothesis. The null hypothesis states that there is no true association between an agent and a disease. Thus, the epidemiologist begins by technically assuming that the relative risk is 1.0 and seeks to develop data that may disprove the hypothesis.[59]

1. False positive error and statistical significance

When a study results in a positive association (i.e., a relative risk greater than 1.0), epidemiologists try to determine whether that outcome represents a true association or is the result of random error.[60] Random error is illustrated by a fair coin yielding five heads out of five tosses,[61] an occurrence that would result, purely by chance, in about 3% of a series of five tosses. Thus, even though the true relative risk is 1.0, an epidemiologic study may find a relative risk greater than 1.0 because of random error. An erroneous conclusion that the null hypothesis is false (i.e., a conclusion that there is a difference in risk when no difference actually exists) owing to random error is called a false positive error or type I error or alpha error.

Common sense leads one to believe that a large enough sample of individuals must be studied if the study is to identify a relationship between exposure to an agent and disease that truly exists. Common sense also suggests that by enlarging the sample size (the size of the study group), researchers can form a more accurate conclusion and reduce the chance of random error in their results. Both statements are correct and can be illustrated by a test to determine if a coin is fair. A test in which a coin is tossed 1,000 times is more helpful than a test in which the coin is tossed only 10 times. Common sense dictates that it is far more likely that a test of a fair coin with 10 tosses will come up, for example, with

58. *See, e.g.*, Daubert v. Merrell Dow Pharms., Inc., 509 U.S. 579, 593 (1993) (scientific methodology involves generating and testing hypotheses). We should explain that this null-hypothesis testing model may be misleading. The reality is that the vast majority of epidemiologic studies are conducted because the researcher suspects that there is a causal effect and seeks to demonstrate that causal relationship. Nevertheless, epidemiologists prepare their study designs and test the plausibility that any association found in a study was the result of sampling error by using the null hypothesis.

59. *See* DeLuca v. Merrell Dow Pharms., Inc., 911 F.2d 941, 945 (3d Cir. 1990); Stephen E. Fienberg et al., *Understanding and Evaluating Statistical Evidence in Litigation*, 36 Jurimetrics J. 1, 21–24 (1995).

60. Hypothesis testing is one of the most counterintuitive techniques in statistics. Given a set of epidemiologic data, one wants to ask the straightforward, obvious question, What is the probability that the difference between two samples reflects a real difference between the populations from which they were taken? Unfortunately, there is no way to answer this question directly or to calculate the probability. Instead, statisticians—and epidemiologists—address a related but very different question: If there really is no difference between the populations, how probable is it that one would find a difference at least as large as the observed difference between the samples? *See* Expert Evidence: A Practitioner's Guide to Law, Science, and the FJC Manual 91 (Bert Black & Patrick W. Lee eds., 1997).

61. *DeLuca*, 911 F.2d at 946–47.

80% heads than will a test with 1,000 tosses. For if the test is conducted with larger numbers (1,000 tosses), the stability of the outcome of the test is less likely to be influenced by random error, and the researcher would have greater confidence in the inferences drawn from the data.[62]

One means for evaluating the possibility that an observed association could have occurred as a result of random error is by calculating a *p*-value.[63] A *p*-value represents the probability that a positive association would result from random error if no association were in fact present.[64] Thus, a *p*-value of .1 means that there is a 10% chance that if the true relative risk is 1.0, the observed relative risk (greater than 1.0) in the study was due to random error.[65]

To minimize false positive error, epidemiologists use a convention that the *p*-value must fall below some selected level known as alpha or significance level for the results of the study to be statistically significant.[66] Thus, an outcome is statistically significant when the observed *p*-value for the study falls below the preselected significance level. The most common significance level, or alpha,

62. This explanation of numerical stability was drawn from Brief Amicus Curiae of Professor Alvan R. Feinstein in Support of Respondent at 12–13, Daubert v. Merrell Dow Pharms., Inc., 509 U.S. 579 (1993) (No. 92-102). *See also* Allen v. United States, 588 F. Supp. 247, 417–18 (D. Utah 1984), *rev'd on other grounds*, 816 F.2d 1417 (10th Cir. 1987), *cert. denied*, 484 U.S. 1004 (1988). The *Allen* court observed that although "[s]mall communities or groups of people are deemed 'statistically unstable'" and "data from small populations must be handled with care [, it] does not mean that [the data] cannot provide substantial evidence in aid of our effort to describe and understand events."

63. *See also* David H. Kaye & David A. Freedman, Reference Guide on Statistics § IV.B, in this manual (*p*-value reflects the implausibility of the null hypothesis).

64. Technically, a *p*-value represents the probability that the study's association or a larger one would occur as a result of sampling error where no association (or, equivalently, the null hypothesis) is the true situation. This means that if one conducted an examination of 20 associations in which the true RR = 1, on average one of those examinations would result in a statistically significant, yet spurious, association.

Unfortunately, some have failed to appreciate the difference between a statement of the probability that the study's outcome would occur as a result of random error (the correct understanding of a *p*-value) if the true association were RR equal to 1 and a statement of the probability that the study's outcome was due to random error (an incorrect understanding of a *p*-value). *See, e.g., In re* TMI Cases Consol. II, 922 F. Supp. 997, 1017 (M.D. Pa. 1996); Barnes v. Secretary of Dep't of Health & Human Servs., No. 92-0032V, 1997 U.S. Claims LEXIS 212, at *22 (Fed. Cl. Sept. 15, 1997) ("The *P* value . . . [measures] the probability that the results could have happened by chance alone."). Conventional statistical methodology does not permit calculation of the latter probability. However, the *p*-value is used to assess the plausibility that a positive association should be taken to disprove the null hypothesis and permit an inference, after assessing the factors discussed in section V *infra*, that the agent causes disease.

65. Technically, a *p*-value of .1 means that if in fact there is no association, 10% of all similar studies would be expected to yield an association the same as, or greater than, the one found in the study due to random error.

66. *Allen*, 588 F. Supp. at 416–17 (discussing statistical significance and selection of a level of alpha); *see also* Sanders, *supra* note 13, at 343–44 (explaining alpha, beta, and their relationship to sample size); *Developments in the Law—Confronting the New Challenges of Scientific Evidence*, 108 Harv. L. Rev. 1481, 1535–36, 1540–46 (1995) [hereinafter *Developments in the Law*].

used in science is .05.[67] A .05 value means that the probability is 5% of observing an association at least as large as that found in the study when in truth there is no association.[68] Although .05 is often the significance level selected, other levels can and have been used.[69] Thus, in its study of the effects of secondhand smoke, the Environmental Protection Agency (EPA) used a .10 standard for significance testing.[70]

67. A common error made by lawyers, judges, and academics is to equate the level of alpha with the legal burden of proof. Thus, one will often see a statement that using an alpha of .05 for statistical significance imposes a burden of proof on the plaintiff far higher than the civil burden of a preponderance of the evidence (i.e., greater than 50%). *See, e.g.*, Ethyl Corp. v. United States Envtl. Protection Agency, 541 F.2d 1, 28 n.58 (D.C. Cir.), *cert. denied*, 426 U.S. 941 (1976); Hodges v. Secretary of Dep't of Health & Human Servs., 9 F.3d 958, 967, 970 (Fed. Cir. 1993) (Newman, J., dissenting); Edward J. Imwinkelried, *The Admissibility of Expert Testimony in* Christophersen v. Allied-Signal Corp.*: The Neglected Issue of the Validity of Nonscientific Reasoning by Scientific Witnesses*, 70 Denv. U. L. Rev. 473, 478 (1993).

This claim is incorrect, although the reasons are a bit complex and a full explanation would require more space and detail than is feasible here. Nevertheless, we sketch out a brief explanation: First, alpha does not address the likelihood that a plaintiff's disease was caused by exposure to the agent; the magnitude of the association bears on that question. *See infra* § VII. Second, significance testing only bears on whether the observed magnitude of association arose as a result of random chance, not on whether the null hypothesis is true. Third, using stringent significance testing to avoid false positive error comes at a complementary cost of inducing false negative error. *See* DeLuca v. Merrell Dow Pharms., Inc., 911 F.2d 941, 947 (3d Cir. 1990). Fourth, using an alpha of .5 would not be equivalent to saying that the probability the association found is real is 50%, and the probability that it is a result of random error is 50%. Statistical methodology does not permit assessments of those probabilities. *See* Green, *supra* note 39, at 686; Michael D. Green, *Science Is to Law as the Burden of Proof Is to Significance Testing*, 37 Jurimetrics J. 205 (1997) (book review); *see also* David H. Kaye, *Apples and Oranges: Confidence Coefficients and the Burden of Persuasion*, 73 Cornell L. Rev. 54, 66 (1987); David H. Kaye & David A. Freedman, Reference Guide on Statistics § IV.B.2, in this manual; *Developments in the Law*, *supra* note 66, at 1551–56; Allen v. United States, 588 F. Supp. 247, 417 (D. Utah 1984) ("Whether a correlation between a cause and a group of effects is more likely than not—particularly in a legal sense—is a different question from that answered by tests of statistical significance . . . ."), *rev'd on other grounds*, 816 F.2d 1417 (10th Cir. 1987), *cert. denied*, 484 U.S. 1004 (1988); Turpin v. Merrell Dow Pharms., Inc., 959 F.2d 1349, 1357 n.2 (6th Cir.), *cert. denied*, 506 U.S. 826 (1992); *cf. DeLuca*, 911 F.2d at 959 n.24 ("The relationship between confidence levels and the more likely than not standard of proof is a very complex one . . . and in the absence of more education than can be found in this record, we decline to comment further on it.").

68. This means that if one conducted an examination of a large number of associations in which the true RR equals 1, on average 1 in 20 associations found to be statistically significant at a .05 level would be spurious. When researchers examine many possible associations that might exist in their data—known as data dredging—we should expect that even if there are no associations, those researchers will find statistically significant associations in 1 of every 20 associations examined. *See* Rachel Nowak, *Problems in Clinical Trials Go Far Beyond Misconduct*, 264 Science 1538, 1539 (1994).

69. A significance test can be either one-tailed or two-tailed, depending on the null hypothesis selected by the researcher. Since most investigators of toxic substances are only interested in whether the agent increases the incidence of disease (as distinguished from providing protection from the disease), a one-tailed test is often viewed as appropriate. For an explanation of the difference between one-tailed and two-tailed tests, see David H. Kaye & David A. Freedman, Reference Guide on Statistics § IV.C.2, in this manual.

70. U.S. Envtl. Protection Agency, Respiratory Health Effects of Passive Smoking: Lung Cancer and Other Disorders (1992); *see also Turpin*, 959 F.2d at 1353–54 n.1 (confidence level frequently set at

Statistical significance is a term that speaks only to the question of sampling error—it does not address the magnitude of any association found in a study.[71] A study may be statistically significant but may find only a very weak association; conversely, a study with small sample sizes may find a high relative risk but still not be statistically significant.[72]

There is some controversy among epidemiologists and biostatisticians about the appropriate role of significance testing.[73] To the strictest significance testers, any study whose *p*-value is not less than the level chosen for statistical significance should be rejected as inadequate to disprove the null hypothesis. Others are

95%, though 90% (which corresponds to an alpha of .10) is also used; selection of the value is "somewhat arbitrary").

71. Unfortunately, some courts have been confused about the relationship between statistical significance and the magnitude of the association. *See In re* Joint E. & S. Dist. Asbestos Litig., 827 F. Supp. 1014, 1041 (S.D.N.Y. 1993), *rev'd on other grounds*, 52 F.3d 1124 (2d Cir. 1995) (concluding that any relative risk less than 1.50 is statistically insignificant).

72. *See* Cole, *supra* note 53, at 10282. While statistical significance and association are two distinct concepts, whether a study's results are statistically significant does depend, in part, on the incidence of disease and the magnitude of any association found in the study. In other words, the more common the disease and the greater the association between an agent and the disease, the more likely that a study's outcome will be statistically significant, all other things being equal. Also critical to alpha is the number of persons participating in the study. As the disease becomes more infrequent, the sample sizes decrease, and the associations found are weaker, it is less likely that the results will be statistically significant.

73. Similar controversy exists among the courts that have confronted the issue of whether statistically significant studies are required to satisfy the burden of production. The leading case advocating statistically significant studies is *Brock v. Merrell Dow Pharmaceuticals, Inc.*, 874 F.2d 307, 312 (5th Cir.), *amended*, 884 F.2d 167 (5th Cir. 1989), *cert. denied*, 494 U.S. 1046 (1990). Overturning a jury verdict for the plaintiff in a Bendectin case, the court observed that no statistically significant study had been published that found an increased relative risk for birth defects in children whose mothers had taken Bendectin. The court concluded: "[W]e do not wish this case to stand as a bar to future Bendectin cases in the event that new and statistically significant studies emerge which would give a jury a firmer basis on which to determine the issue of causation." Brock v. Merrell Dow Pharms., Inc., 884 F.2d 167, 167 (5th Cir. 1989).

A number of courts have followed the *Brock* decision or have indicated strong support for significance testing as a screening device. *See* Kelley v. American Heyer-Schulte Corp., 957 F. Supp. 873, 878 (W.D. Tex. 1997) (lower end of confidence interval must be above 1.0—equivalent to requiring that a study be statistically significant—before a study may be relied upon by an expert), *appeal dismissed*, 139 F.3d 899 (5th Cir. 1998); Renaud v. Martin Marietta Corp., 749 F. Supp. 1545, 1555 (D. Colo. 1990) (quoting *Brock* approvingly), *aff'd*, 972 F.2d 304 (10th Cir. 1992); Thomas v. Hoffman-LaRoche, Inc., 731 F. Supp. 224, 228 (N.D. Miss. 1989) (granting judgment n.o.v. and observing that "there is a total absence of any statistically significant study to assist the jury in its determination of the issue of causation"), *aff'd on other grounds*, 949 F.2d 806 (5th Cir.), *cert. denied*, 504 U.S. 956 (1992); Daubert v. Merrell Dow Pharms., Inc., 727 F. Supp. 570, 575 (S.D. Cal. 1989), *aff'd on other grounds*, 951 F.2d 1128 (9th Cir. 1991), *vacated*, 509 U.S. 579 (1993); Wade-Greaux v. Whitehall Labs., Inc., 874 F. Supp. 1441 (D.V.I. 1994); Merrell Dow Pharms., Inc. v. Havner, 953 S.W.2d 706, 724 (Tex. 1997).

By contrast, a number of courts appear more cautious about using significance testing as a necessary condition, instead recognizing that assessing the likelihood of random error is important in determining the probative value of a study. In *Allen v. United States*, 588 F. Supp. 247, 417 (D. Utah 1984), the court stated, "The cold statement that a given relationship is not 'statistically significant' cannot be read to mean there is no probability of a relationship." The Third Circuit described confidence intervals (i.e., the range of values within which the true value is thought to lie, with a specified level of confidence) critical of using strict significance testing, which rejects all studies with an observed *p*-value below that specified level. Epidemiologic studies have become increasingly sophisticated in addressing the issue of random error and examining the data from studies to ascertain what information they may provide about the relationship between an agent and a disease, without the rejection of all studies that are not statistically significant.[74]

Calculation of a confidence interval permits a more refined assessment of appropriate inferences about the association found in an epidemiologic study.[75] A confidence interval is a range of values calculated from the results of a study, within which the true value is likely to fall; the width of the interval reflects random error. The advantage of a confidence interval is that it displays more information than significance testing. What a statement about whether a result is statistically significant does not provide is the magnitude of the association found in the study or an indication of how statistically stable that association is. A confidence interval for any study shows the relative risk determined in the study as a point on a numerical axis. It also displays the boundaries of relative risk

and their use as an alternative to statistical significance in *DeLuca v. Merrell Dow Pharmaceuticals, Inc.*, 911 F.2d 941, 948–49 (3d Cir. 1990). *See also* Turpin v. Merrell Dow Pharms., Inc., 959 F.2d 1349, 1357 (6th Cir.) ("The defendant's claim overstates the persuasive power of these statistical studies. An analysis of this evidence demonstrates that it is possible that Bendectin causes birth defects even though these studies do not detect a significant association."), *cert. denied*, 506 U.S. 826 (1992); *In re* Bendectin Prod. Liab. Litig., 732 F. Supp. 744, 748–49 (E.D. Mich. 1990) (rejecting defendant's claim that plaintiff could not prevail without statistically significant epidemiologic evidence); Berry v. CSX Transp., Inc., 709 So. 2d 552, 570 (Fla. Dist. Ct. App. 1998) (refusing to hold studies that were not statistically significant inadmissible).

Although the trial court had relied in part on the absence of statistically significant epidemiologic studies, the Supreme Court in *Daubert v. Merrell Dow Pharmaceuticals, Inc.*, 509 U.S. 579 (1993), did not explicitly address the matter. The Court did, however, refer to "the known or potential rate of error" in identifying factors relevant to the scientific validity of an expert's methodology. *Id.* at 594. The Court did not address any specific rate of error, although two cases that it cited affirmed the admissibility of voice spectrograph results that the courts reported were subject to a 2%–6% chance of error owing to either false matches or false eliminations. One commentator has concluded, "*Daubert* did not set a threshold level of statistical significance either for admissibility or for sufficiency of scientific evidence." *Developments in the Law*, *supra* note 66, at 1535–36, 1540–46. The Supreme Court in *General Electric Co. v. Joiner*, 522 U.S. 136, 145–47 (1997), adverted to the lack of statistical significance in one study relied on by an expert as a ground for ruling that the district court had not abused its discretion in excluding the expert's testimony.

74. *See* Sanders, *supra* note 13, at 342 (describing the improved handling and reporting of statistical analysis in studies of Bendectin after 1980).

75. Kenneth Rothman, Professor of Public Health at Boston University and Adjunct Professor of Epidemiology at the Harvard School of Public Health, is one of the leaders in advocating the use of confidence intervals and rejecting strict significance testing. In *DeLuca*, 911 F.2d at 947, the Third Circuit discussed Rothman's views on the appropriate level of alpha and the use of confidence intervals. In *Turpin*, 959 F.2d at 1353–54 n.1, the court discussed the relationship among confidence intervals, alpha, and power. The use of confidence intervals in evaluating sampling error more generally than in the epidemiologic context is discussed in David H. Kaye & David A. Freedman, Reference Guide on Statistics § IV.A, in this manual.

consistent with the data found in the study based on one or several selected levels of alpha or statistical significance. An example of two confidence intervals that might be calculated for a study is displayed in Figure 4.

Figure 4. Confidence Intervals

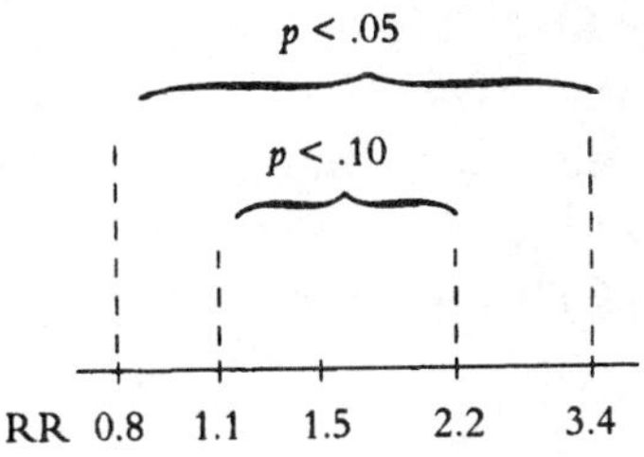

The confidence interval shown in Figure 4 represents a study that found a relative risk of 1.5, with boundaries of 0.8 to 3.4 for alpha equal to .05 (equivalently, a confidence level of .95) and boundaries of 1.1 to 2.2 for alpha equal to .10 (equivalently, a confidence level of .90). Because the boundaries of the confidence interval with alpha set at .05 encompass a relative risk of 1.0, the study is not statistically significant at that level. By contrast, since the confidence boundaries for alpha equal to .10 do not include a relative risk of 1.0, the study does have a positive finding that is statistically significant at that level of alpha. The larger the sample size in a study (all other things being equal), the narrower the confidence boundaries will be (indicating greater statistical stability), thereby reflecting the decreased likelihood that the association found in the study would occur if the true association is 1.0.[76]

76. Where multiple epidemiologic studies are available, a technique known as meta-analysis (*see infra* § VI) may be used to combine the results of the studies to reduce the numerical instability of all the studies. *See generally* Diana B. Petitti, Meta-analysis, Decision Analysis, and Cost-Effectiveness Analysis: Methods for Quantitative Synthesis in Medicine (2d ed. 2000). Meta-analysis is better suited to pooling results from randomly controlled experimental studies, but if carefully performed it may also be helpful for observational studies, such as those in the epidemiologic field. *See* Zachary B. Gerbarg & Ralph I. Horwitz, *Resolving Conflicting Clinical Trials: Guidelines for Meta-Analysis*, 41 J. Clinical Epidemiology 503 (1988).

In *In re Paoli Railroad Yard PCB Litigation*, 916 F.2d 829, 856–57 (3d Cir. 1990), *cert. denied*, 499 U.S. 461 (1991), the court discussed the use and admissibility of meta-analysis as a scientific technique. Overturning the district court's exclusion of a report using meta-analysis, the Third Circuit observed that meta-analysis is a regularly used scientific technique. The court recognized that the technique might be poorly performed, and it required the district court to reconsider the validity of the expert's work in performing the meta-analysis. *See also* E.R. Squibb & Sons, Inc. v. Stuart Pharms., No. 90-1178, 1990 U.S. Dist. LEXIS 15788, at *41 (D.N.J. Oct. 16, 1990) (acknowledging the utility of meta-analysis but rejecting its use in that case because one of the two studies included was poorly performed); Tobin v. Astra Pharm. Prods., Inc., 993 F.2d 528, 538–39 (6th Cir. 1992) (identifying an error in the performance of a meta-analysis, in which the Food and Drug Administration (FDA) pooled data from

2. *False negative error*

False positives can be reduced by adopting more stringent values for alpha. Using a level of .01 or .001 will result in fewer false positives than using an alpha of .05. The trade-off for reducing false positives is an increase in false negative errors (also called beta errors or type II errors). This concept reflects the possibility that a study will be interpreted not to disprove the null hypothesis when in fact there is a true association of a specified magnitude.[77] The beta for any study can be calculated only based on a specific alternative hypothesis about a given positive relative risk and a specific level of alpha selected;[78] that is, beta, or the likelihood of erroneously failing to reject the null hypothesis, depends on the selection of an alternative hypothesis about the magnitude of association and the level of alpha chosen.

3. *Power*

When a study fails to find a statistically significant association, an important question is whether the result tends to exonerate the agent's toxicity or is essentially inconclusive with regard to toxicity. The concept of power can be helpful in evaluating whether a study's outcome is exonerative or inconclusive.[79]

The power of a study expresses the probability of finding a statistically significant association of a given magnitude (if it exists) in light of the sample sizes used in the study. The power of a study depends on several factors: the sample size; the level of alpha, or statistical significance, specified; the background incidence of disease; and the specified relative risk that the researcher would like to detect.[80] Power curves can be constructed that show the likelihood of finding any given relative risk in light of these factors. Often power curves are used in the design of a study to determine what size the study populations should be.[81]

The power of a study is the complement of beta ($1 - \beta$). Thus, a study with a likelihood of .25 of failing to detect a true relative risk of 2.0[82] or greater has a power of .75. This means the study has a 75% chance of detecting a true relative risk of 2.0. If the power of a negative study to find a relative risk of 2.0 or greater

control groups in different studies in which some gave the controls a placebo and others gave the controls an alternative treatment), *cert. denied*, 510 U.S. 914 (1993).

77. *See also* DeLuca v. Merrell Dow Pharms., Inc., 911 F.2d 941, 947 (3d Cir. 1990).

78. *See* Green, *supra* note 39, at 684–89.

79. *See* Fienberg et al., *supra* note 59, at 22–23.

80. *See* Malcolm Gladwell, *How Safe Are Your Breasts?*, New Republic, Oct. 24, 1994, at 22, 26.

81. For examples of power curves, see Kenneth J. Rothman, Modern Epidemiology 80 (1986); Pagano & Gauvreau, *supra* note 47, at 223.

82. We use a relative risk of 2.0 for illustrative purposes because of the legal significance some courts have attributed to this magnitude of association. *See infra* § VII.

is low, it has significantly less probative value than a study with similar results but a higher power.[83]

B. What Biases May Have Contributed to an Erroneous Association?

Systematic error or bias can produce an erroneous association in an epidemiologic study. Bias may arise in the design or conduct of a study, data collection, or data analysis. When scientists use the term *bias*, it does not necessarily carry an imputation of prejudice or other subjective factors, such as the researcher's desire for a particular outcome. The meaning of scientific bias differs from conventional (and legal) usage, in which bias refers to a partisan point of view.[84] Bias refers to anything (other than random sampling error) that results in error in a study and thereby compromises its validity. The two main classes of bias are selection bias (inappropriate selection of study subjects) and information bias (a flaw in measuring exposure or disease in the study groups).

Most epidemiologic studies have some degree of bias that may affect the outcome. If major bias is present it may invalidate the study results. Finding the bias, however, can be difficult if not impossible. In reviewing the validity of an epidemiologic study, the epidemiologist must identify potential biases and analyze the amount or kind of error that might have been induced by the bias. Often the direction of error can be determined; depending on the specific type of bias, it may exaggerate the real association, dilute it, or even completely mask it.

1. Selection bias

Selection bias refers to the error in an observed association that is due to the method of selection of cases and controls (in a case-control study) or exposed and unexposed individuals (in a cohort study).[85] The selection of an appropriate

83. *See also* David H. Kaye & David A. Freedman, Reference Guide on Statistics § IV.C.1, in this manual.

84. A Dictionary of Epidemiology 15 (John M. Last ed., 3d ed. 1995); Edmond A. Murphy, The Logic of Medicine 239–62 (1976).

85. Selection bias is defined as "[e]rror due to systematic differences in characteristics between those who are selected for study and those who are not." A Dictionary of Epidemiology, *supra* note 84, at 153.

In *In re "Agent Orange" Product Liability Litigation*, 597 F. Supp. 740, 783 (E.D.N.Y. 1985), *aff'd*, 818 F.2d 145 (2d Cir. 1987), *cert. denied*, 484 U.S. 1004 (1988), the court expressed concern about selection bias. The exposed cohort consisted of young, healthy men who served in Vietnam. Comparing the mortality rate of the exposed cohort and that of a control group made up of civilians might have resulted in error that was due to selection bias. Failing to account for health status as an independent variable tends to understate any association between exposure and disease in studies in which the exposed cohort is healthier.

control group has been described as the Achilles' heel of a case-control study.[86] Selecting members of the control group (those without disease) is problematic in case-control studies if the control participants were selected for reasons that are related to their having the exposure or potential risk factor being studied.

Hospital-based studies, which are relatively common among researchers located in medical centers, illustrate the problem. Suppose an association is found between coffee drinking and coronary heart disease in a study using hospital patients as controls. The problem is that the hospitalized control group may include individuals who had been advised against drinking coffee for medical reasons, such as to prevent aggravation of a peptic ulcer. In other words, the controls may become eligible for the study because of their medical condition, which is in turn related to their exposure status—their likelihood of avoiding coffee. If this is true, the amount of coffee drinking in the control group would understate the extent of coffee drinking expected in people who do not have the disease, and thus bias upwardly (i.e., exaggerate) any odds ratio observed.[87] Bias in hospital studies may also understate the true odds ratio when the exposures at issue led to the cases' hospitalizations and also contributed to the controls' chances of hospitalization.

Just as case-control study controls should be selected independently of their exposure status, in cohort studies, unexposed controls should be selected independently of their disease risk. For example, in a cohort study of cervical cancer, those who are not at risk for the disease—women who have had their cervices removed and men—should be excluded from the study population. Inclusion of such individuals as controls in a cohort study could result in erroneous findings by overstating the association between the agent and the disease.

A further source of selection bias occurs when those selected to participate refuse to participate or drop out before the study is completed. Many studies have shown that individuals who participate in studies differ significantly from those who do not. If a significant portion of either study group refuses to participate in the study, the researcher should investigate reasons for refusal and whether those who refused are different from those who agreed. The researcher can show that those in the study are not a biased sample by comparing relevant characteristics of individuals who refused to participate with those of individuals who participated to show the similarity of the groups or the degree of differences. Similarly, if a significant number of subjects drop out of a study before completion, there may be a problem in determining whether the remaining subjects are representative of the original study populations. The researcher should

86. William B. Kannel & Thomas R. Dawber, *Coffee and Coronary Disease*, 289 New Eng. J. Med. 100 (1973) (editorial).

87. Hershel Jick et al., *Coffee and Myocardial Infarction*, 289 New Eng. J. Med. 63 (1973).

examine whether the study groups are still representative of the original study populations.

The fact that a study may suffer from selection bias does not in itself invalidate its results. A number of factors may suggest that a bias, if present, had only limited effect. If the association is particularly strong, for example, bias is less likely to account for all of it. In addition, in studies with multiple control groups, the consistent finding of an association when cases are compared with different control groups suggests that possible biases applicable to a particular control group are not invalidating.

2. *Information bias*

Information bias refers to the bias resulting from inaccurate information about the study participants regarding either their disease or exposure status. In a case-control study, potential information bias is an important consideration because the researcher depends on information from the past to determine exposure and disease and their temporal relationship. In some situations the researcher is required to interview the subjects about past exposures, thus relying on the subjects' memories. Research has shown that individuals with disease (cases) may more readily recall past exposures than individuals with no disease (controls);[88] this creates a potential for bias called recall bias.

For example, consider a case-control study conducted to examine the cause of congenital malformations. The epidemiologist is interested in whether the malformations were caused by an infection during the mother's pregnancy.[89] A group of mothers of malformed infants (cases) and a group of mothers of infants with no malformation (controls) are interviewed regarding infections during pregnancy. Mothers of children with malformations may recall an inconsequential fever or runny nose during pregnancy that readily would be forgotten by a mother who had a normal infant. Even if in reality the infection rate in mothers of malformed children is no different from the rate in mothers of normal children, the result in this study would be an apparently higher rate of infection in the mothers of the children with the malformations solely on the basis of recall differences between the two groups. The issue of recall bias can sometimes be evaluated by finding a second source of data to validate the subject's response

88. Steven S. Coughlin, *Recall Bias in Epidemiologic Studies*, 43 J. Clinical Epidemiology 87 (1990).

89. *See* Brock v. Merrell Dow Pharms., Inc., 874 F.2d 307, 311–12 (5th Cir. 1989) (discussion of recall bias among women who bear children with birth defects), *cert. denied*, 494 U.S. 1046 (1990). We note that the court was mistaken in its assertion that a confidence interval could correct for recall bias, or for any bias for that matter. Confidence intervals are a statistical device for analyzing error that may result from random sampling. Systematic errors (bias) in the design or data collection are not addressed by statistical methods, such as confidence intervals or statistical significance. *See* Green, *supra* note 39, at 667–68; Vincent M. Brannigan et al., *Risk, Statistical Inference, and the Law of Evidence: The Use of Epidemiological Data in Toxic Tort Cases*, 12 Risk Analysis 343, 344–45 (1992).

(e.g., blood test results from prenatal visits or medical records that document symptoms of infection).[90] Alternatively, the mothers' responses to questions about other exposures may shed light on the presence of a bias affecting the recall of the relevant exposures. Thus, if mothers of cases do not recall greater exposure than controls' mothers to pesticides, children with German measles, and so forth, then one can have greater confidence in their recall of illnesses.

Bias may also result from reliance on interviews with surrogates, individuals other than the study subjects. This is often necessary when, for example, a subject (in a case-control study) has died of the disease under investigation.

There are many sources of information bias that affect the measure of exposure, including its intensity and duration. Exposure to the agent can be measured directly or indirectly.[91] Sometimes researchers use a biological marker as a direct measure of exposure to an agent—an alteration in tissue or body fluids that occurs as a result of an exposure and that can be detected in the laboratory. Biological markers are only available for a small number of toxins and only reveal whether a person was exposed. Biological markers rarely help determine the intensity or duration of exposure.[92]

Monitoring devices also can be used to measure exposure directly but often are not available for exposures that occurred in the past. For past exposures, epidemiologists often use indirect means of measuring exposure, such as interviewing workers and reviewing employment records. Thus, all those employed to install asbestos insulation may be treated as having been exposed to asbestos during the period that they were employed. However, there may be a wide variation of exposure within any job, and these measures may have limited applicability to a given individual. If the agent of interest is a drug, medical or hospital records can be used to determine past exposure. Thus, retrospective

90. Two researchers who used a case-control study to examine the association between congenital heart disease and the mother's use of drugs during pregnancy corroborated interview data with the mother's medical records. *See* Sally Zierler & Kenneth J. Rothman, *Congenital Heart Disease in Relation to Maternal Use of Bendectin and Other Drugs in Early Pregnancy*, 313 New Eng. J. Med. 347, 347–48 (1985).

91. *See In re* Paoli R.R. Yard PCB Litig., No. 86-2229, 1992 U.S. Dist LEXIS 18430, at *9–*11 (E.D. Pa. Oct. 21, 1992) (discussing valid methods of determining exposure to chemicals).

92. Dose generally refers to the intensity or magnitude of exposure multiplied by the time exposed. *See* Sparks v. Owens-Illinois, Inc., 38 Cal. Rptr. 2d 739, 742 (Ct. App. 1995). For a discussion of the difficulties of determining dose from atomic fallout, see *Allen v. United States,* 588 F. Supp. 247, 425–26 (D. Utah 1984), *rev'd on other grounds,* 816 F.2d 1417 (10th Cir. 1987), *cert. denied,* 484 U.S. 1004 (1988). The timing of exposure may also be critical, especially if the disease of interest is a birth defect. In *Smith v. Ortho Pharmaceutical Corp.*, 770 F. Supp. 1561, 1577 (N.D. Ga. 1991), the court criticized a study for its inadequate measure of exposure to spermicides. The researchers had defined exposure as receipt of a prescription for spermicide within 600 days of delivery, but this definition of exposure is too broad because environmental agents are only likely to cause birth defects during a narrow band of time.

A different, but related, problem often arises in court. Determining the plaintiff's exposure to the alleged toxic substance always involves a retrospective determination and may involve difficulties simioccupational or environmental measurements of exposure are usually less accurate than prospective studies or follow-up studies, especially ones in which a drug or medical intervention is the independent variable being measured.

The route (e.g., inhalation or absorption), duration, and intensity of exposure are important factors in assessing disease causation. Even with environmental monitoring, the dose measured in the environment generally is not the same as the dose that reaches internal target organs. If the researcher has calculated the internal dose of exposure, the scientific basis for this calculation should be examined for soundness.[93]

In assessing whether the data may reflect inaccurate information, one must assess whether the data were collected from objective and reliable sources. Medical records, government documents, employment records, death certificates, and interviews are examples of data sources that are used by epidemiologists to measure both exposure and disease status.[94] The accuracy of a particular source may affect the validity of a research finding. If different data sources are used to collect information about a study group, differences in the accuracy of those sources may affect the validity of the findings. For example, using employment records to gather information about exposure to narcotics probably would lead to inaccurate results, since employees tend to keep such information private. If the researcher uses an unreliable source of data, the study may not be useful to the court.

The kinds of quality-control procedures used may affect the accuracy of the data. For data collected by interview, quality-control procedures should probe the reliability of the individual and whether the information is verified by other sources. For data collected and analyzed in the laboratory, quality-control procedures should probe the validity and reliability of the laboratory test.

Information bias may also result from inaccurate measurement of disease status. The quality and sophistication of the diagnostic methods used to detect a

lar to those faced by an epidemiologist planning a study. Thus, in *Christophersen v. Allied-Signal Corp.*, 939 F.2d 1106, 1113 (5th Cir. 1991), *cert. denied*, 503 U.S. 912 (1992), the court criticized the plaintiff's expert, who relied on an affidavit of a co-worker to determine the dose of nickel and cadmium to which the decedent had been exposed.

In asbestos litigation, a number of courts have adopted a requirement that the plaintiff demonstrate (1) regular use by an employer of the defendant's asbestos-containing product; (2) the plaintiff's proximity to that product; and (3) exposure over an extended period of time. *See, e.g.*, Lohrmann v. Pittsburgh Corning Corp., 782 F.2d 1156, 1162–64 (4th Cir. 1986).

93. *See also* Bernard D. Goldstein & Mary Sue Henifin, Reference Guide on Toxicology § I.D, in this manual.

94. Even these sources may produce unanticipated error. Identifying the causal connection between asbestos and mesothelioma, a rare form of cancer, was complicated and delayed because doctors who were unfamiliar with mesothelioma erroneously identified other causes of death in death certificates. *See* David E. Lilienfeld & Paul D. Gunderson, *The "Missing Cases" of Pleural Malignant Mesothelioma in Minnesota, 1979–81: Preliminary Report*, 101 Pub. Health Rep. 395, 397–98 (1986).

disease should be assessed. The proportion of subjects who were examined also should be questioned. If, for example, many of the subjects refused to be tested, the fact that the test used was of high quality would be of relatively little value.

The scientific validity of the research findings is influenced by the reliability of the diagnosis of disease or health status.[95] For example, a researcher interested in studying spontaneous abortion in the first trimester needs to test women for pregnancy. Diagnostic criteria that are accepted by the medical community should be used to make the diagnosis. If a diagnosis is made using an unreliable home pregnancy kit known to have a high rate of false positive results (indicating pregnancy when the woman is not pregnant), the study will overestimate the number of spontaneous abortions.

Misclassification bias is a form of information bias in which, because of problems with the information available, individuals in the study may be misclassified with regard to exposure status or disease status. Misclassification bias has been subdivided into differential misclassification and nondifferential misclassification. Nondifferential misclassification occurs when inaccuracies in determining exposure are independent of disease status or when inaccuracies in diagnoses are independent of exposure status. This is a common problem resulting from the limitations of data collection. Generally, nondifferential misclassification bias leads to a shift in the odds ratio toward one, or, in other words, toward a finding of no effect. Thus, if the errors are nondifferential, it is generally misguided to criticize an apparent association between an exposure and disease on the grounds that data were inaccurately classified. Instead, nondifferential misclassification generally serves to reduce the observed association below its true magnitude.

Differential misclassification refers to the differential error in determining exposure in cases as compared with controls, or disease status in unexposed cohorts relative to exposed cohorts. In a case-control study this would occur, for example, if, in the process of anguishing over the possible causes of the disease, parents of ill children recalled more exposures to a particular agent than actually occurred, or if parents of the controls, for whom the issue was less emotionally charged, recalled fewer. This can also occur in a cohort study in which, for example, birth control users, the exposed cohort, are monitored more closely for potential side effects, leading to a higher rate of disease identification in that cohort than in the unexposed cohort. Depending on how the misclassification occurs, a differential bias can produce an error in either direction—the exaggeration or understatement of an association.

95. In *In re Swine Flu Immunization Products Liability Litigation*, 508 F. Supp. 897, 903 (D. Colo. 1981), *aff'd sub nom.* Lima v. United States, 708 F.2d 502 (10th Cir. 1983), the court critically evaluated a study relied on by an expert whose testimony was stricken. In that study, determination of whether a patient had Guillain-Barré syndrome was made by medical clerks, not physicians who were familiar with diagnostic criteria.

3. Other conceptual problems

Sometimes studies are flawed because of flawed definitions or premises that do not fall under the rubric of selection bias or information bias. For example, if the researcher defines the disease of interest as all birth defects, rather than a specific birth defect, he or she must have a scientific basis to hypothesize that the effects of the agent being investigated could be so varied. If the effect is in fact more limited, the result of this conceptualization error could be to dilute or mask any real effect that the agent might have on a specific type of birth defect.[96]

Examining a study for potential sources of bias is an important task that helps determine the accuracy of a study's conclusions. In addition, when a source of bias is identified, it may be possible to determine whether the error tended to exaggerate or understate the true association. Thus, bias may exist in a study that nevertheless has probative value.

Even if one concludes that the findings of a study are statistically stable and that biases have not created significant error, additional considerations remain. As repeatedly noted, an association does not necessarily mean a causal relationship exists. To make a judgment about causation, a knowledgeable expert must consider the possibility of confounding factors. The expert must also evaluate several criteria to determine whether an inference of causation is appropriate. These matters are discussed below.

C. Could a Confounding Factor Be Responsible for the Study Result?[97]

Even when an association exists, researchers must determine whether the exposure causes the disease or whether the exposure and disease are caused by some other confounding factor. A confounding factor is both a risk factor for the disease and a factor associated with the exposure of interest. For example, researchers may conduct a study that finds individuals with gray hair have a higher rate of death than those with hair of another color. Instead of hair color having an impact on death, the results might be explained by the confounding factor of age. If old age is associated differentially with the gray-haired group (those with gray hair tend to be older), old age may be responsible for the association found between hair color and death.[98] Researchers must separate the relationship be-

96. In *Brock v. Merrell Dow Pharmaceuticals, Inc.*, 874 F.2d 307, 312 (5th Cir. 1989), *cert. denied*, 494 U.S. 1046 (1990), the court discussed a reanalysis of a study in which the effect was narrowed from all congenital malformations to limb reduction defects. The magnitude of the association changed by 50% when the effect was defined in this narrower fashion. *See* Rothman & Greenland, *supra* note 49, at 132 ("Unwarranted assurances of a lack of any effect can easily emerge from studies in which a wide range of etiologically unrelated outcomes are grouped.").

97. *See* Grassis v. Johns-Manville Corp., 591 A.2d 671, 675 (N.J. Super. Ct. App. Div. 1991) (discussing the possibility that confounders may lead to an erroneous inference of a causal relationship).

98. This example is drawn from Kahn & Sempos, *supra* note 25, at 63.

tween gray hair and risk of death from that of old age and risk of death. When researchers find an association between an agent and a disease, it is critical to determine whether the association is causal or the result of confounding.[99] Some epidemiologists classify confounding as a form of bias. However, confounding is a reality—that is, the observed association of a factor and a disease is actually the result of an association with a third, confounding factor. Failure to recognize confounding can introduce a bias—error—into the findings of the study.

In 1981, Dr. Brian MacMahon, Professor and Chairman of the Department of Epidemiology at the Harvard School of Public Health, reported an association between coffee drinking and cancer of the pancreas in the *New England Journal of Medicine.*[100] This observation caused a great stir, and in fact, one coffee distributor ran a large advertisement in the *New York Times* refuting the findings of the study. What could MacMahon's findings mean? One possibility is that the association is causal and that drinking coffee causes an increased risk of cancer of the pancreas. However, there is also another possibility. We know that smoking is an important risk factor for cancer of the pancreas. We also know that it is difficult to find a smoker who does not drink coffee. Thus, drinking coffee and smoking are associated. An observed association between coffee consumption and an increased risk of cancer of the pancreas could reflect the fact that smoking causes cancer of the pancreas and that smoking also is associated closely with coffee consumption. The association MacMahon found between drinking coffee and pancreatic cancer could be due to the confounding factor of smoking. To be fair to MacMahon, we must note that he was aware of the possibility of confounding and took it into account in his study design by gathering and analyzing data separately for smokers and nonsmokers. The association between coffee and pancreatic cancer remained even when smoking was taken into account.

The main problem in many observational studies such as MacMahon's is that the individuals are not assigned randomly to the groups being compared.[101] As discussed above, randomization maximizes the possibility that exposures other

99. Confounding can bias a study result by either exaggerating or diluting any true association. One example of a confounding factor that may result in a study's outcome understating an association is vaccination. Thus, if a group exposed to an agent has a higher rate of vaccination for the disease under study than the unexposed group, the vaccination may reduce the rate of disease in the exposed group, thereby producing an association that is less than the true association without the confounding of vaccination.

100. Brian MacMahon et al., *Coffee and Cancer of the Pancreas,* 304 New Eng. J. Med. 630 (1981).

101. Randomization attempts to ensure that the presence of a characteristic, such as coffee drinking, is governed by chance, as opposed to being determined by the presence of an underlying medical condition. For additional comments on randomization and confounding, see the Glossary of Terms.

than the one under study are evenly distributed between the exposed and the control cohorts.[102] In observational studies, by contrast, other forces, including self-selection, determine who is exposed to other (possibly causal) factors. The lack of randomization leads to the potential problem of confounding. Thus, for example, the exposed cohort might consist of those who are exposed at work to an agent suspected of being an industrial toxin. The members of this cohort may, however, differ from controls by residence, socioeconomic status, age, or other extraneous factors.[103] These other factors may be causing the disease, but because of potential confounding, an apparent (yet false) association of the disease with exposure to the agent may appear. Confounders, like smoking in the MacMahon study, do not reflect an error made by the investigators; rather, they reflect the inherently "uncontrolled" nature of observational studies. When they can be identified, confounders should be taken into account. Confounding factors that are suspected or known in advance can be controlled during the study design through study-group selection. Unanticipated confounding factors that are suspected after data collection can sometimes be controlled during data analysis, if data have been gathered about them.

MacMahon's study found that coffee drinkers had a higher rate of pancreatic cancer than those who did not drink coffee. To evaluate whether smoking is a confounding factor, the researcher would divide each of the exposed and control groups into smoking and nonsmoking subgroups to examine whether subjects' smoking status affects the study results. If the outcome in the smoking subgroups is the same as that in the nonsmoking subgroups, smoking is not a confounding factor. If the subjects' smoking status affects the outcome, then smoking is a confounder, for which adjustment is required. If the association between coffee drinking and pancreatic cancer completely disappears when the subjects' smoking status is considered, then smoking is a confounder that fully accounts for the association with coffee observed. Table 4 reveals a hypothetical study's results, with smoking being a weak confounding factor, which, when accounted for, does not eliminate the association between coffee drinking and cancer.

102. *See* Rothman & Greenland, *supra* note 49, at 124; *see also supra* § II.A.

103. *See, e.g.*, *In re* "Agent Orange" Prod. Liab. Litig., 597 F. Supp. 740, 783 (E.D.N.Y. 1984) (discussing the problem of confounding that might result in a study of the effect of exposure to Agent Orange on Vietnam servicemen), *aff'd*, 818 F.2d 145 (2d Cir. 1987), *cert. denied*, 484 U.S. 1004 (1988).

Table 4. Pancreatic Cancer Study Data

Pancreatic Cancer Status	All Subjects		Smokers >1 Pack per Day		Nonsmokers	
	Controls	Coffee Drinkers	Controls	Coffee Drinkers	Controls	Coffee Drinkers
Cancer	14	17	8	11	6	6
No Cancer	1,393	476	733	263	660	213
RR	1.1	3.9	1.2	4.6	1.0	3.1

Note: RR = relative risk.

There is always a real risk that an undiscovered or unrecognized confounding factor may contribute to a study's findings, by either magnifying or reducing the observed association.[104] It is, however, necessary to keep that risk in perspective. Often the mere possibility of uncontrolled confounding is used to call into question the results of a study. This was certainly the strategy of those seeking, or unwittingly helping, to undermine the implications of the studies persuasively linking cigarette smoking to lung cancer. The critical question is whether it is plausible that the findings of a given study could indeed be due to unrecognized confounders.

1. *What techniques can be used to prevent or limit confounding?*

Choices in the design of a research project (e.g., methods for selecting the subjects) can prevent or limit confounding. When a factor or factors, such as age, sex, or even smoking status, are considered potential confounders in a study, investigators can limit the differential distribution of these factors in the study groups by selecting controls to "match" cases (or the exposed group) in terms of these variables. If the two groups are matched, for example, by age, then any association observed in the study cannot be due to age, the matched variable.[105]

Restricting the persons who are permitted as subjects in a study is another method to control for confounders. If age or sex is suspected as a confounder, then the subjects enrolled in a study can be limited to those of one sex and those who are within a specified age range. When there is no variance among subjects in a study with regard to a potential confounder, confounding as a result of that variable is eliminated.

104. Rothman & Greenland, *supra* note 49, at 120; *see also supra* § II.A.

105. Selecting a control population based on matched variables necessarily affects the representativeness of the selected controls and may affect how generalizable the study results are to the population at large. However, for a study to have merit, it must first be internally valid, that is, it must not be subject to unreasonable sources of bias or confounding. Only after a study has been shown to meet this standard does its universal applicability or generalizability to the population at large become an issue. When a study population is not representative of the general or target population, existing scientific knowledge may permit reasonable inferences about the study's broader applicability, or additional confirmatory studies of other populations may be necessary.

2. *What techniques can be used to identify confounding factors?*

Once the study data are ready to be analyzed, the researcher must assess a range of factors that could influence risk. In the case of MacMahon's study, the researcher would evaluate whether smoking is a confounding factor by comparing the risk of pancreatic cancer in all coffee drinkers (including smokers) with the risk in nonsmoking coffee drinkers. If the risk is substantially the same, smoking is not a confounding factor (e.g., smoking does not distort the relationship between coffee drinking and the development of pancreatic cancer), which is what MacMahon found. If the risk is substantially different, but still exists in the nonsmoking group, then smoking is a confounder, but doesn't wholly account for the association with coffee. If the association disappears, then smoking is a confounder that fully accounts for the association with coffee observed.

3. *What techniques can be used to control for confounding factors?*

To control for confounding factors during data analysis, researchers can use one of two techniques: stratification or multivariate analysis.

Stratification reduces or eliminates confounding by evaluating the effect of an exposure at different levels (strata) of exposure to the confounding variable. Statistical methods then can be applied to combine the results of exposure at each stratum into an overall single estimate of risk. For example, in MacMahon's study of smoking and pancreatic cancer, if smoking had been a confounding factor, the researchers could have stratified the data by creating subgroups based on how many cigarettes each subject smoked a day (e.g., a nonsmoking group, a light smoking group, a medium smoking group, and a heavy smoking group). When different rates of pancreatic cancer for people in each group who drink the same amount of coffee are compared, the effect of smoking on pancreatic cancer is revealed. The effect of the confounding factor can then be removed from the study results.

Multivariate analysis controls for the confounding factor through mathematical modeling. Models are developed to describe the simultaneous effect of exposure and confounding factors on the increase in risk.[106]

Both of these methods allow for "adjustment" of the effect of confounders. They both modify an observed association to take into account the effect of risk factors that are not the subject of the study and that may distort the association between the exposure being studied and the disease outcomes.

If the association between exposure and disease remains after the researcher completes the assessment and adjustment for confounding factors, the researcher then applies the guidelines described in section V to determine whether an inference of causation is warranted.

106. For a more complete discussion, of multivariate analysis, see Daniel L. Rubinfeld, Reference Guide on Multiple Regression, in this manual.

V. General Causation: Is an Exposure a Cause of the Disease?

Once an association has been found between exposure to an agent and development of a disease, researchers consider whether the association reflects a true cause–effect relationship. When epidemiologists evaluate whether a cause–effect relationship exists between an agent and disease, they are using the term causation in a way similar to, but not identical with, the way the familiar "but for," or sine qua non, test is used in law for cause in fact. "An act or an omission is not regarded as a cause of an event if the particular event would have occurred without it."[107] This is equivalent to describing the act or occurrence as a necessary link in a chain of events that results in the particular event.[108] Epidemiologists use causation to mean that an increase in the incidence of disease among the exposed subjects would not have occurred had they not been exposed to the agent. Thus, exposure is a necessary condition for the increase in the incidence of disease among those exposed.[109] The relationship between the epidemiologic concept of cause and the legal question of whether exposure to an agent caused an individual's disease is addressed in section VII.

As mentioned in section I, epidemiology cannot objectively prove causation; rather, causation is a judgment for epidemiologists and others interpreting the epidemiologic data. Moreover, scientific determinations of causation are inherently tentative. The scientific enterprise must always remain open to reassessing the validity of past judgments as new evidence develops.

In assessing causation, researchers first look for alternative explanations for the association, such as bias or confounding factors, which were discussed in section IV. Once this process is completed, researchers consider how guidelines

107. W. Page Keeton et al., Prosser and Keeton on the Law of Torts 265 (5th ed. 1984); *see also* Restatement (Second) of Torts § 432(1) (1965).

When multiple causes are each operating and capable of causing an event, the but-for, or necessary-condition, concept for causation is problematic. This is the familiar "two-fires" scenario in which two independent fires simultaneously burn down a house and is sometimes referred to as overdetermined cause. Neither fire is a but-for, or necessary condition, for the destruction of the house, because either fire would have destroyed the house. *See id.* § 432(2). This two-fires situation is analogous to an individual being exposed to two agents, each of which is capable of causing the disease contracted by the individual. A difference between the disease scenario and the fire scenario is that, in the former, one will have no more than a probabilistic assessment of whether each of the exposures would have caused the disease in the individual.

108. *See supra* note 8.

109. *See* Rothman & Greenland, *supra* note 49, at 8 ("We can define a cause of a specific disease event as an antecedent event, condition, or characteristic that was necessary for the occurrence of the disease at the moment it occurred, given that other conditions are fixed."); Allen v. United States, 588 F. Supp. 247, 405 (D. Utah 1984) (quoting a physician on the meaning of the statement that radiation causes cancer), *rev'd on other grounds*, 816 F.2d 1417 (10th Cir. 1987), *cert. denied*, 484 U.S. 1004 (1988).

for inferring causation from an association apply to the available evidence. These guidelines consist of several key inquiries that assist researchers in making a judgment about causation.[110] Most researchers are conservative when it comes to assessing causal relationships, often calling for stronger evidence and more research before a conclusion of causation is drawn.[111]

The factors that guide epidemiologists in making judgments about causation are

1. temporal relationship;
2. strength of the association;
3. dose–response relationship;
4. replication of the findings;
5. biological plausibility (coherence with existing knowledge);
6. consideration of alternative explanations;
7. cessation of exposure;
8. specificity of the association; and
9. consistency with other knowledge.

There is no formula or algorithm that can be used to assess whether a causal inference is appropriate based on these guidelines. One or more factors may be absent even when a true causal relationship exists. Similarly, the existence of some factors does not ensure that a causal relationship exists. Drawing causal inferences after finding an association and considering these factors requires judgment and searching analysis, based on biology, of why a factor or factors may be absent despite a causal relationship, and vice-versa. While the drawing of causal inferences is informed by scientific expertise, it is not a determination that is made by using scientific methodology.

110. *See* Mervyn Susser, Causal Thinking in the Health Sciences: Concepts and Strategies in Epidemiology (1973); *In re* Joint E. & S. Dist. Asbestos Litig., 52 F.3d 1124, 1128–30 (2d Cir. 1995) (discussing lower courts' use of factors to decide whether an inference of causation is justified when an association exists).

111. Berry v. CSX Transp., Inc., 709 So. 2d 552, 568 n.12 (Fla. Dist. Ct. App. 1998) ("Almost all genres of research articles in the medical and behavioral sciences conclude their discussion with qualifying statements such as 'there is still much to be learned.' This is not, as might be assumed, an expression of ignorance, but rather an expression that all scientific fields are open-ended and can progress from their present state . . . ."); Hall v. Baxter Healthcare Corp., 947 F. Supp. 1387 App. B. at 1446–51 (D. Or. 1996) (report of Merwyn R. Greenlick, court-appointed epidemiologist). In *Cadarian v. Merrell Dow Pharmaceuticals, Inc.,* 745 F. Supp. 409 (E.D. Mich. 1989), the court refused to permit an expert to rely on a study that the authors had concluded should not be used to support an inference of causation in the absence of independent confirmatory studies. The court did not address the question whether the degree of certainty used by epidemiologists before making a conclusion of cause was consistent with the legal standard. *See* DeLuca v. Merrell Dow Pharms., Inc., 911 F.2d 941, 957 (3d Cir. 1990) (standard of proof for scientific community is not necessarily appropriate standard for expert opinion in civil litigation); Wells v. Ortho Pharm. Corp., 788 F.2d 741, 745 (11th Cir.), *cert. denied,* 479 U.S. 950 (1986).

These guidelines reflect criteria proposed by the U.S. Surgeon General in 1964[112] in assessing the relationship between smoking and lung cancer and expanded upon by A. Bradford Hill in 1965.[113]

A. Is There a Temporal Relationship?

A temporal, or chronological, relationship must exist for causation. If an exposure causes disease, the exposure must occur before the disease develops.[114] If the exposure occurs after the disease develops, it cannot cause the disease. Although temporal relationship is often listed as one of many factors in assessing whether an inference of causation is justified, it is a necessary factor: Without exposure before disease, causation cannot exist.

B. How Strong Is the Association Between the Exposure and Disease?[115]

The relative risk is one of the cornerstones for causal inferences.[116] Relative risk measures the strength of the association. The higher the relative risk, the greater the likelihood that the relationship is causal.[117] For cigarette smoking, for example, the estimated relative risk for lung cancer is very high, about 10.[118] That is, the risk of lung cancer in smokers is approximately ten times the risk in nonsmokers.

A relative risk of 10, as seen with smoking and lung cancer, is so high that it is extremely difficult to imagine any bias or confounding factor that might account for it. The higher the relative risk, the stronger the association and the lower the chance that the effect is spurious. Although lower relative risks can

112. U.S. Dep't of Health, Educ., and Welfare, Public Health Serv., Smoking and Health: Report of the Advisory Committee to the Surgeon General (1964).

113. A. Bradford Hill, *The Environment and Disease: Association or Causation?*, 58 Proc. Royal Soc'y Med. 295 (1965) (Hill acknowledged that his factors could only serve to assist in the inferential process: "None of my nine viewpoints can bring indisputable evidence for or against the cause-and-effect hypothesis and none can be required as a *sine qua non*.").

114. *See* Carroll v. Litton Sys., Inc., No. B-C-88-253, 1990 U.S. Dist. LEXIS 16833, at *29 (W.D.N.C. Oct. 29, 1990) ("[I]t is essential for . . . [the plaintiffs' medical experts opining on causation] to know that exposure preceded plaintiffs' alleged symptoms in order for the exposure to be considered as a possible cause of those symptoms . . . .").

115. Assuming that an association is determined to be causal, the strength of the association plays an important role legally in determining the specific causation question—whether the agent caused an individual plaintiff's injury. *See infra* § VII.

116. *See supra* § III.A.

117. *See* Cook v. United States, 545 F. Supp. 306, 316 n.4 (N.D. Cal. 1982); Landrigan v. Celotex Corp., 605 A.2d 1079, 1085 (N.J. 1992). The use of the strength of the association as a factor does not reflect a belief that weaker effects occur less frequently than stronger effects. *See* Green, *supra* note 39, at 652–53 n.39. Indeed, the apparent strength of a given agent is dependent on the prevalence of the other necessary elements that must occur with the agent to produce the disease, rather than on some inherent characteristic of the agent itself. *See* Rothman & Greenland, *supra* note 49, at 9–11.

118. *See* Doll & Hill, *supra* note 7.

reflect causality, the epidemiologist will scrutinize such associations more closely because there is a greater chance that they are the result of uncontrolled confounding or biases.

C. Is There a Dose–Response Relationship?

A dose–response relationship means that the more intense the exposure, the greater the risk of disease. Generally, higher exposures should increase the incidence (or severity) of disease. However, some causal agents do not exhibit a dose–response relationship when, for example, there is a threshold phenomenon (i.e., an exposure may not cause disease until the exposure exceeds a certain dose).[119] Thus, a dose–response relationship is strong, but not essential, evidence that the relationship between an agent and disease is causal.

D. Have the Results Been Replicated?

Rarely, if ever, does a single study conclusively demonstrate a cause–effect relationship.[120] It is important that a study be replicated in different populations and by different investigators before a causal relationship is accepted by epidemiologists and other scientists.

The need to replicate research findings permeates most fields of science. In epidemiology, research findings often are replicated in different populations.[121] Consistency in these findings is an important factor in making a judgment about causation. Different studies that examine the same exposure–disease relationship

119. The question whether there is a no-effect threshold dose is a controversial one in a variety of toxic substances areas. *See, e.g.*, Irving J. Selikoff, Disability Compensation for Asbestos-Associated Disease in the United States: Report to the U.S. Department of Labor 181–220 (1981); Paul Kotin, *Dose–Response Relationships and Threshold Concepts*, 271 Annals N.Y. Acad. Sci. 22 (1976); K. Robock, *Based on Available Data, Can We Project an Acceptable Standard for Industrial Use of Asbestos? Absolutely*, 330 Annals N.Y. Acad. Sci. 205 (1979); Ferebee v. Chevron Chem. Co., 736 F.2d 1529, 1536 (D.C. Cir.) (dose–response relationship for low doses is "one of the most sharply contested questions currently being debated in the medical community"), *cert. denied*, 469 U.S. 1062 (1984); *In re* TMI Litig. Consol. Proc., 927 F. Supp. 834, 844–45 (M.D. Pa. 1996) (discussing low-dose extrapolation and no-dose effects for radiation exposure).

Moreover, good evidence to support or refute the threshold-dose hypothesis is exceedingly unlikely because of the inability of epidemiology or animal toxicology to ascertain very small effects. *Cf.* Arnold L. Brown, *The Meaning of Risk Assessment*, 37 Oncology 302, 303 (1980). Even the shape of the dose–response curve—whether linear or curvilinear, and if the latter, the shape of the curve—is a matter of hypothesis and speculation. *See* Allen v. United States, 588 F. Supp. 247, 419–24 (D. Utah 1984), *rev'd on other grounds*, 816 F.2d 1417 (10th Cir. 1987), *cert. denied*, 484 U.S. 1004 (1988); Troyen A. Brennan & Robert F. Carter, *Legal and Scientific Probability of Causation for Cancer and Other Environmental Disease in Individuals*, 10 J. Health Pol'y & L. 33, 43–44 (1985).

120. In *Kehm v. Procter & Gamble Co.*, 580 F. Supp. 890, 901 (N.D. Iowa 1982), *aff'd sub nom.* Kehm v. Procter & Gamble Mfg. Co., 724 F.2d 613 (8th Cir. 1983), the court remarked on the persuasive power of multiple independent studies, each of which reached the same finding of an association between toxic shock syndrome and tampon use.

121. *See* Cadarian v. Merrell Dow Pharms., Inc., 745 F. Supp. 409, 412 (E.D. Mich. 1989) (hold-

generally should yield similar results. While inconsistent results do not rule out a causal nexus, any inconsistencies signal a need to explore whether different results can be reconciled with causality.

E. Is the Association Biologically Plausible (Consistent with Existing Knowledge)?[122]

Biological plausibility is not an easy criterion to use and depends upon existing knowledge about the mechanisms by which the disease develops. When biological plausibility exists, it lends credence to an inference of causality. For example, the conclusion that high cholesterol is a cause of coronary heart disease is plausible because cholesterol is found in atherosclerotic plaques. However, observations have been made in epidemiologic studies that were not biologically plausible at the time but subsequently were shown to be correct. When an observation is inconsistent with current biological knowledge, it should not be discarded, but the observation should be confirmed before significance is attached to it. The saliency of this factor varies depending on the extent of scientific knowledge about the cellular and subcellular mechanisms through which the disease process works. The mechanisms of some diseases are understood better than the mechanisms of others.

F. Have Alternative Explanations Been Considered?

The importance of considering the possibility of bias and confounding and ruling out the possibilities was discussed above.[123]

G. What Is the Effect of Ceasing Exposure?

If an agent is a cause of a disease one would expect that cessation of exposure to that agent ordinarily would reduce the risk of the disease. This has been the case, for example, with cigarette smoking and lung cancer. In many situations, however, relevant data are simply not available regarding the possible effects of ending the exposure. But when such data are available and eliminating exposure reduces the incidence of disease, this factor strongly supports a causal relationship.

ing a study on Bendectin insufficient to support an expert's opinion, because "the study's authors themselves concluded that the results could not be interpreted without independent confirmatory evidence").

122. A number of courts have adverted to this criterion in the course of their discussions of causation in toxic substances cases. *E.g.*, Cook v. United States, 545 F. Supp. 306, 314–15 (N.D. Cal. 1982) (discussing biological implausibility of a two-peak increase of disease when plotted against time); Landrigan v. Celotex Corp., 605 A.2d 1079, 1085–86 (N.J. 1992) (discussing the existence vel non of biological plausibility). *See also* Bernard D. Goldstein & Mary Sue Henifin, Reference Guide on Toxicology, § III.E, in this manual.

123. *See supra* § IV.B–C.

H. Does the Association Exhibit Specificity?

An association exhibits specificity if the exposure is associated only with a single disease or type of disease.[124] The vast majority of agents do not cause a wide variety of effects. For example, asbestos causes mesothelioma and lung cancer and may cause one or two other cancers, but there is no evidence that it causes any other types of cancers. Thus, a study that finds that an agent is associated with many different diseases should be examined skeptically. Nevertheless, there may be causal relationships in which this guideline is not satisfied. Cigarette manufacturers have long claimed that because cigarettes have been linked to lung cancer, emphysema, bladder cancer, heart disease, pancreatic cancer, and other conditions, there is no specificity and the relationships are not causal. There is, however, at least one good reason why inferences about the health consequences of tobacco do not require specificity: because tobacco and cigarette smoke are not in fact single agents but consist of numerous harmful agents, smoking represents exposure to multiple agents, with multiple possible effects. Thus, while evidence of specificity may strengthen the case for causation, lack of specificity does not necessarily undermine it where there is a plausible biological explanation for its absence.

I. Are the Findings Consistent with Other Relevant Knowledge?

In addressing the causal relationship of lung cancer to cigarette smoking, researchers examined trends over time for lung cancer and for cigarette sales in the United States. A marked increase in lung cancer death rates in men was observed, which appeared to follow the increase in sales of cigarettes. Had the increase in lung cancer deaths followed a decrease in cigarette sales, it might have given researchers pause. It would not have precluded a causal inference, but the inconsistency of the trends in cigarette sales and lung cancer mortality would have had to be explained.

124. This criterion reflects the fact that although an agent causes one disease, it does not necessarily cause other diseases. *See, e.g.*, Nelson v. American Sterilizer Co., 566 N.W.2d 671, 676–77 (Mich. Ct. App. 1997) (affirming dismissal of plaintiff's claims that chemical exposure caused her liver disorder, but recognizing that evidence supported claims for neuropathy and other illnesses); Sanderson v. International Flavors & Fragrances, Inc., 950 F. Supp. 981, 996–98 (C.D. Cal. 1996).

VI. What Methods Exist for Combining the Results of Multiple Studies?

Not infrequently, the court may be faced with a number of epidemiologic studies whose findings differ. These may be studies in which one shows an association and the other does not, or studies which report associations, but of different magnitude. In view of the fact that epidemiologic studies may disagree and that often many of the studies are small and lack the statistical power needed for definitive conclusions, the technique of meta-analysis was developed.[125] Meta-analysis is a method of pooling study results to arrive at a single figure to represent the totality of the studies reviewed. It is a way of systematizing the time-honored approach of reviewing the literature, which is characteristic of science, and placing it in a standardized framework with quantitative methods for estimating risk. In a meta-analysis, studies are given different weights in proportion to the sizes of their study populations and other characteristics.[126]

Meta-analysis is most appropriate when used in pooling randomized experimental trials, because the studies included in the meta-analysis share the most significant methodological characteristics, in particular, use of randomized assignment of subjects to different exposure groups. However, often one is confronted with non-randomized observational studies of the effects of possible toxic substances or agents. A method for summarizing such studies is greatly needed, but when meta-analysis is applied to observational studies—either case-control or cohort—it becomes more problematic. The reason for this is that often methodological differences among studies are much more pronounced than they are in randomized trials. Hence, the justification for pooling the results and deriving a single estimate of risk, for example, is not always apparent.

A number of problems and issues arise in meta-analysis. Should only published papers be included in the meta-analysis, or should any available studies be used, even if they have not been peer reviewed? How can the problem of differences in the quality of the studies reviewed be taken into account? Can the results of the meta-analysis itself be reproduced by other analysts? When there

125. *See In re* Paoli R.R. Yard PCB Litig., 916 F.2d 829, 856 (3d Cir. 1990), *cert. denied*, 499 U.S. 961 (1991); Hines v. Consolidated Rail Corp., 926 F.2d 262, 273 (3d Cir. 1991); Allen v. International Bus. Mach. Corp., No. 94-264-LON, 1997 U.S. Dist. LEXIS 8016, at *71–*74 (meta-analysis of observational studies is a controversial subject among epidemiologists). Thus, contrary to the suggestion by at least one court, multiple studies with small numbers of subjects may be pooled to reduce the possibility that sampling error is biasing the outcome. *See In re* Joint E. & S. Dist. Asbestos Litig., 827 F. Supp. 1014, 1042 (S.D.N.Y. 1993) ("[N]o matter how many studies yield a positive but statistically insignificant SMR for colorectal cancer, the results remain statistically insignificant. Just as adding a series of zeros together yields yet another zero as the product, adding a series of positive but statistically insignificant SMRs together does not produce a statistically significant pattern."), *rev'd*, 52 F.3d 1124 (2d Cir. 1995); *see also supra* note 76.

126. Petitti, *supra* note 76.

are several meta-analyses of a given relationship, why do the results of different meta-analyses often disagree? Another consideration is that often the differences among the individual studies included in a meta-analysis and the reasons for the differences are important in themselves and need to be understood; however, they may be masked in a meta-analysis. A final problem with meta-analyses is that they generate a single estimate of risk and may lead to a false sense of security regarding the certainty of the estimate. People often tend to have an inordinate belief in the validity of the findings when a single number is attached to them, and many of the difficulties that may arise in conducting a meta-analysis, especially of observational studies like epidemiologic ones, may consequently be overlooked.[127]

VII. What Role Does Epidemiology Play in Proving Specific Causation?

Epidemiology is concerned with the incidence of disease in populations and does not address the question of the cause of an individual's disease.[128] This question, sometimes referred to as specific causation, is beyond the domain of the science of epidemiology. Epidemiology has its limits at the point where an

127. Much has been written about meta-analysis recently, and some experts consider the problems of meta-analysis to outweigh the benefits at the present time. For example, Bailar has written the following:

> [P]roblems have been so frequent and so deep, and overstatements of the strength of conclusions so extreme, that one might well conclude there is something seriously and fundamentally wrong with the method. For the present . . . I still prefer the thoughtful, old-fashioned review of the literature by a knowledgeable expert who explains and defends the judgments that are presented. We have not yet reached a stage where these judgments can be passed on, even in part, to a formalized process such as meta-analysis.

John C. Bailar III, *Assessing Assessments*, 277 Science 528, 529 (1997) (reviewing Morton Hunt, How Science Takes Stock (1997)); *see also Point/Counterpoint: Meta-analysis of Observational Studies*, 140 Am. J. Epidemiology 770 (1994).

128. *See* DeLuca v. Merrell Dow Pharms., Inc., 911 F.2d 941, 945 & n.6 (3d Cir. 1990) ("Epidemiological studies do not provide direct evidence that a particular plaintiff was injured by exposure to a substance."); Smith v. Ortho Pharm. Corp., 770 F. Supp. 1561, 1577 (N.D. Ga. 1991); Grassis v. Johns-Manville Corp., 591 A.2d 671, 675 (N.J. Super. Ct. App. Div. 1991); Michael Dore, *A Commentary on the Use of Epidemiological Evidence in Demonstrating Cause-in-Fact*, 7 Harv. Envtl. L. Rev. 429, 436 (1983).

There are some diseases that do not occur without exposure to a given toxic agent. This is the same as saying that the toxic agent is a necessary cause for the disease, and the disease is sometimes referred to as a signature disease (also, the agent is pathognomonic), because the existence of the disease necessarily implies the causal role of the agent. *See* Kenneth S. Abraham & Richard A. Merrill, *Scientific Uncertainty in the Courts*, Issues Sci. & Tech., Winter 1986, at 93, 101. Asbestosis is a signature disease for asbestos, and adenocarcinoma (in young adult women) is a signature disease for in utero DES exposure. *See In re* "Agent Orange" Prod. Liab. Litig., 597 F. Supp. 740, 834 (E.D.N.Y. 1984) (Agent Orange allegedly caused a wide variety of diseases in Vietnam veterans and their offspring), *aff'd*, 818 F.2d 145 (2d Cir. 1987), *cert. denied*, 484 U.S. 1004 (1988).

inference is made that the relationship between an agent and a disease is causal (general causation) and where the magnitude of excess risk attributed to the agent has been determined; that is, epidemiology addresses whether an agent can cause a disease, not whether an agent did cause a specific plaintiff's disease.[129]

Nevertheless, the specific causation issue is a necessary legal element in a toxic substance case. The plaintiff must establish not only that the defendant's agent is capable of causing disease but also that it did cause the plaintiff's disease. Thus, a number of courts have confronted the legal question of what is acceptable proof of specific causation and the role that epidemiologic evidence plays in answering that question.[130] This question is not a question that is addressed by epidemiology.[131] Rather, it is a legal question a number of courts have grappled with. An explanation of how these courts have resolved this question follows. The remainder of this section should be understood as an explanation of judicial opinions, not as epidemiology.

Before proceeding, one last caveat is in order. This section assumes that epidemiologic evidence has been used as proof of causation for a given plaintiff. The discussion does not address whether a plaintiff must use epidemiologic evidence to prove causation.[132]

Two legal issues arise with regard to the role of epidemiology in proving individual causation: admissibility and sufficiency of evidence to meet the burden of production. The first issue tends to receive less attention by the courts but nevertheless deserves mention. An epidemiologic study that is sufficiently rigorous to justify a conclusion that it is scientifically valid should be admissible,[133] as it tends to make an issue in dispute more or less likely.[134]

129. *Cf. "Agent Orange,"* 597 F. Supp. at 780.

130. In many instances causation can be established without epidemiologic evidence. When the mechanism of causation is well understood, the causal relationship is well established, or the timing between cause and effect is close, scientific evidence of causation may not be required. This is frequently the situation when the plaintiff suffers traumatic injury rather than disease. This section addresses only those situations in which causation is not evident and scientific evidence is required.

131. Nevertheless, an epidemiologist may be helpful to the fact finder in answering this question. Some courts have permitted epidemiologists (or those who use epidemiologic methods) to testify about specific causation. *See* Ambrosini v. Labarraque, 101 F.3d 129, 137–41 (D.C. Cir. 1996), *cert. dismissed*, 520 U.S. 1205 (1997); Zuchowicz v. United States, 870 F. Supp. 15 (D. Conn. 1994); Landrigan v. Celotex Corp., 605 A.2d 1079, 1088–89 (N.J. 1992). In general, courts seem more concerned with the basis of an expert's opinion than with whether the expert is an epidemiologist or clinical physician. *See* Porter v. Whitehall, 9 F.3d 607, 614 (7th Cir. 1992) ("curb side" opinion from clinician not admissible); Wade-Greaux v. Whitehall Labs., 874 F. Supp. 1441, 1469–72 (D.V.I.) (clinician's multiple bases for opinion inadequate to support causation opinion), *aff'd*, 46 F.3d 1120 (3d Cir. 1994); *Landrigan*, 605 A.2d at 1083–89 (permitting both clinicians and epidemiologists to testify to specific causation provided the methodology used is sound).

132. *See* Green, *supra* note 39, at 672–73; 2 Modern Scientific Evidence, *supra* note 2, § 28-1.3.2 to -1.3.3, at 306–11.

133. *See DeLuca*, 911 F.2d at 958; *cf.* Kehm v. Procter & Gamble Co., 580 F. Supp. 890, 902 (N.D. Iowa 1982) ("These [epidemiologic] studies were highly probative on the issue of causation—they all

Far more courts have confronted the role that epidemiology plays with regard to the sufficiency of the evidence and the burden of production. The civil burden of proof is described most often as requiring the fact finder to "believe that what is sought to be proved . . . is more likely true than not true."[135] The relative risk from epidemiologic studies can be adapted to this 50% plus standard to yield a probability or likelihood that an agent caused an individual's disease.[136] An important caveat is necessary, however. The discussion below speaks in terms of the magnitude of the relative risk or association found in a study. However, before an association or relative risk is used to make a statement about the probability of individual causation, the inferential judgment, described in section V, that the association is truly causal rather than spurious is required: "[A]n agent cannot be considered to cause the illness of a specific person unless

concluded that an association between tampon use and menstrually related TSS [toxic shock syndrome] cases exists."), *aff'd sub nom.* Kehm v. Procter & Gamble Mfg. Co., 724 F.2d 613 (8th Cir. 1984).

Hearsay concerns may limit the independent admissibility of the study (*see supra* note 3), but the study could be relied on by an expert in forming an opinion and may be admissible pursuant to Fed. R. Evid. 703 as part of the underlying facts or data relied on by the expert.

In *Ellis v. International Playtex, Inc.*, 745 F.2d 292, 303 (4th Cir. 1984), the court concluded that certain epidemiologic studies were admissible despite criticism of the methodology used in the studies. The court held that the claims of bias went to the studies' weight rather than their admissibility. *Cf.* Christophersen v. Allied-Signal Corp., 939 F.2d 1106, 1109 (5th Cir. 1991) ("As a general rule, questions relating to the bases and sources of an expert's opinion affect the weight to be assigned that opinion rather than its admissibility . . . . "), *cert. denied*, 503 U.S. 912 (1992).

134. Even if evidence is relevant, it may be excluded if its probative value is substantially outweighed by prejudice, confusion, or inefficiency. Fed. R. Evid. 403. However, exclusion of an otherwise relevant epidemiologic study on Rule 403 grounds is unlikely.

In *Daubert v. Merrell Dow Pharmaceuticals, Inc.*, 509 U.S. 579, 591 (1993), the Court invoked the concept of "fit," which addresses the relationship of an expert's scientific opinion to the facts of the case and the issues in dispute. In a toxic substance case in which cause in fact is disputed, an epidemiologic study of the same agent to which the plaintiff was exposed that examined the association with the same disease from which the plaintiff suffers would undoubtedly have sufficient "fit" to be a part of the basis of an expert's opinion. The Court's concept of "fit," borrowed from *United States v. Downing*, 753 F.2d 1224, 1242 (3d Cir. 1985), appears equivalent to the more familiar evidentiary concept of probative value, albeit one requiring assessment of the scientific reasoning the expert used in drawing inferences from methodology or data to opinion.

135. 2 Edward J. Devitt & Charles B. Blackmar, Federal Jury Practice and Instruction § 71.13 (3d ed. 1977); *see also* United States v. Fatico, 458 F. Supp. 388, 403 (E.D.N.Y. 1978) ("Quantified, the preponderance standard would be 50%+ probable."), *aff'd*, 603 F.2d 1053 (2d Cir. 1979), *cert. denied*, 444 U.S. 1073 (1980).

136. An adherent of the frequentist school of statistics would resist this adaptation, which may explain why so many epidemiologists and toxicologists also resist it. To take the step identified in the text of using an epidemiologic study outcome to determine the probability of specific causation requires a shift from a frequentist approach, which involves sampling or frequency data from an empirical test, to a subjective probability about a discrete event. Thus, a frequentist might assert, after conducting a sampling test, that 60% of the balls in an opaque container are blue. The same frequentist would resist the statement, "The probability that a single ball removed from the box and hidden behind a screen is blue is 60%." The ball is either blue or not, and no frequentist data would permit the latter statement. "[T]here is no logically rigorous definition of what a statement of probability means with reference to an individual instance . . . ." Lee Loevinger, *On Logic and Sociology*, 32 Jurimetrics J. 527, 530 (1992); *see*

it is recognized as a cause of that disease in general."[137] The following discussion should be read with this caveat in mind.[138]

The threshold for concluding that an agent was more likely than not the cause of an individual's disease is a relative risk greater than 2.0. Recall that a relative risk of 1.0 means that the agent has no effect on the incidence of disease. When the relative risk reaches 2.0, the agent is responsible for an equal number of cases of disease as all other background causes. Thus, a relative risk of 2.0 (with certain qualifications noted below) implies a 50% likelihood that an exposed individual's disease was caused by the agent. A relative risk greater than 2.0 would permit an inference that an individual plaintiff's disease was more likely than not caused by the implicated agent.[139] A substantial number of courts in a variety of toxic substances cases have accepted this reasoning.[140]

also Steve Gold, Note, *Causation in Toxic Torts: Burdens of Proof, Standards of Persuasion and Statistical Evidence*, 96 Yale L.J. 376, 382–92 (1986). Subjective probabilities about discrete events are the product of adherents to Bayes Theorem. *See* Kaye, *supra* note 67, at 54–62; David H. Kaye & David A. Freedman, Reference Guide on Statistics § IV.D, in this manual.

137. Cole, *supra* note 53, at 10284.

138. We emphasize this caveat, both because it is not intuitive and because some courts have failed to appreciate the difference between an association and a causal relationship. *See, e.g.*, Forsyth v. Eli Lilly & Co., Civ. No. 95-00185 ACK, 1998 U.S. Dist. LEXIS 541, at *26–*31 (D. Haw. Jan. 5, 1998). *But see* Berry v. CSX Transp., Inc., 709 So. 2d 552, 568 (Fla. Dist. Ct. App. 1998) ("From epidemiological studies demonstrating an association, an epidemiologist may or may not infer that a causal relationship exists.").

139. *See* Davies v. Datapoint Corp., No. 94-56-P-DMC, 1995 U.S. Dist. LEXIS 21739, at *32–*35 (D. Me. Oct. 31, 1995) (holding that epidemiologist could testify about specific causation, basing such testimony on the probabilities derived from epidemiologic evidence).

140. *See* DeLuca v. Merrell Dow Pharms., Inc., 911 F.2d 941, 958–59 (3d Cir. 1990) (Bendectin allegedly caused limb reduction birth defects); *In re* Joint E. & S. Dist. Asbestos Litig., 964 F.2d 92 (2d Cir. 1992) (relative risk less than 2.0 may still be sufficient to prove causation); Daubert v. Merrell Dow Pharms., Inc., 43 F.3d 1311, 1320 (9th Cir.) (requiring that plaintiff demonstrate a relative risk of 2), *cert. denied*, 516 U.S. 869 (1995); Pick v. American Med. Sys., Inc., 958 F. Supp. 1151, 1160 (E.D. La. 1997) (recognizing that a relative risk of 2 implies a 50% probability of specific causation, but recognizing that a study with a lower relative risk is admissible, although ultimately it may be insufficient to support a verdict on causation); Sanderson v. International Flavors & Fragrances, Inc., 950 F. Supp. 981, 1000 (C.D. Cal. 1996) (acknowledging a relative risk of 2 as a threshold for plaintiff to prove specific causation); Manko v. United States, 636 F. Supp. 1419, 1434 (W.D. Mo. 1986) (swine flu vaccine allegedly caused Guillain-Barré syndrome), *aff'd in part*, 830 F.2d 831 (8th Cir. 1987); Marder v. G.D. Searle & Co., 630 F. Supp. 1087, 1092 (D. Md. 1986) (pelvic inflammatory disease allegedly caused by Copper 7 IUD), *aff'd without op. sub nom.* Wheelahan v. G.D. Searle & Co., 814 F.2d 655 (4th Cir. 1987); *In re* "Agent Orange" Prod. Liab. Litig., 597 F. Supp. 740, 835–37 (E.D.N.Y. 1984) (Agent Orange allegedly caused a wide variety of diseases in Vietnam veterans and their offspring), *aff'd*, 818 F.2d 145 (2d Cir. 1987), *cert. denied*, 484 U.S. 1004 (1988); Cook v. United States, 545 F. Supp. 306, 308 (N.D. Cal. 1982) (swine flu vaccine allegedly caused Guillain-Barré syndrome); Landrigan v. Celotex Corp., 605 A.2d 1079, 1087 (N.J. 1992) (relative risk greater than 2.0 "support[s] an inference that the exposure was the probable cause of the disease in a specific member of the exposed population"); Merrell Dow Pharms., Inc. v. Havner, 953 S.W.2d 706, 718 (Tex. 1997) ("The use of scientifically reliable epidemiological studies and the requirement of more than a doubling of the risk strikes a balance between the needs of our legal system and the limits of science."). *But cf. In re* Fibreboard Corp., 893 F.2d 706, 711–12 (5th Cir. 1990) (The court disapproved a trial in which several representative

An alternative, yet similar, means to address probabilities in individual cases is use of the attributable risk parameter.[141] The attributable risk is a measurement of the excess risk that can be attributed to an agent, above and beyond the background risk that is due to other causes.[142] When the attributable risk exceeds 50% (equivalent to a relative risk greater than 2.0), this logically might lead one to believe that the agent was more likely than not the cause of the plaintiff's disease.

The discussion above contains a number of assumptions: that the study was unbiased, sampling error and confounding were judged unlikely or minimal, the causal factors discussed in section V point toward causation, and the relative risk found in the study is a reasonably accurate measure of the extent of disease caused by the agent. It also assumes that the plaintiff in a given case is comparable to the subjects who made up the exposed cohort in the epidemiologic study and that there are no interactions with other causal agents.[143]

Evidence in a given case may challenge one or more of those assumptions. Bias in a study may suggest that the outcome found is inaccurate and should be estimated to be higher or lower than the actual result. A plaintiff may have been exposed to a dose of the agent in question that is greater or lower than that to which those in the study were exposed.[144] A plaintiff may have individual factors, such as higher age than those in the study, that make it less likely that

cases would be tried and the results extrapolated to a class of some 3,000 asbestos victims, without consideration of any evidence about the individual victims. The court remarked that under Texas law, general causation, which ignores any proof particularistic to the individual plaintiff, could not be substituted for cause in fact.).

141. *See supra* § III.C.

142. Because cohort epidemiologic studies compare the incidences (rates) of disease, measures like the relative risk and attributable risk are dependent on the time period during which disease is measured in the study groups. Exposure to the agent may either accelerate the onset of the disease in a subject who would have contracted the disease at some later time—all wrongful death cases entail acceleration of death—or be the cause of disease that otherwise would never have occurred in the subject. This creates some uncertainty (when pathological information does not permit determining which of the foregoing alternatives is the case) and ambiguity about the proper calculation of the attributable risk, that is, whether both alternatives should be included in the excess risk or just the latter. *See* Sander Greenland & James M. Robins, *Conceptual Problems in the Definition and Interpretation of Attributable Fractions*, 128 Am. J. Epidemiology 1185 (1988). If information were available, the legal issue with regard to acceleration would be the characterization of the harm and the appropriate amount of damages when a defendant's tortious conduct accelerates development of the disease. *See* Restatement (Second) of Torts § 924 cmt. e (1977); Keeton et al., *supra* note 107, § 52, at 353–54; Robert J. Peaslee, *Multiple Causation and Damages*, 47 Harv. L. Rev. 1127 (1934).

143. *See* Greenland & Robins, *supra* note 142, at 1193.

144. *See supra* § V.C; *see also* Ferebee v. Chevron Chem. Co., 736 F.2d 1529, 1536 (D.C. Cir.) ("The dose–response relationship at low levels of exposure for admittedly toxic chemicals like paraquat is one of the most sharply contested questions currently being debated in the medical community."), *cert. denied*, 469 U.S. 1062 (1984); *In re* Joint E. & S. Dist. Asbestos Litig., 774 F. Supp. 113, 115 (S.D.N.Y. 1991) (discussing different relative risks associated with different doses), *rev'd on other grounds*, 964 F.2d 92 (2d Cir. 1992).

exposure to the agent caused the plaintiff's disease. Similarly, an individual plaintiff may be able to rule out other known (background) causes of the disease, such as genetics, that increase the likelihood that the agent was responsible for that plaintiff's disease. Pathological-mechanism evidence may be available for the plaintiff that is relevant to the cause of the plaintiff's disease.[145] Before any causal relative risk from an epidemiologic study can be used to estimate the probability that the agent in question caused an individual plaintiff's disease, consideration of these (and similar) factors is required.[146]

Having additional evidence that bears on individual causation has led a few courts to conclude that a plaintiff may satisfy his or her burden of production even if a relative risk less than 2.0 emerges from the epidemiologic evidence.[147] For example, genetics might be known to be responsible for 50% of the incidence of a disease independent of exposure to the agent.[148] If genetics can be ruled out in an individual's case, then a relative risk greater than 1.5 might be sufficient to support an inference that the agent was more likely than not responsible for the plaintiff's disease.[149]

145. *See* Tobin v. Astra Pharm. Prods., Inc., 993 F.2d 528 (6th Cir.) (plaintiff's expert relied predominantly on pathogenic evidence), *cert. denied*, 510 U.S. 914 (1993).

146. *See* Merrell Dow Pharms., Inc. v. Havner, 953 S.W.2d 706, 720 (Tex. 1997); Mary Carter Andrues, Note, *Proof of Cancer Causation in Toxic Waste Litigation*, 61 S. Cal. L. Rev. 2075, 2100–04 (1988). An example of a judge sitting as fact finder and considering individual factors for a number of plaintiffs in deciding cause in fact is contained in *Allen v. United States*, 588 F. Supp. 247, 429–43 (D. Utah 1984), *rev'd on other grounds*, 816 F.2d 1417 (10th Cir. 1987), *cert. denied*, 484 U.S. 1004 (1988); *see also* Manko v. United States, 636 F. Supp. 1419, 1437 (W.D. Mo. 1986), *aff'd*, 830 F.2d 831 (8th Cir. 1987).

147. *See, e.g.*, Grassis v. Johns-Manville Corp., 591 A.2d 671, 675 (N.J. Super. Ct. App. Div. 1991): "The physician or other qualified expert may view the epidemiological studies and factor out other known risk factors such as family history, diet, alcohol consumption, smoking . . . or other factors which might enhance the remaining risks, even though the risk in the study fell short of the 2.0 correlation." *See also In re* Joint E. & S. Dist. Asbestos Litig., 52 F.3d 1124 (2d Cir. 1995) (holding that plaintiff could provide sufficient evidence of causation without proving a relative risk greater than 2); *In re* Joint E. & S. Dist. Asbestos Litig., 964 F.2d 92, 97 (2d Cir. 1992), *rev'g* 758 F. Supp. 199, 202–03 (S.D.N.Y. 1991) (requiring relative risk in excess of 2.0 for plaintiff to meet burden of production); Jones v. Owens-Corning Fiberglas Corp., 672 A.2d 230 (N.J. Super. Ct. App. Div. 1996).

148. *See In re* Paoli R.R. Yard PCB Litig., 35 F.3d 717, 758–59 (3d Cir. 1994) (discussing the technique of differential diagnosis to rule out other known causes of a disease for a specific individual).

149. The use of probabilities in excess of .50 to support a verdict results in an all-or-nothing approach to damages that some commentators have criticized. The criticism reflects the fact that defendants responsible for toxic agents with a relative risk just above 2.0 may be required to pay damages not only for the disease that their agents caused, but also for all instances of the disease. Similarly, those defendants whose agents increase the risk of disease by less than a doubling may not be required to pay damages for any of the disease that their agents caused. *See, e.g.*, 2 American Law Inst., Reporter's Study on Enterprise Responsibility for Personal Injury: Approaches to Legal and Institutional Change 369–75 (1991). To date, courts have not adopted a rule that would apportion damages based on the probability of cause in fact in toxic substances cases.

Glossary of Terms

The following terms and definitions were adapted from a variety of sources, including A Dictionary of Epidemiology (John M. Last et al. eds. 3d ed. 1995); 1 Joseph L. Gastwirth, Statistical Reasoning in Law and Public Policy (1988); James K. Brewer, Everything You Always Wanted To Know About Statistics, But Didn't Know How To Ask (1978); and R.A. Fisher, Statistical Methods for Research Workers (1973).

adjustment. Methods of modifying an observed association to take into account the effect of risk factors that are not the focus of the study and that distort the observed association between the exposure being studied and the disease outcome. See also direct age adjustment, indirect age adjustment.

agent. Also, risk factor. A factor, such as a drug, microorganism, chemical substance, or form of radiation, whose presence or absence can result in the occurrence of a disease. A disease may be caused by a single agent or a number of independent alternative agents, or the combined presence of a complex of two or more factors may be necessary for the development of the disease.

alpha. The level of statistical significance chosen by a researcher to determine if any association found in a study is sufficiently unlikely to have occurred by chance (as a result of random sampling error) if the null hypothesis (no association) is true. Researchers commonly adopt an alpha of .05, but the choice is arbitrary and other values can be justified.

alpha error. Also called type I error and false positive error, alpha error occurs when a researcher rejects a null hypothesis when it is actually true (i.e., when there is no association). This can occur when an apparent difference is observed between the control group and the exposed group, but the difference is not real (i.e., it occurred by chance). A common error made by lawyers, judges, and academics is to equate the level of alpha with the legal burden of proof.

association. The degree of statistical relationship between two or more events or variables. Events are said to be associated when they occur more or less frequently together than one would expect by chance. Association does not necessarily imply a causal relationship. Events are said not to have an association when the agent (or independent variable) has no apparent effect on the incidence of a disease (the dependent variable). This corresponds to a relative risk of 1.0. A negative association means that the events occur less frequently together than one would expect by chance, thereby implying a preventive or protective role for the agent (e.g., a vaccine).

attributable proportion of risk (PAR). This term has been used to denote the fraction of risk that is attributable to exposure to a substance (e.g., *X*% of lung cancer is attributable to cigarettes). Synonymous terms include attributable fraction, attributable risk, and etiologic fraction. See attributable risk.

attributable risk. The proportion of disease in exposed individuals that can be attributed to exposure to an agent, as distinguished from the proportion of disease attributed to all other causes.

background risk of disease. Background risk of disease (or background rate of disease) is the rate of disease in a population that has no known exposures to an alleged risk factor for the disease. For example, the background risk for all birth defects is 3%–5% of live births.

beta error. Also called type II error and false negative error, beta error occurs when a researcher fails to reject a null hypothesis when it is incorrect (i.e., when there is an association). This can occur when no statistically significant difference is detected between the control group and the exposed group, but a difference does exist.

bias. Any effect at any stage of investigation or inference tending to produce results that depart systematically from the true values. In epidemiology, the term bias does not necessarily carry an imputation of prejudice or other subjective factor, such as the experimenter's desire for a particular outcome. This differs from conventional usage, in which bias refers to a partisan point of view.

biological marker. A physiological change in tissue or body fluids that occurs as a result of an exposure to an agent and that can be detected in the laboratory. Biological markers are only available for a small number of chemicals.

biological plausibility. Consideration of existing knowledge about human biology and disease pathology to provide a judgment about the plausibility that an agent causes a disease.

case-comparison study. See case-control study.

case-control study. Also, case-comparison study, case history study, case referent study, retrospective study. A study that starts with the identification of persons with a disease (or other outcome variable) and a suitable control (comparison, reference) group of persons without the disease. Such a study is often referred to as retrospective because it starts after the onset of disease and looks back to the postulated causal factors.

case group. A group of individuals who have been exposed to the disease, intervention, procedure, or other variable whose influence is being studied.

causation. Causation, as we use the term, denotes an event, condition, characteristic, or agent's being a necessary element of a set of other events that can produce an outcome, such as a disease. Other sets of events may also cause the disease. For example, smoking is a necessary element of a set of events that result in lung cancer, yet there are other sets of events (without smoking) that cause lung cancer. Thus, a cause may be thought of as a necessary link in at least one causal chain that results in an outcome of interest. Epidemiologists generally speak of causation in a group context; hence, they will inquire whether an increased incidence of a disease in a cohort was "caused" by exposure to an agent.

clinical trial. An experimental study that is performed to assess the efficacy and safety of a drug or other beneficial treatment. Unlike observational studies, clinical trials can be conducted as experiments and use randomization, because the agent being studied is thought to be beneficial.

cohort. Any designated group of persons followed or traced over a period of time to examine health or mortality experience.

cohort study. The method of epidemiologic study in which groups of individuals can be identified who are, have been, or in the future may be differentially exposed to an agent or agents hypothesized to influence the probability of occurrence of a disease or other outcome. The groups are observed to find out if the exposed group is more likely to develop disease. The alternative terms for a cohort study (concurrent study, follow-up study, incidence study, longitudinal study, prospective study) describe an essential feature of the method, which is observation of the population for a sufficient number of person-years to generate reliable incidence or mortality rates in the population subsets. This generally implies study of a large population, study for a prolonged period (years), or both.

confidence interval. A range of values calculated from the results of a study within which the true value is likely to fall; the width of the interval reflects random error. Thus, if a confidence level of .95 is selected for a study, 95% of similar studies would result in the true relative risk falling within the confidence interval. The width of the confidence interval provides an indication of the precision of the point estimate or relative risk found in the study; the narrower the confidence interval, the greater the confidence in the relative risk estimate found in the study. Where the confidence interval contains a relative risk of 1.0, the results of the study are not statistically significant.

confounding factor. Also, confounder. A factor that is both a risk factor for the disease and a factor associated with the exposure of interest. Confounding refers to a situation in which the effects of two processes are not separated. The distortion can lead to an erroneous result.

control group. A comparison group comprising individuals who have not been exposed to the disease, intervention, procedure, or other variable whose influence is being studied.

cross-sectional study. A study that examines the relationship between disease and variables of interest as they exist in a population at a given time. A cross-sectional study measures the presence or absence of disease and other variables in each member of the study population. The data are analyzed to determine if there is a relationship between the existence of the variables and disease. Because cross-sectional studies examine only a particular moment in time, they reflect the prevalence (existence) rather than the incidence (rate) of disease and can offer only a limited view of the causal association between the variables and disease. Because exposures to toxic agents often change over time, cross-sectional studies are rarely used to assess the toxicity of exogenous agents.

data dredging. Jargon that refers to results identified by researchers who, after completing a study, pore through their data seeking to find any associations that may exist. In general, good research practice is to identify the hypotheses to be investigated in advance of the study; hence, data dredging is generally frowned on. In some cases, however, researchers conduct exploratory studies designed to generate hypotheses for further study.

demographic study. See ecological study.

dependent variable. The outcome that is being assessed in a study based on the effect of another characteristic—the independent variable. Epidemiologic studies attempt to determine whether there is an association between the independent variable (exposure) and the dependent variable (incidence of disease).

differential misclassification. A form of bias that is due to the misclassification of individuals or a variable of interest when the misclassification varies among study groups. This type of bias occurs when, for example, individuals in a study are incorrectly determined to be unexposed to the agent being studied when in fact they are exposed. See nondifferential misclassification.

direct adjustment. A technique used to eliminate any difference between two study populations based on age, sex, or some other parameter that might result in confounding. Direct adjustment entails comparison of the study group with a large reference population to determine the expected rates based on the characteristic, such as age, for which adjustment is being performed.

dose. Dose generally refers to the intensity or magnitude of exposure to an agent multiplied by the duration of exposure. Dose may be used to refer only to the intensity of exposure.

dose–response relationship. A relationship in which a change in amount, intensity, or duration of exposure to an agent is associated with a change—either an increase or a decrease—in risk of disease.

double-blinding. A characteristic used in experimental studies in which neither the individuals being studied nor the researchers know during the study whether any individual has been assigned to the exposed or control group. Double-blinding is designed to prevent knowledge of the group to which the individual was assigned from biasing the outcome of the study.

ecological fallacy. An error that occurs when a correlation between an agent and disease in a group (ecological) is not reproduced when individuals are studied. For example, at the ecological (group) level, a correlation has been found in several studies between the quality of drinking water and mortality rates from heart disease; it would be an ecological fallacy to infer from this alone that exposure to water of a particular level of hardness necessarily influences the individual's chances of contracting or dying of heart disease.

ecological study. Also, demographic study. A study of the occurrence of disease based on data from populations, rather than from individuals. An ecological study searches for associations between the incidence of disease and suspected disease-causing agents in the studied populations. Researchers often conduct ecological studies by examining easily available health statistics, making these studies relatively inexpensive in comparison with studies that measure disease and exposure to agents on an individual basis.

epidemiology. The study of the distribution and determinants of disease or other health-related states and events in populations and the application of this study to control of health problems.

error. Random error (sampling error) is the error that is due to chance when the result obtained for a sample differs from the result that would be obtained if the entire population (universe) were studied.

etiologic factor. An agent that plays a role in causing a disease.

etiology. The cause of disease or other outcome of interest.

experimental study. A study in which the researcher directly controls the conditions. Experimental epidemiology studies (also clinical studies) entail random assignment of participants to the exposed and control groups (or some other method of assignment designed to minimize differences between the groups).

exposed, exposure. In epidemiology, the exposed group (or the exposed) is used to describe a group whose members have been exposed to an agent that may be a cause of a disease or health effect of interest, or possess a characteristic that is a determinant of a health outcome.

false negative error. See beta error.

false positive error. See alpha error.

follow-up study. See cohort study.

general causation. General causation is concerned with whether an agent increases the incidence of disease in a group and not whether the agent caused any given individual's disease. Because of individual variation, a toxic agent generally will not cause disease in every exposed individual.

generalizable. A study is generalizable when the results are applicable to populations other than the study population, such as the general population.

in vitro. Within an artificial environment, such as a test tube (e.g., the cultivation of tissue in vitro).

in vivo. Within a living organism (e.g., the cultivation of tissue in vivo).

incidence rate. The number of people in a specified population falling ill from a particular disease during a given period. More generally, the number of new events (e.g., new cases of a disease in a defined population) within a specified period of time.

incidence study. See cohort study.

independent variable. A characteristic that is measured in a study and that is suspected to have an effect on the outcome of interest (the dependent variable). Thus, exposure to an agent is measured in a cohort study to determine whether that independent variable has an effect on the incidence of disease, which is the dependent variable.

indirect adjustment. A technique employed to minimize error that might result when comparing two populations because of differences in age, sex, or another parameter that may affect the rate of disease in the populations. The rate of disease in a large reference population, such as all residents of a country, is calculated and adjusted for any differences in age between the reference population and the study population. This adjusted rate is compared with the rate of disease in the study population and provides a standardized mortality (or morbidity) ratio, which is often referred to as SMR.

inference. The intellectual process of making generalizations from observations. In statistics, the development of generalizations from sample data, usually with calculated degrees of uncertainty.

information bias. Also, observational bias. Systematic error in measuring data that results in differential accuracy of information (such as exposure status) for comparison groups.

interaction. Risk factors interact, or there is interaction among risk factors, when the magnitude or direction (positive or negative) of the effect of one risk factor differs depending on the presence or level of the other. In interaction, the effect of two risk factors together is different (greater or less) than their individual effects.

meta-analysis. A technique used to combine the results of several studies to enhance the precision of the estimate of the effect size and reduce the plausibility that the association found is due to random sampling error. Meta-analysis is best suited to pooling results from randomly controlled experimental studies, but if carefully performed, it also may be useful for observational studies.

misclassification bias. The erroneous classification of an individual in a study as exposed to the agent when the individual was not, or incorrectly classifying a study individual with regard to disease. Misclassification bias may exist in all study groups (nondifferential misclassification) or may vary among groups (differential misclassification).

morbidity rate. Morbidity is the state of illness or disease. Morbidity rate may refer to the incidence rate or prevalence rate of disease.

mortality rate. Mortality refers to death. The mortality rate expresses the proportion of a population that dies of a disease or of all causes. The numerator is the number of individuals dying; the denominator is the total population in which the deaths occurred. The unit of time is usually a calendar year.

model. A representation or simulation of an actual situation. This may be either (1) a mathematical representation of characteristics of a situation that can be manipulated to examine consequences of various actions; (2) a representation of a country's situation through an "average region" with characteristics resembling those of the whole country; or (3) the use of animals as a substitute for humans in an experimental system to ascertain an outcome of interest.

multivariate analysis. A set of techniques used when the variation in several variables has to be studied simultaneously. In statistics, any analytic method that allows the simultaneous study of two or more independent factors or variables.

nondifferential misclassification. A form of bias that is due to misclassification of individuals or a variable of interest into the wrong category when the misclassification varies among study groups. This bias may result from limitations in data collection and will often produce an underestimate of the true association. See differential misclassification.

null hypothesis. A hypothesis that states that there is no true association between a variable and an outcome. At the outset of any observational or experimental study, the researcher must state a proposition that will be tested in the study. In epidemiology, this proposition typically addresses the existence of an association between an agent and a disease. Most often, the null hypothesis is a statement that exposure to Agent A does not increase the occurrence of Disease D. The results of the study may justify a conclusion that the null hypothesis (no association) has been disproved (e.g., a study that finds a strong association between smoking and lung cancer). A study may fail to disprove the null hypothesis, but that alone does not justify a conclusion that the null hypothesis has been proved.

observational study. An epidemiologic study in situations in which nature is allowed to take its course, without intervention from the investigator. For example, in an observational study the subjects of the study are permitted to determine their level of exposure to an agent.

odds ratio (OR). Also, cross-product ratio, relative odds. The ratio of the odds that a case (one with the disease) was exposed to the odds that a control (one without the disease) was exposed. For most purposes the odds ratio from a case-control study is quite similar to a risk ratio from a cohort study.

pathognomonic. An agent is pathognomonic when it must be present for a disease to occur. Thus, asbestos is a pathognomonic agent for asbestosis. See signature disease.

placebo controlled. In an experimental study, providing an inert substance to the control group, so as to keep the control and exposed groups ignorant of their status.

***p*(probability), *p*-value.** The *p*-value is the probability of getting a value of the test outcome equal to or more extreme than the result observed, given that the null hypothesis is true. The letter *p*, followed by the abbreviation "n.s." (not significant) means that $p > .05$ and that the association was not statistically significant at the .05 level of significance. The statement "$p < .05$" means that *p* is less than 5%, and, by convention, the result is deemed statistically significant. Other significance levels can be adopted, such as .01 or .1. The lower the *p*-value, the less likely that random error would have produced the observed relative risk if the true relative risk is 1.

power. The probability that a difference of a specified amount will be detected by the statistical hypothesis test, given that a difference exists. In less formal terms, power is like the strength of a magnifying lens in its capability to identify an association that truly exists. Power is equivalent to one minus type II error. This is sometimes stated as Power $= 1 - \beta$.

prevalence. The percentage of persons with a disease in a population at a specific point in time.

prospective study. In a prospective study, two groups of individuals are identified: (1) individuals who have been exposed to a risk factor and (2) individuals who have not been exposed. Both groups are followed for a specified length of time, and the proportion that develops disease in the first group is compared with the proportion that develops disease in the second group. See cohort study.

random. The term implies that an event is governed by chance. See randomization.

randomization. Assignment of individuals to groups (e.g., for experimental and control regimens) by chance. Within the limits of chance variation, randomization should make the control group and experimental group similar at the start of an investigation and ensure that personal judgment and prejudices of the investigator do not influence assignment. Randomization should not be confused with haphazard assignment. Random assignment follows a predetermined plan that usually is devised with the aid of a table of random numbers. Randomization cannot ethically be used where the exposure is known to cause harm (e.g., cigarette smoking).

randomized trial. See clinical trial.

recall bias. Systematic error resulting from differences between two groups in a study in accuracy of memory. For example, subjects who have a disease may recall exposure to an agent more frequently than subjects who do not have the disease.

relative risk (RR). The ratio of the risk of disease or death among people exposed to an agent to the risk among the unexposed. For instance, if 10% of all people exposed to a chemical develop a disease, compared with 5% of people who are not exposed, the disease occurs twice as frequently among the exposed people. The relative risk is 10%/5% = 2. A relative risk of 1 indicates no association between exposure and disease.

research design. The procedures and methods, predetermined by an investigator, to be adhered to in conducting a research project.

risk. A probability that an event will occur (e.g., that an individual will become ill or die within a stated period of time or by a certain age).

sample. A selected subset of a population. A sample may be random or nonrandom.

sample size. The number of subjects who participate in a study.

secular-trend study. Also, time-line study. A study that examines changes over a period of time, generally years or decades. Examples include the decline of tuberculosis mortality and the rise, followed by a decline, in coronary heart disease mortality in the United States in the past fifty years.

selection bias. Systematic error that results from individuals being selected for the different groups in an observational study who have differences other than the ones that are being examined in the study.

sensitivity, specificity. Sensitivity measures the accuracy of a diagnostic or screening test or device in identifying disease (or some other outcome) when it truly exists. For example, assume that we know that 20 women in a group of 1,000 women have cervical cancer. If the entire group of 1,000 women is tested for cervical cancer and the screening test only identifies 15 (of the known 20) cases of cervical cancer, the screening test has a sensitivity of 15/20, or 75%. Specificity measures the accuracy of a diagnostic or screening test in identifying those who are disease free. Once again, assume that 980 women out of a group of 1,000 women do not have cervical cancer. If the entire group of 1,000 women is screened for cervical cancer and the screening test only identifies 900 women as without cervical cancer, the screening test has a specificity of 900/980, or 92%.

signature disease. A disease that is associated uniquely with exposure to an agent (e.g., asbestosis and exposure to asbestos). See also pathognomonic.

significance level. A somewhat arbitrary level selected to minimize the risk that an erroneous positive study outcome that is due to random error will be accepted as a true association. The lower the significance level selected, the less likely that false positive error will occur.

specific causation. Whether exposure to an agent was responsible for a given individual's disease.

standardized morbidity ratio (SMR). The ratio of the incidence of disease observed in the study population to the incidence of disease that would be expected if the study population had the same incidence of disease as some selected standard or known population.

standardized mortality ratio (SMR). The ratio of the incidence of death observed in the study population to the incidence of death that would be expected if the study population had the same incidence of death as some selected standard or known population.

statistical significance. A term used to describe a study result or difference that exceeds the type I error rate (or *p*-value) that was selected by the researcher at the outset of the study. In formal significance testing, a statistically significant result is unlikely to be the result of random sampling error and justifies rejection of the null hypothesis. Some epidemiologists believe that formal significance testing is inferior to using a confidence interval to express the results of a study. Statistical significance, which addresses the role of random sampling error in producing the results found in the study, should not be confused with the importance (for public health or public policy) of a research finding.

stratification. The process of or result of separating a sample into several subsamples according to specified criteria, such as age or socioeconomic status. Researchers may control the effect of confounding variables by stratifying the analysis of results. For example, lung cancer is known to be associated with smoking. To examine the possible association between urban atmospheric pollution and lung cancer, the researcher may divide the population into strata according to smoking status, thus controlling for smoking. The association between air pollution and cancer then can be appraised separately within each stratum.

study design. See research design.

systematic error. See bias.

teratogen. An agent that produces abnormalities in the embryo or fetus by disturbing maternal health or by acting directly on the fetus in utero.

teratogenicity. The capacity for an agent to produce abnormalities in the embryo or fetus.

threshold phenomenon. A certain level of exposure to an agent below which disease does not occur and above which disease does occur.

time-line study. See secular-trend study.

toxicology. The science of the nature and effects of poisons. Toxicologists study adverse health effects of agents on biological organisms.

toxic substance. A substance that is poisonous.

true association. Also, real association. The association that really exists between exposure to an agent and a disease and that might be found by a perfect (but nonetheless nonexistent) study.

Type I error. Rejecting the null hypothesis when it is true. See alpha error.

Type II error. Failing to reject the null hypothesis when it is false. See beta error.

validity. The degree to which a measurement measures what it purports to measure; the accuracy of a measurement.

variable. Any attribute, condition, or other item in a study that can have different numerical characteristics. In a study of the causes of heart disease, blood pressure and dietary fat intake are variables that might be measured.

References on Epidemiology

Causal Inferences (Kenneth J. Rothman ed., 1988).

William G. Cochran, Sampling Techniques (1977).

A Dictionary of Epidemiology (John M. Last et al. eds., 3d ed. 1995).

Anders Ahlbom & Steffan Norell, Introduction to Modern Epidemiology (2d ed. 1990).

Joseph L. Fleiss, Statistical Methods for Rates and Proportions (1981).

Leon Gordis, Epidemiology (2d ed. 2000).

Morton Hunt, How Science Takes Stock: The Story of Meta-Analysis (1997).

Harold A. Kahn, An Introduction to Epidemiologic Methods (1983).

Harold A. Kahn & Christopher T. Sempos, Statistical Methods in Epidemiology (1989).

David E. Lilienfeld, *Overview of Epidemiology,* 3 Shepard's Expert & Sci. Evid. Q. 25 (1995).

David E. Lilienfeld & Paul D. Stolley, Foundations of Epidemiology (3d ed. 1994).

Judith S. Mausner & Anita K. Bahn, Epidemiology: An Introductory Text (1974).

Marcello Pagano & Kimberlee Gauvreau, Principles of Biostatistics (1993).

Richard K. Riegelman & Robert A. Hirsch, Studying a Study and Testing a Test: How to Read the Health Science Literature (3d ed. 1996).

Bernard Rosner, Fundamentals of Biostatistics (4th ed. 1995).

Kenneth J. Rothman & Sander Greenland, Modern Epidemiology (2d ed. 1998).

James J. Schlesselman, Case-Control Studies: Design, Conduct, Analysis (1982).

Mervyn Susser, Epidemiology, Health and Society: Selected Papers (1987).

References on Law and Epidemiology

2 American Law Institute, Reporters' Study on Enterprise Responsibility for Personal Injury (1991).

Bert Black & David H. Hollander, Jr., *Unraveling Causation: Back to the Basics,* 3 U. Balt. J. Envtl. L. 1 (1993).

Bert Black & David Lilienfeld, *Epidemiologic Proof in Toxic Tort Litigation,* 52 Fordham L. Rev. 732 (1984).

Gerald Boston, *A Mass-Exposure Model of Toxic Causation: The Content of Scientific Proof and the Regulatory Experience,* 18 Colum. J. Envtl. L. 181 (1993).

Vincent M. Brannigan et al., *Risk, Statistical Inference, and the Law of Evidence: The Use of Epidemiological Data in Toxic Tort Cases*, 12 Risk Analysis 343 (1992).

Troyen Brennan, *Causal Chains and Statistical Links: The Role of Scientific Uncertainty in Hazardous-Substance Litigation*, 73 Cornell L. Rev. 469 (1988).

Troyen Brennan, *Helping Courts with Toxic Torts: Some Proposals Regarding Alternative Methods for Presenting and Assessing Scientific Evidence in Common Law Courts*, 51 U. Pitt. L. Rev. 1 (1989).

Philip Cole, *Causality in Epidemiology, Health Policy, and Law*, [1997] 27 Envtl. L. Rep. (Envtl. L. Inst.) 10279 (June1997).

Comment, *Epidemiologic Proof of Probability: Implementing the Proportional Recovery Approach in Toxic Exposure Torts*, 89 Dick. L. Rev. 233 (1984).

George W. Conk, *Against the Odds: Proving Causation of Disease with Epidemiological Evidence*, 3 Shepard's Expert & Sci. Evid. Q. 85 (1995).

Carl F. Cranor et al., *Judicial Boundary Drawing and the Need for Context-Sensitive Science in Toxic Torts After* Daubert v. Merrell Dow Pharmaceuticals, Inc., 16 Va. Envtl. L.J. 1 (1996).

Richard Delgado, *Beyond Sindell: Relaxation of Cause-in-Fact Rules for Indeterminate Plaintiffs*, 70 Cal. L. Rev. 881 (1982).

Michael Dore, *A Commentary on the Use of Epidemiological Evidence in Demonstrating Cause-in-Fact*, 7 Harv. Envtl. L. Rev. 429 (1983).

Jean Macchiaroli Eggen, *Toxic Torts, Causation, and Scientific Evidence After* Daubert, 55 U. Pitt. L. Rev. 889 (1994).

Daniel A. Farber, *Toxic Causation*, 71 Minn. L. Rev. 1219 (1987).

Heidi Li Feldman, *Science and Uncertainty in Mass Exposure Litigation*, 74 Tex. L. Rev. 1 (1995).

Stephen E. Fienberg et al., *Understanding and Evaluating Statistical Evidence in Litigation*, 36 Jurimetrics J. 1 (1995).

Joseph L. Gastwirth, Statistical Reasoning in Law and Public Policy (1988).

Herman J. Gibb, *Epidemiology and Cancer Risk Assessment*, *in* Fundamentals of Risk Analysis and Risk Management 23 (Vlasta Molak ed., 1997).

Steve Gold, Note, *Causation in Toxic Torts: Burdens of Proof, Standards of Persuasion and Statistical Evidence*, 96 Yale L.J. 376 (1986).

Leon Gordis, *Epidemiologic Approaches for Studying Human Disease in Relation to Hazardous Waste Disposal Sites*, 25 Hous. L. Rev. 837 (1988).

Michael D. Green, *Expert Witnesses and Sufficiency of Evidence in Toxic Substances Litigation: The Legacy of Agent Orange and Bendectin Litigation*, 86 Nw. U. L. Rev. 643 (1992).

Khristine L. Hall & Ellen Silbergeld, *Reappraising Epidemiology: A Response to Mr. Dore*, 7 Harv. Envtl. L. Rev. 441 (1983).

Jay P. Kesan, *Drug Development: Who Knows Where the Time Goes?: A Critical Examination of the Post-*Daubert *Scientific Evidence Landscape*, 52 Food Drug Cosm. L.J. 225 (1997).

Constantine Kokkoris, Comment, DeLuca v. Merrell Dow Pharmaceuticals, Inc.: *Statistical Significance and the Novel Scientific Technique*, 58 Brook. L. Rev. 219 (1992).

James P. Leape, *Quantitative Risk Assessment in Regulation of Environmental Carcinogens*, 4 Harv. Envtl. L. Rev. 86 (1980).

David E. Lilienfeld, *Overview of Epidemiology*, 3 Shepard's Expert & Sci. Evid. Q. 23 (1995).

Junius McElveen, Jr., & Pamela Eddy, *Cancer and Toxic Substances: The Problem of Causation and the Use of Epidemiology*, 33 Clev. St. L. Rev. 29 (1984).

2 Modern Scientific Evidence: The Law and Science of Expert Testimony (David L. Faigman et al. eds.,1997).

Note, *The Inapplicability of Traditional Tort Analysis to Environmental Risks: The Example of Toxic Waste Pollution Victim Compensation*, 35 Stan. L. Rev. 575 (1983).

Susan R. Poulter, *Science and Toxic Torts: Is There a Rational Solution to the Problem of Causation?*, 7 High Tech. L.J. 189 (1992).

Jon Todd Powell, Comment, *How to Tell the Truth with Statistics: A New Statistical Approach to Analyzing the Data in the Aftermath of* Daubert v. Merrell Dow Pharmaceuticals, 31 Hous. L. Rev. 1241 (1994).

David Rosenberg, *The Causal Connection in Mass Exposure Cases: A Public Law Vision of the Tort System*, 97 Harv. L. Rev. 849 (1984).

Joseph Sanders, *The Bendectin Litigation: A Case Study in the Life-Cycle of Mass Torts*, 43 Hastings L.J. 301 (1992).

Joseph Sanders, *Scientific Validity, Admissibility, and Mass Torts After* Daubert, 78 Minn. L. Rev. 1387 (1994).

Richard W. Wright, *Causation in Tort Law*, 73 Cal. L. Rev. 1735 (1985).

Development in the Law—Confronting the New Challenges of Scientific Evidence, 108 Harv. L. Rev. 1481 (1995).

Reference Guide on Toxicology

BERNARD D. GOLDSTEIN AND MARY SUE HENIFIN

Bernard D. Goldstein, M.D., is Director, Environmental & Occupational Health Sciences Institute, Piscataway, New Jersey, and Chairman, Department of Environmental & Community Medicine, UMDNJ–Robert Wood Johnson Medical School, Piscataway, New Jersey.

Mary Sue Henifin, J.D., M.P.H., is a partner with Buchanan Ingersoll, P.C., Princeton, New Jersey, and Adjunct Professor of Public Health Law, Department of Environmental & Community Medicine, UMDNJ–Robert Wood Johnson Medical School, Piscataway, New Jersey.

CONTENTS

I. Introduction

Toxicology classically is known as the science of poisons. A modern definition is "the study of the adverse effects of chemicals on living organisms."[1] Although it is an age-old science, toxicology has only recently become a discipline distinct from pharmacology, biochemistry, cell biology, and related fields.

There are three central tenets of toxicology. First, "the dose makes the poison"; this implies that all chemical agents are intrinsically hazardous—whether they cause harm is only a question of dose.[2] Even water, if consumed in large quantities, can be toxic. Second, each chemical agent tends to produce a specific pattern of biological effects that can be used to establish disease causation.[3] Third, the toxic responses in laboratory animals are useful predictors of toxic responses in humans. Each of these tenets, and their exceptions, are discussed in greater detail in this reference guide.

The science of toxicology attempts to determine at what doses foreign agents produce their effects. The foreign agents of interest to toxicologists are all chemicals (including foods) and physical agents in the form of radiation, but not living organisms that cause infectious diseases.[4]

The discipline of toxicology provides scientific information relevant to the following questions:

1. What hazards does a chemical or physical agent present to human populations or the environment?
2. What degree of risk is associated with chemical exposure at any given dose?

Toxicological studies, by themselves, rarely offer direct evidence that a disease in any one individual was caused by a chemical exposure. However, toxicology can provide scientific information regarding the increased risk of contracting a disease at any given dose and help rule out other risk factors for the disease. Toxicological evidence also explains how a chemical causes a disease by describing metabolic, cellular, and other physiological effects of exposure.

1. Casarett and Doull's Toxicology: The Basic Science of Poisons 13 (Curtis D. Klaassen ed., 5th ed. 1996).

2. A discussion of more modern formulations of this principle, which was articulated by Paracelsus in the sixteenth century, can be found in Ellen K. Silbergeld, *The Role of Toxicology in Causation: A Scientific Perspective,* 1 Cts. Health Sci. & L. 374, 378 (1991).

3. Some substances, such as central nervous system toxicants, can produce complex and nonspecific symptoms, such as headaches, nausea, and fatigue.

4. Forensic toxicology, a subset of toxicology generally concerned with criminal matters, is not addressed in this reference guide, since it is a highly specialized field with its own literature and methodologies which do not relate directly to toxic tort or regulatory issues.

A. Toxicology and the Law

The growing concern about chemical causation of disease is reflected in the public attention devoted to lawsuits alleging toxic torts, as well as in litigation concerning the many federal and state regulations related to the release of potentially toxic compounds into the environment. These lawsuits inevitably involve toxicological evidence.

Toxicological evidence frequently is offered in two types of litigation: tort and regulatory. In tort litigation, toxicologists offer evidence that either supports or refutes plaintiffs' claims that their diseases or injuries were caused by chemical exposures.[5] In regulatory litigation, toxicological evidence is used to either support or challenge government regulations concerning a chemical or a class of chemicals. In regulatory litigation, toxicological evidence addresses the issue of how exposure affects populations rather than addressing specific causation, and agency determinations are usually subject to the court's deference.[6]

B. Purpose of the Reference Guide on Toxicology

This reference guide focuses on scientific issues that arise most frequently in toxic tort cases. Where it is appropriate, the reference guide explores the use of regulatory data and how the courts treat such data. The reference guide provides an overview of the basic principles and methodologies of toxicology and offers a scientific context for proffered expert opinion based on toxicological data.[7] The reference guide describes research methods in toxicology and the relationship between toxicology and epidemiology, and it provides model questions for evaluating the admissibility and strength of an expert's opinion. Following each question is an explanation of the type of toxicological data or information that is offered in response to the question, as well as a discussion of its significance.

5. *See, e.g.*, General Elec. Co. v. Joiner, 522 U.S. 136 (1997); Daubert v. Merrell Dow Pharms., Inc., 509 U.S. 579 (1993).

6. *See, e.g.*, Troy Corp. v. Browner, 129 F.3d 1290 (D.C. Cir. 1997) (EPA's decision to list chemical under Emergency Planning and Community Right to Know Act supported by substantial evidence in that animal studies demonstrated significant increases in pathology); AFL-CIO v. OSHA, 965 F.2d 962, 969–70 (11th Cir. 1992) (determinations of the Secretary of Labor are conclusive if supported by substantial evidence); Simpson v. Young, 854 F.2d 1429, 1435 (D.C. Cir. 1988) (toxicology research methods approved by the Food and Drug Administration (FDA) given deference by the court).

7. The use of toxicological evidence in regulatory decision making is discussed in more detail in Richard A. Merrill, *Regulatory Toxicology*, *in* Casarett and Doull's Toxicology: The Basic Science of Poisons, *supra* note 1, at 1011. For a more general discussion of issues that arise in considering expert testimony, see Margaret A. Berger, The Supreme Court's Trilogy on the Admissibility of Expert Testimony § IV, in this manual.

C. Toxicological Research Design

Toxicological research usually involves exposing laboratory animals (in vivo research) or cells or tissues (in vitro research) to chemicals, monitoring the outcomes (such as cellular abnormalities, tissue damage, organ toxicity, or tumor formation), and comparing the outcomes with those for unexposed control groups. As explained below,[8] the extent to which animal and cell experiments accurately predict human responses to chemical exposures is subject to debate.[9] However, because it is often unethical to experiment on humans by exposing them to known doses of chemical agents, animal toxicological evidence often provides the best scientific information about the risk of disease from a chemical exposure.[10]

In contrast to their exposure to drugs, only rarely are humans exposed to environmental chemicals in a manner that permits a quantitative determination of adverse outcomes.[11] This area of toxicological research, known as clinical toxicology, may consist of individual or multiple case reports, or even experimental studies in which individuals or groups of individuals have been exposed to a chemical under circumstances that permit analysis of dose–response relationships, mechanisms of action, or other aspects of toxicology. For example, individuals occupationally or environmentally exposed to polychlorinated biphenyls (PCBs) prior to prohibitions on their use have been studied to determine the routes of absorption, distribution, metabolism, and excretion for this chemical. Human exposure occurs most frequently in occupational settings where workers are exposed to industrial chemicals like lead or asbestos; however, even under these circumstances, it is usually difficult, if not impossible, to quantify the amount of exposure. Moreover, human populations are exposed to many other chemicals and risk factors, making it difficult to isolate the increased risk of a disease that is due to any one chemical.[12]

Toxicologists use a wide range of experimental techniques, depending in part on their area of specialization. Some of the more active areas of toxicological research are classes of chemical compounds, such as solvents and metals; body system effects, such as neurotoxicology, reproductive toxicology, and immunotoxicology; and effects on physiological processes, including inhalation toxicology, dermatotoxicology, and molecular toxicology (the study of how chemicals

8. *See infra* §§ I.D, III.A.

9. The controversy over the use of toxicological evidence in tort cases is described in Silbergeld, *supra* note 2, at 378.

10. *See, e.g.*, Office of Tech. Assessment, U.S. Congress, Reproductive Health Hazards in the Workplace 8 (1985).

11. However, it is from drug studies in which multiple animal species are compared directly with humans that many of the principles of toxicology have been developed.

12. *See, e.g.*, Office of Tech. Assessment, U.S. Congress, *supra* note 10, at 8.

interact with cell molecules). Each of these areas of research includes both in vivo and in vitro research.[13]

1. In vivo research

Animal research in toxicology generally falls under two headings: safety assessment and classic laboratory science, with a continuum in between. As explained in section I.E, safety assessment is a relatively formal approach in which a chemical's potential for toxicity is tested in vivo or in vitro using standardized techniques often prescribed by regulatory agencies, such as the Environmental Protection Agency (EPA) and the Food and Drug Administration (FDA).

The roots of toxicology in the science of pharmacology are reflected in an emphasis on understanding the absorption, distribution, metabolism, and excretion of chemicals. Basic toxicological laboratory research also focuses on the mechanisms of action of external chemical and physical agents. It is based on the standard elements of scientific studies, including appropriate experimental design using control groups and statistical evaluation. In general, toxicological research attempts to hold all variables constant except for that of the chemical exposure.[14] Any change in the experimental group not found in the control group is assumed to be perturbation caused by the chemical. An important component of toxicological research is dose–response relationships. Thus, most toxicological studies generally test a range of doses of the chemical.[15]

a. Dose–response relationships

Animal experiments are conducted to determine the dose–response relationships of a compound by measuring the extent of any observed effect at various doses and diligently searching for a dose that has no measurable physiological effect. This information is useful in understanding the mechanisms of toxicity and extrapolating data from animals to humans.[16]

b. Acute toxicity testing—lethal dose 50 (LD50)

To determine the dose–response relationship for a compound, a short-term lethal dose 50 (LD50) is derived experimentally. The LD50 is the dose at which a compound kills 50% of laboratory animals within a period of days to weeks.

13. *See infra* §§ I.C.1, I.C.2.

14. *See generally* Alan Poole & George B. Leslie, A Practical Approach to Toxicological Investigations (1989); Principles and Methods of Toxicology (A. Wallace Hayes ed., 2d ed. 1989); *see also* discussion on acute, short-term, and long-term toxicity studies and acquisition of data in Frank C. Lu, Basic Toxicology: Fundamentals, Target Organs, and Risk Assessment 77–92 (2d ed. 1991).

15. Rolf Hartung, *Dose–Response Relationships, in* Toxic Substances and Human Risk: Principles of Data Interpretation 29 (Robert G. Tardiff & Joseph V. Rodricks eds., 1987).

16. *See infra* §§ I.D, III.A.

The use of this easily measured end point for acute toxicity is being abandoned, in part because recent advances in toxicology have provided other pertinent end points, and in part because of pressure from animal rights activists to reduce or replace the use of animals in laboratory research.

c. No observable effect level (NOEL)

A dose–response study also permits determination of another important characteristic of the biological action of a chemical—the no observable effect level (NOEL).[17] The NOEL sometimes is called a threshold, since it is the level above which observable effects in test animals are believed to occur and below which no toxicity is observed.[18] Of course, since the NOEL is dependent on the ability to observe the effect, the level is sometimes lowered once more sophisticated methods of detection are developed.

d. No threshold model and determination of cancer risk

Certain genetic mutations, such as those leading to cancer and some inherited disorders, are believed to occur without any threshold. In theory, the cancer-causing mutation to the genetic material of the cell can be produced by any one molecule of certain chemicals. The no threshold model led to the development of the one hit theory of cancer risk, in which each molecule of a cancer-causing chemical has some finite possibility of producing the mutation that leads to cancer. This risk is very small, since it is unlikely that any one molecule of a potentially cancer-causing agent will reach that one particular spot in a specific cell and result in the change that then eludes the body's defenses and leads to a

17. For example, undiluted acid on the skin can cause a horrible burn. As the acid is diluted to lower and lower concentrations less and less of an effect occurs until there is a concentration sufficiently low (e.g., one drop in a bathtub of water, or a sample with less than the acidity of vinegar) that no effect occurs. This no observable effect concentration differs from person to person. For example, a baby's skin is more sensitive than that of an adult, and skin that is irritated or broken responds to the effects of an acid at a lower concentration. However, the key point is that there is some concentration that is completely harmless to the skin. *See, e.g.*, Paul Kotin, *Dose–Response Relationships and Threshold Concepts*, 271 Annals N.Y. Acad. Sci. 22 (1976).

18. The significance of the NOEL was relied on by the court in *Graham v. Canadian National Railway Co.*, 749 F. Supp. 1300 (D. Vt. 1990), in granting judgment for the defendants. The court found the defendant's expert, a medical toxicologist, persuasive. The expert testified that the plaintiffs' injuries could not have been caused by herbicides, since their exposure was well below the reference dose, which he calculated by taking the NOEL and decreasing it by a safety factor to ensure no human effect. *Id.* at 1311–12 & n.11. *But see* Louderback v. Orkin Exterminating Co., 26 F. Supp. 2d 1298 (D. Kan. 1998) (failure to consider threshold levels of exposure does not necessarily render expert's opinion unreliable where temporal relationship, scientific literature establishing an association between exposure and various symptoms, plaintiffs' medical records and history of disease, and exposure to or the presence of other disease-causing factors were all considered). For additional background on the concept of NOEL, see Robert G. Tardiff & Joseph V. Rodricks, *Comprehensive Risk Assessment, in* Toxic Substances and Human Risk: Principles of Data Interpretation, *supra* note 15, at 391.

clinical case of cancer. However, the risk is not zero. The same model also can be used to predict the risk of inheritable mutational events.[19]

e. Maximum tolerated dose (MTD) and chronic toxicity tests

Another type of study uses different doses of a chemical agent to establish over a 90-day period what is known as the maximum tolerated dose (MTD) (the highest dose that does not cause significant overt toxicity). The MTD is important because it enables researchers to calculate the dose of a chemical that an animal can be exposed to without reducing its life span, thus permitting evaluation of the chronic effects of exposure.[20] These studies are designed to last the lifetime of the species.

Chronic toxicity tests evaluate carcinogenicity or other types of toxic effects. Federal regulatory agencies frequently require carcinogenicity studies on both sexes of two species, usually rats and mice. A pathological evaluation is done on the tissues of animals that died during the study and those that are sacrificed at the conclusion of the study.

19. For further discussion of the no threshold model of carcinogenesis, see Office of Tech. Assessment, U.S. Congress, Assessment of Technologies for Determining the Cancer Risks from the Environment (1981); Henry C. Pitot III & Yvonne P. Dragan, *Chemical Carcinogenesis, in* Casarett and Doull's Toxicology: The Basic Science of Poisons, *supra* note 1, at 201, 254–55. *But see* Marvin Goldman, *Cancer Risk of Low-Level Exposure,* 271 Science 1821 (1996); V.P. Bond et al., *Current Misinterpretations of the Linear No-Threshold Hypothesis,* 70 Health Physics 877 (1996).

The no threshold model, as adopted by the Occupational Safety and Health Administration (OSHA) in its regulation of workplace carcinogens, has been upheld. Public Citizen Health Research Group v. Tyson, 796 F.2d 1479, 1498 (D.C. Cir. 1986) (as set forth in 29 C.F.R. § 1990.143(h) (1985), "no determination will be made that a 'threshold' or 'no effect' level of exposure can be established for a human population exposed to carcinogens in general, or to any specific substance"), *clarified sub nom.* Public Citizen Health Research Group v. Brock, 823 F.2d 626, 628 (D.C. Cir. 1987). *But see* Sutera v. Perrier Group of Am., Inc., 986 F. Supp. 655, 666–67 (D. Mass. 1997) (no scientific evidence that linear no-safe threshold analysis is an acceptable scientific technique as used by experts in this case to determine causation).

While the one hit model explains the response to most carcinogens, there is accumulating evidence that for certain cancers there is in fact a multistage process and that some cancer-causing agents act through nonmutational processes, so-called epigenetic or nongenotoxic agents. Committee on Risk Assessment Methodology, National Research Council, Issues in Risk Assessment 34–35, 187, 198–201 (1993). For example, the multistage cancer process may explain the carcinogenicity of benzo(a)pyrene (produced by the combustion of hydrocarbons such as oil) and chlordane (a termite pesticide). However, nonmutational responses to asbestos, dioxin, and estradiol cause their carcinogenic effects. What the appropriate mathematical model is to depict the dose–response relationship for such carcinogens is still a matter of debate. *Id.* at 197–201.

20. Even the determination of the MTD can be fraught with controversy. *See, e.g.,* Simpson v. Young, 854 F.2d 1429, 1431 (D.C. Cir. 1988) (petitioners unsuccessfully argued that the FDA improperly certified color additive Blue No. 2 dye as safe because researchers failed to administer the MTD to research animals, as required by FDA protocols). *See generally* David P. Rall, *Laboratory and Animal Toxicity and Carcinogenesis Testing: Underlying Concepts, Advantages and Constraints,* 534 Annals N.Y. Acad. Sci. 78 (1988); Frank B. Cross, Environmentally Induced Cancer and the Law: Risks, Regulation, and Victim Compensation 54–57 (1989).

The rationale for using the MTD in chronic toxicity tests, such as carcinogenicity bioassays, often is misunderstood. It is preferable to use realistic doses of carcinogens in all animal studies. However, this leads to a loss of statistical power, thereby limiting the ability of the test to detect carcinogens or other toxic compounds. Consider the situation in which a realistic dose of a chemical causes a tumor in 1 in 100 laboratory animals. If the lifetime background incidence of tumors in animals without exposure to the chemical is 6 in 100, a toxicological test involving 100 control animals and 100 exposed animals who were fed the realistic dose would be expected to reveal 6 control animals and 7 exposed animals with the cancer. This difference is too small to be recognized as statistically significant. However, if the study started with ten times the realistic dose, the researcher would expect to get 16 cases in the exposed group and 6 cases in the control group, a significant difference that is unlikely to be overlooked.

Unfortunately, even this example does not demonstrate the difficulties of determining risk.[21] Regulators are responding to public concern about cancer by regulating risks often as low as 1 in a million—not 1 in 100, as in the example given above. To test risks of 1 in a million, a researcher would have to either increase the lifetime dose from 10 times to 100,000 times the realistic dose or expand the numbers of animals under study into the millions. However, increases of this magnitude are beyond the world's animal-testing capabilities and are also prohibitively expensive. Inevitably, then, animal studies must trade statistical power for extrapolation from higher doses to lower doses.

Accordingly, proffered toxicological expert opinion on potentially cancer-causing chemicals almost always is based on a review of research studies that extrapolate from animal experiments involving doses significantly higher than that to which humans are exposed.[22] Such extrapolation is accepted in the regulatory arena. However, in toxic tort cases, experts often use additional background information[23] to offer opinions about disease causation and risk.[24]

21. *See, e.g.*, Committee on Risk Assessment Methodology, National Research Council, *supra* note 19, at 43–51.

22. *See, e.g.*, James Huff, *Chemicals and Cancer in Humans: First Evidence in Experimental Animals,* 100 Envtl. Health Persp. 201, 204 (1993); International Agency for Research on Cancer, World Health Org., *Preamble, in* 63 IARC Monographs on the Evaluation of Carcinogenic Risks to Humans 9, 17 (1995).

23. Researchers have developed numerous biomathematical formulas to provide statistical bases for extrapolation from animal data to human exposure. *See generally* Pitot & Dragen, *supra* note 19, at 255–57; Animal Models in Toxicology (Shayne Cox Gad & Christopher P. Chengelis eds., 1992); V.A. Filov et al., Quantitative Toxicology: Selected Topics (1979). *See also infra* §§ IV, V.

24. Policy arguments concerning extrapolation from low doses to high doses are explored in Troyen A. Brennan & Robert F. Carter, *Legal and Scientific Probability of Causation of Cancer and Other Environmental Disease in Individuals,* 10 J. Health Pol. Pol'y & L. 33 (1985).

2. *In vitro research*

In vitro research concerns the effects of a chemical on human or animal cells, bacteria, yeast, isolated tissues, or embryos. Thousands of in vitro toxicological tests have been described in the scientific literature. Many tests are for mutagenesis in bacterial or mammalian systems. There are short-term in vitro tests for just about every physiological response and every organ system, such as perfusion tests and DNA studies. Relatively few of these tests have been validated by replication in many different laboratories or by comparison with outcomes in animal studies to determine if they are predictive of whole-animal or human toxicity.[25]

Criteria of reliability for an in vitro test include the following: (1) whether the test has come through a published protocol in which many laboratories used the same in vitro method on a series of unknown compounds prepared by a reputable organization (such as the National Institutes of Health (NIH) or the International Agency for Research on Cancer (IARC)) to determine if the test consistently and accurately measures toxicity; (2) whether the test has been adopted by a U.S. or international regulatory body; and (3) whether the test is predictive of in vivo outcomes related to the same cell or target organ system.

D. *Extrapolation from Animal and Cell Research to Humans*

Two types of extrapolation must be considered: from animal data to humans and from higher doses to lower doses. In qualitative extrapolation, one can usually rely on the fact that a compound causing an effect in one mammalian species will cause it in another species. This is a basic principle of toxicology and pharmacology. If a heavy metal, such as mercury, causes kidney toxicity in laboratory animals, it is highly likely to do so at some dose in humans. However, the dose at which mercury causes this effect in laboratory animals is modified by many internal factors, and the exact dose–response curve may be different from that for humans. Through the study of factors that modify the toxic effects of chemicals, including absorption, distribution, metabolism, and excretion, researchers can improve the ability to extrapolate from laboratory animals to humans and from higher to lower doses.[26] Mathematical depiction of the process by which an external dose moves through various compartments in the body

25. *See generally* In Vitro Toxicity Testing: Applications to Safety Evaluation (John M. Frazier ed., 1992); In Vitro Methods in Toxicology (C.K. Atterwill & C.E. Steele eds., 1987) (discussion of the strengths and weaknesses of specific in vitro tests). Use of in vitro data for evaluating human mutagenicity and teratogenicity is described in John M. Rogers & Robert J. Kavlock, *Developmental Toxicology, in* Casarett and Doull's Toxicology: The Basic Science of Poisons, *supra* note 1, at 301, 319–21; George R. Hoffman, *Genetic Toxicology, in* Casarett and Doull's Toxicology: The Basic Science of Poisons, *supra* note 1, at 269, 277–93. For a critique of expert testimony using in vitro data, see *Wade-Greaux v. Whitehall Laboratories, Inc.*, 874 F. Supp. 1441, 1480 (D.V.I.), *aff'd*, 46 F.3d 1120 (3d Cir. 1994).

26. For example, benzene undergoes a complex metabolic sequence that results in toxicity to the

until it reaches the target organ is often called physiologically based pharmacokinetics.[27]

Extrapolation from studies in nonmammalian species to humans is much more difficult and can only be done if there is sufficient information on similarities in absorption, distribution, metabolism, and excretion; quantitative determinations of human toxicity based on in vitro studies usually are not considered appropriate. As discussed in section I.F, in vitro or animal data for elucidating mechanisms of toxicity are more persuasive when positive human epidemiological data also exist.[28]

E. Safety and Risk Assessment

Toxicological expert opinion also relies on formal safety and risk assessments. Safety assessment is the area of toxicology relating to the testing of chemicals and drugs for toxicity. It is a relatively formal approach in which the potential for toxicity of a chemical is tested in vivo or in vitro using standardized techniques. The protocols for such studies usually are developed through scientific consensus and are subject to oversight by governmental regulators or other watchdog groups.

After a number of bad experiences, including outright fraud, government agencies have imposed codes on laboratories involved in safety assessment, including industrial, contract, and in-house laboratories.[29] Known as Good Laboratory Practice (GLP), these codes govern many aspects of laboratory standards,

bone marrow in all species, including humans. Robert Snyder et al., *The Toxicology of Benzene,* 100 Envtl. Health Persp. 293 (1993). The exact metabolites responsible for this bone-marrow toxicity are the subject of much interest but remain unknown. Mice are more susceptible to benzene than are rats. If researchers could determine the differences between mice and rats in their metabolism of benzene, they would have a useful clue as to which portion of the metabolic scheme is responsible for benzene toxicity to the bone marrow. *See, e.g.*, Karl K. Rozman & Curtis D. Klaassen, *Absorption, Distribution, and Excretion of Toxicants, in* Casarett and Doull's Toxicology: The Basic Science of Poisons, *supra* note 1, at 91; Andrew Parkinson, *Biotransformation of Xenobiotics, in* Casarett and Doull's Toxicology: The Basic Science of Poisons, *supra* note 1, at 113.

27. For an analysis of methods used to extrapolate from animal toxicity data to human health effects, see, e.g., Robert E. Menzer, *Selection of Animal Models for Data Interpretation, in* Toxic Substances and Human Risk: Principles of Data Interpretation, *supra* note 15, at 133; Thomas J. Slaga, *Interspecies Comparisons of Tissue DNA Damage, Repair, Fixation and Replication,* 77 Envtl. Health Persp. 73 (1988); Lorenzo Tomatis, *The Predictive Value of Rodent Carcinogenicity Tests in the Evaluation of Human Risks,* 19 Ann. Rev. Pharmacol. & Toxicol. 511 (1979); Willard J. Visek, *Issues and Current Applications of Interspecies Extrapolation of Carcinogenic Potency as a Component of Risk Assessment,* 77 Envtl. Health Persp. 49 (1988); Gary P. Carlson, *Factors Modifying Toxicity, in* Toxic Substances and Human Risk: Principles of Data Interpretation, *supra* note 15, at 47; Michael D. Hogan & David G. Hoel, *Extrapolation to Man, in* Principles and Methods of Toxicology, *supra* note 14, at 879; James P. Leape, *Quantitative Risk Assessment in Regulation of Environmental Carcinogens,* 4 Harv. Envtl. L. Rev. 86 (1980).

28. *See, e.g.*, Goewey v. United States, 886 F. Supp. 1268, 1280–81 (D.S.C. 1995) (extrapolation of neurotoxic effects from chickens to humans unwarranted without human confirmation).

29. A dramatic case of fraud involving a toxicology laboratory that performed tests to assess the

including such details as the number of animals per cage, dose and chemical verification, and the handling of tissue specimens. GLP practices are remarkably similar across agencies, but the tests called for differ depending on mission. For example, there are major differences between the FDA's and the EPA's required procedures for testing drugs and environmental chemicals.[30] The FDA requires and specifies both efficacy and safety testing of drugs in humans and animals. Carefully controlled clinical trials using doses within the expected therapeutic range are required for premarket testing of drugs because exposures to prescription drugs are carefully controlled and should not exceed specified ranges or uses. However, for environmental chemicals and agents, no premarket testing in humans is required by the EPA. Moreover, since exposures are less predictable, a wider range of doses usually is given in the animal tests.[31]

Since exposures to environmental chemicals may continue over the lifetime and affect both young and old, test designs called lifetime bioassays have been developed in which relatively high doses are given to experimental animals. Interpretation of results requires extrapolation from animals to humans, from high to low doses, and from short exposures to multiyear estimates. It must be emphasized that less than 1% of the 60,000–75,000 chemicals in commerce have been subjected to a full safety assessment, and there are significant toxicological data on only 10%–20%.

Risk assessment is an approach increasingly used by regulatory agencies to estimate and compare the risks of hazardous chemicals and to assign priority for avoiding their adverse effects.[32] The National Academy of Sciences defines four components of risk assessment: hazard identification, dose–response estimation, exposure assessment, and risk characterization.[33]

Although risk assessment is not an exact science, it should be viewed as a

safety of consumer products is described in *United States v. Keplinger*, 776 F.2d 678 (7th Cir. 1985), *cert. denied*, 476 U.S. 1183 (1986). Keplinger and the other defendants in this case were toxicologists who were convicted of falsifying data on product safety by underreporting animal morbidity and mortality and omitting negative data and conclusions from their reports.

30. *See, e.g.*, 40 C.F.R. §§ 160, 792 (1993); Lu, *supra* note 14, at 89.

31. It must be appreciated that the development of a new drug inherently requires searching for an agent that at useful doses has a biological effect (e.g., decreasing blood pressure), whereas those developing a new chemical for consumer use (e.g., a house paint) hope that at usual doses no biological effects will occur. There are other compounds, such as pesticides and antibacterial agents, for which a biological effect is desired, but it is intended that at usual doses humans will not be affected. These different expectations are part of the rationale for the differences in testing information available for assessing toxicological effects.

32. Committee on Risk Assessment Methodology, National Research Council, *supra* note 19, at 1.

33. *See generally* National Research Council, Risk Assessment in the Federal Government: Managing the Process (1983); Bernard D. Goldstein, *Risk Assessment/Risk Management Is a Three-Step Process: In Defense of EPA's Risk Assessment Guidelines*, 7 J. Am. C. Toxicol. 543 (1988); Bernard D. Goldstein, *Risk Assessment and the Interface Between Science and Law*, 14 Colum. J. Envtl. L. 343 (1989).

useful estimate on which policy making can be based. In recent years, codification of the methodology used to assess risk has increased confidence that the process can be reasonably free of bias; however, significant controversy remains, particularly when actual data are limited and generally conservative default assumptions are used.[34]

While risk assessment information about a chemical can be somewhat useful in a toxic tort case, at least in terms of setting reasonable boundaries as to the likelihood of causation, the impetus for the development of risk assessment has been the regulatory process, which has different goals.[35] Because of their use of appropriately prudent assumptions in areas of uncertainty and their use of default assumptions when there are limited data, risk assessments intentionally encompass the upper range of possible risks.

F. Toxicology and Epidemiology

Epidemiology is the study of the incidence and distribution of disease in human populations. Clearly, both epidemiology and toxicology have much to offer in elucidating the causal relationship between chemical exposure and disease.[36] These sciences often go hand in hand in assessments of the risks of chemical exposure, without artificial distinctions being drawn between them. However, although courts generally rule epidemiological expert opinion admissible, admissibility of toxicological expert opinion has been more controversial because of uncertain-

34. An example of conservative default assumptions can be found in Superfund risk assessment. The EPA has determined that Superfund sites should be cleaned up to reduce cancer risk from 1 in 10,000 to 1 in 1,000,000. A number of assumptions can go into this calculation, including conservative assumptions about intake, exposure frequency and duration, and cancer-potency factors for the chemicals at the site. *See, e.g.*, Robert H. Harris & David E. Burmaster, *Restoring Science to Superfund Risk Assessment*, 6 Toxics L. Rep. (BNA) 1318 (Mar. 25, 1992).

35. *See, e.g.*, Ellen Relkin, *Use of Governmental and Industrial Standards of Exposure and Toxicological Data in Toxic Tort Litigation, reprinted in* Proving Causation of Disease: Update 1996, at 199 (New Jersey Inst. for Continuing Legal Educ. 1996); Steven Shavell, *Liability for Harm Versus Regulation of Safety*, 13 J. Legal Stud. 357 (1984). Risk assessment has been heavily criticized on a number of grounds. The major argument of industry has been that it is overly conservative and thus greatly overstates the actual risk. The rationale for conservatism is in part the prudent public health approach of "above all, do no harm." The conservative approach is also used, especially in regard to cancer risk, because it is sometimes more feasible to extrapolate to a plausible upper boundary for a risk estimate than it is to estimate a point of maximum likelihood. For a sample of the debate over risk assessment, see Bruce N. Ames & Lois S. Gold, *Too Many Rodent Carcinogens: Mitogenesis Increases Mutagenesis*, 249 Science 970 (1990); Jean Marx, *Animal Carcinogen Testing Challenged*, 250 Science 743 (1990); Philip H. Abelson, *Incorporation of a New Science into Risk Assessment*, 250 Science 1497 (1990); Frederica P. Perera, *Letter to the Editor: Carcinogens and Human Health, Part 1*, 250 Science 1644 (1990); Bruce N. Ames & Lois S. Gold, *Response*, 250 Science 1645 (1990); David P. Rall, *Letter to the Editor: Carcinogens and Human Health, Part 2*, 251 Science 10 (1991); Bruce N. Ames & Lois S. Gold, *Response*, 251 Science 12 (1991); John C. Bailar III et al., *One-Hit Models of Carcinogenesis: Conservative or Not?*, 8 Risk Analysis 485 (1988).

36. *See* Michael D. Green et al., Reference Guide on Epidemiology § V, in this manual.

ties regarding extrapolation from animal and in vitro data to humans. This particularly has been true in cases in which relevant epidemiological research data exist. However, the methodological weaknesses of some epidemiological studies, including their inability to accurately measure exposure and their small numbers of subjects, render these studies difficult to interpret.[37] In contrast, since animal and cell studies permit researchers to isolate the effects of exposure to a single chemical or to known mixtures, toxicological evidence offers unique information concerning dose–response relationships, mechanisms of action, specificity of response, and other information relevant to the assessment of causation.[38]

Even though there is little toxicological data on many of the 75,000 compounds in general commerce, there is far more information from toxicological studies than from epidemiological studies.[39] It is much easier, and more economical, to expose an animal to a chemical or to perform in vitro studies than it is to perform epidemiological studies. This difference in data availability is evident even for cancer causation, for which toxicological study is particularly expensive and time-consuming. Of the perhaps two dozen chemicals that reputable international authorities agree are known human carcinogens based on positive epidemiological studies, arsenic is the only one not known to be an animal carcinogen. Yet, there are more than 100 known animal carcinogens for which there is no valid epidemiological database, and a handful of others for which the epidemiological database is equivocal (e.g., butadiene).[40] To clarify

37. *Id.*

38. Both commonalities and differences between animal responses and human responses to chemical exposures were recognized by the court in *International Union, United Automobile, Aerospace and Agricultural Implement Workers of America v. Pendergrass,* 878 F.2d 389 (D.C. Cir. 1989). In reviewing the results of both epidemiological and animal studies on formaldehyde, the court stated: "Humans are not rats, and it is far from clear how readily one may generalize from one mammalian species to another. But in light of the epidemiological evidence [of carcinogenicity] that was not the main problem. Rather it was the absence of data at low levels." *Id.* at 394. The court remanded the matter to OSHA to reconsider its findings that formaldehyde presented no specific carcinogenic risk to workers at exposure levels of 1 part per million or less. *See also* Hopkins v. Dow Corning Corp., 33 F.3d 1116 (9th Cir. 1994); Ambrosini v. Labarraque, 101 F.3d 129, 141 (D.C. Cir. 1996).

39. *See generally* National Research Council, *supra* note 33. *See also* Lorenzo Tomatis et al., *Evaluation of the Carcinogenicity of Chemicals: A Review of the Monograph Program of the International Agency for Research on Cancer,* 38 Cancer Res. 877, 881 (1978); National Research Council, Toxicity Testing: Strategies to Determine Needs and Priorities (1984); Myra Karstadt & Renee Bobal, *Availability of Epidemiologic Data on Humans Exposed to Animal Carcinogens,* 2 Teratogenesis, Carcinogenesis & Mutagenesis 151 (1982).

40. The absence of epidemiological data is due, in part, to the difficulties in conducting cancer epidemiology studies, including the lack of suitably large groups of individuals exposed for a sufficient period of time, long latency periods between exposure and manifestation of disease, the high variability in the background incidence of many cancers in the general population, and the inability to measure actual exposure levels. These same concerns have led some researchers to conclude that "many negative epidemiological studies must be considered inconclusive" for exposures to low doses or weak carcinogens. Pitot & Dragan, *supra* note 19, at 240–41.

any findings, regulators can require a repeat of an equivocal two-year animal toxicological study or the performance of additional laboratory studies in which animals deliberately are exposed to the chemical. Such deliberate exposure is not possible in humans. As a general rule, equivocally positive epidemiological studies reflect prior workplace practices that led to relatively high levels of chemical exposure for a limited number of individuals and that, fortunately, in most cases no longer occur now. Thus, an additional prospective epidemiological study often is not possible, and even the ability to do retrospective studies is constrained by the passage of time.

II. Expert Qualifications

The basis of the toxicologist's expert opinion in a specific case is a thorough review of the research literature and treatises concerning effects of exposure to the chemical at issue. To arrive at an opinion, the expert assesses the strengths and weaknesses of the research studies. The expert also bases an opinion on fundamental concepts of toxicology relevant to understanding the actions of chemicals in biological systems.

As the following series of questions indicates, no single academic degree, research specialty, or career path qualifies an individual as an expert in toxicology. Toxicology is a heterogeneous field. A number of indicia of expertise can be explored, however, which are relevant to both the admissibility and weight of the proffered expert opinion.

A. Does the Proposed Expert Have an Advanced Degree in Toxicology, Pharmacology, or a Related Field? If the Expert Is a Physician, Is He or She Board Certified in a Field Such As Occupational Medicine?

A graduate degree in toxicology demonstrates that the proposed expert has a substantial background in the basic issues and tenets of toxicology. Many universities have established graduate programs in toxicology only recently. These programs are administered by the faculties of medicine, pharmacology, pharmacy, or public health.

Given the relatively recent establishment of academic toxicology programs, a number of highly qualified toxicologists are physicians or hold doctoral degrees in related disciplines (e.g., pharmacology, biochemistry, environmental health, or industrial hygiene). For a person with this type of background, a single course in toxicology is unlikely to provide sufficient background for developing expertise in the field.

A proposed expert should be able to demonstrate an understanding of the discipline of toxicology, including statistics, toxicological research methods, and disease processes. A physician without particular training or experience in toxicology is unlikely to have sufficient background to evaluate the strengths and weaknesses of toxicological research.[41] Most practicing physicians have little knowledge of environmental and occupational medicine. Generally, physicians are quite knowledgeable about identification of effects and their treatment. The cause of these effects, particularly if they are unrelated to the treatment of the disease, is generally of little concern to the practicing physician. Subspecialty physicians may have particular knowledge of a cause-and-effect relationship (e.g., pulmonary physicians have knowledge of the relationship between asbestos exposure and asbestosis),[42] but most physicians have little training in chemical toxicology and lack an understanding of exposure assessment and dose–response relationships. An exception is a physician who is certified in medical toxicology by the American Board of Medical Toxicology, based on substantial training in toxicology and successful completion of rigorous examinations.

Some physicians who are occupational health specialists also have training in toxicology. Knowledge of toxicology is particularly strong among those who work in the chemical, petrochemical, and pharmaceutical industries, in which surveillance of workers exposed to chemicals is a major responsibility. Of the occupational physicians practicing today, only about 1,000 have successfully completed the board examination in occupational medicine, which contains some questions about chemical toxicology.[43]

41. *See* Mary Sue Henifin et al., Reference Guide on Medical Testimony, § II, in this manual.

42. *See, e.g.*, Moore v. Ashland Chem., Inc., 126 F.3d 679, 701 (5th Cir. 1997) (treating physician's opinion admissible as to causation of reactive airway disease); McCullock v. H.B. Fuller Co., 61 F.3d 1038, 1044 (2d Cir. 1995) (treating physician's opinion admissible as to effect of fumes from hot-melt glue on throat, where physician was board certified in otolaryngology and based his opinion on medical history and treatment, pathological studies, differential etiology, and scientific literature); Benedi v. McNeil-P.P.C., Inc., 66 F.3d 1378, 1384 (4th Cir. 1995) (treating physician's opinion admissible as to causation of liver failure by mixture of alcohol and acetaminophen, based on medical history, physical examination, lab and pathology data, and scientific literature—the same methodologies used daily in the diagnosis of patients).

Treating physicians also become involved in considering cause-and-effect relationships when they are asked whether a patient can return to a situation in which an exposure has occurred. The answer is obvious if the cause-and-effect relationship is clearly known. However, this relationship is often uncertain, and the physician must consider the appropriate advice. In such situations, the physician will tend to give advice as if the causality was established, both because it is appropriate caution and because of fears concerning medicolegal issues.

43. Clinical ecologists, another group of physicians, have offered opinions regarding multiple-chemical hypersensitivity and immune-system responses to chemical exposures. These physicians generally have a background in the field of allergy, not toxicology, and their theoretical approach is derived in part from classic concepts of allergic responses and immunology. This theoretical approach has often led clinical ecologists to find cause-and-effect relationships or low-dose effects that are not generally accepted by toxicologists. Clinical ecologists often belong to the American Academy of Environmental Medicine.

B. Has the Proposed Expert Been Certified by the American Board of Toxicology, Inc., or Does He or She Belong to a Professional Organization, Such As the Academy of Toxicological Sciences or the Society of Toxicology?

As of January 1999, 1,631 individuals from twenty-one countries had received board certification from the American Board of Toxicology, Inc. To sit for the examination, which has a pass rate of less than 75%, the candidate must be involved full-time in the practice of toxicology, including designing and managing toxicological experiments or interpreting results and translating them to identify and solve human and animal health problems. To become certified, the candidate must pass all three parts of the examination within two years. Diplomates must be recertified through examination every five years.

The Academy of Toxicological Sciences (ATS) was formed to provide credentials in toxicology through peer review only. It does not administer examinations for certification.

The Society of Toxicology (SOT), the major professional organization for the field of toxicology, was founded in 1961 and has grown dramatically in recent years; it currently has 4,672 members.[44] It has reasonably strict criteria for membership. Qualified people must have conducted and published original research in some phase of toxicology (excluding graduate work) or be generally recognized as expert in some phase of toxicology and be approved by a majority vote of the board of directors. Many environmental toxicologists who meet these qualifications belong to SOT.

Physician toxicologists can join the American College of Medical Toxicology and the American Academy of Clinical Toxicologists. Other organizations in the field are the American College of Toxicology, which has less stringent criteria for membership; the International Society of Regulatory Toxicology and Pharmacology; and the Society of Occupational and Environmental Health. The last two organizations require only the payment of dues for membership.

In 1991, the Council on Scientific Affairs of the American Medical Association concluded that until "accurate, reproducible, and well-controlled studies are available, . . . multiple chemical sensitivity should not be considered a recognized clinical syndrome." Council on Scientific Affairs, American Med. Ass'n, Council Report on Clinical Ecology 6 (1991). In *Bradley v. Brown*, 42 F.3d 434, 438 (7th Cir. 1994), the court considered the admissibility of an expert opinion based on clinical ecology theories. The court ruled the opinion inadmissible, finding that it was "hypothetical" and based on anecdotal evidence as opposed to scientific research. *See also* Coffin v. Orkin Exterminating Co., 20 F. Supp. 2d 107, 110 (D. Me. 1998); Frank v. New York, 972 F. Supp. 130, 132 n.2 (N.D.N.Y 1997). *But see* Elam v. Alcolac, Inc., 765 S.W.2d 42, 86 (Mo. Ct. App. 1988) (expert opinion based on clinical ecology theories admissible), *cert. denied*, 493 U.S. 817 (1989).

44. There are currently fifteen specialty sections of SOT that represent the different types of research needed to understand the wide range of toxic effects associated with chemical exposures. These sections include mechanisms, molecular biology, inhalation toxicology, metals, neurotoxicology, carcinogenesis, risk assessment, and immunotoxicology.

C. What Other Criteria Does the Proposed Expert Meet?

The success of academic scientists in toxicology, as in other biomedical sciences, usually is measured by the following types of criteria: the quality and number of peer-reviewed publications, the ability to compete for research grants, service on scientific advisory panels, and university appointments.

Publication of articles in peer-reviewed journals indicates an expertise in toxicology. The number of articles, their topics, and whether the individual is the principal author are important factors in determining the expertise of a toxicologist.[45]

Most research grants from government agencies and private foundations are highly competitive. Successful competition for funding and publication of the research findings indicate competence in an area.

Selection for local, national, and international regulatory advisory panels usually implies recognition in the field. Examples of such panels are the National Institutes of Health Toxicology Study Section and panels convened by the EPA, the FDA, the World Health Organization (WHO), and the IARC. Recognized industrial organizations, including the American Petroleum Institute, Electric Power Research Institute, and Chemical Industry Institute of Toxicology, and public interest groups, such as the Environmental Defense Fund and the Natural Resources Defense Council, employ toxicologists directly and as consultants and enlist academic toxicologists to serve on advisory panels. Because of a growing interest in environmental issues, the demand for scientific advice has outgrown the supply of available toxicologists. It is thus common for reputable toxicologists to serve on advisory panels.

Finally, a university appointment in toxicology, risk assessment, or a related field signifies an expertise in that area, particularly if the university has a graduate education program in that area.

45. Examples of reputable, peer-reviewed journals are the *Journal of Toxicology and Environmental Health*; *Toxicological Sciences*; *Toxicology and Applied Pharmacology*; *Science*; *British Journal of Industrial Medicine*; *Clinical Toxicology*; *Archives of Environmental Health*; *Journal of Occupational Medicine*; *Annual Review of Pharmacology and Toxicology*; *Teratogenesis, Carcinogenesis and Mutagenesis*; *Fundamental and Applied Toxicology*; *Inhalation Toxicology*; *Biochemical Pharmacology*; *Toxicology Letters*; *Environmental Research*; *Environmental Health Perspectives*; and *American Journal of Industrial Medicine*.

III. Demonstrating an Association Between Exposure and Risk of Disease

Once the expert has been qualified, he or she is expected to offer an opinion on whether the plaintiff's disease was caused by exposure to a chemical. To do so, the expert relies on the principles of toxicology to provide a scientifically valid methodology for establishing causation and then applies the methodology to the facts of the case.

An opinion on causation should be premised on three preliminary assessments. First, the expert should analyze whether the disease can be related to chemical exposure by a biologically plausible theory. Second, the expert should examine if the plaintiff was exposed to the chemical in a manner that can lead to absorption into the body. Third, the expert should offer an opinion as to whether the dose to which the plaintiff was exposed is sufficient to cause the disease.

The following questions help evaluate the strengths and weaknesses of toxicological evidence.

A. On What Species of Animals Was the Compound Tested? What Is Known About the Biological Similarities and Differences Between the Test Animals and Humans? How Do These Similarities and Differences Affect the Extrapolation from Animal Data in Assessing the Risk to Humans?

All living organisms share a common biology that leads to marked similarities in the responsiveness of subcellular structures to toxic agents. Among mammals, more than sufficient common organ structure and function readily permit the extrapolation from one species to another in most instances. Comparative information concerning factors that modify the toxic effects of chemicals, including absorption, distribution, metabolism, and excretion, in the laboratory test animals and humans enhances the expert's ability to extrapolate from laboratory animals to humans.[46]

The expert should review similarities and differences in the animal species in which the compound has been tested and in humans. This analysis should form the basis of the expert's opinion as to whether extrapolation from animals to humans is warranted.[47]

46. *See generally supra* notes 26–27 and accompanying text; Animal Models in Toxicology, *supra* note 23; Edward J. Calabrese, Principles of Animal Extrapolation (1983); Human Risk Assessment: The Role of Animal Selection and Extrapolation (M. Val Roloff ed., 1987); Filov et al., *supra* note 23.

47. The failure to review similarities and differences in metabolism in performing cross-species extrapolation has led to the exclusion of opinions based on animal data. *See* Hall v. Baxter Healthcare Corp., 947 F. Supp. 1387, 1410 (D. Or. 1996); Nelson v. American Sterilizer Co., 566 N.W.2d 671 (Mich. Ct. App. 1997). *But see In re* Paoli R.R. Yard PCB Litig., 35 F.3d 717, 779–80 (3d Cir. 1994)

In general, there is an overwhelming similarity in the biology of all living things and a particularly strong similarity among mammals. Of course, laboratory animals differ from humans in many ways. For example, rats do not have gall bladders. Thus, rat data would not be pertinent to the possibility that a compound produces human gall bladder toxicity.[48] Note that many subjective symptoms are poorly modeled in animal studies. Thus, complaints that a chemical has caused nonspecific symptoms, such as nausea, headache, and weakness, for which there are no objective manifestations in humans are difficult to test in laboratory animals.

B. Does Research Show That the Compound Affects a Specific Target Organ? Will Humans Be Affected Similarly?

Some toxic agents affect only specific organs and not others. This organ specificity may be due to particular patterns of absorption, distribution, metabolism, and excretion; the presence of specific receptors; or organ function. For example, organ specificity may reflect the presence in the organ of relatively high levels of an enzyme capable of metabolizing or changing a compound to a toxic form of the compound known as a metabolite, or it may reflect the relatively low level of an enzyme capable of detoxifying a compound. An example of the former is liver toxicity caused by inhaled carbon tetrachloride, which affects the liver but not the lungs because of extensive metabolism to a toxic metabolite within the liver but relatively little such metabolism in the lung.[49]

Some chemicals, however, may cause nonspecific effects or even multiple effects. Lead is an example of a toxic agent that affects many organ systems, including red blood cells, the central and peripheral nervous systems, the reproductive system, and the kidneys.

The basis of specificity often reflects the function of individual organs. For

(noting that humans and monkeys are likely to show similar sensitivity to PCBs), *cert. denied sub nom.* General Elec. Co. v. Ingram, 513 U.S. 1190 (1995).

As the Supreme Court noted in *General Electric Co. v. Joiner,* 522 U.S. 136, 144 (1997), the issue as to admissibility is not whether animal studies are ever admissible to establish causation, but whether the particular studies relied upon by plaintiff's experts were sufficiently supported. *See* Carl F. Cranor et al., *Judicial Boundary Drawing and the Need for Context-Sensitive Science in Toxic Torts After* Daubert v. Merrell Dow Pharmaceuticals, Inc., 16 Va. Envtl. L.J. 1, 38 (1996).

48. *See, e.g.*, Calabrese, *supra* note 46, at 583–89 tbl.14-1. Species differences that produce a qualitative difference in response to xenobiotics are well known. Sometimes understanding the mechanism underlying the species difference can allow one to predict whether the effect will occur in humans. Thus, carbaryl, an insecticide commonly used for gypsy moth control, among other things, produces fetal abnormalities in dogs but not in hamsters, mice, rats, and monkeys. Dogs lack the specific enzyme involved in metabolizing carbaryl; the other species tested all have this enzyme, as do humans. Therefore, it has been assumed that humans are not at risk for fetal malformations produced by carbaryl.

49. Brian Jay Day et al., *Potentiation of Carbon Tetrachloride-Induced Hepatotoxicity and Pneumotoxicity by Pyridine,* 8 J. Biochemical Toxicol. 11 (1993).

example, the thyroid is particularly susceptible to radioactive iodine in atomic fallout because thyroid hormone is unique within the body in that it requires iodine. Through evolution a very efficient and specific mechanism has developed which concentrates any absorbed iodine preferentially within the thyroid, thus rendering the thyroid particularly at risk from radioactive iodine. In a test tube the radiation from radioactive iodine can affect the genetic material obtained from any cell in the body, but in the intact laboratory animal or human, only the thyroid is at risk.

The unfolding of the human genome is already beginning to provide information pertinent to understanding the wide variation in human risk to environmental chemicals. The impact of this understanding on toxic tort causation issues remains to be explored.[50]

C. What Is Known About the Chemical Structure of the Compound and Its Relationship to Toxicity?

Understanding of the structural aspects of chemical toxicology has led to the use of structure activity relationships (SAR) as a formal method of predicting the potential toxicity of new chemicals. This technique compares the chemical structure of compounds with known toxicity and the chemical structure of compounds with unknown toxicity. Toxicity then is estimated based on molecular similarities between the two compounds. Although SAR is used extensively by the EPA in evaluating many new chemicals required to be tested under the registration requirements of the Toxic Substances Control Act (TSCA), its reliability has a number of limitations.[51]

50. The wide range in the rate of metabolism of chemicals is at least partly under genetic control. A recent study in China found approximately a doubling of risk in people with high levels of either an enzyme that increased the rate of formation of a toxic metabolite or an enzyme that decreased the rate of detoxification of this metabolite. There was a sevenfold increase in risk for those who had both genetically determined variants. *See* Frederica P. Perera, *Molecular Epidemiology: Insights into Cancer Susceptibility, Risk Assessment, and Prevention,* 88 J. Nat'l Cancer Inst. 496 (1996).

51. For example, benzene and the alkyl benzenes (which include toluene, xylene, and ethyl benzene) share a similar chemical structure. SAR works exceptionally well in predicting the acute central nervous system anesthetic-like effects of both benzene and the alkyl benzenes. Although there are slight differences in dose–response relationships, they are readily explained by the interrelated factors of chemical structure, vapor pressure, and lipid solubility (the brain is highly lipid). National Research Council, The Alkyl Benzenes (1981). However, only benzene produces damage to the bone marrow and leukemia; the alkyl benzenes do not have this effect. This difference is the result of specific toxic metabolic products of benzene in comparison with the alkyl benzenes. Thus, SAR is predictive of neurotoxic effects but not bone-marrow effects. *See* Hoffman, *supra* note 25, at 277.

In *Daubert v. Merrell Dow Pharmaceuticals, Inc.*, 509 U.S. 579 (1993), the Court rejected a per se exclusion of SAR, animal data, and reanalyses of previously published epidemiological data where there were negative epidemiological data. However, as the court recognized in *Sorensen v. Shaklee Corp.*, 31 F.3d 638, 646 n.12 (8th Cir. 1994), the problem with SAR is that "'[m]olecules with minor structural differences can produce very different biological effects.'" (quoting Joseph Sanders, *From Science to Evidence: The Testimony on Causation in the Bendectin Cases,* 46 Stan. L. Rev. 1, 19 (1993)).

D. Has the Compound Been the Subject of In Vitro Research, and If So, Can the Findings Be Related to What Occurs In Vivo?

Cellular and tissue-culture research can be particularly helpful in identifying mechanisms of toxic action and potential target-organ toxicity. The major barrier to use of in vitro results is the frequent inability to relate doses that cause cellular toxicity to doses that cause whole-animal toxicity. In many critical areas, knowledge that permits such quantitative extrapolation is lacking.[52] Nevertheless, the ability to quickly test new products through in vitro tests, using human cells, provides invaluable "early warning systems" for toxicity.[53]

E. Is the Association Between Exposure and Disease Biologically Plausible?

No matter how strong the temporal relationship between exposure and development of disease, or the supporting epidemiological evidence, it is difficult to accept an association between a compound and a health effect when no mechanism can be identified by which the chemical exposure leads to the putative effect.[54]

IV. Specific Causal Association Between an Individual's Exposure and the Onset of Disease

An expert who opines that exposure to a compound caused a person's disease engages in deductive clinical reasoning.[55] In most instances, cancers and other diseases do not wear labels documenting their causation.[56] The opinion is based on an assessment of the individual's exposure, including the amount, the temporal relationship between the exposure and disease, and other disease-causing

52. In Vitro Toxicity Testing: Applications to Safety Evaluation, *supra* note 25, at 8. Despite its limitations, in vitro research can strengthen inferences drawn from whole-animal bioassays and can support opinions regarding whether the association between exposure and disease is biologically plausible. *See* Hoffman, *supra* note 25, at 278–93; Rogers & Kavlock, *supra* note 25, at 319–23.

53. Graham v. Playtex Prods., Inc., 993 F. Supp. 127, 131–32 (N.D.N.Y. 1998) (opinion based on in vitro experiments showing that rayon tampons were associated with higher risk of toxic shock syndrome was admissible in the absence of epidemiological evidence).

54. However, theories of bioplausibility, without additional data, have been found to be insufficient to support a finding of causation. *See, e.g.*, Hall v. Baxter Healthcare Corp., 947 F. Supp. 1387, 1414 (D. Or. 1996); Golod v. Hoffman La Roche, 964 F. Supp. 841, 860–61 (S.D.N.Y. 1997).

55. For an example of deductive clinical reasoning based on known facts about the toxic effects of a chemical and the individual's pattern of exposure, see Bernard D. Goldstein, *Is Exposure to Benzene a Cause of Human Multiple Myeloma?*, 609 Annals N.Y. Acad. Sci. 225 (1990).

56. Research still in the preliminary stages shows that certain cancers do wear labels in the form of DNA adducts and mutational spectra. *See generally* National Research Council, Biologic Markers in Reproductive Toxicology (1989).

factors. This information is then compared with scientific data on the relationship between exposure and disease. The certainty of the expert's opinion depends on the strength of the research data demonstrating a relationship between exposure and the disease at the dose in question and the absence of other disease-causing factors (also known as confounding factors).[57]

Particularly problematic are generalizations made in personal injury litigation from regulatory positions. For example, if regulatory standards are discussed in toxic tort cases to provide a reference point for assessing exposure levels, it must be recognized that there is a great deal of variability in the extent of evidence required to support different regulations.[58] The extent of evidence required to support regulations depends on

1. the law (e.g., the Clean Air Act has language focusing regulatory activity for primary pollutants on adverse health consequences to sensitive populations with an adequate margin of safety and with no consideration of economic consequences, whereas regulatory activity under TSCA clearly asks for some balance between the societal benefits and risks of new chemicals[59]);
2. the specific end point of concern (e.g., consider the concern caused by cancer and adverse reproductive outcomes versus almost anything else); and
3. the societal impact (e.g., the public's support for control of an industry that causes air pollution versus the public's desire to alter personal automobile use patterns).

These three concerns, as well as others, including costs, politics, and the virtual certainty of litigation challenging the regulation, have an impact on the level of scientific proof required by the regulatory decision maker.[60]

57. Causation issues are discussed in Michael D. Green et al., Reference Guide on Epidemiology, § V, and Mary Sue Henifin et al., Reference Guide on Medical Testimony, § IV, in this manual. *See also* Joseph Sanders, *Scientific Validity, Admissibility and Mass Torts After* Daubert, 78 Minn. L. Rev. 1387 (1994); Susan R. Poulter, *Science and Toxic Torts: Is There a Rational Solution to the Problem of Causation?*, 7 High Tech. L.J. 189 (1992); Troyen A. Brennan, *Causal Chains and Statistical Links: The Role of Scientific Uncertainty in Hazardous-Substance Litigation*, 73 Cornell L. Rev. 469 (1988); Orrin E. Tilevitz, *Judicial Attitudes Towards Legal and Scientific Proof of Cancer Causation*, 3 Colum. J. Envtl. L. 344, 381 (1977); David L. Bazelon, *Science and Uncertainty: A Jurist's View*, 5 Harv. Envtl. L. Rev. 209 (1981).

58. The relevance of regulatory standards to toxic tort litigation is explored in Silbergeld, *supra* note 2; Relkin, *supra* note 35; *In re* Paoli R.R. Yard PCB Litig., 35 F.3d 717, 781 (3d Cir. 1994) (district court abused its discretion in excluding animal studies relied upon by the EPA), *cert. denied sub nom.* General Elec. Co. v. Ingram, 513 U.S. 1190 (1995); John Endicott, *Interaction Between Regulatory Law and Tort Law in Controlling Toxic Chemical Exposure*, 47 SMU L. Rev. 501 (1994).

59. *See, e.g.*, Clean Air Act Amendments of 1990, 42 U.S.C. § 7412(f) (1994); Toxic Substances Control Act, 15 U.S.C. § 2605 (1994).

60. These concerns are discussed in Stephen Breyer, Breaking the Vicious Circle: Toward Effective Risk Regulation (1993).

In addition, regulatory standards traditionally include protective factors to reasonably ensure that susceptible individuals are not put at risk. Furthermore, standards are often based on the risk that is due to lifetime exposure. Accordingly, the mere fact that an individual has been exposed to a level above a standard does not necessarily mean that an adverse effect has occurred.

A. Was the Plaintiff Exposed to the Substance, and If So, Did the Exposure Occur in a Manner That Can Result in Absorption into the Body?

Evidence of exposure is essential in determining the effects of harmful substances. Basically, potential human exposure is measured in one of three ways. First, when direct measurements cannot be made, exposure can be measured by mathematical modeling, in which one uses a variety of physical factors to estimate the transport of the pollutant from the source to the receptor. For example, mathematical models take into account such factors as wind variations to allow calculation of the transport of radioactive iodine from a federal atomic research facility to nearby residential areas. Second, exposure can be directly measured in the medium in question—air, water, food, or soil. When the medium of exposure is water, soil, or air, hydrologists or meteorologists may be called upon to contribute their expertise to measuring exposure. The third approach directly measures human receptors through some form of biological monitoring, such as blood tests to determine blood lead levels or urinalyses to check for a urinary metabolite, which shows pollutant exposure. Ideally, both environmental testing and biological monitoring are performed; however, this is not always possible, particularly in instances of past exposure.[61]

The toxicologist must go beyond understanding exposure to determine if the individual was exposed to the compound in a manner that can result in absorption into the body. The absorption of the compound is a function of its physiochemical properties, its concentration, and the presence of other agents or conditions that assist or interfere with its uptake. For example, inhaled lead is absorbed almost totally, whereas ingested lead is taken up only partially into the body. Iron deficiency and low nutritional calcium intake, both common conditions of inner-city children, increase the amount of ingested lead that is absorbed in the gastrointestinal tract and passes into the bloodstream.

61. *See, e.g., In re* Three Mile Island Litig. Consol. Proceedings, 927 F. Supp. 834, 870 (M.D. Pa. 1996) (plaintiffs failed to present direct or indirect evidence of exposure to cancer-inducing levels of radiation); Mitchell v. Gencorp Inc., 165 F.3d 778, 781 (10th Cir. 1999) ("[g]uesses, even if educated, are insufficient to prove the level of exposure in a toxic tort case"). *See also* Wright v. Willamette Indus., Inc., 91 F.3d 1105, 1107 (8th Cir. 1996); Valentine v. Pioneer Chlor Alkali Co., 921 F. Supp. 666, 678 (D. Nev. 1996).

B. Were Other Factors Present That Can Affect the Distribution of the Compound Within the Body?

Once a compound is absorbed into the body through the skin, lungs, or gastrointestinal tract, it is distributed throughout the body through the bloodstream. Thus, the rate of distribution depends on the rate of blood flow to various organs and tissues. Distribution and resulting toxicity are also influenced by other factors, including the dose, the route of entry, tissue solubility, lymphatic supplies to the organ, metabolism, and the presence of specific receptors or uptake mechanisms within body tissues.

C. What Is Known About How Metabolism in the Human Body Alters the Toxic Effects of the Compound?

Metabolism is the alteration of a chemical by bodily processes. It does not necessarily result in less toxic compounds being formed. In fact, many of the organic chemicals that are known human cancer-causing agents require metabolic transformation before they can cause cancer. A distinction often is made between direct-acting agents, which cause toxicity without any metabolic conversion, and indirect-acting agents, which require metabolic activation before they can produce adverse effects. Metabolism is complex, since a variety of pathways compete for the same agent; some produce harmless metabolites, and others produce toxic agents.[62]

D. What Excretory Route Does the Compound Take, and How Does This Affect Its Toxicity?

Excretory routes are urine, feces, sweat, saliva, expired air, and lactation. Many inhaled volatile agents are eliminated primarily by exhalation. Small water-soluble compounds are usually excreted through urine. Higher-molecular-weight compounds are often excreted through the biliary tract into the feces. Certain fat-soluble, poorly metabolized compounds, such as PCBs, may persist in the body for decades, although they can be excreted in the milk fat of lactating women.

E. Does the Temporal Relationship Between Exposure and the Onset of Disease Support or Contradict Causation?

In acute toxicity, there is usually a short time period between cause and effect. However, in some situations, the length of basic biological processes necessitates a longer period of time between initial exposure and the onset of observable

62. Courts have explored the relationship between metabolic transformation and carcinogenesis. *See, e.g.*, Stites v. Sundstrand Heat Transfer, Inc., 660 F. Supp. 1516, 1519 (W.D. Mich. 1987).

disease. For example, in acute myelogenous leukemia, the adult form of acute leukemia, at least one to two years must elapse from initial exposure to radiation, benzene, or cancer chemotherapy before the manifestation of a clinically recognizable case of leukemia. A toxic tort claim alleging a shorter time period between cause and effect is scientifically untenable. Much longer time periods are necessary for the manifestation of solid tumors caused by asbestos.[63]

F. If Exposure to the Substance Is Associated with the Disease, Is There a No Observable Effect, or Threshold, Level, and If So, Was the Individual Exposed Above the No Observable Effect Level?

For agents that produce effects other than through mutations, it is assumed that there is some level that is incapable of causing harm. If the level of exposure was below this no observable effect, or threshold, level, a relationship between the exposure and disease cannot be established.[64] When only laboratory animal data are available, the expert extrapolates the NOEL from animals to humans by calculating the animal NOEL based on experimental data and decreasing this level by one or more safety factors to ensure no human effect.[65] The NOEL can also be calculated from human toxicity data if they exist. This analysis, however, is not applied to substances that exert toxicity by causing mutations leading to cancer. Theoretically, any exposure at all to mutagens may increase the risk of cancer, although the risk may be very slight and not achieve medical probability.[66]

63. The temporal relationship between exposure and causation is discussed in *Cavallo v. Star Enterprise*, 892 F. Supp. 756, 769–74 (E.D. Va. 1995) (expert testimony based primarily on temporal connection between exposure to jet fuel and onset of symptoms, without other evidence of causation, ruled inadmissible). *But see* National Bank of Commerce v. Dow Chem. Co., 965 F. Supp. 1490, 1525 (E.D. Ark. 1996) ("[T]here may be instances where the temporal connection between exposure to a given chemical and subsequent injury is so compelling as to dispense with the need for reliance on standard methods of toxicology.").

64. *See, e.g.*, Allen v. Pennsylvania Eng'g Corp., 102 F.3d 194, 199 (5th Cir. 1996) ("Scientific knowledge of the harmful level of exposure to a chemical, plus knowledge that the plaintiff was exposed to such quantities, are minimal facts necessary to sustain the plaintiff's burden in a toxic tort case."); Redland Soccer Club, Inc. v. Department of Army, 55 F.3d 827, 847 (3d Cir. 1995) (summary judgment for defendant precluded where exposure above cancer threshold level could be calculated from soil samples).

65. *See, e.g.*, *supra* notes 18–19 and accompanying text; Tardiff & Rodricks, *supra* note 18, at 391; Joseph V. Rodricks, Calculated Risks 165–70, 193–96 (1992); Lu, *supra* note 14, at 84.

66. *See* sources cited *supra* note 19.

V. Medical History

A. Is the Medical History of the Individual Consistent with the Toxicologist's Expert Opinion Concerning the Injury?

One of the basic and most useful tools in diagnosis and treatment of disease is the patient's medical history.[67] A thorough, standardized patient information questionnaire would be particularly useful for identifying the etiology, or causation, of illnesses related to toxic exposures; however, there is currently no validated or widely used questionnaire that gathers all pertinent information.[68] Nevertheless, it is widely recognized that a thorough medical history involves the questioning and examination of the patient as well as appropriate medical testing. The patient's written medical records should also be examined.

The following information is relevant to a patient's medical history: past and present occupational and environmental history and exposure to toxic agents; lifestyle characteristics (e.g., use of nicotine and alcohol); family medical history (i.e., medical conditions and diseases of relatives); and personal medical history (i.e., present symptoms and results of medical tests as well as past injuries, medical conditions, diseases, surgical procedures, and medical test results).

In some instances, the reporting of symptoms can be in itself diagnostic of exposure to a specific substance, particularly in evaluating acute effects.[69] For example, individuals acutely exposed to organophosphate pesticides report headaches, nausea, and dizziness accompanied by anxiety and restlessness. Other reported symptoms are muscle twitching, weakness, and hypersecretion with sweating, salivation, and tearing.[70]

B. Are the Complaints Specific or Nonspecific?

Acute exposure to many toxic agents produces a constellation of nonspecific symptoms, such as headaches, nausea, lightheadedness, and fatigue. These types of symptoms are part of human experience and can be triggered by a host of medical and psychological conditions. They are almost impossible to quantify or document beyond the patient's report. Thus, these symptoms can be attributed

67. For a thorough discussion of the methods of clinical diagnosis, see Mary Sue Henifin et al., Reference Guide on Medical Testimony, § IV.B–C, in this manual. *See also* Jerome P. Kassirer & Richard I. Kopelman, Learning Clinical Reasoning (1991). A number of cases have considered the admissibility of the treating physician's opinion based, in part, on medical history, symptomatology, and laboratory and pathology studies. *See* cases cited *supra* note 42.

68. Office of Tech. Assessment, U.S. Congress, *supra* note 10, at 365–89.

69. *But see* Moore v. Ashland Chem., Inc., 126 F.3d 679, 693 (5th Cir. 1997) (discussion of relevance of symptoms within forty-five minutes of exposure).

70. Environmental Protection Agency, Recognition and Management of Pesticide Poisonings (4th ed. 1989).

mistakenly to an exposure to a toxic agent or discounted as unimportant when in fact they reflect a significant exposure.[71]

In taking a careful medical history, the expert focuses on the time pattern of symptoms and disease manifestations in relation to any exposure and on the constellation of symptoms to determine causation. It is easier to establish causation when a symptom is unusual and rarely is caused by anything other than the suspect chemical (e.g., such rare cancers as hemangiosarcoma, associated with vinyl chloride exposure, and mesothelioma, associated with asbestos exposure). However, many cancers and other conditions are associated with several causative factors, thus complicating proof of causation.[72]

C. Do Laboratory Tests Indicate Exposure to the Compound?

Two types of laboratory tests can be considered: tests that are routinely used in medicine to detect changes in normal body status, and specialized tests, which are used to detect the presence of the chemical or physical agent.[73] For the most part, tests used to demonstrate the presence of a toxic agent are frequently unavailable from clinical laboratories. Even when available from a hospital or a clinical laboratory, a test such as that for carbon monoxide combined to hemoglobin is done so rarely that it may raise concerns as to its accuracy. Other tests, such as the test for blood lead levels, are required for routine surveillance of potentially exposed workers. However, if a laboratory is certified for the testing of blood lead in workers, for which the OSHA action level is 40 micrograms per deciliter (μg/dl), it does not necessarily mean that it will give reliable data on blood lead levels at the much lower Centers for Disease Control and Prevention (CDC) action level of 10 μg/dl.

D. What Other Causes Could Lead to the Given Complaint?

With few exceptions, acute and chronic diseases, including cancer, can be caused by either a single toxic agent or a combination of agents or conditions. In taking a careful medical history, the expert examines the possibility of competing causes, or confounding factors, for any disease, which leads to a differential diagnosis. In

71. The issue of whether development of nonspecific symptoms may be related to pesticide exposure was considered in *Kannankeril v. Terminix International, Inc.*, 128 F.3d 802 (3d Cir. 1997). The court ruled that the trial court abused its discretion in excluding expert opinion that considered, and rejected, a negative laboratory test. *Id.* at 808–09.

72. Failure to rule out other potential causes of symptoms may lead to a ruling that the expert's report is inadmissible. *See, e.g.*, Hall v. Baxter Healthcare Corp., 947 F. Supp. 1387, 1413 (D. Or. 1996); Rutigliano v. Valley Bus. Forms, 929 F. Supp. 779, 786 (D.N.J. 1996).

73. *See, e.g.*, Kannankeril v. Terminix Int'l, Inc., 128 F.3d 802, 807 (3d Cir. 1997).

addition, ascribing causality to a specific source of a chemical requires that a history be taken concerning other sources of the same chemical. The failure of a physician to elicit such a history or of a toxicologist to pay attention to such a history raises questions about competence and leaves open the possibility of competing causes of the disease.[74]

E. Is There Evidence of Interaction with Other Chemicals?

An individual's simultaneous exposure to more than one chemical may result in a response that differs from that which would be expected from exposure to only one of the chemicals.[75] When the effect of multiple agents is that which would be predicted by the sum of the effects of individual agents, it is called an additive effect; when it is greater than this sum, it is known as a synergistic effect; when one agent causes a decrease in the effect produced by another, the result is termed antagonism; and when an agent that by itself produces no effect leads to an enhancement of the effect of another agent, the response is termed potentiation.[76]

Three types of toxicological approaches are pertinent to understanding the effects of mixtures of agents. One is based on the standard toxicological evaluation of common commercial mixtures, such as gasoline. The second approach is from studies in which the known toxicological effect of one agent is used to explore the mechanism of action of another agent, such as using a known specific inhibitor of a metabolic pathway to determine whether the toxicity of a second agent depends on this pathway. The third approach is based on an understanding of the basic mechanism of action of the individual components of the mixture, thereby allowing prediction of the combined effect, which can then be tested in an animal model.[77]

74. *See, e.g.*, Bell v. Swift Adhesives, Inc., 804 F. Supp. 1577, 1580 (S.D. Ga. 1992) (expert's opinion that workplace exposure to methylene chloride caused plaintiff's liver cancer, without ruling out plaintiff's infection with hepatitis B virus, a known liver carcinogen, was insufficient to withstand motion for summary judgment for defendant).

75. *See generally* Edward J. Calabrese, Multiple Chemical Interactions (1991).

76. Courts have been called on to consider the issue of synergy. In *International Union, United Automobile, Aerospace & Agricultural Implement Workers of America v. Pendergrass*, 878 F.2d 389, 391 (D.C. Cir. 1989), the court found that OSHA failed to sufficiently explain its findings that formaldehyde presented no significant carcinogenic risk to workers at exposure levels of 1 part per million or less. The court particularly criticized OSHA's use of a linear low-dose risk curve rather than a risk-adverse model after the agency had described evidence of synergy between formaldehyde and other substances that workers would be exposed to, especially wood dust. *Id.* at 395.

77. *See generally* Calabrese, *supra* note 75.

F. Do Humans Differ in the Extent of Susceptibility to the Particular Compound in Question? Are These Differences Relevant in This Case?

Individuals who exercise inhale more than sedentary individuals and therefore are exposed to higher doses of airborne environmental toxins. Similarly, differences in metabolism, which are inherited or caused by external factors, such as the levels of carbohydrates in a person's diet, may result in differences in the delivery of a toxic product to the target organ.[78]

Moreover, for any given level of a toxic agent that reaches a target organ, damage may be greater because of a greater response of that organ. In addition, for any given level of target-organ damage, there may be a greater impact on particular individuals. For example, an elderly individual or someone with preexisting lung disease is less likely to tolerate a small decline in lung function caused by an air pollutant than is a healthy individual with normal lung function.

A person's level of physical activity, age, sex, and genetic makeup, as well as exposure to therapeutic agents (such as prescription or over-the-counter drugs), affect the metabolism of the compound and hence its toxicity.[79] Advances in human genetics research are providing information about susceptibility to environmental agents that may be relevant to determining the likelihood that a given exposure has a specific effect on an individual.[80]

G. Has the Expert Considered Data That Contradict His or Her Opinion?

Multiple avenues of deductive reasoning based on research data lead to scientific acceptance of causation in any field, particularly in toxicology. However, the basis for this deductive reasoning is also one of the most difficult aspects of causation to describe quantitatively. If animal studies, pharmacological research on mechanisms of toxicity, in vitro tissue studies, and epidemiological research all document toxic effects of exposure to a compound, an expert's opinion about causation in a particular case is much more likely to be true.[81]

78. *Id.*

79. The problem of differences in chemical sensitivity was addressed by the court in *Gulf South Insulation v. United States Consumer Product Safety Commission*, 701 F.2d 1137 (5th Cir. 1983). The court overturned the commission's ban on urea-formaldehyde foam insulation because the commission failed to document in sufficient detail the level at which segments of the population were affected and whether their responses were slight or severe: "Predicting how likely an injury is to occur, at least in general terms, is essential to a determination of whether the risk of that injury is unreasonable." *Id.* at 1148.

80. *See supra* note 50.

81. Consistency of research results was considered by the court in *Marsee v. United States Tobacco Co.*, 639 F. Supp. 466, 469–70 (W.D. Okla. 1986). The defendant, the manufacturer of snuff alleged to

The more difficult problem is how to evaluate conflicting research results. When different research studies reach different conclusions regarding toxicity, the expert must be asked to explain how those results have been taken into account in the formulation of the expert's opinion.

cause oral cancer, moved to exclude epidemiological studies conducted in Asia that demonstrate a link between smokeless tobacco and oral cancer. The defendant also moved to exclude evidence demonstrating that the nitrosamines and polonium 210 contained in the snuff are cancer-causing agents in some forty different species of laboratory animals. The court denied both motions, finding:

> There was no dispute that both nitrosamines and polonium 210 are present in defendant's snuff products. Further, defendant conceded that animal studies have accurately and consistently demonstrated that these substances cause cancer in test animals. Finally, the Court found evidence based on experiments with animals particularly valuable and important in this litigation since such experiments with humans are impossible. Under all these circumstances, the Court found this evidence probative on the issue of causation.

Id. See also sources cited *supra* note 7.

Glossary of Terms

The following terms and definitions were adapted from a variety of sources, including Office of Technology Assessment, U.S. Congress, Reproductive Health Hazards in the Workplace (1985); Casarett and Doull's Toxicology: The Basic Science of Poisons (Curtis D. Klaassen ed., 5th ed. 1996); National Research Council, Biologic Markers in Reproductive Toxicology (1989); Committee on Risk Assessment Methodology, National Research Council, Issues in Risk Assessment (1993); M. Alice Ottoboni, The Dose Makes the Poison: A Plain-Language Guide to Toxicology (2d ed. 1991); Environmental and Occupational Health Sciences Institute, Glossary of Environment Health Terms (1989).

absorption. The taking up of a chemical into the body either orally, through inhalation, or through skin exposure.

acute toxicity. An immediate toxic response following a single or short-term exposure to an agent or dosing.

additive effect. When exposure to more than one toxic agent results in the same effect as would be predicted by the sum of the effects of exposure to the individual agents.

antagonism. When exposure to one toxic agent causes a decrease in the effect produced by another toxic agent.

bioassay. A test for measuring the toxicity of an agent by exposing laboratory animals to the agent and observing the effects.

biological monitoring. Measurement of toxic agents or the results of their metabolism in biological materials, such as blood, urine, expired air, or biopsied tissue, to test for exposure to the toxic agents, or the detection of physiological changes that are due to exposure to toxic agents.

biologically plausible theory. A biological explanation for the relationship between exposure to an agent and adverse health outcomes.

carcinogen. A chemical substance or other agent that causes cancer.

carcinogenicity bioassay. Limited or long-term tests using laboratory animals to evaluate the potential carcinogenicity of an agent.

chronic toxicity. A toxic response to long-term exposure or dosing with an agent.

clinical ecologists. Physicians who believe that exposure to certain chemical agents can result in damage to the immune system, causing multiple-chemical hypersensitivity and a variety of other disorders. Clinical ecologists often have a background in the field of allergy, not toxicology, and their theoretical approach is derived in part from classic concepts of allergic responses and immunology. There has been much resistance in the medical community to accepting their claims.

clinical toxicology. The study and treatment of humans exposed to chemicals and the quantification of resulting adverse health effects. Clinical toxicology includes the application of pharmacological principles to the treatment of chemically exposed individuals and research on measures to enhance elimination of toxic agents.

compound. In chemistry, the combination of two or more different elements in definite proportions, which when combined, acquire different properties than the original elements.

confounding factors. Variables that are related to both exposure to a toxic agent and the outcome of the exposure. A confounding factor can obscure the relationship between the toxic agent and the adverse health outcome associated with that agent.

differential diagnosis. A physician's consideration of alternative diagnoses that may explain a patient's condition.

direct-acting agents. Agents that cause toxic effects without metabolic activation or conversion.

distribution. Movement of a toxic agent throughout the organ systems of the body (e.g., the liver, kidney, bone, fat, and central nervous system). The rate of distribution is usually determined by the blood flow through the organ and the ability of the chemical to pass through the cell membranes of the various tissues.

dose, dosage. The measured amount of a chemical that is administered at one time, or that an organism is exposed to in a defined period of time.

dose–response curve. A graphic representation of the relationship between the dose of a chemical administered and the effect produced.

dose–response relationships. The extent to which a living organism responds to specific doses of a toxic substance. The more time spent in contact with a toxic substance, or the higher the dose, the greater the organism's response. For example, a small dose of carbon monoxide will cause drowsiness; a large dose can be fatal.

epidemiology. The study of the occurrence and distribution of disease among people. Epidemiologists study groups of people to discover the cause of a disease, or where, when, and why disease occurs.

epigenetic. Pertaining to nongenetic mechanisms by which certain agents cause diseases, such as cancer.

etiology. A branch of medical science concerned with the causation of diseases.

excretion. The process by which toxicants are eliminated from the body, including through the kidney and urinary tract, the liver and biliary system, the fecal excretor, the lungs, sweat, saliva, and lactation.

exposure. The intake into the body of a hazardous material. The main routes of exposure to substances are through the skin, mouth, and lungs.

extrapolation. The process of estimating unknown values from known values.

Good Laboratory Practice (GLP). Codes developed by the federal government in consultation with the laboratory-testing industry that govern many aspects of laboratory standards.

hazard identification. In risk assessment, the qualitative analysis of all available experimental animal and human data to determine whether and at what dose an agent is likely to cause toxic effects.

hydrogeologists, hydrologists. Scientists who specialize in the movement of ground and surface waters and the distribution and movement of contaminants in those waters.

immunotoxicology. A branch of toxicology concerned with the effects of toxic agents on the immune system.

indirect-acting agents. Agents that require metabolic activation or conversion before they produce toxic effects in living organisms.

inhalation toxicology. The study of the effect of toxic agents that are absorbed into the body through inhalation, including their effects on the respiratory system.

in vitro. A research or testing methodology that uses living cells in an artificial or test tube system, or is otherwise performed outside of a living organism.

in vivo. A research or testing methodology that uses living organisms.

lethal dose 50 (LD50). The dose at which 50% of laboratory animals die within days to weeks.

lifetime bioassay. A bioassay in which doses of an agent are given to experimental animals throughout their lifetime. See bioassay.

maximum tolerated dose (MTD). The highest dose of an agent that an organism can be exposed to without causing death or significant overt toxicity.

metabolism. The sum total of the biochemical reactions that a chemical produces in an organism.

molecular toxicology. The study of how toxic agents interact with cellular molecules, including DNA.

multiple-chemical hypersensitivity. A physical condition whereby individuals react to many different chemicals at extremely low exposure levels.

multistage events. A model for understanding certain diseases, including some cancers, based on the postulate that more than one event is necessary for the onset of disease.

mutagen. A substance that causes physical changes in chromosomes or biochemical changes in genes.

mutagenesis. The process by which agents cause changes in chromosomes and genes.

neurotoxicology. A branch of toxicology concerned with the effects of exposure to toxic agents on the central nervous system.

no observable effect level (NOEL). The highest level of exposure to an agent at which no effect is observed. It is the experimental equivalent of a threshold.

no threshold model. A model for understanding disease causation which postulates that any exposure to a harmful chemical (such as a mutagen) may increase the risk of disease.

one hit theory. A theory of cancer risk in which each molecule of a chemical mutagen has a possibility, no matter how tiny, of mutating a gene in a manner that may lead to tumor formation or cancer.

pharmacokinetics. A mathematical model that expresses the movement of a toxic agent through the organ systems of the body, including to the target organ and to its ultimate fate.

potentiation. The process by which the addition of one agent, which by itself has no toxic effect, increases the toxicity of another agent when exposure to both agents occurs simultaneously.

reproductive toxicology. The study of the effect of toxic agents on male and female reproductive systems, including sperm, ova, and offspring.

risk assessment. The use of scientific evidence to estimate the likelihood of adverse effects on the health of individuals or populations from exposure to hazardous materials and conditions.

risk characterization. The final step of risk assessment, which summarizes information about an agent and evaluates it in order to estimate the risks it poses.

safety assessment. Toxicological research that tests the toxic potential of a chemical in vivo or in vitro using standardized techniques required by governmental regulatory agencies or other organizations.

structure activity relationships (SAR). A method used by toxicologists to predict the toxicity of new chemicals by comparing their chemical structures with those of compounds with known toxic effects.

synergistic effect. When two toxic agents acting together have an effect greater than that predicted by adding together their individual effects.

target organ. The organ system that is affected by a particular toxic agent.

target-organ dose. The dose to the organ that is affected by a particular toxic agent.

teratogen. An agent that changes eggs, sperm, or embryos, thereby increasing the risk of birth defects.

teratogenic. The ability to produce birth defects. (Teratogenic effects do not pass on to future generations.) See teratogen.

threshold. The level above which effects will occur and below which no effects occur. See no observable effect level.

toxic. Of, relating to, or caused by a poison—or a poison itself.

toxic agent or toxicant. An agent or substance that causes disease or injury.

toxicology. The science of the nature and effects of poisons, their detection, and the treatment of their effects.

References on Toxicology

Edward J. Calabrese, Multiple Chemical Interactions (1991).

Edward J. Calabrese, Principles of Animal Extrapolation (1983).

Casarett and Doull's Toxicology: The Basic Science of Poisons (Curtis D. Klaassen ed., 5th ed. 1996).

Committee on Risk Assessment Methodology, National Research Council, Issues in Risk Assessment (1993).

Genetic Toxicology of Complex Mixtures (Michael D. Waters et al. eds., 1990).

Human Risk Assessment: The Role of Animal Selection and Extrapolation (M. Val Roloff ed., 1987).

In Vitro Toxicity Testing: Applications to Safety Evaluation (John M. Frazier ed., 1992).

Michael A. Kamrin, Toxicology: A Primer on Toxicology Principles and Applications (1988).

Frank C. Lu, Basic Toxicology: Fundamentals, Target Organs, and Risk Assessment (2d ed. 1991).

Methods for Biological Monitoring (Theodore J. Kneip & John V. Crable eds., 1988).

National Research Council, Biologic Markers in Reproductive Toxicology (1989).

M. Alice Ottoboni, The Dose Makes the Poison: A Plain-Language Guide to Toxicology (2d ed. 1991).

Alan Poole & George B. Leslie, A Practical Approach to Toxicological Investigations (1989).

Principles and Methods of Toxicology (A. Wallace Hayes ed., 3d ed. 1994).

Joseph V. Rodricks, Calculated Risks (1992).

Short-Term Toxicity Tests for Nongenotoxic Effects (Philippe Bourdeau et al. eds., 1990).

Statistical Methods in Toxicology: Proceedings of a Workshop During Eurotox '90, Leipzig, Germany, September 12–14, 1990 (L. Hutnom ed., 1990).

Toxic Interactions (Robin S. Goldstein et al. eds., 1990).

Toxic Substances and Human Risk: Principles of Data Interpretation (Robert G. Tardiff & Joseph V. Rodricks eds., 1987).

Toxicology and Risk Assessment: Principles, Methods, and Applications (Anna M. Fan & Louis W. Chang eds., 1996).

Reference Guide on Medical Testimony

MARY SUE HENIFIN, HOWARD M. KIPEN, AND SUSAN R. POULTER

Mary Sue Henifin, J.D., M.P.H., is a partner with Buchanan Ingersoll, P.C., Princeton, New Jersey, and Adjunct Professor of Public Health Law, Department of Environmental & Community Medicine, UMDNJ–Robert Wood Johnson Medical School, Piscataway, New Jersey.

Howard M. Kipen, M.D., M.P.H., is Professor and Director of Occupational Health, Environmental and Occupational Health Sciences Institute, UMDNJ–Robert Wood Johnson Medical School in Piscataway, New Jersey.

Susan R. Poulter, J.D., Ph.D., is Professor of Law, University of Utah College of Law, Salt Lake City, Utah.

The authors are listed alphabetically. The authors greatly appreciate the excellent research assistance provided by Sue Elwyn, Dean Miletich, Marie Leary, Ross Jurewitz, and Fazil Khan.

CONTENTS

I. Introduction

Testimony by physicians is one of the most common forms of expert testimony in the courtroom today.[1] Medical testimony is routinely offered in both civil and criminal cases, including assault and battery,[2] rape,[3] workers' compensation proceedings,[4] and personal injury suits.[5] In the civil arena alone, medical testimony is frequently offered as part of medical malpractice cases,[6] Employee Retirement Income Security Act (ERISA) suits on coverage of health care plans,[7] Americans with Disabilities Act litigation,[8] product liability suits,[9] and toxic injury cases, such as breast implant and environmental contamination claims.[10] In

1. Samuel R. Gross, *Expert Evidence*, 1991 Wis. L. Rev. 1113, 1119 (a survey of trials revealed that over half of the testifying experts were physicians or medical professionals). Two unpublished surveys by the Federal Judicial Center, one in 1991 and another in 1998, found that physicians and medical experts comprised approximately 40 percent of the testifying experts in federal civil trials.

2. *See* United States v. Drapeau, 110 F.3d 618, 619–20 (8th Cir. 1997) (medical testimony of the examining doctor of the infant victim refuted the possibility that the child's injuries were the result of a fall from his bed); United States v. Talamante, 981 F.2d 1153, 1158 & n.7 (10th Cir. 1992) (physician testified that the victim's eye was not completely blind at the time of the assault, supporting a finding of serious bodily injury).

3. *See* United States v. Pike, 36 F.3d 1011, 1012–13 (10th Cir. 1994) (in a case of sexual abuse of a minor, the testimony of the examining physician need not be preferred over the testimony of the victim where the physician's testimony neither supports nor refutes the victim's testimony).

4. Medical testimony will almost always be offered on the diagnosis of the plaintiff's injury or disease, and often on other issues as well. *See* Silmon v. Can Do II, Inc., 89 F.3d 240, 241 (5th Cir. 1996) (testimony of three doctors as to the cause of the plaintiff's ruptured disc; the employer denied liability under the Jones Act, alleging that the plaintiff's injury was caused by illegal intravenous drug use); Bertram v. Freeport McMoran, Inc., 35 F.3d 1008, 1018 (5th Cir. 1994) (upholding the district court's discretion to give greater weight to the medical testimony of the plaintiff's primary treating physician where the plaintiff sued under the Jones Act for injuries arising from a workplace accident on a drilling barge).

5. *See* DiPirro v. United States, 43 F. Supp. 2d 327, 331–39 (W.D.N.Y. 1999) (recounting the court's findings of fact based upon the testimony of five physicians for the plaintiff and five physicians for the defendant concerning plaintiff's alleged injuries caused by an accident involving a U.S. Postal Service vehicle).

6. *See* Murray v. United States, 36 F. Supp. 2d 713, 716 (E.D. Va. 1999) (plaintiff's expert medical witness testified that the care provided fell well below that standard applicable to emergency room physicians).

7. *See* Dodson v. Woodmen of the World Ins. Soc'y, 109 F.3d 436, 438 (8th Cir. 1997) (treating physician testified that the plaintiff was mentally disabled prior to the expiration of his ERISA policy).

8. Price v. National Bd. of Med. Exam'rs, 966 F. Supp. 419 (S.D. W. Va. 1997) (medical testimony offered as to whether plaintiff had attention deficit hyperactivity disorder that caused disability as defined by the Americans with Disabilities Act).

9. *See* Demaree v. Toyota Motor Corp., 37 F. Supp. 2d 959 (W.D. Ky. 1999) (plaintiff's examining physician testified regarding injuries allegedly caused by a deploying air bag); Toole v. McClintock, 999 F.2d 1430, 1431 & n.2 (11th Cir. 1993) (reporting that five surgeons, including the plaintiff's treating physician, testified regarding surgery that caused breast implant rupture).

10. *See* Satterfield v. J.M. Huber Corp., 888 F. Supp. 1567, 1571 (N.D. Ga. 1995) (plaintiff's doctors testified that the plaintiff's symptoms were also consistent with exposure to secondary sources of

many instances, medical testimony or medical evidence is an indispensable part of the inquiry.

A. *Applicability of* Daubert v. Merrell Dow Pharmaceuticals, Inc.

Since the U.S. Supreme Court issued its opinion in *Daubert v. Merrell Dow Pharmaceuticals, Inc.*,[11] many courts have assessed the reliability of medical testimony according to *Daubert*'s standards. More recently, in *Kumho Tire Co. v. Carmichael*,[12] the Court held that *Daubert*'s reliability requirement and the trial judge's gatekeeping role apply to all expert testimony.

Although *Kumho* resolved any uncertainty as to the applicability of *Daubert*'s standards to medical testimony, there is still uncertainty over *how* courts will apply these standards, given the different approaches taken by the courts to consideration of the admissibility of medical evidence.[13] Two recent cases illustrate this diversity. In *Moore v. Ashland Chemical, Inc.*,[14] a case decided before *Kumho* that applied *Daubert* standards, the Fifth Circuit, sitting en banc, upheld the trial court's exclusion of a physician–expert's opinion on the cause of the plaintiff's reactive airway disease. The witness had offered the opinion, without citing published research indicating that fumes from toluene and a mixture of other chemicals from a leaking drum could cause reactive airway disease. The Fifth Circuit held that the trial court had not abused its discretion in its application of the *Daubert* factors, noting that expert testimony must be based on at least "some objective, independent validation of the expert's methodology. The expert's assurances that he has utilized generally accepted scientific methodology [are] insufficient."[15]

chemical emissions identified by the defendant and stated that they had no opinion on whether plaintiff's complaints were related to air contamination from defendant's plant).

11. 509 U.S. 579 (1993).

12. 119 S. Ct. 1167 (1999). *Kumho* concerned a tire-failure expert who gave an opinion on the cause of a tire failure based on his examination of the tire and experience in examining tires. *Id.* at 1176–78. Similarly, medical testimony will almost always rely in part on clinical examination, though often in conjunction with other sources of information.

13. *See* Margaret A. Berger, The Supreme Court's Trilogy on the Admissibility of Expert Testimony § IV.C.2.b, in this manual.

14. 151 F.3d 269 (5th Cir. 1998) (en banc), *cert. denied*, 119 S. Ct. 1454 (1999). In a panel decision, the U.S. Court of Appeals for the Fifth Circuit had held that medical testimony in a toxic injury case was not subject to the factors *Daubert* suggests for scientific knowledge. Moore v. Ashland Chem., Inc., 126 F.3d 679 (5th Cir. 1997). The court reconsidered that decision en banc, affirming the trial court's exclusion of the witness based on *Daubert*. 151 F.3d at 277–79. The en banc decision concluded that the trial court did not abuse its discretion, applying *General Electric Co. v. Joiner*, 522 U.S. 136 (1997). *Id.*

15. 151 F.3d at 276. *See also* Black v. Food Lion, Inc., 171 F.3d 308 (5th Cir. 1999) (trial court should not have admitted a physician's testimony that trauma from a slip and fall had caused the plaintiff's fibromyalgia).

In contrast, the Third Circuit's decision in *Heller v. Shaw Industries, Inc.*,[16] also a case decided before *Kumho* that applied *Daubert* standards, illustrates a much different approach. In *Heller*, as in *Moore*, the plaintiff complained of respiratory symptoms, which in this case coincided with exposure to a new carpet in her home. As in *Moore*, the trial court excluded the plaintiff's expert testimony because of the absence of published studies linking fumes from the carpet to allergic reactions. The Third Circuit stated that the trial court erred in so holding, noting the witness's reliance on "differential diagnosis."[17] The court nonetheless upheld the exclusion of the witness's testimony on other grounds.

These two cases illustrate the range of approaches taken by courts in considering testimony on causation, including issues related to testimony on "differential diagnosis" or "differential etiology" (as witnesses and courts use these terms), the necessity of research literature to support opinions on causation, and the importance of temporal relationships. While these issues may be intertwined, they represent different facets of the courts' approaches.[18]

B. Medical versus Legal Terminology

Perhaps because medical testimony is so common and yet not entirely accessible to the lay public, courts have come to use certain medical terms, such as *differential diagnosis* and *differential etiology* in ways that differ from their common usage in the medical profession. For example, although environmental and occupational health physicians may use the term "differential diagnosis" to include the process of determining whether an environmental or occupational exposure caused the patient's disease,[19] most physicians use the term to describe the process of determining which of several *diseases* is causing a patient's *symptoms*.

Expert witnesses and courts, however, frequently use the term "differential

16. 167 F.3d 146 (3d Cir. 1999).

17. *Id.* at 153–57. In this reference guide, the use of quotation marks around the terms *differential diagnosis* and *differential etiology* indicates the witness's or court's use of the terminology, which may differ from usage in the medical profession and from use elsewhere in this manual. *See infra* § I.B.

18. The appellate standard of review is also a critical factor in the analysis of the cases. The Supreme Court has twice instructed that a deferential abuse-of-discretion standard be applied to trial courts' admissibility decisions under Rule 702 of the Federal Rules of Evidence, including both rulings as to admissibility and the manner in which the trial court evaluates the proffered testimony. In *General Electric Co. v. Joiner*, 522 U.S. 136, 143 (1997), the Supreme Court held that an abuse-of-discretion standard applies to decisions on admissibility of expert testimony under *Daubert*. The Court reiterated that holding in *Kumho Tire Co. v. Carmichael*, 119 S. Ct. 1167, 1176 (1999), holding that abuse-of-discretion review applies to *how* the trial court assesses reliability.

19. The demonstration of causation has been described as a part of the process of diagnosing an environmental disease. *See* Mark R. Cullen et al., *Clinical Approach and Establishing a Diagnosis of an Environmental Medical Disorder, in* Environmental Medicine 217, 220 (Stuart M. Brooks et al. eds., 1995) [hereinafter Environmental Medicine]. The typical process of differential diagnosis is described more fully in section IV.B.

diagnosis" to describe the process by which causes of the patient's condition are identified, particularly causes external to the patient.[20] Additionally, courts sometimes characterize causal reasoning as "differential etiology," a term not used in medical practice, but one that more closely suggests the determination of cause.[21] For the sake of clarity and consistency, this reference guide uses the term "differential diagnosis" in its traditional medical sense, that is, referring to the diagnosis of disease, and refers to the process of identifying external causes of diseases and conditions as "determining cause," "determining external cause," or some similar phrase, as the circumstances warrant.

To add a further level of complexity, courts also use the terms *general causation* and *specific causation*. General causation is established by demonstrating, often through a review of scientific and medical literature, that exposure to a substance can cause a particular disease (e.g., that smoking cigarettes can cause lung cancer). Specific, or individual, causation, however, is established by demonstrating that a given exposure is the cause of an individual's disease (e.g., that a specific plaintiff's lung cancer was caused by his smoking).[22] Physicians may offer expert opinion on both specific and general causation,[23] although perhaps more commonly on specific causation as it relates to a patient's medical condi-

20. *See, e.g.*, Kannankeril v. Terminix Int'l, Inc., 128 F.3d 802, 807 (3d Cir. 1997) (court recognized differential diagnosis "as a technique that involves assessing causation with respect to a particular individual" (citing *In re* Paoli R.R. Yard PCB Litig., 35 F.3d 717, 758 (3d Cir. 1994), *cert. denied*, 513 U.S. 1190 (1995))); National Bank of Commerce v. Associated Milk Producers, Inc., 22 F. Supp. 2d 942, 963 (E.D. Ark. 1998) (plaintiff could not show, under differential diagnosis approach, that contaminated milk caused his cancer), *aff'd*, 191 F.3d 858 (8th Cir. 1999); Mancuso v. Consolidated Edison Co., 967 F. Supp. 1437, 1453 (S.D.N.Y. 1997) (proffered expert failed to conduct a differential diagnosis to exclude exposure to substances other than PCBs as the cause of plaintiffs' ailments).

21. *See, e.g.*, Westberry v. Gummi, 178 F.3d 257, 262 (4th Cir. 1999) (differential etiology analysis of talc as the cause of sinus problems); Synder v. Upjohn Co., 172 F.3d 58 (9th Cir. 1999) (unpublished table decision) (text at No. 97-55912, 1999 WL 77975 (9th Cir. Feb. 12, 1999)) (differential etiology analysis of Halcion as the cause of criminal behavior).

22. The issues of general causation and specific causation are addressed in detail in Michael D. Green et al., Reference Guide on Epidemiology §§ V, VII, and Bernard D. Goldstein & Mary Sue Henifin, Reference Guide on Toxicology §§ III–IV, in this manual. The distinction between general causation and specific causation is discussed in *Zwillinger v. Garfield Slope Housing Corp.*, No. CV 94-4009, 1998 WL 623589, at *19–*20 (E.D.N.Y. Aug. 17, 1998) (plaintiff's expert did not offer general causation evidence that outgassing from carpet could cause ailments suffered by plaintiff); National Bank of Commerce v. Associated Milk Producers, Inc., 22 F. Supp. 2d 942, 963 (E.D. Ark. 1998) (although differential diagnosis "'is undoubtedly important to the question of 'specific causation,''" plaintiff must provide expert opinion on the issue of "'general causation'" based on a scientifically valid methodology (quoting Cavallo v. Star Enter., 892 F. Supp. 756, 771 (E.D. Va. 1995), *aff'd in part, rev'd in part*, 100 F.3d 1150 (4th Cir. 1996), *cert. denied*, 522 U.S. 1044 (1998))), *aff'd*, 191 F.3d 858 (8th Cir. 1999).

23. *See In re* Joint E. & S. Dist. Asbestos Litig., 964 F.2d 92, 96 (2d Cir. 1992); Landrigan v. Celotex Corp., 605 A.2d 1079, 1086 (N.J. 1992) (permitting clinician to testify to specific causation based on epidemiology). *But see* Sutera v. Perrier Group of Am., Inc., 986 F. Supp. 655, 662 (D. Mass. 1997) (physician not qualified to testify on epidemiology). *See* Michael D. Green et al., Reference Guide on Epidemiology, § VII, in this manual.

tion. When physicians offer expert opinion on general causation, it is frequently incorporated into proffered testimony on specific causation.

C. Relationship of Medical Testimony to Legal Rules

In litigation, the form and content of medical testimony is shaped by a number of factors, first and foremost of which is the legal issue on which it is offered. In terms of content, in a traditional personal injury claim, the physician may be asked to opine on the actual cause of the patient's illness or injury. Newer theories of tort, however, such as claims for fear of future injury (e.g., "cancerphobia"),[24] increased risk of injury,[25] or medical monitoring,[26] require testimony on the patient's risk of future disease, rather than the actual cause.[27]

The form of testimony, whatever the issue, tends to be shaped by requirements of the applicable legal rules. For example, courts and lawyers will be familiar with various formulations of the causation issue, including the "but for" and "substantial factor" tests. A physician testifying on causation issues will be asked to opine in the form dictated by the legal rule.

Legal rules on the sufficiency of proof will also shape the physician's testimony. In a personal injury case, physicians are often asked to testify on one or more of the ultimate issues in the case, such as causation. Thus, their testimony will be shaped by the applicable substantive rule on the burden of proof. For example, a physician may testify that a plaintiff's disease is "more likely than not"[28] due to a chemical exposure or that causation exists to a "reasonable medical certainty."[29] This reference guide, however, consistent with the purpose of this manual, focuses on the methods and reasoning governing physicians' decisions and opinions, not the differing legal rules and theories on which medical

24. *See* Sterling v. Velsicol Chem. Corp., 855 F.2d 1188 (6th Cir. 1988); *see generally* Glen Donath, Comment, *Curing Cancerphobia Phobia: Reasonableness Redefined*, 62 U. Chi. L. Rev. 1113 (1995).

25. *See* Gideon v. Johns-Manville Sales Corp., 761 F.2d 1129, 1137–38 (5th Cir. 1985) (recognizing a claim for increased risk of contracting cancer where the likelihood is a "reasonable medical probability" or "more likely to occur than not").

26. *See In re* Paoli R.R. Yard PCB Litig., 916 F.2d 829 (3d Cir. 1990), *cert. denied*, 499 U.S. 961 (1991). *But see* Metro-North Commuter R.R. v. Buckley, 521 U.S. 424 (1997) (rejecting medical monitoring claim under the Federal Employers Liability Act). *Metro-North* also rejected a claim for negligent infliction of emotional distress based on fear of asbestos-related cancer. *Id.* at 437.

27. *See* National Bank of Commerce v. Associated Milk Producers, Inc., 22 F. Supp. 2d 942 (E.D. Ark. 1998) (fear of future injury may be an element of damages, requiring expert opinion governed by *Daubert* standards), *aff'd*, 191 F.3d 858 (8th Cir. 1999).

28. *See, e.g.*, Cavallo v. Star Enter., 892 F. Supp. 756, 771 (E.D. Va. 1995), *aff'd in part, rev'd in part*, 100 F.3d 1150 (4th Cir. 1996), *cert. denied*, 522 U.S. 1044 (1998).

29. *See, e.g.*, Black v. Food Lion, Inc., 171 F.3d 308, 310 (5th Cir. 1999) (plaintiff's burden was to prove that her fall caused fibromyalgia "to a reasonable degree of medical certainty, based on a reasonable medical probability and scientifically reliable evidence"). *See generally* Jeff L. Lewin, *The Genesis and Evolution of Legal Uncertainty About "Reasonable Medical Certainty,"* 57 Md. L. Rev. 380 (1998).

testimony is offered, or the standards courts have applied in reviewing medical testimony.[30]

This reference guide also does not address admissibility of testimony on the standard of care in medical malpractice cases. There are several reasons for this exclusion. First, medical malpractice cases are usually (though not exclusively) litigated in state courts rather than federal courts. Second, in most jurisdictions, the standard of care for physicians (like that for other professionals) is the customary level of care provided by competent physicians in the same field.[31] Thus, testimony on the standard of care usually concerns what other physicians do in similar situations, rather than whether the defendant–physician's diagnosis and treatment are based on good medical science (although customary physician practice and good medical science will generally coincide). As a result, the admissibility of expert opinion on the standard of care is decided according to whether the witness is qualified to opine on the same field as the malpractice defendant.[32]

Within the limitations described above, the next four sections of this reference guide explain medical practice, with an emphasis on how physicians apply medical and scientific knowledge, clinical experience, and patient history and examination to the process of diagnosis of disease and selection of appropriate treatment.

30. It is worth reminding readers that this guide is not intended to instruct judges concerning what medical testimony should be admissible as evidence. This chapter and the other reference guides attempt to contribute to the development of the law by clarifying scientific and professional practice in an area, thereby informing the development of consistent legal doctrines as courts consider individual cases. *See* the preface to this manual. This constraint, set by the Board of the Federal Judicial Center, is especially notable in this chapter. The lack of commentary on various standards should not be misunderstood as indicating that the authors have not given considerable thought to the manner in which such conflicts should be resolved. *See generally* Joan E. Bertin & Mary S. Henifin, *Science, Law, and the Search for the Truth in the Courtroom*, 22 J.L. Med. & Ethics 6 (1994); Susan R. Poulter, *Science and Toxic Torts: Is There a Rational Solution to the Problem of Causation?*, 7 High Tech. L.J. 189 (1992); Susan R. Poulter, *Medical and Scientific Evidence of Causation: Guidelines for Evaluating Medical Opinion Evidence, in* Expert Witnessing: Explaining and Understanding Science 186 (Carl Meyer ed., 1998). A summary of different approaches in applying evidentiary rules to medical testimony is offered in Margaret A. Berger, The Supreme Court's Trilogy on the Admissibility of Expert Testimony, § IV.C.2.b, in this manual. Moreover, proposed changes to Rule 702 by the Judicial Conference Advisory Committee on Evidence Rules, if enacted, may also affect the legal analysis of medical testimony.

31. 4 Lane Medical Litigation Guide §§ 40.21–.28, at 73-101 (Fred Lane & David A. Birnbaum eds., 1993 & Supp. 1996).

32. 1 *id.* § 4.15, at 18–20 (1994 & Supp. 1996). In some jurisdictions, the witness must be qualified to testify about the standard of care in a similar or even the same locality. 4 *id.* § 40.23, at 86–92 (1993 & Supp. 1996).

II. The Medical Doctor As an Expert

A. What Is a Physician?

In the United States, a physician is someone who has met the rigorous requirements of a four-year program and graduated from a credentialed medical or osteopathic school. However, as explained below, this training is not sufficient to qualify a physician to practice medicine.[33]

The courses in medical school are generally similar from school to school, and they focus on basic medical sciences (e.g., microbiology, pharmacology, and pathology) as well as clinical training in medical diagnosis and treatment (e.g., internal medicine, cardiology, pulmonology, surgery, psychiatry, dermatology). All medical curricula include some basic training in epidemiology and biostatistics. There is relatively little structured study of public health, occupational medicine, and toxicology in a traditional curriculum, although a number of medical schools offer joint degree programs leading to a Master of Public Health degree (M.P.H.), with enhanced training in epidemiology, toxicology, and other aspects of public health. Furthermore, it is not uncommon for physicians to undertake further study and become proficient in epidemiological research in their particular fields. Most physicians have substantial training and experience in pharmacology, a subject closely related to toxicology that concerns the effects of therapeutic drugs.[34]

In most states, physicians are required to complete a minimum of one additional year of hospital-based "residency" training, the first year of which is called an "internship," in an approved program before they can be licensed to practice medicine. After completing the internship year, a physician may apply for state licensure to practice medicine. However, specialization requires further training in an approved residency program beyond the internship year. For example, surgery requires at least four additional years; family or internal medicine, pediatrics, or neurology requires two additional years. A physician may pursue subspecialty training, which usually requires a further one- to three-year "fellowship" focusing on a particular organ or system (e.g., pulmonology, cardiology, gastroenterology, rheumatology, endocrinology, hematology) or type of disease (e.g., infectious disease, oncology, or neurological movement disorders or electrophysiology).[35]

33. *See* World Health Org., World Directory of Medical Schools 274–75 (6th ed. 1988 & Supp. 1997).

34. *See, e.g.*, Association of Am. Med. Colleges, Curriculum Directory 1998–99, at 104–05 (27th ed. 1998) (listing required courses for Johns Hopkins University School of Medicine).

35. *See* World Health Org., *supra* note 33, at 274–75.

After a physician has completed a residency or fellowship in a specialty, he or she is eligible to take an examination given by that medical specialty's "board." There are twenty-three specialty and subspecialty boards administered by the American Board of Medical Specialists (ABMS), as well as a number of other boards not under ABMS with more idiosyncratic criteria for certification. Passing such an exam makes the physician "board certified" in the field or subspecialty—a marker of substantial proficiency within the particular area of medicine and a credential often required by hospitals for appointment to their medical staff.[36] Other indicia of expertise include academic appointments, published articles in peer-reviewed journals, grant awards, and appointment to peer review panels.[37]

After the conclusion of formal medical education, including internship and residency, physicians continue to acquire medical knowledge through clinical experience, hospital-based lectures and training programs, review of medical literature, and continuing medical education courses that provide information in various specialties. A number of states have moved toward requiring continuing medical education for license renewal.[38] An increasing number of medical specialties require passage of the board examination at regularly scheduled intervals to maintain board certification.

To practice at a hospital, a physician must pass review by a "credentialing committee" that examines the credentials of the physician, as well as legal and state board records concerning the physician. A physician who clears the credentialing committee may become a member of the hospital's medical staff, otherwise known as an "attending physician," and may admit patients to the hospital for treatment. A hospital may revoke staff and admitting privileges for

36. Although it may be helpful in establishing the witness's credentials for opinion testimony, courts usually do not apply a strict requirement of specialization or board certification for most purposes. *See, e.g.*, Holbrook v. Lykes Bros. S.S. Co., 80 F.3d 777, 782–83 (3d Cir. 1996) (physician board certified in pulmonary medicine not required to be a specialist in oncology and radiation to testify on causation of mesothelioma). In contrast, admissibility of testimony on the medical standard of care in medical malpractice cases is typically controlled through screening of the witness's qualifications. *See, e.g.*, Marquardt v. Joseph, 173 F.3d 855 (6th Cir. 1999) (unpublished table decision) (text at No. 98-5163, 1999 WL 196569 (6th Cir. Mar. 30, 1999) (dentist who was not an oral surgeon was not qualified to testify on the standard of care for oral surgery)); Carroll v. Morgan, 17 F.3d 787, 790 (5th Cir. 1994) (cardiologist with many years of experience need not be a specialist in pathology to testify on the relationship between heart problems and death).

37. The American Medical Association (AMA) has taken an interest in the quality of medical expert testimony. After reviewing cases involving testimony by physicians who had falsified their credentials, the AMA issued a 1998 report to its Board of Trustees recommending that the AMA encourage state licensing boards to develop disciplinary measures for physicians who provide fraudulent testimony. The House of Delegates adopted an amended version of the report. *See* Michael Higgins, *Docking Doctors? AMA Eyes Discipline for Physicians Giving 'False' Testimony*, A.B.A. J., Sept. 1998, at 20.

38. Jeoffrey K. Stross & Thomas J. DeKornfeld, *A Formal Audit of Continuing Medical Education Activity for License Renewal*, 264 JAMA 2421 (1990) (audit of continuing medical education activities of

cause.[39] Some hospital physicians are also members of the teaching staff, charged with the training of interns and residents in their medical specialties. Most, but not all, teaching staff have joint academic appointments at a medical school.

B. Physicians' Roles in Patient Care

After completion of training, a physician may be involved in various aspects of medicine. While the public tends to think of a physician as directly involved in patient care, a practicing physician may also serve as a "consulting physician," conduct medical research, or have an academic appointment.[40] Although the lines between these different roles often blur, understanding the range of activities undertaken by physicians is helpful.

A treating physician's primary role is the examination, diagnosis, and treatment of patients.[41] The physician is expected to do one or more of the following: diagnose the patient's conditions, recommend or provide appropriate treatments, and monitor the patient's progress. The treating physician may also, as appropriate, counsel patients on the management of diseases, as well as on dietary habits, genetic and familial risks and other aspects of a patient's life relevant to preventing disease, maintaining health, or managing disease or injury. A treating physician may be a specialist or nonspecialist. Some members of a treating team of physicians, such as radiologists or pathologists, perform primarily diagnostic roles and rarely prescribe treatment.

A consulting physician is someone who is asked for recommendations for diagnosis and treatment or a "second opinion," based on his or her more specialized knowledge and experience. Examples include a cardiologist brought in to assist the primary physician with the care of someone after a heart attack and a pulmonary specialist brought in to assist with the management of a patient with asthma. The consulting physician may rely, in whole or in part, on information developed by other medical practitioners contained in the patient's medical records, such as medical history, laboratory tests, and x-rays. More often, the consulting physician will also conduct an examination of the patient and under-

physicians licensed in Michigan to assess compliance with a law mandating participation in 150 hours of continuing medical education every three years).

39. Chouteau v. Enid Mem'l Hosp., 992 F.2d 1106, 1109 & n.2 (10th Cir. 1993) (upholding the district court's grant of summary judgment, finding that sufficient justification existed for the defendant hospital to lawfully terminate the plaintiff's staff privileges).

40. *See* Alvan R. Feinstein, Clinical Judgment 21 (photo. reprint 1985) (1967).

41. Treating physicians are generally permitted to testify, although contentions are sometimes made that their testimony should be limited. In *Holbrook v. Lykes Bros. Steamship Co.*, 80 F.3d 777 (3d Cir. 1995), the trial court had excluded the treating physician's testimony on his diagnosis of mesothelioma and a pathology report because the physician was not a pathologist or oncologist. The Third Circuit reversed the decision, noting that treating physicians' testimony is often given greater weight than testimony from physicians who have not examined the patient. *Id.* at 782–83.

take additional tests and investigations. While consulting physicians are often an integral part of the team of treating physicians, in some instances they may not be involved in treatment, instead providing opinions for employers, insurers, litigants, or courts.

C. Medical Research and Academic Appointments

In addition to traditional patient care and consultation as to diagnosis and treatment, physicians may be involved in medical research in a variety of areas (e.g., epidemiology, pharmacology, and toxicology) as their primary activity, or in conjunction with patient-oriented medical practice. For example, physicians may be involved in clinical trials to evaluate new drugs or other therapies. They also may participate in studies on the causes of disease. The physician may be the principal investigator, who is primarily responsible for such studies, or may participate as a coinvestigator or collaborator, or simply by referring patients to the studies. Many physicians involved in medical research also have a teaching position at a medical school or a large teaching hospital.

D. Physicians As Expert Witnesses

In contrast to the traditional medical roles they fill as outlined above, physicians frequently act as witnesses in court, either for the parties or, on occasion, as court-appointed experts. Physician–witnesses may testify based on their activities as treating or consulting physicians or more generally about medical and scientific knowledge and its application to the issues in a case. In the former role, they may be characterized as "fact" witnesses, but they will also be applying medical expertise to a greater or lesser degree in assessing the significance of the patient's signs and symptoms and medical history, making a diagnosis, opining on proper treatment and prognosis, and the like. In some medical fields, such as clinical toxicology or occupational medicine, this dual role is quite common. In other instances, the physician is applying his or her expertise solely to offer an expert opinion, relying on factual clinical information developed by treating physicians or from hospital records or other sources.[42]

A physician may be asked to testify about the physical condition of a plaintiff, diagnosis, treatment, causes of the plaintiff's condition, or prognosis. A physician may also be asked to interpret epidemiological or industrial hygiene data if they are within his or her scope of expertise. Such testimony may be important

42. Howard Hu & Frank E. Speizer, ***Influence of Environmental and Occupational Hazards on Disease***, *in* 1 Harrison's Principles of Internal Medicine 18, 19 (Anthony S. Fauci et al. eds., 14th ed. 1998) [hereinafter Principles of Internal Medicine].

both in a factual sense—what happened and when—and as a basis for expert opinion on such issues as the following:

1. Is the diagnosis correct? (assessing what injury the plaintiff suffered);
2. Were the appropriate treatments prescribed? (assessing the issues of standard of care in a medical malpractice case or damages in a tort case);
3. What is the prognosis or the likely course of the plaintiff's condition? (assessing future damages);
4. Was the patient exposed to the substance in question? (assessing exposure through patient symptoms and reports, such as eye burning, the detection of an odor, or a headache, which provide indications as to the concentration of an irritant or other agent);
5. Is there an increased risk of future disease? (assessing damages by predicting future consequences of an existing condition; assessing a claim for increased risk of future disease; assessing the reasonableness of a claim for fear of disease (e.g., cancerphobia); or assessing the propriety of medical surveillance in a medical monitoring claim); and
6. What caused the plaintiff's medical condition? (assessing general and specific causation).

As set forth later in this reference guide,[43] physicians do not always use the same approach in evaluating these issues as the legal system does. For example, in tort cases, liability will often turn on the identification of one or more causes of the plaintiff's condition. A physician, independent of legal issues, typically uses the term *causation* or *etiology* to refer to the various levels of underlying abnormality that have substantially led to the next higher level of abnormality, disease, or diagnosis. This "chain," or web, of causation is considered the "pathogenesis" or pathophysiology of a disease. For instance, a heart attack may be due to a sudden blockage of a coronary artery, which was facilitated by a preexisting cholesterol plaque in the artery, which in turn is due to the patient's high level of blood cholesterol, which is due to genetics, diet, a sedentary lifestyle, and smoking, which contributes at many levels.[44] Most physicians are familiar with the general importance, if not specific degrees of risk, of the listed internal biochemical and mechanical factors in a heart attack, and with many other areas in the web of causation, such as the common external factors listed above.[45]

43. *See infra* § IV and accompanying footnotes.

44. Elliot M. Antman & Eugene Braunwald, *Acute Myocardial Infraction, in* 1 Principles of Internal Medicine, *supra* note 42, at 1352, 1352–53. In this guide, the term *internal* is used to refer to causal factors and conditions internal to the patient's body, such as genetic predisposition to coronary artery disease, to distinguish them from causal factors that are *external* to the body, such as smoking and diet.

45. For a general discussion of the process used to infer internal and external causation, see Feinstein, *supra* note 40, at 80–83. *See, e.g.*, Carroll v. Morgan, 17 F.3d 787, 791 (5th Cir. 1994) (discussing multiple causes of plaintiff's coronary disease).

While physicians dealing with diagnosis and treatment tend to think in terms of both internal and external causation, courts are usually asked to determine the role of causes that are external to the individual. Generally, physicians focus on causal elements that can be addressed through medical treatment or through changes in lifestyle or diet; courts focus primarily on causal elements for which a litigant or other party might be held responsible. For example, a workers' compensation case might concern the role of physiological stress at work in causing underlying heart disease, or the role of carbon monoxide in triggering a specific heart attack.[46] Identification of those kinds of causes depends on information concerning quantification of risks in the workplace environment, as well as on the medical literature on causation, including the psychological, toxicological, and epidemiological literature.[47] To determine general causation, the expert must review the pertinent literature, as familiarity with this literature is key to expert opinion. For example, since many cardiologists advise patients on returning to work after a heart attack, they will often be familiar with the literature on work-based risks and cardiovascular disease, whereas most other physicians, who deal with this question less frequently, would need to devote some time to study before evaluating such a special consideration.

III. Information Utilized by Physicians

Physicians rely on the following diverse sources of information in arriving at a diagnosis, determining a course of treatment, and exploring causation: the patient history (information derived directly from the patient), patient records, physical examination, and diagnostic tests.[48]

A. Patient History (from the Patient)

The patient history is one of the primary and most useful tools in the practice of clinical medicine. It is usually divided into present illness (including both subjective reports and medical documentation) and past medical problems, with or without medical documentation.[49]

As obtained by the examining physician, the patient history is extremely important in evaluating the patient's condition, determining what medical tests may be warranted, arriving at a diagnosis, and recommending an appropriate

46. *See, e.g.*, Fiore v. Consolidated Freightways, 659 A.2d 436 (N.J. 1995) (truck driver's workers' compensation case claiming that his heart disease was caused by occupational exposure to carbon monoxide fumes remanded so that parties could provide more reliable exposure evidence).

47. *See* Cullen et al., *supra* note 19, at 220–21.

48. *See* Jerome P. Kassirer & Richard I. Kopelman, Learning Clinical Reasoning 4 (1991).

49. Barbara Bates et al., A Guide to Physical Examination and History Taking 2–3 (6th ed. 1995).

course of treatment. Even in this era of sophisticated medical testing protocols, it is estimated that 70% of significant patient problems can be identified, although not necessarily confirmed, by a thorough patient history.[50]

A thorough patient history includes not only present illness and past medical problems, but also aspects of medical, occupational, personal, and familial background that are relevant to the present problem. Moreover, patient histories may identify common patterns of illness among individuals with a common lifestyle or exposure element, such as reproductive problems in individuals occupationally exposed to lead. Although patient histories are important in determining a diagnosis, and useful in epidemiological studies of both acute and chronic diseases, there is no validated and widely used patient history questionnaire with which to begin the diagnostic process,[51] perhaps because the history-taking process is so iterative and intertwined with hypothesis testing.

Despite the absence of a standard patient history questionnaire, there is general agreement that a useful adult patient history includes the following information:

1. identification (e.g., name, sex, age);
2. chief complaint and history of the present illness;
3. medical history (e.g., injuries, medical conditions and diseases, surgical procedures);
4. lifestyle characteristics (e.g., use of nicotine, alcohol, and other drugs; exposures in the home);
5. familial health (e.g., medical conditions and diseases of relatives); and
6. occupational history (e.g., present and previous employment, exposures).[52]

While more recent events or those that more directly appear pertinent to the particular presenting symptoms of a patient will usually be given the most attention, historic events or familial history may provide insight into diagnosis and prognosis.[53] This is particularly true when the physician is considering exposure–disease relationships with a long latency, such as in asbestos-related disease or inherited predispositions for malignancy.[54]

1. Symptomatology

Symptoms are by definition subjective, since they are self-reported by the patient in his or her own words. Because symptoms that preoccupy the patient are not always the most relevant to diagnosis, the physician will often need to ask

50. *See* Mark H. Swartz, Textbook of Physical Diagnosis: History and Examination 667 (3d ed. 1998).

51. Office of Tech. Assessment, U.S. Congress, Reproductive Health Hazards in the Workplace app. B at 365 (1985).

52. *See, e.g.,* Bates et al., *supra* note 49, at 3–7, 16–17.

53. *See, e.g., id.* at 637–39.

54. *See* Thomas E. Andreoli et al., Cecil Essentials of Medicine 152 (3d ed. 1993).

the patient about symptoms that are particularly useful for diagnosis, but not of particular concern to the patient. Generally, patients will be asked to characterize symptoms by their location, intensity, frequency, exacerbating factors, ameliorating factors, and novelty.[55]

As a report of the patient's own experience, symptoms are uniquely valuable, but they are also subject to various sources of bias and error, both intentional and unintentional. A competent diagnostician can take sources of error into account, but for some symptoms, such as severity of pain, or when the first severe attack of shortness of breath occurred, it is usually not possible to objectively verify the patient's reports. The physician's skill, knowledge, and experience with the particular area of concern is critical in obtaining an accurate and meaningful history.[56] Physicians are accustomed to reaching a subjective conclusion regarding the quality and reliability of the history they obtain from the patient.

2. Environmental and Occupational History

Consideration of occupational and environmental causation in diagnosis has long been recommended to physicians, but more specific attention to the environmental and occupational history as part of the medical workup has recently been emphasized, with the degree of detail depending on the clinical situation.[57]

If the medical workup indicates a potential occupational or environmental disease, the physician should explore the patient's potential exposures in more detail.[58] Although the physician often will not have measures of environmental exposure, information about the level of exposure can be inferred in certain instances from the description of the workplace and work processes; the duration of exposure; correlates, such as eye irritation, headache, or odor; the size of a room or other enclosure; the presence of windows or other ventilation; and other activities occurring nearby.[59]

55. *See, e.g.*, Bates et al., *supra* note 49, at 635, 645–47.

56. *See* Anthony S. Fauci et al., *The Practice of Medicine, in* 1 Principles of Internal Medicine, *supra* note 42, at 1, 2; Lee Goldman, *Quantitative Aspects of Clinical Reasoning, in* 1 Principles of Internal Medicine, *supra* note 42, at 9, 9.

57. *See* Hu & Speizer, *supra* note 42, at 19; Environmental Medicine: Integrating a Missing Element into Medical Education 5–11 (Andrew M. Pope & David P. Rall eds., 1995).

58. Establishing exposure is usually deemed necessary to a plaintiff's toxic injury claim, and the existence or degree of exposure to the agent is often at issue. *See, e.g.*, *In re* Paoli R.R. Yard PCB Litig., 916 F.2d 829 (3d Cir. 1990) (environmental exposure to polychlorinated biphenyls (PCBs) contested), *cert. denied*, 499 U.S. 961 (1991).

59. *See* Hu & Speizer, *supra* note 42, at 19; Frank E. Speizer, *Environmental Lung Diseases, in* 2 Principles of Internal Medicine, *supra* note 42, at 1429, 1429–30; Peter Casten, Jr., & Katherine Loftfield, *The Eyes and Vision, in* Environmental Medicine, *supra* note 19, at 240, 242. Exposure to chemical agents typically found in certain work environments can sometimes be inferred based on industrial hygiene studies of particular occupations. For example, employment as an asbestos insulator has been associated with significant levels of asbestos exposure.

Information about exposure may also be available from workplace industrial hygiene records or a police report. Other sources of information may include governmental agency or private consultant records and insurance inspections. However, physicians usually have to evaluate environmental or occupational diseases in the absence of quantitative exposure levels. Even in situations in which there are measurements of personal breathing-zone exposures, such data may not take into account various other factors, such as the level of a patient's exertion, which may change the actual dose to make it greater or lower than theoretical calculations; the performance of ventilation equipment; or the fit of a respirator.[60]

3. Other Risk Factors

In addition to information about environmental and occupational exposures, a patient's history should include information about other known risk factors, such as the patient's family history, smoking history, amount of exercise, alcohol use, use of medications or illicit drugs, and exposures to chemicals in the home or from hobbies.[61]

B. Past and Present Patient Records and Exposure-Related Records

Although time-consuming and bureaucratically cumbersome, an examination of patient records from former treating physicians, clinics, and hospitals can often be crucial for accurate diagnosis, for determination of the onset of an illness or symptom, and to provide information about external exposures. Patient records may reveal the course of an illness and the results of prior tests, and they can help gauge the reliability of patient-reported information. Unfortunately, because obtaining multiple patient medical records from various institutions in a timely manner is often difficult, much medical care is rendered in their absence. More complete records are often gathered once litigation has begun.

C. Physical Examination[62]

The physical examination is a routine procedure for evaluating the patient and determining a diagnosis. The physical examination identifies approximately 20%

60. For the effect of exercise, see, e.g., Joseph D. Brain et al., *The Effects of Exercise on Inhalation of Particles and Gases, in* Variations in Susceptibility to Inhaled Pollutants: Identification, Mechanisms, and Policy Implications 204, 210 (Joseph D. Brain et al. eds., 1988); for other variables affecting an individual's exposure and response to inhaled gases or particles, see, e.g., Speizer, *supra* note 59, at 1430.

61. *See* Bates et al., *supra* note 49, at 16–19; Speizer, *supra* note 59, at 1429–30.

62. Courts sometimes attach importance to the physician–witness's examination of the patient. *See, e.g., In re* Paoli R.R. Yard PCB Litig., 35 F.3d 717, 771 (3d Cir. 1994) (physician's testimony on causation admitted as to patients the witness examined), *cert. denied*, 513 U.S. 1190 (1995); *In re* "Agent Orange" Prod. Liab. Litig., 611 F. Supp. 1223, 1235, 1243–47 (E.D.N.Y. 1985), *aff'd*, 818 F.2d 187

of significant medical problems.[63] The physical exam has standard components with which physicians, depending on their degree of specialization, may be more or less proficient. For example, while most physicians will hear a loud heart murmur or identify a severe tremor, subtle signs of heart disease or neurological disease may be missed by those without specialty training in cardiology[64] or neurology, respectively. Greater proficiency can be expected from a specialist, because doctors in specialized fields focus their examinations on the system in question, do more tests within an area, are more skilled in performing the exam, and are better able to distinguish between significant and insignificant deviations from normal.

The findings from the physical exam as well as radiographic imaging studies, noninvasive functional tests, and blood tests are referred to as "signs" of illness, as contrasted with symptoms, which are subjectively reported by the patient. Although signs are more objective than symptoms, they still depend on the physician's skill and objectivity, degree of attention to detail, and level of concern. Physical signs assume enhanced significance when they demonstrate the presence of a functional or structural change already suggested by the patient history.[65]

A thorough physical exam begins with the taking of vital signs (temperature, heart rate, respiratory rate, and blood pressure). Next is a description of the patient's general appearance and whether the patient was able to cooperate with the exam. This is followed by examination of each region and organ system (skin, head, ears, eyes, nose, mouth and throat, neck, chest, lungs, heart and cardiovascular system, abdomen, genitourinary system, extremities and musculoskeletal system, and nervous system). Psychological assessments are sometimes then provided.[66] However, many specialists may perform only a portion of the exam; and, because of time constraints, many practitioners focus on only one aspect of a patient at a given time.[67]

Physicians are taught to record their findings on a physical exam in a routinized but not necessarily standardized fashion. A thorough exam will include

(2d Cir. 1987), *cert. denied*, 487 U.S. 1234 (1988). Courts have also recognized that physicians may present testimony based on examinations and tests performed by others, as well as on medical records. *See, e.g.*, Kannankeril v. Terminix Int'l, Inc., 128 F.3d 802, 809 (3d Cir. 1997); Sementilli v. Trinidad Corp., 155 F.3d 1130 (9th Cir.) (per curiam) (physician could present testimony on plaintiff's condition based on medical records and knowledge, experience, training, and education), *dissenting opinion amended*, 162 F.3d 1015 (9th Cir. 1998).

63. *See* Swartz, *supra* note 50, at 667.

64. *See, e.g.*, Feinstein, *supra* note 40, at 2.

65. *See* Fauci et al., *supra* note 56, at 2.

66. *See* Bates et al., *supra* note 49, at 118–21.

67. *Id.* at 117.

"findings" as opposed to merely notes indicating that an observation was "within normal limits" or "negative." However, the emphasis is on the accuracy of the observation, rather than the degree of detail that may be presented. How the findings of the physical exam fit into context with other data in the case is a key item in assessing the exam's reliability.[68]

As discussed above, specialists are generally better able than generalists to elicit patient history information, ascertain physical findings, and interpret lab results within their area of expertise. Findings that may have limited clinical meaning but may inform decisions regarding external causation in legal proceedings, such as the bilateral asymptomatic stable pleural thickening in someone with a history of asbestos exposure, are sometimes not mentioned by a treating physician, such as a radiologist. Thus, the absence of such findings from the treating physician's records should not necessarily be taken as an indication of disagreement between the treating physician and the specialist.

D. Diagnostic Tests

For diagnosis of more serious conditions, especially cancer, physicians are taught always to seek a tissue biopsy.[69] This is often referred to as a gold standard, because it is regarded as highly accurate or at least the most definitive indicator of a particular condition. For other conditions, the definitive test may be a radiological test (e.g., a pulmonary angiogram for diagnosis of pulmonary embolism)[70] or a microbiological test (e.g., a sputum culture for diagnosis of tuberculosis).[71]

Sometimes physicians and patients will be satisfied with a diagnosis even though the gold standard test for that diagnosis was not performed. There may be too much risk associated with such a test (e.g., if it is invasive or involves intentional exposure to a possible allergen), its costs may outweigh the benefit of achieving a more definitive diagnosis, or it may be superfluous because other data are so consistent and convincing.[72] As always, the various cost–benefit and risk–benefit equations are interpreted relative to the individual patient, physician, and medical circumstances, as well as institutional capabilities.

68. *Id.* at 649–52.

69. *See, e.g.*, Dan L. Longo, *Approach to the Patient with Cancer*, *in* 1 Principles of Internal Medicine, *supra* note 42, at 493, 494.

70. *See* Steven E. Weinberger & Jeffrey M. Drazen, *Diagnostic Procedures in Respiratory Disease*, *in* 2 Principles of Internal Medicine, *supra* note 42, at 1417, 1418.

71. *See* Matthew E. Levinson, *Pneumonia, Including Necrotizing Pulmonary Infections (Lung Abscess)*, *in* 2 Principles of Internal Medicine, *supra* note 42, at 1437, 1440.

72. *See* Kassirer & Kopelman, *supra* note 48, at 217–22.

In modern medical practice, tests and procedures are critical to confirming most diagnoses. These include radiological examination, laboratory tests, physiological tests of lung or nerve function, pathological examination of tissue, and invasive diagnostic tests, such as cardiac catheterization. A physician's decision whether to order a diagnostic test for specified clinical indications should take into consideration expense, risk, accuracy, and predictive value. Tests are limited by their inherent sensitivity and specificity, the fallibility of the instrumentation, and the variation in skills of the individuals who perform or interpret the tests. Error rates for diagnostic tests, as discussed below,[73] in terms of sensitivity and specificity are generally available, but the all-important predictive values[74] vary with the particular disorder and with the population (i.e., demographics, background rate of disease) on whom the test is performed or the population from which a tested individual is derived. While pathological examination of tissue biopsies is considered the gold standard of diagnostic tests, even it has an error rate.[75]

In general, laboratory tests do not have a paramount role in establishing the external etiology of many chronic and acute illnesses. Major exceptions to this are microbiological evaluations for causes of infectious diseases, and cases of toxic substance intoxication, such as lead poisoning or alcohol or drug poisoning.[76]

Depending on the diagnosis being considered and whether the exposure truly leaves a reliable "signature" or "residue,"[77] a biopsy may or may not have great utility for exogenous causal diagnosis. Invasive tissue biopsies are not routinely performed for purposes of establishing causation because of the risk involved with the procedure to obtain the tissue. Sometimes such test results are incidentally available because they may have been used to establish the diagnosis, particularly in the case of lung disorders.

73. *See infra* note 105 and accompanying text.

74. *See infra* notes 107–108 and accompanying text.

75. *See* Fauci et al., *supra* note 56, at 3; Goldman, *supra* note 56, at 10; Kassirer & Kopelman, *supra* note 48, at 23.

76. *See* Christopher H. Linden & Frederick H. Lovejoy, Jr., *Poisoning and Drug Overdose, in* 2 Principles of Internal Medicine, *supra* note 42, at 2523, 2523–25.

77. Certain persistent toxic agents can sometimes be detected in laboratory tests. *See, e.g.*, Hose v. Chicago Northwestern Transp. Co., 70 F.3d 968 (8th Cir. 1995) (laboratory tests showed elevated manganese in plaintiff's body; MRI indicated manganese in brain). The interpretation of such tests has been at issue in a number of cases. *See, e.g.*, *In re* Paoli R.R. Yard PCB Litig., 35 F.3d 717 (3d Cir. 1994) (dispute over whether PCB levels in plaintiffs' adipose tissue exceeded background levels), *cert. denied*, 513 U.S. 1190 (1995); Wright v. Willamette Indus., Inc., 91 F.3d 1105 (8th Cir. 1996) (presence of wood dust fibers at plaintiffs' residence and in tissue samples insufficient to establish exposure to formaldehyde at levels known to cause plaintiffs' symptoms).

1. Laboratory Tests

Laboratory tests are usually tests in which a specimen, usually blood or another body fluid, is submitted to a laboratory for a chemical or microbiological analysis. For many of the routine chemical assays for levels of proteins, fats, electrolytes, enzymes, or hormones in blood, there are established normal ranges for a given laboratory or test manufacturer, and for given subpopulations (e.g., men or women, children or adults). The results are interpreted as being either within or outside of normal limits. Not all deviation from normal limits is pathological, particularly if the individual is otherwise without complaint. For example, the results of liver function tests often fluctuate outside of the normal range in those without liver disease or hepatotoxin exposure. Based on standard statistical techniques for defining normal ranges, one in twenty test results can be expected to be abnormal (i.e., outside the normal range) in a healthy individual.[78]

Common laboratory tests include x-rays, routine blood chemistries, and blood counts. More specialized tests include computerized axial tomography (CAT) scans, magnetic resonance imaging (MRIs), and angiograms.[79] All of these tests are used in one of three ways as part of the diagnostic process. The first and most common use is to clarify a disease process or pathology or pathophysiology.[80] A second and less common use of laboratory tests is for estimation of exposure to potentially toxic substances. These tests include measures of an agent in the body (e.g., blood lead levels) or in an excretory product (e.g., urine mercury). Understanding that such tests only determine exposure and not disease or health effect is critical.[81] A third and fairly uncommon type of laboratory test is used to substantiate an exposure–effect relationship.[82] Many, if not most, such tests are actually tests of allergic sensitization (e.g., to a metal or other potential cause of allergic asthma). The expert should be clear about what type of information is being inferred from a given test and about the basis in the literature for using the test for that purpose.[83]

78. *See* Cullen et al., *supra* note 19, at 223–24. For an overview of available blood tests, fluid analysis studies, and urinalyses, see, e.g., Kathleen Deska Pagana & Timothy James Pagana, Mosby's Manual of Diagnostic and Laboratory Tests 7–9, 557, 859–73 (1998).

79. *See* Fauci et al., *supra* note 56, at 3; for uses of laboratory tests in environmental disease, see Cullen et al., *supra* note 19, at 222–23 and Arthur Frank, *The Environmental History*, *in* Environmental Medicine, *supra* note 19, at 232. *See also In re* Paoli R.R. Yard PCB Litig., 916 F.2d 829 (3d Cir. 1990), *cert. denied*, 499 U.S. 961 (1991).

80. For a case involving the use of laboratory tests in diagnosis, see *Cella v. United States*, 998 F.2d 418 (7th Cir. 1993).

81. *See, e.g.*, Linden & Lovejoy, *supra* note 76, at 2523.

82. *See* Cullen et al., *supra* note 19, at 223.

83. *See id.* at 228. For an example of laboratory tests used to rule out alternative diagnoses and causes, see *Hose v. Chicago Northwestern Transportation Co.*, 70 F.3d 968, 973, 975 (8th Cir. 1995) (supporting a diagnosis of manganese encephalopathy, medical witnesses cited a positron emission tomography (PET) scan to rule out alcoholism, stroke, and Alzheimer's disease, and an MRI to exclude copper, calcium, and other harmful exposures).

Physicians are taught to think about clinical testing in terms of the clinical significance (particularly, predictive value) of a given test in a given situation. Small or inconsistent changes in values do not necessarily indicate a clinically important effect and should be confirmed by repeat testing before being otherwise investigated. On the other hand, important effects may not drive an individual's values outside of the population reference range. For instance, someone previously at the upper limit of the normal range exposed to a chlorine leak might suffer a reduction in rate of airflow. Although the subsequent rate was within the normal range, it would not be normal in this individual.[84] Unfortunately, baseline data on an individual prior to exposure are usually not available. Thus, making inferences from other diagnostic and exposure information may be useful in understanding the impact of exposure on that individual.

2. *Pathology Tests*

Pathology tests are conducted by taking a sample of body tissue (obtained during surgery or a biopsy) and submitting it for microscopic evaluation by a specialist physician (pathologist). The pathologist makes a determination as to whether the tissue appears normal for the organ from which it was taken. If it does not appear normal, then a determination of the pattern of abnormality, such as inflammation, malignancy, or scarring, is sought.[85]

Sometimes the etiology of the abnormality is apparent, as when special stains are used for determination of the presence of microorganisms that can cause a given infection. On the other hand, most cancers, whether of lung or breast or bone marrow, have no features that allow the histopathologist to discern a toxic, viral, or hereditary etiology. Clues from molecular biology analysis have been experimentally reported, but are not yet available clinically.[86]

Pathology, typically felt to be the gold standard, often is found wanting when external etiology needs to be determined. Some conditions, such as neuropsychiatric diseases that may be related to metal or solvent exposure, do not have established pathological abnormalities.[87]

3. *Clinical Tests*

Clinical tests are physiological determinations of organ function. Common examples are pulmonary (lung) function tests, which have well-established normal

84. Cullen et al., *supra* note 19, at 223.

85. For specific examples, see Ivan Damjanov, Histopathology: A Color Atlas and Textbook 23–24, 36, 58, 64 (1996).

86. *See* Bernard D. Goldstein & Mary Sue Henifin, Reference Guide on Toxicology § IV, in this manual.

87. *See* Howard Hu, *Heavy Metal Poisoning*, *in* 2 Principles of Internal Medicine, *supra* note 42, at 2564, 2565–66.

ranges, but are quite dependent on patient effort; nerve and muscle function tests, which are largely effort-independent and have reasonably well-established reference ranges, but are sensitive to interlaboratory variation, and electrocardiograms (EKGs), which are interpreted with a combination of objective measures and more subjective recognition of patterns resulting from inidividual expertise.[88]

All tests have strengths and limitations for their use in reaching a certain diagnosis or making a causal inference. The expert should be able to address strengths and weaknesses of various approaches based on the situation at hand. Why was one test chosen or preferable to another? If available, what is the sensitivity, specificity, and validity for the test in general, and what are its predictive values in the population (characterized by age group, gender, comorbid diseases, workplace exposures) from which the individual comes?[89]

Mostly these predictive values will be available in the medical literature, but there are many disappointing gaps. Given inevitable inconsistencies in the patient's data, a qualified expert will usually be able to interpret and explain these inconsistencies in a satisfactory manner.

IV. Physician Decision Making

A. Introduction

For the treating physician, "[c]linical reasoning is the essential function of the physician; optimal patient care depends on keen diagnostic acumen and thoughtful analysis of the trade-offs between the benefits and risks of tests and treatments."[90] Beyond assessing the presence or absence of disease, and defining appropriate treatment or prevention, the physician must be able to skillfully communicate information to the patient and other interested parties.[91]

Moreover, a physician may be asked to determine the causation of disease, in order, for example, to offer a patient advice on continuing activities that may cause, contribute to, or exacerbate or ameliorate the disease. The physician may also be asked to determine causality as an expert in a legal proceeding.[92] In undertaking all of these activities, the physician is grounded in the art and science of clinical reasoning, which we describe below in general terms.

88. For specific tests of pulmonary, nerve and muscle function, and electrocardiography, respectively, see Pagana & Pagana, *supra* note 78, at 1016–21, 490–92, 486–89, 478–82.

89. *See infra* § IV and accompanying footnotes.

90. Kassirer & Kopelman, *supra* note 48, at 2.

91. *See* Cullen et al., *supra* note 19, at 217.

92. *See* Hu & Speizer, *supra* note 42, at 19, 20.

The physician is trained to recognize diseases as coherent deviations from normal structure or function that affect a certain part of the body or type of tissue. Physicians recognize the characteristic symptoms, signs, and laboratory manifestations of given diseases, although a relatively small number of discrete symptoms and signs are shared by a much larger number of coherent diseases. In fact, diseases result from one or a combination of only ten or so general pathophysiological processes (congenital, infectious, neoplastic, toxic, genetic, vascular, immunologic, inflammatory, endocrine, and traumatic). The goal of the physician is to distinguish which specific type of disorder (disease) is causing a patient's symptoms and signs.[93]

One of the difficulties in recognizing diseases is the absence of an accepted metric for establishing new disease entities. Thus, when a possible new set of characteristic symptoms, signs, and laboratory manifestations is described, there is no one method for developing consensus on whether a new disease entity exists.[94] For example, when the characteristic symptoms, signs, and laboratory test results of acquired immunodeficiency syndrome (AIDS) were first described in the early 1980s, prior to the identification of the human immunodeficiency virus (HIV), there was considerable controversy over whether a new disease entity had manifested itself. Development of a test for infection with the specific virus cemented recognition of the disease. There have also been analogous, but largely unresolved, controversies over chronic fatigue syndrome, fibromyalgia, multiple-chemical sensitivity, and Gulf War syndrome.[95]

93. For an example of how a symptom may be common to a number of diseases, compare Jeffrey A. Gelfand & Charles A. Dinarello, *Fever and Hyperthermia*, *in* 1 Principles of Internal Medicine, *supra* note 42, at 84, 88 tbl.17-1; Elaine T. Kaye & Kenneth M. Kaye, *Fever and Rash*, *in* 1 Principles of Internal Medicine, *supra* note 42, at 90, 91–96 tbl.18-1; Robert B. Daroff & Joseph B. Martin, *Faintness, Syncope, Dizziness, and Vertigo*, *in* 1 Principles of Internal Medicine, *supra* note 42, at 100, 100 tbl.20-1; Patrick T. O'Gara & Eugene Braunwald, *Approach to the Patient with a Heart Murmur*, *in* 1 Principles of Internal Medicine, *supra* note 42, at 198, 199 tbl. 34-1.

94. *See, e.g.*, Khalida Ismail et al., *Is There a Gulf War Syndrome?*, 353 Lancet 179, 179 (1999) ("For an illness to be recognised as a new disorder it must be sufficiently different from other recognised disorders . . . . There is no formal process to investigate whether a set of symptoms are unique to a new illness."). For an explication of several methods that can be used to determine whether a new disease entity exists, see also David H. Wegman et al., *Invited Commentary: How Would We Know a Gulf War Syndrome If We Saw One?*, 146 Am. J. Epidemiology 704 (1997).

95. The recognition of multiple-chemical sensitivity as a disease was at issue in *Zwillinger v. Garfield Slope Housing Corp.*, No. CV 94-4009, 1998 WL 623589 (E.D.N.Y. Aug. 17, 1998). *See also* Howard M. Kipen & Nancy Fiedler, *Invited Commentary: Sensitivities to Chemicals—Context and Implications*, 150 Am. J. Epidemiology 13 (1999).

B. Diagnosis

Clinical diagnosis has been described as a process of "iterative hypothesis testing." It relies on both analysis and synthesis of data. When making a diagnosis, a clinician makes inferences about types of malfunctions of the patient's organs or chemistry that would lead to the observed abnormalities. The basis for the inferences are facts (information) that have been collected about the patient. The clinician applies inferential (also known as inductive) reasoning, considering the specific historical, physical, and laboratory facts, until a diagnosis that coherently describes the patient's condition can be hypothesized. Such a working diagnosis is sometimes called, or corresponds to, a syndrome, which is a clustering of signs and symptoms of abnormal function.[96] Syndromes and working diagnoses do not identify precise underlying internal causes. To arrive at an underlying internal cause, the physician must process the multiple symptoms and signs from the working diagnosis into a single diagnosis or disease, such as multiple vascular strokes as an explanation for dementia.

In the process of performing a differential diagnosis, the physician determines which of two or more diseases with similar clinical findings is the one that the patient is suffering from.[97] The physician does this by developing a list of all of the possible diseases that could produce the observed signs and symptoms, and then comparing the expected clinical findings for each with those exhibited by the patient.[98]

While working through a differential diagnosis, the clinician will often have generated a number of diagnostic hypotheses of what specific underlying diseases might be the cause of the patient's problem. Initially these hypotheses are colored by the patient's demographic characteristics (e.g., age, gender, race) as well as appearance and chief (or presenting) complaints, because all of these

96. For example, dementia is a syndrome of impaired memory, thinking, language, and judgment (all of which are symptoms that can actually also be measured as signs) related to destruction or malfunction of specific parts of the brain. In congestive heart failure, shortness of breath (symptom), trouble lying down flat (symptom), swollen ankles (symptom or sign), weight gain (sign), swollen neck veins (sign), crackling noises heard in the lungs (sign), and galloping heart sounds (sign) are attributable to one pathophysiological dysfunction—inadequate pumping of blood by the heart. In Cushing's syndrome, an abnormally round face (moon face), diabetes mellitus (high blood sugar causing a syndrome of its own), bone thinning (osteoporosis), and high blood pressure are all due to excessive amounts of certain hormones, glucocorticoids, resulting from either excess glandular secretion by the body or overuse as a medication. Fauci et al., *supra* note 56, at 3.

97. *See* Stedman's Medical Dictionary 474 (26th ed. 1995) (definition of *differential diagnosis*); Kassirer & Kopelman, *supra* note 48, at 16.

98. Diagnosis is at issue in many kinds of cases, including medical malpractice and other personal injury claims. *See, e.g.*, Bates et al., *supra* note 49, at 635–48; Samuels v. Secretary of Dep't of Health & Human Servs., No. 91-127V, 1995 WL 809884 (Fed. Cl. Aug. 1, 1995) (diagnosis of a neurological disorder at issue in claim under the National Vaccine Injury Compensation Program); Alex v. Dr. X, 692 So. 2d 499 (La. Ct. App. 1997) (diagnosis of tuberculosis at issue).

affect the probabilities of developing specific illnesses and are also easily observable.[99] For instance, lung cancer and heart attacks are relatively rare in individuals under age 40 and would not usually be at the top of a list of preliminary hypotheses for patients in this age group even if they did complain of cough or chest pain, respectively. Sometimes the diagnostic hypotheses will be greatly influenced by a single piece of physical or laboratory data. As the physician develops and considers hypotheses during the history-taking, he or she may modify the questions asked of the patient to probe specific areas that test and rule out a succession of hypotheses.[100]

The initial, or working, diagnosis provides a context or template for gathering further information and specifying tests to confirm or refute the working diagnosis. Each working diagnosis implies the presence of certain symptoms or test results and the absence of others if the patient has the given disorder. The physician modifies and refines the working diagnosis as additional information is gathered, generating new diagnoses as the old ones are pushed aside by inconsistent findings.[101] In essence a physician thinks the patient probably has Condition X and orders tests that will verify or refute this diagnosis. If the diagnosis is refuted, the physician reshapes the diagnostic hypothesis and orders additional tests that may be required. Experienced physicians select and test the most probable hypothesis first. This is the generally accepted (though seldom formally acknowledged) methodology that physicians employ to arrive at a diagnosis.

The goal of the clinician is to arrive at a diagnosis that can be used to develop a rational plan for further investigation, observation, or treatment, and ultimately to predict the course of the patient's illness (prognosticate). To do this, the clinician must verify or validate the diagnostic hypothesis.[102] Validation of a diagnostic hypothesis requires an assessment of coherency of the hypothesis (i.e., do the patient's physiology, risk factor profile, and complications sufficiently match those expected from the suspected disease?). The presence of each such symptom or sign that matches those expected for a given condition is known as a "pertinent positive" for that diagnosis. Determining the adequacy of the diagnostic hypothesis requires assessment of the converse (i.e., does the suspected disease encompass or satisfactorily explain enough of the patient's normal and abnormal findings?). The absence of each symptom or sign characteristic of a particular condition is known as a "pertinent negative" for that condition and tends to make that condition less likely. Finally, the principle of parsimony requires asking whether the suspected disease is a simple explanation for all of the patient's important findings. Although it is not always correct or possible, an

99. *See* Kassirer & Kopelman, *supra* note 48, at 7; Bates et al., *supra* note 49, at 637–38.

100. *See* Kassirer & Kopelman, *supra* note 48, at 9; Bates et al., *supra* note 49, at 646–47.

101. *See* Kassirer & Kopelman, *supra* note 48, at 11, 32–33.

102. *See id.* at 32–33.

explanation of all of the patient's signs and symptoms with a single underlying condition or disease process is desirable. Of course, some patients, especially the elderly, may have more than one underlying disease (e.g., heart disease, osteoporosis, and chronic renal failure). Sometimes two common conditions will be a more logical explanation than one complex and unusual disease that could also explain all of the observed manifestations. Physicians also consider competing hypotheses, to ascertain that no other disease is present that better explains the current hypothesis or findings.[103]

All diagnostic hypotheses represent probabilistic judgments that are based on observed medical facts that have variable probabilities of being correct. Each fact (symptom, sign, or test abnormality) also has only a variable probability of being found in a given condition that is typically characterized by its presence. If the diagnosis is based on inconsistent records or observations, the physician should explain how the inconsistencies affected the assessment being offered.[104]

C. Probabilistic Basis of Diagnosis

Medical diagnosis is not an exact science. As indicated above, physicians make probabilistic judgments on a day-to-day basis, even when they can supplement a patient's history and physical with the results of extensive laboratory tests. Laboratory, clinical, and physiological tests are important for any given disease and may be characterized in terms of their "sensitivity" and "specificity," which indicate the usefulness of the test results in making a particular disease diagnosis. For a given test, sensitivity, which is also known as the true positive rate, is the percentage of positive tests in patients who actually have the disease. Test results in those who have a disease but are incorrectly identified as not having the disease because of the test's insensitivity are "false negatives." Thus, a test that is positive in 80% of actual cases of asthma (80% sensitivity) will fail to indicate asthma, or be falsely negative, in 20% of actual cases.

Specificity is the percentage of negative test results in individuals who are free of a given disease, also known as the true negative rate. Test results in those who are free of the disease who are incorrectly identified as having the condition are "false positives." Thus, a test that indicates abnormal bronchial reactivity in 15% of individuals without asthma would have a false positive rate of 15%; their test results were positive, but they are free of the condition.[105] For example, a physician may order a chest x-ray as a test to rule out lung cancer for a 60-year-old man who just began to cough up flecks of blood but has a normal physical exam.

103. *See id.*

104. *See id.* at 16; Bates et al., *supra* note 49, at 635–74.

105. *See* Bates et al., *supra* note 49, at 641; Goldman, *supra* note 56, at 10–11; Kassirer & Kopelman, *supra* note 48, at 18–19; Michael D. Green et al., Reference Guide on Epidemiology § V.H, and David H. Kaye & David A. Freedman, Reference Guide on Statistics §§ III.A.3, IV.B.2, IV.C, in this manual.

If the x-ray does not show any evidence of lung cancer (is negative for a finding consistent with lung cancer), that diminishes the probability of lung cancer, but it does not rule it out. A cancer may actually be present but not show up on the x-ray because it is too small or because it is in an unobservable location. The physician will be aware of the possibility of such a false-negative result and, especially for a high-risk individual (see below), may order a follow-up exam in a few months or immediately order a more sensitive test, such as a CAT scan or bronchoscopy. A false-positive result that was due to the imperfect specificity of the chest x-ray would occur if the x-ray showed an abnormality that suggested cancer, but when biopsied (the gold standard of tissue diagnosis) turned out to be an old scar resulting from a dormant injection.

Sensitivity and specificity provide information about the usefulness of a piece of data (a symptom, sign, or test) for diagnostic reasoning in any population of patients. However, they do not give complete information for predicting or excluding disease in individual patients. For that, information about the patient, and the population that he or she represents, must be incorporated.[106]

Physicians must interpret the predictive value of a test in assessing the presence or absence of disease in a specific patient. The predictive value of a test for a specific individual is based not only on the sensitivity and specificity of the test, but also on the prevalence of disease in the population from which the patient comes, such as age group, gender group, racial group, and groups with occupational exposures.[107] In the previous example, if the 60-year-old man was a smoker and had been occupationally exposed to a lung carcinogen, such as asbestos, a negative x-ray might be viewed more suspiciously than if he was free of additional risks.

If sensitivity and specificity are known in general for a particular test, sign, or symptom, and the overall prevalence of the condition is known for the population group from which the patient comes, then one can actually calculate a good approximation of the predictive value of the test, sign, or symptom for that person and condition according to a rule known as Bayes' theorem. These calculations have actually been translated into nomograms (tables) for general use.[108] Few clinicians actually calculate such probabilities, but they use an analogous reasoning process on a routine basis. This Bayesian reasoning is a major tool of

106. *See* Bates et al., *supra* note 49, at 645–46.

107. "Positive predictive value" is the frequency of disease among patients with positive results, and "negative predictive value" is the frequency of absence of disease among individuals with negative test results. For a test with a given sensitivity and specificity, positive predictive value is higher when a condition is common in a population, and negative predictive value is higher when the condition is rare. Bates et al., *supra* note 49, at 642. *See also* David H. Kaye & David A. Freedman, Reference Guide on Statistics §§ III.A.3, IV.C, in this manual.

108. *See* Swartz, *supra* note 50, at 675–76 & fig.25-3. *See generally* David H. Kaye & David A. Freedman, Reference Guide on Statistics § IV.D, app., in this manual.

physicians in thinking through a differential diagnosis. For instance, heart attacks are very rare in 25-year-olds and relatively more common in 75-year-olds. In analyzing a patient with chest pain and borderline abnormal EKG changes, the physician is much more likely to suspect a heart attack as the cause of the pain in the 75-year-old, and admit the patient to a hospital, at least for monitoring.[109]

Diagnostic reasoning is usually more complex than the examples given because it is simultaneously based on multiple symptoms, signs, and test results (e.g., family history, physical exam). These findings are not all truly independent of one another, thus preventing straightforward addition of the probabilities as in a Bayesian model. This lack of independence limits the ability of physicians to make accurate calculations of the results of multiple simultaneous predictive values. However, physicians must routinely make such estimations, albeit often implicitly and without numerical quantification, as part of clinical care. Thus, physicians frequently rely on the principles of Bayesian reasoning when deciding on a diagnosis.[110] Doctors combine probabilities of disease (prevalence) with their knowledge of the frequency of signs and symptoms in a given disease and competing diseases to progressively modify and ultimately arrive at their view of the likelihood of the disease under consideration.

D. Causal Reasoning

During the diagnostic process, the physician employs causal reasoning to integrate the various clinical variables into an understanding of the cause-and-effect relationships among them, based on an understanding of how the various systems of the human body interact and react to external stressors. Causal reasoning allows the clinician to conceptualize the possible course of the patient's disease and predict the effects of treatment, and is important in evaluating the coherency of a diagnosis. For example, if the patient is experiencing chest pain on exertion and has a history of high blood cholesterol levels, the physician might posit a causal model that involves cholesterol plaque substantially obstructing coronary arteries, resulting in inadequate blood flow to the heart muscle during exercise causing chest pain. This model might then suggest that the physician first investigate the degree of occlusion in the coronary arteries, and second

109. The positive predictive value of a symptom of chest pain for a heart attack is very low in a 25-year-old because advanced atherosclerotic cardiovascular disease is rare in this age group and other causes of chest pain are more common. Similarly, interstitial fibrosis on a chest x-ray, whatever the x-ray's sensitivity and specificity for a true underlying finding of pathologic fibrosis, has a much higher predictive value for a diagnosis of asbestosis in a person known to come from an asbestos-exposed population than in someone with no known occupational exposure to asbestos.

110. *See* Kassirer & Kopelman, *supra* note 48, at 19–24; Steven N. Goodman, *Toward Evidence-Based Medical Statistics. 2: The Bayes Factor,* 130 Annals Internal Med. 1005, 1011 (1999).

consider measures such as smoking cessation, dietary modification, medications, and even angioplasty or surgery if the level of occlusion proves to be substantial and a likely explanation for the pain.

As the process of refinement of diagnostic hypotheses unfolds, the consideration of several causal models may be necessary, because consistency of the model with observed findings does not necessarily prove that a model is correct. In the example above, another model that would explain the findings is exposure to high levels of carbon monoxide from a faulty furnace at home, producing a blood carboxyhemoglobin level of 18% (the normal for a nonsmoker is less than 1%) and reducing the blood's oxygen-carrying capacity. In conjunction with only mild coronary artery obstruction by plaque, this exposure then leads to inadequate oxygen delivery to the heart muscle and chest pain. The model combines general causation models for coronary artery disease with information on the levels of carbon monoxide and coronary artery obstruction specific to this patient. Thus, the physician applies general medical knowledge about the relationship of various factors to symptoms and then refines the appropriate causal model in accordance with the specific patient's condition. Although carbon monoxide intoxication can cause chest pain that is due to inadequate oxygen delivery to the heart, it requires a blood carboxyhemoglobin level of at least 5% to 10%, and its impact is enhanced by the presence of underlying mechanical obstruction of the coronary arteries. Hence, the physician must usually consider and assess alternative and more specific causal models before accepting a particular model as the preferred explanation. Like the probabilistic reasoning described above, this kind of reasoning is rarely made explicit.

E. Evaluation of External Causation

For the physician, both causal and probabilistic reasoning are the basis for establishing external causation, which is the relationship between environmental factors (work, chemical exposures, lifestyle, medications) and illness, as well as for making the more common analysis of internal causation as discussed earlier in section IV.B. The physician may be asked to determine external causation by the patient or a third party, such as a lawyer, insurance company, or governmental agency. A key element of determining causation is gaining access to all information available about the patient's condition.

Figure 1 provides examples of the diverse types of information that may be available for review in determining external causation. In any given case, much of the listed information is normally not available.[111] Determining external causation also generally occurs in a stepwise fashion. In the first step the physician

111. For a somewhat different illustration of the interaction of such factors, see Cullen et al., *supra* note 19, at 230 fig.18-2.

Figure 1. Determining External Causation

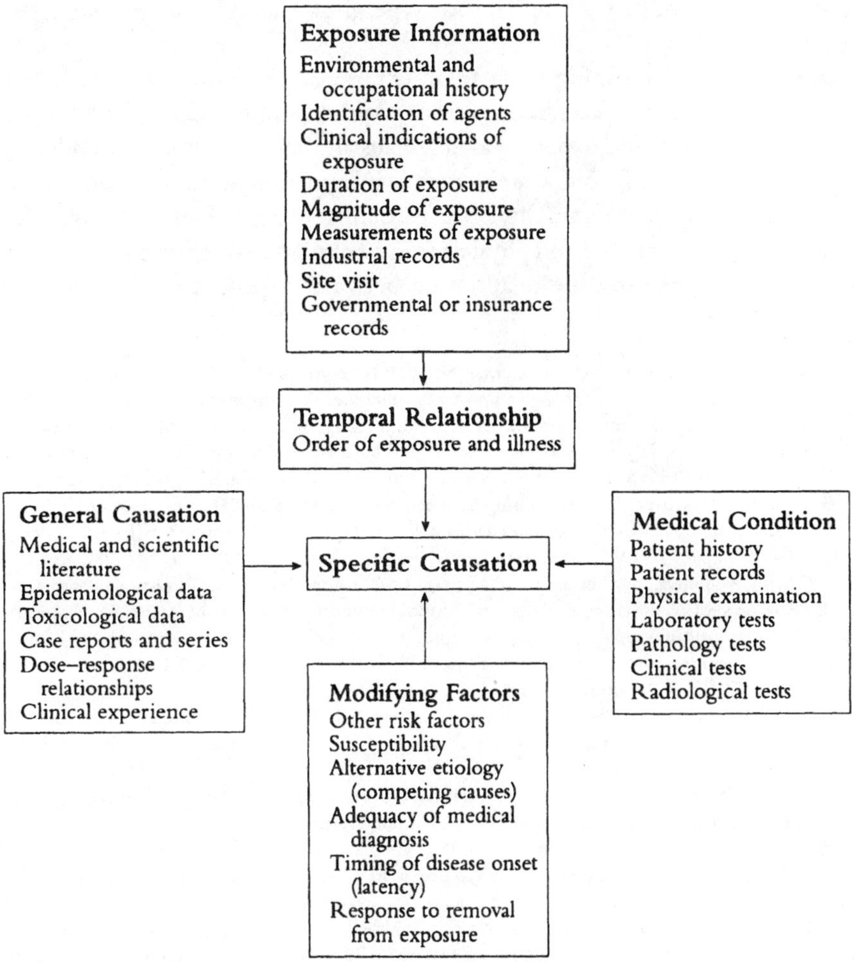

must establish the characteristics of the medical condition. Second, he or she carefully defines the nature and amount of the environmental exposure. The third step is to demonstrate that the medical and scientific literature provides evidence that in some circumstances the exposure under consideration can cause the outcome under consideration. This step is synonymous with establishment of general causation. As part of this step, the clinician attempts to establish the relationship between dose and response, including whether thresholds exist, ultimately defining the clinical toxicology of the exposure. The fourth step is to apply this general knowledge to the specific circumstances of the case at hand, incorporating the specifics of exposure, mitigating or exacerbating influences, individual susceptibilities, competing or synergistic causes, and any other relevant data.[112]

Many conditions resulting from toxic exposures are similar or identical in clinical manifestations to conditions arising from nontoxic causes.[113] Physicians rely on their training and expertise as clinicians and scientists when considering the medical and scientific literature as well as information about a patient's condition to best determine causality in a particular patient. Definitive tests for causality are actually rare,[114] and physicians must almost always use an element of judgment in determining the relationship between exposure and disease in a

112. Many cases involving issues of external causation have involved witnesses who testify to having arrived at an opinion on cause through a process of ruling out or eliminating other causes, a process frequently referred to by the courts and witnesses as "differential diagnosis" or "differential etiology" (for explanation of the differences between medical and legal uses of terminology, see section I.B., *supra*). Not infrequently, this form of testimony is implicitly or explicitly offered to satisfy the applicable burden of proof on causation. The relationship between the "more probable than not burden of proof" and "differential diagnosis" was discussed in *Cavallo v. Star Enterprise*, 892 F. Supp. 756 (E.D. Va. 1995), *aff'd in part, rev'd in part*, 100 F.3d 1150 (4th Cir. 1996), *cert. denied*, 522 U.S. 1044 (1998), a case in which the witness opined on whether a spill of aircraft fuel caused the plaintiff's rash. The court explained, "The process of differential diagnosis is undoubtedly important to the question of 'specific causation.' If other possible causes of an injury cannot be ruled out, or at least the probability of their contribution to causation minimized, then the 'more likely than not' threshold for proving causation may not be met." *Id.* at 771 (footnote omitted).

Courts differ on whether opinion based on such "differential diagnosis" or "differential etiology" of cause is admissible. *Compare* Westberry v. Gummi, 178 F.3d 257, 263 (4th Cir. 1999) (reliable "differential diagnosis" provides a valid basis for an expert opinion), Anderson v. Quality Stores, Inc., 181 F.3d 86 (4th Cir. 1999) (per curiam) (opinion on spray paint causing pulmonary problems should have been admitted based on "differential diagnosis" and temporal relationship), *In re* Paoli R.R. Yard PCB Litig., 35 F.3d 717 (3d Cir. 1994) (approving opinion based on "differential diagnosis"), *cert. denied*, 513 U.S. 1190 (1995), McCullock v. H.B. Fuller Co., 61 F.3d 1038, 1042–44 (2d Cir. 1995) (accepting opinion based on "differential etiology"), *and* Zuchowicz v. United States, 140 F.3d 381, 387–91 (2d Cir. 1998) (accepting witness's "differential etiology" opinion of causes of pulmonary hypertension), *with* Raynor v. Merrell Pharms., Inc., 104 F.3d 1371, 1375–76 (D.C. Cir. 1997) ("differential diagnosis" of cause of birth defect inadmissible where general causation proof absent), Cavallo v. Star Enter., 892 F. Supp. 756, 771–73 (E.D. Va. 1995) ("differential diagnosis" of cause inadmissible where general causation not established), *aff'd in part, rev'd in part*, 100 F.3d 1150 (4th Cir. 1996), *cert. denied*, 522 U.S. 1044 (1998), Hall v. Baxter Healthcare Corp., 947 F. Supp. 1387, 1412–14 (D. Or. 1996) ("differential diagnosis" and specific causation require proof of general causation; witness did not explain how he ruled out other causes), Haggerty v. Upjohn Co., 950 F. Supp. 1160, 1166–67 (S.D. Fla. 1996) ("differential diagnosis" testimony inadmissible where another cause could explain all of plaintiff's symptoms), *aff'd*, 158 F.3d 588 (11th Cir. 1998) (unpublished table decision), *and* Austin v. Children's Hosp. Med. Ctr., 92 F.3d 1185 (6th Cir. 1996) (unpublished table decision) (text at No. 95-3880, 1996 WL 422484, at *3 (6th Cir. July 26, 1996)) (expert unable to show that defendant, rather than other sources, "more likely than not" infected plaintiff's son with fatal virus).

113. *See, e.g.*, Herbert Y. Reynolds, *Interstitial Lung Disease*, *in* 2 Principles of Internal Medicine, *supra* note 42, at 1460, 1460–63 & tbl.259-1.

114. For a discussion of the difficulty of establishing causation, see Feinstein, *supra* note 40, at 266–74.

given patient. For instance, if a substance is suspected to cause an allergic or toxic condition, it may be necessary for diagnostic purposes to remove a patient from the workplace on a trial basis. On the other hand, determinations of external causation in patients with cancer may be irrelevant to treatment decisions as treatment is usually unaffected by assignment of cause.[115]

Physicians use both causal and probabilistic reasoning in determining both internal and external causation in regard to a particular illness. Methods for determination of some special external causes of disease may be found in occupational and environmental medical texts and journals[116] and generally are analogous to methods used for assessment of internal disease causation.[117] The difference is essentially in the body of medical, toxicological, epidemiological, and industrial hygiene knowledge that is relevant and needs to be incorporated.

For instance, in an elderly patient with chronic shortness of breath, the treating physician may use differential diagnosis to determine that chronic bronchitis is the best explanation as the underlying cause of symptoms, having excluded heart disease, anemia, lung fibrosis, and emphysema. The treating physician will rarely consider the external causes of the chronic bronchitis, beyond consideration of whether the patient smoked cigarettes.[118] The specific contribution of environmental or workplace exposures is rarely assessed as a part of clinical care in an elderly nonworking patient, since it does not affect diagnosis, treatment, and prognosis of this particular disease.[119] However, such determination of external causation may be essential to determination of a contested workers' compensation award.[120]

The key factor for the courts to recognize is that, while similar underlying reasoning is used in determination of both internal and external causation, and

115. However, exceptions may be cited, including the need to determine if there is a genetic (familial) risk of cancer that may require notification and screening of family members (e.g., certain forms of colon cancer and breast cancer), or if other family members or workers may be at remediable risk.

116. *See, e.g.*, Howard Hu & Frank E. Speizer, *Specific Environmental and Occupational Hazards, in* 2 Principles of Internal Medicine, *supra* note 42, at 2521, 2521–22; Linden & Lovejoy, *supra* note 76, at 2523–25; Hu, *supra* note 87, at 2565–67.

117. *See, e.g.*, peer review case studies published by the Agency for Toxic Substances and Disease Registry (ATSDR), a branch of the Centers for Disease Control and Prevention. For the most part, these case studies discuss the diagnosis and treatment of environmental illness, and in a number of instances discuss the reasoning involved in assessing the causal role of an environmental exposure. Selected ATSDR case studies are included in Environmental Medicine: Integrating a Missing Element into Medical Education, *supra* note 57, at app. C.

118. *See* Eric G. Honig & Ronald H. Ingram, Jr., *Chronic Bronchitis, Emphysema, and Airways Obstruction, in* 2 Principles of Internal Medicine, *supra* note 42, at 1451, 1452.

119. In a working patient, the contribution of workplace conditions may be taken into account in advising the patient on the advisability of returning to or remaining in the work environment if there are conditions present that may exacerbate the patient's respiratory condition. *Id.* at 1456.

120. *See, e.g.*, Fiore v. Consolidated Freightways, 659 A.2d 436 (N.J. 1995).

physicians routinely make limited determinations of external causation, many of the facts relevant to a determination of external causation rely on a body of scientific literature that is not routinely used by treating physicians. As a corollary, an expert's opinion on diagnosis and his or her opinion on external causation should generally be assessed separately, since the bases for such opinions are often quite different.

1. Exposure

Critical to a determination of causation is characterizing exposure. Exposure to a toxic substance can sometimes be established by a review of the patient's history and various available indicators of exposure, as discussed in section III. There are four "cardinal" pieces of exposure information:

1. The material or agent in the environmental exposure should be identified.
2. The magnitude or concentration of an exposure should be estimated, including use of clinical inference.
3. The temporal aspects of the exposure should be determined—whether the exposure was short-term and lasted a few minutes, days, weeks, or months, or was long-term and lasted for years. Similarly, the latency between exposure and disease onset is often critical.
4. If possible, the impact on disease or symptoms should be defined.[121]

In many instances, the desired information will be incomplete,[122] but it can often be inferred from the literature that a given amount of time in a particular industry is well associated with disease-producing potential. Progressive pulmonary fibrosis (accelerated silicosis) can develop in as little as ten months in workers involved in manufacturing abrasive soaps, tunneling in rock that has a high quartz content, or carrying out sandblasting in small, enclosed spaces, although

121. *See* Cullen et al., *supra* note 19, at 224.

122. The courts vary in the degree of certainty they require in exposure estimates. Many courts accept exposure evidence as sufficient without proof of specific levels. *See, e.g.*, Kannankeril v. Terminix Int'l, Inc., 128 F.3d 802, 808–09 (3d Cir. 1997). Other courts have required more particularized proof. *See, e.g.*, Curtis v. M&S Petroleum, Inc., 174 F.3d 661, 671–72 (5th Cir. 1999) (exposure evidence sufficient for opinion on causation where expert testified that refinery workers were exposed to at least 100 parts per million (ppm), and probably several hundred ppm, of benzene). Based on these measurements, *Curtis* distinguishes another Fifth Circuit case, *Moore v. Ashland Chemical, Inc.*, 151 F.3d 269 (5th Cir. 1998) (en banc), *cert. denied*, 119 S. Ct. 1454 (1999), in which exposure evidence was found insufficient to support an opinion on causation because the expert had a "'paucity of facts'" on which to base an opinion and did not testify to any specific levels of exposure. 174 F.3d at 670 (quoting *Moore*, 151 F.3d at 279 n.10). Exposure levels have been at issue in a number of other cases. *See, e.g.*, *In re* Paoli R.R. Yard PCB Litig., 916 F.2d 829 (3d Cir. 1990), *cert. denied*, 499 U.S. 961 (1991); *In re* "Agent Orange" Prod. Liab. Litig., 611 F. Supp. 1223 (E.D.N.Y. 1985), *aff'd*, 818 F.2d 187 (2d Cir. 1987), *cert. denied*, 487 U.S. 1234 (1988).

simple silicosis is much more commonly a chronic illness resulting from years of exposure.[123] In other situations, exposure estimates will be based on methods beyond the scope of medical expertise, such as physical or chemical analyses, or chemical fate-and-transport modeling (i.e., using mathematical models to project the movement of chemicals in air, water, and soil).

In determining causation, the physician may have particular insight into clinical clues related to exposure, such as clinical indicators of degree of exposure, temporal relationships, and the effect of removal from the toxic substance.[124] The physician also has particular insight into the role that preexisting illnesses may play in causing an exacerbation, recurrence, or complication of a clinical condition independent of any exposure to toxic products, or in concert with a toxic exposure.[125]

2. *Reviewing the Medical and Scientific Literature*

After characterizing exposure and the nature of the patient's disease, the physician expert witness must determine if the medical and research literature supports a determination of environmental causation.[126] The research literature in-

123. *See* Speizer, *supra* note 59, at 1431–32.

124. An appropriate temporal relationship—the time that elapsed between exposure and onset of disease or symptoms—is a necessary but often insufficient basis for an opinion on causation. Courts frequently warn against reasoning based on the premise "*post hoc, ergo propter hoc.*" *See, e.g.*, Whiting v. Boston Edison Co., 891 F. Supp. 12, 23 n.52 (D. Mass. 1995) (rejecting opinion on cause of acute lymphocytic leukemia following radiation exposure). In some cases, courts have permitted opinions on causation based primarily on temporal proximity between exposure and development of the disease, but many of these cases involved symptoms or diseases that closely followed the exposure asserted to be the cause. *See, e.g.*, Curtis v. M&S Petroleum, Inc., 174 F.3d 661, 670 (5th Cir. 1999); Anderson v. Quality Stores, Inc., 181 F.3d 86 (4th Cir. 1999) (unpublished table decision) (text at No. 98-2240, 1999 WL 387827, at *2 (4th Cir. June 14, 1999) (per curiam)). Other courts have excluded opinions on causation based primarily on temporal proximity. In *Moore v. Ashland Chemical, Inc.*, 151 F.3d 269, 278 (5th Cir. 1998) (en banc), *cert. denied*, 119 S. Ct. 1454 (1999), for example, the Fifth Circuit found that the expert's reliance on the temporal relationship between the exposure and the onset of symptoms was entitled to little weight in the absence of supporting medical literature. *See also* Rosen v. Ciba-Geigy Corp., 78 F.3d 316, 319 (7th Cir.) (rejecting expert testimony on nicotine patch as cause of heart attack that occurred after three days of wearing patch), *cert. denied*, 519 U.S. 819 (1996); Porter v. Whitehall Labs., Inc., 9 F.3d 607, 614 (7th Cir. 1993) (rejecting clinical observations and temporal relationship between drug ingestion and renal failure as bases for opinion on causation where scientific studies unavailable). On occasion, a temporal relationship that does not fit the expected pattern may be a basis for ruling out the suspected cause. *See, e.g.*, Heller v. Shaw Indus., Inc., 167 F.3d 146, 157–58 (3d Cir. 1999) (temporal relationships may be important in supporting an opinion on causation, but expert's reliance on temporal relationship is flawed in this case). *See generally* Speizer, *supra* note 59, at 1429–36; Honig & Ingram, *supra* note 118, at 1452, 1456.

125. *See* Cullen et al., *supra* note 19, at 227.

126. The courts differ on the question whether the witness giving an opinion on causation must support his or her opinion with references to medical or scientific studies supporting a causal link between the toxic exposure and the plaintiff's disease. A number of courts have answered this question in the affirmative. *See, e.g.*, Moore v. Ashland Chem., Inc., 151 F.3d 269, 277–78 (5th Cir. 1998) (en banc), *cert. denied*, 119 S. Ct. 1454 (1999); Rosen v. Ciba-Geigy Corp., 78 F.3d 316, 319 (7th Cir.)

cludes epidemiological studies and toxicology studies. The physician should be guided by the methods set forth in the Reference Guides on Epidemiology and Toxicology in evaluating this literature and its relevance to the patient's exposure and condition.[127]

Physicians also have access to case reports or case series in the medical literature. These are reports in medical journals describing clinical events involving one individual or a few individuals. They report unusual or new disease presentations, treatments, or manifestations, or suspected associations between two diseases, effects of medication, or external causes of diseases. For example, the association between asbestos and lung cancer was first reported in a 1933 case report, although the first controlled epidemiological study on the association was not published until the 1950s.[128] There are a number of other instances in which epidemiological studies have confirmed associations between a specific exposure and a disease first reported in case studies (e.g., benzene and leukemia; vinyl chloride and hepatic angiosarcoma),[129] but there are also instances in which controlled studies have failed to substantially confirm the initial case reports (e.g., the alleged connection between coffee and pancreatic and bladder cancer or the infectious etiology of Hodgkins disease).[130]

(witness cited no scientific or medical literature, or other explanation of asserted causal relationship between nicotine patch and heart attack), *cert. denied*, 519 U.S. 819 (1996); Porter v. Whitehall Labs., Inc., 9 F.3d 607, 615 (7th Cir. 1993) (medical literature did not establish link between ibuprofen and plaintiff's kidney ailment; medical theories had not been tested). Other courts have upheld the admission of medical opinion based solely on clinical observations and reasoning, sometimes with reference to the physician's experience with similar kinds of patients or cases. *See, e.g.*, Heller v. Shaw Indus., Inc., 167 F.3d 146, 153–57 (3d Cir. 1999); Westberry v. Gummi, 178 F.3d 257, 262–66 (4th Cir. 1999) (affirmed trial court's admission of expert testimony on talc as cause of plaintiff's sinus problems despite absence of supporting medical literature); Fadelalla v. Secretary of the Dep't of Health & Human Servs., No. 97-05730, 1999 WL 270423, at *6 (Fed. Cl. Apr. 15, 1999) (while clinical experience may be sufficient to establish causal relationship, in this case expert had insufficient clinical experience on which to base an opinion on causation); Becker v. National Health Prods., Inc., 896 F. Supp. 100, 103 (N.D.N.Y. 1995) (absence of published literature on relationship between diet supplement and diverticulosis not fatal to plaintiff's case where expert relied on "differential etiology").

127. *See* Michael D. Green et al., Reference Guide on Epidemiology, §§ V–VII, and Bernard D. Goldstein & Mary Sue Henifin, Reference Guide on Toxicology, §§ III–V, in this manual.

128. *See* Michael Gochfeld, *Asbestos Exposure in Buildings, in* Environmental Medicine, *supra* note 19, at 438, 440.

129. *See* Michael Gochfeld, *Chemical Agents, in* Environmental Medicine, *supra* note 19, at 592, 600 (vinyl chloride); Howard M. Kipen & Daniel Wartenberg, *Lymphohematopoietic Malignancies, in* Textbook of Clinical Occupational and Environmental Medicine 555, 560 (Linda Rosenstock & Mark R. Cullen eds., 1994) (benzene).

130. Kristin E. Anderson et al., *Pancreatic Cancer, in* Cancer Epidemiology and Prevention 725, 740–41 (David Schottenfeld & Joseph F. Fraumeni, Jr., eds., 2d ed. 1996); Debra T. Silverman et al., *Bladder Cancer, in* Cancer Epidemiology and Prevention, *supra*, at 1156, 1165–66.

Case reports lack controls and thus do not provide as much information as controlled epidemiological studies do.[131] However, case reports are often all that is available on a particular subject because they usually do not require substantial, if any, funding to accomplish, and human exposure may be rare and difficult to study. Causal attribution based on case studies must be regarded with caution. However, such studies may be carefully considered in light of other information available, including toxicological data.[132]

3. Clinical Evaluation of Information Affecting Dose–Response Relationships

Assessing the role of external causes in the patient's condition requires the integration of the information described in the preceding sections, with particular attention to dose–response relationships. The toxicological law of dose–response, that is, that "the dose makes the poison," refers to the general tendency for greater doses of a toxin to cause greater severity of responses in individuals, as well as greater frequency of response in populations.[133] Clinically, there are some instances in which the general rule does not hold. For agents that cause an allergic response through an immunologic mechanism, the dose–response relationship is often less straightforward. Many people who are not prone or able to develop an allergic reaction, for genetic or other reasons, will not respond adversely to the substance at any dose. However, those who are susceptible are more likely to become specifically reactive (sensitized) to the specific agent as the dose increases. After sensitization has occurred, severe reactions may occur with exposures that are much lower than the previous level required for sensitization.[134]

Although some diseases (e.g., pneumonia that is due to influenza) are frequently considered to be unifactorial, the possibility of multiple causes of a clini-

131. *See generally* Michael D. Green et al., Reference Guide on Epidemiology § II.A, in this manual.

132. *See* Cullen et al., *supra* note 19, at 226. Courts have given varying treatment to case reports. *Compare* Haggerty v. Upjohn Co., 950 F. Supp. 1160, 1165 (S.D. Fla. 1996) (case reports are "no substitute for a scientifically designed and conducted inquiry" (citing Casey v. Ohio Med. Prods., 877 F. Supp. 1380, 1385 (N.D. Cal. 1995))), *aff'd*, 158 F.3d 588 (11th Cir. 1998) (unpublished table decision), *and* Hall v. Baxter Healthcare Corp., 947 F. Supp. 1387, 1411 (D. Or. 1996) (case reports "cannot be the basis of an opinion based on scientific knowledge"), *with* Pick v. American Med. Sys., Inc., 958 F. Supp. 1151, 1160–62, 1178 (E.D. La. 1997) (case studies on gel implants admissible in case on penile implant; theory developed by single physician not admissible), Glaser v. Thompson Med. Co., 32 F.3d 969, 975 (6th Cir. 1994) (ordering trial based on witness who relied on case reports and his own research in rendering opinion on diet pills as cause of intracranial bleeding and fall), *and* Cella v. United States, 998 F.2d 418, 426 (7th Cir. 1993) (in claim under Jones Act, medical opinion on cause of polymyositis based in part on case reports).

133. *See* Michael Gochfeld, *Principles of Toxicology*, *in* Environmental Medicine, *supra* note 19, at 65, 71–72.

134. *See* Cullen et al., *supra* note 19, at 228–29.

cal condition is a critical concern. At some level most diseases have multiple host and environmental factors that contribute to their presence. A commonly held misconception is that the presence of a nontoxic or other toxic cause for a condition automatically excludes a role for the toxin being considered as an external cause.[135] While this is sometimes true, in reality the converse can also be true. For example, epidemiology studies dealing with occupational asbestos exposure and cigarette smoking indicate that together they result in much higher rates of lung cancer than either one causes on its own.[136] Thus, two toxic agents have been found to interact in a synergistic manner so that their combined effects are much greater than even the sum of their individual effects.[137]

Even if causal factors do not interact synergistically, several may contribute in an incremental fashion to a disease and should not be assumed to be mutually exclusive.[138] Accordingly, the common statement that "alternative causes of disease must be ruled out" before causation is attributed can be more accurately refined to say that "the role of other causes must be adequately considered." If there is a significant rate of disease of unknown etiology (i.e., other causes or risk factors have not been identified), the determination of external causation

135. Some courts have stated that the plaintiff must offer a "differential diagnosis" to rule out other causes, whereas other courts have rejected such a requirement. *Compare* Wheat v. Pfizer, Inc., 31 F.3d 340, 342 (5th Cir. 1994) (witness failed to rule out hepatitis C and another drug as causes of plaintiff's liver disease), Mancuso v. Consolidated Edison Co., 967 F. Supp. 1437, 1446 (S.D.N.Y. 1997) ("differential diagnosis" required to rule out other possible causes; plaintiff's complaints were commonplace ailments), *and* National Bank of Commerce v. Dow Chem. Co., 965 F. Supp. 1490 (E.D. Ark. 1996) (case dismissed because, inter alia, plaintiffs failed to exclude other causes), *aff'd*, 133 F.3d 1132 (8th Cir. 1998), *with* Curtis v. M&S Petroleum, Inc., 174 F.3d 661, 670–72 (5th Cir. 1999) (rejecting requirement of "differential diagnosis" to rule out other causes), *and* Heller v. Shaw Indus., Inc., 167 F.3d 146, 153–57 (3d Cir. 1999) (existence of possible alternative causes goes to weight, not admissibility).

136. Occupational asbestos exposure in nonsmokers increases the risk of lung cancer by a factor of about five, from about 11 per 100,000, for nonsmoking industrial workers not exposed to asbestos to about 58 per 100,000 for nonsmoking asbestos workers; a significant smoking history increases the rate of lung cancer by a factor of at least ten. *See* U.S. Surgeon Gen., U.S. Dep't of Health & Human Servs., The Health Consequences of Smoking: Cancer and Chronic Lung Disease in the Workplace 216 (1985); *see also* Rodolfo Saracci, *The Interactions of Tobacco Smoking and Other Agents in Cancer Etiology*, 9 Epidemiologic Revs. 175, 176–80 (1987). Because the effects of smoking and asbestos are multiplicative for lung cancer, the population of smoking asbestos workers has a lung cancer incidence of 5 times 10, or 50 times the background rates, rather than the 15-fold increase predicted by adding the separate risks. *See* U.S. Surgeon Gen., U.S. Dep't of Health & Human Servs., *supra*, at 216–17.

137. *See* Gochfeld, *supra* note 133, at 73.

138. For example, both occupational asthma and smoking can lead to impairment of pulmonary function, and the presence of one does not rule out a causal role for the other. *See* John H. Holbrook, *Nicotine Addiction, in* 2 Principles of Internal Medicine, *supra* note 42, at 2516, 2518; E.R. McFadden, Jr., *Asthma, in* 2 Principles of Internal Medicine, *supra* note 42, at 1419, 1419–21. *Cf.* Wheat v. Pfizer, Inc., 31 F.3d 340 (5th Cir. 1994), which involved a victim who died of hepatitis after taking two drugs known to cause liver damage. As to her claim against Pfizer, the manufacturer of one of the drugs, the court found the evidence inadequate, in part, for failing to exclude the possibility that her disease was caused by the other drug. *Id.* at 343. The plaintiff's witness offered the possibility that the hepatitis

may be complicated.[139] In general, if a patient is not subject to other known risk factors for a disease, it is more likely that the external cause is a factor in causing the patient's illness.[140]

Differences in individual susceptibility are commonly cited as the reason why one person gets sick from an environmental exposure while other persons are not affected. True individual susceptibility is based on genetic differences, such as immunologic reactivity, enzyme metabolism, and gender.[141] A number of other acquired factors, such as age, body mass, interacting simultaneous exposures, and preexisting disease, may also contribute to susceptibility.[142] Reliable and accurate information is available about the effects on some diseases of age, body mass, gender, and other factors; however, information on genetic susceptibility is available for only a few diseases, and information on the relation between genetic susceptibility and particular toxic exposures, for even fewer.[143]

resulted from the combined action of the two drugs, which the court rejected because the witness cited no study of the combined effects of the drugs. *Id.* The court also faulted the plaintiff for failing to rule out hepatitis C as a cause of the liver damage, though there was no test for the condition at that time. *Id.* at 342. *But see* Benedi v. McNeil-PPC, Inc., 66 F.3d 1378, 1384 (4th Cir. 1995) (upholding plaintiff's recovery for liver damage caused by Tylenol and alcohol consumption).

139. The problem of unidentified risks (often termed "background cases of unknown etiology") has been recognized in a number of decisions. For example, in *In re Breast Implant Litigation*, 11 F. Supp. 2d 1217 (D. Colo. 1998), the court disapproved of a physician's identification of silicone as the cause of the plaintiff's disease through "differential diagnosis," stating: "As a practical matter, the cause of many diseases remains unknown; therefore, a clinician who suspects that a substance causes a disease in some patients very well might conclude that the substance caused the disease in the plaintiff simply because the clinician has no other explanation." *Id.* at 1230. *See also* National Bank of Commerce v. Dow Chem. Co., 965 F. Supp. 1490 (E.D. Ark. 1996) (rejecting testimony that pesticide caused birth defect where witness acknowledged that causes are unknown for 70% to 80% of birth defects), *aff'd*, 133 F.3d 1132 (8th Cir. 1998); Whiting v. Boston Edison Co., 891 F. Supp. 12 (D. Mass. 1995) (in case alleging radiation caused power plant worker's acute lymphocytic leukemia, witness's acknowledgement that 90% of cases are of unknown cause cast doubt on "differential diagnosis" of cause); *In re* "Agent Orange" Prod. Liab. Litig., 611 F. Supp. 1223, 1250 (E.D.N.Y. 1985) ("Central to the inadequacy of plaintiffs' case is their inability to exclude other possible causes of plaintiffs' illnesses—those arising out of their service in Vietnam as well as those that all of us face in military and civilian life."), *aff'd*, 818 F.2d. 187 (2d Cir. 1987), *cert. denied*, 487 U.S. 1234 (1988). The plaintiff may be able to rely on inferences from epidemiological, toxicological, or other evidence, however. *See* Michael D. Green et al., Reference Guide on Epidemiology, and Bernard D. Goldstein & Mary Sue Henifin, Reference Guide on Toxicology, in this manual; *In re* Hanford Nuclear Reservation Litig., No. CV-91-3015-AAM, 1998 WL 775340 (E.D. Wash. Aug. 21, 1998).

140. This kind of reasoning is discussed in *In re Paoli Railroad Yard PCB Litigation*, 35 F.3d 717, 760 n.30 (3d Cir. 1994), *cert. denied*, 513 U.S. 1190 (1995).

141. *See* Stuart M. Brooks et al., *Types and Sources of Environmental Hazards*, *in* Environmental Medicine, *supra* note 19, at 9, 15–17; Daniel W. Nebert et al., *Genetic Epidemiology of Environmental Toxicity and Cancer Susceptibility: Human Allelic Polymorphisms in Drug-Metabolizing Enzyme Genes, Their Functional Importance, and Nomenclature Issues*, 31 Drug Metabolism Revs. 467 (1999); Maurizio Taningher et al., *Drug Metabolism Polymorphisms as Modulators of Cancer Susceptibility*, 436 Mutation Res. 227 (1999).

142. *See* Karen Reiser, *General Principles of Susceptibility*, *in* Environmental Medicine, *supra* note 19, at 351, 351–52, 358.

143. *See id.* at 357.

In almost all instances, integration of all the above factors into an opinion on causality cannot be reduced to mathematical formulas. There are inevitable gaps in information, as well as lack of knowledge regarding individual characteristics, such as susceptibility and resistance. Thus, clinical judgment is critical to opinions on diagnosis and causation for the individual patient even when the scientific population basis for general causation may be quite strong.

V. Treatment Decisions

Following diagnosis, most physicians are concerned with applying appropriate treatment to either cure or ameliorate a patient's condition. Such treatment may be surgical (e.g., removal of a diseased organ), ablative (e.g., radiotherapy aimed at a tumor), chemotherapeutic (e.g., use of pharmacological agents with a host of different actions), rehabilitative (e.g., physical therapy), interdictive (e.g., removal of the patient from a toxic or allergenic exposure), behavioral (e.g., counseling), or something else.[144] Some of the recommended therapies for different conditions found in the textbooks and professional literature are reified as practice guidelines by various organizations and the government. Some recommended therapies have demonstrated their effectiveness in randomized controlled trials, whereas others, both old and new, have much less scientific support.

Treatment options for an individual patient must be assessed in light of the nature and severity of the particular disease (e.g., people whose lung cancer is metastatic are not often candidates for removal of the primary tumor), and the likelihood of unacceptable complications from the treatment (e.g., removal of a lung to cure cancer in someone with severe emphysema may not leave enough remaining lung tissue to allow the patient to walk, even if his or her cancer is cured).[145] Prediction of the effects, both positive and negative, of a course of therapy is based on the professional literature and consideration of a patient's specific situation. For example, a patient with underlying kidney disease may not be an appropriate candidate for some radiographic tests and therapies that use dye that runs a high risk of causing further damage to the kidneys. Use of an effective antibiotic to which a patient "may possibly" have had a previous aller-

144. *See* Kassirer & Kopelman, *supra* note 48, at 11, 32–33.

145. A physician's selection of appropriate treatment is often at issue in medical malpractice cases (*see supra* notes 31–32 and accompanying text), but it also is at issue in other kinds of cases, including claims that medical treatment was "necessary" and therefore covered in insurance litigation under ERISA (*see, e.g.*, McGraw v. Prudential Ins. Co., 137 F.3d 1253, 1258–1263 (10th Cir. 1998)), claims that treatment was improperly withheld from prisoners under the Eighth Amendment (*see, e.g.*, Kulas v. Roberson, 202 F.3d 278 (9th Cir. 1999) (unpublished table decision) (text at No. 98-16954, 1999 WL 1054663 (9th Cir. Nov. 19, 1999) (mem.)), and medical monitoring claims (*see, e.g.*, *In re* Paoli R.R. Yard PCB Litig., 916 F.2d 829, 852 (3d Cir. 1990), *cert. denied*, 499 U.S. 961 (1991)).

gic reaction should be weighed against the use of alternative antibiotics that may be less effective against the infection. The physician may also consider the likely severity of a reaction and the ability to prevent or treat it with additional medication. Thus, although treatment recommendations are often written down as a precise series of sequential decisions (often called algorithms), making decisions for actual patients is generally more complex and requires consideration of many individual factors.

VI. Medical Testimony: Looking to the Future

It is likely that medical testimony will continue to be one of the most common forms of expert testimony in the future. While many commentators have focused attention on medical testimony in toxic injury cases, particularly testimony offered on issues of external causation, a growing number of cases concern ERISA suits challenging coverage under health care plans and claims of unlawful discrimination under the Americans with Disabilities Act. As the health care system continues to evolve, there will be growing numbers of cases, particularly on coverage issues, requiring medical testimony. Also, advances in the medical sciences, including medical genetics and biotechnology, will present new challenges to courts in cases requiring medical testimony.

With this forecast, courts will continue to grapple with issues of admissibility of medical testimony for the foreseeable future. As the cases we have used to illustrate this chapter demonstrate, there are great and unresolved differences in how various courts treat the admissibility of medical testimony. While this reference guide does not propose legal standards to govern admissibility of medical evidence,[146] it does provide a framework for legal analysis by describing the scientific and professional practices of physicians as they perform their professional duties and offer opinions on diagnosis, treatment, and internal and external causation. It is challenging to encourage consistent use of medical terminology and make explicit the extensive knowledge base and reasoning process that physicians implicitly employ in evaluating medical problems. Further work in these areas will improve the transferability of medical knowledge into the courts and other arenas.

146. *See supra* note 30.

Glossary of Terms

adequacy of diagnostic hypothesis. Diagnostic sufficiency. To be considered adequate, a diagnostic hypothesis must explain the patient's normal findings as well as abnormal findings.

attending physician. A physician formally attached to (credentialed at) the hospital in which the patient is being treated.

Bayes' theorem. An algebraic formula that allows the pretest and posttest clinical data to be expressed in terms of probabilities. By integrating the pretest probability of a disease or set of diseases with the result of a given test (and taking into account the sensitivity and specificity of that test), the physician is able to calculate a posttest probability of a disease or set of diseases. This approach can be useful in certain circumstances, but many clinical situations can be so complex that it is impractical to apply Bayes' theorem.

case report/case series. The most basic type of descriptive study of an individual (case report) or a series of individuals (case series), usually including such factors as gender, age, and exposure or treatment, but without controlled assessment of the relationship between exposure or treatment and disease or outcome.

clinical tests. Noninvasive tests of the function of an organ system, including tests of pulmonary function, muscle function, endurance, and heart function.

coherency of a diagnostic hypothesis. In a coherent diagnostic hypothesis, the patient's findings (signs, symptoms, test results), risk factors, and complications match the expectations for the disease.

consulting physician. A physician brought in to give an expert opinion or a second opinion, who may or may not be involved in treatment. He or she may rely on information contained in the patient's medical records, patient history, laboratory tests, x-rays, and so forth, or may combine these facts with his or her own examination of the patient and any additional tests considered advisable.

diagnosis. The determination of which disease is most likely present in a given patient, as indicated by the patient's various symptoms, signs, and test results.

diagnostic hypothesis. One or more disease entities, conditions, or syndromes postulated to be responsible for causing a patient's clinical presentation. See working diagnosis.

diagnostic tests. Any tests (clinical, laboratory, or pathologic) whose results may assist the physician in making his or her diagnosis.

differential diagnosis. The term used by physicians to refer to the process of determining which of two or more diseases with similar symptoms and signs the patient is suffering from, by means of comparing the various competing diagnostic hypotheses with the clinical findings.

differential etiology. A term used on occasion by expert witnesses or courts to describe the investigation and reasoning that leads to a determination of external causation, sometimes more specifically described by the witness or court as a process of identifying external causes by a process of elimination.

disease. Coherent deviation from normal in structure or function that affects a certain part or parts of the body or type of tissue.

dose–response relationship. The general tendency to observe greater responses in individuals when they are given greater doses of a drug or toxic substance. The presence of such a relationship supports an inference of a causal relationship between exposure and response (disease).

external causation. As used herein, an underlying cause of a given disease in a given individual that stems from a source outside the individual's body. A hereditary disease such as Tay-Sachs disease or hemophilia would not be due to external causation; cirrhosis of the liver resulting from excessive alcohol intake or ataxia resulting from lead poisoning would be due to external causation.

general causation. General causation is established by demonstrating (usually by reference to a scientific publication) that exposure to the substance in question causes (or is capable of causing) disease; for example, smoking cigarettes causes lung cancer.

inductive reasoning. See inferential reasoning.

inferential reasoning. The reasoning process by which a physician assimilates the various findings on a given patient and forms hypotheses that lead to testing and further hypotheses until a coherent diagnosis is reached.

invasive procedure. A procedure (surgery, test, etc.) in which the body of the patient is invaded by an instrument of some sort. Invasive procedures may be as minimal as the biopsy of a lesion on the skin or as traumatic as open-heart surgery.

laboratory tests. Analyses of fluids or other substances collected from the body of the patient, including blood samples, urine samples, and fecal samples.

multiplicative interaction. A process that occurs when two toxic agents (or two disease states) interact in the patient in such a manner that the magnitude of their combined effects is equal to the product of the effect of each agent (or disease) working in isolation. This is a special instance of synergism.

noninvasive procedure. A procedure (usually a test procedure) that does not invade the body of the patient, including exercise and stress tests, electrocardiograms, CAT scans, and MRIs.

parsimony in a diagnostic hypothesis. A preference for the simplest way to coherently and adequately explain all of the patient's findings, normal and abnormal.

pathogenesis. The mode of origin or development of any disease or morbid process.

pathology test. Microscopic analysis of a piece of body tissue obtained during surgery or by biopsy, in which an expert determines whether the tissue appears to be normal for the organ form from which it was taken. If it does not appear normal, the expert then attempts to determine what the pattern of abnormality is (scarring, malignancy, inflammation, etc.)

pathophysiology. The derangement of function seen in disease; alteration in function as distinguished from structural disease.

patient history. An interview conducted by the treating physician with the patient, in which the physician elicits from the patient the symptoms he or she is suffering from, as well as information about past and present medical history and treatment, personal information on family status and lifestyle, environmental information about habitation and employment, and the like.

physical exam. A noninvasive, largely external examination of the patient's body in which the physician looks for signs of normal and abnormal function. The physician may do a physical examination of a healthy individual to fulfill the requirements of an employer or insurance company, or of a patient who is ill to substantiate or refute the symptoms obtained from a patient during the taking of the patient history.

predictive value. The extent to which a given test will predict the presence or absence of a given disease. The positive predictive value of a test or observation refers to the proportion of all positive results that are "true" positive test results in a particular population. The negative predictive value of a test or observation refers to the proportion of "true" negative results in a population.

sensitivity. The percentage of patients with positive test results for a disease who actually have the disease (called a "true positive" result). Test results for those who have a disease but are incorrectly identified as not having the disease because of the test's insensitivity are called "false negatives." A test with high sensitivity given to people suffering from the disease it tests for will have a high proportion of true positives and only a few false negatives. A test with low sensitivity will reveal a considerable number of false negatives and fewer true positives.

sensitization. The initial exposure of a person to a specific antigen (any substance that is capable of inducing an immune reaction in an individual and of reacting with the products of that response); repeated exposure to the same antigen may then result in a much stronger immune response (e.g., an individual stung by a bee on one occasion may have a stronger response if stung again, and if subjected to sufficient numbers of bee stings, may eventually react by going into anaphylactic shock).

sign. A physical condition observed in a patient by the physician in the course of a physical examination, such as fever, cardiac murmur, enlarged lymph nodes, suspicious breast mass.

specific causation. Specific, or individual, causation is established by demonstrating that a given exposure is the cause of an individual's disease (for example, that a given plaintiff's lung cancer was caused by smoking).

specificity. The percentage of negative test results in individuals who are free of a given disease, also known as the "true negative" rate. Test results in those who are free of the disease who are incorrectly identified as having the condition are called "false positives." Thus, a test that indicates abnormal bronchial reactivity in 15% of individuals without asthma would have a false positive rate of 15%; their test results were positive, but they are free of the condition.

susceptibility. The propensity of an individual to be harmed by an agent (e.g., a person who has a high susceptibility to irritant gases will suffer from bronchitis or asthma more than a person with a low susceptibility). Susceptibility tends to be influenced by age, gender, and genetics as well as the individual's state of health and history of prior exposure.

symptom. A patient's subjective report of physical abnormality as described to the physician during the taking of the patient history. Symptoms may include reports of pain in various parts of the body, sensations such as dizziness or fatigue, fever or chills, or swelling or suspicious nodules. If a symptom, such as fever or the existence of a suspicious breast nodule, is verified by the physician during the physical exam, it is considered a sign.

syndrome. A clustering of the symptoms, signs, and laboratory findings that indicate a specific disease state.

synergistic interaction. The joint action of two or more agents such that their combined effect is greater than the sum of the effects of each agent working separately. See multiplicative interaction.

threshold. The lowest dose of any substance at which a measurable response occurs. For a substance that produces more than one effect, the threshold may vary according to the effect. For instance, with a neurotoxin that can produce dizziness, convulsion, coma, and death, the thresholds for the different effects can vary from quite low for dizziness to relatively high for death.

treating physician. A physician in charge of diagnosis and therapy for a given patient. The treating physician is likely to be an attending physician at the hospital to which the patient has been admitted. Many physicians will act as treating physicians with patients for whom they provide primary care, but may be called upon to act as consulting physicians at the request of colleagues or the patients of other physicians.

working diagnosis. A diagnostic hypothesis sufficiently convincing to form the basis for planning the next step in patient management. A working diagnosis may provide a rationale for the physician to order further tests, to forecast a likely clinical course for the patient, to refrain from further testing and simply to observe the patient for a given time, or to initiate a course of treatment. If a working diagnosis proves to be correct, either by subsequent testing or by patient response, it may become the final diagnosis.

References on Medical Testimony

Thomas E. Andreoli et al., Cecil Essentials of Medicine (3d ed. 1993).

Barbara Bates et al., A Guide to Physical Examination and History Taking (6th ed. 1995).

Joan E. Bertin & Mary S. Henifin, *Science, Law, and the Search for the Truth in the Courtroom,* 22 J.L. Med. & Ethics 6 (1994).

Environmental Medicine (Stuart M. Brooks et al. eds., 1995).

1 & 2 Harrison's Principles of Internal Medicine (Anthony S. Fauci et al. eds., 14th ed. 1998).

Alvan R. Feinstein, Clinical Judgment (1967).

Michael D. Green, Bendectin and Birth Defects: The Challenges of Mass Toxic Substances Litigation (1996).

Jerome P. Kassirer & Richard I. Kopelman, Learning Clinical Reasoning (1991).

Susan R. Poulter, *Medical and Scientific Evidence of Causation: Guidelines for Evaluating Medical Opinion Evidence, in* Expert Witnessing: Explaining and Understanding Science 186 (Carl Meyer ed., 1999).

Susan R. Poulter, *Science and Toxic Torts: Is There a Rational Solution to the Problem of Causation?* 7 High Tech. L.J. 189 (1992).

Reference Guide on DNA Evidence

DAVID H. KAYE AND GEORGE F. SENSABAUGH, JR.

David H. Kaye, M.A., J.D., is Regents' Professor of Law, Arizona State University College of Law, Tempe, Arizona

George F. Sensabaugh, Jr., D. Crim., is Professor, School of Public Health, University of California, Berkeley, California.

CONTENTS

I. Introduction

Deoxyribonucleic acid, or DNA, is a molecule that encodes the genetic information in all living organisms. Its chemical structure was elucidated in 1954. More than thirty years later, samples of human DNA began to be used in the criminal justice system, primarily in cases of rape or murder. The evidence has been the subject of extensive scrutiny by lawyers, judges, and the scientific community.[1] It is now admissible in virtually all jurisdictions, but debate lingers over the safeguards that should be required in testing samples and in presenting the evidence in court.[2] Moreover, there are many types of DNA analysis, and still more are being developed.[3] New problems of admissibility arise as advancing methods of analysis and novel applications of established methods are introduced.

This reference guide addresses technical issues that arise in considering the admissibility of and weight to be accorded analyses of DNA, and it identifies legal issues whose resolution requires scientific information.[4] The goal is to present the essential background information and to provide a framework for resolving the possible disagreements among scientists or technicians who testify as to the results and import of forensic DNA comparisons.

A. Summary of Contents

Section I lists the major objections that can be raised to the admission of DNA evidence. It also outlines the types of scientific expertise that go into the analysis of DNA samples.

1. At the request of various government agencies, the National Research Council empaneled two committees for the National Academy of Sciences that produced book-length reports on forensic DNA technology, with recommendations for enhancing the rigor of laboratory work and improving the presentation of the evidence in court. Committee on DNA Technology in Forensic Science, National Research Council, DNA Technology in Forensic Science (1992) [hereinafter NRC I]; Committee on DNA Forensic Science: An Update, National Research Council, The Evaluation of Forensic DNA Evidence (1996) [hereinafter NRC II]. One author of this guide served on both committees, the other served on the second committee (NRC II), and we have drawn on those reports. We also have relied extensively on the version of this reference guide on DNA evidence by Judith A. McKenna, Joe S. Cecil, and Pamela Coukos that appeared in the 1994 edition of the *Reference Manual on Scientific Evidence*.

2. *See* D.H. Kaye, *DNA, NAS, NRC, DAB, RFLP, PCR, and More: An Introduction to the Symposium on the 1996 NRC Report on Forensic DNA Evidence*, 37 Jurimetrics J. 395 (1997); William C. Thompson, *Guide to Forensic DNA Evidence*, *in* Expert Evidence: A Practitioner's Guide to Law, Science, and the *FJC Manual* 185 (Bert Black & Patrick W. Lee eds., 1997).

3. Emerging systems of DNA analysis are described and contrasted to the established methods and markers in National Comm'n on the Future of DNA Evidence Research & Dev. Working Group, Report to the Commission (forthcoming 2000).

4. Leading cases are collected in tables in NRC II, *supra* note 1, at 205–11. For subsequent developments, see D.H. Kaye, *DNA Identification in Criminal Cases: Lingering and Emerging Evidentiary Issues*, *in* Proceedings of the Seventh International Symposium on Human Identification 12 (1997).

Section II gives an overview of the scientific principles behind DNA typing. It describes the structure of DNA and how this molecule differs from person to person. These are basic facts of molecular biology. The section also defines the more important scientific terms. It explains at a general level how DNA differences are detected. These are matters of analytical chemistry and laboratory procedure. Finally, the section indicates how it is shown that these differences permit individuals to be identified. This is accomplished with the methods of probability and statistics.

Sections III and IV outline basic methods used in DNA testing. Section III describes methods that begin by using the polymerase chain reaction (PCR) to make many copies of short segments of DNA. Section IV examines the theory and technique of the older procedure of variable number tandem repeat (VNTR) profiling.

Section V considers issues of sample quantity and quality common to all methods of DNA profiling. Section VI deals with laboratory performance. It outlines the types of information that a laboratory should produce to establish that it can analyze DNA reliably and that it has adhered to established laboratory protocols.

Section VII examines issues in the interpretation of laboratory results. To assist the courts in understanding the extent to which the results incriminate the defendant, it enumerates the hypotheses that need to be considered before concluding that the defendant is the source of the crime-scene samples, and it explores the issues that arise in judging the strength of the evidence. It focuses on questions of statistics, probability, and population genetics.

Section VIII takes up novel applications of DNA technology, such as the forensic analysis of non-human DNA. It identifies questions that can be useful in judging whether a new method or application has the scientific merit and power claimed by the proponent of the evidence.

An appendix provides detail on technical material, and a glossary defines selected terms and acronyms encountered in genetics, molecular biology, and forensic DNA work.[5]

B. Objections to DNA Evidence

The usual objective of forensic DNA analysis is to detect variations in the genetic material that differentiate individuals one from another.[6] Laboratory techniques for isolating and analyzing DNA have long been used in scientific research and medicine. Applications of these techniques to forensic work usually

5. The glossary also defines a number of other terms that may be used by experts in these fields.

6. Biologists accept as a truism the proposition that, except for identical twins, human beings are genetically unique.

involve comparing a DNA sample obtained from a suspect with a DNA sample obtained from the crime scene. Often, a perpetrator's DNA in hair, blood, saliva, or semen can be found at a crime scene,[7] or a victim's DNA can be found on or around the perpetrator.[8]

In many cases, defendants have objected to the admission of testimony of a match or its implications.[9] Under *Daubert v. Merrell Dow Pharmaceuticals, Inc.*,[10] the district court, in its role as "gatekeeper" for scientific evidence, then must ensure that the expert's methods are scientifically valid and reliable. Because the basic theory and most of the laboratory techniques of DNA profiling are so widely accepted in the scientific world, disputed issues involve features unique to their forensic applications or matters of laboratory technique. These include the extent to which standard techniques have been shown to work with crime-scene samples exposed to sunlight, heat, bacteria, and chemicals in the environment; the extent to which the specific laboratory has demonstrated its ability to follow protocols that have been validated to work for crime-scene samples; possible ambiguities that might interfere with the interpretation of test results; and the validity and possible prejudicial impact of estimates of the probability of a match between the crime-scene samples and innocent suspects.

C. Relevant Expertise

DNA identification can involve testimony about laboratory findings, about the statistical interpretation of these findings, and about the underlying principles of molecular biology. Consequently, expertise in several fields might be required to establish the admissibility of the evidence or to explain it adequately to the jury. The expert who is qualified to testify about laboratory techniques might

7. *E.g.*, United States v. Beasley, 102 F.3d 1440 (8th Cir. 1996) (two hairs were found in a mask used in a bank robbery and left in the abandoned get-away car); United States v. Two Bulls, 918 F.2d 56 (8th Cir. 1990), *vacated for reh'g en banc, app. dismissed due to death of defendant*, 925 F.2d 1127 (1991) (semen stain on victim's underwear).

8. *E.g.*, United States v. Cuff, 37 F. Supp. 2d 279 (S.D.N.Y. 1999) (scrapings from defendant's fingernails); State v. Bible, 858 P.2d 1152 (Ariz. 1993) (bloodstains on defendant's shirt); People v. Castro, 545 N.Y.S.2d 985 (Bronx Co. Sup. Ct. 1989) (bloodstains on defendant's watch). For brevity, we refer only to the typical case of a perpetrator's DNA at a crime scene. The scientific and legal issues in both situations are the same.

9. Exclusion of the testimony can be sought before or during trial, depending on circumstances and the court's rules regarding pretrial motions. Pretrial requests for discovery and the appointment of experts to assist the defense also can require judicial involvement. *See, e.g.*, Dubose v. State, 662 So. 2d 1189 (Ala. 1995) (holding that due process was violated by the failure to provide an indigent defendant with funds for an expert); Paul C. Giannelli, *The DNA Story: An Alternative View*, 88 J. Crim. L. & Criminology 380, 414–17 (1997) (book review) (criticizing the reluctance of state courts to appoint defense experts and to grant discovery requests); Paul C. Giannelli, *Criminal Discovery, Scientific Evidence, and DNA*, 44 Vand. L. Rev. 791 (1991); NRC II, *supra* note 1, at 167–69.

10. 509 U.S. 579 (1993).

not be qualified to testify about molecular biology, to make estimates of population frequencies, or to establish that an estimation procedure is valid.[11]

Trial judges ordinarily are accorded great discretion in evaluating the qualifications of a proposed expert witness, and the decisions depend on the background of each witness. Courts have noted the lack of familiarity of academic experts—who have done respected work in other fields—with the scientific literature on forensic DNA typing,[12] and on the extent to which their research or teaching lies in other areas.[13] Although such concerns may give trial judges pause, they rarely result in exclusion of the testimony on the ground that the witness simply is not qualified as an expert.[14]

The scientific and legal literature on the objections to DNA evidence is extensive.[15] By studying the scientific publications, or perhaps by appointing a special master or expert adviser to assimilate this material, a court can ascertain where a party's expert falls in the spectrum of scientific opinion. Furthermore, an expert appointed by the court under Rule 706 could testify about the scientific literature generally or even about the strengths or weaknesses of the particular arguments advanced by the parties.[16]

11. *See* 1 McCormick on Evidence § 203, at 875 n.40 (John W. Strong ed., 1992). Nevertheless, if previous cases establish that the testing and estimation procedures are legally acceptable, and if the computations are essentially mechanical, then highly specialized statistical expertise might not be essential. Reasonable estimates of DNA characteristics in major population groups can be obtained from standard references, and many quantitatively literate experts could use the appropriate formulae to compute the relevant profile frequencies or probabilities. NRC II, *supra* note 1, at 170. Limitations in the knowledge of a technician who applies a generally accepted statistical procedure can be explored on cross-examination. *E.g.*, State v. Colbert, 896 P.2d 1089 (Kan. 1995) (in view of general acceptance of databases, estimate of probability was admissible despite an expert's concessions that he was not a population geneticist and was not qualified to explain how the databases applied to the town of Coffeyville); State v. Harvey, 699 A.2d 596, 637 (N.J. 1997) (statistician not required).

12. *E.g.*, State v. Copeland, 922 P.2d 1304, 1318 n.5 (Wash. 1996) (noting that defendant's statistical expert "was also unfamiliar with publications in the area," including studies by "a leading expert in the field" whom he thought was "a guy in a lab somewhere").

13. *E.g.*, *id.* (noting that defendant's population genetics expert "had published little in the field of human genetics, only one non-peer reviewed chapter in a general text, had two papers in the area rejected, was uninformed of the latest articles in the field, had misused a statistical model . . . , had no graduate students working under him, had not received any awards in his field in over ten years, had not received a research grant in about eight years, and made about $100,000 testifying as an expert in 1990–91").

14. *E.g.*, Commonwealth v. Blasiolli, 685 A.2d 151 (Pa. Super. Ct. 1996) (professor of ecology and evolutionary biology was said to be qualified, but "barely").

15. *See, e.g.*, Bruce S. Weir, *A Bibliography for the Use of DNA in Human Identification, in* Human Identification: The Use of DNA Markers 179–213 (Bruce S. Weir ed., 1995); NRC II, *supra* note 1, at 226–39 (list of references).

16. Some courts have appointed experts to address general questions relating to DNA profiling. *E.g.*, United States v. Bonds, 12 F.3d 540 (6th Cir. 1993); United States v. Porter, Crim. No. F06277-89, 1994 WL 742297 (D.C. Super. Ct. Nov. 17, 1994) (mem.). Whether a court should appoint its own expert instead of an expert for the defense when there are more specific disputes is more controversial.

II. Overview of Variation in DNA and Its Detection

A. DNA, Chromosomes, Sex, and Genes

DNA is a complex molecule that contains the "genetic code" of organisms as diverse as bacteria and humans.[17] The molecule is made of subunits that include four nucleotide bases, whose names are abbreviated to A, T, G, and C.[18] The physical structure of DNA is described more fully in the appendix, but for general purposes it suffices to say that a DNA molecule is like a long sequence of these four letters, where the chemical structure that corresponds to each letter is known as a base pair.

Most human DNA is tightly packed into structures known as chromosomes, which are located in the nuclei of most cells.[19] If the bases are like letters, then each chromosome is like a book written in this four-letter alphabet, and the nucleus is like a bookshelf in the interior of the cell. All the cells in one individual contain copies of the same set of books. This library, so to speak, is the individual's genome.[20]

In human beings, the process that produces billions of cells with the same genome starts with sex. Every sex cell (a sperm or ovum) contains 23 chromosomes. When a sperm and ovum combine, the resulting fertilized cell contains 23 pairs of chromosomes, or 46 in all. It is as if the father donates half of his collection of 46 books, and the mother donates a corresponding half of her collection. During pregnancy, the fertilized cell divides to form two cells, each of which has an identical copy of the 46 chromosomes. The two then divide to form four, the four form eight, and so on. As gestation proceeds, various cells specialize to form different tissues and organs. In this way, each human being has immensely many copies[21] of the original 23 pairs of chromosomes from the fertilized egg, one member of each pair having come from the mother and one from the father.

All told, the DNA in the 23 chromosomes contains over three billion letters (base pairs) of genetic "text."[22] About 99.9% is identical between any two individuals. This similarity is not really surprising—it accounts for the common features that make humans an identifiable species. The remaining 0.1% is particular to an individual (identical twins excepted). This variation makes each

17. Some viruses use a related nucleic acid, RNA, instead of DNA to encode genetic information.

18. The full names are adenine, thymine, guanine, and cytosine.

19. A few types of cells, such as red blood cells, do not contain nuclei.

20. Originally, "genome" referred to the set of base pairs in an egg or sperm, but the term also is used to designate the ordered set in the fertilized cell.

21. The number of cells in the human body has been estimated at more than 10^{15} (a million billion).

22. If the base pairs were listed as letters in a series of books, one piled on top of the other, the pile would be as high as the Washington Monument.

person genetically unique.

A gene is a particular DNA sequence, usually from 1,000 to 10,000 base pairs long, that "codes" for an observable characteristic.[23] For example, a tiny part of the sequence that directs the production of the human group-specific complement protein (GC)[24] is

G C A A A A T T G C C T G A T G C C A C A C C C A A G G A A C T G G C A[25]

This gene always is located at the same position, or locus, on chromosome number 4. As we have seen, most individuals have two copies of each gene at a given locus—one from the father and one from the mother.

A locus where almost all humans have the same DNA sequence is called monomorphic ("of one form"). A locus at which the DNA sequence varies among individuals is called polymorphic ("of many forms"). The alternative forms are called alleles. For example, the GC protein gene sequence has three common alleles that result from single nucleotide polymorphisms (SNPs, pronounced "snips")—substitutions in the base that occur at a given point.[26] In the scientific literature, the three alleles are designated Gc*1F, Gc*1S, and Gc*2, and the sequences at the variable sites are shown in Figure 1.

Figure 1. The variable sequence region of the group-specific component gene. The base substitutions that define the alleles are shown in bold.

Allele *2: G C A A A A T T G C C T G A T G C C A C A C C C A A G G A A C T G G C A
Allele *1F: G C A A A A T T G C C T G A T G C C A C A C C C A **C** G G A A C T G G C A
Allele *1S: G C A A A A T T G C C T G A **G** G C C A C A C C C A **C** G G A A C T G G C A

In terms of the metaphor of DNA as text, the gene is like an important paragraph in the book; a SNP is a change in a letter somewhere within that paragraph, and the two versions of the paragraph that result from this slight change are the alleles. An individual who inherits the same allele from both parents is

23. The genetic code consists of "words" that are three nucleotides long and that determine the structure of the proteins that are manufactured in cells. *See, e.g.*, Elaine Johnson Mange & Arthur P. Mange, Basic Human Genetics 107 (2d ed. 1999).

24. This "GC" stands for "group-specific component," and not for the bases guanine and cytosine.

25. The full GC gene is nearly 42,400 base pairs in length. The product of this gene is also known as vitamin D–binding protein. GC is one of the five loci included in the polymarker (PM) typing kit, which is widely used in forensic testing.

26. *See* R.L. Reynolds & G.F. Sensabaugh, *Use of the Polymerase Chain Reaction for Typing Gc Variants, in* 3 Advances in Forensic Haemogenetics 158 (H.F. Polesky & W.R. Mayr eds. 1990); Andreas Braun et al., *Molecular Analysis of the Gene for the Human Vitamin-D-binding Protein (Group-specific Component): Allelic Differences of the Common Genetic GC Types*, 89 Hum. Genetics 401 (1992). These are examples of *point mutations*.

called a homozygote.[27] An individual with distinct alleles is termed a heterozygote.[28]

Regions of DNA used for forensic analysis usually are not genes, but parts of the chromosome without a known function. The "non-coding" regions of DNA have been found to contain considerable sequence variation, which makes them particularly useful in distinguishing individuals. Although the terms "locus," "allele," "homozygous," and "heterozygous" were developed to describe genes, the nomenclature has been carried over to describe all DNA variation—coding and non-coding alike—for both types are inherited from mother and father in the same fashion.

B. Types of Polymorphisms and Methods of Detection

By determining which alleles are present at strategically chosen loci, the forensic scientist ascertains the genetic profile, or genotype, of an individual. Genotyping does not require "reading" the full DNA sequence; indeed, direct sequencing is technically demanding and time-consuming.[29] Rather, most genetic typing focuses on identifying only those variations that define the alleles and does not attempt to "read out" each and every base as it appears.[30]

For instance, simple sequence variation, such as that for the GC locus, is conveniently detected using a sequence-specific oligonucleotide (SSO) probe. With GC typing, probes for the three common alleles (which we shall call A_1, A_2, and A_3) are attached to designated locations on a membrane. When DNA with a given allele (say, A_1) comes in contact with the probe for that allele, it sticks.[31] To get a detectable quantity of DNA to stick, many copies of the variable sequence region of the GC gene in the DNA sample have to be made.[32] All this DNA then is added to the membrane. The DNA fragments with the allele A_1 in them stick to the spot with the A_1 probe. To permit these fragments to be seen, a chemical "label" that catalyses a color change at the spot where the DNA

27. For example, someone with the Gc*2 allele on both number 4 chromosomes is homozygous at the GC locus. This homozygous GC genotype is designated as 2,2 (or simply 2).

28. For example, someone with the Gc*2 allele on one chromosome and the Gc*1F allele on the other is heterozygous at the GC locus. This heterozygous genotype is designated as 2,1F.

29. However, automated machinery for direct sequencing has been developed and is used at major research centers engaged in the international endeavor to sequence the human genome (and the genomes of other organisms). *See* R. Waterston & J.E. Sulston, *The Human Genome Project: Reaching the Finish Line*, 282 Science 53 (1998).

30. For example, genetic typing at the GC locus focuses on the sequence region shown in Figure 1; the remainder of the 42,300 base pairs of the GC gene sequence is the same for almost all individuals and is ignored for genetic typing purposes.

31. This process of hybridization is described in Part B of the Appendix.

32. The polymerase chain reaction (PCR) is used to make many copies of the DNA that is to be typed. PCR is roughly analogous to copying and pasting a section of text with a word processor. *See infra* the Appendix, Part D.

binds to its probe can be attached when the copies are made. A colored spot showing that the A_1 allele is present thus should appear on the membrane.[33]

Another category of polymorphism is characterized by the insertion of a variable number of tandem repeats (VNTR) at a locus.[34] The core unit of a VNTR is a particular short DNA sequence that is repeated many times end-to-end. This repetition gives rise to alleles with length differences; regions of DNA containing more repeats are larger than those containing fewer repeats. Genetic typing of polymorphic VNTR loci employs electrophoresis, a technique that separates DNA fragments based on size.[35]

The first polymorphic VNTRs to be used in genetic and forensic testing had core repeat sequences of 15–35 base pairs. Alleles at VNTR loci of this sort generally are too long to be measured precisely by electrophoretic methods—alleles differing in size by only a few repeat units may not be distinguished. Although this makes for complications in deciding whether two length measurements that are close together result from the same allele, these loci are quite powerful for the genetic differentiation of individuals, for they tend to have many alleles that occur relatively rarely in the population. At a locus with only twenty such alleles (and most loci typically have many more), there are 210 possible genotypes.[36] With five such loci, the number of possible genotypes is 210^5, which is more than 400 billion. Thus, VNTRs are an extremely discriminating class of DNA markers.

More recently, the attention of the genetic typing community has shifted to repetitive DNA characterized by short core repeats, two to seven base pairs in length. These non-coding DNA sequences are known as short tandem repeats (STRs).[37] Because STR alleles are much smaller than VNTR alleles, electrophoretic detection permits the exact number of base pairs in an STR to be determined, permitting alleles to be defined as discrete entities. Figure 2 illustrates the nature of allelic variation at a polymorphic STR locus. The first allele has nine tandem repeats, the second has ten, and the third has eleven.[38]

Figure 2. Three Alleles of an STR with the Core Sequence ATTT

ATTTATTTATTTATTTATTTATTTATTTATTTATTT

ATTTATTTATTTATTTATTTATTTATTTATTTATTTATTT

ATTTATTTATTTATTTATTTATTTATTTATTTATTTATTTATTT

33. This approach can be miniaturized and automated with hybridization chip technology. *See infra* Glossary of Terms ("chip").

34. VNTR polymorphisms also are referred to as minisatellites.

35. We describe one form of electrophoresis often used with VNTR loci *infra* § IV.

36. There are 20 homozygous genotypes and another (20 × 19)/2 = 190 heterozygous ones.

37. They also are known as microsatellites.

38. To conserve space, the figure uses alleles that are unrealistically short. A typical STR is in the range of 50–350 base pairs in length. In contrast, a typical VNTR is thousands of base pairs long.

Although there are fewer alleles per locus for STRs than for VNTRs, there are many STRs, and they can be analyzed simultaneously.[39] As more STR loci are included, STR testing becomes more revealing than VNTR profiling at four or five loci.[40]

Full DNA sequencing is employed at present only for mitochondrial DNA (mtDNA).[41] Mitochondria are small structures found inside the cell. In these organelles, certain molecules are broken down to supply energy. Mitochondria have a small genome that bears no relation to the chromosomal genome in the cell nucleus.[42] Mitochondrial DNA has three features that make it useful for forensic DNA testing. First, the typical cell, which has but one nucleus, contains hundreds of identical mitochondria.[43] Hence, for every copy of chromosomal DNA, there are hundreds of copies of mitochondrial DNA. This means that it is possible to detect mtDNA in samples containing too little nuclear DNA for conventional typing.[44] Second, the mtDNA contains a sequence region of about a thousand base pairs that varies greatly among individuals. Finally, mitochondria are inherited mother to child,[45] so that siblings, maternal half-siblings, and others related through maternal lineage possess the same mtDNA sequence.[46] This last feature makes mtDNA particularly useful for associating persons related through their maternal lineage—associating skeletal remains to a family, for example.[47]

39. The procedures for simultaneous detection are known as multiplex methods. *See infra* Glossary of Terms ("capillary electrophoresis," "chip"). Mass spectrometry also can be applied to detect STR fragments. *Id.*

40. Usually, there are between seven and fifteen STR alleles per locus. Thirteen loci that have ten STR alleles each can give rise to 55^{13}, or 42 billion trillion, possible genotypes.

41. The first use of this mtDNA analysis as evidence in a criminal case occurred in Tennessee in *State v. Ware*, No. 03C01-9705CR00164, 1999 WL 233592 (Tenn. Crim. App. Apr. 20, 1999). *See* Mark Curriden, *A New Evidence Tool: First Use of Mitochondrial DNA Test in a U.S. Criminal Trial*, A.B.A.J., Nov. 1996, at 18.

42. In contrast to the haploid nuclear genome of over three billion base pairs, the mitochondrial genome is a circular molecule 16,569 base pairs long.

43. There are from 75 to 1,000 or so mitochondria per cell.

44. Even so, because the mitochondrial genome is so much shorter than the nuclear genome, it is a tiny fraction of the total mass of DNA in a cell.

45. Although sperm have mitochondria, these are not passed to the ovum at fertilization. Thus the only mitochondria present in the newly fertilized cell originate from the mother.

46. Evolutionary studies suggest an average mutation rate for the mtDNA control region of one nucleotide difference every 300 generations, or one difference every 6,000 years. Consequently, one would not expect to see many examples of nucleotide differences between maternal relatives. On the other hand, differences in the bases at a specific sequence position among the copies of the mtDNA within an individual have been seen. This heteroplasmy, which is more common in hair than other tissues, counsels against declaring an exclusion on the basis of a single base pair difference between two samples.

47. *See, e.g.*, Peter Gill et al., *Identification of the Remains of the Romanov Family by DNA Analysis*, 6 Nature Genetics 130 (1994).

Just as genetic variation in mtDNA can be used to track maternal lineages, genetic variations on the Y chromosome can be used to trace paternal lineages. Y chromosomes, which contain genes that result in development as a male rather than a female, are found only in males and are inherited father to son.[48] Markers on this chromosome include STRs and SNPs,[49] and they have been used in cases involving semen evidence.[50]

In sum, DNA contains the genetic information of an organism. In humans, most of the DNA is found in the cell nucleus, where it is organized into separate chromosomes. Each chromosome is like a book, and each cell has the same library of books of various sizes and shapes. There are two copies of each book of a particular size and shape, one that came from the father, the other from the mother. Thus, there are two copies of the book entitled "Chromosome One," two copies of "Chromosome Two," and so on. Genes are the most meaningful paragraphs in the books, and there are differences (polymorphisms) in the spelling of certain words in the paragraphs of different copies of each book. The different versions of the same paragraph are the alleles. Some alleles result from the substitution of one letter for another. These are SNPs. Others come about from the insertion or deletion of single letters, and still others represent a kind of stuttering repetition of a string of extra letters. These are the VNTRs and STRs. In addition to the 23 pairs of books in the cell nucleus, another page or so of text resides in each of the mitochondria, the power plants of the cell.

The methods of molecular biology permit scientists to determine which alleles are present. The next two sections describe how this is done. Section III discusses the procedures that can distinguish among all the known alleles at certain loci. Section IV deals with the "RFLP" procedures that measure the lengths of DNA fragments at a scale that is not fine enough to resolve all the possible alleles.

48. *See infra* note 110.

49. *See, e.g.*, M.F. Hammer et al., *The Geographic Distribution of Human Y Chromosome Variation*, 145 Genetics 787 (1997). The Y chromosome is used in evolutionary studies along with mtDNA to learn about human migration patterns. *Id.*; Michael F. Hammer & Stephen L. Zegura, *The Role of the Y Chromosome in Human Evolutionary Studies*, 5 Evolutionary Anthropology 116 (1996). The various markers are inherited as a single package (known as a haplotype).

50. They also were used in a family study to ascertain whether President Thomas Jefferson fathered a child of his slave, Sally Hemings. *See* Eugene A. Foster et al., *Jefferson Fathered Slave's Last Child*, 396 Nature 27 (1998); Eliot Marshall, *Which Jefferson Was the Father?*, 283 Science 153 (1999).

III. DNA Profiling with Loci Having Discrete Alleles

Simple sequence variations and STRs occur within relatively short fragments of DNA. These polymorphisms can be analyzed with so-called PCR-based tests (PCR = polymerase chain reaction). The three steps of PCR-based typing are (1) DNA extraction, (2) amplification, and (3) detection of genetic type using a method appropriate to the polymorphism. This section discusses the scientific and technological foundations of these three steps and the basis for believing that the DNA characteristics identified in the laboratory can help establish who contributed the potentially incriminating DNA.[51]

A. DNA Extraction and Amplification

DNA usually can be found in biological materials such as blood, bone, saliva, hair, semen, and urine.[52] A combination of routine chemical and physical methods permit DNA to be extracted from cell nuclei and isolated from the other chemicals in a sample.[53] Thus, the premise that DNA is present in many biological samples and can be removed for further analysis is firmly established.[54]

Just as the scientific foundations of DNA extraction are clear, the procedures for amplifying DNA sequences within the extracted DNA are well established. The first National Academy of Sciences committee on forensic DNA typing described the amplification step as "simple . . . analogous to the process by which cells replicate their DNA."[55] Details of this process, which can make millions of copies of a single DNA fragment, are given in the Appendix.

51. The problem of drawing an inference about the source of the evidence DNA, which is common to all forms of DNA profiling, is taken up in section VII.

52. *See, e.g.*, NRC I, *supra* note 1, at 28, tbl.1.1.

53. *See, e.g.*, Michael L. Baird, *DNA Profiling: Laboratory Methods*, *in* 1 Modern Scientific Evidence: The Law and Science of Expert Testimony § 16-2.2, at 667 (David L. Faigman et al. eds., 1997) [hereinafter Modern Scientific Evidence]; Catherine T. Comey et al., *DNA Extraction Strategies for Amplified Fragment Length Polymorphism Analysis*, 39 J. Forensic Sci. 1254 (1994); Atsushi Akane et al., *Purification of Forensic Specimens for the Polymerase Chain Reaction (PCR) Analysis*, 38 J. Forensic Sci. 691 (1993).

54. *See, e.g.*, NRC I, *supra* note 1, at 149 (recommending judicial notice of the proposition that "DNA polymorphisms can, in principle, provide a reliable method for comparing samples," "although the actual discriminatory power of any particular DNA test will depend on the sites of DNA variation examined"); NRC II, *supra* note 1, at 9 ("DNA typing, with its extremely high power to differentiate one human being from another, is based on a large body of scientific principles and techniques that are universally accepted.").

55. NRC I, *supra* note 1, at 40. The second committee used similar language, reporting that "[t]he PCR process is relatively simple and easily carried out in the laboratory." NRC II, *supra* note 1, at 70. *But see* NRC I, *supra*, at 63 ("Although the basic exponential amplification procedure is well understood, many technical details are not, including why some primer pairs amplify much better than others, why some loci cause systematically unfaithful amplification, and why some assays are much more sensitive to variations in conditions."). For these reasons, PCR-based procedures are validated by experiment.

For amplification to work properly and yield copies of only the desired sequence, however, care must be taken to achieve the appropriate biochemical conditions and to avoid excessive contamination of the sample.[56] A laboratory should be able to demonstrate that it can faithfully amplify targeted sequences with the equipment and reagents that it uses[57] and that it has taken suitable precautions to avoid or detect handling or carryover contamination.[58]

B. DNA Analysis

To determine whether the DNA sample associated with a crime could have come from a suspect, the genetic types as determined by analysis of the DNA amplified from the crime-scene sample are compared to the genetic types as determined for the suspect. For example, Figure 3 shows the results of STR typing at four loci in a sexual assault case.[59]

Figure 3. Sexual Assault Case (CTTA)

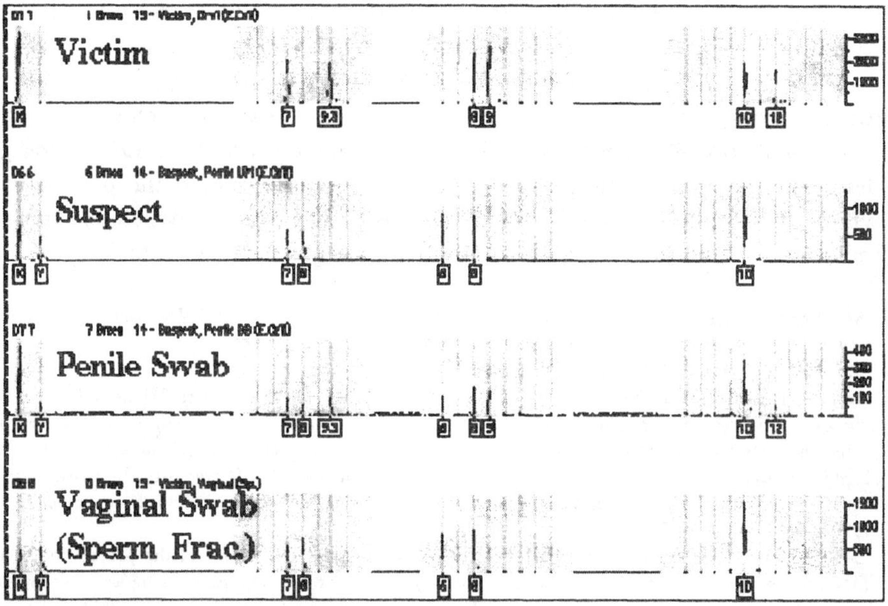

56. *See* NRC I, *supra* note 1, at 63–67; NRC II, *supra* note 1, at 71.

57. *See* NRC I, *supra* note 1, at 63–64.

58. Carryover occurs when the DNA product of a previous amplification contaminates samples or reaction solutions. *See id.* at 66.

59. The initials CTTA refer to these loci, which are known as CPO, TPO, THO, and amelogenin.

The peaks result from DNA fragments of different sizes.[60] The bottom row shows the profile of sperm DNA isolated from a vaginal swab. These sperm have two alleles at the first locus (indicating that both X and Y chromosomes are present),[61] two alleles at the second locus (consisting of 7 and 8 repeat units), two at the third locus (a 6 and an 8), and one (a 10 on each chromosome) at the fourth.[62] The same profile also appears in the DNA taken from the suspect. DNA from a penile swab from the suspect is consistent with a mixture of DNA from the victim and the suspect.

Regardless of the kind of genetic system used for typing—STRs, Amp-FLPs,[63] SNPs, or still other polymorphisms[64]—some general principles and questions can be applied to each system that is offered for courtroom use. As a beginning, the nature of the polymorphism should be well characterized. Is it a simple sequence polymorphism or a fragment length polymorphism? This information should be in the published literature or in archival genome databanks.[65]

Second, the published scientific literature also can be consulted to verify claims that a particular method of analysis can produce accurate profiles under various conditions.[66] Although such validation studies have been conducted for all the discrete-allele systems ordinarily used in forensic work, determining the point at which the empirical validation of a particular system is sufficiently convincing to pass scientific muster may well require expert assistance.

Finally, the population genetics of the marker should be characterized. As new marker systems are discovered, researchers typically analyze convenient collections of DNA samples from various human populations[67] and publish studies

60. The height of (more, precisely, the area under) each peak is related to the amount of DNA in the gel.

61. The X-Y typing at the first locus is simply used to verify the sex of the source of the DNA. XY is male, and XX is female. *See infra* note 110. That these markers show that the victim is female and the suspect male helps demonstrate that a valid result has been obtained.

62. Although each sperm cell contains only one set of chromosomes, a collection of many sperm cells from the same individual contains both sets of chromosomes. *See infra* note 90.

63. "Amp-FLP" is short for "Amplified Fragment Length Polymorphism." The DNA fragment is produced by amplifying a longish sequence with a PCR primer. The longer Amp-FLPs, such as DS180, overlap the shorter VNTRs. In time, PCR methods will be capable of generating longer Amp-FLPs.

64. *See supra* § II; *infra* Appendix, Part C (Table A-1).

65. Primary data regarding gene sequence variation is increasingly being archived in publicly accessible computer databanks, such as GenBank, rather than in the print literature. *See* Victor A. McKusick, *The Human Genome Project: Plans, Status, and Applications in Biology and Medicine*, *in* Gene Mapping: Using Law and Ethics as Guides 18, 35 (George J. Annas & Sherman Elias eds., 1992). This trend is driven by an explosion of new data coupled with the fact that most of the detected variation has no known biological significance and hence is not particularly noteworthy.

66. *Cf.* NRC I, *supra* note 1, at 72 ("Empirical validation of a DNA typing procedure must be published in appropriate scientific journals.").

67. The samples come from diverse sources, such as blood banks, law enforcement personnel, paternity cases, and criminal cases. Reliable inferences probably can be drawn from these samples. *See infra* note 178.

of the relative frequencies of each allele in these population samples. These database studies give a measure of the extent of genetic variability at the polymorphic locus in the various populations, and thus of the potential probative power of the marker for distinguishing between individuals.

At this point, the existence of PCR-based procedures that can ascertain genotypes accurately cannot be doubted.[68] Of course, the fact that scientists have shown that it is possible to extract DNA, to amplify it, and to analyze it in ways that bear on the issue of identity does not mean that a particular laboratory has adopted a suitable protocol and is proficient in following it. These laboratory-specific issues are considered in section VI.[69]

IV. VNTR Profiling

VNTR profiling, described in section II, was the first widely used method of forensic DNA testing. Consequently, its underlying principles, its acceptance within the scientific community, and its scientific soundness have been discussed in a great many opinions.[70] Because so much has been written on VNTR profiling, only the basic steps of the procedure will be outlined here.

68. *See, e.g.*, United States v. Shea, 159 F.3d 37 (1st Cir. 1998) (DQA, Polymarker, D1S80), *cert. denied*, 119 S. Ct. 1480 (1999); United States v. Lowe, 145 F.3d 45 (1st Cir. 1998) (DQA, Polymarker, D1S80); United States v. Beasley, 102 F.3d 1440, 1448 (8th Cir. 1996) (DQA, Polymarker); United States v. Hicks, 103 F.3d 837 (9th Cir. 1996) (DQA); United States v. Gaines, 979 F. Supp. 1429 (S.D. Fla. 1997) (DQA, Polymarker, D1S80); State v. Hill, 895 P.2d 1238 (Kan. 1995) (DQA); Commonwealth v. Rosier, 685 N.E.2d 739 (Mass. 1997) (STRs); Commonwealth v. Vao Sok, 683 N.E.2d 671 (Mass. 1997) (DQA, Polymarker, D1S80); State v. Moore, 885 P.2d 457 (Mont. 1994) (DQA), *overruled on other grounds in* State v. Gollehon, 906 P.2d 697 (Mont. 1995); State v. Harvey, 699 A.2d 596 (N.J. 1997) (DQA, Polymarker); State v. Lyons, 924 P.2d 802 (Or. 1996) (DQA); State v. Moeller, 548 N.W.2d 465 (S.D. 1996) (DQA); State v. Begley, 956 S.W.2d 471 (Tenn. 1997) (DQA); State v. Russell, 882 P.2d 747, 768 (Wash. 1994) (DQA).

69. Some commentators have assumed or argued that some or all of these issues are aspects of admissibility under Federal Rule of Evidence 702. *E.g.*, Edward J. Imwinkelried, *The Debate in the DNA Cases over the Foundation for the Admission of Scientific Evidence: The Importance of Human Error as a Cause of Forensic Misanalysis*, 69 Wash. U. L.Q. 19 (1991); Barry C. Scheck, *DNA and* Daubert, 15 Cardozo L. Rev.. 1959, 1979–87 (1994); William C. Thompson, *Accepting Lower Standards: The National Research Council's Second Report on Forensic DNA Evidence*, 37 Jurimetrics J. 405, 417 (1997). This reading of *Daubert* is rejected in *United States v. Shea*, 957 F. Supp. 331, 340–41 (D.N.H. 1997), but the protocols of a specific laboratory and the proficiency of its analysts are factors that affect probative value under Federal Rule of Evidence 403. *See* Margaret A. Berger, *Laboratory Error Seen Through the Lens of Science and Policy*, 30 U.C. Davis L. Rev. 1081 (1997); Edward J. Imwinkelried, *The Case Against Evidentiary Admissibility Standards that Attempt to "Freeze" the State of a Scientific Technique*, 67 U. Colo. L. Rev. 887 (1996).

70. *See* NRC II, *supra* note 1, at 205–11 (listing leading cases and status as of 1995, by jurisdiction). The first reported appellate opinion is *Andrews v. State*, 533 So. 2d 841 (Fla. Dist. Ct. App. 1988).

1. Like profiling by means of discrete allele systems,[71] VNTR profiling begins with the extraction of DNA from a crime-scene sample. (Because this DNA is not amplified, however, larger quantities of higher quality DNA[72] are required.)

2. The extracted DNA is "digested" by a restriction enzyme that recognizes a particular, very short sequence; the enzyme cuts the DNA at these restriction sites. When a VNTR falls between two restriction sites, the resulting DNA fragments will vary in size depending on the number of core repeat units in the VNTR region.[73] (These VNTRs are thus referred to as a restriction fragment length polymorphism, or RFLP.)

3. The digested DNA fragments are then separated according to size by gel electrophoresis. The digest sample is placed in a well at the end of a lane in an agarose gel, which is a gelatin-like material solidified in a slab. Digested DNA from the suspect is placed in another well on the same gel. Typically, control specimens of DNA fragments of known size, and, where appropriate, DNA specimens obtained from a victim, are run on the same gel. Mild electric current applied to the gel slowly separates the fragments in each lane by length, as shorter fragments travel farther in a fixed time than longer, heavier fragments.

4. The resulting array of fragments is transferred for manageability to a sheet of nylon by a process known as Southern blotting.[74]

5. The restriction fragments representing a particular polymorphic locus are "tagged" on the membrane using a sequence-specific probe labeled with a radioactive or chemical tag.[75]

6. The position of the specifically bound probe tag is made visible, either by autoradiography (for radioactive labels) or by a chemical reaction (for chemical labels). For autoradiography, the washed nylon membrane is placed between

71. *See supra* § III.

72. "Quality" refers to the extent to which the original, very long strands of DNA are intact. When DNA degrades, it forms shorter fragments. RFLP testing requires fragments that are on the order of at least 20,000–30,000 base pairs long.

73. *See supra* § II.

74. This procedure is named after its inventor, Edwin Southern. Either before or during this transfer, the DNA is denatured ("unzipped") by alkali treatment, separating each double helix (*see infra* Appendix, Figure A-1) into two single strands. The weak bonds that connect the two members of a base pair are easily broken by heat or chemical treatment. The bonds that hold a base to the backbone and keep the backbone intact are much stronger. Thus, the double-stranded helix separates neatly into two single strands, with one base at each position.

75. This locus-specific probe is a single strand of DNA that binds to its complementary sequence of denatured DNA in the sample. *See supra* § II.B. The DNA locus identified by a given probe is found by experimentation, and individual probes often are patented by their developers. Different laboratories may use different probes (i.e., they may test for alleles at different loci). Where different probes (or different restriction enzymes) are used, test results are not comparable.

two sheets of photographic film. Over time, the radioactive probe material exposes the film where the biological probe has hybridized with the DNA fragments.[76] The result is an autoradiograph, or an autorad, a visual pattern of bands representing specific DNA fragments. An autorad that shows two bands in a single lane indicates that the individual who is the source of the DNA is a heterozygote at that locus. If the autorad shows only one band, the person may be homozygous for that allele (that is, each parent contributed the same allele), or the second band may be present but invisible for technical reasons. The band pattern defines the person's genotype at the locus associated with the probe.

Once an appropriately exposed autorad is obtained, the probe is stripped from the membrane, and the process is repeated with a separate probe for each locus tested. Three to five probes are typically used, the number depending in part on the amount of testable DNA recovered from the crime-scene sample. The result is a set of autorads, each of which shows the results of one probe.[77] If the crime-scene and suspect samples yield bands that are closely aligned on each autorad, the VNTR profiles[78] from the two samples are considered to match.[79]

A. Validity of the Underlying Scientific Theory

The basic theory underlying VNTR profiling is textbook knowledge. The molecular structure of DNA,[80] the presence of highly polymorphic VNTR loci,[81] and the existence of methods to produce VNTR fragments and measure their lengths are not in doubt.[82] Indeed, some courts have taken judicial notice of

76. One film per probe is checked during the process to see whether the process is complete. Because this can weaken the image, the other film is left undisturbed, and it is used in comparing the positions of the bands.

77. For a photograph of an autorad, see, e.g., NRC II, *supra* note 1, at 68 fig. 2.4.

78. Each autorad reveals a single-locus genotype. The collection of single-locus profiles, one for each single-locus probe, sometimes is called a multi-locus VNTR profile. A "multi-locus probe," however, is a single probe that produces bands on a single autorad by hybridizing with VNTRs from many loci at the same time. It is, in other words, like a cocktail of single-locus probes. Because it is more difficult to interpret autoradiographs from multi-locus probes, these probes are no longer used in criminal cases in the United States.

79. Issues that arise in interpreting autoradiographs and declaring matches are considered *infra* § IV.

80. *See supra* § II.

81. Studies of the population genetics of VNTR loci are reviewed in NRC II, *supra* note 1. *See also infra* § VII.

82. *See, e.g.*, NRC I, *supra* note 1, at 149 (recommending judicial notice of the proposition that "DNA polymorphisms can, in principle, provide a reliable method for comparing samples," but cautioning that "the actual discriminatory power of any particular DNA test will depend on the sites of DNA variation examined"); NRC II, *supra* note 1, at 9 ("DNA typing, with its extremely high power to differentiate one human being from another, is based on a large body of scientific principles and techniques that are universally accepted."); *id.* at 36 ("Methods of DNA profiling are firmly grounded in molecular technology. When profiling is done with appropriate care, the results are highly reproducible.").

these scientific facts.[83] In short, the ability to discriminate between human DNA samples using a relatively small number of VNTR loci is widely accepted.

B. Validity and Reliability of the Laboratory Techniques

The basic laboratory procedures for VNTR analysis have been used in other settings for many years: "The complete process—DNA digestion, electrophoresis, membrane transfer, and hybridization—was developed by Edwin Southern in 1975 . . . . These procedures are routinely used in molecular biology, biochemistry, genetics, and clinical DNA diagnosis . . . ."[84] Thus, "no scientific doubt exists that [these technologies] accurately detect genetic differences."[85]

Before concluding that a particular enzyme-probe combination produces accurate profiles as applied to crime-scene samples at a particular laboratory, however, courts may wish to consider studies concerning the effects of environmental conditions and contaminants on VNTR profiling as well as the laboratory's general experience and proficiency with these probes.[86] And the nature of the sample and other considerations in a particular case can affect the certainty of the profiling. The next two sections outline the type of inquiry that can help assess the accuracy of a profile in a specific case.

V. Sample Quantity and Quality

The primary determinants of whether DNA typing can be done on any particular sample are (1) the quantity of DNA present in the sample and (2) the extent to which it is degraded. Generally speaking, if a sufficient quantity of reasonable quality DNA can be extracted from a crime-scene sample, no matter what the

83. *See, e.g.*, State v. Fleming, 698 A.2d 503, 507 (Me. 1997) (taking judicial notice that "the overall theory and techniques of DNA profiling [are] scientifically reliable if conducted in accordance with appropriate laboratory standards and controls"); State v. Davis, 814 S.W.2d 593, 602 (Mo. 1991); People v. Castro, 545 N.Y.S.2d 985, 987 (N.Y. Sup. Ct. 1989); cases cited, NRC II, *supra* note 1, at 172 n.15.

84. NRC I, *supra* note 1, at 38.

85. Office of Tech. Assessment, Genetic Witness: Forensic Uses of DNA Tests 59 (1990). The 1992 NRC report therefore recommends that courts take judicial notice that:

> [t]he current laboratory procedure for detecting DNA variation (specifically, single-locus probes analyzed on Southern blots without evidence of band shifting) is fundamentally sound, although the validity of any particular implementation of the basic procedure will depend on proper characterization of the reproducibility of the system (e.g., measurement variation) and the inclusion of all necessary scientific controls.

NRC I, *supra* note 1, at 149. The 1996 report reiterates the conclusion that "[t]he techniques of DNA typing [including RFLP analysis] are fully recognized by the scientific community." NRC II, *supra* note 1, at 50. It insists that "[t]he state of the profiling technology and the methods for estimating frequencies and related statistics have progressed to the point where the admissibility of properly collected and analyzed DNA data should not be in doubt." *Id.* at 36.

86. *See supra* note 69.

nature of the sample, DNA typing can be done without problem. Thus, DNA typing has been performed successfully on old blood stains, semen stains, vaginal swabs, hair, bone, bite marks, cigarette butts, urine, and fecal material. This section discusses what constitutes sufficient quantity and reasonable quality in the contexts of PCR-based genetic typing[87] and VNTR analysis by Southern blotting.[88] Complications due to contaminants and inhibitors also are discussed. Finally, the question of whether the sample contains DNA from two or more contributors is considered.

A. Did the Sample Contain Enough DNA?

The amount of DNA in a cell varies from organism to organism. The DNA in the chromosomes of a human cell, for example, is about two thousand times greater than that in a typical bacterium.[89] Within an organism, however, DNA content is constant from cell to cell. Thus, a human hair root cell contains the same amount of DNA as a white cell in blood or a buccal cell in saliva.[90] Amounts of DNA present in some typical kinds of samples are indicated in Table A-2 of the Appendix. These vary from a trillionth or so of a gram for a hair shaft to several millionths of a gram for a post-coital vaginal swab. RFLP typing requires a much larger sample of DNA than PCR-based typing. As a practical matter, RFLP analysis requires a minimum of about 50 billionths of a gram of relatively non-degraded DNA,[91] while most PCR test protocols recommend samples on the order of one to five billionths of a gram for optimum yields.[92] Thus, PCR tests can be applied to samples containing ten to five hundred-fold less nuclear

87. *See supra* § III.

88. *See supra* § IV.

89. A human egg or sperm cell contains half as much DNA; hence, the haploid human genome is about one thousand times larger than the typical bacterial genome.

90. A human cell contains about six picograms of DNA. (A picogram (pg) is one trillionth (1/1,000,000,000,000) of a gram.) Sperm cells constitute a special case, for they contain half a genetic complement (that which the father passes along to an offspring) and so contain half as much DNA (about 3 pg). The 3 pg of DNA varies from sperm cell to sperm cell because each such cell has a randomly drawn half of the man's chromosomes. The DNA in a semen sample contains many of these cells; being a mixture of the many combinations, it contains all the man's alleles.

91. RFLP analysis has been performed successfully on smaller amounts of DNA but at a cost of longer autoradiograph exposure times. From the standpoint of the reliability of the typing, what is important is the strength of the banding pattern on the autoradiograph or lumigraph. Threshold amounts of DNA may result in weak bands, and some bands could be missed because they are too weak to be observed.

92. Although the polymerase chain reaction can amplify DNA from the nucleus of a single cell, chance effects may result in one allele being amplified much more than another. To avoid preferential amplification, a lower limit of about ten to fifteen cells' worth of DNA has been determined to give balanced amplification. PCR tests for nuclear genes are designed to yield no detectable product for samples containing less than about 20 cell equivalents (100–200 pg) of DNA. This result is achieved by limiting the number of amplification cycles.

DNA than that required for RFLP tests.[93] Moreover, mitochondrial DNA analysis works reliably with DNA from even fewer cells. As noted in section II, cells contain only one nucleus, but hundreds of mitochondria. Consequently, even though there rarely is sufficient DNA in a hair shaft to allow testing with nuclear DNA markers, the mitochondrial DNA often can be analyzed.[94]

These sample-size requirements help determine the approach to be taken for a DNA typing analysis. Samples which, from experience, are expected to contain at least fifty to one hundred billionths of a gram of DNA typically are subjected to a formal DNA extraction followed by characterization of the DNA for quantity and quality. This characterization typically involves gel electrophoresis of a small portion of the extracted DNA. This test, however, does not distinguish human from non-human DNA. Since the success of DNA typing tests depends on the amount of human DNA present, it may be desirable to test for the amount of human DNA in the extract.[95] For samples that typically contain small amounts of DNA, the risk of DNA loss during extraction may dictate the use of a different extraction procedure.[96]

Whether a particular sample contains enough human DNA to allow typing cannot always be predicted in advance. The best strategy is to try; if a result is obtained, and if the controls (samples of known DNA and blank samples) have behaved properly, then the sample had enough DNA.

B. Was the Sample of Sufficient Quality?

The primary determinant of DNA quality for forensic analysis is the extent to which the long DNA molecules are intact. Within the cell nucleus, each molecule of DNA extends for millions of base pairs. Outside the cell, DNA spontaneously degrades into smaller fragments at a rate that depends on temperature,

93. The great sensitivity of PCR for the detection of DNA, even under these "safe" conditions, is illustrated by the successful genetic typing of DNA extracted from fingerprints. Roland A.H. van Oorschot & Maxwell K. Jones, *DNA Fingerprints from Fingerprints*, 387 Nature 767 (1997).

94. *E.g.*, M.R. Wilson et al., *Extraction, PCR Amplification, and Sequencing of Mitochondrial DNA from Human Hair Shafts*, 18 Biotechniques 662 (1995). Of course, mitochondrial DNA analysis can be done with other sources of mtDNA.

95. This test entails measuring the amount of a human-specific DNA probe that binds to the DNA in the extract. This test is particularly important in cases where the sample extract contains a mixture of human and microbial DNA. Vaginal swabs, for example, are expected to contain microbial DNA from the vaginal flora as well as human DNA from the female and sperm donor. Similarly, samples that have been damp for extended periods of time often contain significant microbial contamination; indeed, in some cases, little or no human DNA can be detected even though the extract contains significant amounts of DNA.

96. Boiling a sample for a few minutes releases DNA, and this DNA is used directly for PCR without first characterizing the DNA. The boiling step usually is conducted in the presence of a resin that adsorbs inhibitors of PCR.

exposure to oxygen, and, most importantly, the presence of water.[97] In dry biological samples, protected from air, and not exposed to temperature extremes, DNA degrades very slowly. In fact, the relative stability of DNA has made it possible to extract usable DNA from samples hundreds to thousands of years old.[98]

RFLP analysis requires relatively non-degraded DNA, and testing DNA for degradation is a routine part of the protocol for VNTR analysis. In RFLP testing, a restriction enzyme cuts long sequences of DNA into smaller fragments. If the DNA is randomly fragmented into very short pieces to begin with, electrophoresis and Southern blotting will produce a smear of fragments rather than a set of well-separated bands.[99]

In contrast, PCR-based tests are relatively insensitive to degradation. Testing has proved effective with old and badly degraded material such as the remains of the Tsar Nicholas family (buried in 1918, recovered in 1991)[100] and the Tyrolean Ice Man (frozen for some 5,000 years).[101] The extent to which degradation affects a PCR-based test depends on the size of the DNA segment to be amplified. For example, in a sample in which the bulk of the DNA has been degraded to fragments well under 1,000 base pairs in length, it may be possible to amplify a 100 base-pair sequence, but not a 1,000 base-pair target. Consequently, the shorter alleles may be detected in a highly degraded sample, but the larger ones may be missed.[102] As with RFLP analysis, this possibility would have to be considered in the statistical interpretation of the result.

97. Other forms of chemical alteration to DNA are well studied, both for their intrinsic interest and because chemical changes in DNA are a contributing factor in the development of cancers in living cells. Most chemical modification has little effect on RFLP analysis. Some forms of DNA modification, such as that produced by exposure to ultraviolet radiation, inhibit the amplification step in PCR-based tests, while other chemical modifications appear to have no effect. George F. Sensabaugh & Cecilia von Beroldingen, *The Polymerase Chain Reaction: Application to the Analysis of Biological Evidence*, *in* Forensic DNA Technology 63 (Mark A. Farley & James J. Harrington eds., 1991).

98. This has resulted in a specialized field of inquiry dubbed "ancient DNA." Ancient DNA: Recovery and Analysis of Genetic Material from Paleontological, Archaeological, Museum, Medical, and Forensic Specimens (Bernd Herrmann & Susanne Hummel eds., 1993); Svante Paabo, *Ancient DNA: Extraction, Characterization, Molecular Cloning, and Enzymatic Amplification*, 86 Proc. Nat'l Acad. Sci. USA 1939 (1989).

99. Practically speaking, RFLP analysis can yield interpretable results if the bulk of the DNA in a sample exceeds 20,000–30,000 base pairs in length. Partial degradation of the DNA can result in the weakening or loss of the signal from large restriction fragments. This effect is usually evident from the appearance of the restriction fragment banding pattern. Another indication of degradation is smearing in the background of the banding pattern. If there is evidence that degradation has affected the banding pattern, the statistical interpretation of a match should account for the possibility that some allelic bands might not have been detected.

100. Gill et al., *supra* note 47.

101. Oliva Handt et al., *Molecular Genetic Analyses of the Tyrolean Ice Man*, 264 Science 1775 (1994).

102. For example, typing at a genetic locus such as D1S80, for which the target allelic sequences range in size from 300 to 850 base pairs, may be affected by the non-amplification of the largest alleles ("allelic dropout").

Allelic dropout of this sort does not seem to be a problem for STR loci, presumably because the size differences between alleles at a locus are so small (typically no more than 50 base pairs). If there is a degradation effect on STR typing, it is "locus dropout": in cases involving severe degradation, loci yielding smaller PCR products (less than 180 base pairs) tend to amplify more efficiently than loci yielding larger products (greater than 200 base pairs).[103]

Surprising as it may seem, DNA can be exposed to a great variety of environmental insults without any effect on its capacity to be typed correctly. Exposure studies have shown that contact with a variety of surfaces, both clean and dirty, and with gasoline, motor oil, acids, and alkalis either have no effect on DNA typing or, at worst, render the DNA untypable.[104]

Although contamination with microbes generally does little more than degrade the human DNA,[105] other problems sometimes can occur with both RFLP[106] and PCR-based analyses.[107] Nevertheless, there are procedures that identify or avoid these anomalies.[108] Therefore, the validation of DNA typing

103. J.P. Whitaker et al., *Short Tandem Repeat Typing of Bodies from a Mass Disaster: High Success Rate and Characteristic Amplification Patterns in Highly Degraded Samples*, 18 Biotechniques 670 (1995).

104. Dwight E. Adams et al., *Deoxyribonucleic Acid (DNA) Analysis by Restriction Fragment Length Polymorphisms of Blood and Other Body Fluid Stains Subjected to Contamination and Environmental Insults*, 36 J. Forensic Sci. 1284 (1991); Roland A.H. van Oorschot et al., *HUMTH01 Validation Studies: Effect of Substrate, Environment, and Mixtures*, 41 J. Forensic Sci. 142 (1996). Most of the effects of environmental insult readily can be accounted for in terms of basic DNA chemistry. For example, some agents produce degradation or damaging chemical modifications. Other environmental contaminants inhibit restriction enzymes or PCR. (This effect sometimes can be reversed by cleaning the DNA extract to remove the inhibitor.) But environmental insult does not result in the selective loss of an allele at a locus or in the creation of a new allele at that locus.

105. Michael B.T. Webb et al., *Microbial DNA Challenge Studies of Variable Number Tandem Repeat (VNTR) Probes Used for DNA Profiling Analysis*, 38 J. Forensic Sci. 1172 (1993).

106. Autoradiograms sometimes show many bands that line up with the molecular weight sizing ladder bands. (The "ladder" is a set of DNA fragments of known lengths that are placed by themselves in one or more lanes of the gel. The resulting set of bands provides a benchmark for determining the weights of the unknown bands in the samples.) These extra bands can result from contamination of the sample DNA with ladder DNA at the time the samples are loaded onto the electrophoresis gel. Alternatively, the original sample may have been contaminated with a microbe infected with lambda phage, the virus that is used for the preparation of the sizing ladder.

107. Although PCR primers designed to amplify human gene sequences would not be expected to recognize microbial DNA sequences, much less amplify them, such amplification has been reported with the D1S80 typing system. A. Fernández-Rodríguez et al., *Microbial DNA Challenge Studies of PCR-based Systems in Forensic Genetics*, *in* 6 Advances in Forensic Haemogenetics 177 (A. Carracedo et al., eds., 1996).

108. Whatever the explanation for the extra sizing bands mentioned *supra* note 106, the lambda origin of the bands can be demonstrated by an additional probing with the ladder probe alone or with a human specific probe without the ladder probe. Likewise, the spurious PCR products observed by Fernández-Rodríguez et al., *supra* note 107, can be differentiated from the true human PCR products, and the same authors have described a modification to the D1S80 typing system that removes all question of the non-human origin of the spurious PCR products. A. Fernández-Rodríguez et al., *D1S80 Typing in Casework: A Simple Strategy to Distinguish Non-specific Microbial PCR Products from Human Alleles*, 7 Progress in Forensic Genetics 18 (1998).

systems should include tests for interference with a variety of microbes to see if artifacts occur; if artifacts are observed, then control tests should be applied to distinguish between the artifactual and the true results.

C. Does a Sample Contain DNA from More Than One Person?

DNA from a single individual can have no more than two alleles at each locus. This follows from the fact that individuals inherit chromosomes in pairs, one from each parent.[109] An individual who inherits the same allele from each parent (a homozygote) can contribute only that one allele to a sample, and an individual who inherits a different allele from each parent (a heterozygote) will contribute those two alleles.[110] Finding three or more alleles at a locus therefore indicates a mixture of DNA from more than one person.[111]

Some kinds of samples, such as post-coital vaginal swabs and blood stains from scenes where several persons are known to have bled, are expected to be mixtures. Sometimes, however, the first indication the sample has multiple contributors comes from the DNA testing. The chance of detecting a mixture by finding extra alleles depends on the proportion of DNA from each contributor as well as the chance that the contributors have different genotypes at one or more loci. As a rule, a minor contributor to a mixture must provide at least 5% of the DNA for the mixture to be recognized.[112] In addition, the various contributors must have some different alleles. The chance that multiple contributors will differ at one or more locus increases with the number of loci tested and the genetic diversity at each locus. Unless many loci are examined, genetic markers with low to moderate diversities do not have much power to detect multiple contributors. Genetic markers that are highly polymorphic are much better at detecting mixtures. Thus, STRs and especially VNTRs are sensitive to mixtures.

109. *See supra* § II.

110. Loci on the sex chromosomes constitute a special case. Females have two X chromosomes, one from each parent; as with loci on the other chromosomes, they can be either homozygous or heterozygous at the X-linked loci. Males, on the other hand, have one X and one Y chromosome; hence, they have only one allele at the X-linked loci and one allele at the Y-linked loci. In cases of trisomy, such as XXY males, multiple copies of loci on the affected chromosome will be present, but this condition is rare and often lethal.

111. On very rare occasions, an individual exhibits a phenotype with three alleles at a locus. This can be the result of a chromosome anomaly (such as a duplicated gene on one chromosome or a mutation). A sample from such an individual is usually easily distinguished from a mixed sample. The three-allele variant is seen at only the affected locus, whereas with mixtures, more than two alleles typically are evident at several loci.

112. With RFLP testing, alleles from a contributor of as little as one percent can be detected at the price of overexposing the pattern from the major contributor. Studies in which DNA from different individuals is combined in differing proportions show that the intensity of the bands reflects the proportions of the mixture. Thus, if bands in a crime-scene sample have different intensities, it may be possible to assign alleles to major and minor contributors. However, if bands are present in roughly equal

VI. Laboratory Performance

A. Quality Control and Assurance

DNA profiling is valid and reliable, but confidence in a particular result depends on the quality control and quality assurance procedures in the laboratory. Quality control refers to measures to help ensure that a DNA-typing result (and its interpretation) meets a specified standard of quality. Quality assurance refers to monitoring, verifying, and documenting laboratory performance.[113] A quality assurance program helps demonstrate that a laboratory is meeting its quality control objectives and thus justifies confidence in the quality of its product.

Professional bodies within forensic science have described procedures for quality assurance. Guidelines have been prepared by two FBI-appointed groups—the Technical Working Group on DNA Analysis Methods (TWGDAM)[114] and the DNA Advisory Board (DAB).[115] The DAB also has encouraged forensic DNA laboratories to seek accreditation,[116] and at least two states require forensic DNA laboratories to be accredited.[117] The American Society of Crime Laboratory Directors–Laboratory Accreditation Board (ASCLD–LAB) accredits forensic laboratories.[118]

proportions, this allocation cannot be made, and the statistical interpretation of the observed results must include all possible combinations. *See infra* note 220.

113. For general descriptions of quality assurance programs, see NRC II, *supra* note 1, at ch. 3 ("Ensuring High Standards of Laboratory Performance"); NRC I, *supra* note 1, at ch. 4.

114. *See* Technical Working Group on DNA Analysis Methods, *Guidelines for a Quality Assurance Program for DNA Analysis*, 22 Crime Laboratory Dig. 21 (1995) [hereinafter TWGDAM Guidelines], 18 Crime Laboratory Dig. 44 (1991).

115. *See* Federal Bureau of Investigation, Quality Assurance Standards for Forensic DNA Testing Laboratories, July 15, 1998 [hereinafter DAB Standards]; *see also Recommendations of the DNA Commission of the International Society for Forensic Haemogenetics Relating to the Use of PCR-based Polymorphisms*, 64 Vox Sang. 124 (1993); *1991 Report Concerning Recommendations of the DNA Commission of the International Society for Forensic Haemogenetics Relating to the Use of DNA Polymorphism*, 63 Vox Sang. 70 (1992).

Under the DNA Identification Act of 1994, Pub. L. No. 103-322, 108 Stat. 2065 (codified at 42 U.S.C. § 13701 (1994)), to qualify for federal laboratory improvement funds, a forensic DNA laboratory must meet the quality assurance standards recommended by the DAB and issued by the director of the FBI. The DAB membership includes molecular geneticists, population geneticists, an ethicist, and representatives from federal, state, and local forensic DNA laboratories, private sector DNA laboratories, the National Institute of Standards and Technology, and the judiciary. Its recommendations closely follow the 1995 TWGDAM Guidelines.

116. DAB Standards, *supra* note 115, at 1 (preface).

117. *N.Y. Executive Law* § 995-b (McKinney 1999); Cal. DNA and Forensic Identification Data Base and Data Bank Act of 1998, Cal. Penal Code § 297 (West 1999).

118. *See* American Society of Crime Laboratory Directors—Laboratory Accreditation Board, ASCLD-LAB Accreditation Manual, Jan. 1997. As of mid-1998, ASCLD-LAB had accredited laboratories in Australia, New Zealand, and Hong Kong as well as laboratories in the United States and Canada. The ASCLD-LAB accreditation program does not allow laboratories to obtain accreditation only for particular services—a laboratory seeking accreditation must qualify for the full range of services it offers. This constraint has slowed some forensic DNA labs from seeking accreditation. As an interim solution,

Documentation. The quality assurance guidelines promulgated by TWGDAM, the DAB, and ASCLD-LAB call for laboratories to document laboratory organization and management, personnel qualifications and training, facilities, evidence control procedures, validation of methods and procedures, analytical procedures, equipment calibration and maintenance, standards for case documentation and report writing, procedures for reviewing case files and testimony, proficiency testing, corrective actions, audits, safety programs, and review of sub-contractors. Of course, maintaining even such extensive documentation and records does not guarantee the correctness of results obtained in any particular case. Errors in analysis or interpretation might occur as a result of a deviation from an established procedure, analyst misjudgement, or an accident. Although case-review procedures within a laboratory should be designed to detect errors before a report is issued, it is always possible that some incorrect result will slip through. Accordingly, determination that a laboratory maintains a strong quality assurance program does not eliminate the need for case-by-case review.

Validation. The validation of procedures is central to quality assurance. "Developmental" validation is undertaken to determine the applicability of a new test to crime-scene samples; it defines conditions that give reliable results and identifies the limitations of the procedure. For example, a new genetic marker being considered for use in forensic analysis will be tested to determine if it can be typed reliably in both fresh samples and in samples typical of those found at crime scenes. The validation would include testing samples originating from different tissues—blood, semen, hair, bone, samples containing degraded DNA, samples contaminated with microbes, samples containing DNA mixtures, and so on. Developmental validation of a new marker also includes the generation of population databases and the testing of allele and genotype distributions for independence. Developmental validation normally results in publication in the scientific literature, but a new procedure can be validated in multiple laboratories well ahead of publication.

"Internal" validation, on the other hand, involves the verification by a laboratory that it can reliably perform an established procedure that already has undergone developmental validation. Before adopting a new procedure, the laboratory should verify its ability to use the system in a proficiency trial.

Both forms of validation build on the accumulated body of knowledge and experience. Thus, some aspects of validation testing need be repeated only to the extent required to verify that previously established principles apply. One

the National Forensic Science Technology Center (NFSTC) has an agreement with ASCLD-LAB to perform certification audits on DNA sections of laboratories for compliance with DAB and ASCLD-LAB standards; this service is available to private sector DNA laboratories as well as government laboratories.

need not validate the principle of the internal combustion engine every time one brings out a new model of automobile.

Proficiency Testing. Proficiency testing in forensic genetic testing is designed to ascertain whether an analyst can correctly determine genetic types in a sample the origin of which is unknown to the analyst but is known to a tester. Proficiency is demonstrated by making correct genetic typing determinations in repeated trials, and not by opining on whether the sample originated from a particular individual. Proficiency tests also require laboratories to report random-match probabilities to determine if proper calculations are being made.

An internal proficiency trial is conducted within a laboratory. One person in the laboratory prepares the sample and administers the test to another person in the laboratory. An external trial is one in which the test sample originates from outside the laboratory—from another laboratory, a commercial vendor, or a regulatory agency. In a declared (or open) proficiency trial the analyst knows the sample is a proficiency sample. In contrast, in a blind (or more properly "full-blind") trial, the sample is submitted so that the analyst does not recognize it as a proficiency sample.[119] It has been argued that full-blind trials provide a better indication of proficiency because the analyst will not give the trial sample any special attention.[120] On the other hand, full-blind proficiency trials for forensic DNA analysis entail considerably more organizational effort and expense than open proficiency trials. Obviously, the "evidence" samples prepared for the trial have to be sufficiently realistic that the laboratory does not suspect the legitimacy of the submission. A police agency and prosecutor's office have to submit the "evidence" and respond to laboratory inquiries with information about the "case." Finally, the genetic profile from a proficiency test must not be entered into regional and national databases.[121]

119. There is potential confusion over nomenclature with regard to open and blind trials. All proficiency tests are blind in the sense that the analyst does not know the composition of the test sample. In some disciplines, any trial in which the analyst receives "unknowns" from a tester is referred to as a blind trial. With regard to proficiency testing in the forensic area, however, the convention is to distinguish "open" and "blind" trials as described here.

120. *See, e.g.*, Scheck, *supra* note 69, at 1980. Another argument for the full-blind trial is that it tests a broader range of laboratory operations, from submission of the evidence to the laboratory through the analysis and interpretation stages to the reporting out to the submitting agency. However, these aspects of laboratory operations also can be evaluated, at much less cost, by mechanisms such as laboratory audits and random review of case files.

121. The feasibility of mounting a national, full-blind proficiency trial program is under study as a part of the DNA Identification Act of 1994, Pub. L. No. 103-322, 108 Stat. 2065 (codified at 42 U.S.C. § 13701 (1994)). The results of this study, funded by the National Institute of Justice, are to be reported to the DAB with subsequent recommendations made to the director of the FBI.

The DAB recommends that every analyst undergo regular external, open proficiency testing[122] and that the laboratory take "corrective action whenever proficiency testing discrepancies [or] casework errors are detected."[123] Certification by the American Board of Criminalistics as a specialist in forensic biology DNA analysis requires one proficiency trial per year. Accredited laboratories must maintain records documenting compliance with required proficiency test standards.[124]

B. Handling Samples

Sample mishandling, mislabeling, or contamination, whether in the field or in the laboratory, is more likely to compromise a DNA analysis than an error in genetic typing. For example, a sample mixup due to mislabeling reference blood samples taken at the hospital could lead to incorrect association of crime-scene samples to a reference individual or to incorrect exclusions. Similarly, packaging two items with wet blood stains into the same bag could result in a transfer of stains between the items, rendering it difficult or impossible to determine whose blood was originally on each item. Contamination in the laboratory may result in artifactual typing results or in the incorrect attribution of a DNA profile to an individual or to an item of evidence. Accordingly, it is appropriate to look at the procedures that have been prescribed and implemented to guard against such error.

Mislabeling or mishandling can occur when biological material is collected in the field, when it is transferred to the laboratory, when it is in the analysis stream in the laboratory,[125] when the analytical results are recorded, or when the recorded results are transcribed into a report. Mislabeling and mishandling can happen with any kind of physical evidence and are of great concern in all fields of forensic science. Because forensic laboratories often have little or no control over the handling of evidence prior to its arrival in the laboratory, checkpoints should be established to detect mislabeling and mishandling along the line of

122. Standard 13.1 specifies that these tests are to be performed at least as frequently as every 180 days. DAB Standards, *supra* note 115, at 16. TWGDAM recommended two open proficiency tests per year per analyst. TWGDAM Guidelines, *supra* note 114.

123. DAB Standards, *supra* note 115, at 17 (standard 14.1).

124. Proficiency test results from laboratories accredited by ASCLD-LAB are reported also to an ASCLD-LAB Proficiency Review Committee. The committee independently reviews test results and verifies compliance with accreditation requirements. ASCLD-LAB specifies the vendors whose proficiency tests it accepts for accreditation purposes. Since accreditation can be suspended or withdrawn by unacceptable proficiency trial performance, the proficiency test vendors must meet high standards with respect to test-sample preparation and documentation. Yet, in some instances vendors have provided mislabeled or contaminated test samples. *See* TWGDAM & ASCLD-LAB Proficiency Review Comm., *Guidelines for DNA Proficiency Test Manufacturing and Reporting*, 21 Crime Laboratory Dig. 27–32 (1994).

125. *E.g.*, United States v. Cuff, 37 F. Supp. 2d 279, 283 (S.D.N.Y. 1999).

evidence flow.[126] Investigative agencies should have guidelines for evidence collection and labeling so that a chain of custody is maintained. Similarly, there should be guidelines, produced with input from the laboratory, for handling biological evidence in the field. These principles remain the same as in the pre-DNA era.[127]

TWGDAM guidelines and DAB recommendations require documented procedures to ensure sample integrity and to avoid sample mixups, labeling errors, recording errors, and the like. They also mandate case review to identify inadvertent errors before a final report is released. Finally, laboratories must retain, when feasible, portions of the crime-scene samples and extracts to allow reanalysis.[128] However, retention is not always possible. For example, retention of original items is not to be expected when the items are large or immobile (for example, a wall or sidewalk). In such situations, a swabbing or scraping of the stain from the item would typically be collected and retained. There also are situations where the sample is so small that it will be consumed in the analysis.[129]

Assuming appropriate chain-of-custody and evidence-handling protocols are in place, the critical question is whether there are deviations in the particular case. This may require a review of the total case documentation as well as the laboratory findings.[130]

As the 1996 NRC Report emphasizes, an important safeguard against error due to mislabeling and mishandling is the opportunity to retest original evidence items or the material extracted from them.[131] Should mislabeling or mishandling have occurred, reanalysis of the original sample and the intermediate extracts should detect not only the fact of the error but also the point at which

126. NRC II, *supra* note 1, at 80–82.

127. Samples (particularly those containing wet stains) should not be packaged together, and samples should be dried or refrigerated as soon as possible. Storage in the dry state and at low temperatures stabilizes biological material against degradation. George F. Sensabaugh, *Biochemical Markers of Individuality, in* 1 Forensic Science Handbook 338, 385 (Richard Saferstein ed., 1982). The only precaution to have gained force in the DNA era is that evidence items should be handled with gloved hands to protect against handling contamination and inadvertent sample-to-sample transfers.

128. Forensic laboratories have a professional responsibility to preserve retained evidence so as to minimize degradation. *See* TWGDAM Guidelines, *supra* note 114, at 30 para. 6.3. Furthermore, failure to preserve potentially exculpatory evidence has been treated as a denial of due process and grounds for suppression. People v. Nation, 604 P.2d 1051 (Cal. 1980). In *Arizona v. Youngblood*, 488 U.S. 51 (1988), however, the Supreme Court held that a police agency's failure to preserve evidence not known to be exculpatory does not constitute a denial of due process unless "bad faith" can be shown.

129. When small samples are involved, whether it is necessary to consume the entire sample is a matter of scientific judgment.

130. Such a review is best undertaken by someone familiar with police procedures, forensic DNA analysis, and forensic laboratory operations. Case review by an independent expert should be held to the same scientific standard as the work under review. Any possible flaws in labeling or in evidence handling should be specified in detail, with consideration given to the consequence of the possible error.

131. NRC II, *supra* note 1, at 81.

it occurred. It is even possible in some cases to detect mislabeling at the point of sample collection if the genetic typing results on a particular sample are inconsistent with an otherwise consistent reconstruction of events.[132]

Contamination describes any situation in which foreign material is mixed with a sample of DNA. Contamination by non-biological materials, such as gasoline or grit, can cause test failures, but they are not a source of genetic typing errors. Similarly, contamination with non-human biological materials, such as bacteria, fungi, or plant materials, is generally not a problem. These contaminants may accelerate DNA degradation, but they do not contribute spurious genetic types.[133]

Consequently, the contamination of greatest concern is that resulting from the addition of human DNA. This sort of contamination can occur three ways:[134]

1. The crime-scene samples by their nature may contain a mixture of fluids or tissues from different individuals. Examples include vaginal swabs collected as sexual assault evidence[135] and blood stain evidence from scenes where several individuals shed blood.[136]
2. The crime-scene samples may be inadvertently contaminated in the course of sample handling in the field or in the laboratory. Inadvertent contamination of crime-scene DNA with DNA from a reference sample could lead to a false inclusion.[137]

132. For example, a mislabeling of husband and wife samples in a paternity case might result in an apparent maternal exclusion, a very unlikely event. The possibility of mislabeling could be confirmed by testing the samples for gender and ultimately verified by taking new samples from each party under better controlled conditions.

133. Validation of new genetic markers includes testing on a variety of non-human species. The probes used in VNTR analysis and the PCR-based tests give results with non-human primate DNA samples (apes and some monkeys). This is not surprising given the evolutionary proximity of the primates to humans. As a rule, the validated test systems give no results with DNA from animals other than primates, from plants, or from microbes. An exception is the reaction of some bacterial DNA samples in testing for the marker D1S80. Fernández-Rodríguez et al., *supra* note 107. However, this could be an artifact of the particular D1S80 typing system, since other workers have not been able to replicate fully their results, and an alternative D1S80 typing protocol gave no spurious results. Shamsah Ebrahim et al., Investigation of the Specificity of STR and D1S80 Primers on Microbial DNA Samples, Presentation B84, 50th Annual Meeting of the American Academy of Forensic Sciences, San Francisco (Feb. 1998).

134. NRC II, *supra* note 1, at 82–84; NRC I, *supra* note 1, at 65–67; George F. Sensabaugh & Edward T. Blake, *DNA Analysis in Biological Evidence: Applications of the Polymerase Chain Reaction*, *in* 3 Forensic Science Handbook 416, 441 (Richard Saferstein ed., 1993); Sensabaugh & von Beroldingen, *supra* note 97, at 63, 77.

135. These typically contain DNA in the semen from the assailant and in the vaginal fluid of the victim. The standard procedure for analysis allows the DNA from sperm to be separated from the vaginal epithelial cell DNA. It is thus possible not only to recognize the mixture but also to assign the DNA profiles to the different individuals.

136. Such mixtures are detected by genetic typing that reveals profiles of more than one DNA source. *See supra* § V.C.

137. This source of contamination is a greater concern when PCR-based typing methods are to be used due to the capacity of PCR to detect very small amounts of DNA. However, experiments de-

3. Carry-over contamination in PCR-based typing can occur if the amplification products of one typing reaction are carried over into the reaction mix for a subsequent PCR reaction. If the carry-over products are present in sufficient quantity, they could be preferentially amplified over the target DNA.[138] The primary strategy used in most forensic laboratories to protect against carry-over contamination is to keep PCR products away from sample materials and test reagents by having separate work areas for pre-PCR and post-PCR sample handling, by preparing samples in controlled air-flow biological safety hoods, by using dedicated equipment (such as pipetters) for each of the various stages of sample analysis, by decontaminating work areas after use (usually by wiping down or by irradiating with ultraviolet light), and by having a one-way flow of sample from the pre-PCR to post-PCR work areas.[139] Additional protocols are used to detect any carry-over contamination.[140]

In the end, whether a laboratory has conducted proper tests and whether it conducted them properly depends both on the general standard of practice and on the questions posed in the particular case. There is no universal checklist, but the selection of tests and the adherence to the correct test procedures can be reviewed by experts and by reference to professional standards, such as the TWGDAM and DAB guidelines.

signed to introduce handling contamination into samples have been unsuccessful. *See* Catherine Theisen Comey & Bruce Budowle, *Validation Studies on the Analysis of the HLA DQα Locus Using the Polymerase Chain Reaction*, 36 J. Forensic Sci. 1633 (1991). Of course, it remains important to have evidence-handling procedures to safeguard against this source of contamination. Police agencies should have documented procedures for the collection, handling, and packaging of biological evidence in the field and for its delivery to the laboratory that are designed to minimize the chance of handling contamination. Ideally, these procedures will have been developed in coordination with the laboratory, and training in the use of these procedures will have been provided. Similarly, laboratories should have procedures in place to minimize the risk of this kind of contamination. *See* DAB Standards, *supra* note 115; TWGDAM Guidelines, *supra* note 114. In particular, these procedures should specify the safeguards for keeping evidence samples separated from reference samples.

138. Carry-over contamination is not an issue in RFLP analysis, which involves no amplification steps.

139. Some laboratories with space constraints separate pre-PCR and post-PCR activities in time rather than space. The other safeguards can be used as in a space-separated facility.

140. Standard protocols include the amplification of blank control samples—those to which no DNA has been added. If carry-over contaminants have found their way into the reagents or sample tubes, these will be detected as amplification products. Outbreaks of carry-over contamination can also be recognized by monitoring test results. Detection of an unexpected and persistent genetic profile in different samples indicates a contamination problem. When contamination outbreaks are detected, appropriate corrective actions should be taken, and both the outbreak and the corrective action should be documented. *See* DAB Standards, *supra* note 115; TWGDAM Guidelines, *supra* note 114.

VII. Interpretation of Laboratory Results

The results of DNA testing can be presented in various ways. With discrete allele systems, it is natural to speak of "matching" and "non-matching" profiles. If the genetic profile obtained from the biological sample taken from the crime scene or the victim (the "trace evidence sample") matches that of a particular individual, then that individual is included as a possible source of the sample. But other individuals also might possess a matching DNA profile. Accordingly, the expert should be asked to provide some indication of how significant the match is. If, on the other hand, the genetic profiles are different, then the individual is excluded as the source of the trace evidence. Typically, proof tending to show that the defendant is the source incriminates the defendant, while proof that someone else is the source exculpates the defendant.[141]

This section elaborates on these ideas, indicating issues that can arise in connection with an expert's testimony interpreting the results of a DNA test.

A. Exclusions, Inclusions, and Inconclusive Results

When the DNA from the trace evidence clearly does not match the DNA sample from the suspect, the DNA analysis demonstrates that the suspect's DNA is not in the forensic sample. Indeed, if the samples have been collected, handled, and analyzed properly, then the suspect is excluded as a possible source of the DNA in the forensic sample. Even a single allele that cannot be explained as a laboratory artifact or other error can suffice to exclude a suspect.[142] As a practical matter, such exclusionary results normally would keep charges from being filed against the excluded suspect.[143]

In some cases, however, DNA testing is inconclusive, in whole or in part. The presence or absence of a discrete allele can be in doubt, or the existence or location of a VNTR band may be unclear.[144] For example, when the trace evidence sample is extremely degraded, VNTR profiling might not show all the

141. Whether being the source of the forensic sample is incriminating depends on other facts in the case. *See infra* note 155. Likewise, whether someone else being the source is exculpatory depends on the circumstances. For example, a suspect who might have committed the offense without leaving the trace evidence sample still could be guilty. In a rape case with several rapists, a semen stain could fail to incriminate one assailant because insufficient semen from that individual is present in the sample.

142. Due to heteroplasmy, a single sequence difference in mtDNA samples would not be considered an exclusion. *See supra* note 46. With testing at many polymorphic loci, however, it would be unusual to find two unrelated individuals whose DNA matches at all but one locus.

143. *But see* State v. Hammond, 604 A.2d 793 (Conn. 1992).

144. *E.g.*, State v. Fleming, 698 A.2d 503, 506 (Me. 1997) ("The fourth probe was declared uninterpretable."); People v. Leonard, 569 N.W.2d 663, 666–67 (Mich. Ct. App. 1997) ("There was a definite match of defendant's DNA on three of the probes, and a match on the other two probes could not be excluded."). In some cases, experts have disagreed as to whether extra bands represented a mixture or resulted from partial digestion of the forensic sample. *E.g.*, State v. Marcus, 683 A.2d 221 (N.J. Super. Ct. App. Div. 1996).

alleles that would be present in a sample with more intact DNA. If the quantity of DNA to be amplified for sequence-specific tests is too small, the amplification might not yield enough product to give a clear signal. Thus, experts sometimes disagree as to whether a particular band is visible on an autoradiograph or whether a dot is present on a reverse dot blot.[145]

Furthermore, even when RFLP bands are clearly visible, the entire pattern of bands can be displaced from its true location in a systematic way (a phenomenon known as band-shifting).[146] Recognizing this phenomenon, analysts might deem some seemingly matching patterns as inconclusive.[147]

145. *E.g.*, People v. Leonard, 569 N.W.2d 663, 667 (Mich. Ct. App.) (prosecution's academic expert concluded that there was a match at all bands rather than just the three that the state laboratory considered to match), *app. denied*, 570 N.W.2d 659 (Mich. 1997); State v. Jobe, 486 N.W.2d 407 (Minn. 1992) (one FBI examiner found a match on the basis of two of four probes, with the other two being inconclusive; another examiner found no match; another scientist called the profiles a "very, very, very significant match"); State v. Marcus, 683 A.2d 221 (N.J. Super. Ct. App. 1996) (defendant's academic expert questioned the results of one probe); State v. Gabriau, 696 A.2d 290, 292 n.3 (R.I. 1997) ("According to [a university geneticist] the laboratory technician had not considered two loci as matches where he himself would have."). In *United States v. Perry*, No. CR 91-395-SC (D.N.M. Sept. 7, 1995), the district court found a defense expert's suggestions of "lab technicians manipulating samples to achieve false matches" and of an analyst's sizing a band "when no band existed" to be "particularly unprincipled," "the stuff of mystery novels, not science." But bona fide disagreements of this sort would certainly go to the weight of the evidence and might bear on its admissibility through Federal Rule of Evidence 403.

It also can be argued that such disagreements pertain to admissibility under *Daubert*—to the extent that "adequate scientific care" necessitates "an objective and quantitative procedure for identifying the pattern of a sample," and that "[p]atterns must be identified separately and independently in suspect and evidence samples." The quoted language appears in NRC I, *supra* note 1, at 53, and it refers to VNTR profiles. Because the lengths of the VNTRs cannot be determined precisely, statistical criteria must be used if a statement as to whether bands "match" is to be made. Such criteria are discussed below, and they might be all that the committee had in mind when it called for an "objective and quantitative procedure." *Cf.* NRC II, *supra* note 1, at 142 ("the use of visual inspection other than as a screen before objective measurement . . . usually should be avoided"). In any event, courts have not been inclined to treat procedures that allow for subjective judgment in ascertaining the location of VNTR bands as fatal to admissibility. *E.g.*, United States v. Perry, No. CR 91-395-SC (D.N.M. Sept. 7, 1995) (stating that "the autorad is a permanent record, and anyone, including defense experts, can conduct an independent measurement of band size . . . "); State v. Jobe, 486 N.W.2d 407, 420 (Minn. 1992) (observing that "each sample is also examined by a second trained examiner and ultimately the 'match' is confirmed or rejected through computer analysis using wholly objective criteria"); State v. Copeland, 922 P.2d 1304, 1323 (Wash. 1996) (suggesting that "complaints about the analyst's ability to override the computer in placing the cursor at the center of a band . . . would be the type of human error going to weight, not admissibility"); *cf.* NRC II, *supra* ("if for any reason the analyst by visual inspection overrides the conclusion from the measurements, that should be clearly stated and reasons given").

146. *See* NRC II, *supra* note 1, at 142 ("[D]egraded DNA sometimes migrates farther on a gel than better quality DNA. . . . "). Band-shifting produces a systematic error in measurement. Random error is also present. *See infra* § VII.A.4.

147. *See* NRC II, *supra* note 1, at 142 ("[A]n experienced analyst can notice whether two bands from a heterozygote are shifted in the same or in the opposite direction from the bands in another lane containing the DNA being compared. If the bands in the two lanes shift a small distance in the same direction, that might indicate a match with band-shifting. If they shift in opposite directions, that is

At the other extreme, the genotypes at a large number of loci can be clearly identical, and the fact of a match not in doubt. In these cases, the DNA evidence is quite incriminating, and the challenge for the legal system lies in explaining just how probative it is. Naturally, as with exclusions, inclusions are most powerful when the samples have been collected, handled, and analyzed properly. But there is one logical difference between exclusions and inclusions. If it is accepted that the samples have different genotypes, then the conclusion that the DNA in them came from different individuals is essentially inescapable. In contrast, even if two samples have the same genotype, there is a chance that the forensic sample came—not from the defendant—but from another individual who has the same genotype. This complication has produced extensive arguments over the statistical procedures for assessing this chance or related quantities. This problem of describing the significance of an unequivocal match is taken up later in this section.

The classification of patterns into the two mutually exclusive categories of exclusions and inclusions is more complicated for VNTRs than for discrete alleles. Determining that DNA fragments from two different samples are the same size is like saying that two people are the same height. The height may well be similar, but is it identical? Even if the same person is measured repeatedly, we expect some variation about the true height due to the limitations of the measuring device. A perfectly reliable device gives the same measurements for all repeated measurements of the same item, but no instrument can measure a quantity like height with both perfect precision and perfect reproducibility. Consequently, measurement variability is a fact of life in ascertaining the sizes of VNTRs.[148]

The method of handling measurement variation that has been adopted by most DNA profilers is statistically inelegant,[149] but it has the virtue of simplic-

probably not a match, but a simple match rule or simple computer program might declare it as a match.").

At least one laboratory has reported matches of bands that lie outside its match window but exhibit a band-shifting pattern. It uses monomorphic probes to adjust for the band-shifting. *Compare* Caldwell v. State, 393 S.E.2d 436, 441 (Ga. 1990) (admissible as having reached the "scientific stage of verifiable certainty") *and* State v. Futch, 860 P.2d 264 (Or. Ct. App. 1993) (admissible under a *Daubert*-like standard), *with* Hayes v. State, 660 So. 2d 257 (Fla. 1995) (too controversial to be generally accepted), State v. Quatrevingt, 670 So. 2d 197 (La. 1996) (not shown to be valid under *Daubert*), *and* People v. Keene, 591 N.Y.S.2d 733 (N.Y. Sup. Ct. 1992) (holding that the procedure followed in the case, which did not use the nearest monomorphic probe to make the corrections, was not generally accepted).

148. In statistics, this variability often is denominated "measurement error." The phrase does not mean that a mistake has been made in performing the measurements, but rather that even measurements that are taken correctly fluctuate about the true value of the quantity being measured.

149. *See* NRC II, *supra* note 1, at 139 ("[T]he most accurate statistical model for the interpretation of VNTR analysis would be based on a continuous distribution. . . . If models for measurement uncertainty become available that are appropriate for the wide range of laboratories performing DNA analy-

ity.[150] Analysts typically are willing to declare that two fragments match if the bands appear to match visually, and if they fall within a specified distance of one another. For example, the FBI laboratory declares matches within a ±5% match window—if two bands are within ±5% of their average length, then the alleles can be said to match.[151]

Whether the choice of ±5% (or any other figure) as an outer limit for matches is scientifically acceptable depends on how the criterion operates in classifying pairs of samples of DNA.[152] The ±5% window keeps the chance of a false exclusion for a single allele quite small, but at a cost. The easier it is to declare a match between bands at different positions, the easier it is to declare a match between two samples with *different* genotypes. Therefore, deciding whether a match window is reasonable involves an examination of the probability not merely of a false exclusion but also of a false inclusion: "[t]he match window should not be set so small that true matches are missed. At the same time, the window should not be so wide that bands that are clearly different are declared to match."[153]

ses and if those analyses are sufficiently robust with respect to departures from the models, we would recommend such methods. Indeed, . . . we expect that any problems in the construction of such models will be overcome, and we encourage research on those models."). Forcing a continuous variable like the positions of the bands on an autoradiogram into discrete categories is not statistically efficient. It results in more matching bands being deemed inconclusive or non-matching than more sophisticated statistical procedures. *See, e.g.*, D.A. Berry et al., *Statistical Inference in Crime Investigations Using Deoxyribonucleic Acid Profiling*, 41 Applied Stat. 499 (1992); I.W. Evett et al., *An Illustration of the Advantages of Efficient Statistical Methods for RFLP Analysis in Forensic Science*, 52 Am. J. Hum. Genetics 498 (1993). Also, it treats matches that just squeak by the match windows as just as impressive as perfect matches.

150. NRC II, *supra* note 1, at 139.

151. The FBI arrived at this match window by experiments involving pairs of measurements of the same DNA sequences. It found that this window was wide enough to encompass all the differences seen in the calibration experiments. Other laboratories use smaller percentages for their match windows, but comparisons of the percentage figures can be misleading. *See* D.H. Kaye, Science in Evidence 192 (1997). Because different laboratories can have different standard errors of measurement, profiles from two different laboratories might not be considered inconsistent even though some corresponding bands are outside the match windows of both laboratories. The reason: there is more variability in measurements on different gels than on the same gel, and still more in different gels from different laboratories. *See* Satcher v. Netherland, 944 F. Supp. 1222, 1265 (E.D. Va. 1996).

152. The use of this window was attacked unsuccessfully in *United States v. Yee*, 134 F.R.D. 161 (N.D. Ohio 1991), *aff'd sub nom. United States v. Bonds*, 12 F.3d 540 (6th Cir. 1993); *United States v. Jakobetz*, 747 F. Supp. 250 (D. Vt. 1990), *aff'd*, 955 F.2d 786 (2d Cir. 1992); and *United States v. Perry*, No. CR 91-395-SC (D.N.M. Sept. 7, 1995). For assessments of these arguments, see David H. Kaye, *DNA Evidence: Probability, Population Genetics, and the Courts*, 7 Harv. J.L. & Tech. 101 (1993); D.H. Kaye, *The Relevance of "Matching" DNA: Is the Window Half Open or Half Shut?*, 85 J. Crim. L. & Criminology 676 (1995); William C. Thompson, *Evaluating the Admissibility of New Genetic Tests: Lessons from the "DNA War,"* 84 J. Crim. L. & Criminology 22 (1993); Hans Zeisel & David Kaye, Prove It with Figures: Empirical Methods in Law and Litigation 204–06 (1997).

153. NRC II, *supra* note 1, at 140. Assuming that the only source of error is the statistical uncertainty in the measurements, this error probability is simply the chance that the two people whose DNA is tested have profiles so similar that they satisfy the matching criterion. With genotypes consisting of four or five VNTR loci, that probability is much smaller than the chance of a false exclusion. *Id.* at 141.

Viewed in this light, the ±5% match window is easily defended—it keeps the probabilities of *both* types of errors very small.[154]

B. Alternative Hypotheses

If the defendant is the source of DNA of sufficient quantity and quality found at a crime scene, then a DNA sample from the defendant and the forensic sample should have the same profile. The inference required in assessing the evidence, however, runs in the opposite direction. The forensic scientist reports that the sample of DNA from the crime scene and a sample from the defendant have the same genotype. To what extent does this tend to prove that the defendant is the source of the forensic sample?[155] Conceivably, other hypotheses could account for the matching profiles. One possibility is laboratory error—the genotypes are not actually the same even though the laboratory thinks that they are. This situation could arise from mistakes in labeling or handling samples or from cross-contamination of the samples.[156] As the 1992 NRC report cautioned, "[e]rrors happen, even in the best laboratories, and even when the analyst is certain that every precaution against error was taken."[157] Another possibility is that the laboratory analysis is correct—the genotypes are truly identical—but the forensic sample came from another individual. In general, the true source might be a close relative of the defendant[158] or an unrelated person who, as luck would have it, just happens to have the same profile as the defendant. The former hypothesis we shall refer to as kinship, and the latter as coincidence. To infer that the defendant is the source of the crime scene DNA, one must reject these alternative hypotheses of laboratory error, kinship, and coincidence. Table 1 summarizes the logical possibilities.

154. NRC II, *supra* note 1, at 140–41; Bernard Devlin & Kathryn Roeder, *DNA Profiling: Statistics and Population Genetics, in* 1 Modern Scientific Evidence, *supra* note 53, § 18-3.1.2, at 717–18.

155. That the defendant is the source does not necessarily mean that the defendant is guilty of the offense charged. Aside from issues of intent or knowledge that have nothing to do with DNA, there remains, for instance, the possibility that the two samples match because someone framed the defendant by putting a sample of defendant's DNA at the crime scene or in the container of DNA thought to have come from the crime scene. *See generally* United States v. Chischilly, 30 F.3d 1144 (9th Cir. 1994) (dicta on "source probability"); Jonathan J. Koehler, *DNA Matches and Statistics: Important Questions, Surprising Answers*, 76 Judicature 222 (1993). For reports of state police planting fingerprint and other evidence to incriminate arrestees, see John Caher, *Judge Orders New Trial in Murder Case*, Times Union (Albany), Jan. 8, 1997, at B2; John O'Brien & Todd Lightly, *Corrupt Troopers Showed No Fear*, The Post-Standard (Syracuse), Feb. 4, 1997, at A3 (an investigation of 62,000 fingerprint cards from 1983–1992 revealed 34 cases of planted evidence among one state police troop).

156. *See supra* § VI.

157. NRC I, *supra* note 1, at 89.

158. A close relative, for these purposes, would be a brother, uncle, nephew, etc. For relationships more distant than second cousins, the probability of a chance match is nearly as small as for persons of the same ethnic subgroup. Devlin & Roeder, *supra* note 154, § 18-3.1.3, at 724. For an instance of the "evil twin" defense, see Hunter v. Harrison, No. 71723, 1997 WL 578917 (Ohio Ct. App. Sept. 18, 1997) (unpublished paternity case).

Table 1. Hypotheses that Might Explain a Match Between Defendant's DNA and DNA at a Crime Scene[159]

IDENTITY:	same genotype, defendant's DNA at crime scene
NON-IDENTITY:	
lab error	different genotypes mistakenly found to be the same
kinship	same genotype, relative's DNA at crime scene
coincidence	same genotype, unrelated individual's DNA

Some scientists have urged that probabilities associated with false positive error, kinship, or coincidence be presented to juries. While it is not clear that this goal is feasible, scientific knowledge and more conventional evidence can help in assessing the plausibility of these alternative hypotheses. If laboratory error, kinship, and coincidence can be eliminated as explanations for a match, then only the hypothesis of identity remains. We turn, then, to the considerations that affect the chances of a reported match when the defendant is not the source of the trace evidence.

1. *Error*

Although many experts would concede that even with rigorous protocols, the chance of a laboratory error exceeds that of a coincidental match,[160] quantifying the former probability is a formidable task. Some commentary proposes using the proportion of false positives that the particular laboratory has experienced in blind proficiency tests or the rate of false positives on proficiency tests averaged across all laboratories.[161] Indeed, the 1992 NRC Report remarks that "proficiency tests provide a measure of the false-positive and false-negative rates of a laboratory."[162] Yet, the same report recognizes that "errors on proficiency tests do not necessarily reflect permanent probabilities of false-positive or false-negative results,"[163] and the 1996 NRC report suggests that a probability of a false-positive error that would apply to a specific case cannot be estimated objectively.[164] If the false-positive probability were, say, 0.001, it would take tens of thousands of proficiency tests to estimate that probability accurately, and the application of an historical industry-wide error rate to a particular laboratory at a later time would be debatable.[165]

159. *Cf.* N.E. Morton, *The Forensic DNA Endgame*, 37 Jurimetrics J. 477, 480 tbl. 1 (1997).

160. *E.g.*, Devlin & Roeder, *supra* note 154, § 18-5.3, at 743.

161. *E.g.*, Jonathan J. Koehler, *Error and Exaggeration in the Presentation of DNA Evidence at Trial*, 34 Jurimetrics J. 21, 37–38 (1993); Scheck, *supra* note 69, at 1984 n.93.

162. NRC I, *supra* note 1, at 94.

163. *Id.* at 89.

164. NRC II, *supra* note 1, at 85–87.

165. *Id.* at 85–86; Devlin & Roeder, *supra* note 154, § 18-5.3, at 744–45. Such arguments have not persuaded the proponents of estimating the probability of error from industry-wide proficiency testing.

Most commentators who urge the use of proficiency tests to estimate the probability that a laboratory has erred in a particular case agree that blind proficiency testing cannot be done in sufficient numbers to yield an accurate estimate of a small error rate. However, they maintain that proficiency tests, blind or otherwise, should be used to provide a conservative estimate of the false-positive error probability.[166] For example, if there were no errors in 100 tests, a 95% confidence interval would include the possibility that the error rate could be almost as high as 3%.[167]

Instead of pursuing a numerical estimate, the second NAS committee and individual scientists who question the value of proficiency tests for estimating case-specific laboratory-error probabilities suggest that each laboratory document all the steps in its analyses and reserve portions of the DNA samples for independent testing whenever feasible. Scrutinizing the chain of custody, examining the laboratory's protocol, verifying that it adhered to that protocol, and conducting confirmatory tests if there are any suspicious circumstances can help to eliminate the hypothesis of laboratory error,[168] whether or not a case-specific probability can be estimated.[169] Furthermore, if the defendant has had a meaningful opportunity to retest a sample but has been unable or unwilling to obtain an inconsistent result, the relevance of a statistic based on past proficiency tests might be questionable.

2. Kinship

With enough genetic markers, all individuals except for identical twins should be distinguishable, but this ideal is not always attainable with the limited number of loci typically used in forensic testing.[170] Close relatives have more genes in common than unrelated individuals, and various procedures have been pro-

E.g., Jonathan J. Koehler, *Why DNA Likelihood Ratios Should Account for Error (Even When a National Research Council Report Says They Should Not)*, 37 Jurimetrics J. 425 (1997).

166. *E.g.*, Koehler, *supra* note 155, at 228; Richard Lempert, *After the DNA Wars: Skirmishing with NRC II*, 37 Jurimetrics J. 439, 447–48, 453 (1997).

167. *See* NRC II, *supra* note 1, at 86 n.1. For an explanation of confidence intervals, see David H. Kaye & David A. Freedman, Reference Guide on Statistics, § IV.A.2, in this manual.

168. *E.g.*, Jonathan J. Koehler, *On Conveying the Probative Value of DNA Evidence: Frequencies, Likelihood Ratios, and Error Rates*, 67 U. Colo. L. Rev. 859, 866 (1996) ("In the *Simpson* case, [l]aboratory error was unlikely because many blood samples were tested at different laboratories using two different DNA typing methods."); William C. Thompson, *DNA Evidence in the O.J. Simpson Trial*, 67 U. Colo. L. Rev. 827, 827 (1996) ("the extensive use of duplicate testing in the *Simpson* case greatly reduced concerns (that are crucial in most other cases) about the potential for false positives due to poor scientific practices of DNA laboratories").

169. *See* Berger, *supra* note 69.

170. *See, e.g.*, B.S. Weir, *Discussion of "Inference in Forensic Identification,"* 158 J. Royal Stat. Soc'y Ser. A 49, 50 (1995) ("the chance that two unrelated individuals in a population share the same 16-allele [VNTR] profile is vanishingly small, and even for full sibs the chance is only 1 in very many thousands").

posed for dealing with the possibility that the true source of the forensic DNA is not the defendant but a close relative.[171] Often, the investigation, including additional DNA testing, can be extended to all known relatives.[172] But this is not feasible in every case, and there is always the chance that some unknown relatives are included in the suspect population.[173] Formulae are available for computing the probability that any person with a specified degree of kinship to the defendant also possesses the incriminating genotype.[174] For example, the probability that an untested brother (or sister) would match at four loci (with alleles that each occur in 5% of the population) is about 0.006; the probability that an aunt (or uncle) would match is about 0.0000005.[175]

171. *See* Thomas R. Belin et al., *Summarizing DNA Evidence When Relatives are Possible Suspects*, 92 J. Am. Stat. Ass'n 706, 707–08 (1997). Recommendation 4.4 of the 1996 NRC report reads:

> If possible contributors of the evidence sample include relatives of the suspect, DNA profiles of those relatives should be obtained. If these profiles cannot be obtained, the probability of finding the evidence profile in those relatives should be calculated with [specified formulae].

NRC II, *supra* note 1, at 6.

172. NRC II, *supra* note 1, at 113.

173. When that population is very large, however, the presence of a few relatives will have little impact on the probability that a suspect drawn at random from that population will have the incriminating genotype. *Id.* Furthermore, it has been suggested that the effect of relatedness is of practical importance only for very close relatives, such as siblings. JFY Brookfield, *The Effect of Relatives on the Likelihood Ratio Associated with DNA Profile Evidence in Criminal Cases*, 34 J. Forensic Sci. Soc'y 193 (1994).

174. *E.g.*, Brookfield, *supra* note 173; David J. Balding & Peter Donnelly, *Inference in Forensic Identification*, 158 J. Royal Stat. Soc'y Ser. A 21 (1995); Ian W. Evett & Bruce S. Weir, Interpreting DNA Evidence: Statistical Genetics for Forensic Scientists 108–18 (1998); Morton, *supra* note 159, at 484; NRC II, *supra* note 1, at 113. *But see* NRC I, *supra* note 1, at 87 (giving an incorrect formula for siblings). Empirical measures that are not directly interpretable as probabilities also have been described. Belin et al., *supra* note 171.

175. The large discrepancy between two siblings on the one hand, and an uncle and nephew on the other, reflects the fact that the siblings have far more shared ancestry. All their genes are inherited through the same two parents. In contrast, a nephew and an uncle inherit from two unrelated mothers, and so will have few maternal alleles in common. As for paternal alleles, the nephew inherits not from his uncle, but from his uncle's brother, who shares by descent only about one-half of his alleles with the uncle.

One commentator has proposed that unless the police can eliminate all named relatives as possible culprits, "the defendant should be allowed to name any close relative whom he thinks might have committed the crime," and the state should use the probability "that at least one named relative has DNA like the defendant's" as the sole indication of the plausibility of the hypothesis of kinship. Lempert, *supra* note 166, at 461. For example, if the defendant named two brothers and two uncles as possible suspects, then the probability that at least one shares the genotype would be about (2 x .006) + (2 x .0000005), or about 0.012. Whether such numbers should be introduced even when there is no proof that a close relative might have committed the crime is, of course, a matter to be evaluated under Federal Rules of Evidence 104(b), 401, and 403. *See, e.g.*, Taylor v. Commonwealth, No. 1767-93-1, 1995 WL 80189 (Va. Ct. App. Feb. 28, 1995) (unpublished) ("Defendant argues that this evidence did not consider the existence of an identical twin or close relative to defendant, a circumstance which would diminish the probability that he was the perpetrator. While this hypothesis is conceivable, it has no basis in the record and the Commonwealth must only exclude hypotheses of innocence that reasonably flow from the evidence, not from defendant's imagination.").

3. Coincidence

Another rival hypothesis is coincidence: The defendant is not the source of the crime scene DNA, but happens to have the same genotype as an unrelated individual who is the true source. Various procedures for assessing the plausibility of this hypothesis are available. In principle, one could test all conceivable suspects. If everyone except the defendant has a non-matching profile, then the conclusion that the defendant is the source is inescapable. But exhaustive, error-free testing of the population of conceivable suspects is almost never feasible. The suspect population normally defies any enumeration, and in the typical crime where DNA evidence is found, the population of possible perpetrators is so huge that even if all its members could be listed, they could not all be tested.[176]

An alternative procedure would be to take a sample of people from the suspect population, find the relative frequency of the profile in this sample, and use that statistic to estimate the frequency in the entire suspect population. The smaller the frequency, the less likely it is that the defendant's DNA would match if the defendant were not the source of trace evidence. Again, however, the suspect population is difficult to define, so some surrogate must be used. The procedure commonly followed is to estimate the relative frequency of the incriminating genotype in a large population. But even this cannot be done directly because each possible multilocus profile is so rare that it is not likely to show up in any sample of a reasonable size.[177] However, the frequencies of most alleles can be determined accurately by sampling the population[178] to construct

176. In the United Kingdom and Europe, mass DNA screenings in small towns have been undertaken. *See, e.g.*, Kaye, *supra* note 151, at 222–26.

177. NRC II, *supra* note 1, at 89–90 ("A very small proportion of the trillions of possible profiles are found in any database, so it is necessary to use the frequencies of individual alleles to estimate the frequency of a given profile."). The 1992 NRC report proposed reporting the occurrences of a profile in a database, but recognized that "such estimates do not take advantage of the full potential of the genetic approach." NRC I, *supra* note 1, at 76. For further discussion of the statistical inferences that might be drawn from the absence of a profile in a sample of a given size, see NRC II, *supra*, at 159–60 (arguing that "the abundant data make [the direct counting method] unnecessary").

178. Ideally, a probability sample from the population of interest would be taken. Probability sampling is described in David H. Kaye & David A. Freedman, Reference Guide on Statistics, § II.B, and Shari Seidman Diamond, Reference Guide on Survey Research, § III.C, in this manual. Indeed, a few experts have testified that no meaningful conclusions can be drawn in the absence of random sampling. *E.g.*, People v. Soto, 88 Cal. Rptr. 2d 34 (1999); State v. Anderson, 881 P.2d 29, 39 (N.M. 1994).

Unfortunately, a list of the people who comprise the entire population of possible suspects is almost never available; consequently, probability sampling from the directly relevant population is generally impossible. Probability sampling from a proxy population is possible, but it is not the norm in studies of the distributions of genes in populations. Typically, convenience samples are used. The 1996 NRC report suggests that for the purpose of estimating allele frequencies, convenience sampling should give results comparable to random sampling, and it discusses procedures for estimating the random sampling error. NRC II, *supra* note 1, at 126–27, 146–48, 186. For an analysis of case law on the need for random sampling in this area, see D.H. Kaye, Bible *Reading: DNA Evidence in Arizona*, 28 Ariz. St. L.J. 1035 (1996).

databases that reveal how often each allele occurs.[179] Principles of population genetics then can be applied to combine the estimated allele frequencies into an estimate of the probability that a person born in the population will have the multilocus genotype. This probability often is referred to as the random match probability. Three principal methods for computing the random match probability from allele frequencies have been developed. This section describes these methods; the next section considers other quantities that have been proposed as measures of the probative value of the DNA evidence.

a. The Basic Product Rule

The basic product rule estimates the frequency of genotypes in an infinite population of individuals who choose their mates and reproduce independently of the alleles used to compare the samples. Although population geneticists describe this situation as random mating, these words are terms of art. Geneticists know that people do not choose their mates by a lottery, and they use "random mating" to indicate that the choices are uncorrelated with the specific alleles that make up the genotypes in question.[180]

In a randomly mating population, the expected frequency of a pair of alleles at each locus depends on whether the two alleles are distinct. If a different allele is inherited from each parent, the expected single-locus genotype frequency is twice the product of the two individual allele frequencies.[181] But if the offspring happens to inherit the same allele from each parent, the expected single-locus genotype frequency is the square of the allele frequency.[182] These proportions

179. In the formative years of forensic DNA testing, defendants frequently contended that the size of the forensic databases were too small to give accurate estimates, but this argument generally proved unpersuasive. *E.g.*, United States v. Shea, 937 F. Supp. 331 (D.N.H. 1997); People v. Soto, 88 Cal. Rptr. 2d 34 (1999); State v. Dishon, 687 A.2d 1074, 1090 (N.J. Super. Ct. App. 1997); State v. Copeland, 922 P.2d 1304, 1321 (Wash. 1996).

To the extent that the databases are comparable to random samples, confidence intervals are a standard method for indicating the amount of error due to sample size. *E.g.*, Kaye, *supra* note 152. Unfortunately, the meaning of a confidence interval is subtle, and the estimate commonly is misconstrued. *See* David H. Kaye & David A. Freedman, Reference Guide on Statistics, § IV.A.2, in this manual.

180. *E.g.*, NRC II, *supra* note 1, at 90:

> In the simplest population structure, mates are chosen at random. Clearly, the population of the United States does not mate at random; a person from Oregon is more likely to mate with another from Oregon than with one from Florida. Furthermore, people often choose mates according to physical and behavioral attributes, such as height and personality. But they do not choose each other according to the markers used for forensic studies, such as VNTRs and STRs. Rather, the proportion of matings between people with two marker genotypes is determined by their frequencies in the mating population. If the allele frequencies in Oregon and Florida are the same as those in the nation as a whole, then the proportion of genotypes in the two states will be the same as those for the United States, even though the population of the whole country clearly does not mate at random.

181. In more technical terms, when the frequencies of two alleles are p_1 and p_2, the single-locus genotype frequency for the corresponding heterozygotes is expected to be $2p_1p_2$.

182. The expected proportion is p_1^2 for allele 1, and p_2^2 for allele 2. With VNTRs, a complication arises with apparent homozygotes. A single band on an autoradiogram might really be two bands that

are known as Hardy-Weinberg proportions. Even if two populations with distinct allele frequencies are thrown together, within the limits of chance variation, random mating produces Hardy-Weinberg equilibrium in a single generation. An example is given in this footnote.[183]

Once the proportion of the population that has each of the single-locus genotypes for the forensic profile has been estimated in this way, the proportion of the population that is expected to share the combination of them—the multilocus profile frequency—is given by multiplying the single-locus proportions. This multiplication is exactly correct when the single-locus genotypes are statistically independent. In that case, the population is said to be in linkage equilibrium.

Extensive litigation and scientific commentary have considered whether the occurrences of alleles at each locus are independent events (Hardy-Weinberg equilibrium), and whether the loci are independent (linkage equilibrium). Beginning around 1990, several scientists suggested that the equilibrium frequencies do not follow the simple model of a homogeneous population mating without regard to the loci used in forensic DNA profiling. They suggested that the major racial populations are composed of ethnic subpopulations whose members tend to mate among themselves.[184] Within each ethnic subpopulation, mating still can be random, but if, say, Italian-Americans have allele frequencies that are markedly different than the average for all whites, and if Italian-Americans only mate among themselves, then using the average frequencies for all whites in the basic product formula could understate—or overstate—a multilocus profile frequency for the subpopulation of Italian-Americans.[185] Similarly, using the popu-

are close together, or a second band that is relatively small might have migrated to the edge of the gel during the electrophoresis. Forensic laboratories therefore make a "conservative" assumption. They act as if there is a second, unseen band, and they use the excessively large value of p_2 = 100% for the frequency of the presumably unseen allele. With this modification, the genotype frequency for apparent homozygotes becomes $P = 2p_1$. If the single-banded pattern is a true homozygote, this 2p convention overstates the frequency of the single-locus genotype because 2p is greater than p^2 for any possible proportion p. For instance, if p = 0.05, then 2p = 0.10, which is 40 times greater than $p^2 = 0.0025$.

183. Suppose that 10% of the sperm in the gene pool of the population carry allele 1 (A_1), and 50% carry allele 2 (A_2). Similarly, 10% of the eggs carry A_1, and 50% carry A_2. (Other sperm and eggs carry other types.) With random mating, we expect 10% x 10% = 1% of all the fertilized eggs to be A_1A_1, and another 50% x 50% = 25% to be A_2A_2. These constitute two distinct homozygote profiles. Likewise, we expect 10% x 50% = 5% of the fertilized eggs to be A_1A_2 and another 50% x 10% = 5% to be A_2A_1. These two configurations produce indistinguishable profiles—a band, dot, or the like for A_1 and another mark for A_2. So the expected proportion of heterozygotes A_1A_2 is 5% + 5% = 10%.

Oddly, some courts and commentators have written that the expected heterozygote frequency for this example is only 5%. *E.g.*, William C. Thompson & Simon Ford, *DNA Typing: Acceptance and Weight of the New Genetic Identification Tests*, 75 Va. L. Rev. 45, 81–82 (1989). For further discussion, see Kaye, *supra* note 178; David H. Kaye, *Cross-Examining Science*, 36 Jurimetrics J. vii (Winter 1996).

184. The most prominent expression of this position is Richard C. Lewontin & Daniel L. Hartl, *Population Genetics in Forensic DNA Typing*, 254 Science 1745 (1991).

185. On average, the use of population-wide allele frequencies overstates the genotype frequencies within defendant's subpopulation. *See* Dan E. Krane et al., *Genetic Differences at Four DNA Typing Loci*

lation frequencies could understate—or overstate—the profile frequencies in the white population itself.[186]

Consequently, if we want to know the frequency of an incriminating profile among Italian-Americans, the basic product rule applied to the white allele frequencies could be in error; and there is some chance that it will understate the profile frequency in the white population as a whole. One might presume that the extent of the error could be determined by looking to the variations across racial groups,[187] but, for a short time, a few scientists insisted that variations from one ethnic group to another within a race were larger than variations from one race to another.[188] In light of this literature[189] courts had grounds to conclude that the basic product rule, used with broad population frequencies, was not universally accepted for estimating profile frequencies within subpopulations. Yet, few courts recognized that there was much less explicit dissension over the ability of the rule to estimate profile frequencies in a general population.[190] Particularly in *Frye* jurisdictions, a substantial number of appellate courts began to exclude DNA evidence for want of a generally accepted method of estimating profile frequencies in both situations.[191]

in Finnish, Italian, and Mixed Caucasian Populations, 89 Proc. Nat'l Acad. Sci. 10583 (1992); Stanley Sawyer et al., *DNA Fingerprinting Loci Do Show Population Differences: Comments on Budowle et al.*, 59 Am. J. Hum. Genetics 272 (1996) (letter). This mean overestimation occurs because (1) the use of population-wide frequencies rather than subpopulation frequencies underestimates homozygote frequencies and overestimates heterozygote frequencies, and (2) heterozygosity far exceeds homozygosity.

186. The use of the population-wide allele frequencies usually overstates genotype frequencies in the population as a whole, thereby benefitting most defendants. *See* Kaye, *supra* note 152, at 142.

187. On the problems in defining racial populations, compare C. Loring Brace, *Region Does Not Mean "Race"—Reality Versus Convention in Forensic Anthropology*, 40 J. Forensic Sci. 171 (1995), with Kenneth A.R. Kennedy, *But Professor, Why Teach Race Identification if Races Don't Exist?*, 40 J. Forensic Sci. 797 (1995).

188. *Compare* Lewontin & Hartl, *supra* note 184, at 1745 ("there is, on average, one-third more genetic variation among Irish, Spanish, Italians, Slavs, Swedes, and other subpopulations than there is, on average, between Europeans, Asians, Africans, Amerindians, and Oceanians"), *with* Richard C. Lewontin, *Discussion*, 9 Stat. Sci. 259, 260 (1994) ("all parties agree that differentiation among [major ethnic groups] is as large, if not larger than, the difference among tribes and national groups [within major ethnic groups]"). Other population geneticists dismissed as obviously untenable the early assertions of greater variability across the ethnic subpopulations of a race than across races. *E.g.*, B. Devlin et al., *NRC Report on DNA Typing*, 260 Science 1057 (1993); N.E. Morton et al., *Kinship Bioassay on Hypervariable Loci in Blacks and Caucasians*, 90 Proc. Nat'l Acad. Sci. USA 1892, 1896 (1993) (Gene frequencies cited by Lewontin & Hartl are atypical, and "[l]ess than 2% of the diversity selected by Lewontin and Hartl is due to the national kinship to which they attribute it, little of which persists in regional forensic samples.").

189. The literature on genetic differences across the globe is reviewed in, *e.g.*, Devlin & Roeder, *supra* note 154, § 18–3.2.1, at 725–28 (suggesting that this body of research indicates that the extent of the variation across subpopulations is relatively small).

190. *See* Kaye, *supra* note 152, at 146. The general perception was that ethnic stratification within the major racial categories posed a problem regardless of whether the relevant population for estimating the random match probability was a broad racial group or a narrow, inbred ethnic subpopulation.

191. *See* cases cited, Kaye, *supra* note 152. Courts applying *Daubert* or similar standards were more

b. The Product Rule with Ceilings

In 1992, the National Academy of Sciences' Committee on DNA Technology in Forensic Science assumed arguendo that population structure was a serious threat to the basic product rule and proposed a variation to provide an upper bound on a profile frequency within any population or subpopulation.[192] The interim ceiling method uses the same general formulas as the basic product rule,[193] but with different values of the frequencies. Instead of multiplying together the allele frequencies from any single, major racial database, the procedure picks, for each allele in the DNA profile, the largest value seen in *any* race.[194] If that value is less than 10%, the procedure inflates it to 10%. Those values are then multiplied as with the basic product rule. Thus, the ceiling method employs a mix-and-match, inflate, and multiply strategy. The result, it is widely believed, is an extremely conservative estimate of the profile frequency that more than compensates for the possibility of any population structure that might undermine the assumptions of Hardy-Weinberg and linkage equilibria in the major racial populations.[195]

receptive to the evidence. *E.g.*, United States v. Jakobetz, 955 F.2d 786 (2d Cir. 1992), *aff'g*, 747 F. Supp. 250 (D. Vt. 1990); United States v. Bonds, 12 F.3d 540 (6th Cir. 1993), *aff'g*, United States v. Yee, 134 F.R.D. 161 (N.D. Ohio 1991); United States v. Chischilly, 30 F.3d 1144 (9th Cir. 1994); United States v. Davis, 40 F.3d 1069 (10th Cir. 1994).

192. *See* NRC I, *supra* note 1, at 91–92; *id.* at 80 ("Although mindful of the controversy, the committee has chosen to assume for the sake of discussion that population substructure may exist and provide a method for estimating population [genotype] frequencies in a manner that adequately accounts for it."). The report was unclear as to whether its "interim ceiling principle" was a substitute for or merely a supplement to the usual basic product rule. Years later, one member of the committee opined that the committee intended the latter interpretation. Eric S. Lander & Bruce Budowle, *Commentary: DNA Fingerprinting Dispute Laid to Rest*, 371 Nature 735 (1994). In any event, the interim ceiling principle was proposed as a stopgap measure, to be supplanted by another ceiling principle that could be used after sampling many "[g]enetically homogeneous populations from various regions of the world." NRC I, *supra*, at 84.

193. Applied to a single racial group like whites, the basic product rule estimates the frequency of the multilocus genotype as the product of the single-locus frequencies, and it estimates each single-locus frequency as $2p_1p_2$ for heterozygotes or as a quantity exceeding p^2 for homozygotes, where p refers to frequencies estimated from the database for that race.

194. Actually, an even larger figure is used—the upper 95% confidence limit on the allele frequency estimate for that race. This is intended to account for sampling error due to the limited size of the databases. NRC I, *supra* note 1, at 92.

195. *See, e.g.*, NRC II, *supra* note 1, at 156 ("sufficiently conservative to accommodate the presence of substructure . . . a lower limit on the size of the profile frequency"); NRC I, *supra* note 1, at 91 ("conservative calculation"). This modification of the basic product rule provoked vociferous criticism from many scientists, and it distressed certain prosecutors and other law enforcement personnel who perceived the 1992 NRC report as contributing to the rejection of DNA evidence in many jurisdictions. *See, e.g.*, Kaye, *supra* note 2, at 396. The judicial impact of the NRC report and the debate among scientists over the ceiling method are reviewed in D.H. Kaye, *The Forensic Debut of the National Research Council's DNA Report: Population Structure, Ceiling Frequencies and the Need for Numbers*, 34 Jurimetrics J. 369 (1994) (suggesting that because the disagreement about the ceiling principle is a dispute about legal

c. The Product Rule for a Structured Population

The 1996 NRC Report distinguishes between cases in which the suspect population is a broad racial population and those in which that population is a genetically distinct subgroup. In the former situation, Recommendation 4.1 endorses the basic product rule:

> In general, the calculation of a profile frequency should be made with the product rule. If the race of the person who left the evidence-sample DNA is known, the database for the person's race should be used; if the race is not known, calculations for all the racial groups to which possible suspects belong should be made.[196]

"For example," the committee wrote, "if DNA is recovered from semen in a case in which a woman hitchhiker on an interstate highway has been raped by a white man, the product rule with the 2*p* rule can be used with VNTR data from a sample of whites to estimate the frequency of the profile among white males. If the race of the rapist were in doubt, the product rule could still be used and the results given for data on whites, blacks, Hispanics, and east Asians."[197] However, "[w]hen there are partially isolated subgroups in a population, the situation is more complex; then a suitably altered model leads to slightly different estimates of the quantities that are multiplied together in the formula for the frequency of the profile in the population."[198] Thus, the committee's Recommendation 4.2 urges that:

> If the particular subpopulation from which the evidence sample came is known, the allele frequencies for the specific subgroup should be used as described in Recommendation 4.1.

policy rather than scientific knowledge, the debate among scientists does not justify excluding ceiling frequencies).

By 1995, however, many courts were concluding that because a consensus that ceiling estimates are conservative had emerged, these estimates are admissible. At the same time, other courts that only a short while ago had held basic product estimates to be too controversial to be admissible decided that there was sufficient agreement about the basic product rule for it to be used. *See* State v. Johnson, 922 P.2d 294, 300 (Ariz. 1996); State v. Copeland, 922 P.2d 1304, 1318 (Wash. 1996) ("Although at one time a significant dispute existed among qualified scientists, from the present vantage point we are able to say that the significant dispute was short-lived."); Kaye, *supra* note 4.

In 1994, a second NAS committee was installed to review the criticism and the studies that had accumulated in the aftermath of the 1992 report. In 1996, it reported that the ceiling method is an unnecessary and extravagant way to handle the likely extent of population structure. NRC II, *supra* note 1, at 158, 162.

196. NRC II, *supra* note 1, at 5. The recommendation also calls for modifications to the Hardy-Weinberg proportion for apparent homozygotes. The modifications depend on whether the alleles are discrete (as in PCR-based tests) or continuous (as in VNTR testing). *Id.* at 5 n.2.

197. *Id.* at 5 (note omitted). *See also* C. Thomas Caskey, *Comments on DNA-based Forensic Analysis*, 49 Am. J. Hum. Genetics 893 (1991) (letter). For a case with comparable facts, see *United States v. Jakobetz*, 747 F. Supp. 250 (D. Vt. 1990), *aff'd*, 955 F.2d 786 (2d Cir. 1992).

198. NRC II, *supra* note 1, at 5.

199. *Id.* at 5–6.

If allele frequencies for the subgroup are not available, although data for the full population are, then the calculations should use the population-structure equations 4.10 for each locus, and the resulting values should be multiplied.[199]

The "suitably altered model" is a generalization of the basic product rule. In this affinal model, as it is sometimes called,[200] the "population-structure equations" are similar to those for multiplying single-locus frequencies. However, they involve not only the individual allele frequencies, but also a quantity that measures the extent of population structure.[201] The single-locus frequencies are multiplied together as in the basic product rule to find the multilocus frequency. Although few reported cases have analyzed the admissibility of random match probabilities estimated with the product rule for structured populations, the validity of the affinal model of a structured population has not been questioned in the scientific literature.[202]

The committee recommended that the population-structure equations be used in special situations,[203] but they could be applied to virtually all cases. The report suggests conservative values of the population-structure constant might be used for broad suspect populations as well as values for many partially isolated subpopulations.[204] The population-structure equations always give more conservative probabilities than the basic product rule when both formulae are applied to the same database, and they are usually conservative relative to calculations based on the subpopulation of the defendant.[205]

200. Devlin & Roeder, *supra* note 154, § 18–3.1.3, at 723.

201. NRC II, *supra* note 1, at 114–15 (equations 4.10a & 4.10b). *See also* papers cited, Devlin & Roeder, *supra* note 154, § 18-3.1.3, at 723 n.37. This quantity usually is designated θ. *See generally* Evett & Weir, *supra* note 174, at 94–107, 118–23, 156–62.

202. The district court in *United States v. Shea*, 957 F. Supp. 331, 343 (D.N.H. 1997), held that a random match probability using an F_{ST} adjustment satisfies *Daubert*. *See also* United States v. Gaines, 979 F. Supp. 1429 (S.D. Fla. 1997).

203. The report explains that the recommendation to use the population-structure equations "deals with the case in which the person who is the source of the evidence DNA is known to belong to a particular subgroup of a racial category." NRC II, *supra* note 1, at 6. It offers this illustration:

> For example, if the hitchhiker was not on an interstate highway but in the midst of, say, a small village in New England and we had good reason to believe that the rapist was an inhabitant of the village, the product rule could still be used (as described in Recommendation 4.1) if there is a reasonably large database on the villagers.
>
> If specific data on the villagers are lacking, a more complex model could be used to estimate the random-match probability for the incriminating profile on the basis of data on the major population group (whites) that includes the villagers.

Id. For further discussion of when Recommendation 4.1 applies, see *infra* note 208.

204. *Id.* at 115, 116 ("typical values for white and black populations are less than 0.01, usually about 0.002. Values for Hispanics are slightly higher . . . .") ("For urban populations, 0.01 is a conservative value. A higher value—say 0.03—could be used for isolated villages."); *cf.* Devlin & Roeder, *supra* note 154, § 18–3.1.3, at 723–24 ("For [VNTR] markers, θ is generally agreed to lie between 0 and .02 for most populations.").

205. Devlin & Roeder, *supra* note 154, § 18–3.1.3, at 723.

In a few situations, however, very little data on either the larger population or the specific subpopulation will be available.[206] To handle such cases, Recommendation 4.3 provides:

> If the person who contributed the evidence sample is from a group or tribe for which no adequate database exists, data from several other groups or tribes thought to be closely related to it should be used. The profile frequency should be calculated as described in Recommendation 4.1 for each group or tribe.[207]

Similar procedures have been followed in a few cases where the issue has surfaced.[208]

206. *See, e.g.*, People v. Atoigue, DCA No. CR 91-95A, 1992 WL 245628 (D. Guam App. Div. 1992), *aff'd without deciding whether admission of DNA evidence was error*, No. 92-10589, 1994 WL 477518 (9th Cir. 1994) (unpublished).

207. NRC II, *supra* note 1, at 6. The committee explained that:

> This recommendation deals with the case in which the person who is the source of the evidence DNA is known to belong to a particular subgroup of a racial category but there are no DNA data on either the subgroup or the population to which the subgroup belongs. It would apply, for example, if a person on an isolated Indian reservation in the Southwest, had been assaulted by a member of the tribe, and there were no data on DNA profiles of the tribe. In that case, the recommendation calls for use of the product rule (as described in Recommendation 4.1) with several other closely related tribes for which adequate databases exist.

Id.

208. A variation on this procedure was used in *United States v. Chischilly*, 30 F.3d 1144, 1158 n.29 (9th Cir. 1994), to handle the concern that the FBI had insufficient data on VNTR allele frequencies among Navajos. In *Government of the Virgin Islands v. Byers*, 941 F. Supp. 513 (D.V.I. 1996), two black men in St. Thomas engaged in "a four-month crime spree" of rape, robbery, kidnapping, and burglary. *Id.* at 514. After one woman was raped a second time by the pair, she identified one as Byers. Byers pled guilty to various charges and testified against an acquaintance, whom the FBI linked to three victims by a three-locus VNTR profile. *Id.* Random match probabilities for African-Americans, whites, and Hispanics were estimated from the FBI's databases, which did not include inhabitants of St. Thomas. The defendant argued that because the African-American database did not include Afro-Caribbeans, the probabilities were inadmissible. *Id.* at 515. The district court reasoned that:

> [A]s the 1996 NRC Report concluded, population subgrouping is important only if we know that the suspect is a member of a particular subgroup. All that was known about the suspect in this case was his race. The victims did not indicate whether he was a transplanted North American, a native St. Thomian, or an immigrant from one of the other Caribbean islands. As recommended by the 1996 NRC Report, the FBI's database for Blacks was used in comparing the defendant's DNA profile since the suspect's race is known in this case. Because investigators did not know the subgroup to which the suspect belonged, there was no need to compare the defendant's DNA profile with any subgroup. The FBI procedure of giving DNA frequency estimations for several different racial groups was more than adequate under the circumstances.

Id. at 522. In our view, the court's reliance on Recommendation 4.1 of the 1996 report was misplaced. Although the victims could not know with certainty whether their assailants were African-American or Afro-Caribbean, the locale of the crimes indicates that the suspect population was dominated by the latter, and that group is not a subpopulation of the African-American population for which a database is available. Consequently, Recommendation 4.3 would seem to apply. Nevertheless, by crediting FBI testimony that the distribution of VNTR alleles in African-Americans is similar to that in Afro-Caribbeans, the court followed the substance of Recommendation 4.3. *Id.*; *see also* Government of Virgin Islands v. Penn, 838 F. Supp. 1054, 1071 (D.V.I. 1993) ("any concern that the St. Thomas black population's bin frequencies are drastically different from those of the United States' black population is unwarranted").

d. Adjusting for a Database Search

Whatever variant of the product rule might be used to find the probability of the genotype in a population, subpopulation, or relative, the number is useful only insofar as it establishes (1) that the DNA profile is sufficiently discriminating to be probative, and (2) that the same DNA profile in the defendant and the crime-scene stain is unlikely to occur if the DNA came from someone other than the defendant. Yet, unlikely events happen all the time. An individual wins the lottery even though it was very unlikely that the particular ticket would be a winner. The chance of a particular supertanker running aground and producing a massive spill on a single trip may be very small, but the Exxon Valdez did just that.

The apparent paradox of supposedly low-probability events being ubiquitous results from what statisticians call a "selection effect" or "data mining." If we pick a lottery ticket at random, the probability p that we have the winning ticket is negligible. But if we search through all the tickets, sooner or later we will find the winning one. And even if we search through some smaller number N of tickets, the probability of picking a winning ticket is no longer p, but Np.[209]

Likewise, there may be a small probability p that a randomly selected individual who is not the source of the forensic sample has the incriminating genotype. That is somewhat like having a winning lottery ticket.[210] If N people are included in the search for a person with the matching DNA, then the probability of a match in this group is not p, but some quantity that could be as large as Np.[211] This type of reasoning led the second NRC committee to recommend that "[w]hen the suspect is found by a search of DNA databases, the random-match probability should be multiplied by N, the number of persons in the database."[212]

The first NAS committee also felt that "[t]he distinction between finding a match between an evidence sample and a suspect sample and finding a match between an evidence sample and one of many entries in a DNA profile databank

209. If there are T tickets and one winning ticket, then the probability that a randomly selected ticket is the winner is $p = 1/T$, and the probability that a set of N randomly selected tickets includes the winner is $N/T = Np$, where $1 \leq N \leq T$.

210. The analysis of the DNA database search is more complicated than the lottery example suggests. In the simple lottery, there was exactly one winner. In the database case, we do not know how many "winners" there are, or even if there are any. The situation is more like flipping a coin N times, where the coin has a probability p of heads on each independent toss.

211. *See* NRC II, *supra* note 1, at 163–65. Assuming that the individual who left the trace evidence sample is not in a database of unrelated people, the probability of at least one match is $1 - (1-p)N$, which is equal to or less than Np.

212. NRC II, *supra* note 1, at 161 (Recommendation 5.1). The DNA databases that are searched usually consist of profiles of offenders convicted of specified crimes. *See, e.g.*, Boling v. Romer, 101 F.3d 1336 (10th Cir. 1996); Rise v. Oregon, 59 F.3d 1556 (9th Cir. 1995); Jones v. Murray, 962 F.2d 302 (4th Cir. 1992); Landry v. Attorney General, 709 N.E.2d 1085 (Mass. 1999) (all rejecting constitutional challenges to compelling offenders to provide DNA samples for databases).

is important."[213] Rather than proposing a statistical adjustment to the match probability, however, that committee recommended using only a few loci in the databank search, then confirming the match with additional loci, and presenting only "the statistical frequency associated with the additional loci. . . ."[214]

A number of statisticians reject the committees' view that the random match probability should be inflated, either by a factor of N or by ignoring the loci used in the database search.[215] They argue that, if anything, the DNA evidence against the defendant is slightly stronger when not only has the defendant been shown to possess the incriminating profile, but also a large number of other individuals have been eliminated as possible sources of the crime scene DNA.[216] They conclude that no adjustment is required.

At its core, the statistical debate turns on how the problem is framed and what type of statistical reasoning is accepted as appropriate. The NAS committees ask how surprising it would be to find a match in a large database if the database does not contain the true source of the trace evidence. The more surprising the result, the more it appears that the database does contain the source. Because it would be more surprising to find a match in a test of a single innocent suspect than it would be to find a match by testing a large number of innocent suspects, the NAS committees conclude that the single-test match is more convincing evidence than the database search match.

The critics do not deny the mathematical truism that examining more innocent individuals increases the chance of finding a match, but they maintain that the committees have asked the wrong question. They emphasize that the question of interest to the legal system is not whether the database contains the culprit, but whether the one individual whose DNA matches the trace evidence DNA is the source of that trace; and they note that as the size of a database approaches that of the entire population, finding one and only one matching individual should be more, not less, convincing evidence against that person.[217] Thus, instead of looking at how surprising it would be to find a match in a group of innocent suspects, the "no-adjustment" school asks how much the result of the database search enhances the probability that the individual so identified is the source. They reason that the many exclusions in a database search reduce the number of people who might have left the trace evidence if

213. It used the same N*p* formula in a numerical example to show that "[t]he chance of finding a match in the second case is considerably higher, because one . . . fishes through the databank, trying out many hypotheses." NRC I, *supra* note 1, at 124.

214. *Id.* The second NAS Committee did not object to this procedure. It proposed the N*p* adjustment as an alternative that might be useful when there were very few typable loci in the trace evidence sample.

215. *E.g.*, Peter Donnelly & Richard D. Friedman, *DNA Database Searches and the Legal Consumption of Scientific Evidence*, 97 Mich. L. Rev. 931 (1999); authorities cited, *id.* at 933 n.13.

216. *Id.* at 933, 945, 948, 955, 957; Evett & Weir, *supra* note 174, at 219–22.

217. *See, e.g.*, Donnelly & Friedman, *supra* note 215, at 952–53.

the suspect did not. This additional information, they conclude, increases the likelihood that the defendant is the source, although the effect is indirect and generally small.[218]

C. Measures of Probative Value

Sufficiently small probabilities of a match for close relatives and unrelated members of the suspect population undermine the hypotheses of kinship and coincidence. Adequate safeguards and checks for possible laboratory error make that explanation of the finding of matching genotypes implausible. The inference that the defendant is the source of the crime scene DNA is then secure. But this mode of reasoning by elimination is not the only way to analyze DNA evidence. This section discusses two alternatives that some statisticians prefer—likelihoods and posterior probabilities. In the next section, we review all the statistics that relate to rival hypotheses and probative value and consider the legal doctrine that must be considered in deciding the admissibility of the various types of presentations.

1. Likelihood Ratios

To choose between two competing hypotheses, one can compare how probable the evidence is under each hypothesis. Suppose that the probability of a match in a well-run laboratory is close to 1 when the samples both contain only the defendant's DNA, while the probability of a coincidental match and the probability of a match with a close relative are close to 0. In these circumstances, the DNA profiling result strongly supports the claim that the defendant is the source, for the observed outcome—the match—is many times more probable when the defendant is the source than when someone else is. How many times more probable? Suppose that there is a 1% chance that the laboratory would miss a true match, so that the probability of its finding a match when the defendant is the source is 0.99. Suppose further that $p = 0.00001$ is the random match probability. Then the match is 0.99/0.00001, or 99,000 times more likely to be seen if the defendant is the source than if an unrelated individual is. Such a ratio is called a likelihood ratio, and a likelihood ratio of 99,000 means that the DNA profiling supports the claim of identity 99,000 times more strongly than it supports the hypothesis of coincidence.[219]

Likelihood ratios are particularly useful for VNTRs and for trace evidence samples that contain DNA from more than one person.[220] With VNTRs, the

218. *Id.* at 245.

219. *See* NRC II, *supra* note 1, at 100; Kaye, *supra* note 152.

220. *See supra* § V. Mixed samples arise in various ways—blood from two or more persons mingled at the scene of a crime, victim and assailant samples on a vaginal swab, semen from multiple sexual assailants, and so on. In many cases, one of the contributors—for example, the victim—is known, and

procedure commonly used to estimate the allele frequencies that are combined via some version of the product rule is called binning.[221] In the simplest and most accurate version, the laboratory first forms a "bin" that stretches across the range of fragment lengths in the match window surrounding an evidence band. For example, if a 1,000 base-pair (bp) band is seen in the evidence sample, and the laboratory's match window is ±5%, then the bin extends from 950 to 1,050 bp. The laboratory then finds the proportion of VNTR bands in its database that fall within this bin. If 7% of the bands in the database lie in the 950–1,050 bp range, then 7% is the estimated allele frequency for this band. The two-stage procedure of (1) declaring matches between two samples when all the corresponding bands lie within the match window and (2) estimating the frequency of a band in the population by the proportion that lie within the corresponding bin is known as match-binning.[222]

As noted in section VII.A, match-binning is statistically inefficient. It ignores the extent to which two samples match and gives the same coincidence probability to a close match as it does to a marginal one. Other methods obviate the need for matching by simultaneously combining the probability of the observed degree of matching with the probability of observing bands that are that close together. These "similarity likelihood ratios" dispense with the somewhat arbitrary dichotomy between matches and nonmatches.[223] They have been advocated on the ground that they make better use of the DNA data,[224] but they

the genetic profile of the unknown portion is readily deduced. In those situations, the analysis of a remaining single-person profile can proceed in the ordinary fashion. "However, when the contributors to a mixture are not known or cannot otherwise be distinguished, a likelihood-ratio approach offers a clear advantage and is particularly suitable." NRC II, *supra* note 1, at 129. *Contra* R.C. Lewontin, *Population Genetic Issues in the Forensic Use of DNA, in* 1 Modern Scientific Evidence, The Law and Science of Expert Testimony, *supra* note 53, § 17-5.0, at 703–05; Thompson, *supra* note 168, at 855–56. For an exposition of this likelihood ratio approach, see Evett & Weir, *supra* note 174, at 188–205.

221. There are two types of binning in use. *Floating bins* are conceptually simpler and more appropriate than *fixed bins*, but the latter can be justified as an approximation to the former. For the details of binning and suggestions for handling some of the complications that have caused disagreements over certain aspects of fixed bins, see NRC II, *supra* note 1, at 142–45.

222. Likelihood ratios for match-binning results are identical to those for discrete allele systems. If the bin frequencies reveal that a proportion p of the population has DNA whose bands each fall within the match window of the corresponding evidence bands, then the match-binning likelihood ratio is $1/p$.

223. The methods produce likelihood ratios tailored to the observed degree of matching. Two more or less "matching" bands would receive less weight when the measured band lengths differ substantially, and more weight when the lengths differ very little. Devlin & Roeder, *supra* note 154, § 18-3.1.4, at 724. And, bands that occur in a region where relatively few people have VNTRs contribute more to the likelihood ratio than if they occur in a zone where VNTRs are common.

224. *See* NRC II, *supra* note 1, at 161 ("VNTR data are essentially continuous, and, in principle, a continuous model should be used to analyze them."); authorities cited, *id.* at 200; A. Collins & N.E. Morton, *Likelihood Ratios for DNA Identification*, 91 Proc. Nat'l Acad. Sci. USA 6007 (1994); Devlin & Roeder, *supra* note 154, § 18-3.1.4, at 724.

have been attacked, primarily on the ground that they are complicated and difficult for nonstatisticians to understand.[225]

2. Posterior Probabilities

The likelihood ratio expresses the relative strength of an hypothesis, but the judge or jury ultimately must assess a different type of quantity—the probability of the hypothesis itself. An elementary rule of probability theory known as Bayes' theorem yields this probability. The theorem states that the odds in light of the data (here, the observed profiles) are the odds as they were known prior to receiving the data times the likelihood ratio: *posterior odds = likelihood ratio x prior odds*.[226] For example, if the relevant match probability[227] were 1/100,000, and if the chance that the laboratory would report a match between samples from the same source were 0.99, then the likelihood ratio would be 99,000, and the jury could be told how the DNA evidence raises various prior probabilities that the defendant's DNA is in the evidence sample.[228] It would be appropriate to explain that these calculations rest on many premises, including the premise that the genotypes have been correctly determined.[229]

One difficulty with this use of Bayes' theorem is that the computations consider only one alternative to the claim of identity at a time. As indicated in § VII(B), however, several rival hypotheses might apply in a given case. If it is not defendant's DNA in the forensic sample, is it from his father, his brother, his uncle, et cetera? Is the true source a member of the same subpopulation? A member of a different subpopulation in the same general population? In principle the likelihood ratio can be generalized to a likelihood function that takes on suitable values for every person in the world, and the prior probability for each person can be cranked into a general version of Bayes' rule to yield the posterior probability that the defendant is the source. In this vein, a few commentators suggest that Bayes' rule be used to combine the various likelihood

225. *E.g.*, Lewontin, *supra* note 220, § 17–5.0, at 705.

226. Odds and probabilities are two ways to express chances quantitatively. If the probability of an event is P, the odds are P/(1 – P). If the odds are O, the probability is O/(O + 1). For instance, if the probability of rain is 2/3, the odds of rain are 2 to 1 because (2/3) / (1 – 2/3) = (2/3) / (1/3) = 2. If the odds of rain are 2 to 1, then the probability is 2/(2 + 1) = 2/3.

227. By "relevant match probability," we mean the probability of a match given a specified type of kinship or the probability of a random match in the relevant suspect population. For relatives more distantly related than second cousins, the probability of a chance match is nearly as small as for persons of the same subpopulation. Devlin & Roeder, *supra* note 154, § 18–3.1.3, at 724.

228. For further discussion of how Bayes' rule might be used in court with DNA evidence, see, *e.g.*, Kaye, *supra* note 152; NRC II, *supra* note 1, at 201–03.

229. *See* Richard Lempert, *The Honest Scientist's Guide to DNA Evidence*, 96 Genetica 119 (1995). If the jury accepted these premises and also decided to accept the hypothesis of identity over those of kinship and coincidence, it still would be open to the defendant to offer explanations of how the forensic samples came to include his or her DNA even though he or she is innocent.

ratios for all possible degrees of kinship and subpopulations.[230] However, it is not clear how this ambitious proposal would be implemented.[231]

D. Which Probabilities or Statistics Should Be Presented?

Up to this point, we have described probabilities that can be used in evaluating the extent to which the discovery that the trace evidence sample contains DNA of the same type as the defendant's establishes that this DNA came from the defendant. We have concentrated on the methods that are available to compute the probabilities, and we have examined the concerns that have been voiced about the validity of these methods. This section discusses the legal question regarding which of the various scientifically defensible probabilities should be admissible in court. Assuming that the probabilities are computed according to a method that meets *Daubert*'s demand for scientific validity and reliability and thus satisfies Rule 702, the major issue arises under Rule 403: To what extent will the presentation assist the jury to understand the meaning of a match so that the jury can give the evidence the weight it deserves? This question involves psychology and law, and we summarize the assertions and analyses that have been offered with respect to the various probabilities and statistics that can be used to indicate the probative value of DNA evidence.

1. Should Match Probabilities Be Excluded?

Are small frequencies or probabilities inherently prejudicial? The most common form of expert testimony about matching DNA takes the form of an explanation of how the laboratory ascertained that the defendant's DNA has the profile of the forensic sample plus an estimate of the profile frequency or random match probability. Many arguments have been offered against this entrenched practice. First, it has been suggested that jurors do not understand probabilities in general,[232] and infinitesimal match probabilities[233] will so bedazzle jurors that they will not appreciate the other evidence in the case or any innocent explanations for the

230. *See* Balding & Donnelly, *supra* note 174.

231. A related proposal in Lempert, *supra* note 166, suffers from the same difficulty of articulating the composition of the suspect population and the prior probabilities for its members. Professor Lempert reasons that "the relevant match statistic, if it could be derived, is an average that turns on the number of people in the suspect population and a likelihood that each has DNA matching the defendant's DNA, weighted by the probability that each committed the crime if the defendant did not." *Id.* at 458. He concludes that although this "weighted average statistic" does not directly state how likely it is "that the defendant and not some third party committed the crime," it is superior to "the 'random man' match statistic" in that it "tells the jury how surprising it would be to find a DNA match if the defendant is innocent." *Id.*

232. *E.g.*, R.C. Lewontin, *Forensic DNA Typing Dispute*, 372 Nature 398 (1994).

233. There have been cases in which the reported population frequencies are measured in the billionths or even trillionths. *E.g.*, Perry v. State, 606 So. 2d 224, 225 (Ala. Crim. App. 1992) ("one in 12

match.[234] Empirical research into this hypothesis has been limited and inconclusive,[235] and remedies short of exclusion are available.[236] Thus, no jurisdiction currently excludes all match probabilities on this basis.[237]

A more sophisticated variation on this theme is that the jury will misconstrue the random match probability—by thinking that it gives the probability that the match is random.[238] Suppose that the random match probability *p* is some very small number such as one in a billion. The words are almost identical, but the probabilities can be quite different. The random match probability is the probability that (A) the requisite genotype is in the sample from the individual tested *if* (B) the individual tested has been selected at random. In contrast, the probability that the match is random is the probability that (B) the individual tested has been selected at random *given that* (A) the individual has the requisite genotype. In general, for two events A and B, P(A *given* B) does not equal P(B *given*

billion"); Snowden v. State, 574 So. 2d 960, 960 (Ala. Crim. App. 1990) ("'approximately one in eleven billion,' with a 'minimum value' of one in 2.5 billion and a 'maximum' value of one in 27 trillion"); State v. Bible, 858 P.2d 1152, 1191 (Ariz. 1993) (between one in 60 million and one in 14 billion); State v. Daughtry, 459 S.E.2d 747, 758–59 (N.C. 1995) ("one in 5.5 billion for each of the caucasion, African-American, and Lumbee populations in North Carolina"); State v. Buckner, 890 P.2d 460, 460 (Wash. 1995) ("one Caucasian in 19.25 billion").

234. *Cf.* Government of the Virgin Islands v. Byers, 941 F. Supp. 513, 527 (D.V.I. 1996) ("Vanishingly small probabilities of a random match may tend to establish guilt in the minds of jurors and are particularly suspect."); Commonwealth v. Curnin, 565 N.E.2d 440, 441 (Mass. 1991) ("evidence of this nature [a random-match probability of 1 in 59 million] . . . , having an aura of infallibility, must have a strong impact on a jury").

235. *See* NRC II, *supra* note 1, at 197; Jason Schklar & Shari Seidman Diamond, *Juror Reactions to DNA Evidence: Errors and Expectancies*, 23 Law & Hum. Behav. 159, 181–82 (1999).

236. Suitable cross-examination, defense experts, and jury instructions might reduce the risk that small estimates of the match probability will produce an unwarranted sense of certainty and lead a jury to disregard other evidence. NRC II, *supra* note 1, at 197

237. *E.g.*, United States v. Chischilly, 30 F.3d 1144 (9th Cir. 1994) (citing cases); Martinez v. State, 549 So. 2d 694, 694–95 (Fla. Dist. Ct. App. 1989) (rejecting the argument that testimony that "one individual in 234 billion" would have the same banding pattern was "so overwhelming as to deprive the jury of its function"); State v. Weeks, 891 P.2d 477, 489 (Mont. 1995) (rejecting the argument that "the exaggerated opinion of the accuracy of DNA testing is prejudicial, as juries would give undue weight and deference to the statistical evidence" and "that the probability aspect of the DNA analysis invades the province of the jury to decide the guilt or innocence of the defendant"); State v. Schweitzer, 533 N.W.2d 156, 160 (S.D. 1995) (reviewing cases).

238. Numerous opinions or experts present the random match probability in this manner. Compare the problematic characterizations in, *e.g.*, *United States v. Martinez*, 3 F.2d 1191, 1194 (8th Cir. 1993) (referring to "a determination of the probability that someone other than the contributor of the known sample could have contributed the unknown sample"), and *State v. Foster*, 910 P.2d 848 (Kan. 1996) (a DNA analyst testified that "the probability of another person in the Caucasian population having the same banding pattern was 1 in 100,000"), with the more accurate comments of an FBI examiner in *State v. Freeman*, No. A-95-1027, 1996 WL 608328, at *7 (Neb. Ct. App. Oct. 22, 1996), *aff'd*, 571 N.W.2d 276 (Neb. 1997), that "[t]he probability of randomly selecting an unrelated individual from the Caucasian population who would have the same DNA profile as I observed in the K2 sample for Mr. Freeman was approximately one in 15 million." For more examples of mischaracterizations of the random match probability, see cases and authorities cited, NRC II, *supra* note 1, at 198 n.92.

A). The claim that it does is known as the fallacy of the transposed conditional.[239]

To appreciate that the equation is fallacious, consider the probability that a lawyer picked at random from all lawyers in the United States is a federal judge. This "random judge probability" is practically zero. But the probability that a person randomly selected from the current federal judiciary is a lawyer is one. The "random judge probability" P(judge *given* lawyer) does not equal the transposed probability P(lawyer *given* judge). Likewise, the random match probability P(genotype *given* unrelated source) does not necessarily equal P(unrelated source *given* genotype).

To avoid this fallacious reasoning by jurors, some defense counsel have urged the exclusion of random match probabilities, and some prosecutors have suggested that it is desirable to avoid testimony or argument about probabilities, and instead to present the statistic as a simple frequency—an indication of how rare the genotype is in the relevant population.[240] The 1996 NRC report noted that "few courts or commentators have recommended the exclusion of evidence merely because of the risk that jurors will transpose a conditional probability,"[241] and it observed that "[t]he available research indicates that jurors may be more likely to be swayed by the 'defendant's fallacy' than by the 'prosecutor's fallacy.' When advocates present both fallacies to mock jurors, the defendant's fallacy dominates."[242] Furthermore, the committee suggested that "if the initial presentation of the probability figure, cross-examination, and opposing testimony all fail to clarify the point, the judge can counter both fallacies by appropriate instructions to the jurors that minimize the possibility of cognitive errors."[243]

239. It is also called the "inverse fallacy," or the "prosecutor's fallacy." The latter expression is rare in the statistical literature, but it is common in the legal literature on statistical evidence. For an exposition of related errors, see Koehler, *supra* note 161.

240. George W. Clark, *Effective Use of DNA Evidence in Jury Trials*, Profiles in DNA, Aug. 1997, at 7, 8 ("References to probabilities should normally be avoided, inasmuch as such descriptions are frequently judicially equated with disfavored "probabilities of guilt. . . . [T]he purpose of frequency data is simply to provide the factfinder with a guide to the relative rarity of a DNA match . . . .").

241. NRC II, *supra* note 1, at 198 (citing McCormick on Evidence, *supra* note 11, § 212).

242. *Id.* The "defendant's fallacy" consists of dismissing or undervaluing the matches with high likelihood ratios because other matches are to be expected in unrealistically large populations of potential suspects. For example, defense counsel might argue that (1) even with a random match probability of one in a million, we would expect to find ten unrelated people with the requisite genotypes in a population of 10 million; (2) the defendant just happens to be one of these ten, which means that the chances are nine out of ten that someone unrelated to the defendant is the source; so (3) the DNA evidence does nothing to incriminate the defendant. The problem with this argument is that in a case involving both DNA and non-DNA evidence against the defendant, it is unrealistic to assume that there are 10 million equally likely suspects.

243. *Id.* (footnote omitted). The committee suggested the following instruction to define the random match probability:

> In evaluating the expert testimony on the DNA evidence, you were presented with a number indicating the

To date, no federal court has excluded a random match probability (or, for that matter, an estimate of the small frequency of a DNA profile in the general population) as unfairly prejudicial just because the jury might misinterpret it as a posterior probability that the defendant is the source of the forensic DNA. One court, however, noted the need to have the concept "properly explained,"[244] and prosecutorial misrepresentations of the random match probabilities for other types of evidence have produced reversals.[245]

Are small match probabilities irrelevant? Second, it has been maintained that match probabilities are logically irrelevant when they are far smaller than the probability of a frame-up, a blunder in labeling samples, cross-contamination, or other events that would yield a false positive.[246] The argument is that the jury should concern itself only with the chance that the forensic sample is reported to match the defendant's profile even though the defendant is not the source. Such a report could happen either because another person who is the source of the forensic sample has the same profile or because fraud or error of a kind that falsely incriminates the defendant occurs in the collection, handling, or analysis of the DNA samples. Match probabilities do not express this chance of a match being reported when the defendant is not the source unless the probability of a false-positive report is essentially zero.

Both theoretical and practical rejoinders to this argument about relevance have been given. At the theoretical level, some scientists question a procedure that would prevent the jury from reasoning in a stepwise, eliminative fashion. In their view, a rational juror might well want to know that the chance that another person selected at random from the suspect population has the incriminating genotype is negligible, for this would enable the juror to eliminate the hy-

> probability that another individual drawn at random from the [specify] population would coincidentally have the same DNA profile as the [blood stain, semen stain, etc.]. That number, which assumes that no sample mishandling or laboratory error occurred, indicates how distinctive the DNA profile is. It does not by itself tell you the probability that the defendant is innocent.

Id. at 198 n.93. *But see* D.H. Kaye, *The Admissibility of "Probability Evidence" in Criminal Trials—Part II*, 27 Jurimetrics J. 160, 168 (1987) ("Nevertheless, because even without misguided advice from counsel, the temptation to compute the probability of criminal identity [by transposition] seems strong, and because the characterization of the population proportion as a [random match probability] does little to make the evidence more intelligible, it might be best to bar the prosecution from having its expert state the probability of a coincidental misidentification, as opposed to providing [a simpler] estimate of the population proportion.").

244. United States v. Shea, 957 F. Supp. 331, 345 (D.N.H. 1997).

245. *E.g.*, United States v. Massey, 594 F.2d 676, 681 (8th Cir. 1979) (in closing argument about hair evidence, "the prosecutor 'confuse[d] the probability of concurrence of the identifying marks with the probability of mistaken identification'").

246. *E.g.*, Jonathan J. Koehler et al., *The Random Match Probability in DNA Evidence: Irrelevant and Prejudicial?*, 35 Jurimetrics J. 201 (1995); Lewontin & Hartl, *supra* note 184, at 1749 ("probability estimates like 1 in 738,000,000,000,000 . . . are terribly misleading because the rate of laboratory error is not taken into account").

potheses of kinship or coincidence.[247] If the juror concludes that there is little chance that the same genotype would exist in the forensic sample if the DNA originated from anyone but the defendant, then the juror can proceed to consider whether that genotype is present because someone has tried to frame the defendant, or whether it is not really present but was reported to be there because DNA samples were mishandled or misanalyzed.[248] These probabilities, they add, are not amenable to objective modeling and should not be mixed with probabilities that are derived from verifiable models of genetics.[249]

At the practical level, there is disagreement about the adequacy of the estimates that have been proposed to express the probability of a false positive result. The opponents of match probabilities usually argue that an error rate somewhat higher than that observed in a series of proficiency tests should be substituted for the match probability,[250] but the extent to which any such figure applies to the case at bar has been questioned.[251] No reported cases have excluded statistics on proficiency tests administered at a specific laboratory as too far removed from the case at bar to be relevant,[252] but neither has it been held that these statistics must be used in place of random match or kinship probabilities.[253]

247. *E.g.*, NRC II, *supra* note 1, at 85; NRC I, *supra* note 1, at 88; Russell Higuchi, *Human Error in Forensic DNA Typing*, 48 Am. J. Hum. Genetics 1215 (1991) (letter). Of course, if the defense were to stipulate that a true DNA match establishes identity, there would be no need for probabilities that would help the jury to reject the rival hypotheses of coincidence or kinship.

248. *E.g.*, Devlin & Roeder, *supra* note 154, § 18–5.3, at 743–44 ("One way to handle the possibility of a laboratory error, which follows the usual presentation of similar types of evidence, is to present the evidence in two stages: Does the evidence suggest that the samples were obtained from the same individual? If so, is there a harmless reason? Either formal calculations or informal analysis could be used to evaluate the possibility of a laboratory error, both of which should be predicated on the facts of the specific case.").

249. *E.g.*, Morton, *supra* note 159, at 480–81; *cf.* NRC I, *supra* note 1, at 88 ("Coincidental identity and laboratory error are different phenomena, so the two cannot and should not be combined in a single estimate.").

250. *But see* Thompson, *supra* note 69, at 417 (suggesting that "DNA evidence" should be excluded as "unacceptable scientifically if the probability of an erroneous match cannot be quantified").

251. *See, e.g.*, David J. Balding, *Errors and Misunderstandings in the Second NRC Report*, 37 Jurimetrics J. 469, 475–76, 476 n.21 (1997) ("report[ing] a match probability which adds error rates to profile frequencies . . . would clearly be unacceptable since overall error rates are not directly relevant: jurors must assess on the basis of the evidence presented to them the chance that an error has occurred in the particular case at hand," but "[e]rror rates observed in blind trials may well be helpful to jurors"); Berger, *supra* note 69. *But cf.* Thompson, *supra* note 69, at 421 ("While it makes little sense to present a single number derived from proficiency tests as *the* error rate in every case, it makes less sense to exclude quantitative estimates of the error altogether.").

252. *But see* United States v. Shea, 957 F. Supp. 331, 344 n.42 (D.N.H. 1997) ("The parties assume that error rate information is admissible at trial. This assumption may well be incorrect. Even though a laboratory or industry error rate may be logically relevant, a strong argument can be made that such evidence is barred by Fed. R. Evid. 404 because it is inadmissible propensity evidence.").

253. *See* Armstead v. State, 673 A.2d 221 (Md. 1996) (rejecting the argument that the introduction of a random match probability deprives the defendant of due process because the error rate on proficiency

Are match probabilities unfairly prejudicial when they are smaller than the probability of laboratory error? It can be argued that very small match probabilities are relevant but unfairly prejudicial. Such prejudice could occur if the jury did not simply use a small match probability to reject the hypotheses of coincidence or kinship, but was so impressed with this single number that it neglected or underweighted the probability of a match arising due to a false-positive laboratory error.[254] Some commentators believe that this prejudice is so likely and so serious that "jurors ordinarily should receive *only* the laboratory's false positive rate . . . ."[255] The 1996 NRC report is skeptical of this view, especially when the defendant has had a meaningful opportunity to retest the DNA at a laboratory of his or her choice, and it suggests that judicial instructions can be crafted to avoid this form of prejudice.[256]

Are small match probabilities unfairly prejudicial when not accompanied by an estimated probability of a laboratory error? Rather than excluding small match probabilities entirely, a court might require the expert who presents them also to report a probability that the laboratory is mistaken about the profiles.[257] Of course, some experts would deny that they can provide a meaningful statistic for the case at hand, but they could report the results of proficiency tests and leave it to the jury to use this figure as best it can in considering whether a false-positive error has occurred.[258] To assist the jury in making sense of two num-

tests is many orders of magnitude greater than the match probability); Williams v. State, 679 A.2d 1106 (Md. 1996) (reversing because the trial court restricted cross-examination about the results of proficiency tests involving other DNA analysts at the same laboratory).

254. *E.g.*, Koehler et al., *supra* note 246; Thompson, *supra* note 69, at 421–22.

255. Richard Lempert, *Some Caveats Concerning DNA as Criminal Identification Evidence: With Thanks to the Reverend Bayes*, 13 Cardozo L. Rev. 303, 325 (1991) (emphasis added); *see also* Lempert, *supra* note 166, at 447; Scheck, *supra* note 69, at 1997.

256. NRC II, *supra* note 1, at 199 (notes omitted):

> The argument that jurors will make better use of a single figure for the probability that an innocent suspect would be reported to match has never been tested adequately. The argument for a single figure is weak in light of this lack of research into how jurors react to different ways of presenting statistical information, and its weakness is compounded by the grave difficulty of estimating a false-positive error rate in any given case. But efforts should be made to fill the glaring gap in empirical studies of such matters.

The district court in *United States v. Shea*, 957 F. Supp. 331, 334–45 (D.N.H. 1997), discussed some of the available research and rejected the argument that separate figures for match and error probabilities are prejudicial. For more recent research, see Schklar & Diamond, *supra* note 235, at 179 (concluding that separate figures are desirable in that "[j]urors . . . may need to know the disaggregated elements that influence the aggregated estimate as well as how they were combined in order to evaluate the DNA test results in the context of their background beliefs and the other evidence introduced at trial").

257. Koehler, *supra* note 155, at 229 ("A good argument can be made for requiring DNA laboratories to provide fact finders with conservatively high estimates of their false positive error rates when they provide evidence about genetic matches. By the same token, laboratories should be required to divulge their estimated false negative error rate in cases where exclusions are reported."). This argument has prevailed in a few cases. *E.g.*, United States v. Porter, Crim. No. F06277-89, 1994 WL 742297 (D.C. Super. Ct. Nov. 17, 1994) (mem.). Other courts have rejected it. *E.g.*, United States v. Lowe, 954 F. Supp. 401, 415 (D. Mass. 1997), *aff'd*, 145 F.3d 45 (1st Cir. 1998).

258. *See* NRC I, *supra* note 1, at 94 ("Laboratory error rates should be measured with appropriate

bers, however, it has been suggested that an expert take the additional step of reporting how the probability that a matching genotype would be found coincidentally *or* erroneously changes given the random match probability and various values for the probability of a false-positive error.[259]

2. *Should Likelihood Ratios Be Excluded?*

Likelihood ratios associated with DNA evidence were discussed in section VII.C.1. The 1996 NRC Report offers the following analysis of their admissibility:

> Although LRs [likelihood ratios] are rarely introduced in criminal cases, we believe that they are appropriate for explaining the significance of data and that existing statistical knowledge is sufficient to permit their computation. None of the LRs that have been devised for VNTRs can be dismissed as clearly unreasonable or based on principles not generally accepted in the statistical community. Therefore, legal doctrine suggests that LRs should be admissible unless they are so unintelligible that they provide no assistance to a jury or so misleading that they are unduly prejudicial. As with frequencies and match probabilities, prejudice might exist because the proposed LRs do not account for laboratory error, and a jury might misconstrue even a modified version that did account for it as a statement of the odds in favor of S [the claim that the defendant is the source of the forensic DNA sample]. [But] the possible misinterpretation of LRs as the odds in favor of identity . . . is a question of jury ability and performance to which existing research supplies no clear answer.[260]

proficiency tests and should play a role in the interpretation of results of forensic DNA typing. . . . A laboratory's overall rate of incorrect conclusions due to error should be reported with, but separately from, the probability of coincidental matches in the population. Both should be weighed in evaluating evidence."); NRC II, *supra* note 1, at 87 ("[A] calculation that combines error rates with match probabilities is inappropriate. The risk of error is properly considered case by case, taking into account the record of the laboratory performing the tests, the extent of redundancy, and the overall quality of the results."). The district court in *Government of the Virgin Islands v. Byers*, 941 F. Supp. 513 (D.V.I. 1996), declined to require proficiency test results as a precondition for admissibility. *See also* Berger, *supra* note 69, at 1093 ("the rationale for [requiring the prosecution to introduce a pooled error rate] is weak, and . . . such a shift would be inconsistent with significant evidentiary policies").

259. *See* Thompson, *supra* note 69, at 421–22 (footnote omitted):

> For example, an expert could say that if the probability of a random match is .00000001 and the probability of an erroneous match is .001, then the overall probability of a false match is approximately .001. . . . If the probability of an erroneous match is unclear or controversial (as it undoubtedly will be in many cases), then illustrative combinations could be performed for a range of hypothetical probabilities.

This procedure could lead to arguments about the relevance of the values for the "probability of an erroneous match." Depending on such factors as the record of the laboratory on proficiency tests, the precautions observed in processing the samples, and the availability of the samples for independent testing, the prosecution could contend that the .001 figure in this example has no foundation in the evidence.

260. NRC II, *supra* note 1, at 200–01. A footnote adds that:

> Likelihood ratios were used in State v. Klindt, 389 N.W.2d 670 (Iowa 1986) . . . , and are admitted routinely in parentage litigation, where they are known as the 'paternity index' . . . . Some state statutes use them to create a presumption of paternity . . . . The practice of providing a paternity index has been carried over into criminal cases in which genetic parentage is used to indicate the identity of the perpetrator of an offense. . . . .

Id. at 200 n.97.

Notwithstanding the lack of adequate empirical research, other commentators believe that the danger of prejudice (in the form of the transposition fallacy) warrants the exclusion of likelihood ratios.[261]

3. Should Posterior Probabilities Be Excluded?

Match probabilities state the chance that certain genotypes would be present conditioned on specific hypotheses about the source of the DNA (a specified relative, or an unrelated individual in a population or subpopulation). Likelihood ratios express the relative support that the presence of the genotypes in the defendant gives to these hypotheses compared to the claim that the defendant is the source. Posterior probabilities or odds express the chance that the defendant is the source (conditioned on various assumptions). These probabilities, if they are meaningful and accurate, would be of great value to the jury.

Experts have been heard to testify to posterior probabilities. In *Smith v. Deppish*,[262] for example, the state's "DNA experts informed the jury that . . . there was more than a 99 percent probability that Smith was a contributor of the semen,"[263] but how such numbers are obtained is not apparent. If they are instances of the transposition fallacy, then they are scientifically invalid (and objectionable under Rule 702) and unfairly prejudicial (under Rule 403).

However, a meaningful posterior probability can be computed with Bayes' theorem.[264] Ideally, one would enumerate every person in the suspect population, specify the prior odds that each is the source of the forensic DNA and weight those prior odds by the likelihoods (taking into account the familial relationship of each possible suspect to the defendant) to arrive at the posterior odds that the defendant is the source of the forensic sample. But this hardly seems practical. The 1996 NRC Report therefore discusses a somewhat different implementation of Bayes' theorem. Assuming that the hypotheses of kinship and error could be dismissed on the basis of other evidence, the report focuses on "the variable-prior-odds method," by which:

> an expert neither uses his or her own prior odds nor demands that jurors formulate their prior odds for substitution into Bayes's rule. Rather, the expert presents the jury with a

261. *See* Koehler, *supra* note 168, at 880; Thompson, *supra* note 168, at 850; *cf.* Koehler et al., *supra* note 246 (proposing the use of a likelihood ratio that incorporates laboratory error).

262. 807 P.2d 144 (Kan. 1991).

263. *See also* Thomas v. State, 830 S.W.2d 546, 550 (Mo. Ct. App. 1992) (a geneticist testified that "the likelihood that the DNA found in Marion's panties came from the defendant was higher than 99.99%"); Commonwealth v. Crews, 640 A.2d 395, 402 (Pa. 1994) (an FBI examiner who at a preliminary hearing had estimated a coincidental-match probability for a VNTR match "at three of four loci" reported at trial that the match made identity "more probable than not").

264. *See supra* § VII.C.2.

table or graph showing how the posterior probability changes as a function of the prior probability.[265]

This procedure, it observes, "has garnered the most support among legal scholars and is used in some civil cases."[266] Nevertheless, "very few courts have considered its merits in criminal cases."[267] In the end, the report concludes:

> How much it would contribute to jury comprehension remains an open question, especially considering the fact that for most DNA evidence, computed values of the likelihood ratio (conditioned on the assumption that the reported match is a true match) would swamp any plausible prior probability and result in a graph or table that would show a posterior probability approaching 1 except for very tiny prior probabilities.[268]

E. Which Verbal Expressions of Probative Value Should Be Presented?

Having surveyed various views about the admissibility of the probabilities and statistics indicative of the probative value of DNA evidence, we turn to a related issue that can arise under Rules 702 and 403: Should an expert be permitted to offer a non-numerical judgment about the DNA profiles?

Inasmuch as most forms of expert testimony involve qualitative rather than quantitative testimony, this may seem an odd question. Yet, many courts have held that a DNA match is inadmissible unless the expert attaches a scientifically valid number to the figure.[269] In reaching this result, some courts cite the statement in the 1992 NRC report that "[t]o say that two patterns match, without providing any scientifically valid estimate (or, at least, an upper bound) of the frequency with which such matches might occur by chance, is meaningless."[270]

265. NRC II, *supra* note 1, at 202 (footnote omitted).

266. *Id.*

267. *Id.* (footnote omitted).

268. *Id.* For arguments said to show that the variable-prior-odds proposal is "a bad idea," see Thompson, *supra* note 69, at 422–23.

269. *E.g.*, Commonwealth v. Daggett, 622 N.E.2d 272, 275 n.4 (Mass. 1993) (plurality opinion insisting that "[t]he point is not that this court should require a numerical frequency, but that the scientific community clearly does"); State v. Carter, 524 N.W.2d 763, 783 (Neb. 1994) ("evidence of a DNA match will not be admissible if it has not been accompanied by statistical probability evidence that has been calculated from a generally accepted method"); State v. Cauthron, 846 P.2d 502 (Wash. 1993) ("probability statistics" must accompany testimony of a match); *cf.* Commonwealth v. Crews, 640 A.2d 395, 402 (Pa. 1994) ("The factual evidence of the physical testing of the DNA samples and the matching alleles, even without statistical conclusions, tended to make appellant's presence more likely than it would have been without the evidence, and was therefore relevant.").

270. NRC I, *supra* note 1, at 74. For criticism of this statement, see Kaye, *supra* note 195, at 381–82 (footnote omitted):

> [I]t would not be 'meaningless' to inform the jury that two samples match and that this match makes it more probable, in an amount that is not precisely known, that the DNA in the samples comes from the same person. Nor, when all estimates of the frequency are in the millionths or billionths, would it be meaningless

The 1996 report phrases the scientific question somewhat differently. Like the 1992 report, it states that "[b]efore forensic experts can conclude that DNA testing has the power to help identify the source of an evidence sample, it must be shown that the DNA characteristics vary among people. Therefore, it would not be scientifically justifiable to speak of a match as proof of identity in the absence of underlying data that permit some reasonable estimate of how rare the matching characteristics actually are."[271] However, the 1996 report then explains that "determining whether quantitative estimates should be presented to a jury is a different issue. Once science has established that a methodology has some individualizing power, the legal system must determine whether and how best to import that technology into the trial process."[272]

Since the loci typically used in forensic DNA identification have been shown to have substantial individualizing power, it is scientifically sound to introduce evidence of matching profiles. Nonetheless, even evidence that meets the scientific soundness standard of *Daubert* is not admissible if its prejudicial effect clearly outweighs its probative value. Unless some reasonable explanation accompanies testimony that two profiles match, it is surely arguable that the jury will have insufficient guidance to give the scientific evidence the weight that is deserves.[273]

Instead of presenting frequencies or match probabilities obtained with quantitative methods, however, a scientist would be justified in characterizing every four-locus VNTR profile, for instance, as "rare," "extremely rare," or the like.[274] At least one state supreme court has endorsed this qualitative approach as a substitute to the presentation of more debatable numerical estimates.[275]

The most extreme case of a purely verbal description of the infrequency of a profile arises when that profile can be said to be unique. The 1992 report cautioned that "an expert should—given . . . the relatively small number of loci

to inform the jury that there is a match that is known to be extremely rare in the general population. Courts may reach differing results on the legal propriety of qualitative as opposed to quantitative assessments, but they only fool themselves when they act as if scientific opinion automatically dictates the correct answer.

271. NRC II, *supra* note 1, at 192. As indicated in earlier sections, these "underlying data" have been collected and analyzed for many genetic systems.

272. *Id.*

273. *Id.* at 193 ("Certainly, a judge's or juror's untutored impression of how unusual a DNA profile is could be very wrong. This possibility militates in favor of going beyond a simple statement of a match, to give the trier of fact some expert guidance about its probative value.").

274. *Cf. id.* at 195 ("Although different jurors might interpret the same words differently, the formulas provided . . . produce frequency estimates for profiles of three or more loci that almost always can be conservatively described as 'rare.'").

275. State v. Bloom, 516 N.W.2d 159, 166–67 (Minn. 1994) ("Since it may be pointless to expect ever to reach a consensus on how to estimate, with any degree of precision, the probability of a random match, and that given the great difficulty in educating the jury as to precisely what that figure means and does not mean, it might make sense to simply try to arrive at a fair way of explaining the significance of the match in a verbal, qualitative, non-quantitative, nonstatistical way."); *see also* Kenneth R. Kreiling, Review-Comment, *DNA Technology in Forensic Science*, 33 Jurimetrics J. 449 (1993).

used and the available population data—avoid assertions in court that a particular genotype is unique in the population."[276] Following this advice in the context of a profile derived from a handful of single-locus VNTR probes, several courts initially held that assertions of uniqueness are inadmissible,[277] while others found such testimony less troublesome.[278]

With the advent of more population data and loci, the 1996 NRC report pointedly observed that "we are approaching the time when many scientists will wish to offer opinions about the source of incriminating DNA."[279] Of course, the uniqueness of any object, from a snowflake to a fingerprint, in a population that cannot be enumerated never can be proved directly. The committee therefore wrote that "[t]here is no 'bright-line' standard in law or science that can pick out exactly how small the probability of the existence of a given profile in more than one member of a population must be before assertions of uniqueness are justified . . . . There might already be cases in which it is defensible for an expert to assert that, assuming that there has been no sample mishandling or laboratory error, the profile's probable uniqueness means that the two DNA samples come from the same person."[280]

276. NRC I, *supra* note 1, at 92.

277. *See* State v. Hummert, 905 P.2d 493 (Ariz. Ct. App. 1994), *rev'd*, 933 P.2d 1187 (1997); State v. Cauthron, 846 P.2d 502, 516 (Wash. 1993) (experts presented no "probability statistics" but claimed that the DNA could not have come from anyone else on earth), *overruled*, State v. Copeland, 922 P.2d 1304 (Wash. 1996); State v. Buckner, 890 P.2d 460, 462 (Wash. 1995) (testimony that the profile "would occur in only one Caucasian in 19.25 billion" and that because "this figure is almost four times the present population of the Earth, the match was unique" was improper), *aff'd on reconsideration*, 941 P.2d 667 (Wash. 1997).

278. State v. Zollo, 654 A.2d 359, 362 (Conn. App. Ct. 1995) (testimony that the chance "that the DNA sample came from someone other than the defendant was 'so small that . . . it would not be worth considering'" was not inadmissible as an opinion on an ultimate issue in the case "because his opinion could reasonably have aided the jury in understanding the [complex] DNA testimony"); Andrews v. State, 533 So. 2d 841, 849 (Fla. Ct. App. 1988) (geneticist "concluded that to a reasonable degree of scientific certainty, appellant's DNA was present in the vaginal smear taken from the victim"); People v. Heaton, 640 N.E.2d 630, 633 (Ill. App. Ct. 1994) (an expert who used the product rule to estimate the frequency at 1/52,600 testified over objection to his opinion that the "defendant was the donor of the semen"); State v. Pierce, No. 89-CA-30, 1990 WL 97596, at *2–3 (Ohio Ct. App. July 9, 1990) (affirming admission of testimony that the probability would be one in 40 billion "that the match would be to a random occurrence," and "[t]he DNA is from the same individual"), *aff'd*, 597 N.E.2d 107 (Ohio 1992); *cf.* State v. Bogan, 905 P.2d 515, 517 (Ariz. Ct. App. 1995) (it was proper to allow a molecular biologist to testify, on the basis of a PCR-based analysis that he "was confident the seed pods found in the truck originated from" a palo verde tree near a corpse); Commonwealth v. Crews, 640 A.2d 395, 402 (Pa. 1994) (testimony of an FBI examiner that he did not know of a single instance "where different individuals that are unrelated have been shown to have matching DNA profiles for three or four probes" was admissible under *Frye* despite an objection to the lack of a frequency estimate, which had been given at a preliminary hearing as 1/400).

279. NRC II, *supra* note 1, at 194.

280. As an illustration, the committee cited *State v. Bloom*, 516 N.W.2d 159, 160 n.2 (Minn. 1994), a case in which a respected population geneticist was prepared to testify that "in his opinion the nine-locus match constituted 'overwhelming evidence that, to a reasonable degree of scientific certainty, the

The report concludes that "[b]ecause the difference between a vanishingly small probability and an opinion of uniqueness is so slight, courts may choose to allow the latter along with, or instead of the former, when the scientific findings support such testimony."[281] Confronted with an objection to an assertion of uniqueness, a court may need to verify that a large number of sufficiently polymorphic loci have been tested.[282]

DNA from the victim's vaginal swab came from the [defendant], to the exclusion of all others.'" NRC II, *supra* note 1, at 194–95 n.84. *See also* People v. Hickey, 687 N.E.2d 910, 917 (Ill. 1997) (given the results of nine VNTR probes plus PCR-based typing, two experts testified that a semen sample originated from the defendant).

281. NRC II, *supra* note 1, at 195. If an opinion as to uniqueness were simply tacked on to a statistical presentation, it might be challenged as cumulative. *Cf. id.* ("Opinion testimony about uniqueness would simplify the presentation of evidence by dispensing with specific estimates of population frequencies or probabilities. If the basis of an opinion were attacked on statistical grounds, however, or if frequency or probability estimates were admitted, this advantage would be lost.").

282. The NAS committee merely suggested that a sufficiently small random match probability compared to the earth's population could justify a conclusion of uniqueness. The committee did not propose any single figure, but asked: "Does a profile frequency of the reciprocal of twice the earth's population suffice? Ten times? One hundred times?" *Id.* at 194. Another approach would be to consider the probability of recurrence in a close relative. *Cf.* Belin et al., *supra* note 171.

The FBI uses a slightly complex amalgam of such approaches. Rather than ask whether a profile probably is unique in the world's population, the examiner focuses on smaller populations that might be the source of the evidentiary DNA. When the surrounding evidence does not point to any particular ethnic group, the analyst takes the random match probability and multiplies it by ten (to account for any uncertainty due to population structure). The analyst then asks what the probability of generating a population of unrelated people as large as that of the entire U.S. (290 million people) that contains no duplicate of the evidentiary profile would be. If that "no-duplication" probability is one percent or less, the examiner must report that the suspect "is the source of the DNA obtained from [the evidentiary] specimen . . . ." Memorandum from Jenifer A.L. Smith to Laboratory, Oct. 1, 1997, at 3. Similarly, the FBI computes the no-duplication probability in each ethnic or racial subgroup that may be of interest. If that probability is 1% or less, the examiner must report that the suspect is the source of the DNA. *Id.* Finally, if the examiner thinks that a close relative could be the source, and these individuals cannot be tested, standard genetic formulae are used to find the probability of the same profile in a close relative, that probability is multiplied by ten, and the resulting no-duplication probability for a small family (generally ten or fewer individuals) is computed. Once again, if the no-duplication probability is no more than 1%, the examiner reports that the suspect is the source. *Id.* at 3–4. In an apparent genuflection to older cases requiring testifying physicians to have "a reasonable degree of medical certainty," the analyst must add the phrase "to a reasonable degree of scientific certainty" to the ultimate opinion that the suspect is the source. *Id.* at 2–4. This type of testimony is questioned in Evett & Weir, *supra* note 174, at 244.

VIII. Novel Applications of DNA Technology

Most routine applications of DNA technology in the forensic setting involve the identification of human beings— suspects in criminal cases, missing persons, or victims of mass disasters. However, inasmuch as DNA technology can be applied to the analysis of any kind of biological evidence containing DNA, and because the technology is advancing rapidly, unusual applications are inevitable. In cases in which the evidentiary DNA is of human origin, new methods of analyzing DNA will come into at least occasional use, and new loci or DNA polymorphisms will be used for forensic work. In other cases, the evidentiary DNA will come from non-human organisms—household pets,[283] wild animals,[284] insects,[285] even bacteria[286] and viruses.[287] These applications are directed either at distinguishing among species or at distinguishing among individuals (or subgroups) within a species. These two tasks can raise somewhat different scientific issues, and no single, mechanically applied test can be formulated to assess the validity of the diversity of applications and methods that might be encountered.

Instead, this section outlines and describes four factors that may be helpful in deciding whether a new application is scientifically sound. These are the novelty of the application, the validity of the underlying scientific theory, the validity of any statistical interpretations, and the relevant scientific community to consult in assessing the application. We illustrate these considerations in the context of three novel, recent applications of DNA technology to law enforcement:

- Although federal law prohibits the export of bear products, individuals in this country have offered to supply bear gall bladder for export to Asia, where it is prized for its supposed medicinal properties. In one investigation, the National Fish and Wildlife Forensic Laboratory, using DNA test-

283. Ronald K. Fitten, *Dog's DNA May Be Key in Murder Trial: Evidence Likely to Set Court Precedent*, Seattle Times, Mar. 9, 1998, at A1, *available in* 1998 WL 3142721 (reporting a trial court ruling in favor of admitting evidence linking DNA found on the jackets of two men to a pit bull that the men allegedly shot and killed, along with its owners).

284. For example, hunters sometimes claim that they have cuts of beef rather than the remnants of illegally obtained wildlife. These claims can be verified or refuted by DNA analysis. *Cf.* State v. Demers, 707 A.2d 276, 277–78 (Vt. 1997) (unspecified DNA analysis of deer blood and hair helped supply probable cause for search warrant to look for evidence of illegally hunted deer in defendant's home).

285. Felix A.H. Sperling et al., *A DNA-Based Approach to the Identification of Insect Species Used for Postmortem Interval Estimation*, 39 J. Forensic Sci. 418 (1994).

286. DNA testing of bacteria in food can help establish the source of outbreaks of food poisoning and thereby facilitate recalls of contaminated foodstuffs. *See* Jo Thomas, *Outbreak of Food Poisoning Leads to Warning on Hot Dogs and Cold Cuts*, N.Y. Times, Dec. 24, 1998.

287. *See* State v. Schmidt, 699 So. 2d 448 (La. Ct. App. 1997) (where the defendant was a physician accused of murdering his former lover by injecting her with the AIDS virus, the state's expert witnesses established that PCR-based analysis of human HIV can be used to identify HIV strains so as to satisfy *Daubert*).

ing, determined that the material offered for export actually came from a pig, absolving the suspect of any export law violations.[288]

- In *State v. Bogan*,[289] a woman's body was found in the desert, near several palo verde trees. A detective noticed two seed pods in the bed of a truck that the defendant was driving before the murder. A biologist performed DNA profiling on this type of palo verde and testified that the two pods "were identical" and "matched completely with" a particular tree and "didn't match any of the [other] trees," and that he felt "quite confident in concluding that" the tree's DNA would be distinguishable from that of "any tree that might be furnished" to him. After the jury convicted the defendant of murder, jurors reported that they found this testimony very persuasive.[290]
- In *R. v. Beamish*, a woman disappeared from her home on Prince Edward Island, on Canada's eastern seaboard. Weeks later a man's brown leather jacket stained with blood was discovered in a plastic bag in the woods. In the jacket's lining were white cat hairs. After the missing woman's body was found in a shallow grave, her estranged common-law husband was arrested and charged. He lived with his parents and a white cat. Laboratory analysis showed the blood on the jacket to be the victim's, and the hairs were ascertained to match the family cat at ten STR loci. The defendant was convicted of the murder.[291]

A. Is the Application Novel?

The more novel and untested an application is, the more problematic is its introduction into evidence. In many cases, however, an application can be new to the legal system but be well established in the field of scientific inquiry from which it derives. This can be ascertained from a survey of the peer-reviewed scientific literature and the statements of experts in the field.[292]

288. Interview with Dr. Edgard Espinoza, Deputy Director, National Fish and Wildlife Forensic Laboratory, in Ashland, Ore. (June 1998). Also, FDA regulations do not prohibit mislabeling of pig gall bladder.

289. 905 P.2d 515 (Ariz. Ct. App. 1995).

290. Brent Whiting, *Tree's DNA "Fingerprint" Splinters Killer's Defense*, Ariz. Republic, May 28, 1993, at A1, *available in* 1993 WL 8186972; *see also* Carol Kaesuk Yoon, *Forensic Science: Botanical Witness for the Prosecution*, 260 Science 894 (1993).

291. *DNA Testing on Cat Hairs Helped Link Man to Slaying*, Boston Globe, Apr. 24, 1997, *available in* 1997 WL 6250745; Gina Kolata, *Cat Hair Finds Way into Courtroom in Canadian Murder Trial*, N.Y. Times, Apr. 24, 1997, at A5; Marilyn A. Menott-Haymond et al., *Pet Cat Hair Implicates Murder Suspect*, 386 Nature 774 (1997).

292. Even though some applications are represented by only a few papers in the peer-reviewed literature, they may be fairly well established. The breadth of scientific inquiry, even within a rather specialized field, is such that only a few research groups may be working on any particular problem. A better gauge is the extent to which the genetic typing technology is used by researchers studying related

Applications designed specially to address an issue before the court are more likely to be truly novel and thus may be more difficult to evaluate. The studies of the gall bladder, palo verde trees, and cat hairs exemplify such applications in that each was devised solely for the case at bar.[293] In such cases, there are no published, peer-reviewed descriptions of the particular application to fall back on, but the analysis still could give rise to "scientific knowledge" within the meaning of *Daubert*.[294]

The novelty of an unusual application of DNA technology involves two components—the novelty of the analytical technique, and the novelty of applying that technique to the samples in question.[295] With respect to the analytical method, forensic DNA technology in the last two decades has been driven in part by the development of many new methods for the detection of genetic variation between species and between individuals within a species. The approaches outlined in table A-1 for the detection of genetic variation in humans—RFLP analysis of VNTR polymorphism, PCR, detection of VNTR and STR polymorphism by electrophoresis, and detection of sequence variation by probe hybridization or direct sequence analysis—have been imported from other research contexts. Thus, their use in the detection of variation in nonhuman species and of variation among species involves no new technology. DNA technology transcends organismal differences.

Some methods for the characterization of DNA variation widely used in studies of other species, however, are not used in forensic testing of human DNA. These are often called "DNA fingerprint" approaches. They offer a snapshot characterization of genomic variation in a single test, but they essentially presume that the sample DNA originates from a single individual, and this presumption cannot always be met with forensic samples.

The original form of DNA "fingerprinting" used electrophoresis, Southern blotting, and a multilocus probe that simultaneously recognizes many sites in the genome.[296] The result is comparable to what would be obtained with a

problems and the existence of a general body of knowledge regarding the nature of the genetic variation at issue.

293. Of course, such evidence hardly is unique to DNA technology. *See, e.g.*, Coppolino v. State, 223 So. 2d 68 (Fla. Dist. Ct. App.), *appeal dismissed*, 234 So. 2d 120 (Fla. 1968) (holding admissible a test for the presence of succinylcholine chloride first devised for this case to determine whether defendant had injected a lethal dose of this curare-like anesthetic into his wife).

294. 509 U.S. 579, 590 (1993) ("to qualify as 'scientific knowledge,' an inference or assertion must be derived by the scientific method").

295. From its inception, both these aspects of forensic DNA testing have been debated. *See, e.g.*, 1 McCormick on Evidence, *supra* note 11, § 205, at 902; Thompson & Ford, *supra* note 183.

296. The probes were pioneered by Alec Jeffreys. *See, e.g.*, Alec J. Jeffreys et al., *Individual-specific "Fingerprints" of Human DNA*, 316 Nature 76 (1985). In the 1980s, the "Jeffreys probes" were used for forensic purposes, especially in parentage testing. *See, e.g.*, D.H. Kaye, *DNA Paternity Probabilities*, 24 Fam. L.Q. 279 (1990).

"cocktail" of single-locus probes—one complex banding pattern sometimes analogized to a bar-code.[297] Probes for DNA fingerprinting are widely used in genetic research in non-human species.[298]

With the advent of PCR as the central tool in molecular biology, PCR-based "fingerprinting" methods have been developed. The two most widely used are the random amplified polymorphic DNA (RAPD) method[299] and the amplified fragment length polymorphism (AFLP) method.[300] Both give bar code-like patterns.[301] In RAPD analysis, a single, arbitrarily constructed, short primer amplifies many DNA fragments of unknown sequence.[302] AFLP analysis begins with a digestion of the sample DNA with a restriction enzyme followed by amplification of selected restriction fragments.[303]

Although the DNA fingerprinting procedures are not likely to be used in the analysis of samples of human origin, new approaches to the detection of genetic variation in humans as well as other organisms are under development. On the horizon are methods based on mass spectrometry and hybridization chip technology. As these or other methods come into forensic use, the best measure of scientific novelty will be the extent to which the methods have found their way into the scientific literature. Use by researchers other than those who developed them indicates some degree of scientific acceptance.

The second aspect of novelty relates to the sample analyzed. Two questions are central: Is there scientific precedent for testing samples of the sort tested in the particular case? And, what is known about the nature and extent of genetic variation in the tested organism and in related species? *Beamish*, the Canadian case involving cat hairs, illustrates both points. The nature of the sample—cat

297. As with RFLP analysis in general, this RFLP fingerprinting approach requires a relatively good quality sample DNA. Degraded DNA results in a loss of some of the bars in the barcode-like pattern.

298. *E.g.*, DNA Fingerprinting: State of the Science (S.D.J. Pena et al. eds., 1993). The discriminating power of a probe must be determined empirically in each species. The probes used by Jeffreys for human DNA fingerprinting, for instance, are less discriminating for dogs. A.J. Jeffreys & D.B. Morton, *DNA Fingerprints of Dogs and Cats*, 18 Animal Genetics 1 (1987).

299. John Welsh & Michael McClelland, *Fingerprinting Genomes Using PCR with Arbitrary Primers*, 18 Nucleic Acids Res. 7213 (1990); John G.K. Williams et al., *DNA Polymorphisms Amplified by Arbitrary Primers Are Useful as Genetic Markers*, 18 Nucleic Acids Res. 6531 (1990).

300. Pieter Vos et al., *AFLP: A New Technique for DNA Fingerprinting*, 23 Nucleic Acids Res. 4407 (1995).

301. The identification of the seed pods in *State v. Bogan*, 905 P.2d 515 (Ariz. Ct. App. 1995), was accomplished with RAPD analysis. The general acceptance of this technique in the scientific community was not seriously contested. Indeed, the expert for the defense conceded the validity of RAPD in genetic research and testified that the state's expert had correctly applied the procedure. *Id.* at 520.

302. Primers must be validated in advance to determine which give highly discriminating patterns for a particular species in question.

303. Both the RAPD and AFLP methods provide reproducible results within a laboratory, but AFLP is more reproducible across laboratories. *See, e.g.*, C.J. Jones et al., *Reproducibility Testing of RAPD, AFLP and SSR Markers in Plants by a Network of European Laboratories*, 3 Molecular Breeding 381 (1997). This may be an issue if results from different laboratories must be compared.

hairs—does not seem novel, for there is ample scientific precedent for doing genetic tests on animal hairs.[304] But the use of STR testing to identify a domestic cat as the source of particular hairs was new. Of course, this novelty does not mean that the effort was scientifically unsound; indeed, as explained in the next section, the premise that cats show substantial microsatellite polymorphism is consistent with other scientific knowledge.

B. Is the Underlying Scientific Theory Valid?

Daubert does not banish novel applications of science from the courtroom, but it does demand that trial judges assure themselves that the underlying science is sound, so that the scientific expert is presenting scientific knowledge rather than speculating or dressing up unscientific opinion in the garb of scientific fact.[305] The questions that might be asked to probe the scientific underpinnings extend the line of questions asked about novelty: What is the principle of the testing method used? What has been the experience with the use of the testing method? What are its limitations? Has it been used in applications similar to those in the instant case—for instance, for the characterization of other organisms or other kinds of samples? What is known of the nature of genetic variability in the organism tested or in related organisms? Is there precedent for doing any kind of DNA testing on the sort of samples tested in the instant case? Is there anything about the organism, the sample, or the context of testing that would render the testing technology inappropriate for the desired application?[306] To illustrate the usefulness of these questions, we can return to the cases involving pig gall bladders, cat hairs, and palo verde seed pods.

Deciding whether the DNA testing is valid is simplest in the export case. The question there was whether the gall bladders originated from bear or from some other species. The DNA analysis was based on the approach used by evolutionary biologists to study relationships among vertebrate species. It relies on sequence variation in the mitochondrial cytochrome b gene. DNA sequence analysis is a routine technology, and there is an extensive library of cytochrome b sequence data representing a broad range of vertebrate species.[307] As for the sample

304. *E.g.*, Russell Higuchi et al., *DNA Typing from Single Hairs*, 332 Nature 543, 545 (1988). Collection of hair is non-invasive and is widely used in wildlife studies where sampling in the field would otherwise be difficult or impossible. Hair also is much easier to transport and store than blood, a great convenience when working in the field. *Id.*

305. *See* Daubert v. Merrell Dow Pharmaceuticals, Inc., 509 U.S. 579, 590 (1993) ("The adjective 'scientific' implies a grounding in the methods and procedures of science. Similarly, the word 'knowledge' connotes more than subjective belief or unsupported speculation.").

306. *But cf.* NRC I, *supra* note 1, at 72 (listing seven "requirements" for new forensic DNA tests to achieve "the highest standards of scientific rigor").

307. If the bear cytochrome b gene sequence were not in the database, it would be obligatory for the proponents of the application to determine it and add it to the database, where it could be checked by other researchers.

material—the gall bladder—such cells may not have been used before, but gall bladder is simply another tissue from which DNA can be extracted.[308] Thus, although the application was novel in that an approach had to be devised to address the question at hand, each segment of the application rests on a solid foundation of scientific knowledge and experience. No great inferential leap from the known to the unknown was required to reach the conclusion that the gall bladder was from a pig rather than a bear.

The DNA analysis in *Beamish* required slightly more extrapolation from the known to the unknown. As indicated in the previous section, the use of cat hairs as a source of DNA was not especially novel, and the very factors that reveal a lack of novelty also suggest that it is scientifically valid to test the DNA in cat hairs. But we also observed that the use of STR typing to distinguish among cats was novel. Is such reasoning too great a leap to constitute scientific knowledge? A great deal is known about the basis and extent of genetic variation in cats and other mammals. In particular, microsatellite polymorphism is extensive in all mammalian species that have been studied, including other members of the cat family. Furthermore, by testing small samples from two cat populations, the researchers verified the loci they examined were highly polymorphic.[309] Thus, the novelty in using STR analysis to identify cats is not scientifically unsettling; rather, it extends from and fits with everything else that is known about cats and mammals in general. However, as one moves from well-studied organisms to ones about which little is known, one risks crossing the line between knowledge and speculation.

The DNA testing in *State v. Bogan*[310] pushes the envelope further. First, the genetic variability of palo verde trees had not been previously studied. Second, it was not known whether enough DNA could be extracted from seed pods to perform a genetic analysis. Both of these questions had to be answered by new testing. RAPD analysis, a well-established method for characterizing genetic variation within a species, demonstrated that palo verde trees were highly variable. Seed pods were shown to contain adequate DNA for RAPD analysis. Finally, a blind trial showed that RAPD profiles correctly identified individual

308. There is a technical concern that the DNA extracted from a gall bladder might contain inhibitors that would interfere with the subsequent sequence analysis; however, this merely affects whether the test will yield a result, and not the accuracy of any result.

309. One sample consisted of nineteen cats in Sunnyside, Prince Edward Island, where the crime occurred. *See* Commentary, *Use of DNA Analysis Raises Some Questions* (CBS radio broadcast, Apr. 24, 1997), *transcript available in* 1997 WL 5424082 ("19 cats obtained randomly from local veterinarians on Prince Edward Island"); Marjorie Shaffer, *Canadian Killer Captured by a Whisker from Parents' Pet Cat*, Biotechnology Newswatch, May 5, 1997, *available in* 1997 WL 8790779 ("the Royal Canadian Mounted Police rounded up 19 cats in the area and had a veterinarian draw blood samples"). The other sample consisted of nine cats from the United States. *DNA Test on Parents' Cat Helps Put Away Murderer*, Chi. Trib., Apr. 24, 1997, *available in* 1997 WL 3542042.

310. 905 P.2d 515 (Ariz. Ct. App. 1995).

palo verde trees.[311] In short, the lack of pre-existing data on DNA fingerprints of palo verde trees was bridged by scientific experimentation that established the validity of the specific application.

The DNA analyses in all three situations rest on a coherent and internally consistent body of observation, experiment, and experience. That information was mostly pre-existing in the case of the gall bladder testing. Some information on the population genetics of domestic cats on Prince Edward's Island had to be generated specifically for the analysis in *Beamish*, and still more was developed expressly for the situation in the palo verde tree testing in *Bogan*. A court, with the assistance of suitable experts, can make a judgment as to scientific validity in these cases because the crucial propositions are open to critical review by others in the scientific community and are subject to additional investigation if questions are raised. Where serious doubt remains, a court might consider ordering a blind trial to verify the analytical laboratory's ability to perform the identification in question.[312]

C. Has the Probability of a Chance Match Been Estimated Correctly?

The significance of a human DNA match in a particular case typically is presented or assessed in terms of the probability that an individual selected at random from the population would be found to match. A small random match probability renders implausible the hypothesis that the match is just coincidental.[313] In *Beamish*, the random match probability was estimated to be one in many millions,[314] and the trial court admitted evidence of this statistic.[315] In

311. The DNA in the two seed pods could not be distinguished by RAPD testing, suggesting that they fell from the same tree. The biologist who devised and conducted the experiments analyzed samples from the nine trees near the body and another nineteen trees from across the county. He "was not informed, until after his tests were completed and his report written, which samples came from" which trees. *Bogan*, 905 P.2d at 521. Furthermore, unbeknownst to the experimenter, two apparently distinct samples were prepared from the tree at the crime scene that appeared to have been abraded by the defendant's truck. The biologist correctly identified the two samples from the one tree as matching, and he "distinguished the DNA from the seed pods in the truck bed from the DNA of all twenty-eight trees except" that one. *Id.*

312. *Cf. supra* note 311. The blind trial could be devised and supervised by a court-appointed expert, or the parties could be ordered to agree on a suitable experiment. *See* 1 McCormick on Evidence, *supra* note 11, § 203, at 867.

313. *See supra* § VII.

314. David N. Leff, *Killer Convicted by a Hair: Unprecedented Forensic Evidence from Cat's DNA Convinced Canadian Jury*, Bioworld Today, Apr. 24, 1997, *available in* 1997 WL 7473675 ("the frequency of the match came out to be on the order of about one in 45 million," quoting Steven O'Brien); *All Things Considered: Cat DNA* (NPR broadcast, Apr. 23, 1997), *available in* 1997 WL 12832754 ("it was less than one in two hundred million," quoting Steven O'Brien).

315. *See also* Tim Klass, *DNA Tests Match Dog, Stains in Murder Case*, Portland Oregonian, Aug. 7, 1998, at D06 (reporting expert testimony in a Washington murder case that "the likelihood of finding

State v. Bogan,[316] the random match probability was estimated by the state's expert as one in a million and by the defense expert as one in 136,000, but the trial court excluded these estimates because of the then-existing controversy over analogous estimates for human RFLP genotypes.[317]

Estimating the probability of a random match or related statistics requires a sample of genotypes from the relevant population of organisms. As discussed in section VII, the most accurate estimates combine the allele frequencies seen in the sample according to formulae that reflect the gene flow within the population. In the simplest model for large populations of sexually reproducing organisms, mating is independent of the DNA types under investigation, and each parent transmits half of his or her DNA to the progeny at random. Under these idealized conditions, the basic product rule gives the multilocus genotype frequency as a simple function of the allele frequencies.[318] The accuracy of the estimates thus depends on the accuracy of the allele frequencies in the sample database and the appropriateness of the population genetics model.

1. *How Was the Database Obtained?*

Since the allele frequencies come from sample data, both the method of sampling and the size of the sample can be crucial. The statistical ideal is probability sampling, in which some objective procedure provides a known chance that each member of the population will be selected. Such random samples tend to be representative of the population from which they are drawn. In wildlife biology, however, the populations often defy enumeration, and hence strict random sampling rarely is possible. Still, if the method of selection is uncorrelated with the alleles being studied, then the sampling procedure is tantamount to random sampling with respect to those alleles.[319] Consequently, the key question about the method of sampling for a court faced with estimates based on a database of cats, dogs, or any such species, is whether that sample was obtained in some biased way—a way that would systematically tend to include (or exclude) organisms with particular alleles or genotypes from the database.

a 10-for-10 match in the DNA of a randomly chosen dog of any breed or mix would be one in 3 trillion, and the odds for a nine-of-10 match would be one in 18 billion").

316. 905 P.2d 515 (Ariz. Ct. App. 1995).

317. *Id.* at 520. The Arizona case law on this subject is criticized in Kaye, *supra* note 178.

318. More complicated models account for the population structure that arises when inbreeding is common, but they require some knowledge of how much the population is structured. *See supra* § VII.

319. Few people would worry, for example, that the sample of blood cells taken from their vein for a test of whether they suffer from anemia is not, strictly speaking, a random sample. The use of convenience samples from human populations to form forensic databases is discussed in, *e.g.*, NRC II, *supra* note 1, at 126–27, 186. Case law is collected *supra* note 179.

2. How Large Is the Sampling Error?

Assuming that the sampling procedure is reasonably structured to give representative samples with respect to those genotypes of forensic interest, the question of database size should be considered. Larger samples give more precise estimates of allele frequencies than smaller ones, but there is no sharp line for determining when a database is too small.[320] Instead, just as pollsters present their results within a certain margin of error, the expert should be able to explain the extent of the statistical error that arises from using samples of the size of the forensic database.[321]

3. How Was the Random Match Probability Computed?

As we have indicated, the theory of population genetics provides the framework for combining the allele frequencies into the final profile frequency. The frequency estimates are a mathematical function of the genetic diversity at each locus and the number of loci tested. The formulas for frequency estimates depend on the mode of reproduction and the population genetics of the species. For outbreeding sexually reproducing species,[322] under conditions that give rise to Hardy-Weinberg and linkage equilibrium, genotype frequencies can be estimated with the basic product rule.[323] If a species is sexually reproducing but given to inbreeding, or if there are other impediments to Hardy-Weinberg or linkage equilibrium, such genotype frequencies may be incorrect. Thus, the reasonableness of assuming Hardy-Weinberg equilibrium and linkage equilibrium depends on what and how much is known about the population genetics of the species.[324] Ideally, large population databases can be analyzed to verify independence of alleles.[325] Tests for deviations from the single-locus genotype

320. The 1996 NRC Report refers to "at least several hundred persons," but it has been suggested that relatively small databases, consisting of fifty or so individuals, allow statistically acceptable frequency estimation for the common alleles. NRC II, *supra* note 1, at 114. A new, specially constructed database is likely to be small, but alleles can be a assigned a minimum value, resulting in conservative genotype frequency estimates. Ranajit Chakraborty, *Sample Size Requirements for Addressing the Population Genetic Issues of Forensic Use of DNA Typing*, 64 Human Biology 141, 156–57 (1992). Later, the NAS committee suggests that the uncertainty that arises "[i]f the database is small . . . can be addressed by providing confidence intervals on the estimates." NRC II, *supra* note 1, at 125.

321. Bruce S. Weir, *Forensic Population Genetics and the NRC*, 52 Am. J. Hum. Genetics 437 (1993) (proposing interval estimate of genotype frequency); *cf.* NRC II, *supra* note 1, at 148 (remarking that "calculation of confidence intervals is desirable," but also examining the error that could be associated with the choice of a database on an empirical basis).

322. Outbreeding refers to the propensity for individuals to mate with individuals who are not close relations.

323. *See supra* § VII.

324. In *State v. Bogan*, 905 P.2d 515 (Ariz. Ct. App. 1995), for example, the biologist who testified for the prosecution consulted with botanists who assured him that palo verde trees were an outcrossing species. *Id.* at 523–24.

325. However, large, pre-existing databases may not be available for the populations of interest in

frequencies expected under Hardy-Weinberg equilibrium will indicate if population structure effects should be accorded serious concern. These tests, however, are relatively insensitive to minor population structure effects, and adjustments for possible population structure might be appropriate.[326] For sexually reproducing species believed to have local population structure, a sampling strategy targeting the relevant population would be best. If this is not possible, estimates based on the larger population might be presented with appropriate caveats. If data on the larger population are unavailable, the uncertainty implicit in basic product rule estimates should not be ignored, and less ambitious alternatives to the random match probability as a means for conveying the probative value of a match might be considered.[327]

A different approach may be called for if the species is not an outbreeding, sexually reproducing species. For example, many plants, some simple animals, and bacteria reproduce asexually. With asexual reproduction, most offspring are genetically identical to the parent. All the individuals that originate from a common parent constitute, collectively, a clone. The major source of genetic variation in asexually reproducing species is mutation.[328] When a mutation occurs, a new clonal lineage is created. Individuals in the original clonal lineage continue to propagate, and two clonal lineages now exist where before there was one. Thus, in species that reproduce asexually, genetic testing distinguishes clones, not individuals, and the product rule cannot be applied to estimate genotype frequencies for individuals. Rather, the frequency of a particular clone in a population of clones must be determined by direct observation. For example, if a rose thorn found on a suspect's clothing were to be identified as originating from a particular cultivar of rose, the relevant question becomes how common that variety of rose bush is and where it is located in the community.

these more novel cases. Analyses of the smaller, ad hoc databases are unlikely to be decisive. In *Beamish*, for instance, two cat populations were sampled. The sample of nineteen cats from Sunnyside, in Prince Edward Island, and the sample of nine cats from the United States revealed considerable genetic diversity; moreover, most of the genetic variability was between individual cats, not between the two populations of cats. There was no statistically significant evidence of population substructure, and there was no statistically significant evidence of linkage disequilibrium in the Sunnyside population. The problem is that with such small samples, the statistical tests for substructure are not very sensitive; hence, the failure to detect it is not strong proof that either the Sunnyside or the North American cat population is unstructured.

326. A standard correction for population structure is to incorporate a population structure parameter F_{ST} into the calculation. Such adjustments are described *supra* § VII. However, appropriate values for F_{ST} may not be known for unstudied species.

327. The "tree lineup" in *Bogan* represents one possible approach. Adapting it to *Beamish* would have produced testimony that the researchers were able to exclude all the other (28) cats presented to them. This simple counting, however, is extremely conservative.

328. Bacteria also can exchange DNA through several mechanisms unrelated to cell division, including conjugation, transduction, and transformation. Bacterial species differ in their susceptibility to undergo these forms of gene transfer.

In short, the approach for estimating a genotype frequency depends on the reproductive pattern and population genetics of the species. In cases involving unusual organisms, a court will need to rely on experts with sufficient knowledge of the species to verify that the method for estimating genotype frequencies is appropriate.

D. What Is the Relevant Scientific Community?

Even the most scientifically sophisticated court may find it difficult to judge the scientific soundness of a novel application without questioning appropriate scientists.[329] Given the great diversity of forensic questions to which DNA testing might be applied, it is not possible to define specific scientific expertises appropriate to each. If the technology is novel, expertise in molecular genetics or biotechnology might be necessary. If testing has been conducted on a particular organism or category of organisms, expertise in that area of biology may be called for. If a random match probability has been presented, one might seek expertise in statistics as well as the population biology or population genetics that goes with the organism tested. Given the penetration of molecular technology into all areas of biological inquiry, it is likely that individuals can be found who know both the technology and the population biology of the organism in question. Finally, where samples come from crime scenes, the expertise and experience of forensic scientists can be crucial. Just as highly focused specialists may be unaware of aspects of an application outside their field of expertise, so too scientists who have not previously dealt with forensic samples can be unaware of case-specific factors that can confound the interpretation of test results.

329. *See supra* § I.C.

Appendix

A. Structure of DNA

DNA is a complex molecule made of subunits known as nucleotides that link together to form a long, spiraling strand. Two such strands are intertwined around each other to form a double helix as shown in Figure A-1. Each strand has a "backbone" made of sugar and phosphate groups and nitrogenous bases attached to the sugar groups.[330] There are four types of bases, abbreviated A, T, G, and C, and the two strands of DNA in the double helix are linked by weak chemical bonds such that the A in one strand is always paired to a T in the other strand and the G in one strand is always paired to a C in the other.[331] The A:T and G:C complementary base pairing means that knowledge of the sequence of one strand predicts the sequence of the complementary strand. The sequence of the nucleotide base pairs carries the genetic information in the DNA molecule—it is the genetic "text." For example, the sequence ATT on one strand (or TAA on the other strand) "means" something different than GTT (or CAA).

Figure A-1. A Schematic Diagram of the DNA Molecule

The bases in the nucleotide (denoted C, G, A, and T) are arranged like the rungs in a spiral staircase.

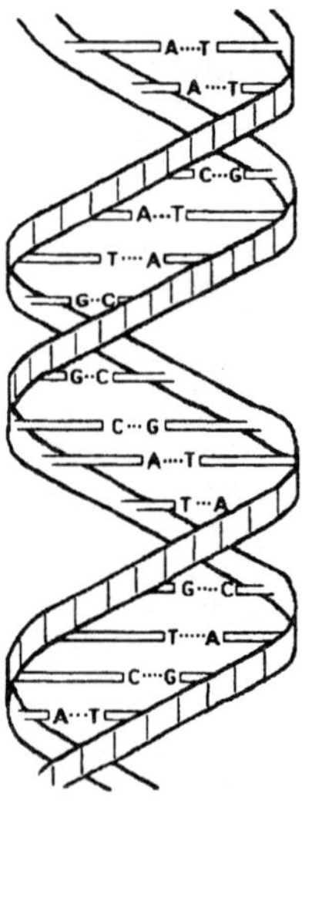

330. For more details about DNA structure, see, *e.g.*, Anthony J.F. Griffiths et al., An Introduction to Genetic Analysis (6th ed. 1996); Mange & Mange, *supra* note 23, at 95.

331. The bonds that connect the complementary bases are known as *hydrogen bonds*.

B. DNA Probes

A sequence specific oligonucleotide (SSO) probe is a short segment of single-stranded DNA with bases arranged in a particular order. The order is chosen so that the probe will bind to the complementary sequence on a DNA fragment, as sketched in Figure A-2.

Figure A-2. A Sequence-Specific Probe Links (Hybridizes) to the Targeted Sequence on a Single Stand of DNA

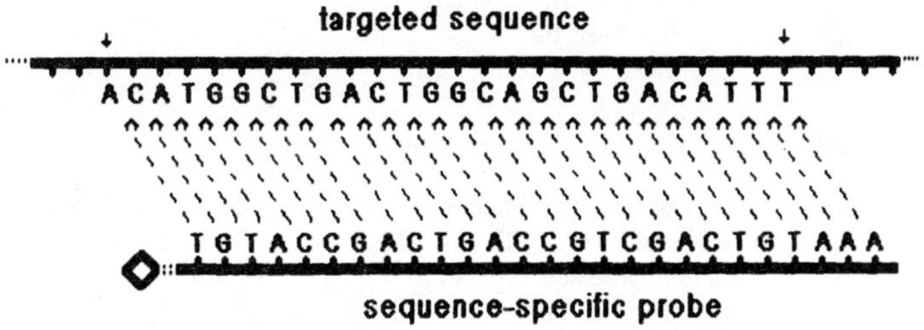

C. Examples of Genetic Markers in Forensic Identification

Table A-1 offers examples of the major types of genetic markers used in forensic identification.[332] As noted in the table, simple sequence polymorphisms, some variable number tandem repeat (VNTR) polymorphisms, and nearly all short tandem repeat (STR) polymorphisms are detected using polymerase chain reaction (PCR) as a starting point. Most VNTRs containing long core repeats are too large to be amplified reliably by PCR and are instead characterized by restriction fragment length polymorphism (RFLP) analysis using Southern blotting. As a result of the greater efficiency of PCR-based methods, VNTR typing by RFLP analysis is fading from use.

332. The table is adapted from NRC II, *supra* note 1, at 74.

Table A-1. Genetic Markers Used in Forensic Identification

Nature of variation at locus

Locus example	Method of detection	Number of alleles
Variable number tandem repeat (VNTR) loci contain repeated core sequence elements, typically 15–35 base pairs (bp) in length. Alleles differ in the number of repeats and are distinguished on the basis of size.		
D2S44 (core repeat 31 bp)	Intact DNA digested with restriction enzyme, producing fragments that are separated by gel electrophoresis; alleles detected by Southern blotting followed by probing with locus-specific radioactive or chemiluminescent probe	At least 75 (size range is 700–8500 bp); allele size distribution is essentially continuous
D1S80 (core repeat 16 bp)	Amplification of allelic sequences by PCR; discrete allelic products separated by electrophoresis and visualized directly	About 30 (size range is 350–1000 bp); alleles can be discretely distinguished
Short tandem repeat (STR) loci are VNTR loci with repeated core sequence elements 2–6 bp in length. Alleles differ in the number of repeats and are distinguished on the basis of size.		
HUMTHO1 (tetranucleotide repeat)	Amplification of allelic sequences by PCR; discrete allelic products separated by electrophoresis on sequencing gels and visualized directly, by capillary electrophoresis, or by other methods	8 (size range 179–203 bp); alleles can be discretely distinguished
Simple sequence variation (nucleotide substitution in a defined segment of a sequence)		
DQA (an expressed gene in the histocompatibility complex)	Amplification of allelic sequences by PCR; discrete alleles detected by sequence-specific probes	8 (6 used in DQA kit)
Polymarker (a set of five loci)	Amplification of allelic sequences by PCR; discrete alleles detected by sequence-specific probes	Loci are bi- or tri-allelic; 972 genotypic combinations
Mitochondrial DNA control region (D-loop)	Amplification of control-sequence and sequence determination	Hundreds of sequence variants are known

D. Steps of PCR Amplification

The second National Research Council report provides a concise description of how PCR "amplifies" DNA:

> First, each double-stranded segment is separated into two strands by heating. Second, these single-stranded segments are hybridized with primers, short DNA segments (20–30 nucleotides in length) that complement and define the target sequence to be amplified. Third, in the presence of the enzyme DNA polymerase, and the four nucleotide building blocks (A, C, G, and T), each primer serves as the starting point for the replication of the target sequence. A copy of the complement of each of the separated strands is made, so that there are two double-stranded DNA segments. The three-step cycle is repeated, usually 20–35 times. The two strands produce four copies; the four, eight copies; and so on until the number of copies of the original DNA is enormous. The main difference between this procedure and the normal cellular process is that the PCR process is limited to the amplification of a small DNA region. This region is usually not more than 1,000 nucleotides in length, so PCR methods cannot, at least at present, be used [to amplify] large DNA regions, such as most VNTRs.[333]

Figure A-3 illustrates the steps in the PCR process for two cycles.[334]

Figure A-3. The PCR Process

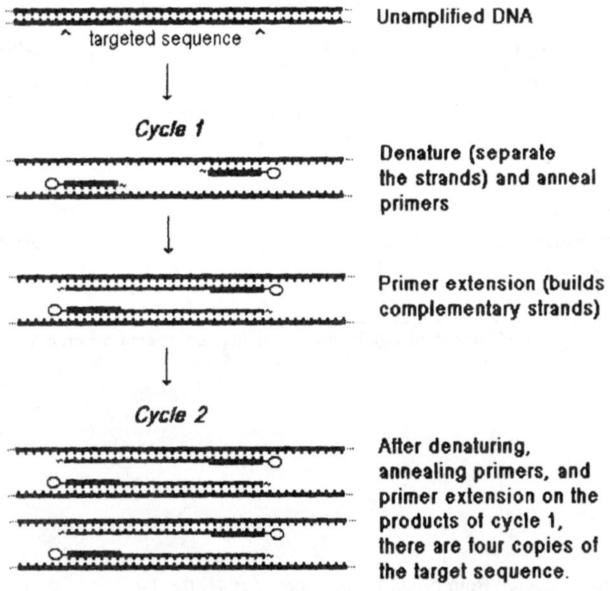

333. NRC II, *supra* note 1, at 69–70.

In principle, PCR amplification doubles the number of double-stranded DNA fragments each cycle. Although there is some inefficiency in practice, the yield from a 30-cycle amplification is generally about one million to ten million copies of the targeted sequence.

E. Quantities of DNA in Forensic Samples

Amounts of DNA present in some typical kinds of evidence samples are indicated in Table A-2. These are approximate, and the quantities of DNA extracted from evidence in particular cases may vary somewhat.[335]

Table A-2. DNA Content of Biological Samples[336] and Genetic Testing Success Rates

Type of Sample	DNA Content	PCR Success Rate
Blood	20,000–40,000 ng/mL	
stain 1 cm x 1 cm	ca. 200 ng	> 95%
stain 1 mm x 1 mm	ca. 2 ng	
Semen	150,000–300,000 ng/mL	
on post-coital vaginal swab	0–3000 ng	>95%
Saliva	1000–10,000 ng/mL	
on a cigarette butt	0–25ng	50–70%
Hair		
root end of pulled hair	1–750 ng	>90%
root end of shed hair	1–12 ng	<20%
hair shaft	0.001–0.040 ng/cm	
Urine	1–20 ng/mL	
Skin cells		
from socks, gloves, or clothing repeatedly used		30–60%
from handled objects (e.g., a doorknob)		<20%

ng = nanogram, or 1/1,000,000,000th of a gram; mL = milliliter; cm = centimeter; mm = millimeter

334. The figure is adapted from NRC I, *supra* note 1, at 41, fig. 1-6.

335. The amounts in the table are given in nanograms (ng) or ng per milliliter (ng/mL). A nanogram is one billionth (1/1,000,000,000) of a gram.

336. Adapted from NRC I, *supra* note 1, at 28 (with additions); PCR genetic test success rate estimates from the New York City Office of the Chief Medical Examiner, Department of Forensic Biology.

Glossary of Terms

adenine (A). One of the four bases, or nucleotides, that make up the DNA molecule. Adenine only binds to thymine. See nucleotide.

affinal method. A method for computing the single locus profile probabilities for a theoretical subpopulation by adjusting the single locus profile probability, calculated with the product rule from the mixed population database, by the amount of heterogeneity across subpopulations. The model is appropriate even if there is no database available for a particular subpopulation, and the formula always gives more conservative probabilities than the product rule applied to the same database.

allele. In classical genetics, an allele is one of several alternative forms of a gene. A biallelic gene has two variants; others have more. Alleles are inherited separately from each parent, and for a given gene, an individual may have two different alleles (heterozygosity) or the same allele (homozygosity). In DNA analysis, the term is applied to any DNA region (whether or not it constitutes a gene) used for analysis.

Alu sequences. A family of short interspersed elements (SINEs) distributed throughout the genomes of primates.

amplification. Increasing the number of copies of a DNA region, usually by PCR.

amplified fragment length polymorphism (AMP-FLP). A DNA identification technique that uses PCR-amplified DNA fragments of varying lengths. The DS180 locus is a VNTR whose alleles can be detected with this technique.

antibody. A protein (immunoglobulin) molecule, produced by the immune system, that recognizes a particular foreign antigen and binds to it; if the antigen is on the surface of a cell, this binding leads to cell aggregation and subsequent destruction.

antigen. A molecule (typically found in the surface of a cell) whose shape triggers the production of antibodies that will bind to the antigen.

autoradiograph (autoradiogram, autorad). In RFLP analysis, the x-ray film (or print) showing the positions of radioactively marked fragments (bands) of DNA, indicating how far these fragments have migrated, and hence their molecular weights.

autosome. A chromosome other than the X and Y sex chromosomes.

band. See autoradiograph.

band shift. Movement of DNA fragments in one lane of a gel at a different rate than fragments of an identical length in another lane, resulting in the same pattern "shifted" up or down relative to the comparison lane. Band-shift does not necessarily occur at the same rate in all portions of the gel.

base pair (bp). Two complementary nucleotides bonded together at the matching bases (A and T or C and G) along the double helix "backbone" of the DNA molecule. The length of a DNA fragment often is measured in numbers of base pairs (1 kilobase (kb) = 1000 bp); base pair numbers also are used to describe the location of an allele on the DNA strand.

Bayes' theorem. An elementary formula that relates certain conditional probabilities. It can be used to describe the impact of new data on the probability that a hypothesis is true.

bin, fixed. In VNTR profiling, a bin is a range of base pairs (DNA fragment lengths). When a database is divided into fixed bins, the proportion of bands within each bin is determined and the relevant proportions are used in estimating the profile frequency.

bins, floating. In VNTR profiling, a bin is a range of base pairs (DNA fragment lengths). In a floating bin method of estimating a profile frequency, the bin is centered on the base pair length of the allele in question, and the width of the bin can be defined by the laboratory's matching rule (e.g., ±5% of band size).

binning. Grouping VNTR alleles into sets of similar sizes because the alleles' lengths are too similar to differentiate.

blind proficiency test. See proficiency test.

capillary electrophoresis. A method for separating DNA fragments (including STRs) according to their lengths. A long, narrow tube is filled with an entangled polymer or comparable sieving medium, and an electric field is applied to pull DNA fragments placed at one end of the tube through the medium. The procedure is faster and uses smaller samples than gel electrophoresis, and it can be automated.

ceiling principle. A procedure for setting a minimum DNA profile frequency proposed in 1992 by a committee of the National Academy of Science. One hundred persons from each of 15–20 genetically homogeneous populations spanning the range of racial groups in the United States are sampled. For each allele, the higher frequency among the groups sampled (or 5%, whichever is larger) is used in calculating the profile frequency. Compare interim ceiling principle.

chip. A miniaturized system for genetic analysis. One such chip mimics capillary electrophoresis and related manipulations. DNA fragments, pulled by small voltages, move through tiny channels etched into a small block of glass, silicon, quartz, or plastic. This system should be useful in analyzing STRs.

Another technique mimics reverse dot blots by placing a large array of oligonucleotide probes on a solid surface. Such hybridization arrays should be useful in identifying SNPs and in sequencing mitochondrial DNA.

chromosome. A rod-like structure composed of DNA, RNA, and proteins. Most normal human cells contain 46 chromosomes, 22 autosomes and a sex chromosome (X) inherited from the mother, and another 22 autosomes and one sex chromosome (either X or Y) inherited from the father. The genes are located along the chromosomes. See also homologous chromosomes.

coding DNA. A small fraction of the human genome contains the "instructions" for assembling physiologically important proteins. The remainder of the DNA is "non-coding."

CODIS (combined DNA index system). A collection of databases on STR and other loci of convicted felons maintained by the FBI.

complementary sequence. The sequence of nucleotides on one strand of DNA that corresponds to the sequence on the other strand. For example, if one sequence is CTGAA, the complementary bases are GACTT.

cytosine (C). One of the four bases, or nucleotides, that make up the DNA double helix. Cytosine only binds to guanine. See nucleotide.

database. A collection of DNA profiles.

degradation. The breaking down of DNA by chemical or physical means.

denature, denaturation. The process of splitting, as by heating, two complementary strands of the DNA double helix into single strands in preparation for hybridization with biological probes.

deoxyribonucleic acid (DNA). The molecule that contains genetic information. DNA is composed of nucleotide building blocks, each containing a base (A, C, G, or T), a phosphate, and a sugar. These nucleotides are linked together in a double helix—two strands of DNA molecules paired up at complementary bases (A with T, C with G). See adenine, cytosine, guanine, thymine.

diploid number. See haploid number.

D-loop. A portion of the mitochrondrial genome known as the "control region" or "displacement loop" instrumental in the regulation and initiation of mtDNA gene products.

DNA polymerase. The enzyme that catalyzes the synthesis of double-stranded DNA.

DNA probe. See probe

DNA profile. The alleles at each locus. For example, a VNTR profile is the pattern of band lengths on an autorad. A multilocus profile represents the combined results of multiple probes. *See* genotype.

DNA sequence. The ordered list of base pairs in a duplex DNA molecule or of bases in a single strand.

DQA. The gene that codes for a particular class of Human Leukocyte Antigen (HLA). This gene has been sequenced completely and can be used for forensic typing. See human leukocyte antigen.

DQ. The antigen that is the product of the DQA gene. *See* DQA, human leukocyte antigen.

EDTA. A preservative added to blood samples.

electrophoresis. See capillary electrophoresis, gel electrophoresis.

endonuclease. An enzyme that cleaves the phosphodiester bond within a nucleotide chain.

environmental insult. Exposure of DNA to external agents such as heat, moisture, and ultraviolet radiation, or chemical or bacterial agents. Such exposure can interfere with the enzymes used in the testing process, or otherwise make DNA difficult to analyze.

enzyme. A protein that catalyzes (speeds up or slows down) a reaction.

ethidium bromide. A molecule that can intercalate into DNA double helices when the helix is under torsional stress. Used to identify the presence of DNA in a sample by its fluorescence under ultraviolet light.

fallacy of the transposed conditional. See transposition fallacy.

false match. Two samples of DNA that have different profiles could be declared to match if, instead of measuring the distinct DNA in each sample, there is an error in handling or preparing samples such that the DNA from a single sample is analyzed twice. The resulting match, which does not reflect the true profiles of the DNA from each sample, is a false match. Some people use "false match" more broadly, to include cases in which the true profiles of each sample are the same, but the samples come from different individuals. Compare true match. See also match, random match.

gel, agarose. A semisolid medium used to separate molecules by electrophoresis.

gel electrophoresis. In RFLP analysis, the process of sorting DNA fragments by size by applying an electric current to a gel. The different-sized fragments move at different rates through the gel.

gene. A set of nucleotide base pairs on a chromosome that contains the "instructions" for controlling some cellular function such as making an enzyme. The gene is the fundamental unit of heredity; each simple gene "codes" for a specific biological characteristic.

gene frequency. The relative frequency (proportion) of an allele in a population.

genetic drift. Random fluctuation allele frequencies from generation to generation.

genetics. The study of the patterns, processes, and mechanisms of inheritance of biological characteristics.

genome. The complete genetic makeup of an organism, comprising roughly 100,000 genes in humans.

genotype. The particular forms (alleles) of a set of genes possessed by an organism (as distinguished from phenotype, which refers to how the genotype expresses itself, as in physical appearance). In DNA analysis, the term is applied to the variations within all DNA regions (whether or not they constitute genes) that are analyzed.

genotype, single locus. The alleles that an organism possesses at a particular site in its genome.

genotype, multilocus. The alleles that an organism possesses at several sites in its genome.

guanine (G). One of the four bases, or nucleotides, that make up the DNA double helix. Guanine only binds to cytosine. See nucleotide.

Hae III. A particular restriction enzyme.

haploid number. Human sex cells (egg and sperm) contain 23 chromosomes each. This is the haploid number. When a sperm cell fertilizes an egg cell, the number of chromosomes doubles to 46. This is the diploid number.

haplotype. A specific combination of linked alleles at several loci.

Hardy-Weinberg equilibrium. A condition in which the allele frequencies within a large, random, intrabreeding population are unrelated to patterns of mating. In this condition, the occurrence of alleles from each parent will be independent and have a joint frequency estimated by the product rule. See independence, linkage disequilibrium.

heteroplasty. The condition in which some copies of mitochondrial DNA in the same individual have different base pairs at certain points.

heterozygous. Having a different allele at a given locus on each of a pair of homologous chromosomes. See allele. Compare homozygous.

homologous chromosomes. The 44 autosomes (non-sex chromosomes) in the normal human genome are in homologous pairs (one from each parent) that share an identical set of genes, but may have different alleles at the same loci.

human leukocyte antigen (HLA). Antigen (foreign body that stimulates an immune system response) located on the surface of most cells (excluding red blood cells and sperm cells). HLAs differ among individuals and are associated closely with transplant rejection. See DQA.

homozygous. Having the same allele at a given locus on each of a pair of homologous chromosomes. See allele. Compare heterozygous.

hybridization. Pairing up of complementary strands of DNA from different sources at the matching base pair sites. For example, a primer with the sequence AGGTCT would bond with the complementary sequence TCCAGA on a DNA fragment.

independence. Two events are said to be independent if one is neither more nor less likely to occur when the other does.

interim ceiling principle. A procedure proposed in 1992 by a committee of the National Academy of Sciences for setting a minimum DNA profile frequency. For each allele, the highest frequency (adjusted upward for sampling error) found in any major racial group (or 10%, whichever is higher), is used in product-rule calculations. Compare ceiling principle.

kilobase (kb). One thousand bases.

linkage. The inheritance together of two or more genes on the same chromosome.

linkage equilibrium. A condition in which the occurrence of alleles at different loci is independent.

locus. A location in the genome, i.e., a position on a chromosome where a gene or other structure begins.

mass spectroscopy. The separation of elements or molecules according to their molecular weight. In the version being developed for DNA analysis, small quantities of PCR-amplified fragments are irradiated with a laser to form gaseous ions that traverse a fixed distance. Heavier ions have longer times of flight, and the process is known as "matrix-assisted laser desorption-ionization time-of-flight mass spectroscopy." MALDI-TOF-MS, as it is abbreviated, may be useful in analyzing STRs.

match. The presence of the same allele or alleles in two samples. Two DNA profiles are declared to match when they are indistinguishable in genetic type. For loci with discrete alleles, two samples match when they display the same set of alleles. For RFLP testing of VNTRs, two samples match when the pattern of the bands is similar and the positions of the corresponding bands at each locus fall within a preset distance. See match window, false match, true match.

match window. If two RFLP bands lie with a preset distance, called the match window, that reflects normal measurement error, they can be declared to match.

microsatellite. Another term for an STR.

minisatellite. Another term for a VNTR.

mitochondria. A structure (organelle) within nucleated (eukaryotic) cells that is the site of the energy producing reactions within the cell. Mitochondria contain their own DNA (often abbreviated as mtDNA), which is inherited only from mother to child.

molecular weight. The weight in grams of one mole of a pure, molecular substance.

monomorphic. A gene or DNA characteristic that is almost always found in only one form in a population.

multilocus probe. A probe that marks multiple sites (loci). RFLP analysis using a multilocus probe will yield an autorad showing a striped pattern of thirty or more bands. Such probes rarely are used now in forensic applications in the United States.

multilocus profile. See profile.

multiplexing. Typing several loci simultaneously.

mutation. The process that produces a gene or chromosome set differing from the type already in the population; the gene or chromosome set that results from such a process.

nanogram (ng). A billionth of a gram.

nucleic acid. RNA or DNA.

nucleotide. A unit of DNA consisting of a base (A, C, G, or T) and attached to a phosphate and a sugar group; the basic building block of nucleic acids. See deoxyribonucleic acid.

nucleus. The membrane-covered portion of a eukaryotic cell containing most of the DNA and found within the cytoplasm.

oligonucleotide. A synthetic polymer made up of fewer than 100 nucleotides; used as a primer or a probe in PCR. See primer.

paternity index. A number (technically, a likelihood ratio) that indicates the support that the paternity test results lend to the hypothesis that the alleged father is the biological father as opposed to the hypothesis that another man selected at random is the biological father. Assuming that the observed phenotypes correctly represent the phenotypes of the mother, child, and alleged father tested, the number can be computed as the ratio of the probability of the phenotypes under the first hypothesis to the probability under the second hypothesis. Large values indicate substantial support for the hypothesis of paternity; values near zero indicate substantial support for the hypothesis that someone other than the alleged father is the biological father; and values near unity indicate that the results do not help in determining which hypothesis is correct.

pH. A measure of the acidity of a solution.

phenotype. A trait, such as eye color or blood group, resulting from a genotype.

polymarker. A commercially marketed set of PCR-based tests for protein polymorphisms.

polymerase chain reaction (PCR). A process that mimics DNA's own replication processes to make up to millions of copies of short strands of genetic material in a few hours.

polymorphism. The presence of several forms of a gene or DNA characteristic in a population.

point mutation. See SNP.

population genetics. The study of the genetic composition of groups of individuals.

population structure. When a population is divided into subgroups that do not mix freely, that population is said to have structure. Significant structure can lead to allele frequencies being different in the subpopulations.

primer. An oligonucleotide that attaches to one end of a DNA fragment and provides a point for more complementary nucleotides to attach and replicate the DNA strand. See oligonucleotide.

probe. In forensics, a short segment of DNA used to detect certain alleles. The probe hybridizes, or matches up, to a specific complementary sequence. Probes allow visualization of the hybridized DNA, either by radioactive tag (usually used for RFLP analysis) or biochemical tag (usually used for PCR-based analyses).

product rule. When alleles occur independently at each locus (Hardy-Weinberg equilibrium) and across loci (linkage equilibrium), the proportion of the population with a given genotype is the product of the proportion of each allele at each locus, times factors of two for heterozygous loci.

proficiency test. A test administered at a laboratory to evaluate its performance. In a blind proficiency study, the laboratory personnel do not know that they are being tested.

prosecutor's fallacy. See transposition fallacy.

protein. A class of biologically important molecules made up of a linear string of building blocks called amino acids. The directions for the synthesis of any particular protein are encoded in the DNA sequence of its gene.

quality assurance. A program conducted by a laboratory to ensure accuracy and reliability.

quality audit. A systematic and independent examination and evaluation of a laboratory's operations.

quality control. Activities used to monitor the ability of DNA typing to meet specified criteria.

random match. A match in the DNA profiles of two samples of DNA, where one is drawn at random from the population. See also random match probability.

random match probability. The chance of a random match. As it is usually used in court, the random match probability refers to the probability of a true match when the DNA being compared to the evidence DNA comes from a person drawn at random from the population. This random true match probability reveals the probability of a true match when the samples of DNA come from different, unrelated people.

random mating. The members of a population are said to mate randomly with respect to particular genes of DNA characteristics when the choice of mates is independent of the alleles.

recombination. In general, any process in a diploid or partially diploid cell that generates new gene or chromosomal combinations not found in that cell or in its progenitors.

reference population. The population to which the perpetrator of a crime is thought to belong.

replication. The synthesis of new DNA from existing DNA. See polymerase chain reaction.

restriction enzyme. Protein that cuts double-stranded DNA at specific base pair sequences (different enzymes recognize different sequences). See restriction site.

restriction fragment length polymorphism (RFLP). Variation among people in the length of a segment of DNA cut at two restriction sites.

restriction fragment length polymorphism (RFLP) analysis. Analysis of individual variations in the lengths of DNA fragments produced by digesting sample DNA with a restriction enzyme.

restriction site. A sequence marking the location at which a restriction enzyme cuts DNA into fragments. See restriction enzyme.

Reverse Dot Blot. A detection method used to identify SNPs in which DNA probes are affixed to a membrane, and amplified DNA is passed over the probes to see if it contains the complementary sequence.

sequence-specific oligonucleotide (SSO) probe. Also, allele-specific oligonucleotide (ASO) probe. Oligonucleotide probes used in a PCR-associated detection technique to identify the presence or absence of certain base pair sequences identifying different alleles. The probes are visualized by an array of dots rather than by the electrophoretograms associated with RFLP analysis.

sequencing. Determining the order of base pairs in a segment of DNA.

short tandem repeat (STR). See variable number tandem repeat.

single-locus probe. A probe that only marks a specific site (locus). RFLP analysis using a single-locus probe will yield an autorad showing one band if the individual is homozygous, two bands if heterozygous.

SNP (single nucleotide polymorphism). A substitution, insertion, or deletion of a single base pair at a given point in the genome.

Southern blotting. Named for its inventor, a technique by which processed DNA fragments, separated by gel electrophoresis, are transferred onto a nylon membrane in preparation for the application of biological probes.

thymine (T). One of the four bases, or nucleotides, that make up the DNA double helix. Thymine only binds to adenine. See nucleotide.

transposition fallacy. Confusing the conditional probability of A given B [P(A | B)] with that of B given A [P(B | A)]. Few people think that the probability that a person speaks Spanish (A) given that he or she is a citizen of Chile (B) equals the probability that a person is a citizen of Chile (B) given that he or she speaks Spanish (A). Yet, many court opinions, newspaper articles, and even some expert witnesses speak of the probability of a matching DNA genotype (A) given that someone other than the defendant is the source of the crime scene DNA (B) as if it were the probability of someone else being the source (B) given the matching profile (A). Transposing conditional probabilities correctly requires Bayes' Theorem.

true match. Two samples of DNA that have the same profile should match when tested. If there is no error in the labeling, handling, and analysis of the samples and in the reporting of the results, a match is a true match. A true match establishes that the two samples of DNA have the same profile. Unless the profile is unique, however, a true match does not conclusively prove that the two samples came from the same source. Some people use "true match" more narrowly, to mean only those matches among samples from the same source. Compare false match. See also match, random match.

variable number tandem repeat (VNTR). A class of RFLPs due to multiple copies of virtually identical base pair sequences, arranged in succession at a specific locus on a chromosome. The number of repeats varies from individual to individual, thus providing a basis for individual recognition. VNTRs are longer than STRs.

window. See match window.

X chromosome. See chromosome.

Y chromosome. See chromosome.

References on DNA

Ian W. Evett & Bruce S. Weir, Interpreting DNA Evidence: Statistical Genetics for Forensic Scientists (1998).

Elaine Johnson Mange & Arthur P. Mange, Basic Human Genetics (2d ed. 1999).

National Research Council Committee on DNA Forensic Science: An Update, The Evaluation of Forensic DNA Evidence (1996).

National Research Council Committee on DNA Technology in Forensic Science, DNA Technology in Forensic Science (1992).

Reference Guide on Engineering Practice and Methods

HENRY PETROSKI

Henry Petroski, Ph.D., P.E., is Aleksandar S. Vesic Professor of Civil Engineering and Professor of History, Duke University, Durham, North Carolina.

CONTENTS

I. Introduction

The products of engineering are everywhere, and it is unlikely that any person can spend a day without depending upon engineering of some kind for basic human needs, including health, food, and shelter. The very foundations of material civilization, in the form of its infrastructure and physical systems, are the results of deliberate engineering design. Even those things that have been in place for virtually the entire twentieth century and that now seem so mundane and are so often taken for granted, like the distribution networks that put clean water and ample electricity at our fingertips, require ongoing engineering monitoring and maintenance to ensure their reliability. Just as we have come to expect water and electricity to be givens of modern society, so we have come to expect automobiles to be in our garages and gasoline to be around the corner. These things would not be so without engineering.

Most people today tend to give scant notice to the marvels of engineering that once awed visitors to great exhibitions and world's fairs. It seems to be only when something goes wrong—a utility service is interrupted, the car does not start, or the computer crashes—that we take notice of engineering. And when something goes really wrong and results in injury or death, engineering tends to be not only noticed but also blamed and its practitioners held responsible. When blame results in litigation, the judge must make an assessment of the testimony offered by engineers in relation to the methods, customs, and practices of the profession.

II. Engineering and Science; Engineers and Scientists

A. Engineering and Science

The distinction between engineering and science, and between engineer and scientist, is not often made, yet it can be clearly stated: Science in its purest form theorizes about nature as it is found; engineering at its most basic re-forms the raw materials of nature into useful things. "The scientist seeks to understand what is; the engineer seeks to create what never was" is an oft-quoted way of putting it. Ironically, the quote is usually attributed to Theodore von Karman, who has been ambiguously identified at different times as a scientist and an engineer.

Many courts have struggled with this distinction. Until just recently the U.S. courts of appeals were split as to whether the *Daubert* standard for analyzing expert testimony of scientific evidence was applicable to engineering evidence.[1]

1. Daubert v. Merrell Dow Pharms., Inc., 509 U.S. 579 (1993).

Six courts held that the standard for scientific evidence should also be used for engineering evidence.[2] Four courts held that two different standards apply,[3] suggesting that scientific evidence and engineering evidence were quite different. The Eleventh Circuit concluded that "the Supreme Court in *Daubert* explicitly limited its holding to cover only the 'scientific context.'"[4] This issue was recently resolved by the Supreme Court in *Kumho Tire Co. v. Carmichael.*[5] The Court held that "[t]he *Daubert* factors *may* apply to the testimony of engineers and other experts who are not scientists."[6] The Court further noted that it would be difficult to distinguish "between 'scientific' knowledge and 'technical' or 'other specialized' knowledge, since there is no clear line dividing the one from the others . . . ."[7]

The fuzziness in the distinction between engineer and scientist can be attributed to the fact that what scientists sometimes do is engineering and the fact that engineers can make things that are not fully understood by scientists. A commonly given example of the former fact is that scientists were engaged in the Manhattan Project, whose purpose was the development of the first atomic bomb. A classic example of the latter fact is that the development of the steam engine by seventeenth- and eighteenth-century inventors (engineers) involved principles of nature that were not fully articulated by scientists until the advancement of thermodynamics in the nineteenth century. Indeed, it was the existence of working steam engines that prompted the development of the science of thermodynamics. For this reason, the science of thermodynamics is even more properly called an engineering science, that is, a science whose objects of study are not those that naturally occur in the universe, but those that are products of engineering, like the steam engine.

2. *See generally* Habecker v. Clark Equip. Co., 36 F.3d 278 (3d Cir. 1994); Freeman v. Case Corp., 118 F.3d 1011 (4th Cir. 1997), *cert. denied*, 522 U.S. 1069 (1998); Watkins v. Telsmith, Inc., 121 F.3d 984 (5th Cir. 1997); Smelser v. Norfolk S. Ry., 105 F.3d 299 (6th Cir.), *cert. denied*, 522 U.S. 817 (1997); DePaepe v. General Motors Corp., 141 F.3d 715 (7th Cir.), *cert. denied*, 525 U.S. 1054 (1998); Dancy v. Hyster Co., 127 F.3d 649 (8th Cir. 1997), *cert. denied*, 523 U.S. 1004 (1998).

3. *See generally* Bogosian v. Mercedes-Benz of N. Am., Inc., 104 F.3d 472 (1st Cir. 1997); McKendall v. Crown Control Corp., 122 F.3d 803 (9th Cir. 1997); Kieffer v. Weston Land, Inc., 90 F.3d 1496 (10th Cir. 1996); Carmichael v. Samyang Tire, Inc., 131 F.3d 1433 (11th Cir. 1997), *cert. granted sub nom.* Kumho Tire Co. v. Carmichael, 524 U.S. 836 (1998).

4. *Carmichael*, 131 F.3d at 1435 (quoting Daubert v. Merrell Dow Pharms., Inc., 509 U.S. 579, 580 n.8 (1993)).

5. 119 S. Ct. 1167 (1999).

6. *Id.* at 1169 (emphasis added).

7. *Id.*

B. Engineers and Scientists

Exactly who is a scientist and who is an engineer, and who is practicing science and who is practicing engineering are not always easy questions to answer. The educational background of individuals is no certain indicator, for it is not uncommon to encounter prominent "engineers" who do not have a single engineering degree, or individuals doing excellent "science" who have all of their degrees in engineering. Thus, on one hand, someone with three degrees in physics might be working on the foremost developments in computer storage devices, which are definitely products of engineering. On the other hand, an engineering faculty member educated as an engineer and specializing in electronic materials might also have a secondary academic appointment in a department of physics, definitely a science, and might be contributing original work to the literature of that field.

It is not uncommon to find, especially in a research-and-development context, an individual's position or title being given according to educational credentials rather than job description and vice versa. Membership in professional societies, however, very often does correlate with educational credentials, not only because individuals develop a loyalty to a profession and its organizations through student chapters but also because membership criteria are most easily satisfied by a degree in the relevant field. In contrast, professional certification, such as registration as a professional engineer, which in the United States is controlled by the individual states, can be obtained on the basis of experience and examination alone, regardless of educational credentials. Thus, for example, Jane Smith, P.E., who is responsible for the structural analysis of water-storage tanks, may have all of her degrees in mathematics. (In other countries, such as those of the British Commonwealth, professional registration is commonly under the auspices of professional societies or institutions.)

The most common route to registration or licensing as a professional engineer is for an individual to earn a bachelor's degree from an accredited engineering program (see section III.A.2). Such an individual can take the Fundamentals of Engineering examination during the senior year of college. Passing this eight-hour examination earns the individual the designation Engineer-in-Training (E.I.T.). The Fundamentals of Engineering is a standardized test, and hence the E.I.T. is recognized in all states of the United States. After gaining sufficient experience in responsible charge of engineering work, a person holding the E.I.T. designation may apply to a particular state board of registration to take a second examination in a specialty area, such as electrical engineering or mechanical engineering. Successful passing of this exam earns the individual the right to identify himself or herself as a Professional Engineer (P.E.) in the specialty area in which the P.E. examination was taken. There is reciprocity among states, but some are known to have more stringent requirements than others, for example, as to whether a new examination must be taken. It is not uncommon for a prominent consulting engineer with a nationwide practice to maintain registration in several dozen states.

An engineer registered as a P.E. is expected to adhere to a code of ethics. The elements of this code are often affixed to the application form that the engineer fills out to begin the registration process, and the engineer acknowledges awareness of the code at the time of application. (Many of the larger engineering societies have their own codes of ethics.) Increasingly, registered professional engineers are expected to participate in continuing professional development to maintain their registration. Whether such continuing professional development is mandatory currently varies from state to state.

Some states have special designations for certain engineering specialties. Thus, California and Illinois, which have special concerns about earthquake-resistant design and skyscraper design and construction, respectively, have separate registration procedures for structural engineers. Licensing and registration as a structural engineer in one of these states earns the individual the right to use the letters S.E. after his or her name.

Some engineering specialties have developed, independent of state registration laws, their own form of recognition and designation of professional practitioners. Thus, the American Academy of Environmental Engineers (AAEE) uses the term Diplomate Environmental Engineer (D.E.E.). The AAEE operates the specialty certification program, in which an engineer qualifies for the designation D.E.E. by holding a professional engineer's license, having at least eight years of progressively responsible civil engineering experience, and passing a peer review and examinations.[8] As another example, the American Institute of Hydrology (AIH), which includes the Society for Certification and Registration of Professional Hydrologists and Hydrogeologists, uses the terms Professional Hydrologist and Professional Hydrogeologist, among others, depending upon expertise, to designate engineers who it certifies and registers. Engineers practicing in such specialty areas may consider these designations to be more important than state registration as a P.E., and they may in fact consider them equivalent to the P.E. designation.[9]

Among the reliable indicators of who has done outstanding engineering are the prizes, awards, and distinguished membership ranks (such as Fellow) administered by professional societies and organizations. Although some of these recognitions are restricted to dues-paying members of the society and are thus of lesser reliability as indicators of true distinction, many of the most distinguished honors bestowed by the societies and institutions are independent of member-

8. *See* American Academy of Envtl. Eng'rs, *Board Certification Identifies Environmental Engineering Experts* (visited July 28, 1999) <http://www.enviro-engrs.org/experts.htm>.

9. *See* American Inst. of Hydrology home page (visited July 28, 1999) <http://www.aihydro.org>.

ship or educational background. Among the highest honors an American engineer can receive is membership in the National Academy of Engineering (NAE). That many of the members of the NAE were educated as scientists and have no degrees in engineering underscores the overlap between engineering and science. Indeed, many members of the NAE, including some who are engineers by education as well as by practice, are also members of the National Academy of Sciences, and a small number of these are also members of the Institute of Medicine.

In spite of this apparent open-mindedness and inclusiveness at the highest ranks of the profession, it is a common complaint among engineers who reflect on the nature of the profession and the public perception of it that science is often credited with technological achievements that are properly termed engineering. Although such observations, like most complaints of interest groups, are usually taken as sour grapes, there appears to be some validity to the engineers' claim, as newspaper stories about technological subjects frequently reveal. When, for example, the Mars Pathfinder mission approached its goal of landing on the red planet and deploying the rock-exploring rover in July 1997, a typical newspaper headline read, "A New Breed of Scientists Studying Mars Takes Control."[10] The scientists who were charged with studying the geology and chemistry of the planet's surface did indeed take over the news conferences and television interviews. The engineers who had conceived and designed the essential spacecraft and the rover it carried were, after some brief initial appearances, relegated to obscurity. A cultural critic writing for the *New York Times* even dismissed the engineers as prosaic and the Mars landing as not a television spectacular.[11] Whether or not it was spectacular, the physical mission was definitely an engineering achievement from which the scientific enterprise of planetary exploration benefited greatly.

Another common irritation among many engineers is when scientists are actually credited with an achievement that is clearly an engineering one. A new airplane, for example, might be heralded in the mass media as a "scientific breakthrough" when in fact it is an engineering one. More irritating to engineers, however, is the perception that when such an airplane crashes, as during a test flight, a headline is more likely than not to describe it as an "engineering failure."

The crediting of scientists over engineers with achievement was strikingly demonstrated when a U.S. postage stamp was issued in 1991 commemorating Theodore von Karman, one of the founders of the Jet Propulsion Laboratory,

10. John Noble Wilford, *A New Breed of Scientists Studying Mars Takes Control*, N.Y. Times, July 14, 1997, at A10.

11. Walter Goodman, *Critic's Notebook: Rocks, in Sharp Focus, but Still Rocks*, N.Y. Times, July 6, 1997, § 1, at 12.

which managed the Pathfinder mission. He was identified on the stamp as an "aerospace scientist," a fact that disappointed many engineers. It was only on the selvage of the stamp that von Karman was acknowledged to be a "gifted aerodynamicist and engineer." Yet von Karman's first degree was in engineering, and it was his desire to build and launch successful rockets—definitely an engineering objective—that drove him to study them as objects of science, just as an astronomer might study the stars as objects of nature, seeking to understand their origin and behavior. Unlike the engineer von Karman, who wanted to understand the behavior of rockets in order to make them do what he desired, however, the astronomer as scientist observes the stars with no further objective than to understand them and their place in the universe. A pure "rocket scientist," in other words, would be interested not in building rockets but in studying them.

C. Some Shared Qualities

Engineering clearly does share some qualities with science, and much of what engineering students study in school is actually mathematics, science, and engineering science. In fact, the graduate engineer's considerable coursework in these theoretical subjects distinguishes him or her more from the engineering technician than from the scientist. With this scientific background, an engineer is expected to be able to design and analyze and predict reliably the behavior of new objects of technology and not just copy and replicate the old. In addition to mathematics, science, and engineering science, however, the engineering student takes courses specifically addressing design, which is what distinguishes engineering from science.

1. Engineering is not merely applied science

That science forms a foundation for engineering is not to say that engineering is merely applied science and that engineers merely apply the laws of science in creating engineering designs. Although "applied science" is a commonly encountered pejorative definition of engineering, sometimes offered by scientists who consider engineering inferior to science and who do not fully appreciate the nature of engineering design, it is a patently false characterization. Engineering in its purest form involves creative leaps of the imagination not unlike those made by a scientist in framing a hypothesis or those made by an artist in conceiving a piece of sculpture.

Rather than following from scientific theory, an engineering design (hypothesis) provides the basis for analysis (testing the hypothesis) within that theory.[12] Engineering designs are not often likened to scientific hypotheses, but in fact

12. *See* Henry Petroski, To Engineer Is Human: The Role of Failure in Successful Design 40–44 (1985).

their origins can be quite similar and the testing of them remarkably analogous. Just as the conception of a scientific hypothesis is often the result of a creative, synthetic mental leap from a mass of data to a testable statement about it, from disorder to order, from wonder to understanding, so the origins of an engineering design can be spontaneous, imaginative, and inductive. Like the testing of the hypothesis, the analysis of the design proceeds in an orderly and deductive way. As in most analogies, however, the parallels are not perfect and the distinctions are not clear-cut. Design and analysis are in fact often intertwined in engineering practice. The design of a bridge may serve as a paradigm.

Imagine that a city wants a bridge to cross a river much wider and deeper than has ever been bridged before. Because the problem is without precedent, there is no existing bridge (no preexisting design) to copy. Engineers will, of course, be aware of plenty of shorter bridges in more shallow water, but can such models be scaled up? Even if it appears that they can technically, would it be practical or economical to do so? When presented with such a problem, the engineer must conceive a solution—a design—not on the basis of mathematics and science alone, but on the basis of extrapolating experience and, if necessary, inventing new types of bridges. The creative engineer will come up with a conceptual design, perhaps little more than a sketch on the back of an envelope, but clear enough in its intention to be debated among colleagues. This is the hypothesis—that the particular kind of bridge sketched can in fact be built and function as a bridge.

It is only when such a conceptual design is articulated that it can be analyzed to see if it will work. If, for example, the bridge proposed is a suspension bridge of a certain scale, it is possible to calculate whether its cables will be strong enough to support themselves, let alone a bridge deck hanging from them and carrying rush-hour traffic. Contrary to conventional lay wisdom, however, bridge designs do not follow from the equations of physics or any other science. Rather, the conceptual bridge design provides the geometrical framework for the engineer to use in applying the equations embodying the theory of structures to determine whether the various parts of the proposed bridge will be able to carry the loads they will have to after construction is complete. When a preliminary analysis determines that the conceptual design is in fact sound, the engineer can carry out more detailed design calculations, checking the minutest details to be sure that the structure will not fail under the expected loads.

The design of less critical and less costly products of engineering follows a similar process. Imagine that a company wants to develop a new product, perhaps because sales of its existing products are dropping off. The company's engineers are thus given the problem of coming up with something new, something better than all existing products, something unprecedented. The engineers, who often work in teams, will, perhaps by some ineffable process, conceive and articulate some new design, some new invention. Their hypothesis is, of course, that this design can be realized and the product sold at a competitive price. Testing the hypothesis may involve years of work, during which the engineers may find themselves faced with new problems of developing new materials and new manufacturing processes to fully and effectively realize the new design for a specified cost. The final product thus may be something that looks quite different from the first sketches of the original conceptual design. The engineers' experience will be not unlike that of scientists finding that they must modify their hypothesis as testing it reveals its weaknesses.

2. Engineering has an artistic component

The act of conceiving an engineering design is akin to the act of conceiving a painting or other work of art. Like the fine artist, the engineer does not proceed in a cultural vacuum, but draws upon experience in creating new work. Given the task of designing a bridge over obstacles between Point A and Point B, the engineer usually begins by sketching, literally or in the mind's eye, possible bridges. These preliminary concepts are likely to look not unlike those of bridges that cross over similar obstacles. Bridge designs that have worked in the past are likely to work in the future, if the new bridge is not too much longer or is not in too much deeper water than the earlier designs. However, each bridge project can also have its unique foundation, approach, or span problems, and the engineer must be prepared to modify the design accordingly, thus creating something that is different from everything that has come before.

Just as the artist chooses a particular block of stone out of which to chisel a figure or a specific size of canvas on which to paint, the engineer engaged in conceptual design also makes a priori choices about how tall a bridge's towers will be or how far its deck will span between piers. There are infinite geometrical combinations of these features of a bridge, as there are for the features of a figure in stone or the painting on canvas. It is the artistic decision of the engineer, no less than that of the artist, that fixes the idea of the form so that it can be analyzed, criticized, and realized by others. A recently published biography of a geotechnical engineer highlights the creative aspect of engineering practice through its subtitle, *The Engineer as Artist*.[13]

D. The Engineering Method

What is known as the engineering method is akin to the scientific method in that it is a rational approach to problem solving. Whereas the fundamental problem addressed via the scientific method is the testing of hypotheses, that ad-

13. Richard E. Goodman, Karl Terzaghi: The Engineer as Artist (1999). The book also provides insight into the many dimensions of personality and temperament—from the artistic to the scientific—that can coexist in an individual engineer.

dressed by the engineering method is the analysis of designs, which, as noted earlier, may be considered hypotheses of a sort. Once a conceptual design has been fixed upon, detailed design work can begin to flesh out the details. The engineering method is the collective means by which an engineer approaches such a problem, not only to achieve a final design but also to do so in such a way that the rationale will be understood by other engineers. Those other engineers might be called upon to check the work with the intention of catching any errors of commission or omission in the assumptions, calculations, and logic employed.

The starting point of much engineering work is in what has previously been done. That is not to say that engineers merely follow examples or use handbooks, for engineers are typically dealing with what has not been encountered before in exactly the same scale, context, or configuration. Yet, just as artists are ever conscious of the traditions of art history, so in the most creative stage of engineering, where conceptual designs are produced, engineers typically rely upon their knowledge of what has and has not worked in the past in coming up with their new designs. The development of these conceptual designs into working artifacts usually involves the greater expenditure of time and visible effort, and it is in this developmental stage that the engineering method most manifests itself.

Many engineering problems begin with shortcomings or downright failures with existing technology. For example, earthquakes in California have revealed weaknesses in prior designs of highway bridges: horizontal ground motion causing road decks to slide off their supports and vertical ground motion causing the support columns themselves to be crushed. To prevent such failures in the future, engineers have proposed a variety of ways to retrofit existing structures. Among the designs is one that wraps reinforced concrete columns in composite materials, with the intention of preventing the concrete from expanding to the point of failure. The idea is attractive because the flexible, textile-like materials could be applied relatively easily and economically to bridges already built. The basic engineering question would be whether it would be economical to wrap enough material around a column to achieve the desired effect.

The engineering method of answering such a question typically involves both theory and experiment. Since the material has a known strength and a known structure, calculations within the broad category of theory of strength of materials can produce answers as to whether the wrapping can contain the pressure of the expanding concrete during an earthquake. The problem and the calculations are complicated by the fact that a composite material is not a simple one, and its containing strength depends upon the structure of the wrapping material. Indeed, the engineering problem can very easily be diverted to one of establishing the best way to manufacture the composite material itself in order to achieve the desired result most efficiently. The calculations themselves will involve hypotheses about how the material is made and how it will perform when called upon to do so. In other words, all the calculations depend to a great extent upon theory and theoretical assumptions. Furthermore, there are fundamental questions about how the material will behave after prolonged exposure to the environment, including pollution and sunlight, which are known to have deleterious effects on certain composite materials. Also, there are questions about the long-term behavior of the composite wrapping when it would be in place on a column which itself was subjected to the repeated loads on the highway it supports. The repeated loading and unloading can cause what is known as fatigue, and what may be strong enough when newly installed may have its strength considerably reduced over the course of time. Experiments on the composite material, its components, and the wrapped column may be necessary to answer questions about the design and the theory upon which its analysis is based. What is central to the engineering method used to approach and attack such problems is its empirical and quantitative nature, and in this regard it is not unlike the scientific method.

While the design of bridges and analysis of proposed means to retrofit them against earthquake damage may appear to involve problems specific to civil engineering, the nature of the design process and the method used to analyze proposed designs is typical of engineering design and the engineering method generally. No engineer can design a crankshaft for an automobile engine or a circuit for an electronic calculator without first having a conceptual design that serves as a basis for the detailed design and development, including the confirming analysis that the thing is going to work when manufactured, installed, or assembled. The difference between a successful design and an unsuccessful one can often be traced to how carefully and thoroughly a design was in fact analyzed and tested—just as if it were a scientific hypothesis.

III. The Nature of Engineering

The practice of engineering is often separated into the two components of design and analysis, and different groups of engineers frequently carry out the distinct but hardly separable activities and pass their results back and forth over what has sometimes been described metaphorically as a wall. It is also a common complaint among engineers that when the designers and analysts have finished their work, they throw the "finished" design over another wall and let the manufacturing engineers worry about how to make the parts and assemble them. This model has historically been especially notorious in the aircraft manufacturing industry, with the notable exception of the Skunk Works operation of the

Lockheed Corporation, in which all engineers and assembly workers carried out their secret and highly successful projects in one big building.[14]

With the advent of computer-aided design and manufacturing, designers and manufacturers scattered around the world were able to combine design, analysis, and manufacturing in a highly integrated manner, as was done very successfully with the design and manufacture of the Boeing 777.[15] For all their importance in being but preludes to manufacturing, however, design and analysis are the aspects of engineering that are most commonly subject to dispute and thus to scrutiny. Indeed, even when there are problems with manufacturing, it is the tools and practices of design and analysis that are called upon to identify the causes of faults and to redesign the artifact or the process that manufactured it.

A. Design Versus Analysis

1. Design

Design, being dominated at its most fundamental level by the artistic component of engineering, and involving a lot of creativity, cannot be easily codified. A conceptual design can thus often be sketched more easily than it can be articulated in words, which is perhaps one of the reasons patents are not easy reading and almost always are accompanied by figures. It is debatable, therefore, whether design can be taught in any definitive way. That is not to say that design cannot be assessed in meaningful ways. Unlike an artistic design, which is often judged principally on the basis of aesthetics and taste, an engineering design is most properly judged by how well it functions. Indeed, engineers sometimes are rightly criticized for apparently seeing function as the only requirement of their designs.

The word *design*, used in an engineering context as a noun, verb, and adjective, has several different meanings, and is often used without distinguishing qualifiers. One engineer's conceptual design of a bridge or machine part is seldom, if ever, sufficiently fleshed out that the artifact can be built or manufactured without further details. This kind of design is high-level design, in the sense that it is typically conceived of or decided upon by someone in a leadership role on a project. With the conceptual design fixed, the engineering or detail design can proceed, usually by individual engineers or teams of engineers. This kind of design can be repetitive and tedious, full of calculations and small iterations, but the computer is increasingly being used to take over such tasks. A typical design task at this level would be to choose the sizes of the individual

14. *See* Ben R. Rich & Leo Janos, Skunk Works: A Personal Memoir of My Years at Lockheed (1994).

15. *See* Henry Petroski, Invention by Design: How Engineers Get from Thought to Thing 129 (1996).

pieces of steel that will make up a bridge or to determine the detailed geometry of a machine part for an engine. The finished product of such tasks can itself be referred to as "the design." This is not to say that the result will be exactly the same no matter what engineer carries out the calculations, for the design process is replete with individual judgments and decisions that cumulatively affect the result.

2. Analysis

Analysis, in contrast, is highly codified and structured. Unlike design problems, which seldom if ever have unique solutions, problems in analysis have only one right or relevant answer. Thus, once produced on paper or computer screen, the design might be checked by analysts using well-established theories of engineering science and mechanics, such as strength of materials, elasticity, or dynamics. Given the now fixed geometry of a structural or machine component and the agreed-upon design loads it is expected to experience, the analyst is able to calculate deflections, natural frequencies, and other responses of the part to the loads. Assuming no errors are made, the value of these responses will not depend upon who does the calculations. The calculated responses serve to check that the design is correct within the specifications of the design problem, and this is one way engineering design proceeds within a system of checks and balances. If the magnitudes of the responses prove to be unacceptable, the design will be sent back to the designers for further iteration. Needless to say, sometimes the designer and the analyst are one and the same individual engineer, in which case the design should ultimately be checked by another engineer.

Because the end result of an analysis is often a single precise number, analysis lends itself more easily to explication in the classroom and to coursework in the curriculum, and, according to some critics, it is taught in engineering schools sometimes almost to the exclusion of design. Indeed, until recently, the Accreditation Board for Engineering and Technology (ABET), which accredits engineering programs in the United States, had specific and distinct minimum requirements for the number of both design and analysis courses in the curriculum. Although this bean-counting approach has been abandoned of late, ABET does expect each program it accredits typically to contain a capstone design course, in which engineering students, usually in their senior year, are involved in a major design project that forces them to draw upon and synthesize the use of the analytical and design skills learned throughout the curriculum.

The usual engineering curriculum in the United States now comprises four years of study leading to a bachelor's degree, typically a Bachelor of Science or a Bachelor of Science in Engineering. Thus, in engineering, unlike in law and medicine, it is common to encounter practitioners with only an undergraduate education, and often a highly specialized, technical one at that. This, along with the fact that engineering has no single membership organization analogous to the American Bar Association or the American Medical Association, has been identified as a reason that the engineering profession is not perceived to have the status of the legal and medical professions, at least in the eyes of many engineers. For decades, there have been ongoing debates within the profession as to whether the first degree in engineering should be a five-year degree,[16] but few serious movements have been made in that direction. Indeed, five-year engineering degrees were more common decades ago, and long-term trends have been to move away from an extended curriculum and even to reduce the requirements for the four-year degree. Increasingly, there has been discussion about expecting a master's degree to be the first professional degree, but this too is far from the universal point of view.

The Ph.D. in engineering is typically a research degree, and the doctoral-level engineer will most often be engaged in analysis rather than design. Indeed, a design-based dissertation is considered an oxymoron in most engineering graduate programs. That is not to say that the engineer with a doctorate will not or cannot do design; he or she will more typically serve in a consulting capacity, engaged in both design and analysis of a nonroutine kind. It is not at all uncommon to find doctoral-level engineers working in research-and-development environments who seldom if ever perform design tasks, however, and they may have had little if any design experience.

B. Design Considerations Are More Than Purely Technical

The considerations that go into judging the success or effectiveness of an engineering design are seldom only technical, and at a minimum they usually involve questions of cost and benefit, and of investment and profit. Other design considerations include aesthetics, environmental impact, ergonomics, ethics, and social impact. Although such implications may not be considered explicitly by every engineer working on every design project, an engineering team collectively is likely to be aware of them. Aesthetics, for example, have been discussed explicitly as a dominant design consideration for bridges of monumental proportions, such as long-span suspension bridges. The ratio of the sag to the span of the main cables, which can be set for aesthetic as well as technical objectives, subsequently can have a profound impact on the forces in the cables themselves and hence the economics of the project.[17]

16. *See, e.g.*, Samuel C. Florman, The Civilized Engineer 205–06 (1987).

17. *See* David P. Billington, The Innovators: The Engineering Pioneers Who Made America Modern 6–12 (1996).

1. Design constraints

Engineering has been defined as design under constraint. Design constraints are among the givens of a problem, the limitations within which the engineer must work. A bridge over a navigable waterway has to provide a clear shipping channel between its piers and sufficient clearance beneath its roadway, and these are thus nonnegotiable design constraints. The specification of such clearances forces the design to have piers at least a certain distance apart and a roadway that is a certain distance above the water. The design of a roof structure over an auditorium has to accommodate the architect's decision that the auditorium will have a given width and ceiling height and have no columns among its seats. Such constraints can have profound implications for the type of bridge chosen and the kind of roof structure devised by the structural designer.

2. Design assumptions

No engineering design can be advanced through analysis unless certain assumptions are made. These design assumptions can be implicit or explicit, and they often involve technical details that affect the difficulty and accuracy of any subsequent analysis. Common design assumptions for long-span suspension bridges in the 1930s were that wind blowing across a deck displaced it sideways only and that wind did not have any aerodynamic effect on the structure. The former was an explicit design assumption that was manifested in the calculation of how stiff the bridge deck had to be in a horizontal plane. The latter assumption was implicit in the sense that it was never considered, but it may be considered an assumption nevertheless, since no calculation or analysis was performed to verify that aerodynamic effects were of no consequence. It was only after the Tacoma Narrows Bridge was destroyed by wind in 1940[18] that the bridge-design community recognized that aerodynamic effects were indeed important and could not be ignored by engineers or anyone else.

3. Design loads

No structural engineering analysis can proceed without the loads on the structure being stated explicitly. This presents a dilemma for the designer who is charged with specifying how large the structural components must be. The components are chosen to support a given load, but the bulk of that load is often the weight of the structural components themselves. For example, the weight of the steel in a long-span bridge may be over 80% of the total load on the structure. The engineer proceeds with the analysis only by first making an educated guess about how much steel will be required for the bridge. Since most bridge design involves familiar spans and types of structures, the educated guess can be

18. *See* Northwestern Mut. Fire Ass'n v. Union Mut. Fire Ins. Co., 144 F.2d 274 (9th Cir. 1944).

guided by experience. After a "design by analysis" based on the assumed weight is carried out, the original assumption about the weight of steel can be checked. If there is not sufficiently close agreement, the guess (assumption) can be modified and an iteration carried out. In other engineering design problems, the design loads may be the electric currents expected in a circuit or the volume of water to be handled by a sewer system, but the nature of the design problem is analogous to that of designing a bridge.

A well-known failure resulting from an improper use of the iterative design process occurred early in the twentieth century in the design and construction of the Quebec Bridge across the Saint Lawrence River.[19] The chief engineer, Theodore Cooper, was approaching the end of a distinguished career when he was given the opportunity to design and build the longest cantilever bridge in the world. His concept was for a slender-looking steel span of 1,800 feet between piers. The detailed design, that is, the sizing of the steel members, was to be carried out by Peter Szlapka, an engineer who worked in the offices of the Phoenix Bridge Company but had no experience in the field. Since Cooper, who was not in good health, did not want to travel to the construction site from his office in New York, he could not heed in time warning signs that the steel was not bearing the load properly, and the bridge collapsed before it was completed. An investigation by a royal commission found that Szlapka had curtailed his iteration prematurely and had underestimated the actual weight of steel on the bridge. As a result, some of his calculations of strength were as much as 20% higher than existed in the actual structure. The Quebec Bridge was redesigned and completed in 1917, but to this day no cantilever bridge has been designed with a longer span.

The weight of a bridge structure itself is known as the dead load.[20] The weight of traffic and snow and the force of wind and earthquakes are known as live loads.[21] These live loads are often specified as design loads, and they involve assumptions about how much traffic the bridge will carry and how extreme nature can be at the location of the bridge. The specification of design loads[22] has a profound impact on the cost of a structure, and hence design loads are

19. *See* Henry Petroski, Engineers of Dreams: Great Bridge Builders and the Spanning of America 101–11 (1995).

20. *See* Space Structures Int'l Corp. v. George Hyman Constr. Co., No. 88-0423, 1989 U.S. Dist. LEXIS 5798, at *5 n.2 (D.D.C. May 24, 1989) (defining "dead load" as the weight of the frame and its components). *See also* Wright v. State Bd. of Eng'g Exam'rs, 250 N.W.2d 412, 414 (Iowa 1977) (defining "dead load" as the weight of the roof itself).

21. *See Space Structures*, 1989 U.S. Dist. LEXIS 5798, at *5 n.2 (defining "live load" as the weight of the snow, rain, and wind that a frame can support). *See also Wright*, 250 N.W.2d at 415 (defining "live load" as the weight of the snow).

22. *See Space Structures*, 1989 U.S. Dist. LEXIS 5798, at *5 n.2 (defining "load" as the weight-bearing capacity of the frame itself).

chosen carefully. A bridge might conceivably have to support bumper-to-bumper traffic consisting entirely of heavy trucks fully loaded, but designing for such a load would make for a heavy, and therefore expensive, bridge. For a wide bridge with many lanes, it is unlikely that trucks would ever occupy every lane equally (indeed, they might be prohibited from doing so at all), and so an engineering judgment is made as to what is a credible design load. Because engineers took into account such considerations, the George Washington Bridge, which was first opened to traffic in 1931, could be designed and built for an affordable price. Otherwise it might not have been built when it was.[23]

Another example involves the construction of library buildings. Whereas libraries built at the beginning of the twentieth century are likely to have the floors of their bookstacks supported by the shelving structure, libraries built after the middle of the twentieth century are more likely to have the bookcases supported by the floors of the building. The space devoted to bookcases in such structures is actually only about one-third of the floor space, since adequate aisle space must be allowed for access. The dead load of the modern library building is that of the structure itself. The bookcases, which can be relocated if necessary, the books they hold, and the library staff and patrons can be considered the live load. A typical design assumption might be that upper-stack floors would carry a live load of about 150 pounds per square foot. Because of the ever-present demands on libraries to find more space for shelving books without constructing a new building or expanding an existing one, compact shelving came to be increasingly considered. However, since such shelving might increase the design live load on a floor to 300 pounds per square foot or more, it could not be installed on upper floors without compromising the factor of safety of the structure (see section III.C.1). Basement floors, on the other hand, which might have been designed at the outset for heavier loads, such as those required for storing larger and heavier library materials like maps and newspapers, could be retrofitted with compact shelving.[24]

Increasingly, bridges, buildings, machine parts, and other engineering structures and components are being designed with computers by a process known as computer-aided design (CAD). Much of the iterative process and the loading considerations described earlier can be incorporated into the computer software and so is invisible to the engineer using the computer. The engineer still plays a central role in the design process, however, especially when specifying what goes into the computer model of the structure or machine part being designed. This input can typically include the overall size of the structure or part, the

23. Jameson W. Doig & David P. Billington, *Ammann's First Bridge: A Study in Engineering, Politics, and Entrepreneurial Behavior*, 35 Tech. & Culture 537 (1994).

24. *See* Henry Petroski, The Book on the Bookshelf 178–80, 206–08 (1999).

specification of loads, the strength of the materials chosen, and the details of connections between interacting parts of the design.

C. "State of the Art"

The term "prior art"[25] is ubiquitous in the patent literature and designates existing technology that is being improved upon by something new, useful, and nonobvious. Virtually everything that is patented improves upon the prior art, and thus the prior art is in an ever-changing state. To work totally within the prior art at a given time is to design something that would be considered routine and thus hardly an invention. Engineers often work within the prior art, as when they design a common highway bridge that is very much like so many other highway bridges up and down the same road. Yet engineers are also often called upon to build bridges in new settings and under new circumstances, and in these cases they often must develop new types of bridges or devise new construction procedures. In such cases they may in fact have to go beyond the prior art and thus come up with something that is patentable.

When engineers are solving problems of an unusual kind or solving routine problems in a new way, they are in fact acting as inventors. Indeed, engineering can be thought of as institutionalized or formalized invention, though the terminologies of invention and engineering are commonly kept distinct. The term "prior art," for example, is seldom used in engineering; the term "state of the art" is used instead. Yet just as the prior art changes with each new patent, the "state of the art" in engineering also means different things at different times. At any given time, however, it designates what is considered the latest and generally agreed upon practice of engineers in a given area, whether that be bridge design, automobile design, or ladder design. To be considered innovative engineering, a new idea or design must not be obvious to someone versed in the state of the art.

To say that an engineer is practicing engineering within the state of the art is not a pejorative characterization, but rather an indication that the engineer is up-to-date in the field. The state of the art is advanced in engineering, as in science, by pioneers (inventors) who see limitations to the state of the art and who find fault with aspects of the state of the art that are not evident to those immersed in the paradigm.

25. *See* 35 U.S.C. § 103(a) (1999) (defining "prior art" as subject matter that as a whole would have been obvious to a person having ordinary skill in the subject area). *See also* Afros S.P.A. v. Krauss-Maffei Corp., 671 F. Supp. 1402, 1412 (D. Del. 1987) (discussing the scope of prior art as "that which is 'reasonably pertinent to the particular problem with which the inventor was involved'" (quoting Stratoflex, Inc. v. Aeroquip Corp., 713 F.2d 1530, 1535 (Fed. Cir. 1983))).

1. *"Factor of safety"*

Engineers recognize that they do not always fully understand the engineering–scientific theory or principles that underlie the functioning of their design. They also recognize that they necessarily have made assumptions in their analysis, and so the design as built will not behave exactly like the theoretical (mathematical) model that served as the basis for their analysis. They recognize further that a design as built does not necessarily have exactly the same details of workmanship or strength of materials as were assumed in the calculations. For these reasons and more, engineering designs are not made exactly to theoretical specifications but rather are made to practical ones.

If a machine part is calculated to carry a certain maximum load when in operation, the part as designed will in theory be able to carry a multiple of that load to allow for an abnormally weak part or batch of material being used, an exceptionally high load being applied, and other unusual but not fully unexpected conditions of use. The multiple is known as a "factor of safety,"[26] or sometimes jocularly (but not totally in jest), a "factor of ignorance" in recognition of the fact that not everything engineers do is fully understood by them and that there are likely to be unanticipated conditions that must somehow be taken into account in design. Although the concept of factor of safety is most readily articulated and understood in the context of loads on structures, the idea of a factor of safety can apply to engineering designs of all kinds.

2. *Conservatism in design*

An engineering design is said to be conservative when it carries an adequate factor of safety.[27] What is adequate may be a matter of judgment. There can actually be several different factors of safety identified with a given design. Thus, an airplane may be designed with one factor of safety against its wings fracturing and falling off and another against its fuselage being dented. A dented fuselage may have a small effect on how efficiently the plane flies, but a fractured wing would obviously jeopardize everyone on board. To apply a greater factor of safety to the wings makes sense even to a nonengineer.

What is an adequate factor of safety in a given application depends upon many things, including the state of the art of the theory underlying the design, the quality of materials that are used, and the quality and reliability of the workmanship that goes into realizing the design. In the middle of the nineteenth century, the theory of iron bridge design was in its infancy, and a responsible

26. *See generally* Baum v. United States, 765 F. Supp. 268, 273 (D. Md. 1991); *In re* Lloyd's Leasing Ltd., 764 F. Supp. 1114, 1127–28 (S.D. Tex. 1990); State *ex rel.* Fruehauf Corp. v. Industrial Comm'n, No. 90AP-393, 1991 Ohio App. LEXIS 2022, at *4 (Ohio Ct. App. 1991).

27. *See generally* Union of Concerned Scientists v. Atomic Energy Comm'n, 499 F.2d 1069, 1086–90 (D.C. Cir. 1974); United States v. Hooker Chem. & Plastics Corp., 607 F. Supp. 1052, 1065 (W.D.N.Y. 1985).

bridge engineer had to rely upon a large factor of safety—a good deal of conservatism—to ensure a safe bridge.

When a bridge over the River Dee collapsed in 1847 and the accident claimed some lives, a royal commission was appointed to look into the use of iron in railroad bridges. As part of the investigation, prominent engineers of the time were asked what factor of safety they applied to their bridges, and the responses ranged from 3 to 7.[28] Robert Stephenson, the engineer of the Dee Bridge, had been using factors between 1 and 2 for bridges like the Dee, and the Dee itself was found to have had a factor of safety of about 1.5.[29]

Dozens of bridges like the Dee, which was a brittle cast-iron beam trussed with malleable wrought iron, had been built in the preceding decade or so, and their successful performance justified to Stephenson, at least, the use of the lower factors of safety. The Dee was, however, the longest such bridge that had ever been attempted, and it collapsed after some heavy gravel was added to its roadway to reduce the possibility of its wooden deck being set afire by hot cinders spewed out of crossing steam engines. (The addition of the gravel also naturally lowered the factor of safety below 1.5.)

Although Stephenson was not as conservative as his contemporaries, he was not found negligent by the royal commission, and he went on to complete the landmark Britannia Bridge, whose design was being developed at the time of the Dee collapse and during its investigation. The Britannia, however, being of a more innovative design than the Dee, and with barely a precedent, was much more conservatively designed. Indeed, it was so conservative in its design that the chains that were to assist in holding up the box girder spans were deemed unnecessary, and so the towers to hold the chains remained a functionless frill on the completed bridge.

3. "Pushing the envelope"

As indicated in Figure 1 on the following page, Robert Stephenson was "pushing the envelope"[30] with his Dee Bridge and related bridges, in the sense that he was designing and building structures that were on the edge of the field of experience.[31] When the main-span length of such bridges was plotted against the year of construction, the data points representing Stephenson's bridges were in extreme positions on the graph.[32] Since the vague but generally smooth border formed by the extreme points in such a plot is known as an envelope of the

28. *See* Petroski, *supra* note 12, at 101.

29. *See* Henry Petroski, Design Paradigms: Case Histories of Error and Judgment in Engineering 85–86 & fig.6.2 (1994).

30. *See generally* Hataway v. Jeep Corp., 679 So. 2d 913, 920 (La. Ct. App. 1996) (defining "pushing the envelope" in the context of vehicle testing).

31. *See* Petroski, *supra* note 29, at 83–84 & fig.6.1.

32. P.G. Sibly, The Prediction of Structural Failures (1977) (unpublished Ph.D. dissertation, University of London).

points, Stephenson's designs represented by the extreme points were "pushing the envelope," that is, bulging it outward however slightly. It should be realized, however, that there are notable examples of successful bridges built well outside the envelope of experience. One was Stephenson's Britannia Bridge, and another famous one is the Forth Bridge, a cantilever bridge that was built at twice the span length of existing examples when there was very little experience with that genre.

Figure 1. The building and length of nineteenth-century trussed-girder bridges

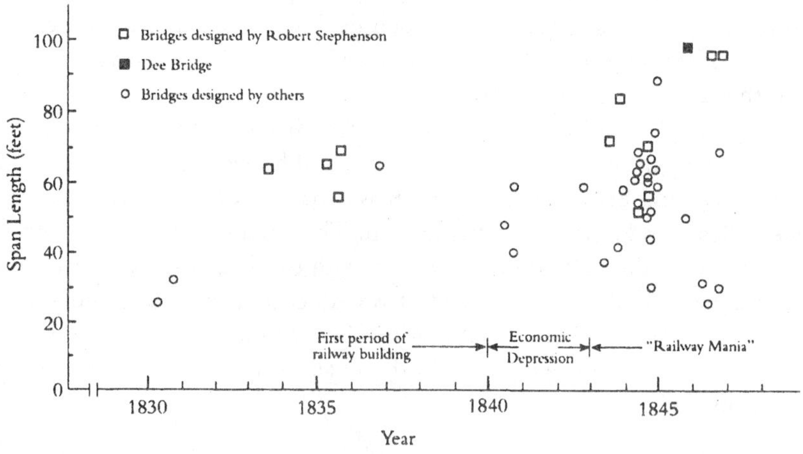

From Petroski, *supra* note 29, at 84 & fig. 6.1 (after Sibly, 1977).

Although the term may be more familiar in aeronautical and aerospace applications, the phenomenon of "pushing the envelope" is a common and natural thing to do in all of engineering. When designs work, there is a natural tendency to pare down those designs to shed excess strength, which usually equates with weight and, therefore, cost. There are several good reasons for the lowering of the factor of safety. With experience comes confidence, not to mention familiarity, with a design, and the design does not command the same sense of conservatism that new and unfamiliar designs do. As familiar designs of a particular kind proliferate, there also tends to evolve a sense that they can be extended to new limits, because prior limitations, which were expressions of conservatism, are thought to be excessive. New materials, construction, and manufacturing techniques; greater theoretical understanding; and improved tools of analysis also argue for less conservatism, lower factors of safety, and the pushing of the envelope.

The development of cable-stayed bridges was following this pattern at the end of the twentieth century. Dating principally from the 1950s in post-war Germany, cable-stayed bridges are attractive design options because they are relatively light and can be constructed relatively quickly, as compared with, say, suspension bridges. Cable-stayed bridges soon proliferated, but their main spans were increased slowly and incrementally, a conservative way to push the envelope. It was generally held that cable-stayed bridges were the span of choice for many applications in the 1,000- to 1,500-foot range; conventional suspension bridges were specified for longer spans. In the 1990s, however, cable-stayed designs with longer spans—some on the order of 3,000 feet—began to be built, increasing the maximum span by about 50% in one fell swoop.[33]

Such severe pushing of the envelope—indeed, going beyond or outside the envelope—is not unheard of. As mentioned earlier, the 1,710-foot Forth Bridge of the cantilever type did so in 1890, and the 3,500-foot George Washington Bridge almost doubled the main span of the longest previous suspension bridge, the 1,800-foot Ambassador Bridge between Detroit and Windsor, Ontario. The Tacoma Narrows Bridge near Seattle was built to the same state of the art as the George Washington, and, with a 2,800-foot main span, was the third largest in the world when completed in 1940. The Tacoma Narrows differed from the George Washington in a significant way, however, in that it was extremely narrow in comparison with its length, something so far outside the envelope of experience that one consulting engineer reviewing the design recommended that the bridge be built only if it were widened.[34] It was not, and the bridge collapsed in a 42-mile-per-hour wind only three months after it was completed.[35] The state of the art had not included analyzing and designing suspension bridges for aerodynamic effects, which were considered irrelevant.

D. Design Experience and Wisdom

The engineer who had most to do with the design of the Tacoma Narrows Bridge, Leon Moisseiff, was among the most distinguished engineers working on suspension bridges at the time. He had had a hand, as consulting engineer, in the design of virtually every record-breaking suspension bridge conceived and built since the turn of the century, and he was responsible for the principal analytical tool that was used in making bridges lighter because the forces in them

33. *See* Petroski, *supra* note 29, at 175 fig.10.3.

34. *See* Petroski, *supra* note 19, at 297–300.

35. *See* Northwestern Mut. Fire Ass'n v. Union Mut. Fire Ins. Co., 144 F.2d 274 (9th Cir. 1944).

could be calculated more accurately. When the critical but much less prominent engineer reviewing the Tacoma Narrows design recommended that it be widened to bring it more in line with demonstrated practice, Moisseiff dismissed the suggestion and essentially pointed to his considerable experience with suspension bridges and the theories of their behavior that he and a colleague had developed as his justification for leaving things as they were. Experience can be a dangerous thing in engineering if it blinds the engineer to the fact that envelopes can be pushed only so far.[36]

Another example of the arrogance of experience occurred in the design and construction of the Quebec Bridge across the Saint Lawrence River, discussed earlier. The chief engineer, Theodore Cooper, had an impeccable reputation, but his confidence seems to have been almost without bounds. The construction of the bridge was not properly monitored, and the incomplete structure collapsed in 1907. It was later found that the weight of the structure had been seriously underestimated in the design calculations and that the principal compression members in the structure were too slender.[37]

The examples of the Tacoma Narrows and Quebec Bridges are not typical of engineering practice, of course, but they are instructive in indicating that experience alone is no substitute for careful, correct, and complete analysis. These examples also illustrate that modes of failure that can be ignored in the design of structures of a certain proportion can be critical in the design of structures of the same genre but a different proportion. In the case of the Tacoma Narrows Bridge, aerodynamic effects that were of little consequence for wider, stiffer bridges like the George Washington proved disastrous for Moisseiff's narrow, flexible design. Similarly, the compression members of heavy, stubby cantilever bridges were not in danger of buckling, but they proved to be the weak links in a light, slender bridge like the Quebec.

E. Conservative Designs

Although it would appear to be a truism that conservative designs well within the state of the art pose little danger of failing, what constitutes conservatism in engineering design can be elusive. Galileo, though commonly thought of as a scientist, was very interested in Renaissance engineering. In fact, the motivation for his mature work, *Dialogues Concerning Two New Sciences*, was in some of the limitations of engineering understanding that led at the time to the spontaneous failure of ships and obelisks, among other things. One story Galileo tells at the beginning of this seminal work on strength of materials is of a long piece of marble that was being kept in storage with a support under each of its ends. Because it was known at the time that long heavy objects like ships and obelisks

36. *See* Petroski, *supra* note 19, at 294–308.

37. *See id.* at 109–18.

could break under such conditions, one observer suggested that a third support be added under the middle of the piece of marble, as indicated in Figure 2. According to Galileo, everyone consulted thought it was a good idea, and it was done. After a while, however, the marble was found to have broken in two, anyway.[38] In their self-satisfaction in taking action to prevent one mode of failure from occurring, the Renaissance engineers did not think to worry about the new mode of failure they were making possible by adding an additional support and thus changing the whole system and enabling it to behave in an unanticipated way.

Figure 2. The two failure modes described by Galileo.

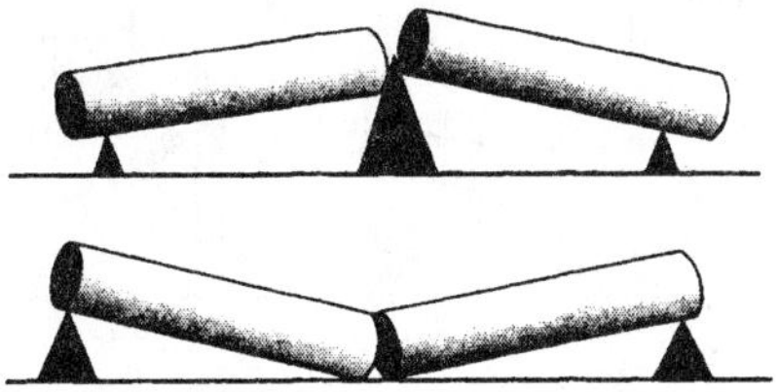

From Petroski, *supra* note 29, at 53 & fig. 4.3 (after Galileo, 1638).

An analogous event happened in 1981 in Kansas City, Missouri, when the elevated walkways of a hotel collapsed, killing 114 people.[39] The recently opened Hyatt-Regency Hotel had an expansive and towering lobby–atrium, and the elevated walkways, or skywalks, crossing it were designed to be supported from above so as to leave the floor of the lobby unobstructed by columns. The original design called for suspending one of the skywalks below another by means of long roof-anchored steel rods that would pass through the beams supporting the top walkway and support the lower one also, as indicated in Figure 3a. During construction, it was suggested that each single long rod be replaced by two shorter rods, one supporting the upper walkway from the roof and the other supporting the lower walkway from the upper. Such a design change could have been viewed as conservative because the unwieldy longer rods could have been bent and damaged during installation, whereas the shorter ones were more likely to survive installation without incident.

38. *See* Petroski, *supra* note 29, at 47–51.

39. *See* Deborah R. Hensler & Mark A. Peterson, *Understanding Mass Personal Injury Litigation: A Socio-Legal Analysis*, 59 Brook. L. Rev. 961, 972–74 (1993) (overviewing the events of the Hyatt-Regency skywalk collapse). *See also In re* Federal Skywalk Cases, 680 F.2d 1175 (8th Cir. 1982); *In re* Federal Skywalk Cases, 97 F.R.D. 380 (W.D. Mo. 1983).

Figure 3. Connection detail of upper suspended walkway in the Kansas City Hyatt Regency Hotel, as originally designed (A) and as built (B).

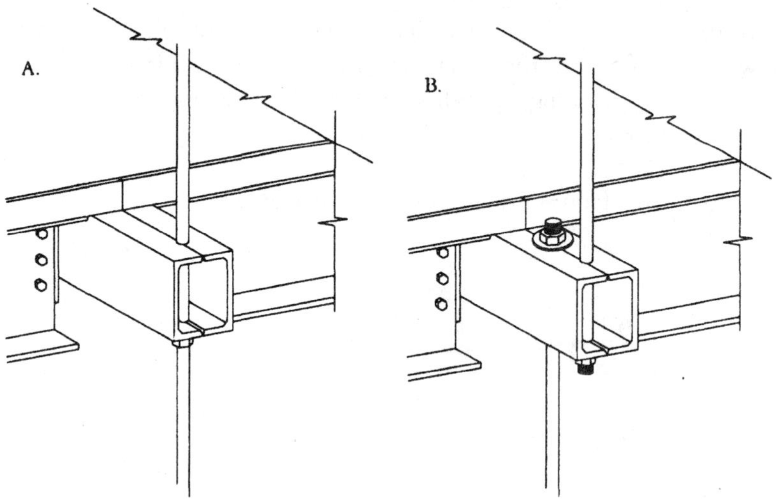

From Petroski, *supra* note 29, at 61 & fig. 4.7 (after Marshall et al., 1982).

When the structural engineers were asked about the change from single rods to double ones, they apparently raised no objection, and the skywalks were built in the changed manner. When the skywalks collapsed, the design change was quickly identified as the structural culprit. Replacing the one-rod design with the two-rod design essentially doubled the bearing stress on the upper walkway beam, because the connection there had to support the weight of not only the upper walkway but also the lower walkway. In the original design, the lower walkway's weight was carried by the rod and not the upper walkway.[40] Thus, what might appear to be relatively simple design changes for the better can drastically alter a system's behavior by introducing failure modes not even possible in the original design. Seemingly simple and innocuous design changes can be among the most pernicious. Had the design change not been made, the skywalks would likely still be in place.

The explosion of the space shuttle *Challenger* might be attributed, at least in part, to an attempt to design a more conservative solid booster rocket than had ever flown. Prior booster rocket designs, such at that of the Titan III, had a single O-ring sealing the gap between mating sections of the rocket casing. The

40. *See* Petroski, *supra* note 12, at 86–88.

Titan design was a very successful and proven one, and this argued for its adoption for space shuttle use. However, to make the design even more reliable, or so it was thought, a second O-ring was added to the joint between the sections, as indicated in Figure 4. This design change must surely have been considered a more conservative approach. It was, however, the complication of having two O-rings, and the difficulty of checking the proper seating of the one hidden by the other from visual inspection, that was a factor in the development of the leak that caused the *Challenger* to explode. Indeed, the supposed conservatism of the double O-ring design might also have contributed to the ill-fated decision to launch the shuttle against the advice of engineers who knew the O-rings were susceptible to damage in cold weather, which prevailed on the morning of the launch.[41]

Figure 4. O-ring designs for Titan III and space shuttle booster rocket.

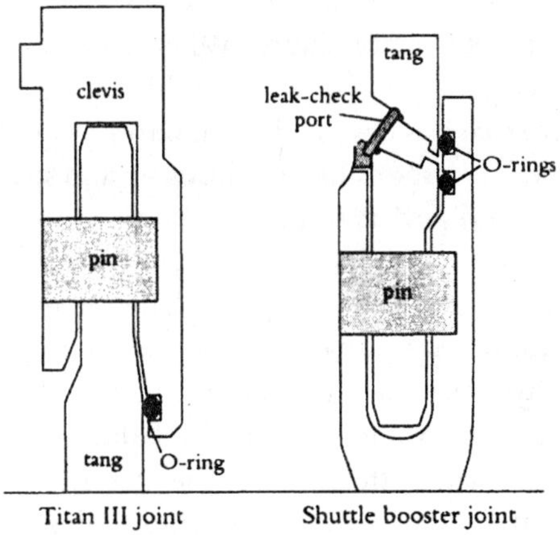

From Petroski, *supra* note 29, at 63 & fig. 4.9 (after Bell & Esch, 1987).

41. *See* Trudy E. Bell & Karl Esch, *The Fatal Flaw in Flight 51-L*, IEEE Spectrum, Feb. 1987, at 36. *See also* Hans Mark, The Space Station: A Personal Journey 218–21 (1987).

F. Daring Designs

If the belief that a design is conservative can be misplaced, so can a fear that any design innovation is doomed to fail. The *Apollo 11* mission to the moon demonstrated that an engineering system design of enormous complexity and novelty, that of the moon lander, could succeed the first time it was tried. Indeed, the history of engineering is full of examples of new designs succeeding the first time they have been attempted. Among the most famous and successful bridges in the world is the Forth Bridge in Scotland, described earlier. This innovative design comprising record-breaking cantilever spans was also the first major bridge to be made entirely of steel.

IV. Success and Failure in Engineering

A. The Role of Failure in Engineering Design

Failure is a central idea in engineering. In fact, one definition of engineering might be that it is the avoidance of failure. When a device, machine, or structure is designed by an engineer, every way in which it might credibly fail must be anticipated to ensure that it is designed to function properly. Thus, in designing a bridge, the engineer is responsible for choosing and specifying the type and size of the piers, beams, and girders so that the bridge does not get undermined by the current in the river the bridge spans, does not collapse under rush-hour traffic, and does not get blown off its supports. The engineer ensures that these and other failures do not occur by analyzing the design on paper, and the objective of the analysis is to calculate the intensity of forces in the structure and compare them with limiting values that define failure. If the calculated force intensities are sufficiently within the limits of the material to be used, the bridge is assumed to be safe, at least with respect to the modes of failure considered. (Each separate mode of failure must be identified and checked individually.)

In a suspension bridge, for example, the total force in the main cable depends upon the geometry of the bridge and the traffic it must carry. The force the cable must resist determines how large the cable must be if a certain type of steel wire is used. Since the steel wire, like every engineering material, has a breaking (failure) point, the engineer calculates how far from the breaking point the cable will be when the bridge is in service. If this difference provides the desired factor of safety, the engineer concludes that the bridge will not fail, at least in the mode of the cable breaking, even if the wire installed is somewhat weaker than average and the traffic load is heavier than normal. Other possible ways in which failure may occur must also be considered, of course. These may include such phenomena as corrosion, ship collision, and earthquakes. The collection of such calculations and considerations constitutes a complete analysis of the design.

B. The Value of Successes and Failures

It is an apparent paradox of science and engineering that more is learned from failures than from successes. Indeed, Karl Popper's philosophy of science holds that a scientific hypothesis must be falsifiable. What this means is that a given hypothesis can be found false by a single counterexample. Thus, if a scientist puts forth a hypothesis that states that no living thing can exist for more than 100 years, the documented existence of a living tree more than 300 years old disproves the hypothesis. If, however, no one can produce a living thing that is more than 100 years old, this does not prove the hypothesis. It merely confirms it as a (true) hypothesis, still subject to being proven false by a single counterexample.

Engineering has hypotheses also, and they are equally refutable by a single counterexample. In the first half of the nineteenth century, it was a commonly held belief (or hypothesis) that a suspension bridge could not safely carry railroad trains. John Roebling explained his reason for studying the failures of suspension bridges that had occurred during that time by stating that he could not know how to design a successful bridge unless he knew what he had to design it against. In the 1850s he designed and built a suspension bridge over the Niagara Gorge that did carry railroad as well as carriage traffic. In other words, Roebling's bridge provided the counterexample to the hypothesis that suspension bridges could not carry railroad trains. At the same time, his successful bridge did not prove that all suspension bridges would be safe.

When a bridge carries traffic successfully or a skyscraper stands steady in the wind, the structure does not reveal much beyond the fact that it is fulfilling its function. Although design claims that the structure would not fail will have been verified by the successful structure, and measurements of how much the structure moves under load will confirm quantitatively what the design calculations predicted, that does not prove that the design analysis was total or complete. If the design calculations did not include aerodynamic effects, for example, like the flutter of a bridge's roadway in the wind, that does not mean the wind cannot bring the structure down, as it did the Tacoma Narrows Bridge. Nature does not ignore what an engineer may have overlooked.

If an unexpected failure occurs, however, such as the collapse of the Tacoma Narrows Bridge, then it provides incontrovertible evidence that the design was improperly (or incompletely) analyzed or something was overlooked. Whereas aerodynamic effects might have been insignificant in bridges that were wide and heavy, like the George Washington Bridge, they could not be ignored in light and narrow structures like the Tacoma Narrows Bridge. Unfortunately, it often takes a catastrophic failure to provide the clear and unambiguous evidence that the design assumptions were faulty.

There were precursors to the collapse of the Tacoma Narrows Bridge, in that several other bridges built in the late 1930s displayed unexpected behavior in the wind. Indeed, engineers were studying the phenomenon, trying to understand and explain it, and debating how properly to retrofit the bridges affected when the landmark failure occurred. It provided the counterexample to the implicit engineering hypothesis under which all such bridges were designed, namely, that the wind did not produce aerodynamic effects in heavy bridge decks sufficient to bring them down. Thus, the failure of the Tacoma Narrows Bridge proved more instructive than the success of all the bridges that had performed satisfactorily—or nearly so—over the preceding decades.

1. Lessons from successful designs

Strictly speaking, a successful design teaches engineers only that that design is successful. It does not prove that another design like it in every way but one will also be successful. For example, there is a size effect in engineering, as in nature, and it appears to have been known, though not necessarily fully understood, for millennia. Vitruvius, who wrote in the first century B.C. what is generally considered to be the oldest work on engineering extant, related the story of the ancient engineer Callias, who convinced the citizens of Rhodes with the aid of a model that he could build a machine to defend their city against any siege the enemy could launch. When the enemy did attack with an unprecedentedly large heliopolis, Callias confessed that he could not defend the city as promised because although his defense machine worked as a model, it would not work at the scale needed to conquer the gigantic heliopolis.

Galileo, writing fifteen centuries later, described how limitations to size were appreciated in the Renaissance, even though still not fully understood. He told of the spontaneous failure of wooden ships upon being launched and of stone obelisks upon being moved. It was Galileo's work that finally explained what was happening. Since the volume of a body, natural or artificial, increases faster than the area of its parts as they are scaled up in a geometrically similar way, there will come a time when the weight is simply too much for material of the body to bear. This, as Galileo explained, is why smaller animals have different proportions than larger ones, and it is also why things in nature grow only so large. So it is with engineered structures.

The phenomenon of the size effect is not the only one that has taken engineers by surprise. The aerodynamic instability manifested in suspension bridges in the late 1930s was absent or insignificant and thus unimportant in early designs of those structures. However, it became dominant and thus significant in evolved designs, which were so much larger, lighter, narrower, or more slender.

Another example relates to metal fatigue, a mechanical phenomenon in which the repeated loading and unloading of a structural component leads to crack growth, which in turn can lead to catastrophic failure of the weakened part.

Metal fatigue had long plagued the railroad industry. In time it came to be understood that if the intensity of loading was kept below a certain threshold, cracks would not develop and thus the structure would not be weakened. When commercial jet aircraft were first developed after the Second World War, metal fatigue was not believed to be relevant, but the mysterious failures of several de Havilland Comets in the 1950s led one engineer to suspect that fatigue was indeed the cause of the mid-air disasters. It was in fact true that the cyclic pressurization and depressurization of the cabin with every takeoff and landing was producing fatigue cracks that grew until the fuselage could no longer hold together. The engineer was able to confirm his hypothesis about fatigue by testing to failure an actual Comet fuselage under controlled conditions.[42]

The phenomenon of fatigue does not affect only large structures made of metal. A fatigue failure of a more modest kind but nevertheless of significant consequence to those who used the device was the breakage of keys on the child's toy Speak & Spell. Introduced by Texas Instruments in the late 1970s, not long after electronic calculators had become embraced by engineers, this remarkable device employed one of the first microelectronic voice synthesizers. Speak & Spell would ask a child to spell a word, and the child responded by pecking out the word letter by letter on the keyboard, each letter appearing as it was typed on the calculator-like display. Upon hitting the enter key, the child was told that the spelling was correct or was asked to try again. Children enjoyed the toy so much that they used it for hours on end, thus flexing the plastic hinges of the letter keys over and over again. This repeated loading and unloading of the plastic hinges led some of them to exhibit fatigue and break off. Children could still fit their little fingers into the keyholes, however, and so they could continue to use the toy, disfigured as it was. What makes the experience with Speak & Spell so instructive as an example of a fatigue failure is that the first key to break was invariably the one used most—the E key. For those Speak & Spells that continued to be used, subsequent keys tended to break in the same sequence as the frequency of letters used in the English language—E, T, A, O, I, N, and so forth—thus demonstrating the fundamental characteristic of fatigue failure, namely, that all other things being equal, the part subjected to the most loadings and unloadings will break first.[43]

The Speak & Spell example also shows how engineering designs are changed in response to repeated failures. In time, a new model of the toy was introduced, one with a redesigned keyboard. In place of the plastic keys that fit individually into recesses there was a flat keyboard printed on a rubbery plastic sheet that overlay all the switches for the letters. Not only did the new design reduce the incidence of key failure, but it also made for a flat surface that was much easier

42. *See* Petroski, *supra* note 12, at 176–84.

43. *Id.* at 22–27.

to clean than the original model, which collected the snack residue that children are likely to leave on their toys. The redesign of the Speak & Spell is a representative example of how engineers are attentive and responsive to failures.

2. *Lessons from failures*

Unanticipated failures may be thought of as unplanned experiments. While failures are also unwanted, of course, the surprise result of any failure is clearly interesting, and it reveals a point of ignorance that engineers must then seek to correct. Thus, when the Tacoma Narrows Bridge collapsed, bridge engineers could no longer argue that they did not have to analyze large suspension bridge designs for their susceptibility to aerodynamic effects. Indeed, it was the unanticipated motion of bridge decks (the failure of them to hang steady in the wind) that prompted wind-tunnel tests of the deck designs for future suspension bridges. Although such model tests were still open to some criticism as to their relevance for the full-scale bridge, comparative wind-tunnel tests could be conducted on alternative deck designs, and such tests led to new designs in the wake of the Tacoma Narrows collapse. The wing-like decks of the Severn and Humber Bridges in Britain are examples of such new designs.

Failures in machine parts are equally revealing of design weaknesses. A bracket that keeps breaking in an automobile engine, for example, indicates a poorly designed detail, and it is likely that this bracket will in time be redesigned to give it greater strength in the vulnerable location. As a result, replacement parts will come to be manufactured in a slightly different form than the original, and later models of the same automobile are likely to come with the redesigned bracket factory-installed.

C. Successful Designs Can Lead to Failure

A major advance in the design and construction of long-span suspension bridges was made in the mid-nineteenth century by John A. Roebling. His career culminated in his design of the Brooklyn Bridge, the completion of which was overseen by his son, Washington A. Roebling, and his wife, Emily Warren Roebling. For half a century from 1883, when the Brooklyn Bridge was opened to traffic, suspension bridges evolved in several directions. The most obvious change was that the length of the main span increased from the 1,595 feet of the Brooklyn Bridge to the 4,200 feet of the Golden Gate Bridge, which was completed in 1937. Another important development was the increasing slenderness of suspension bridges, perhaps best exemplified by the shallow roadway of the George Washington Bridge as completed in 1931 with only a single deck. (The lower deck was not added until the early 1960s.) The evolution to slenderness of suspension bridges culminated in several long-span suspension bridges of the late 1930s, including the Bronx-Whitestone and Deer Isle Bridges, which used shallow plate girders instead of deep deck trusses to support the roadway.

Another important change in the design of suspension bridges after the Brooklyn Bridge was the elimination of the cable stays that radiate from that bridge's Gothic towers to its roadway. In the Brooklyn Bridge this feature results in the web-like pattern of its cables that is characteristic of Roebling designs. John Roebling had incorporated this feature, as well as guy wires steadying the bridge from beneath, in his Niagara Gorge Bridge of 1854, which was the first suspension bridge to carry the heavy and violent loads of railroad trains. As suspension bridges came in time to be built larger, the feature of guy wires was dispensed with, as the effect of the wind on vertical motions of the deck was believed to be insignificant. In this way, the successful designs of more than a half century earlier evolved into the light, narrow, slender, and unadorned Tacoma Narrows Bridge that could not withstand a 42-mile-per-hour wind.

The evolution of bridges is a paradigm for the development of all designed structures and for the evolution of artifacts generally. The more successful a design, the more likely it is to be a model for future designs. But because engineering and construction are influenced by aesthetics, economics, and, yes, ethics or their absence, designs tend to get pared down in time.[44] This paring down can take the form of enlargement in size without a proportional increase in strength, in defiance of the size effect; streamlining in the sense of doing away with what is believed to be superfluous; lightening by the use of stronger materials or materials stressed higher than before; and cheating, which can take the form of leaving out some indicated reinforcement in concrete or deliberately substituting inferior materials for specified ones. The cumulative effect of such paring down of strength is a product that can more readily fail. If the trend continues indefinitely, failure is sure to occur.

When failures do occur, engineers necessarily want to learn the causes. Understanding of the reason for repeated failures—structural or otherwise—that jeopardize the satisfactory use and therefore the reputation of a product typically leads to a redesigned product. Thus, the vulnerability of automobile doors to being dented in parking lots led to the introduction of protective strips along the length of car bodies. The propensity of pencil points to break under relatively light writing pressure led pencil manufacturers in the 1930s to look into the reasons for the failures. When it was found that the pencil lead was not being

44. *See* Baum v. United States, 765 F. Supp. 268, 274 (D. Md. 1991) (noting the often conflicting factors, the court commented that "National Park Service officials have more than safety in mind in determining the design and use of man-made objects such as guardrails and signs along the parkway. These decisions require balancing many factors: safety, aesthetics, environmental impact and available financial resources.").

properly glued to the wood case, research-and-development efforts were initiated to design a more supportive joining process. This led to proprietary pencil manufacturing processes with names such as "Bonded," "Chemi-Sealed," "Pressure Proofed," and "Woodclinched," some of which can be found still stamped on pencils sold today.[45]

Failures that cause more significant property damage or that claim lives are usually the subject of failure analyses conducted by consulting engineers or forensic engineers. Such investigations may be likened to puzzle solving or to design problems worked in reverse, in that the engineer must develop hypotheses and then test them with analysis. However, with direct design there is no unique solution; in a forensic engineering problem, there presumably is a unique cause of a particular failure, but it might not easily be found.

The failure analyst or forensic engineer must essentially come up with a hypothesis of how the particular failure under investigation was initiated and progressed. The hypothesis obviously must be consistent with the evidence, which should be preserved as much as possible in the state in which it existed when the failure occurred. This means, for example, that the configuration of an accident scene should be recorded before anything is moved, that the fracture surfaces of broken parts should not be touched or damaged further, that bent and twisted parts should be left in their as-found condition, and generally that each and every piece of potential evidence should be carefully labeled and handled with care. In other words, the scene of an engineering failure should as much as possible be treated as if it were the scene of a crime. The urgent need to move material objects to reach persons involved in an accident takes precedence, of course, and how this may have affected forensic evidence must itself be taken into account in the analysis of evidence from the accident scene.

There have been attempts to formalize the procedures involved in the investigation of failures, especially those of a recurring nature, such as the collapse of structures.[46] However, with the exception of aircraft accident sites, which are under the control of the National Transportation Safety Board (NTSB), there is no uniform way in which structural failure sites are controlled. In the case of the Kansas City Hyatt-Regency walkways collapse, for example, the owner of the building had the one surviving walkway removed within a day or so of the accident, thus depriving engineers of the opportunity to study an undamaged structure of similar design to see if it provided any clues to the cause of the collapse of the other two walkways.

Regardless of how the failure or accident site is treated, investigating engineers must seek clues to the cause in whatever way they can. The most helpful information naturally comes from the most well-preserved pieces of the puzzle.

45. *See* Henry Petroski, The Pencil: A History of Design and Circumstance 244–45 (1990).

46. *See, e.g.*, Jack R. Janney, Guide to Investigation of Structural Failures (1979).

Thus, broken parts should be handled with care so as not to destroy evidence of how a crack might have begun and propagated or how two broken pieces may or may not fit together. Cracks in metal and plastic generally leave telltale clues as they grow, and the failure-analysis expert can read these clues under a microscope with some degree of certainty. Broken pieces that fit together to produce a part that could be mistaken for new were it not for the fracture indicate that the material was extremely brittle when the part broke, something that may or may not have been appropriate for the design. In contrast, pieces that when fitted together show the part to have been stretched and bent before breaking indicate a ductile material and give some indication of the nature of the loads before the fracture. Such conclusions can be drawn with a high degree of certainty, and the kind of information they yield can often lead to the construction of a very likely scenario for what happened.

Investigators for the NTSB look for such clues, and more of course, when they collect the parts of a crashed plane and assemble them on the floor of a hangar. No matter how sure the board's final conclusion might be, however, it is always presented as a "most likely cause" rather than a proven fact, in recognition that fundamentally the proffered cause is but a hypothesis. Just as scientific hypotheses can be confirmed and verified but never proven with mathematical certainty, so the cause of an engineering failure can only be confirmed and verified by the surviving evidence. The evidence can often be so overwhelmingly convincing, however, that engineers use it to guide their redesigns and future designs.

The more catastrophic and dramatic failures, especially those that claim lives, are often the subject of public and formal investigations. The explosion of the space shuttle *Challenger*, in which all seven astronauts on board died, was investigated by a presidential commission, whose hearings were televised. The collapse of the Quebec Bridge, which claimed the lives of about seventy-five construction workers, was looked into by a royal commission. And the failure of the elevated walkways in the Kansas City Hyatt-Regency Hotel in 1981 was investigated in some detail by what was then the National Bureau of Standards. (The role of the engineers in the collapse of the walkways was the subject of a case presented by the professional engineering licensing board of Missouri before a commissioner.[47]) In all such cases, there have been extensive formal reports, which are often very informative not only about the particular case under consideration but also about the nature of the engineering design process generally. Collectively, such reports can point to patterns regarding failures and thus to generalizations about what engineers might be watchful for in the future.

For example, the history of bridges over the last century and a half reveals a

47. Missouri Bd. of Architects, Prof'l Eng'rs & Land Surveyors v. Duncan, No. AR-84-0239, 1985 Mo. Tax LEXIS 50 (Mo. Admin. Hearing Comm'n Nov. 15, 1985).

disturbing pattern of success leading to failure. Beginning with the Dee Bridge failure in 1847, roughly every 30 years there has been a major bridge failure—each of a different type of bridge—and each failure can be traced to the gradual transformation of a successful bridge design.[48] Among the explanations for this haunting pattern is that novel types of bridges are designed by engineers who take care with the designs, since they have few precedents, and the designs that are successful are copied and in time come to be attempted in longer lengths, in more slender profiles, and with increasing casualness by a younger generation of engineers that is unaware of or does not remember the assumptions that went into the early designs or the limitations of those designs. Such a pattern was being repeated in the late twentieth century for cable-stayed and post-tensioned bridges, and such bridges may well be expected to suffer a catastrophic failure early in the new millennium.

D. Failures Can Lead to Successful Designs

Just as successful designs can lead to failures, so can failures lead to revolutionary successes. The same history of bridge failures described earlier (in section IV.C) also reveals that with a catastrophic failure, a type of bridge or a construction practice falls out of favor. This occurs often more for extratechnical reasons, such as an attempt to regain the public's confidence so that the new bridge will attract the public to a railroad or a toll highway.

If a type of bridge ceases to be used, then a new type must be developed for the building of new bridges. In the wake of a major failure, new engineers are likely to be retained, engineers with solid reputations and impeccable credentials. Furthermore, because a novel type of bridge is being proposed, its design must proceed with deliberate attention to detail and explicit consideration of all relevant modes of failure. In the wake of the failure, the bridge tends to be overdesigned to further ensure its reliability.[49]

E. Engineering History and Engineering Practice

The historical pattern described in the preceding two sections points to the value of history for present and future engineering. As suspension bridges were being designed with ever longer lengths and with ever more slender profiles, engineers of the 1920s and 1930s looked to the history of bridges for aesthetic models. Among the bridges often referred to was the Menai Strait Suspension Bridge in Wales, which was designed and built by Thomas Telford in the 1820s. The stone towers, iron chains, and wooden deck of this classic bridge influenced greatly the bridges of a century later, but the Menai served only as an aesthetic

48. *See* Petroski, *supra* note 29, at 168–69.
49. *Id.* at 176–77.

model and thus only to a limited extent. The repeated destruction in the first half of the nineteenth century of the Menai Strait Bridge's deck in the wind was dismissed as irrelevant to the state of the art of modern bridge building. This was so because it was believed that the force of the wind could not produce the same effects on a heavy steel deck that it did on the Menai Strait's light wooden fabric. This, of course, proved to be a totally unfounded assumption.

The history of engineering, even of ancient engineering as recorded 2,000 years ago by Vitruvius, has a relevance to modern engineering because the fundamental characteristics of the central activity of engineering—design—are essentially the same now as they were then, have been through the intervening millennia, and will be in the new millennium and beyond. Those characteristics are the origins of design in the creative imagination, in the mind's eye, and the fleshing out of designs with the help of experience and analysis, however crude. Furthermore, the evolution of designs appears to have occurred throughout recorded history in the same way, by incremental corrections in response to real and perceived failures in or inadequacies of the existing technology, the prior art. There also is strong evidence in the historical record that engineers and their antecedents in the crafts and trades have always pushed the envelope until failures have occurred, giving the advance of technology somewhat of an epicyclic character. Thus, according to this view, the fundamental characteristics of the creative human activity we call design are independent of technological advances in analytical tools, materials, and the like.

The way artifacts were designed and developed in ancient times remains a model for how they are designed and evolve today. This is illustrated in a story Vitruvius relates of how the contractors and engineers Chersiphron, Metagenes, and his son Paconius used different methods to move heavy pieces of stone from quarry to building site. The method of Chersiphron—which was essentially to use column shafts as wheels, into whose ends hollows were cut to receive the pivots by which a pulling frame was attached, as indicated in Figure 5—worked fine for the cylindrical shapes that were used for columns, but the method failed to be useful to move the prismatic shapes of stones that were used for architraves. Metagenes very cleverly adapted Chersiphron's method by making some evolutionary modifications in how the stone was prepared for hauling. He essentially used an architrave as an axle, around whose ends he constructed wheels out of timber, as indicated in Figure 6. When Paconius was faced with a new problem, however, involving a stone that could not be defaced in the way the earlier methods had to be to receive pivots, he devised a scheme to prepare the stone without damaging it. As indicated in Figure 7, he enclosed the stone in a great timber spool around which a hauling rope could be wound. The method would also appear to be but an incremental evolutionary development from that of his predecessors, but it proved to be a colossal failure because the spool and its cargo could not be kept on a straight path, and all the time and effort spent in getting the spool back to the center of the road led to the bankruptcy of the contracting business. Understanding the way in which Chersiphron's successful method evolved through Metagenes's method to Paconius's dismal failure is a paradigm for the design process. It behooves engineers and those who wish to appreciate the enterprise of engineering to understand through such a paradigm the process independent of the particular application and the state of the art in which it is embedded at any given point in history.[50]

Figure 5. Chersiphron's scheme for transporting circular columns.

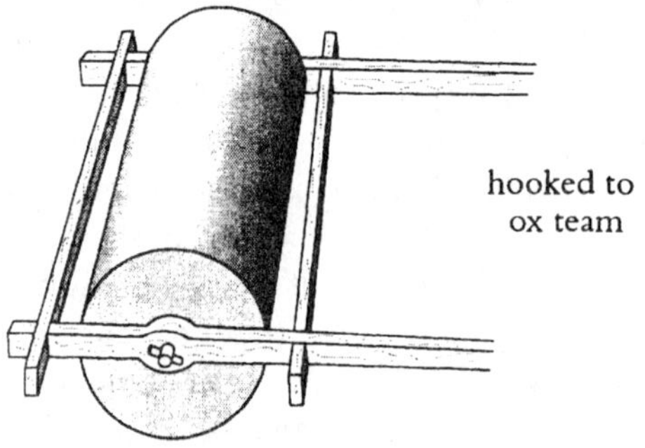

From Petroski, *supra* note 29, at 19 & fig. 2.1 (after Larsen, 1969).

50. *Id.* at 17–26.

Figure 6. Metagenes's scheme for transporting architraves.

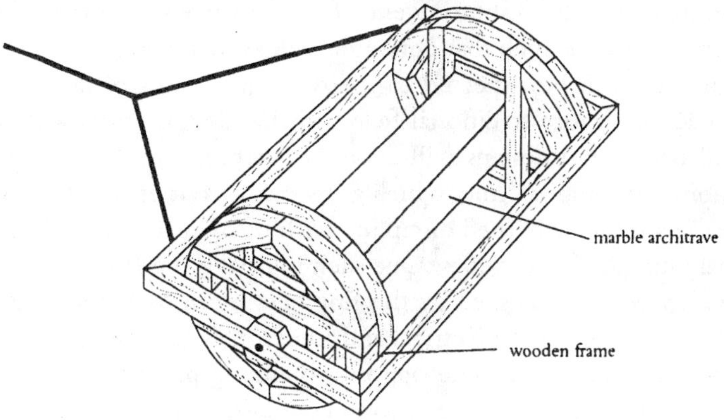

From Petroski, *supra* note 29, at 20 & fig. 2.2 (after Coulten, 1977).

Figure 7. Paconius's scheme for transporting the pedestal for the Statue of Apollo.

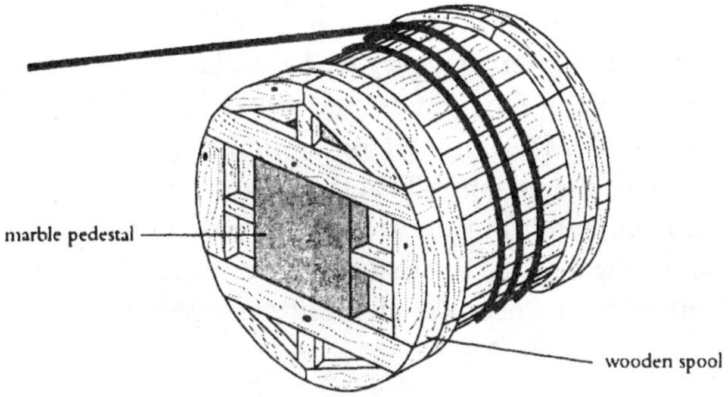

From Petroski, *supra* note 29, at 22 & fig. 2.3 (after Coulten, 1977).

Although the examples in this reference guide are drawn mainly from the fields of civil and mechanical engineering and are largely historical, the principles of design, analysis, and practice that they illustrate are common to all fields of engineering and are relevant to twenty-first century engineering. The nature of engineering design is such that emerging fields like bioengineering and software engineering can be expected to follow similar paths of development as have the older and more traditional fields, in that design errors will be made, failures will occur, and designs will evolve in response to real and perceived failures. Biomedical engineering, which grew mainly out of electrical engineering, is already a well-established discipline with its own academic departments, professional journals, and societies. One such journal is the *IEEE Transactions on Biomedical Engineering*, published by the Engineering in Medicine and Biology Society of the Institution of Electrical and Electronics Engineers.

Although there has been some opposition among professional engineers to the term "software engineering" and to the use of the title "software engineer" by those without engineering degrees, there are clear indications that this opposition is lessening. The State of Texas, for example, now licenses software engineers under that title. The software engineering community itself has for some time felt a kinship to engineering more than to computer science, and the name of their principal professional society, the Association for Computing Machinery (ACM), is certainly more suggestive of an engineering organization than a science one. Software engineering publications have run at least one extensive interview with a prominent bridge designer, and at least one expert on bridge failures has been invited to give keynote addresses at meetings of software engineers. Thus, those engaged in software design and development are recognizing the validity of the analogy between what they and civil engineers do and the lessons to be learned by analogy from structural engineering history and failures. There is also on the Internet a very well-established and closely read Forum on Risks to the Public in Computers and Related Systems (comp.risks), which is operated by the ACM Committee on Computers and Public Policy, and moderated by Peter G. Neumann.[51] That the newest engineering fields share a methodology and an interest in failures with the oldest engineering fields should be no more surprising than the fact that the newest scientific fields share the scientific method with older sciences like chemistry and physics.

51. This publication is available on request from risks-request@csl.sri.com with the single-line message "Subscribe."

V. Summary

In summary, engineering and science share many characteristics and methodologies, but they also have their distinct features and realms of interest. Among the points that have been made in this reference guide that might be considered in evaluating an engineering expert's testimony are the following:

- Engineering and scientific practice share qualities, such as rigor and method, but they remain distinct endeavors.
- Engineering in its purest form seeks to synthesize new things; science seeks to understand what already exists.
- Engineering is more than applied science; engineering has an artistic and creative component that manifests itself in the design process.
- Engineering designs are analogous to scientific hypotheses in that they can be proven wrong by a single counterexample (such as a failure) but cannot ever be proven absolutely correct or safe.
- Engineering always involves an element of risk; it is the engineer's responsibility to minimize that risk to within socially acceptable limits.
- Engineering designs are tested by analysis; it is when engineers are doing analysis that they behave most like scientists.
- Engineering in a climate of repeatedly successful experience can lead to overconfidence and complacency, and this is when errors, accidents, and failures can happen.
- Engineering failures provide reality checks on engineering practice, and the information generated by a failure investigation is very valuable not only to explain the failure itself but also to point to shortcomings in the state of the art.
- Engineering is always striking out in new directions, but that is not to say that new fields of engineering are different in principle from traditional ones.
- Engineering has a rich history, which is dominated by successes but punctuated by some colossal failures, and that history provides great insight into the nature of engineering and its practice today.

Glossary of Terms

ABET. Accreditation Board for Engineering and Technology, a consortium of engineering professional societies that accredits academic engineering and engineering technology programs.

analysis. The study of an engineering system that leads to a usually quantitative understanding of how its constituent parts interact. See also design.

applied science. Science or a scientific endeavor pursued not merely for an understanding of the universe and its materials and structures but with a practical objective in mind. Seeking the fundamental nature of subatomic particles is considered pure science if it has no other objective than an understanding of the nature of matter. Using scientific principles relating to the interaction of atoms to define specifications for a nuclear reactor is applied science. Engineering, which involves a synthesis of science, experience, and judgment, is frequently but mistakenly termed applied science.

computer-aided design (CAD). The use of digital computers to model, analyze, compare, and evaluate how changes in an engineering system affect its behavior, with the objective of establishing an acceptable design. The most sophisticated applications of CAD eliminate much of the paper calculations and drawings long associated with engineering design and allow the data associated with a design to be transferred electronically from the design to the manufacturing stage.

conservatism (in engineering). When choices are encountered in engineering modeling, design, or analysis, choosing the option that makes the design safer or causes the analysis to predict a lower load capacity rather than a higher one.

constraints. Anything outside the designer's control that restricts choices in design is known as a constraint. Thus, if a certain clearance above mean high water or a certain width of channel is required of a bridge, these are design constraints for the bridge. Other constraints may be more abstract, but nonetheless physically meaningful, for example, in the mathematical analysis of two machine parts interacting with one another in a computer model, the constraint that one solid part is not allowed to share the same position in space at the same time as another.

dead load. The load on a structure that is due to the weight of the structure itself.

design. The aspect of engineering that creates new machines, systems, structures, and the like. Design involves an artistic component, in that the design engineer must create something, usually expressed in a sketch or physical model, that can be communicated to other engineers, who can then analyze and criticize it, and flesh it out.

design assumptions. No engineering design can proceed through analysis without some assumptions being made about what its salient features are or what physical phenomena are important to its operation. Thus, it is a common assumption that the series of bolts connecting a steel beam to a column is so tightened that no movement is allowed between the parts. This design assumption defines conditions under which the analysis must proceed.

design constraints. See constraints.

design load. The load that a component of a structure is designed to support.

E.I.T. See Engineer in Training.

Engineer in Training (E.I.T.). An engineer who has passed the Fundamentals of Engineering Examination, the first step in becoming licensed as a professional engineer.

engineering method. Akin to the scientific method, the engineering method uses quantitative tools and experimental procedures to test and refine designs.

engineering science. Disciplines that follow the rigors of the scientific method but have as their objects of study the artifacts of engineering rather than the given objects and phenomena of the universe.

equilibrium state. The condition of an engineering system whereby it is in equilibrium with its surroundings, that is, no change in the system will occur without some change in the forces applied or the configuration obtaining.

"factor of safety." The ratio of a load that causes failure to the design load of a structure.

failure. The condition of not working as designed. A bridge that collapses under a railroad train is obviously a failure of a catastrophic kind. A less dramatic but nonetheless bothersome design failure might be a skyscraper that sways in the wind not so much as to endanger the structure but enough to cause the occupants of upper stories to become sick to their stomachs. A project that goes over budget or is not aesthetically satisfying might also be considered a failure by some engineers.

failure analysis. The determination of the sequence of events and cause of a failure. Failure analysis can involve not only a detailed physical examination of the broken parts of a failed structure or system but also the development of conceptual and computer models to demonstrate how the failure progressed.

failure load. The load at which a structure fails to support the loads imposed on it.

fatigue. The phenomenon whereby a part of a machine or structure develops cracks (fatigue cracks) that grow under continued, repeated loading. When the cracks grow to critical lengths, the machine part or structure can fracture.

forensic engineering. That branch of engineering that deals with the investigation, nature, and causes of failures.

Fundamentals of Engineering Examination. The test that is used to qualify engineers to use the Engineer-in-Training (E.I.T.) designation.

hypothesis. In engineering, a design on paper or in a computer. The design is a hypothesis in the sense that it is an unproven assertion, albeit one that may have a high level of professional experience and judgment backing up its veracity. Also like a scientific hypothesis, an engineering design cannot be proven absolutely to be correct, but can only be falsified. The falsification of an engineering design (hypothesis) is known as a failure.

instability. The phenomenon whereby a small disturbance of an engineering system results in a large change from its equilibrium state or condition of stability. An aluminum beverage can that crumples under a slightly too strong grip could be said to exhibit a buckling instability.

iteration. The engineering design process whereby successive calculations yield successively more accurate predictions of an engineering system's behavior. Iterations often proceed in reaction to the degree to which the latest calculation differs from the previous one, with an increment based on the difference. The process is necessary in steel design, for example, because the principal load on a structure is its dead weight, which naturally depends on the size of the steel members used. The choice of the size of the members, in contrast, depends on the weight of the structure. To begin to iterate toward a fixed design in this vicious circle requires an educated guess at the outset of how heavy the structure must be. The more experienced an engineer, the more accurate the guess is likely to be.

licensing. The process by which engineers progress from E.I.T. to P.E. status.

live load. The load on a structure that is due to things other than the weight of the structure itself. Live loads can include people, furniture, and materials stored in an office building or warehouse, or the traffic on a bridge.

load. In structural engineering, the weight of a structure and the weight of any objects resting upon it or moving across it. See also dead load, design load, live load.

metal fatigue. See fatigue.

mode of failure. The manner in which an engineering system can fail. Most systems have multiple modes of failure, and for design purposes the one that is likely to occur under the smallest load on the system is termed the governing mode of failure.

model. A physical, mathematical, or computer-based representation of an engineering system. Although a model is clearly not identical to the real system, this fact is often forgotten in the interpretation of results from testing a model or running a computer program.

P.E. See Professional Engineer.

prior art. In the field of patents, the technology that is in place at the time a patent is applied for. To be patentable, an invention must not be obvious to one versed in the prior art. See also state of the art.

professional engineer (P.E.). An engineer who has completed a number of years in responsible charge of engineering work and who has passed both the Fundamentals of Engineering and the Professional Engineering Examinations. Under certain circumstances in some states, exemptions to examination may be granted. Abbreviated P.E. in the United States.

"pushing the envelope." Designing beyond engineering experience. Much of engineering is making ever larger, lighter, faster, or smaller things. Such evolutionary developments can, of course, be guided by experience with what has already been made and is operating successfully. All examples of a thing that have been successfully designed are said to be contained within an envelope, which metaphorically encloses them. When data points representing individual engineering systems of a certain kind are plotted on a graph, a smooth curve going through the data points on the fringes of the collection of points is said to be an envelope. To push the envelope is to extend the range of experience, or to add a data point that moves the envelope curve beyond the realm of experience, something that is a natural activity of engineers. When it is done a little at a time, there is little chance that engineers will be surprised by some totally new behavior or not have time to react to it if it does appear to be developing. When the envelope is pushed too violently, however, the design can surprise engineers with totally unexpected and uncontrollable behavior.

scientific method. See engineering method.

S.E. A registered Structural Engineer.

size effect. Something that works fine on a small scale will not necessarily work as well when it is scaled up. In structural engineering this phenomenon has been known since ancient times but was not explained until Galileo did so in the Renaissance. In structural engineering, the phenomenon has to do with the fact that the weight of an object is proportional to its volume, which is related to its size (height, length, or width) to the third power. The strength of an object, however, is only proportional to the area that resists it being pulled apart, and the area is related to size to the second power. There will invariably be a point in the scaling up of a structure geometrically at which the weight exceeds the strength and the structure cannot hold together. Size or scale effects can be exhibited in all kinds of engineering systems, as in a manufacturing process that works fine in the laboratory but is a complete failure when scaled up to factory proportions. It is for this reason that novel power plant designs go through several stages of being scaled up.

stability. An engineering system is said to be stable if it exhibits a small response to a small disturbance. Stable behavior is exhibited when the top of a tall building moves just slightly to the side when the wind increases and returns to its equilibrium position when the wind stops blowing. In contrast, if the top of the building begins moving in an erratic way when the wind increases from 40 to 42 miles per hour, the structure is said to be unstable at that wind speed.

"state of the art." The sum total of knowledge, experience, and techniques that are known and used by those practicing a particular branch of engineering at a given time. See also prior art.

strength of materials. The engineering science that relates how the change of shape of a body is related to the forces that are applied to it, and, by extension, how much resistance it offers to breaking.

structural engineer (S.E). A civil engineer who specializes in the design and analysis of structures, especially large structures like bridges and skyscrapers. A licensed structural engineer is entitled to use the letters S.E. after his or her name.

structure. An assemblage of parts made of a material or materials (steel, concrete, timber, etc.) and designed to carry loads.

truss. An arrangement of structural elements, usually in a series of triangular configurations, used to build up a larger structural component that can span long distances with minimal weight. Trusses are usually made of metal or timber, the former being common in bridges and industrial applications and the latter in domestic roof structures.

wind tunnel. An experimental facility in which models can be placed in a controlled air stream to test their behavior in the wind or the air currents flowing around them. Wind tunnels are commonly used in the development of airplanes and large structures like suspension bridges and skyscrapers, which are likely to be subjected to large wind forces. Prior to the collapse of the Tacoma Narrows Bridge in the wind, bridge decks were not subjected to wind-tunnel testing. Subsequent to the 1940 accident, it became standard practice to test for stability in a wind tunnel the model of any proposed bridge deck design.

References on Engineering Practice and Methods

James L. Adams, Flying Buttresses, Entropy, and O-Rings: The World of an Engineer (1991).

David P. Billington, The Innovators: The Engineering Pioneers Who Made America Modern (1996).

David P. Billington, Robert Maillart's Bridges: The Art of Engineering (1979).

D.I. Blockley, The Nature of Structural Design and Safety (1980).

Kenneth A. Brown, Inventors at Work: Interviews with 16 Notable American Inventors (1988).

Louis L. Bucciarelli, Designing Engineers (1994).

Steven M. Casey, Set Phasers on Stun: And Other True Tales of Design, Technology, and Human Error (1993).

Jacob Feld & Kenneth L. Carper, Construction Failure (2d ed. 1997).

Eugene S. Ferguson, Engineering and the Mind's Eye (1992).

Samuel C. Florman, The Introspective Engineer (1996).

Samuel C. Florman, The Civilized Engineer (1987).

Samuel C. Florman, The Existential Pleasures of Engineering (1976).

Forensic Engineering (Kenneth L. Carper ed., 1989).

Michael J. French, Invention and Evolution: Design in Nature and Engineering (2d ed. 1994).

Gordon L. Glegg, The Development of Design (1981).

Richard E. Goodman, Karl Terzaghi: The Engineer as Artist (1999).

James E. Gordon, Structures, Or, Why Things Don't Fall Down (Da Capo Press 1981) (1978).

Barry B. LePatner & Sidney M. Johnson, Structural and Foundation Failures: A Casebook for Architects, Engineers, and Lawyers (1982).

Matthys Levy & Mario Salvadori, Why Buildings Fall Down: How Structures Fail (1992).

Richard L. Meehan, Getting Sued, and Other Tales of the Engineering Life (1981).

Henry Petroski, The Book on the Bookshelf (1999).

Henry Petroski, Remaking the World: Adventures in Engineering (1997).

Henry Petroski, Invention by Design: How Engineers Get from Thought to Thing (1996).

Henry Petroski, Engineers of Dreams: Great Bridge Builders and the Spanning of America (1995).

Henry Petroski, Design Paradigms: Case Histories of Error and Judgment in Engineering (1994).

Henry Petroski, The Evolution of Useful Things (1992).

Henry Petroski, The Pencil: A History of Design and Circumstance (1990).

Henry Petroski, To Engineer Is Human: The Role of Failure in Successful Design (1985).

Jacob Rabinow, Inventing for Fun and Profit (1990).

Ben R. Rich & Leo Janos, Skunk Works: A Personal Memoir of My Years at Lockheed (1994).

Steven S. Ross, Construction Disasters: Design Failures, Causes, and Prevention (1984).

Mario Salvadori, Why Buildings Stand Up: The Strength of Architecture (McGraw-Hill 1982) (1980).

Charles H. Thornton et al., Exposed Structure in Building Design (1993).

Walter G. Vincenti, What Engineers Know and How They Know It: Analytical Studies from Aeronautical History (1990).

When Technology Fails: Significant Technological Disasters, Accidents, and Failures of the Twentieth Century (Neil Schlager ed., 1994).

Index

About the Federal Judicial Center

The Federal Judicial Center is the research and education agency of the federal judicial system. It was established by Congress in 1967 (28 U.S.C. §§ 620–629), on the recommendation of the Judicial Conference of the United States.

By statute, the Chief Justice of the United States chairs the Center's Board, which also includes the director of the Administrative Office of the U.S. Courts and seven judges elected by the Judicial Conference.

The Director's Office is responsible for the Center's overall management and its relations with other organizations. Its Systems Innovation & Development Office provides technical support for Center education and research. Communications Policy & Design edits, produces, and distributes all Center print and electronic publications, operates the Federal Judicial Television Network, and through the Information Services Office maintains a specialized library collection of materials on judicial administration.

The Judicial Education Division develops and administers education programs and services for judges, career court attorneys, and federal defender office personnel. These include orientation seminars, continuing education programs, and special-focus workshops. The Interjudicial Affairs Office provides information about judicial improvement to judges and others of foreign countries, and identifies international legal developments of importance to personnel of the federal courts.

The Court Education Division develops and administers education and training programs and services for nonjudicial court personnel, such as those in clerks' offices and probation and pretrial services offices, and management training programs for court teams of judges and managers.

The Research Division undertakes empirical and exploratory research on federal judicial processes, court management, and sentencing and its consequences, often at the request of the Judicial Conference and its committees, the courts themselves, or other groups in the federal system. The Federal Judicial History Office develops programs relating to the history of the judicial branch and assists courts with their own judicial history programs.